W9-DEA-221

THE POET
IN AMERICA

1650 to the Present

THE POET IN AMERICA,
1650 to the Present

Edited and with an introduction by
ALBERT J. GELPI
Stanford University

D. C. HEATH AND COMPANY
Lexington, Massachusetts   Toronto   London

ACKNOWLEDGMENTS

Wendell Berry "The Peace of Wild Things" © 1968 by Wendell Berry. Reprinted from his volume *Openings* by permission of Harcourt Brace Jovanovich, Inc.; "The Dead Calf" © 1967 by Wendell Berry. Reprinted from his volume *Openings* by permission of Harcourt Brace Jovanovich, Inc.; "Enriching the Earth" © 1969 by Wendell Berry. Reprinted from his volume *Farming: A Hand Book* by permission of Harcourt Brace Jovanovich, Inc.; "A Wet Time" © 1969 by Wendell Berry. Reprinted from his volume *Farming: A Hand Book* by permission of Harcourt Brace Jovanovich, Inc.; "The Satisfactions of the Mad Farmer" © 1970 by Wendell Berry. Reprinted from his volume *Farming: A Hand Book* by permission of Harcourt Brace Jovanovich, Inc.

John Berryman "Dream Songs" (Nos. 1, 9, 29, 48, 75, 77) reprinted with the permission of Farrar, Straus & Giroux, Inc., from *77 Dream Songs* by John Berryman, copyright © 1959, 1962, 1963, 1964 by John Berryman. Other selections reprinted with the permission of Farrar, Straus & Giroux, Inc. from *Love and Fame* by John Berryman, copyright © 1970 by John Berryman.

Elizabeth Bishop Reprinted with the permission of Farrar, Straus & Giroux, Inc., from *The Complete Poems* by Elizabeth Bishop, copyright © 1957, 1962, 1969 by Elizabeth Bishop.

Edgar Bowers "To the Reader," "The Stoic," "Amor Vincit Omnia," and "The Virgin Mary," from *The Form of Loss* © 1956. Reprinted by permission of The Swallow Press, Chicago; "An Afternoon at the Beach" and "Autumn Shade" (Parts 1, 9, 10) from *The Astronomers* © 1965. Reprinted by permission of The Swallow Press, Chicago.

Hart Crane From *The Collected Poems and Selected Letters and Prose of Hart Crane* by Hart Crane. Permission of Liveright Publishers, N. Y. Copyright © 1933, 1958, 1966 by Liveright Publishing Corp.

Robert Creeley "The Language" (copyright © 1964 Robert Creeley) is reprinted by permission of Charles Scribner's Sons from *Words* by Robert Creeley. "Gemini," "In Secret," and ' "Time" is some sort of hindsight' are reprinted from *Pieces* by

and "The Moon: Passages 5" from *Bending the Bow*. Copyright © 1964, 1968 by Robert Duncan. Reprinted by permission of New Directions Publishing Corporation.

T. S. Eliot "Morning at the Window," "La Figlia Che Piange," "The Waste Land," and "Marina," from *Collected Poems 1909–1962* by T. S. Eliot, copyright, 1936, by Harcourt Brace Jovanovich, Inc.; © 1963, 1964, by T. S. Eliot. Reprinted by permission of the publishers; "The Dry Salvages," from *Four Quartets*, copyright, 1943, by T. S. Eliot. Reprinted by permission of Harcourt Brace Jovanovich, Inc. Canadian rights: reprinted by permission of Faber and Faber, Ltd., from *Collected Poems, 1909–1962*.

William Everson (Brother Antoninus) "We in the Fields," "Bard," "August," "Lava Bed," and "'The Raid," from William Everson, *The Residual Years*. Copyright 1942 by William Everson. Copyright 1948 by New Directions Publishing Corporation. Reprinted by permission of New Directions Publishing Corporation; "A Canticle to the Waterbirds" and "The South Coast" reprinted from William Everson, *Crooked Lines of God*, 1962, by permission of the University of Detroit Press; "The Poet is Dead" by William Everson is reprinted by permission of the author; "The Rose of Solitude" and "The Vision of Felicity" from *The Rose of Solitude* by Brother Antoninus, copyright © 1963, 1966 by Brother Antoninus. Reprinted by permission of Doubleday & Company, Inc.; "The Song the Body Dreamed in the Spirit's Mad Behest," copyright © 1962 by Atlantic Monthly Co., "In All These Acts," copyright © 1962 by Brother Antoninus, from *The Hazards of Holiness* by Brother Antoninus. Reprinted by permission of Doubleday & Company, Inc.

Lawrence Ferlinghetti *Starting from San Francisco*. Copyright © 1961 by Lawrence Ferlinghetti. Reprinted by permission of New Directions Publishing Corporation.

Robert Frost From *The Poetry of Robert Frost* edited by Edward Connery Lathem. Copyright 1916, 1923, 1928, 1930, 1939, 1947, © 1969 by Holt, Rinehart and Winston, Inc. Copyright 1936, 1942, 1944, 1951, © 1956, 1958, 1962 by Robert Frost. Copyright © 1964, 1967, 1970 by Lesley Frost Ballantine. Reprinted by permission of Holt, Rinehart and Winston, Inc.

Allen Ginsberg "Kral Majales" Copyright © 1968 by Allen Ginsberg. Reprinted by permission of City Lights Books; "A Supermarket in California," "Sunflower Sutra," and "America" copyright © 1956, 1959, by Allen Ginsberg. Reprinted by permission of City Lights Books.

Langston Hughes "The Negro Speaks of Rivers," "Dream Variations," and "I, Too," Copyright 1926 by Alfred A. Knopf, Inc., and renewed 1954 by Langston Hughes. Reprinted from *Selected Poems* by Langston Hughes; "Fire," Copyright 1927 by Alfred A. Knopf, Inc., and renewed 1955 by Langston Hughes. Reprinted from *Selected Poems* by Langston Hughes; "Old Walt" and "Down and Out" from *Selected Poems* by Langston Hughes. Copyright © 1959 by Langston Hughes; "Stony Lonesome," Copyright 1942 by Alfred A. Knopf, Inc., and renewed 1970 by Arna Bontemps and George Houston Bass. Reprinted from *Selected Poems* by Langston Hughes; "Bad Morning" from *Selected Poems*, by Langston Hughes. Copyright © 1959 by Langston Hughes. Reprinted by permission of Alfred A. Knopf, Inc.; "Midnight Raffle," Copyright 1948 by Alfred A. Knopf, Inc. Reprinted from *Selected Poems*, by Langston Hughes. All reprinted by permission of Alfred A. Knopf, Inc.

Robinson Jeffers "Divinely Superfluous Beauty" and "To the Stone Cutters," Copyright 1924 and renewed 1952 by Robinson Jeffers. Reprinted from *The Selected Poetry of Robinson Jeffers*; "Shine, Perishing Republic," and "Post Mortem," Copyright 1925 and renewed 1953 by Robinson Jeffers. Reprinted from *The Selected Poetry of Robinson Jeffers*; "Hurt Hawks," Copyright 1928 and renewed 1956 by Robinson Jeffers. Reprinted from *The Selected Poetry of Robinson Jeffers*; "The Bed by the Window," Copyright 1932 and renewed 1960 by Robinson Jeffers. Reprinted

1907 Charles Scribner's Sons; renewal copyright 1935.) and "For a Dead Lady" (Copyright 1909 Charles Scribner's Sons, renewal copyright 1937.) from *The Town Down the River*. "Luke Havergal," "Cliff Klingenhagen," "The Clerks," and "Credo" from *The Children of the Night*; "Eros Turannos" and "Veteran Sirens" reprinted with permission of The Macmillan Company from *Collected Poems*. Copyright 1916 by Edwin Arlington Robinson, renewed 1948 by Ruth Nivison; "The Flying Dutchman" reprinted with permission of The Macmillan Company from *Collected Poems* by Edwin Arlington Robinson. Copyright 1920 by Edwin Arlington Robinson, renewed 1949 by Ruth Nivison; "Mr. Flood's Party," "The Lost Anchors," and "Many Are Called," reprinted with permission of The Macmillan Company from *Collected Poems* by Edwin Arlington Robinson. Copyright 1921 by Edwin Arlington Robinson, renewed 1953 by Ruth Nivison; "The Sheaves," "Karma," "Maya," and "New England," reprinted with permission of The Macmillan Company from *Collected Poems* by Edwin Arlington Robinson. Copyright 1925 renewed 1953 by Ruth Nivison and Barbara R. Holt.

Theodore Roethke "Cuttings," "Cuttings (later)," "Orchids," "Transplanting," "Forcing House," "The Waking," and "Frau Bauman, Frau Schmidt, and Frau Schwartze," copyright 1946, 1948, 1952 by Theodore Roethke, from *Collected Poems of Theodore Roethke*. Reprinted by permission of Doubleday & Company, Inc.; "Weed Puller," "Moss-Gathering," "Child on Top of a Greenhouse," and "Flower Dump," copyright © 1946 by Editorial Publications, Inc., from *Collected Poems of Theodore Roethke*. Reprinted by permission of Doubleday & Company, Inc.; "The Longing," "The Rose," "In a Dark Time," and "The Tree, the Bird," copyright © 1960, 1961, 1962 by Beatrice Roethke as Administratrix of the Estate of Theodore Roethke, from *Collected Poems of Theodore Roethke*. Reprinted by permission of Doubleday & Company, Inc.

Carl Sandburg "Four Preludes on Playthings of the Wind," from *Smoke and Steel* by Carl Sandburg, copyright, 1920, by Harcourt Brace Jovanovich, Inc.; copyright, 1948, by Carl Sandburg. Reprinted by permission of the publisher; "Upstream," from *Slabs of the Sunburnt West*, copyright, 1922, by Harcourt Brace Jovanovich, Inc.; copyright, 1950, by Carl Sandburg. Reprinted by permission of the publisher; *The People, Yes*, Section 107, from *The People, Yes*, by Carl Sandburg, copyright, 1936, by Harcourt Brace Jovanovich, Inc.; copyright, 1964, by Carl Sandburg. Reprinted by permission of the publisher; "Early Copper," "Cheap Rent," "Elm Buds," "Skyscrapers Stand Proud," "Chicago," "Child of the Romans," and "Fog," from *Chicago Poems* by Carl Sandburg, copyright, 1916, by Holt, Rinehart and Winston, Inc.; copyright, 1944, by Carl Sandburg. Reprinted by permission of Harcourt Brace Jovanovich, Inc.; "Wilderness," "Bilbea," "Cool Tombs," and "Grass," from *Cornhuskers* by Carl Sandburg. Copyright 1918 by Holt, Rinehart and Winston, Inc. Copyright 1946 by Carl Sandburg. Reprinted by permission of Holt, Rinehart and Winston, Inc.

W. D. Snodgrass "The Marsh" Copyright © 1957 by W. D. Snodgrass. Reprinted from *Heart's Needle*, by W. D. Snodgrass, by permission of Alfred A. Knopf, Inc.; "Heart's Needle," Selections 1 and 7, Copyright © 1959 by W. D. Snodgrass. Reprinted from *Heart's Needle*, by W. D. Snodgrass, by permission of Alfred A. Knopf, Inc.; Acknowledgement is due to Harper and Row, Publishers, Inc., New York, for permission to reprint the following poems by W. D. Snodgrass: "Mementos, 1," "Leaving the Motel," "Lobsters in the Window."

Gary Snyder From Gary Snyder, *Regarding Wave*. Copyright © by Gary Snyder. Reprinted by permission of New Directions Publishing Corporation.

Wallace Stevens "Domination of Black," "The Snow Man," "A High-Toned Old

This book is for
Barbara
and for
Christopher and Adrienne

FOREWORD

In an anthology like this, the Foreword is a statement of intentions: a kind of fore-warning. I wanted to combine a historical and a critical view of the development of American poetry from the beginning to the present. The real achievement of Ameri-can poetry resides in the major poets of the nineteenth and twentieth centuries, and I have given them as much room in the book as I could. At the same time for histori-cal balance I wanted to include some Puritan poetry, a little from the Revolutionary and Federalist period, and selections from the "household poets" who held sway over cultivated as well as popular tastes through the last century and well into our own. As for contemporary American poetry, its rich diversity is remarkable, and while my choices no doubt reflect my own preferences and judgments, I have made every effort to offer a representative sampling.

Let me add that I hope this anthology can be used as textbook for a variety of purposes in a variety of courses. The selections are wide-ranging enough for a sur-vey of American poetry, while there is enough poetry from the nineteenth century alone or the twentieth century alone to be used in surveys of those periods. The advantage of having it all in one book is that one can look backward or forward and have the references and associations right in hand, at the flip of a few pages.

As for the selections themselves, I tried to include not just necessary and ob-vious titles, but less frequently anthologized pieces that in many cases deserve equal attention. The aim was a "Table of Contents" that gave a truer and fuller image of the poet's work. Often, too, I wanted to play particular poems by different poets off against each other for historical and critical reasons, as they anticipated or extended important attitudes or ideas or techniques. Respect for the integrity of the poem required that I use only those poems I could give in full. The only relaxation of this rule was for the passage from Barlow's long epic, *The Columbiad*, and also for complete poems that are parts of larger wholes, such as several of Pound's *Cantos* and several sections of Hart Crane's *The Bridge*.

The Introduction attempts to raise some general questions about the status of poetry in America in the minds of American poets: questions that have prompted them to reflect on the sources and ends of poetry. The brief introduction to each of the major sections provides a more specific context for the poets included therein by noting movements, tendencies, and divergences. The headnote for each poet pro-vides a schematic biography and points to important or characteristic features of theme or technique. Below the headnote is given the standard text, if there is one. The titles for further references are sometimes essays or letters by the poet that have not been mentioned previously, and sometimes biographical and critical studies, though with no pretence at a bibliography. The footnotes give information helpful in reading the text rather than an interpretation of the text. My notion is to provide the reader, student, and teacher with as much as I can between two covers, while leaving him free to take his own approach, to make his own responses, to come to his own conclusions.

At this time I want to refer the reader to several general studies of American poetry that he will find immensely useful. I am presently at work on a series of chapters on perhaps a dozen poets that, as a book, will trace out strands in the American tradition. The following are books already in print: Alfred Kreymborg, *A History of American Poetry: Our Singing Strength,* (New York: Tudor Publishing Co., 1934); H. H. Wells, *The American Way of Poetry* (New York: Columbia University Press, 1943); Roy Harvey Pearce, *The Continuity of American Poetry* (Princeton: Princeton University Press, 1961); Kenneth Rexroth, *American Poetry in the Twentieth Century* (New York: Herder & Herder, 1971). And the best and most complete history of American poetry is, and will probably remain Hyatt H. Waggoner's *American Poets, from the Puritans to the Present* (Boston: Houghton Mifflin, 1968) now readily available in paperback.

Every anthologist weeps for more space, and his tears are not without cause. Aside from that, I enjoyed working on this book, helped as I was by many people: Stephen Ross, now teaching at Purdue, who served as research assistant for many of the headnotes and put in many hours of creative labor; Don Bevis, who had the seed-idea from which this much longer anthology grew; David Levin of the University of Virginia and Hyatt Waggoner of Brown for suggested additions that have enriched the collection; William Allen and James Knox of the Stanford Library for their boundless and cheerful knowledgeability and aid; Carole Reeves, Christine Gwynn, and Susan Riggs for help in preparing the manuscript; and my students at Harvard and Stanford whose queries and enthusiasms have made me understand American poetry better. The indebtedness closest to my heart is expressed in the dedication.

Albert Gelpi
Stanford University

CONTENTS

Part Two
AMERICAN ROMANTIC POETRY   61

Sidney Lanier (1842–1881)   328

Part Three
THE AMERICAN POETIC RENAISSANCE 347

Robert Frost (1874–1963) 365

Carl Sandburg (1878–1967) 386

Wallace Stevens (1879–1955) 398

Part Four
THE CONTEMPORARY SCENE   605

Charles Olson (1910–1970)   629

Elizabeth Bishop (1911–   )   643

J. V. Cunningham (1911–   )   646

William Everson (Brother Antoninus) (1912–) 655

John Berryman (1914–1972)   675

Robert Lowell (1917–)   682

Robert Duncan (1919–)   702

INTRODUCTION

American poetry, and American arts and letters in general, have been a problem from the beginning. The question in the seventeenth and eighteenth centuries and into the middle of the nineteenth was whether a scattered and disparate people, busy with building a country in a wilderness of continental vastness, would have the time or roots or inspiration to produce art and literature. America was "Nature's nation," but was that an obstacle to artistic development, or a unique opportunity? Was America destined by its unusual circumstances to develop into a new civilization, or was it destined because of those same circumstances to be precluded from significant cultural expression? So swiftly did the pioneers span the continent and so efficiently did the townspeople who followed in their paths impose a booming economy on the open land, that the terms of the question shifted and seemed to invert themselves. Now the question about American culture was whether a society as urban and industrialized as the United States had sufficient vision and humanity and reverence for the land on which its capitals and factories stood to produce art that could move the heart and elevate the spirit. America's history is short but accelerated; its experience has been marked by rapid changes and violent contrasts. However, the difficulty for the artist has been the same: Can a poet or painter find a place for himself in a capitalist republic like the United States? Can American society, spawned in the wilderness by a largely unlettered group of speculators, generate poets and painters and make room for their art amidst the clatter of business?

The principal lines of response to the question of civilization in America were projected at the outset. Upon arriving at the Virgin Queen's virgin land, the Virginians named their settlement Jamestown after her royal successor, and began to model themselves, as closely as conditions and money and education permitted, on the religious, social, and cultural precedents they knew in England. The Puritans emigrated to the New World in resistance to most of the prevailing English models, and despite all the necessary and continuing ties with the mother country, their adaptation to the new circumstances soon made their differences plain. This paradigm may seem too simple to indicate very much, but in point of fact the tensions inherent in the separation and the association between the New World and the Old are crucial to American arts and letters. Virginia kept looking back across the seas more longingly than did Massachusetts, and for that reason Massachusetts, rather than Virginia, began more quickly and decisively to define a native American character—and a literature.

Not at all surprisingly, then, American poetry originated in New England. In art, as in religion and politics, the question was just how "new," or how "English," poets were and should be. Anne Bradstreet, the first American poet, came, almost emblematically, with that first boatload of settlers under Governor Winthrop, and her career is emblematic as well. The friends who published her verse, the first book of American poetry, proclaimed her independence by calling it *The Tenth Muse*

Lately Sprung up in America, but they had it published in London, not Boston. Her poetry does not totally bear out the promise of the title: she dreamed of the English countryside and wrote conventional poems on the four seasons and the four ages of man. There are also, however, the personal lyrics that grew out of her "American experience"—the burning of her house in the forest clearing, the loss of a child, the triumph of love over hard conditions. Edward Taylor, the minister of Westfield, Massachusetts, was the first important American poet, and his career foreshadowed much that has followed. Writing in the manner of metaphysical poets like Donne and Herbert but without the company or challenge of other poets, writing in fact for himself without expectation of fame or influence in a frontier hamlet surrounded by the wilds, he produced poems less skilled and polished, more crude and home-spun—but also bolder and more idiosyncratic—than Donne or Herbert, and in them we can hear American speech and American rhythms emerging from the British tradition. Taylor's poems are not an echo, but a native statement.

Once America had established its political and economic character, thoughtful and cultivated Americans had to face squarely the dilemma of an American civilization. Bradstreet was minor, and unread; Taylor was undiscovered; Americans could look only to Freneau and to the "Connecticut Wits," and their verse, whether political or pastoral, sentimental or epic or bombastic, consisted mostly of tepid imitations of neoclassical models.

In self-doubt and self-justification, early artists and critics had to raise the issue of a national literature. William Cullen Bryant, for example, could not rest in being the "American Wordsworth," and devoted one of his four *Lectures on Poetry* to "Poetry in Its Relation to Our Age and Country" in order to quench the concerns, expressed here and abroad, that American talents were commercial and American circumstances barbarous. He hoped to establish the grounds for a flowering of the arts: "I infer, then, that all the materials of poetry exist in our country, with all the ordinary encouragements and opportunities for making a successful use of them.... If under the circumstances our poetry should finally fail of rivaling that of Europe, it will be because Genius sits idle in the midst of its treasures." At the same time that Melville was aligning himself with the "Young America" group in New York to proclaim a national literary identity and was hailing Hawthorne in the same breath as Shakespeare, Emerson had begun to sound—first from Concord and Boston, then from lecture platforms across the land—the summons for a free and original literature conversant with America's size and spirit: "Our day of dependence, our long apprenticeship to the learning of other lands, draws to a close.... Events, actions arise, that must be sung, that will sing themselves." For in a democracy the poet "is representative of man, in virtue of being the largest power to receive and to impart" impressions, intuitions, visions.

Whitman heard Emerson's call and took as his life's task the prophetic mission of absorbing all the nation's diversities—East and South and West, metropolis and farmland and wide-open spaces—into a mystique that validated the present in the promise of the future. To Englishmen and Europeans, Whitman loomed as the exponent of a new mode of imaginative creation; but Whitman's spiritual heirs had the challenge and burden of maintaining a sense of coherence against the wastefulness and extravagance of American materialism: Ezra Pound pondering the power of money; William Carlos Williams brooding over the slums of Paterson; Hart Crane confronting the Brooklyn Bridge and the plane crash at Cape Hatteras; Allen Gins-

berg howling in the supermarket; Lawrence Ferlinghetti starting back from San Francisco to reach Whitman's Paumanok again. Robinson Jeffers could only move to land's end like the last pioneer, seeking to lose himself in the brute beauty of the California coast and singing a national dirge in "Shine, Perishing Republic" while Carmel's affluence closed round his hand-built tower. Nonetheless, many have refused to accept the end. Crane saw the Bridge as the apotheosis of technology; Frost answered Jeffers that it was "Our Doom to Bloom"; Denise Levertov can still see, for a crucial moment, "Paradise in the dust of a street"; William Everson, Jeffers' only disciple, is tranfixed by the "Vision of Felicity" amidst the crush of Manhattan.

From the very start, of course, some American critics and poets have inveighed against the provincialism of literary nationalists in the name of a shared and ongoing tradition, and this more conservative group includes not just genteel sophisticates like Washington Irving and Henry Wadsworth Longfellow, but some of the nation's strongest literary voices. For them the Tenth Muse would not spring up in the New World spontaneously; she would have to be imported to engender poetry of mixed parentage. Even before Hawthorne wondered whether a prosperous republic provided the materials for a psychological and moral romance (a question to which James would return with Hawthorne in mind before exploring the "international" theme in his fiction), even before Melville had come to ridicule the "Young America" group in *Pierre* shortly before lapsing into his long silence, Poe the Virginian had set out to reduce the chauvinism of New York and New England to its parochial absurdity: the "boisterous and arrogant . . . pride of a too speedily assumed literary freedom" devolves into the "gross paradox of liking a stupid book the better, because, sure enough, its stupidity is American." Poe stands at the head of a long line of indigenous cosmopolites that stretches from Irving and Copley and Cooper, to James and Whistler, to Eliot and Pound and Stevens, to Allen Tate and Yvor Winters and Robert Lowell, each refusing to stake his art to a narrow nationalism.

Poets cannot, needless to say, be sorted out absolutely on this single issue; their specific attitudes and responses are in fact expectedly varied. What is more, each of the two "groups" is constantly taking the opposite position into account in arguing out its own. Pound defined himself against Whitman as his poetic father and Williams as the loyal son, and told Williams that the very fact that Williams could live and write in the United States proved that he was less aware of America, less committed to America—in effect, less "American" than Pound himself was in exile. In turn, Williams defined himself against the internationalism of Pound and Eliot, and warned younger poets like Lowell against the enervation of Europe. The basis of the controversy between Pound and Williams, and of their deep respect for one another, was their unshakable—and shared—concern for the state of American arts and letters; from opposite sides of the Atlantic, they were working for an American Renaissance. So, too, for one very good reason, Williams held Poe, otherwise an uncongenial figure, in the highest esteem: his critical work was a "single gesture . . . to sweep all worthless chaff aside" and to "clear the ground" for serious American writing. Here is the common cause for all American poets, whether nationalist or internationalist, whether challenged by the unpeopled wilderness or by teeming cities, whether sanguine or sceptical about the prospects for American civilization. When critics charged Stevens with escaping into a Frenchified aestheticism, his reply was sharp and clear: the poet contributes to his society because his commitment to the aesthetic order issues in creations that transform our sense of possibilities for individual and collective existence.

It is, therefore, the depth and intensity of the concern about the poet in America—whatever that means to the individual with the pen in his hand—that has produced, some would say against all odds, a body of work so vigorous and original that now, as Melville had hoped, England and Europe must take American poetry into account, and increasingly take their lead from it. However hostile or susceptible to art conditions have been, American poetry is an achieved and growing fact—and a distinctive accomplishment as well. Stevens did not talk about an American language, as Whitman and Williams did, yet for all his affinities with the aesthetes and for all the Romantic echoes in his poems, he recognized that "nothing could be more inappropriate to American literature than its English source since the Americans are not British in sensibility." In his old age Eliot admitted that despite the years in London, his roots were American just as W. H. Auden was still British after decades as an American citizen. And Auden's conclusion as an American Englishman matches Eliot's and Stevens': "from Bryant on there is scarcely one American poet whose work, if unsigned, could be mistaken for that of an Englishman."

II

American poetry, therefore, has developed in relation to, and distinctive from, the European and especially the British tradition: a pattern of dependence, independence, and growing interdependence. At the same time that we begin to trace out strands of a native tradition, we note an equally important fact that seems at first to work against continuities of tradition and that has established the terms on which continuities of sorts have been possible. The plain fact is that the American poet has characteristically found himself alone, thrown back upon his own wits and resources. Each has had to ask the basic questions about his art over again, to answer them for himself, and thereby to establish his own position in relation to, and thus within, the tradition. From his special vantage point Auden has observed that "the situation of the first American poets—Emerson, Thoreau, Poe—was ... doubly difficult" because "they were without status with the majority" in the society while "the cultured minority of which they were members looked to England for its literary standards." While British domination has waned, the American artist still finds himself without an accepted and understood function in the economy, since the nation has developed no cultured class or literary elite. This very isolation has been the source of the limits and the strengths of American poetry: its rude power, its openness to risk and experimentation, its directness and clumsiness, its energy and excesses, its individuality and eccentricity, its honesty and self-absorption.

American poets have had to be honest and self-conscious because they could assume far less about the poetic act than poets of other countries. Each American poet has had to question and test everything about his vocation. In a way that is not true in most other major countries, poets, major and minor, had to determine quite individually, the function and nature of the poet and the form and nature of the poem. Consequently the creative act is not just an urgent concern in critical theory; it is an urgent theme of the poetry itself. It is no accident that our poetry matured in the Romantic Age, when experience was becoming increasingly individualized and awareness was becoming increasingly subjective.

The first and last concern of modern poetry is epistemological: concern for the complexity and validity of perception. But the problems for the American poet were particularly acute because they were peculiarly basic. In poetry, as in economics and politics, the issues of the modern experience present themselves more nakedly in the United States than abroad. For the poet, his assumptions and expectations were at issue, were the issue. More than the English or French or German—or for that matter the Japanese—poet, the American had to begin anew, or at any rate begin again. He was conscious, of course, of older poets and of contemporaries, and he responded to them; but if he was not working in a vacuum, he was nonetheless responsible to and for himself. For this reason the lines of the developing American tradition link similar or analogous or related positions reached, in general, much more independently and painfully than would be true in other cultures.

Still, patterns began to emerge. Emerson, for example, gave rhapsodic expression to a notion of the poet that has found itself explored through different temperaments in a long line of vatic poets: Whitman, Pound, Williams, Carl Sandburg, Hart Crane, Jeffers, William Everson, Allen Ginsberg, Charles Olson, Robert Duncan, Denise Levertov, and others. For Emerson the poet was a visionary and a prophet; in him the divine powers of perception moved more freely, and he was inspired to see things and into things in order to reveal the wholeness of creation to his fellows. Surveying the dead deeds of "the foregoing generations," Emerson cried out: "Why should not we also enjoy an original relation to the universe? Why should not we have a poetry and philosophy of insight and not of tradition, and a religion by revelation to us, and not the history of theirs?" This was the American people's manifest destiny, not merely to occupy the continent. Whitman roared back that the bard was the priest of the modern democracy. To discover the coherence of cosmos, the poet submits to the flow of energy, is open to the promptings and suggestions that emerge from beneath the surfaces of things, even from the depths of his own mind. The poem itself must be equally open and free of prescriptions in order to unfold the particular form this experience takes in its organic verbal structure. Like the oracle at Delphi, or like the new priest of Dionysus, the poet-seer will be gripped by the god and speak; no wonder his verses imply more than they say and only point toward their ultimate meaning.

In good part Emerson was asserting the power of poetry to compensate for the gradual erosion of the orthodox religious and theological formulations that had shaped the verses as well as the devotional prose of Bradstreet and Taylor. But for Poe, bad philosophy made for bad poetry; the universe was chaos, not cosmos, except where the artist had made an aesthetic order through artificial means. The poet needed discipline, training, and conscious craft to devise a poem that would suggest the harmony he lacked and the ideal he hankered after. The arrangement of words, images, and sounds achieved its deliberate effect as "this poem *per se*—this poem which is a poem and nothing more—this poem written solely for the poem's sake." The autonomous art object and the craft that achieved its closed form are saving graces in the face of metaphysical uncertainty, the failure of human relations, and the indifference of nature. The ideal is Apollonian perfection, which transcends the material order by fixing it. The philosophical and aesthetic objections that Poe raised against "the so-called poetry of the so-called transcendentalists" and the consequent vindication of the poem as poem have found themselves echoed and explored in many ways in the work of a long line of formalist poets, all agonizingly aware of loss and limitation: among them Frederick Goddard Tuckerman, Edwin Arlington Robinson, T. S. Eliot, Wallace Stevens, John Crowe Ransom, Allen Tate, Yvor Winters, J. V. Cunningham, W. D. Snodgrass, and Edgar Bowers. Their Romantic *angst* made them anti-Romantic and made some of them imitate the balanced and harmonious "classicism" of Greece or the Middle Ages or the Renaissance.

The contrasts and distinctions of the above sketch are not meant to be categorical or final. They are meant to set forth provisionally the terms of a dialectic that has beset and stimulated American poetry all along the way. At the same time, a reading of many of these poets will quickly reveal that they are too complex and divided within themselves to be summed up neatly or trimmed to an argument, and many stand or waver or negotiate between the extremes. Everyone would rejoice to have Emerson's sense of the correspondence that links mind and matter, but even many fellow-New Englanders could not reach, or sustain, that point of vision. While returning again and again to the Emersonian hypothesis, Tuckerman fell back on the strict conventions of the sonnet; Emily Dickinson depicted the artist as a spider spinning his precise and fragile web out of himself; Frost saw the poet reconstructing things "into a new order with not so much as a ligature clinging to it of the old place where it was organic." If Whitman was "America's poet," then Pound wanted "to drive him into the old world" so that European culture might educate his brash vulgarity, and discipline his poetic method. Yet though Pound proclaimed the axioms of Imagism as a corrective to Romantic sloppiness and expansiveness, his Imagist phase was only a prelude to his life's work in *The Cantos*, the most daring and extended experiment in open form since *Leaves of Grass*.

Moreover, there can be no easy or necessary correlation between optimists and open form and between sceptics and closed form, as the discussion above might seem at first to suggest. Neither optimism nor scepticism is simple, nor is a poet's sense of form. For poets like Marianne Moore and Richard Wilbur, the verse forms, painstakingly achieved, articulate the limits under and through which they come to moral and religious perceptions. Eliot was always a highly conscious craftsman, even while his *vers libre* spoke of disillusionment and fragmentation; but in *Four Quartets,* his most intricately worked and most positively Christian poem, the elaborated structure allowed him to explore the implications of transcendent moments and to build them into a coherent view of life and history. As Robert Lowell moved in the other direction, from Christianity to doubt, his poems became less packed with sound and metaphor, less reliant on rigid structure; they opened up to sift the bits of memory and experience for connection and perspective. E. E. Cummings had to impose his own mannerisms on old forms like the sonnet and the ballad in order to celebrate life on his own terms, while John Berryman had to shake himself loose from traditional conventions in order to find, in a vehicle open but controlled by its own eccentricities, a tragicomic voice for his anxiety. Adrienne Rich learned to refuse the protection of preconceived form in order to expose herself to all the risks and threats of experience. Theodore Roethke alternated between open and closed form; his last volume is built around two sequences, one in Whitmanesque free verse and the other in rhymed and metered stanzas.

And so it goes, response and counter-response. No single or fixed position, but individual responses to those old dilemmas that the American artist has had to face with fewer axiomatic guidelines than others: To what extent is a work of art conscious or unconscious, spontaneous or disciplined? To what extent is a poem given or received? To what extent does language suggest or define, concentrate or expand? To what extent is form imposed or disclosed? Each artist must work it out, again and again, in his own practice and in his reflection on that practice. However, at the extremes stand two radically different kinds of poets holding opposite views of the poem based on contradictory assumptions about the world. Denise Levertov has put the difference this way:

> There are no doubt temperamental differences between poets who use prescribed forms and those who look for new ones—people who need a tight schedule to get anything done, and people who have to have a free hand—but the difference in their conceptions of "content" and "reality" is functionally more important. On the one hand is the idea that content, reality, experience, is essentially fluid and must be given form; on the other, this sense of seeking out inherent, though not immediately apparent, form.

"Basically," as William Everson summed it up, "one kind of poet or artist creates a world of his own making, while another stands witness to a world beyond the world of his making." These archetypes of the poet frame the poems that follow and the range of variations contained therein.

Beyond assumptions and procedures lies the recognition that (in Adrienne Rich's words) "for a poet, in any case, language is always a form of moral behavior." American poetry is distinctive because American poets, even the alienated and the expatriated, even those who found their models abroad, have come to the act of language rooted not just in their individual circumstances but in our collective experience as a people.

Richard Mather, 1596–1669, American Congregational cleric. Woodcut, c. 1670, attributed to John Foster (1648–1681), the earliest portrait engraving known to have been made in America. (Courtesy of The Granger Collection)

Part One

COLONIAL BEGINNINGS

America did not produce much poetry of distinction before the nineteenth century, but this fact is less surprising than the amount of poetry—much of it competent enough—that did come out of the colonial period. This was the time, after all, in which the colonists—many of little or no education and culture— were busy clearing the wilds and setting up a community.

Some American colonists spoke of the New World idealistically: John Winthrop told the Puritans about to land in Massachusetts that their theocratic community would be "a City upon a Hill," watched by people the world over. Others seized upon the economic advantages of an undeveloped country. Though the religious and moral zeal of the New Englanders has remained a powerful factor in the American character, practical concerns soon commanded attention all up and down the coast. Not only were Americans assembling the apparatus for social and economic life with astonishing rapidity, but almost immediately they were beginning to explore the open opportunities stretching westward. In Joel Barlow's epic *The Columbiad*, which sums up much about the mind of America as it took charge of its political destiny, the angel Hesper foretells to Columbus the future "progress of arts in America" with the following priorities: "Fur trade. Fisheries. Productions. Commerce. Education. Philosophical discoveries. Painting. Poetry." Art—quite understandably, in fact—comes last, and theology here receives no mention at all.

1

While the most cultivated of the Virginians read and sometimes turned a hand to translating and imitating the Greek and Latin poets, most of their writing was not just prose but prosaic: documents dealing with administration, geographical surveys, descriptions of land and customs. The Puritans, often stereotyped as anti-aesthetic, produced much more and better poetry. The principle that guided their writing, as well as their architecture and music, is enunciated in William Bradford's statement at the beginning of his history of the Plymouth Plantation: He would use "a plain style, with singular regard unto the simple truth in all things." Yet all the Puritan hesitation about art and literature as fictitious imaginings, all the worry about excess and self-indulgence, all the suspicion of the senses and passions, all the moral commitment to truth above beauty, did not choke off artistic activity; the notion of the plain style provided the guidelines for writing poetry, not prescriptions against it. Thus, Edward Taylor's sternly orthodox theology did not keep him from composing verses notable, even among metaphysical poets, for their passionate energy and sensory detail. Much of the best Puritan poetry—not just Taylor's but Anne Bradstreet's and Philip Pain's as well—was not written for publication, and that assumption of privacy made for a powerful honesty, as it would in Emily Dickinson's poetry and much other American poetry not so strictly private as theirs.

Even before the Revolution Puritan rigor had relented to the point where *belles lettres* held a recognized place in a society that was trying to measure itself against England and the Continent by seeing whether it was capable of "polite writing." During the decades before and after the Revolution, when the polyglot country was trying to argue out its political character and trying to devise from its wranglings the appropriate collective forms and institutions, the word, written and spoken, was devoted mostly to politics and polemics, and the greatest literary figures from this period were public men addressing themselves like good eighteenth-century rationalists to public issues: Jefferson, Adams, Franklin, and so on. Even so, there were poetic voices on both major sides of the political debate. Philip Freneau became the Poet of the American Revolution, attacking British tyranny and exalting American heroism with the same excited sense of high purpose; after the war he spoke as a journalist for the Jeffersonian position while he aspired to be the first democratic poet of the American nation. At the same time, the "Connecticut Wits" established their claim as the first poetic clique in the New World. Cool, academic, consciously English and neoclassical, they settled on a Federalist conservatism that found its political image in Alexander Hamilton and on standards of taste that harkened back to the London of Pope and Swift. Centered in Hartford and at Yale College, they collaborated on such projects in satiric couplets as *The Anarchiad* and *The Echo*. John Trumbull used the rhymed tetrameters of Swift and of Samuel Butler's *Hudibras* for his down-to-earth caricatures in *The Progress of Dulness* (1772–73) and *M'Fingal* (1782). Timothy Dwight composed a ponderous epic called *The Conquest of Canaan* (1785), in which the progress of the Israelites under Joshua toward the promised land described allegorically the progress of the Americans under General Washington toward their national reward; he wrote *Greenfield Hill* (1794) to demonstrate that the new republic could yield pastoral poetry of philosophic seriousness worthy of Thomson and Denham and Goldsmith. The exception among the Wits was Joel Barlow, whose politics shifted under the influence of Paine's radicalism and whose writings showed a more independent spirit: *The Hasty Pudding* (1796) is a genuine American poem for all its literary antecedents, and *The Columbiad* (1807) projected the epic expectations of the new nation.

The opposition between the Connecticut Wits on the one side and Freneau and perhaps Barlow on the other—and more especially their sense of opposition —foreshadows divisions that would distinguish literary nationalists such as Emerson and Melville from American internationalists such as Irving and James; and still later divisions that would separate expatriates like Eliot and Pound and Gertrude Stein from poets like Williams and Hart Crane and Jeffers who made their poetry in and of America; and more contemporary divisions that set the beats and the projectivist poets against the academic formalists. But all of this was to come. Prior to the nineteenth century there are only the first attempts and the isolated achievements, skimmed from the welter of occasional poems: the expected panegyrics, wedding poems, elegies, and devotional verses.

Anne Bradstreet (1612?–1672)

Anne Bradstreet was probably born near Northampton, England, where her father, Thomas Dudley, was steward of the Puritan Earl of Lincoln. At sixteen she was married by arrangement to Simon Bradstreet, and came to America with her father and her husband aboard the *Arbella* under Governor Winthrop in the Great Migration of 1630. Her comment sums up her situation: "I found a new world and new manners, at which my heart rose. But after I was convinced it was the way of God, I submitted to it and joined the church at Boston." Both her husband and father were later governors of the colony.

The Bradstreets soon became pioneers of Ipswich and then of North Andover, Massachusetts. On the frontier Anne wrote long, conventional poems on such subjects as the four seasons and the four ages of man, and poetic tributes to Queen Elizabeth and her favorite poets, Sidney, Spenser, and the French Calvinist du Bartas. In 1650, without her knowledge, friends published a book of her verse under the grandiloquent title *The Tenth Muse Lately Sprung up in America.* It is the first book of poems to emerge from the New World. Anne Bradstreet also wrote prose meditations for her many children, and the lyrics about her husband and family published posthumously in 1678. The emotional depth and honesty of her lyrics transform the conventional conceits and metaphors into a personal statement. Her special place in the Colony is indicated by the number of verse tributes and elegies upon her death.

TEXT

Bradstreet, Anne. *The Works of Anne Bradstreet.* Ed. Jeannine Hensley. Cambridge, Mass.: Harvard University Press, 1967.

REFERENCE

Piercy, Josephine K. *Anne Bradstreet.* New York: Twayne, 1965.
White, Elizabeth Wade. *Anne Bradstreet: The Tenth Muse.* New York: Oxford University Press, 1971.

THE AUTHOR TO HER BOOK

Thou ill-formed offspring of my feeble brain,
Who after birth didst by my side remain,
Till snatched from thence by friends, less wise then[1] true,
Who thee abroad, expos'd to publick view,
5   Made thee in raggs, halting to th' press to trudg,
Where errors were not lessened (all may judge)[.]
At thy return my blushing was not small,
My rambling brat (in print) should mother call,
I cast thee by as one unfit for light,
10   Thy Visage was so irksome in my sight;
Yet being mine own, at length affection would
Thy blemishes amend, if so I could:
I wash'd thy face, but more defects I saw,
And rubbing off a spot still made a flaw.
15   I stretched thy joynts to make thee even feet,
Yet still thou run'st more hobling[2] then is meet;
In better dress to trim thee was my mind,
But nought save homespun Cloth i' th' house I find[.]
In this array 'mongst Vulgars may'st thou roam[.]
20   In Criticks hands, beware thou dost not come;
And take thy way where yet thou are not known,
If for thy Father asked, say, thou hadst none:
And for thy Mother, she alas is poor,
Which caus'd her thus to send thee out of door.

BEFORE THE BIRTH OF ONE OF HER CHILDREN

All things within this fading world hath end,
Adversity doth still our joyes attend;
Not tyes so strong, no friends so dear and sweet,
But with death's parting blow is sure to meet.
5   The sentence past is most irrevocable,
A common thing, yet oh inevitable.
How soon, my Dear, death may my steps attend,
How soon't may be thy Lot to lose thy friend,
We are both ignorant, yet love bids me

---

[1]Regularly the texts of Bradstreet poems have "then" as "than."
[2]Hobbling.

10 These farewell lines to recommend to thee,
    That when that knot's untyd that made us one,
    I may seem thine, who in effect am none.
    And if I see not half my dayes that's due,
    What nature would, God grant to yours and you;
15 The many faults that well you know I have,
    Let be interr'd in my oblivions grave;
    If any worth or virtue were in me,
    Let that live freshly in thy memory
    And when thou feel'st no grief, as I no harms,
20 Yet love thy dead, who long lay in thine arms:
    And when thy loss shall be repaid with gains
    Look to my little babes[,] my dear remains.
    And if thou love thy self, or loved'st me[,]
    These o protect from step Dames injury.
25 And if chance to thine eyes shall bring this verse,
    With some sad sighs honour my absent Herse;[1]
    And kiss this paper for thy loves dear sake,
    Who with salt tears this last Farewel did take.

TO MY DEAR AND LOVING HUSBAND

    If ever two were one, then surely we.
    If ever man were lov'd by wife, then thee;
    If ever wife was happy in a man,
    Compare with me ye women if you can.
5   I prize thy love more then whole Mines of gold,
    Or all the riches that the East doth hold.
    My love is such that Rivers cannot quench,
    Nor ought but love from thee, give recompence.
    Thy love is such I can no way repay,
10 The heavens reward thee manifold I pray.
    Then while we live, in love lets so persever,
    That when we live no more, we may live ever.

[1]Hearse.

A LETTER TO HER HUSBAND, ABSENT UPON PUBLICK EMPLOYMENT

My head, my heart, mine Eyes, my life, nay more,
My joy, my Magazine of earthly store,
If two be one, as surely thou and I,
How stayest thou there, whilst I at *Ipswich* lye?
5 So many steps, head from the heart to sever[,]
If but a neck, soon should we be together:
I[,] like the earth this season, mourn in black,
My Sun is gone so far in's Zodiack,
Whom whilst I 'joyed, nor storms, nor frosts I felt,
10 His warmth such frigid colds did cause to melt.
My chilled limbs now nummed[1] lye forlorn;
Return, return sweet *Sol* from *Capricorn*;[2]
In this dead time, alas, what can I more
Then view those fruits which through thy heat I bore?
15 Which sweet contentment yield me for a space,
True living Pictures of their Fathers face.
O strange effect! now thou art *Southward* gone,
I weary grow, the tedious day so long;
But when thou *Northward* to me shalt return,
20 I with my Sun may never set, but burn
Within the Cancer of my glowing breast,
The welcome house of him my dearest guest.
Where ever, ever stay, and go not thence,
Till natures sad decree shall call thee hence;
25 Flesh of thy flesh, bone of thy bone,
I here, thou there, yet both but one.

[1]Numbed.
[2]Capricorn is a constellation of the Southern Hemisphere and the tenth sign of the astrological zodiac, ruling from late December to late January. Cancer is a constellation of the Northern Hemisphere and the fourth sign of the zodiac, ruling from late June to late July. The tropics of Capricorn and of Cancer are the latitudes marking the southern and northern boundaries of the Torrid Zone, for which the equator is the central latitude. Thus Capricorn and Cancer represent opposites in direction and in season, and are complementary astrological signs, Capricorn being a "masculine" and Cancer a "feminine" sign.

VERSES UPON THE BURNING
OF OUR HOUSE, JULY 10TH, 1966

In silent night when rest I took,
For sorrow neer I did not look,
I waken'd was with thundring nois
And Piteous shrieks of dreadfull voice.
5   That fearfull sound of fire and fire,
Let no man know is my Desire.

I, starting up, the light did spye,
And to my God my heart did cry
To strengthen me in my Distresse
10   And not to leave me succorlesse.
Then coming out beheld a space,
The flame consume my dwelling place.

And, when I could no longer look,
I blest his Name that gave and took,
15   That layd my goods now in the dust:
Yea so it was, and so 'twas just.
It was his own: it was not mine;
Far be it that I should repine.

He might of All justly bereft,
20   But yet sufficient for us left.
When by the Ruines oft I past,
My sorrowing eyes aside did cast,
And here and there the places spye
Where oft I sate, and long did lye.

25   Here stood that Trunk, and there that chest;
There lay that store I counted best:
My pleasant things in ashes lye,
And them behold no more shall I.
Under my roof no guest shall sitt,
30   Nor at thy Table eat a bitt.

No pleasant tale shall 'ere be told,
Nor things recounted done of old.
No Candle 'ere shall shine in Thee,
Nor bridegroom's voice ere heard shall bee.

35 In silence ever shalt thou lye;
Adieu, Adieu; All's vanity.[1]

Then streight I 'gin my heart to chide,
And did thy wealth on earth abide?
Didst fix thy hope on mouldring dust,
40 The arm of flesh didst make thy trust?
Raise up thy thoughts above the skye
That dunghill mists away may flie.

Thou hast an house on high erect,
Fram'd by that mighty Architect,
45 With glory richly furnished,
Stands permanent though this be fled.
It's purchased, and paid for too
By him who hath enough to doe.

A prise[2] so vast as is unknown,
50 Yet, by his Gift, is made thine own.
Ther's wealth enough, I need no more;
Farewell my Pelf, farewell my Store.
The world no longer let me Love,
My hope and Treasure lyes Above.

AS WEARY PILGRIM, NOW AT REST

As weary pilgrim, now at rest,
   Hugs with delight his silent nest[,]
His wasted limbes now lye full soft
   That myrie[1] steps have troden oft[,]
5 Blesses himself to think upon
   His dangers past, and travails done[.]
The burning sun no more shall heat[,]
   Nor stormy rains on him shall beat.
The bryars and thornes no more shall scratch
10   Nor Hungry wolves at him shall catch.
He erring pathes no more shall tread[,]
   Nor wild fruits eate, in stead of bread,

---

[1]Eccles. 1:2: "Vanity of vanities, all is vanity."
[2]Price.

---

[1]Mirey.

For waters cold he doth not long
   For thirst no more shall parch his tongue[.]
15 No rugged stones his feet shall gaule[,]
   Nor stumps nor rocks cause him to fall[.]
All cares and feares, he bids farewell
   And meanes in safity now to dwell.
A pilgrim I, on earth, perplext
20   With sinns with cares and sorrows vext[,]
By age and paines brought to decay
   And my Clay house mouldring away[.]
Oh how I long to be at rest
   And soare on high among the blest.
25 This body shall in silence sleep[,]
   Mine eyes no more shall ever weep[,]
No fainting fits shall me assaile[,]
   Nor grinding paines my body fraile[,]
With cares and fears ne'r cumbred be
30   Nor losses know, nor sorrows see[.]
What though my flesh shall there consume[;]
   It is the bed Christ did perfume[.]
And when a few yeares shall be gone
   This mortal shall be cloth'd upon[.]
35 A Corrupt Carcasse downe it lyes[,]
   A glorious body it shall rise[.]
In weaknes and dishonour sowne[,]
   In power 'tis rais'd by Christ alone[.]
Then soule and body shall unite
40   And of their maker have the sight[.]
Such lasting joyes shall there behold
   As ear ne'r heard nor tongue e'er told[.]
Lord make me ready for that day[;]
   Then Come deare bridgrome[2] Come away.

Aug. 31, 1669.

---

[2]Bridegroom.

Philip Pain (d. 1668?)　Nothing is known about Philip Pain except that as a very young man he "lately suffering Shipwrack, was drowned." Even this we know only from the title page of a slim volume of verse, called *Daily Meditations; or, Quotidian Preparations for, and Considerations of Death and Eternity, Begun July 19, 1666.* Only one copy of the 1668 edition survives, the rest destroyed through popular use. Pain's meditations, which show the reading of George Herbert and Francis Quarles, record a personal struggle: an afflicted spirit wrangling against his fears in the name of religious conviction.

THE PORCH

To live's a Gift, to dye's a Debt that we
Each of us owe unto Mortality.
What, though the dead do ghastly look, and we
Like Children frighted are even but to be
5   Spectators of a dying man or woman?
Yet nothing's to be fear'd that is so common.
It is not *Death* that we in them do see;
It's but the *Mask* wherewith 'twill vailed be.
Yet where's the man or woman that can look
10   Death in the face, as in some pleasing book?
Can we contented be to view our face
In such a dreadful, doleful Looking-glass?
O where's the man or woman that can cry,
Behold I come, Death I desire to die?
15   O where's the man or woman that can say,
Lord, I desire my dissolution day?
And what's the reason 'tis so hard to dye,
To leave this world so full of vanity?
What makes it terrible? nought but the sense
20   Of *guilt & sin:* Break down this potent fence,
And then be sure for aye you shall enjoy
Joyes everlasting, Everlasting joy.

MEDITATION 8

Scarce do I pass a day, but that I hear
Some one or other's dead; and to my ear
Me thinks it is no news: but Oh! did I
Think deeply on it, what it is to dye,
5   My pulses all would beat, I should not be
Drown'd in this Deluge of Security.

MEDITATION 10

Alas, what is the *World?* a Sea of Glass.
Alas, what's *Earth?* it's but an Hower-glass.
The Sea dissolves; the Glass is quickly run:
Behold, with speed man's Life is quickly done.
5   Let me so swim in this Sea, that I may
    With thee live happy in another day.

MEDITATION 62

How is it that I am so careless here,
And never mind how I my Course do steer
For an Eternal Port? and never think
That at the last my leaky Ship will sink?
5   Lord, guard me from those Pirats that would catch
    My Soul, do thou (Lord) be their over-match.

Edward Taylor (1642?–1729)

Taylor was born in Leicestershire during the Civil War, the son of a prosperous yeoman farmer of Puritan convictions. Unwilling to subscribe to the Act of Uniformity after the Restoration, he came to Boston in 1668. By this time his education was already begun, and his appreciation of the metaphysical poets already set. After graduating from Harvard College in 1671, Taylor accepted a call from the frontier hamlet of Westfield and remained minister there until his retirement in 1725. He had a large number of children by each of his two wives. Taylor was known for the staunch orthodoxy of his theological position, and his library of perhaps 200 books was a remarkable collection.

At his death he left a bound 400-page manuscript of his unpublished poetical works, containing several individual poems and two long sequences: *God's Determinations Touching His Elect,* a part-lyric, part-allegorical presentation of the redemption of the elect, written in various meters and probably completed before 1690; and the *Preparatory Meditations Before My Approach to the Lords Supper. Chiefly upon the Doctrine Preached upon the Day of Administration,* written probably on the text of the Sunday sermon, in the same six-line stanza about every two months between 1682 and 1725 before receiving and administering communion to his congregation. The manuscripts were discovered by Thomas H. Johnson in the Yale Library in 1937.

In Taylor's roughness of diction and rhythm, in his sometimes clumsy honesty and sometimes eccentric individuality, we hear the idiom and temper of American poetic speech begin to separate itself from the more restrained and civilized tradition of English verse.

TEXT

Taylor, Edward. *The Poems of Edward Taylor.* Ed. Donald Stanford. New Haven: Yale University Press, 1960.

REFERENCE

Grabo, Norman. *Edward Taylor.* New York: Twayne, 1961.

from **God's Determinations Touching His Elect**

THE PREFACE

Infinity, when all things it beheld
In Nothing, and of Nothing all did build,
Upon what Base was fixt the Lath, wherein
He turn'd this Globe, and riggalld[1] it so trim?
5   Who blew the Bellows of his Furnace Vast?
Or held the Mould wherein the world was Cast?
Who laid its Corner Stone? Or whose Command?
Where stand the Pillars upon which it stands?
Who Lac'de and Fillitted[2] the earth so fine,
10   With Rivers like green Ribbons Smaragdine?
Who made the Sea's its Selvedge,[3] and it[s] locks
Like a Quilt Ball within a Silver Box?
Who Spread its Canopy? Or Curtains Spun?
Who in this Bowling Alley bowld the Sun?
15   Who made it always when it rises set
To go at once both down, and up to get?
Who th' Curtain rods made for this Tapistry?
Who hung the twinckling Lanthorns in the Sky?
Who? who did this? or who is he? Why, know
20   Its Onely Might Almighty this did doe.
His hand hath made this noble worke which Stands
His Glorious Handywork not made by hands.
Who spake all things from nothing and with ease
Can speake all things to nothing, if he please.
25   Whose Little finger at his pleasure Can
Out mete ten thousand worlds with halfe a Span:
Whose Might Almighty can by half a looks
Root up the rocks and rock the hills by th'roots.
Can take this mighty World up in his hande,
30   And shake it like a Squitchen[4] or a Wand.
Whose single Frown will make the Heavens shake
Like as an aspen leafe the Winde makes quake.
Oh! what a might is this Whose single frown
Doth shake the world as it would shake it down?

---

[1]Verb formed from the noun *riggal* "ring-like mark" (or "groove in wood or stone"?). [Most of the definitions of obscure words come from the Glossary provided by Donald E. Stanford in his edition of Taylor's *Poems* cited above.]
[2]Bound or girded with an ornamental band.
[3]Border or edge.
[4]Variant of *scutcheon* ("piece of bark used in grafting").

35   Which All from Nothing fet,[5] from Nothing All:
    Hath All on Nothing set, lets Nothing fall.
    Gave All to nothing Man indeed, whereby
    Through nothing man all might him Glorify.
    In Nothing then inbosst[6] the brightest Gem
40   More pretious than all pretiousness in them.
    But Nothing man did throw down all by Sin:
    And darkened that lightsom Gem in him.
        That now his Brightest Diamond is grown
        Darker by far than any Coalpit Stone.

OUR INSUFFICIENCY TO PRAISE GOD SUITABLY, FOR HIS MERCY

Should all the World so wide to atoms fall
    Should th'Aire be shred to motes, should we
Se all the Earth hackt here so small
        That none Could smaller bee?
5   Should Heaven, and Earth be Atomizd, we guess
The Number of these Motes were numberless.

But should we then a World each Atom deem,
    Where dwell as many pious men
    As all these Motes the world Could teem
10   Were it shred into them?
Each Atom would the World surmount wee guess
Whose men in number would be numberless.

But had each pious man, as many Tongues
    At singing all together then
15   The Praise that to the Lord belongs
        As all these Atoms men?
Each man would sing a World of Praise, we guess,
Whose Tongues in number would be numberless.

And had each Tongue, as many Songs of Praise
20   To sing to the Almighty ALL
    As all these men have Tongues to raise
        To him their Holy Call?

[5]Fetched.
[6]Embossed, or carved with a raised design.

Each Tongue would tune a World of Praise, we guess
Whose songs in number would be numberless.

25 Nay, had each song as many Tunes most sweet
        Or one intwisting in't as many,
        As all these Tongues have songs most meet
            Unparallelld by any?
    Each song a world of Musick makes we guess
30 Whose Tunes in number would be numberless.

    Now should all these Conspire in us that we
        Could breath such Praise to thee, Most High?
        Should we thy Sounding Organs be
            To ring such Melody?
35 Our Musick would the World of Worlds out ring
    Yet be unfit within thine Eares to ting.[1]

    Thou didst us mould, and us new mould when wee
        Were worse than mould we tread upon.
        Nay Nettles made by Sin wee bee.
40   Yet hadst Compassion.
    Thou hast pluckt out our Stings; and by degrees
    Hast of us, lately Wasps, made Lady-Bees.

    Though e're our Tongues thy Praises due can fan
        A Weevle with the World may fly,
45   Yea fly away: and with a span
            We may out mete the Sky.
    Though what we can is but a Lisp, We pray
    Accept thereof. We have no better pay.

from **Preparatory Meditations . . . First Series**

1. MEDITATION

    What Love is this of thine, that Cannot bee
        In thine Infinity, O Lord, Confinde,
    Unless it in thy very Person see,
        Infinity, and Finity Conjoyn'd?
5   What hath thy Godhead, as not satisfide
        Marri'de our Manhood, making it its Bride?

[1]Ring.

    Oh, Matchless Love! filling Heaven to the brim!
      O're running it: all running o're beside
  This World! Nay Overflowing Hell; wherein
10   For thine Elect, there rose a mighty Tide!
      That there our Veans might through thy Person bleed,
      To quench those flames, that else would on us feed.

    Oh! that thy Love might overflow my Heart!
      To fire the same with Love: for Love I would.
15   But oh! my streight'ned Breast! my Lifeless Sparke!
      My Fireless Flame! What Chilly Love, and Cold?
      In measure small! In Manner Chilly! See.
  Lord blow the Coal: Thy Love Enflame in mee.

2. MEDITATION ON CANTICLES' 1:3.
THY NAME IS AN OINTMENT POURED OUT

*[Delicate is the fragrance of your perfume, your
name is ointment poured out, that is why maidens
love you.]*

    My Dear, Deare, Lord I do thee Saviour Call:
      Thou in my very Soul art, as I Deem,
  Soe High, not High enough, Soe Great; too small:
      Soe Deare, not Dear enough in my esteem.
5   Soe Noble, yet So Base: too Low; too Tall:
      Thou Full, and Empty art: Nothing, yet ALL.

    A Precious Pearle, above all price dost 'bide.
      Rubies no Rubies are at all to thee.
  Blushes of burnisht Glory Sparkling Slide
10   From every Square in various Colour'd glee
      Nay Life itselfe in Sparkling Spangles Choice.
      A Precious Pearle thou art above all price.

---

[1]Canticles is another name for The Song of Songs in the Old Testament.

Oh! that my Soul, Heavens Workmanship (within
My Wicker'd Cage,) that Bird of Paradise
15   Inlin'de with Glorious Grace up to the brim
Might be thy Cabbinet, oh Pearle of Price.
Oh! let thy Pearle, Lord, Cabbinet in mee.
I'st then be rich! nay rich enough for thee.

My Heart, oh Lord, for thy Pomander gain.
20   Be thou thyselfe my sweet Perfume therein.
Make it thy Box, and let thy Pretious Name
My Pretious Ointment be emboxt therein.
If I thy box and thou my Ointment bee
I shall be sweet, nay, sweet enough for thee.

25   Enough! Enough! oh! let me eat my Word.
For if Accounts be ballanc'd any way,
Can my poore Eggeshell ever be an Hoard,
Of Excellence enough for thee? Nay: nay.
Yet may I Purse, and thou my Mony bee.
30   I have enough. Enough in having thee.

3. MEDITATION. CANTICLES 1:3.
THY GOOD OINTMENT

How sweet a Lord is mine? If any should
Guarded, Engarden'd, nay, Imbosomed bee
In reechs[1] of Odours, Gales of Spices, Folds
Of Aromaticks, Oh! how sweet was hee?
5   He would be sweet, and yet his sweetest Wave
Compar'de to thee my Lord, no Sweet would have.

A Box of Ointments, broke; sweetness most sweet.
A surge of spices: Odours Common Wealth,
A Pillar of Perfume: a steaming Reech
10   Of Aromatick Clouds: All Saving Health.
Sweetness itselfe thou art: And I presume
In Calling of thee Sweet, who are Perfume.

[1]Reek, odor.

But Woe is mee! who have so quick a Sent
   To Catch perfumes pufft out from Pincks, and Roses
15 And other Muscadalls,[2] as they get Vent,
   Out of their Mothers Wombs to bob our noses.
   And yet thy sweet perfume doth seldom latch
   My Lord, within my Mammulary[3] Catch.

Am I denos'de? or doth the Worlds ill sents
20   Engarison my nosthrills narrow bore?
Or is my smell lost in these Damps it Vents?
   And shall I never finde it any more?
   Or is it like the Hawks, or Hownds whose breed
     Take stincking Carrion for Perfume indeed?

25 This is my Case. All things smell sweet to mee:
   Except thy sweetness, Lord. Expell these damps.
Breake up this Garison: and let me see
   Thy Aromaticks pitching in these Camps.
   Oh! let the Clouds of thy sweet Vapours rise,
30   And both my Mammularies Circumcise.

Shall Spirits thus my Mammularies suck?
   (As Witches Elves their teats,) and draw from thee
My Dear, Dear Spirit after fumes of muck?
   Be Dunghill Damps more sweet than Graces bee?
35   Lord, clear these Caves. These Passes take, and keep.
   And in these Quarters lodge thy Odours sweet.

Lord, breake thy Box of Ointment on my Head;
   Let thy sweet Powder powder all my hair:
My Spirits let with thy perfumes be fed
40   And make thy Odours, Lord, my nosthrills fare.
   My Soule shall in thy sweets then soar to thee:
I'le be thy Love, thou my sweet Lord shalt bee.

---

[2]The grapes from which muscatel wine is made; or the muscadell pears.
[3]Nipple, breast. (In his edition of Taylor's poems, Thomas H. Johnson suggests that Taylor uses the word to refer to the nose and the sense of smell.)

5. MEDITATION. CANTICLES 2:1.
THE LILLY OF THE VALLIES

[I am the rose of Sharon, and the lily of the valleys.]

My Blessed Lord, art thou a Lilly Flower?
  Oh! that my Soul thy Garden were, that so
Thy bowing Head root in my Heart, and poure
  Might of its Seeds, that they therein might grow.
5   Be thou my Lilly, make thou me thy knot:
  Be thou my Flowers, I'le be thy Flower Pot.

My barren heart thy Fruitfull Vally make:
  Be thou my Lilly flouerishing in mee:
Oh Lilly of the Vallies. For thy sake,
10   Let me thy Vally, thou my Lilly bee.
  Then nothing shall me of thyselfe bereave.
  Thou must not me, or must thy Vally leave.

How shall my Vallie's Spangling Glory spred,
  Thou Lilly of the Vallies Spangling
15 There springing up? Upon thy bowing Head
  All Heavens bright Glory hangeth dangling.
  My Vally then with Blissful Beams shall shine,
  Thou Lilly of the Vallys, being mine.

7. MEDITATION. PSALMS 45:2.
GRACE IN THY LIPS IS POURED OUT

[Of all men you are the most handsome, your lips are moist
for God has blessed you forever.]

Thy Humane Frame, my Glorious Lord, I spy,
  A Golden Still with Heavenly Choice drugs filld;
Thy Holy Love, the Glowing heate whereby,
  The Spirit of Grace is graciously distilld.
5   Thy Mouth the Neck through which these spirits still.
  My Soul thy Violl make, and therewith fill.

Thy Speech the Liquour in thy Vessell stands,
  Well ting'd with Grace a blessed Tincture, Loe,
Thy Words distilld, Grace in thy Lips pour'd, and,
10   Give Graces Tinctur in them where they go.
  Thy words in graces tincture stilld, Lord, may
  The Tincture of thy Grace in me Convay.

That Golden Mint of Words, thy Mouth Divine,
  Doth tip[1] these Words, which by my Fall were spoild;
15 And Dub[2] with Gold dug out of Graces mine
  That they thine Image might have in them foild.[3]
  Grace in thy Lips pour'd out's as Liquid Gold.
  Thy Bottle make my Soule, Lord, it to hold.

8. MEDITATION. JOHN 6:51.
I AM THE LIVING BREAD

*[I am the living bread which has come down from
heaven. Anyone who eats this bread will live forever;
and the bread that I give is my flesh, for the life of
the world.]*

I kening[1] through Astronomy Divine
  The Worlds bright Battlement, wherein I spy
A Golden Path my Pensill cannot line,
  From that bright Throne unto my Threshold ly.
5   And while my puzzled thoughts about it pore
  I finde the Bread of Life in't at my doore.

When that this Bird of Paradise put in
  This Wicker Cage (my Corps) to tweedle praise
Had peckt the Fruite forbad:[2] and so did fling
10   Away its Food; and lost its golden dayes;
  It fell into Celestiall Famine sore:
  And never could attain a morsell more.

[1]Cover, decorate.
[2]Array, adorn.
[3]Covered with a thin sheet of metal.

[1]Catching sight of.
[2]Forbidden.

Alas! alas! Poore Birde, what wilt thou doe?
    The Creatures field no food for Souls e're gave.
15 And if thou knock at Angells dores they show
    An Empty Barrell: they no soul bread have.
    Alas! Poore Bird, the Worlds White Loafe is done.
    And cannot yield thee here the smallest Crumb.

In this sad state, Gods Tender Bowells[3] run
20   Our streams of Grace: And he to end all strife
The Purest Wheate in Heaven, his deare-dear Son
    Grinds, and kneads up into this Bread of Life.
    Which Bread of Life from Heaven down came and stands
    Disht on thy Table up by Angells Hands.

25 Did God mould up this Bread in Heaven, and bake,
    Which from his Table came, and to thine goeth?
Doth he bespeake thee thus, This Soule Bread take.
    Come Eate thy fill of this thy Gods White Loafe?
    Its Food too fine for Angells, yet come, take
30   And Eate thy fill. Its Heavens Sugar Cake.

What Grace is this knead in this Loafe? This thing
    Souls are but petty things it to admire.
Yee Angells, help: this fill would to the brim
    Heav'ns whelm'd-down Chrystall meele Bowle, yea and
        higher.
35   This Bread of Life dropt in thy mouth, doth Cry.
    Eate, Eate me, Soul, and thou shalt never dy.

---

[3]The bowels were considered the seat of pity and the gentler emotions in
the body.

23. MEDITATION. CANTICLES 4:8. MY SPOUSE

[Come from Lebanon, my spouse; come from Lebanon, come
on your way.]

Would God I in that Golden City[1] were,
    With Jaspers Walld, all garnisht, and made swash,
With Pretious Stones, whose Gates are Pearles most cleare
    And Street Pure Gold, like to transparent Glass.
5   That my dull Soule, might be inflamde to see
    How Saints and Angells ravisht are in Glee.

Were I but there, and could but tell my Story,
    'Twould rub those Walls of Pretious Stones more bright:
And glaze those Gates of Pearle, with brighter Glory;
10   And pave the golden Street with greater light.
    'Twould in fresh Raptures Saints, and Angells fling.
    But I poore Snake Crawl here, scarce mudwalld in.

May my Rough Voice, and my blunt Tongue but spell
    My Tale (for tune they can't) perhaps there may
15 Some Angell catch an end of't up, and tell
    In Heaven, when he doth return that way,
    He'l make thy Palace, Lord, all over ring,
    With it in Songs, thy Saint, and Angells sing.

I know not how to speak't, it is so good:
20   Shall Mortall, and Immortall marry? nay,
Man marry God? God be a Match for Mud?
    The King of Glory Wed a Worm? mere Clay?
    This is the Case. The Wonder too in Bliss.
    Thy Maker is thy Husband. Hearst thou this?

25 My Maker, he my Husband? Oh! strange joy!
    If Kings wed Worms, and Monarchs Mites wed should,
Glory spouse Shame, a Prince a Snake or Fly
    An Angell Court an Ant, all Wonder would.
    Let such wed Worms, Snakes, Serpents, Divells, Flyes.
30   Less Wonder than the Wedden in our Eyes.

---

[1]Zion, or the City of God. Much of the imagery here, as is true throughout
Taylor's poetry, is derived from Biblical sources.

I am to Christ more base, than to a King
    A Mite, Fly, Worm, Ant, Serpent, Divell is,
Or Can be, being tumbled all in Sin,
    And shall I be his Spouse? How good is this?
35   It is too good to be declar'de to thee.
    But not too good to be believ'de by mee.

Yet to this Wonder, this is found in mee,
    I am not onely base but backward Clay,
When Christ dot Wooe: and till his Spirit bee
40   His Spokes man to Compell me I deny.
    I am so base and Froward to him, Hee
    Appears as Wonders Wonder, wedding mee.

Seing, Dear Lord, its thus, thy Spirit take
    And send thy Spokes man, to my Soul, I pray.
45 Thy Saving Grace my Wedden Garment make:
    Thy Spouses Frame into my Soul Convay.
    I then shall be thy Bride Espousd by thee
    And thou my Bridesgroom Deare Espousde shalt bee.

29. MEDITATION. JOHN 20:17.
MY FATHER, AND YOUR
FATHER, TO MY GOD AND YOUR GOD

*[I am ascending to my Father and your Father, to my
God and your God.]*

My shattred Phancy stole away from mee,
    (Wits run a Wooling over Edens Parke)
And in Gods Garden saw a golden Tree,
    Whose Heart was All Divine, and gold its barke.
5   Whose glorious limbs and fruitful branches strong
    With Saints, and Angells bright are richly hung.

Thou! thou! my Deare-Deare Lord, art this rich Tree
    The Tree of Life Within Gods Paradise.
I am a Withred Twig, dri'de fit to bee

10   A Chat[1] Cast in thy fire, Writh[2] off by Vice.
      Yet if thy Milke white-Gracious Hand will take mee
    And grafft mee in this golden stock, thou'lt make mee.

    Thou'lt make me then its Fruite, and Branch to spring.
      And though a nipping Eastwinde blow, and all
15   Hells Nymps with spite their Dog's sticks thereat ding?[3]
      To Dash the Grafft off, and it's[4] fruits to fall,
      Yet I shall stand thy Grafft, and Fruits that are
      Fruits of the Tree of Life thy Grafft shall beare.

    I being grafft in thee there up do stand
20   In us Relations all that mutuall are.
    I am thy Patient, Pupill, Servant, and
      Thy Sister, Mother, Doove, Spouse, Son, and Heire.
      Thou are my Priest, Physician, Prophet, King,
      Lord, Brother, Bridegroom, Father, Ev'ry thing.

25   I being grafft in thee am graffted here
      Into thy Family, and kindred Claim
    To all in Heaven, God, Saints, and Angells there.
      I thy Relations my Relations name.
      Thy Father's mine, thy God my God, and I
30   With Saints, and Angells draw Affinity.

    My Lord, what is it that thou dost bestow?
      The Praise on this account fills up, and throngs
    Eternity brimfull, doth overflow
      The Heavens vast with rich Angelick Songs.
35   How should I blush? how Tremble at this thing,
      Not having yet my Gam-Ut,[5] learnd to sing.

    But, Lord, as burnish't Sun Beams forth out fly
      Let Angell-Shine forth in my Life out flame,
    That I may grace thy gracefull Family
40   And not to thy Relations be a Shame.
      Make mee thy Grafft, be thou my Golden Stock.
      Thy Glory then I'le make my fruits and Crop.

[1]Small branch.
[2]Writhed.
[3]Hurl.
[4]Its.
[5]Musical scale; technically, the "Great Scale" of all the recognized notes of medieval music.

38. MEDITATION. 1 JOHN 2:1.
AN ADVOCATE WITH THE FATHER

[If anyone should sin, we have our advocate with the
the Father, Jesus Christ, who is just.]

Oh! What a thing is Man? Lord, Who am I?
    That thou shouldst give him Law (Oh! golden Line)
To regulate his Thoughts, Words, Life thereby.
    And judge him Wilt thereby too in thy time.
5   A Court of Justice thou in heaven holdst
    To try his Case while he's here housd on mould.

How do thy Angells lay before thine eye
    My Deeds both White, and Black I dayly doe?
How doth thy Court thou Pannellst there them try?
10   But flesh complains. What right for this? let's know.
    For right, or wrong I can't appeare unto't.
    And shall a sentence Pass on such a suite?

Soft; blemish not this golden Bench, or place.
    Here is no Bribe, nor Colourings to hide
15 Nor Pettifogger to befog the Case
    But Justice hath her Glory here will tri'de.
    Her spotless Law all spotted Cases tends.
    Without Respect or Disrespect them ends.

God's Judge himselfe: and Christ Atturny is,
20   The Holy Ghost Regesterer is founde.
Angells the sergeants are, all Creatures kiss
    The booke, and doe as Evidences abounde.
    All Cases pass according to pure Law
    And in the sentence is no Fret, nor flaw.

25 What saist, my soule? Here all thy Deeds are tri'de.
    Is Christ thy Advocate to pleade thy Cause?
Art thou his Client? Such shall never slide.[1]
    He never lost his Case: he pleads such Laws
    As Carry do the same, nor doth refuse
30   The Vilest sinners Case that doth him Choose.

---

[1]Go unattended without action.

This is his Honour, not Dishonour: nay
   No Habeas-Corpus[2] gainst his Clients came
For all their Fines his Purse doth make down pay.
   He Non-Suites[3] Satan's Suite or Casts[4] the Same.
35   He'l plead thy Case, and not accept a Fee.
   He'l plead Sub Forma Pauperis[5] for thee.

My Case is bad. Lord, be my Advocate.
   My sin is red: I'me under Gods Arrest.
Thou hast the Hint of Pleading; plead my State.
40   Although it's bad thy Plea will make it best.
   If thou wilt plead my Case before the King:
   I'le Waggon Loads of Love, and Glory bring.

from **Preparatory Meditations . . . Second Series**

1. MEDITATION. COLOSSIANS 2:17 WHICH ARE SHADDOWS OF THINGS TO COME AND THE BODY IS CHRIST

[These were only pale reflections of what was coming: the reality is Christ.]

Oh Leaden heeld. Lord, give, forgive I pray.
   Infire my Heart: it bedded is in Snow.
I Chide myselfe seing myselfe decay.
   In heate and Zeale to thee, I frozen grow.
5   File my dull Spirits: make them sharp and bright:
   Them firbush[1] for thyselfe, and thy delight.

---

[2]A writ issued to bring a party before a court or judge; literal translation from the Latin: "You shall have the body."
[3]Brings the case to a "non-suit," in which the judge stops the legal action for the lack of sufficient evidence.
[4]Defeats in a legal action.
[5]Latin: "under the form for a poor person." That is, under provisions for a poor person exempted from paying legal costs.

---

[1]Furbish, polish.

My Stains are such, and sinke so deep, that all
    The Excellency in Created Shells
Too low, and little is to make it fall
10   Out of my leather Coate wherein it dwells.
    This Excellence is but a Shade to that
    Which is enough to make my Stains go back.

The glory of the world slickt up in types[2]
    In all Choise things chosen to typify,
15 His glory upon whom the worke doth light,
    To thine's a Shaddow, or a butterfly.
    How glorious then, my Lord, art thou to mee
    Seing to cleanse me, 's worke alone for thee.

The glory of all Types doth meet in thee.
20   Thy glory doth their glory quite excell:
More than the Sun excells in its bright glee
    A nat, an Earewig, Weevill, Snaile, or Shell.
    Wonders in Crowds start up; your eyes may strut
    Viewing his Excellence, and's bleeding cut.

25 Oh! that I had but halfe an eye to view
    This excellence of thine, undazled: so
Therewith to give my heart a touch anew
    Until I quicknd am, and made to glow.
    All is too little for thee: but alass
30   Most of my little all hath other pass.

Then Pardon, Lord, my fault: and let thy beams
    Of Holiness pierce through this Heart of mine.
Ope to thy Blood a passage through my veans.
    Let thy pure blood my impure blood refine.
35   Then with new blood and spirits I will dub
    My tunes upon thy Excellency good.

---

[2]Originally a person or object or occurrence in the Old Testament that fore-shadowed the New Testament, and so a way of reading the Bible history symbolically; by extension, a prefiguring emblem or symbol. Taylor's sense of the typology of nature itself anticipates and provides the religious basis for a symbolic reading of nature that would characterize many subsequent New England poets.

4. MEDITATION. GALATIANS 4:24.
WHICH THINGS ARE AN ALLEGORIE

[This can be regarded as an allegory: the women stand for the two covenants.]

My Gracious Lord, I would thee glory doe:
  But finde my Garden over grown with weeds:
My Soile is sandy; brambles o're it grow;
  My Stock is stunted; branch no good Fruits breeds.
5   My Garden weed: Fatten my Soile, and prune
My Stock, and make it with thy glory bloome.

O Glorious One, the gloriou'st thought I thincke
  Of thee falls black as Inck upon thy Glory.
The brightest Saints that rose, do Star like, pinck.[1]
10   Nay, Abrams[2] Shine to thee's an Allegory,
  Or fleeting Sparke in th'Smoke, to typify
Thee, and thy Glorious Selfe in mystery.

Should all the Sparks in heaven, the Stars there dance
  A Galliard, Round about the Sun, and stay
15 His Servants (while on Easter morn his prance
  Is o're, which old wives preate of) O brave Play.
Thy glorious Saints thus boss[3] thee round, which stand
Holding thy glorious Types out in their hand.

But can I thinck this Glory greate, its head
20   Thrust in a pitchy cloude, should strangled ly
  Or trucking up its beams should go to bed
  Within the Grave, darke me to glorify?
  This Mighty thought my hearts too streight for, though
  I hold it by the hand, and let not goe.

[1]Peep, wink.
[2]Abraham's. Abraham made the first covenant with God, which established the Israelites as His chosen people. So Abraham is a type of Jesus Christ and the New Covenant. For the meaning of "type" in this sense, see Note 2 to the previous poem
[3]Ornament with bosses—that is, a raised design.

25 Then, my Blesst Lord, let not the Bondmaids⁴ type
        Take place in mee. But thy blesst Promisd Seed.
    Distill thy Spirit through thy royall Pipe
        Into my Soule, and so my Spirits feed,
        Then them, and me still into praises right
30   Into thy Cup where I to swim delight.

    Though I desire so much, I can't o're doe.
        All that my Can contains, to nothing comes
    When summed up, it onely Cyphers grows
        Unless thou set thy Figures to my Sums.
35   Lord set thy Figure 'fore them, greate, or small.
        To make them something, and I'l give thee all.

60. MEDITATION. CORINTHIANS 10.4.
AND ALL DRUNK THE SAME SPIRITUALL DRINKE¹

*[They were all baptized into Moses in this cloud and in
this sea; all ate the same spiritual food and all drank
the same spiritual drink, since they all drank from the
spiritual rock that followed them as they went, and
that rock was Christ.]*

Ye Angells bright, pluck from your Wings a Quill.
    Make me a pen thereof that best will write.
Lende me your fancy, and Angellick skill
    To treate this Theme, more rich than Rubies bright.
5   My muddy Inke, and Cloudy fancy dark,
    Will dull its glory, lacking highest Art.

---

⁴St. Paul's Epistle to the Galatians, 4:22: "It is written that Abraham had two
sons, the one by the bondmaid [Ishmael born of Hagar], the other by a free-
woman [Isaac born of Sarah]. But he who was of the bondwoman was born
after the flesh; but he of the freewoman was by promise." Hence the "alle-
gory" of the text for the poem: the bondwoman's son is a type of the un-
redeemed; the freewoman's son, a type of the redeemed.

---

¹The imagery of the poem brings together various types demonstrating God's
covenant with His people through their leader Moses. "Horeb's rock" is the
mountain in Sinai where God gave the Tablets of the Law to Moses. The other
rock, struck by Moses with his rod, poured out water in the desert for the
Israelites on their exodus from Egypt to find the Promised Land. The poem
then construes the types.

An Eye at Centre righter may describe
   The Worlds Circumferentiall glory vast
As in its nutshell bed it snugs fast tide,
10   Than any angells pen can glory Cast
   Upon this Drink Drawn from the Rock, tapt by
   The Rod of God, in Horeb, typickly.

Sea water straind through Mineralls, Rocks, and Sands
   Well Clarifi'de by Sunbeams, Dulcifi'de,[2]
15 Insipid, Sordid, Swill, Dishwater stands.
   But here's a Rock of Aqua-Vitae[3] tride.
   When once God broacht it, out a River came
   To bath and bibble in, for Israels train.

Some Rocks have sweat. Some Pillars bled out tears.
20   But here's a River in a Rock up tun'd
Not of Sea Water nor of Swill. Its beere.
   No Nectar like it. Yet it once Unbund[4]
   A River down out runs through ages all.
   A Fountain opte,[5] to wash off Sin and Fall.

25   Christ is this Horebs Rock, the streames that slide
   A River is of Aqua Vitae Deare
Yet costs us nothing, gushing from his side.
   Celestiall Wine our Sinsunk souls to cheare.
   This Rock and Water, Sacramentall Cup
30   Are made, Lords Supper Wine for us to sup.

This Rock's the Grape that Zions Vineyard bore
   Which Moses Rod did smiting pound, and press
Untill its blood, the brooke of Life, run ore.
   All Glorious Grace, and Gacious Righteousness.
35   We in this brook must bath: and with faiths quill
   Suck Grace, and Life out of this Rock our fill.

Lord, oynt[6] me with this Petro oyle. I'm sick.
   Make mee drinke Water of the Rock. I'm dry.

[2]Sweetened.
[3]Any brandy or medicinal liquor. Literally "water of life."
[4]Unbound. The compressed construction for: "once it was unbound."
[5]Opened.
[6]Anoint; rub with oil.

Me in this fountain wash. My filth is thick.
40   I'm faint, give Aqua Vitae or I dy.
If in this stream thou cleanse and Chearish mee
My Heart thy Hallelujahs Pipe shall bee.

UPON A WASP CHILD[1] WITH COLD

The Bare[2] that breaths the Northern blast
Did numb, Torpedo like, a Wasp
Whose stiffend limbs encrampt, lay bathing
In Sol's[3] warm breath and shine as saving,
5 Which with her hands she chafes and stands
Rubbing her Legs, Shanks, Thighs, and hands.
Her petty toes, and fingers ends
Nipt with this breath, she out extends
Unto the Sun, in greate desire
10 To warm her digits[4] at that fire.
Doth hold her Temples in this state
Where pulse doth beate, and head doth ake.
Doth turn, and stretch her body small,
Doth Comb her velvet Capitall.[5]
15 As if her little brain pan were
A Volume of Choice precepts cleare.
As if her sattin jacket hot
Contained Apothecaries Shop
Of Natures recepts, that prevails
20 To remedy all her sad ailes,
As if her velvet helmet high
Did turret rationality.[6]
She fans her wing up to the Winde
As if her Pettycoate were lin'de,
25 With reasons fleece, and hoises[7] sails

---

[1]Chilled.
[2]The constellations Ursa Major and Minor, the Greater Bear and the Lesser Bear, both associated with the North. The North Star is the last star in the handle of the Little Dipper, which is part of the Lesser Bear, and the lip of the Big Dipper, which is part of the Greater Bear, points to the North Star.
[3]The Sun's.
[4]Fingers.
[5]From the Latin word for "head."
[6]That is, as if her head were a turret of reason, as if the wasp were a rational creature.
[7]Hoists.

And hu'ming flies in thankfull gails
Unto her dun Curld palace Hall
Her warm thanks offering for all.

Lord cleare my misted sight that I
30 May hence view thy Divinity.
Some sparkes whereof thou up dost hasp
Within this little downy Wasp
In whose small Corporation[8] wee
A school and a schoolmaster see
35 Where we may learn, and easily finde
A nimble Spirit bravely minde
Her worke in e'ry limb: and lace
It up neate with a vitall grace,
Acting each part though ne'er so small
40 Here of this Fustian animall.
Till I enravisht Climb into
The Godhead on this Lather[9] doe.
Where all my pipes inspir'de upraise
An Heavenly musick furrd[10] with praise.

---

[8]From the Latin word for "body."
[9]Ladder.
[10]Trimmed; covered over.

Anonymous (eighteenth century)   The author of *Poems on Several Occasions by a Gentleman of Virginia* is unknown and unidentified, but when his verses were issued in Williamsburg in 1736, with a quotation from Cicero on the title page, he declared them to be "the casual Production of Youth," and concluded that if the reader "finds them unworthy of his Approbation, the Author takes this Opportunity of being the first in giving his Vote, that he never hereafter publish any more." However, some of his imitations of classical and neoclassical models have charm and wit, as the Virginia gentleman turned a graceful verse in his spare time to amuse himself and his friends.

TO SYLVIA. AN IMITATION OF ANACREON[1]

Oft I string the *Lydian*[2] Lyre,
Oft in noble Strains aspire
To sing the Glories of that Face,
Each secret Charm, each nameless Grace;
5   But still the disobedient Strings do move
In softest Notes, and murmur nought but Love.

Oft with witty quaint Conceit,
I vainly strive to celebrate
That, which no Colours can reveal
10   Which we only see, and only feel:
But still the disobedient Strings do move
In softest Notes, and murmur nought but Love.

Farewel, wild impetuous Ode;
Farewel, *Phoebus*,[3] mighty God
15   Of well turn'd Wit; with all your Train,
The frantick Off-spring of the Brain.
But welcome, gentle Lyre, whose Strings do move
In softest Notes, and murmur nought but Love.

Tell her, in soft pathetic Strains,
20   All my Anguish, all my Pains;
Tell her, I love, I rave, I die;
I dare not speak, I cannot fly.
Tell her, all this, ye gentle Strings, that move
In softest Notes, and murmur nought but love.

---

[1]Greek poet, fifth and sixth centuries B.C, famous for poems in praise of love
and wine.
[2]Lydia was an ancient country on the Aegean Sea.
[3]Phoebus Apollo, the god of poetry.

EPIGRAM

Scaurus[1] hates *Greek*, and is become
    Mere *Trojan* in his Spight;
But why so fierce against the Men,
    So learned and polite?

5   The *Trojans* stole, and kept by Force
      A Dame, elop'd from Duty;[2]
    But you can't plead e'en this Pretence
      Of having stole one BEAUTY.

TO A FRIEND, WHO
RECOMMENDED A WIFE TO HIM

I own, the Match, you recommend,
    Is far above my mean Desert;
I own, you've acted like a Friend,
    A hearty, kind, and gen'rous Part.

5   But Marriage, Sir, 's a serious Case;
      Maturest Thought should chuse a Wife;
    Tho' some aver, the wisest Way's
      To think upon it all one's Life.

[1]Apparently a Latin name coined by the author for an acquaintance.
[2]Paris, son of King Priam of Troy, eloped with Helen, wife of King Menelaus of Sparta, thus precipitating the war between Greece and Troy that was the source of much Greek myth and poetry.

Philip Freneau (1752–1832)

Freneau's moderately wealthy New York family moved to an estate called Mount Pleasant, New Jersey, before he entered Princeton. There he wrote "The Power of Fancy" and, with Hugh Brackenridge, "The Rising Glory of America." He graduated in 1771, and after a stint in the West Indies became a soldier and later a blockade runner during the Revolution. His capture provided the vehemence for his verse polemic, "The British Prison Ship" (1781). After the war he became an editor and a sea captain as well as a poet. He ran *The Freeman's Journal* and, with Jefferson's backing, the anti-Federalist *National Gazette,* which attacked Hamilton and his literary counterparts, the Connecticut Wits.

Today, Freneau's public and patriotic poems sound bombastic and unrestrained; his philosophical poems on the benevolence of nature's plan seem almost parodic; his poems about the American Indian sound patronizing and sentimental. However, Freneau had high ambitions for an American literature and for himself as the first major American poet. His last seven years were spent in relative obscurity; he died of exposure after getting lost in a snowstorm, and was buried under a stone that read "Poet's Grave."

TEXT

Freneau, Philip. *Poems of Freneau.* Ed. F. L. Pattee. Princeton, N. J.: The University Library, 1902–1907.

REFERENCE

Axelrad, Jacob. *Philip Freneau: Champion of Democracy.* Austin: University of Texas Press, 1967.

Marsh, Philip M. *Philip Freneau: Poet and Journalist.* Minneapolis: Dillon Press, 1968.

A PICTURE OF THE TIMES[1]

With Occasional Reflections

Still round the world triumphant Discord flies,
Still angry kings to bloody contest rise;
Hosts bright with steel, in dreadful order plac'd,
And ships contending on the watery waste;
5 Distracting demons every breast engage,
Unwearied nations glow with mutual rage;
Still to the charge the routed Briton turns,
The war still rages and the battle burns;
See, man with man in deadly combat join,
10 See, the black navy form the flaming line;
Death smiles alike at battles lot or won—
Art does for him what Nature would have done.
    Can scenes like these delight the human breast?—
Who sees with joy humanity distrest;
15 Such tragic scenes fierce passion might prolong,
But slighted Reason says, they must be wrong.
    Curs'd be the day, how bright soe'er it shin'd,
That first made kings the masters of mankind;
And curs'd the wretch who first with regal pride
20 Their equal rights to equal men deny'd.
But curs'd o'er all, who first to slav'ry broke
Submissive bow'd and own'd a monarch's yoke,
Their servile souls his arrogance ador'd
And basely own'd a brother for a lord;
25 Hence wrath and blood, and feuds and wars began,
And man turned monster to his fellow man.
    Not so that age of innocence and ease
When men, yet social, knew no ills like these;
Then dormant yet, ambition (half unknown)
30 No rival murder'd to possess a throne;
No seas to guard, no empires to defend—
Of some small tribe the father and the friend.
The hoary sage beneath his sylvan shade
Impos'd no laws but those which reason made;
35 On peace not war, on good not ill intent,

---

[1]First published in the July 19, 1782, issue of *The Freeman's Journal*, which Freneau edited, and written between the final defeat of Cornwallis at Yorktown in October 1781, and the signing of the preliminary peace treaty between the Americans and British in November 1782.

He judg'd his brethren by their own consent;
Untaught to spurn those brethren to the dust;
In virtue firm, and obstinately just,
For him no navies rov'd from shore to shore.
40 No slaves were doom'd to dig the glitt'ring ore;
Remote from all the vain parade of state,
No slaves in diamonds saunter'd at his gate,
Nor did his breast the guilty passions tear,
He knew no murder and he felt no fear.
45   Was this the patriarch sage?—Then turn thine eyes
And view the contrast that our age supplies;
Touch'd from the life, I trace no ages fled,
I draw no curtain that conceals the dead;
To distant Britain let thy view be cast,
50 And say the present far exceeds the past;
Of all the plagues that e'er the world have curs'd,
Name George the tyrant, and you name the worst!
What demon, hostile to the human kind,
Planted these fierce disorders in the mind?
55 All urg'd alike, one phantom we pursue,
But what has war with happiness to do?
In death's black shroud this gem can ne'er be found;
Who deals for that the life-destroying wound,
Or pines with grief to see a brother live,
60 That life dissolving which we cannot give?
'Tis thine, Ambition!—Thee these horrors suit:
Lost to the human, she assumes the brute;
She proudly vain or insolently bold,
Her heart revenge, her eye intent on gold,
65 Sway'd by the madness of the present hour
Mistakes for happiness extent of power;
That shining bait which dropt in folly's way
Tempts the weak mind, and leads the heart astray!
Thou happiness! still sought but never found,
70 We, in a circle, chase thy shadow round:
Meant all mankind in different forms to bless,
Which yet possessing, we no more possess:—
Thus far remov'd and painted on the eye
Smooth verdant fields seem blended with the sky,
75 But where they both in fancied contact join
In vain we trace the visionary line;
Still as we chase, the empty circle flies,
Emerge new mountains or new oceans rise.

ON THE EMIGRATION TO AMERICA

And Peopling the Western Country

To western woods, and lonely plains,
Palemon[1] from the crowd departs,
Where Nature's wildest genius reigns,
To tame the soil, and plant the arts—
5   What wonders there shall freedom show,
What mighty states successive grow!

From Europe's proud, despotic shores
Hither the stranger takes his way,
And in our new found world explores
10   A happier soil, a milder sway,
Where no proud despot holds him down,
No slaves insult him with a crown.

What charming scenes attract the eye,
On wild Ohio's savage stream!
15   There Nature reigns, whose works outvie
The boldest pattern art can frame;
There ages past have rolled away,
And forests bloomed but to decay.

From these fair plains, these rural seats,
20   So long concealed, so lately known,
The unsocial Indian far retreats,
To make some other clime his own,
When other streams, less pleasing, flow,
And darker forests round him grow.

25   Great Sire[2] of floods! whose varied wave
Through climes and countries takes its way,
To whom creating Nature gave
Ten thousand streams to swell thy sway!
No longer shall they useless prove,
30   Nor idly through the forests rove;

[1]Possibly adapted from the name of the knight-errant in Chaucer's *Knight's Tale*; here, the western pioneer in search of the place where nature and reason hold sway together.
[2]Freneau's note: the Mississippi.

Nor longer shall your princely flood
From distant lakes be swelled in vain,
Nor longer through a darksome wood
Advance, unnoticed, to the main,
35   Far other ends, the heavens decree—
And commerce plans new freights for thee.

While virtue warms the generous breast,
There heaven-born freedom shall reside,
Nor shall the voice of war molest,
40   Nor Europe's all-aspiring pride—
There Reason shall new laws devise,
And order from confusion rise.

Forsaking kings and regal state,
With all their pomp and fancied bliss,
45   The traveller owns, convinced though late,
No realm so free, so blest as this—
The east is half to slaves consigned,
Where kings and priests enchain the mind.[3]

O come the time, and haste the day,
50   When man shall man no longer crush,
When Reason shall enforce her sway,
Nor these fair regions raise our blush,
Where still the African complains,
And mourns his yet unbroken chains.

55   Far brighter scenes a future age,
The muse predicts, these States will hail,
Whose genius may the world engage,
Whose deeds may over death prevail,
And happier systems bring to view,
60   Than all the eastern sages knew.

[3]Freneau's note: from the 1786 edition: "And half to slavery more revin'd."
The remark seems to include as slaves those trapped in "more refin'd" forms
of economic slavery.

THE WILD HONEY SUCKLE

Fair flower, that dost so comely grow
Hid in this silent, dull retreat,
Untouched thy honied blossoms blow,
Unseen thy little branches greet:
5   No roving foot shall crush thee here,
    No busy hand provoke a tear.

By Nature's self in white arrayed,
She bade thee shun the vulgar eye,
And planted here the guardian shade,
10   And sent soft waters murmuring by;
    Thus quietly thy summer goes,
    Thy days declining to repose.

Smit with those charms, that must decay,
I grieve to see your future doom;
15   They died—nor were those flowers more gay,
The flowers that did in Eden bloom;
    Unpitying frosts, and Autumn's power
    Shall leave no vestige of this flower.

From morning suns and evening dews
20   At first thy little being came:
If nothing once, you nothing lose,
For when you die you are the same;
    The space between, is but an hour,
    The frail duration of a flower.

THE INDIAN BURYING GROUND[1]

In spite of all the learned have said,
    I still my old opinion keep;
The posture, that we give the dead,
    Points out the soul's eternal sleep.

5 Not so the ancients of these lands—
    The Indian, when from life released,

[1]Freneau's note: "The North American Indians bury their dead in a sitting posture; decorating the corpse with wampum, the images of birds, quadrupeds, & c: And (if that of a warrior) with bows, arrows, tomahawks, and other military weapons."

Again is seated with his friends,
    And shares again the joyous feast.

His imaged birds, and painted bowl,
10   And venison, for a journey dressed,
Bespeak the nature of the soul,
    Activity, that knows no rest.

His bow, for action ready bent,
    And arrows, with a head of stone,
15 Can only mean that life is spent,
    And not the old ideas gone.

Thou, stranger, that shalt come this way,
    No fraud upon the dead commit—
Observe the swelling turf, and say
20   They do not lie, but here they sit.

Here still a lofty rock remains,
    On which the curious eye may trace
(Now wasted, half, by wearing rains)
    The fancies of a ruder race.

25 Here still an aged elm aspires,
    Beneath whose far-projecting shade
(And which the shepherd still admires)
    The children of the forest played!

There oft a restless Indian queen
30   (Pale Shebah,² with her braided hair)
And many a barbarous form is seen
    To chide the man that lingers there.

By midnight moons, o'er moistening dews;
    In habit for the chase arrayed,
35 The hunter still the deer pursues,
    The hunter and the deer, a shade!

And long shall timorous fancy see
    The painted chief, and pointed spear,
And Reason's self shall bow the knee
40   To shadows and delusions here.

²Name adapted from the Queen of Sheba, who visited King Solomon (see
I Kings 10); the name for an exotic, foreign queen.

Phillis Wheatley (1753?–1784)

Phillis Wheatley was brought from Africa to Boston in 1761 as a frail slave of about seven years old and bought by John Wheatley, a tailor, for his wife. The young girl was educated by the Wheatleys and encouraged to develop her poetic talents; treated almost as a daughter, she was received in some of the most cultivated parlors of Boston. In 1771 she was baptized at Old South Meeting House. She went to England with one of the Wheatley children in 1773, and met many prominent people, including titled aristocracy, and was to be presented at Court when she was called back to Boston to attend the ailing Mrs. Wheatley. Meanwhile arrangements had been made in London for the publication of *Poems on Various Subjects, Religious and Moral* (1773), probably the first book by an American Negro.

After the death of the Wheatleys, Phillis married John Peters in 1778, and this began a period of poverty, misery, and decline for her. Her poems include a few allusions to her race and origins; for the most part they are occasional poems of greeting or congratulation or elegy, which show her reading of Milton, Gray and, Pope whose translation of Homer was her favorite book aside from the Bible.

TEXT

Wheatley, Phillis. *The Poems of Phillis Wheatley.* Ed. Julian D. Mason, Jr. Chapel Hill: University of North Carolina Press, 1966.

ON BEING BROUGHT
FROM AFRICA TO AMERICA

'Twas mercy brought me from my *Pagan* land,
Taught my benighted soul to understand
That there's a God, that there's a *Saviour* too:
Once I redemption neither sought nor knew.
5   Some view our sable race with scornful eye,
"Their colour is a diabolic die."
Remember, *Christians, Negroes,* black as *Cain*,[1]
May be refin'd, and join th' angelic train.

---

[1]The old notion that blacks were the descendants of Cain, their skin darkened
by the curse that fell on Cain for murdering his brother Abel.

Joel Barlow (1754–1812)

A farmer's son from Redding, Connecticut, Barlow graduated from Yale in 1778 after a public recitation of his first long poem, *The Prospect of Peace*. He served as chaplain to a brigade during the Revolution, and his expectations for the new republic found expression—to his contemporaries sublime and to us inflated—in *The Vision of Columbus* (1787), an epic in couplets heavily flavored with Milton. Meanwhile he had become associated with the Connecticut Wits, a sophisticated group of poets with Federalist convictions, which included Timothy Dwight, his old tutor at Yale, John Trumbull, Lemuel Hopkins and David Humphreys.

From 1788 to 1805 Barlow lived in Europe, writing and learning to be a successful businessman. Under Thomas Paine's influence he shed Federalist conservatism for the liberal attitude that produced *Advice to the Priviledged Orders* (1792, 1796). Abroad he celebrated his country and his region in *The Hasty Pudding* (1796), a mock-pastoral epic about this native New England dish, and in a revision of his epic as *The Columbiad* (1807). On his return Barlow became a literary and financial presence in Washington. In 1811, President Madison appointed him Minister to France to negotiate a commercial treaty with Napoleon, and he died in Poland the next year returning from an unsuccessful attempt to meet the Emperor, now in retreat from Russia.

Of the Wits, Barlow was politically the most egalitarian and poetically the most imaginative in adapting neoclassical and Miltonic models. *The Hasty Pudding* is a vigorous and delightful poem: and, for all the rhetoric of the angel Hesper, *The Columbiad* is the first full-blown effort to project an original epic myth commensurate with the size and ambitions of America.

REFERENCE

Howard, Leon. *The Connecticut Wits*. Chicago: University of Chicago Press, 1943.

Parrington, V. L. (Ed.). *The Connecticut Wits*. New York: Harcourt, Brace, 1926.

Woodress, James L. *A Yankee's Odyssey: The Life of Joel Barlow*. Philadelphia: Lippincott, 1958.

THE HASTY PUDDING[1]

A Poem in Three Cantos

CANTO I

Ye Alps audacious, thro' the Heav'ns that rise,
To cramp the day and hide me from the skies;
Ye Gallic flags, that o'er their heights unfurl'd,
Bear death to kings, and freedom to the world,
5 I sing not you.[2] A softer theme I choose,
A virgin theme, unconscious of the Muse,
But fruitful, rich, well suited to inspire
The purest frenzy of poetic fire.
   Despise it not, ye Bards to terror steel'd,
10 Who hurl your thunders round the epic field;
Nor ye who strain your midnight throats to sing
Joys that the vineyard and the still-house bring;
Or on some distant fair your notes employ,
And speak of raptures that you ne'er enjoy.
15 I sing the sweets I know, the charms I feel,
My morning incense, and my evening meal,
The sweets of Hasty Pudding. Come, dear bowl,
Glide o'er my palate, and inspire my soul.
The milk beside thee, smoking from the kine,
20 Its substance mingled, married in with thine,
Shall cool and temper thy superior heat,
And save the pains of blowing while I eat.
   Oh! could the smooth, the emblematic song
Flow like thy genial juices o'er my tongue,
25 Could those mild morsels in my numbers chime,
And, as they roll in substance, roll in rhyme,
No more thy awkward unpoetic name
Should shun the muse, or prejudice thy fame;
But rising grateful to th' accustom'd ear,
30 All Bards should catch it, and all realms revere!
   Assist me first with pious toil to trace
Thro' wrecks of time, thy lineage and thy race;
Declare what lovely squaw, in days of yore,

---

[1]Corn meal mush; an Indian pudding made by dropping meal or flour into boiling water and stirring while it thickens. It is an old New England favorite.
[2]This mock-epic was written in 1793 when Barlow's homesickness was aroused by being served a bowl of hasty pudding, to his surprised delight, at an inn in Chambéry in Savoy near the French Alps. He dedicated the poem to Mrs. George Washington.

(Ere great Columbus sought thy native shore)
35   First gave thee to the world; her works of fame
Have lived indeed, but lived without a name.
Some tawny Ceres,[3] goddess of her days,
First learn'd with stones to crack the well dried maize,
Through the rough sieve to shake the golden show'r,
40   In boiling water stir the yellow flour:
The yellow flour, bestrew'd and stirr'd with haste,
Swells in the flood and thickens to a paste,
Then puffs and wallops, rises to the brim,
Drinks the dry knobs that on the surface swim;
45   The knobs at last the busy ladle breaks,
And the whole mass its true consistence takes.
     Could but her sacred name, unknown so long,
Rise, like her labors, to the son of song,
To her, to them, I'd consecrate my lays.
50   And blow her pudding with the breath of praise.
If 'twas Oella[4] whom I sang before
I here ascribe her one great virtue more.
Not through the rich Peruvian realms alone
The fame of Sol's sweet daughter should be known,
55   But o'er the world's wide clime should live secure,
Far as his rays extend, as long as they endure.
     Dear Hasty Pudding, what unpromised joy
Expands my heart, to meet thee in Savoy!
Doom'd o'er the world through devious paths to roam,
60   Each clime my country, and each house my home,
My soul is soothed, my cares have found an end,
I greet my long lost, unforgotten friend.
     For thee thro' Paris, that corrupted town,
How long in vain I wandered up and down,
65   Where shameless Bacchus,[5] with his drenching hoard,
Cold from his cave usurps the morning board.
London is lost in smoke and steep'd in tea;
No Yankey there can lisp the name of thee;
The uncouth word, a libel on the town,
70   Would call a proclamation from the crown.[6]

---

[3]The goddess of harvests.
[4]In Books II and III of *The Vision of Columbus* and *The Columbiad*, Barlow
refers to the Peruvian legend that the Incas descended from two children of
the Sun, Manco Capac and his sister-bride Oella.
[5]The god of wine.
[6]Barlow's note: "A certain king, at the time when this was written, was pub-
lishing proclamations to prevent American principles from being propagated
in his country." Obviously he means George III.

From climes oblique, that fear the sun's full rays,
Chill'd in their fogs, exclude the generous maize:
A grain, whose rich, luxuriant growth requires
Short gentle showers, and bright etherial fires.
75   But here, though distant from our native shore,
With mutual glee, we meet and laugh once more,
The same! I know thee by that yellow face,
That strong complexion of true Indian race,
Which time can never change, nor soil impair,
80   Nor Alpine snows, nor Turkey's morbid air;
For endless years, through every mild domain,
Where grows the maize, there thou art sure to reign,
But man, more fickle, the bold license claims,
In different realms to give the different names.
85   Thee the soft nations round the warm Levant
Polanta call, the French of course *Polante.*
E'en in thy native regions, how I blush
To hear the Pennsylvanians call thee *Mush!*
On Hudson's banks, while men of Belgic spawn
90   Insult and eat thee by the name *Suppawn.*
All spurious appellations, void of truth;
I've better known thee from my earliest youth,
Thy name is *Hasty Pudding!* thus our sires
Were wont to greet thee fuming from their fires;
95   And while they argued in thy just defense
With logic clear, they thus explain'd the sense:—
"In *haste* the boiling cauldron o'er the blaze,
Receives and cooks the ready powder'd maize;
In *haste* 'tis serv'd, and then in equal *haste,*
100   With cooling milk, we make the sweet repast.
No carving to be done, no knife to grate
The tender ear, and wound the stony plate;
But the smooth spoon, just fitted to the lip,
And taught with art the yielding mass to dip.
105   By frequent journeys to the bowl well stored,
Performs the *hasty* honors of the board."
Such is thy name, significant and clear,
A name, a sound to every Yankey dear,
But most to me, whose heart and palate chaste
110   Preserve my pure hereditary taste.
There are who strive to stamp with disrepute
The luscious food, because it feeds the brute;
In tropes of high-strain'd wit, while gaudy prigs
Compare thy nursling, man, to pamper'd pigs;

115 With sovereign scorn I treat the vulgar jest,
    Nor fear to share thy bounties with the beast.
    What though the generous cow gives me to quaff
    The milk nutritious: am I then a calf?
    Or can the genius of the noisy swine,
120 Though nursed on pudding, claim a kin to mine?
    Sure the sweet song, I fashion to thy praise,
    Runs more melodious than the notes they raise.
        My song resounding in its grateful glee,
    No merit claims: I praise myself in thee.
125 My father lov'd thee thro' his length of days;
    For thee his fields were shaded o'er with maize;
    From thee what health, what vigor he possess'd,
    Ten sturdy freemen from his loins attest;
    Thy constellation rul'd my natal morn,
130 And all my bones were made of Indian corn.
    Delicious grain! whatever form it take,
    To roast or boil, to smother or to bake,
    In every dish 'tis welcome still to me,
    But most, my Hasty Pudding, most in thee.
135   Let the green succotash with thee contend,
    Let beans and corn their sweetest juices blend,
    Let butter drench them in its yellow tide,
    And a long slice of bacon grace their side;
    Not all the plate, how fam'd soe'er it be,
140 Can please my palate like a bowl of thee.
    Some talk of Hoe-Cake, fair Virginia's pride,
    Rich Johnny-Cake, this mouth has often tri'd;
    Both please me well, their virtues much the same,
    Alike their fabric, as allied their fame,
145 Except in dear New England, where the last
    Receives a dash of pumpkin in the paste,
    To give it sweetness and improve the taste.
    But place them all before me, smoaking hot,
    The big, round dumpling, rolling from the pot,
150 The pudding of the bag, whose quivering breast,
    With suet lin'd leads on the Yankee feast,
    The Charlotte[7] brown, within whose crusty sides
    A belly soft the pulpy apple hides;
    The yellow bread whose face like amber glows,
155 And all of Indian that the bake-pan knows,—
    You tempt me not—my fav'rite greets my eyes,
    To that lov'd bowl my spoon by instinct flies.

[7]An apple or apple custard baked in bread soaked in milk.

CANTO II

To mix the food by vicious rules of art,
To kill the stomach, and to sink the heart
160　To make mankind to social virtue sour,
Cram o'er each dish, and be what they devour;
For this the kitchen muse first fram'd her book,
Commanding sweats to stream from every cook;
Children no more their antic gambols tried,
165　And friends to physic wonder'd why they died.
　　Not so the Yankey—his abundant feast,
With simples furnish'd and with plainness drest,
A numerous offspring gathers round the board,
And cheers alike the servant and the lord;
170　Whose well-bought hunger prompts the joyous taste
And health attends them from the short repast.
　　While the full pail rewards the milk-maid's toil,
The mother sees the morning cauldron boil;
To stir the pudding next demands their care;
175　To spread the table and the bowls prepare;
To feed the household as their portions cool
And send them all to labor or to school.
　　Yet may the simplest dish some rules impart,
For nature scorns not all the aids of art.
180　Ev'n Hasty Pudding, purest of all food.
May still be bad, indifferent, or good,
As sage experience the short process guides,
Or want of skill, or want of care presides.
Whoe'er would form it on the surest plan,
185　To rear the child and long sustain the man;
To shield the morals while it mends the size,
And all the powers of every food supplies,
Attend the lesson that the muse shall bring,
Suspend your spoons, and listen while I sing.
190　　But since, O man! thy life and health demand
Not food alone but labour from thy hand,
First in the field, beneath the sun's strong rays,
Ask of thy mother earth the needful maize;
She loves the race that courts her yielding soil,
195　And gives her bounties to the sons of toil.
　　When now the ox, obedient to thy call,
Repays the loan that fill'd the winter stall,
Pursue his traces o'er the furrow'd plain,
And plant in measur'd hills the golden grain.
200　But when the tender germ begins to shoot,
And the green spire declares the sprouting root,

Then guard your nursling from each greedy foe,
The insidious worm, the all-devouring crow.
A little ashes, sprinkled round the spire,
205 Soon steep'd in rain, will bid the worm retire;
The feather'd robber with his hungry maw
Swift flies the field before your man of straw,
A frightful image, such as school-boys bring,
When met to burn the pope or hang the king.
210   Thrice in the season, through each verdant row
Wield the strong plow-share and the faithful hoe:
The faithful hoe, a double task that takes,
To till the summer corn, and roast the winter cakes.
    Slow springs the blade, while check'd by chilling rains,
215 Ere yet the sun the seat of Cancer gains;
But when his fiercest fires emblaze the land,
Then start the juices, then the roots expand;
Then, like a column of Corinthian mould,
The stalk struts upward and the leaves unfold;
220 The busy branches all the ridges fill,
Entwine their arms, and kiss from hill to hill.
Here cease to vex them, all your cares are done:
Leave the last labors to the parent sun;
Beneath his genial smiles, the well-drest field,
225 When autumn calls, a plenteous crop shall yield.
    Now the strong foliage bears the standards high,
And shoots the tall top-gallants to the sky;
The suckling ears their silky fringes bend,
And pregnant grown, their swelling coats distend;
230 The loaded stalk, while still the burden grows,
O'erhangs the space that runs between the rows;
High as a hop-field waves the silent grove,
A safe retreat for little thefts of love,
When the pledged roasting-ears invite the maid,
235 To meet her swain beneath the new-form'd shade;
His generous hand unloads the cumbrous hill,
And the green spoils her ready basket fill;
Small compensation for the twofold bliss,
The promised wedding, and the present kiss.
240   Slight depredations these; but now the moon
Calls from his hollow tree the sly raccoon;
And while by night he bears his prize away,
The bolder squirrel labors through the day.
Both thieves alike, but provident of time,
245 A virtue rare, that almost hides their crime.
Then let them steal the little stores they can,

And fill their gran'ries from the toils of man;
We've one advantage, where they take no part,—
With all their wiles they ne'er have found the art
250 To boil the Hasty-Pudding; here we shine
Superior far to tenants of the pine;
This envied boon to man shall still belong,
Unshar'd by them, in substance or in song.
   At last the closing season browns the plain,
255 And ripe October gathers in the grain;
Deep loaded carts the spacious corn-house fill,
The sack distended marches to the mill;
The lab'ring mill beneath the burden groans
And show'rs the future pudding from the stones;
260 Till the glad house-wife greets the powder'd gold,
And the new crop exterminates the old.
Ah, who can sing what every wight must feel,
The joy that enters with the bag of meal,
A general jubilee pervades the house,
265 Wakes every child and gladdens every mouse.

CANTO III

   The days grow short; but tho' the falling sun
To the glad swain proclaims his day's work done,
Night's pleasing shades his various tasks prolong,
And yield new subjects to my various song.
270 For now, the corn-house fill'd, the harvest home,
The invited neighbors to the *Husking* come;
A frolic scene, where work, and mirth, and play,
Unite their charms to chace the hours away.
   Where the huge heap lies centered in the hall,
275 The lamp suspended from the cheerful wall,
Brown corn-fed nymphs, and strong hard-handed beaux,
Alternate rang'd, extend in circling rows,
Assume their seats, the solid mass attack;
The dry husks rustle, and the corncobs crack;
280 The song, the laugh, alternate notes resound,
And the sweet cider trips in silence round.
   The laws of Husking every wight can tell;
And sure no laws he ever keeps so well:
For each red ear a general kiss he gains,
285 With each smut ear he smuts[8] the luckless swains;
But when to some sweet maid a prize is cast,
Red as her lips, and taper as her waist,

[8]Blackens or dirties.

She walks the round, and culls one favored beau,
Who leaps, the luscious tribute to bestow.
290 Various the sport, as are the wits and brains
Of well pleas'd lasses and contending swains;
Till the vast mound of corn is swept away,
And he that gets the last ear wins the day.
     Meanwhile the house-wife urges all her care,
295 The well-earn'd feast to hasten and prepare.
The sifted meal already waits her hand,
The milk is strain'd, the bowls in order stand,
The fire flames high; and, as a pool (that takes
The headlong stream that o'er the mill-dam breaks)
300 Foams, roars, and rages with incessant toils,
So the vex'd cauldron rages, roars and boils.
     First with clean salt, she seasons well the food,
Then strews the flour, and thickens all the flood.
Long o'er the simmering fire she lets it stand;
305 To stir it well demands a stronger hand;
The husband takes his turn: and round and round
The ladle flies; at last the toil is crown'd;
When to the board the thronging huskers pour,
And take their seats as at the corn before.
310   I leave them to their feast. There still belong
More useful matters to my faithful song.
For rules there are, tho' ne'er unfolded yet,
Nice rules and wise, how pudding should be ate.
     Some with molasses line the luscious treat,
315 And mix, like bards, the useful with the sweet,
A wholesome dish, and well deserving praise,
A great resource in those bleak wintry days,
When the chill'd earth lies buried deep in snow,
And raging Boreas drives the shivering cow.
320   Blest cow! thy praise shall still my notes employ,
Great source of health, the only source of joy;
Mother of Egypt's god.⁹—but sure, for me,
Were I to leave my God, I'd worship thee.
How oft thy teats these pious hands have prest!
325 How oft thy bounties prove my only feast!
How oft I've fed thee with my favorite grain!
And roar'd, like thee, to find thy children slain!
     Ye swains who know her various worth to prize,
Ah! house her well from winter's angry skies.
330 Potatoes, pumpkins, should her sadness cheer,

---

⁹Nut, the mother of Osiris, was depicted as a cow.

Corn from your crib, and mashes from your beer;
When spring returns, she'll well acquit the loan,
And nurse at once your infants and her own.
     Milk then with pudding I should always choose;
335 To this in future I confine my muse.
Till she in haste some further hints unfold,
Good for the young, nor useless to the old.
First in your bowl the milk abundant take,
Then drop with care along the silver lake
340 Your flakes of pudding; these at first will hide
Their little bulk beneath the swelling tide;
But when their growing mass no more can sink,
When the soft island looms above the brink,
Then check your hand; you've got the portion due,
345 So taught our sires, and what they taught is true.
     There is a choice in spoons. Though small appear
The nice distinction, yet to me 'tis clear.
The deep bowl'd Gallic spoon, contrived to scoop
In ample draughts the thin diluted soup,
350 Performs not well in those substantial things,
Whose mass adhesive to the metal clings;
Where the strong labial muscles must embrace,
The gentle curve, and sweep the hollow space.
With ease to enter and discharge the freight,
355 A bowl less concave, but still more dilate,
Becomes the pudding best. The shape, the size,
A secret rests, unknown to vulgar eyes.
Experienc'd feeders can alone impart
A rule so much above the lore of art.
360 These tuneful lips that thousand spoons have tried,
With just precision could the point decide.
Though not in song; the muse but poorly shines
In cones, and cubes, and geometric lines;
Yet the true form, as near as she can tell,
365 Is that small section of a goose egg shell,
Which in two equal portions shall divide
The distance from the center to the side.
     Fear not to slaver; 'tis no deadly sin:—
Like the free Frenchman, from your joyous chin
370 Suspend the ready napkin; or like me,
Poise with one hand your bowl upon your knee;
Just in the zenith your wise head project,
Your full spoon, rising in a line direct,
Bold as a bucket, heed no drops that fall,
375 The wide mouth'd bowl will surely catch them all!

from **THE COLUMBIAD, BOOK VIII**[1]

    Now had Columbus well enjoy'd the sight
Of armies vanquisht and of fleets in flight,[2]
From all Hesperia's[3] heaven the darkness flown,
And colon[4] crowds to sovereign sages grown.
5 To cast new glories o'er the changing clime,
The guardian Power reversed the flight of time,
Roll'd back the years that led their course before,
Stretch'd out immense the wild uncultured shore;
Then shifts the total scene, and rears to view
10 Arts and the men that useful arts pursue.
As o'er the canvass when the painter's mind
Glows with a future landscape well design'd,
While Panorama's wondrous aid he calls,
To crowd whole realms within his circling walls,
15 Lakes, fields and forests, ports and navies rise,
A new creation to his kindling eyes;
He smiles o'er all; and in delightful strife
The pencil moves and calls the whole to life.
So while Columbia's patriarch stood sublime,
20 And saw rude nature clothe the trackless clime;
The green banks heave, the winding currents pour,
The bays and harbors cleave the yielding shore,
The champaigns spread, the solemn groves arise,
And the rough mountains lengthen round the skies;
25 Thro' all their bounds he traced, with skilful ken,
The unform'd seats and future walks of men;
Mark'd where the field should bloom, the pennon play,
Great cities grow and empires claim their sway;
When, sudden waked by Hesper's waving hand,
30 They rose obedient round the cultured land.
    In western tracts, where still the wildmen tread,
From sea to sea an inland commerce spread;
On the dim streams and thro the gloomy grove

---

[1]The headnote to Book VIII gives this narrative scenario for the passage included here: "Hesper, recurring to his object of showing Columbus the importance of his discoveries, reverses the order of time, and exhibits the continent again in its savage state. He then displays the progress of arts in America." These are lines 431–550.
[2]Book VII had ended with the defeat of Cornwallis at Yorktown and the end of the Revolutionary War, all presented to Columbus, old and imprisoned, by the Angel Hesper, named after the evening or western star.
[3]The land of the West, first used by the Greeks to indicate Italy.
[4]Colonial.

The trading bands their cumbrous burdens move;
35 Furs, peltry, drugs, and all the native store
Of midland realms descended to the shore.
    Where summer suns, along the northern coast,
With feeble force dissolve the chains of frost,
Prolific waves the scaly nations trace,
40 And tempt the toils of man's laborious race.
Tho rich Brazilian strands, beneath the tide,
Their shells of pearl and sparkling pebbles hide,
While for the gaudy prize, a venturous train
Plunge the dark deep and brave the surging main,
45 Drag forth the shining gewgaws into air,
To stud a sceptre or emblaze a star;
Far wealthier stores these genial tides display,
And works less dangerous with their spoils repay.
The Hero saw the hardy crews advance,
50 Cast the long line and aim the barbed lance;
Load the deep floating barks, and bear abroad
To every land the life-sustaining food;
Renascent swarms by nature's care supplied,
Repeople still the shoals and fin the fruitful tide.
55   Where southern streams thro broad savannas bend,
The rice-clad vales their verdant rounds extend;
Tobago's[5] plant its leaf expanding yields,
The maize luxuriant clothes a thousand fields;
Steeds, herds and flocks o'er northern regions rove,
60 Embrown the hill and wanton thro the grove.
The woodlands wide their sturdy honors bend,
The pines, the liveoaks to the shores descend,
There couch the keels, the crooked ribs arise,
Hulls heave aloft and mastheads mount the skies;
65 Launcht on the deep o'er every wave they fly,
Feed tropic isles and Europe's looms supply.
    To nurse the arts and fashion freedom's lore
Young schools of science rise along the shore;
Great without pomp their modest walls expand,
70 Harvard and Yale and Princeton grace the land,
Penn's student halls his youths with gladness greet,
On James's bank Virginian Muses meet,
Manhattan's mart collegiate domes command,
Bosom'd in groves, see growing Dartmouth stand;
75 Bright o'er its realm reflecting solar fires,
On yon tall hill Rhode Island's seat aspires.[6]

[5]Tobacco.
[6]Rhode Island College, now Brown University, in Providence.

Thousands of humbler name around them rise,
Where homebred freedmen seize the solid prize;
Fixt in small spheres, with safer beams to shine,
80 They reach the useful and refuse the fine,
Found, on its proper base, the social plan,
The broad plain truths, the common sense of man,
His obvious wants, his mutual aids discern,
His rights familiarize, his duties learn,
85 Feel moral fitness all its force dilate,
Embrace the village and comprise the state.
Each rustic here who turns the furrow'd soil,
The maid, the youth that ply mechanic toil,
In equal rights, in useful arts inured,
90 Know their just claims, and see their claims secured;
They watch their delegates, each law revise,
Its faults designate and its merits prize,
Obey, but scrutinize; and let the test
Of sage experience prove and fix the best.
95   Here, fired by virtue's animating flame,
The preacher's task persuasive sages claim,
To mould religion to the moral mind,
In bands of peace to harmonize mankind,
To life, to light, to promised joys above
100 The soften'd soul with ardent hope to move.
No dark intolerance blinds the zealous throng,
No arm of power attendant on their tongue;
Vext Inquisition, with her flaming brand,
Shuns their mild march, nor dares approach the land.
105 Tho different creeds their priestly robes denote,
Their orders various and their rites remote,
Yet one their voice, their labors all combined,
Lights of the world and friends of humankind.
So the bright galaxy o'er heaven displays
110 Of various stars the same unbounded blaze;
Where great and small their mingling rays unite,
And earth and skies exchange the friendly light.
   And lo, my son, that other sapient band,
The torch of science flaming in their hand!
115 Thro nature's range their searching souls aspire,
Or wake to life the canvass and the lye.
Fixt in sublimest thought, behold them rise
World after world unfolding to the eyes,
Lead, light, allure them thro the total plan,
120 And give new guidance to the paths of man.

"Snap-the-Whip," wood engraving, 1873, by Winslow Homer (1836–1910). (Courtesy of The Granger Collection)

Part Two

AMERICAN ROMANTIC POETRY

Political independence precipitated the question of literary independence: should Americans work within the European tradition and extend it, should they begin from fresh sources? The question was a highly theoretical one because advocates of both viewpoints were painfully aware of the paucity and thinness of what had been accomplished so far. At the same time, the urgency of the question helped to stimulate the appearance of a number of remarkable writers whose works at least provided an actual focus for the theoretical question. F. O. Matthiessen called this period the "American Renaissance," but it was more properly speaking a first birth. Most of the great figures of the American nineteenth century thought, albeit with some ambivalence, that artists in the United States faced a unique challenge and opportunity. Even Poe's denunciation of American provincialism was intended to produce great American writing. Meanwhile Cooper was turning history into myth; Hawthorne was interiorizing the romance to invest "commonplace prosperity" with the mysterious density of light and shade; Melville's archetypal sailors invested homespun writing with tragic and epic possibilities.

Although the Transcendentalists helped to introduce European poetry and philosophy into America, they spoke up for an expression native to their age and circumstances. Emerson began *Nature* by denouncing his retrospective age for writing "biographies, histories, and criticism" when "there are new lands, new men, new thoughts." His essays on poetry describe a bard who would awaken the New World by opening the psyche to the breathing of the One Spirit through Nature. The Puritans had always construed experience emblematically; Emerson now extended organic symbolism to language itself when he laid down these three interrelated axioms: "1. Words are signs of natural facts. 2. Particular natural facts are symbols of particular spiritual facts. 3. Nature is the symbol of spirit." Thoreau summed up the interaction between man and Nature that lay behind the conception of organic form:

> He would be a poet who could impress the winds and streams into his service, to speak for him; who nailed words to their primitive senses, as farmers drive down stakes in the spring, which the frost has heaved; who derived words as often as he used them—transplanted them to his page with earth adhering to their roots; whose words were so true and fresh and natural that they would appear to expand like the buds at the approach of spring, though they lay half smothered between two musty leaves in a library—aye, to bloom and bear fruit there, after their kind, annually, for the faithful reader, in sympathy with surrounding nature.

This was no mere domestication of Pan or Dionysus; it was an American definition of the poet as oracle, translating wordless truth into symbolic speech. By mid-century Whitman was able to draw on the Transcendentalists' ideas and their first experiments with form to extend the vision from the individual to the society and thereby to link Paumanok and Manhattan in the intuitive and cumulative rhythms of free verse.

There were of course adaptors as well as creators; poets like Bryant and Longfellow and Lowell were treating American landscapes and themes in the traditional forms, and their popularity during the nineteenth century should not cancel out our awareness either of their serious purpose and technical skill, or of their effect on the culture of the country. But they did not represent the real challenge to the revolutionary notion of the seer chanting in open form; nor was the opposition, as it developed, just the urbane condescension of Manhattan to New England zeal or to stuffy Boston amusement at Whitman's "barbaric yawp." Many of Emerson's contemporaries found his ideas about man and nature—and so about the poet and the poem—questionable at best: Poe the Virginian; Melville the New Yorker, and New Englanders like Emily Dickinson, Frederick Goddard Tuckerman, and Jones Very, who were somewhat off the Boston-Concord axis. But, most categorically, it was Poe who stood as Emerson's and Whitman's shadow. With Poe it was not just a matter of difference, but of contradiction. He saw lunacy instead of sanity as the psyche's secret, entropy and not coherence at nature's heart. In challenging Emerson's moral and metaphysical suppositions, he wanted to disprove his artistic axioms too. Poe made a rigid distinction between life and art a century before Stevens conceived of poetry in terms of a "supreme fiction" and before Ransom delineated the principles of the New Criticism from a similar sense of dislocation. The poem was an artificial and self-validating creation, operating by the laws and within the limits set by the poet and posited in the work. Poe's theoretical essays set standards for his contemporaries and anticipated much modern criticism. Moreover, he exemplified a method as well; he came to the poem as craftsman and technician, analyzing texts and evaluating each as a constructed pattern of effects through language.

Poe was the first important Southern poet and critic, but his quarrel was not merely with New England. The image of the poet that Whitman, a working-class New Yorker, developed out of Emerson's notions, was the crucial issue. As William Carlos Williams saw a century later, it threatened "the entire concept of the poetic idea, and from a new viewpoint, a rebel viewpoint, an American viewpoint." The lyric strain that it generated is largely responsible for the international influence of American poetry during the last hundred years, but at the same time it provoked within the United States doubts and denials that made for the internal dialectic of American Romanticism.

The Civil War was a turning point in poetry as in almost every aspect of national life. The political struggle and the horrors of fratricidal battle split American Romanticism wide open and scattered its energies. During the "Gilded Age" between the Civil War and World War I the excitement and controversy centered on the new movements of realism and naturalism, and fiction-writers like Twain, James, Howells, and Norris dominated the scene. But the final and contrasting expressions of nineteenth-century Romanticism, both of which have analogues in the literature of this century, are Lanier's impassioned lyricism and Crane's tight-lipped irony. Otherwise in poetry there was only the enervated gentility of poetasters like E. C. Stedman and Thomas Bailey Aldrich. However, a slack period was perhaps necessary after the great Romantic achievement before American poetry could come unquestionably into its own between 1910 and 1920 with a generation of poets that is one of the marvels of Western literature.

William Cullen Bryant (1794–1878)

Bryant's grandfather was a Calvinist and a Federalist; his father became a Unitarian; he himself became a nature poet and a political liberal. Born in Cummington, Massachusetts, he spent a year at Williams College, then studied privately to become a lawyer. He wrote "Thanatopsis" at the age of seventeen, and many of his best poems were written by 1821, when *Poems* was published. He gave up his law practice and moved to New York in 1825 and soon became editor of the *Evening Post,* a position he held until his death. He made the paper a strong advocate of the laboring man and of the black slave, and eventually of the Republican Party.

Meanwhile Bryant was continuing to compose lyrics, some meditating on American landscapes from the Berkshires to Long Island and from the Hudson River to the Illinois prairies, and others articulating a melancholy optimism. Subsequent volumes include: a new *Poems* (1832), *The Fountain* (1842), *A Forest Hymn* (1860), and *The Flood of Years* (1877). He translated *The Iliad* and *The Odyssey* into blank verse. His *Lectures on Poetry,* delivered to the New York Atheneum in 1825, contain a warm argument for the possibilities of an American literature. Bryant became known as the "American Wordsworth," but his New England spirit made him more like such precursors of Wordsworth as Gray and Thomson, or like the later, more orthodox, Wordsworth.

TEXT

Bryant, William Cullen. *The Poetical Works of William Cullen Bryant.* Ed. Parke Godwin. New York: D. Appleton, 1883.

REFERENCE

Bryant, William Cullen. *Complete Prose Writings of William Cullen Bryant.* Ed. Parke Godwin. New York: D. Appleton, 1884.

McLean, Albert F. *William Cullen Bryant.* New York: Twayne, 1964.

Peckham, H. H. *Gotham Yankee: A Biography of William Cullen Bryant.* New York: Russell and Russell, 1971.

THANATOPSIS[1]

To him who in the love of Nature holds
Communion with her visible forms, she speaks
A various language; for his gayer hours
She has a voice of gladness, and a smile
5   And eloquence of beauty, and she glides
Into his darker musings, with a mild
And healing sympathy, that seals away
Their sharpness, ere he is aware. When thoughts
Of the last bitter hour come like a blight
10   Over thy spirit, and sad images
Of the stern agony, and shroud, and pall.
And breathless darkness, and the narrow house,
Make thee to shudder, and grow sick at heart—
Go forth, under the open sky, and list
15   To Nature's teachings, while from all around—
Earth and her waters, and the depths of air—
Comes a still voice—Yet a few days, and thee
The all-beholding sun shall see no more
In all his course; nor yet in the cold ground,
20   Where thy pale form was laid, with many tears,
Nor in the embrace of ocean, shall exist
Thy image. Earth, that nourished thee, shall claim
Thy growth, to be resolved to earth again,
And, lost each human trace, surrendering up
25   Thine individual being, shalt thou go
To mix for ever with the elements.
To be a brother to the insensible rock
And to the sluggish clod, which the rude swain
Turns with his share,[2] and treads upon. The oak
30   Shall send his roots abroad, and pierce thy mould.

Yet not to thine eternal resting-place
Shalt thou retire alone, nor couldst thou wish
Couch more magnificent. Thou shalt lie down

---

[1]A meditation on death. Bryant said later that he wrote the poem when he was seventeen or eighteen years old and added: "As it was first committed to paper, it began with half-line—'Yet a few days, and thee'—and ended with the beginning of another line with the words—'And make their bed with thee.' The rest of the poem—the introduction and the close—was added some years afterward, in 1821, when I first published a little collection of my poems at Cambridge."

[2]Plowshare.

With patriarchs of the infant world—with kings,
35 The powerful of the earth—the wise, the good,
Fair forms, and hoary seers of ages past,
All in one mighty sepulchre. The hills.
Rock-ribbed and ancient as the sun,—the vales
Stretching in pensive quietness between;
40 The venerable woods—rivers that move
In majesty, and the complaining brooks
That make the meadows green; and, poured round all,
Old Ocean's gray and melancholy waste,—
Are but the solemn decorations all
45 Of the great tomb of man. The golden sun,
The planets, all the infinite host of heaven,
Are shining on the sad abodes of death,
Through the still lapse of ages. All that tread
The globe are but a handful to the tribes
50 That slumber in its bosom.—Take the wings
Of morning, pierce the Barcan[3] wilderness,
Or lose thyself in the continuous woods
Where rolls the Oregon,[4] and hears no sound,
Save his own dashings–yet the dead are there:
55 And millions in those solitudes, since first
The flight of years began, have laid them down
In their last sleep—the dead reign there alone.
So shalt thou rest, and what if thou withdraw
In silence from the living, and no friend
60 Take note of thy departure? All that breathe
Will share thy destiny. The gay will laugh
When thou are gone, the solemn brood of care
Plod on, and each one as before will chase
His favorite phantom; yet all these shall leave
65 Their mirth and their employments, and shall come
And make their bed with thee. As the long train
Of ages glide away, the sons of men,
The youth in life's green spring, and he who goes
In the full strength of years, matron and maid,
70 The speechless babe, and the gray-headed man—
Shall one by one be gathered to thy side,
By those, who in their turn shall follow them.

So live, that when thy summons comes to join

---

[3]Bryant here calls the American desert after the Libyan desert of Barca.
[4]The Indian name for the Columbia River.

The innumerable caravan, which moves
75 To that mysterious realm, where each shall take
His chamber in the silent halls of death,
Thou go not, like the quarry-slave at night,
Scourged to his dungeon, but, sustained and soothed
By an unfaltering trust, approach thy grave,
80 Like one who wraps the drapery of his couch
About him, and lies down to pleasant dreams.[5]

INSCRIPTION FOR THE ENTRANCE TO A WOOD

Stranger, if thou has learned a truth which needs
No school of long experience, that the world
Is full of guilt and misery, and hast seen
Enough of all its sorrows, crimes, and cares,
5 To tire thee of it, enter this wild wood
And view the haunts of Nature. The calm shade
Shall bring a kindred calm, and the sweet breeze
That makes the green leaves dance, shall waft a balm
To thy sick heart. Thou wilt find nothing here
10 Of all that pained thee in the haunts of men,
And made thee loathe thy life. The primal curse[1]
Fell, it is true, upon the unsinning earth,
But not in vengeance. God hath yoked to guilt
Her pale tormentor, misery. Hence, these shades
15 Are still the abodes of gladness; the thick roof
Of green and stirring branches is alive
And musical with birds, that sing and sport
In wantonness of spirit; while below
The squirrel, with raised paws and form erect,
20 Chirps merrily. Throngs of insects in the shade
Try their thin wings and dance in the warm beam
That waked them into life. Even the green trees
Partake the deep contentment; as they bend

[5]Bryant intended the Roman tone of these last lines to reinforce the stoic serenity they are calling for.

[1]The original sin, committed by Adam and Eve in the Garden of Eden, violated the harmony of creation with God, and thereby man and nature "fell" into its present imperfect state. However, nature's fallen state is without consciousness or guilt, whereas man is aware of his condition and of his own generic and personal guilt for his own miserable condition.

To the soft winds, the sun from the blue sky
25   Looks in and sheds a blessing on the scene.
Scarce less the cleft-born wild-flower seems to enjoy
Existence, than the wingèd plunderer
That sucks its sweets. The mossy rocks themselves
And the old and ponderous trunks of prostrate trees
30   That lead from knoll to knoll a causey[2] rude
Or bridge the sunken brook, and their dark roots,
With all their earth upon them, twisting high,
Breathe fixed tranquility. The rivulet
Sends forth glad sounds, and tripping o'er its bed
35   Of pebbly sands, or leaping down the rocks,
Seems, with continuous laughter, to rejoice
In its own being. Softly tread the marge,
Lest from her midway perch thou scare the wren
That dips her bill in water. The cool wind,
40   That stirs the stream in play, shall come to thee,
Like one that loves thee nor will let thee pass
Ungreeted, and shall give its light embrace.

TO A WATERFOWL

Whither, midst falling dew,
While glow the heavens with the last steps of day,
Far, through their rosy depths, dost thou pursue
Thy solitary way?

5   Vainly the fowler's[1] eye
Might mark thy distant flight, to do thee wrong,
As, darkly seen against the crimson sky,
Thy figure floats along.

Seek'st thou the plashy brink
10   Of weedy lake, or marge of river wide,
Or where the rocking billows rise and sink
On the chafed ocean-side?

[2]Causeway.
———
[1]Hunter's.

There is a Power, whose care
Teaches thy way along that pathless coast—
15 The desert and illimitable air—
Lone wandering, but not lost.

All day thy wings have fanned,
At that far height, the cold, thin atmosphere,
Yet stoop not, weary, to the welcome land,
20 Though the dark night is near.

And soon that toil shall end;
Soon shalt thou find a summer home, and rest,
And scream among thy fellows; reeds shall bend,
Soon, o'er thy sheltered nest.

25 Thou'rt gone, the abyss of heaven
Hath swallowed up thy form; yet, on my heart
Deeply has sunk the lesson thou hast given,
And shall not soon depart.

He, who, from zone to zone,
30 Guides through the boundless sky thy certain flight,
In the long way that I must tread alone,
Will lead my steps aright.

AN INDIAN AT THE
BURIAL-PLACE OF HIS FATHERS

It is the spot I came to seek—
My father's ancient burial-place,
Ere from these vales, ashamed and weak,
Withdrew our wasted race.
5 It is the spot—I know it well—
Of which our old traditions tell.

For here the upland bank sends out
A ridge toward the riverside;
I know the shaggy hills about,
10 The meadows smooth and wide,
The plains, that toward the southern sky,
Fenced east and west by mountains lie.

A white man, gazing on the scene,
  Would say a lovely spot was here,
15 And praise the lawns, so fresh and green,
  Between the hills so sheer.
I like it not—I would the plain
Lay in its tall old groves again.

The sheep are on the slopes around,
20   The cattle in the meadows feed,
And laborers turn the crumbling ground,
  Or drop the yellow seed,
And prancing steeds, in trappings gay,
Whirl the bright chariot o'er the way.

25 Methinks it were a nobler sight
    To see these vales in woods arrayed,
Their summits in the golden light,
    Their trunks in grateful shade,
And herds of deer that bounding go
30 O'er hills and prostrate trees below.

And then to mark the lord of all,
  The forest hero, trained to wars,
Quivered and plumed, and lithe and tall,
  And seamed with glorious scars,
35 Walk forth, amid his reign, to dare
The wolf, and grapple with the bear.

This bank, in which the dead were laid,
  Was sacred when its soil was ours;
Hither the silent Indian maid
40   Brought wreaths of beads and flowers,
And the gray chief and gifted seer
Worshipped the god of thunders here.

But now the wheat is green and high
  On clods that hid the warrior's breast,
45 And scattered in the furrows lie
    The weapons of his rest;
And there, in the loose sand, is thrown
Of his large arm the mouldering bone.

Ah, little thought the strong and brave
50   Who bore their lifeless chieftain forth—

Or the young wife that weeping gave
   Her first-born to the earth,
That the pale race who waste us now
Among their bones should guide the plough.

55 They waste us—ay—like April snow
   In the warm noon, we shrink away;
And fast they follow, as we go
   Toward the setting day—
Till they shall fill the land, and we
60 Are driven into the Western sea.

But I behold a fearful sign,
   To which the white men's eyes are blind;
Their race may vanish hence, like mine,
   And leave no trace behind,
65 Save ruins o'er the region spread,
And the white stones above the dead.[3]

Before these fields were shorn and tilled,
   Full to the brim our rivers flowed;
The melody of waters filled
70   The fresh and boundless wood;
And torrents dashed and rivulets played,
And fountains spouted in the shade.

Those grateful sounds are heard no more,
   The springs are silent in the sun;
75 The rivers, by the blackened shore,
   With lessening current run;
The realm our tribes are crushed to get
May be a barren desert yet.

[3]This theme—the cyclic nature of history and consequently the inevitable fall
of the new civilization just establishing itself in the New World—expresses a
doubt and anxiety from the earliest days of the Republic. For example, Thomas
Cole, (see Bryant's sonnet to Cole) painted a series of canvases called "The
Course of Empire" tracing the rise, decline, and fall of a society.

A SCENE ON THE BANKS OF THE HUDSON

Cool shades and dews are round my way,
And silence of the early day;
Mid the dark rocks that watch his bed,
Glitters the mighty Hudson spread,
5   Unrippled, save by drops that fall
From shrubs that fringe his mountain wall;
And o'er the clear still water swells
The music of the Sabbath bells.

All, save this little nook of land
10   Circled with trees, on which I stand;
All, save that line of hills which lie
Suspended in the mimic sky—
Seems a blue void, above, below,
Through which the white clouds come and go,
15   And from the green world's farthest steep
I gaze into the airy deep.

Loveliest of lovely things are they,
On earth, that soonest pass away.
The rose that lives its little hour
20   Is prized beyond the sculptured flower.
Even love, long tried and cherished long,
Becomes more tender and more strong,
At thought of that insatiate grave
From which its yearnings cannot save.

25   River! in this still hour thou hast
Too much of heaven on earth to last;
Nor long may thy still waters lie,
An image of the glorious sky.
Thy fate and mine are not repose,
30   And ere another evening close,
Thou to thy tides shalt turn again,
And I to seek the crowd of men.

TO COLE, THE PAINTER, DEPARTING FOR EUROPE[1]

Thine eyes shall see the light of distant skies:
    Yet, COLE! thy heart shall bear to Europe's strand
    A living image of our own bright land,
Such as upon thy glorious canvas lies;
5   Lone lakes—savannas where the bison roves—
    Rocks rich with summer garlands—sole streams—
    Skies, where the desert eagle wheels and screams—
Spring bloom and autumn blaze of boundless groves.
Fair scenes shall greet thee where thou goest—fair,
10   But different—everywhere the trace of men,
    Paths, homes, graves, ruins, from the lowest glen
To where life shrinks from the fierce Alpine air,
    Gaze on them, till the tears shall dim thy sight,
    But keep that earlier, wilder image bright.

TO THE FRINGED GENTIAN

Thou blossom bright with autumn dew,
And colored with the heaven's own blue,
That openest when the quiet light
Succeeds the keen and frosty night.

5   Thou comest not when violets lean
O'er wandering brooks and springs unseen,
Or columbines, in purple dressed,
Nod o'er the ground-bird's hidden nest.

Thou waitest late and com'st alone,
10   When woods are bare and birds are flown.
And frosts and shortening days portend
The aged year is near his end.

---

[1]Thomas Cole (1801–1848) was the chief painter of the Hudson River School, which painted American landscape to show its beauty and sublimity as a source of the moral character of "Nature's nation." Cole was a friend of Cooper as well as of Bryant.

Then doth thy sweet and quiet eye
Look through its fringes to the sky,
15 Blue—blue—as if that sky let fall
A flower from its cerulean wall.

I would that thus, when I shall see
The hour of death draw near to me,
Hope, blossoming within my heart,
20 May look to heaven as I depart.

HYMN OF THE CITY

Not in the solitude
Alone may man commune with Heaven, or see
Only in savage wood
And sunny vale, the present Deity;
5   Or only hear his voice
Where the winds whisper and the waves rejoice.

Even here do I behold
Thy steps, Almighty!—here, amidst the crowd,
Through the great city[1] rolled,
10 With everlasting murmur deep and loud—
Choking the ways that wind
'Mongst the proud piles, the work of human kind.

Thy golden sunshine comes
From the round heaven, and on their dwellings lies,
15   And lights their inner homes;
For them thou fill'st with air the unbounded skies,
And givest them the stores
Of ocean, and the harvests of its shores.

Thy Spirit is around,
20 Quickening the restless mass that sweeps along;
And this eternal sound—
Voices and footfalls of the numberless throng—
Like the resounding sea,
Or like the rainy tempest, speaks of Thee.

[1]Bryant moved to New York City in 1825.

25   And when the hours of rest
       Come, like a calm upon the mid-sea brine,
          Hushing its billowy breast—
       The quiet of that moment too is thine,
          It breathes of Him who keeps
30   The vast and helpless city while it sleeps.

THE PRAIRIES

     These are the gardens of the Desert, these
     The unshorn fields, boundless and beautiful,
     For which the speech of England has no name—
     The Prairies. I behold them for the first,
5   And my heart swells, while the dilated sight
     Takes in the encircling vastness. Lo! they stretch
     In airy undulations, far away,
     As if the Ocean, in his gentlest swell,
     Stood still, with all his rounded billows fixed,
10   And motionless forever. Motionless?—
     No—they are all unchained again. The clouds
     Sweep over with their shadows, and, beneath,
     The surface rolls and fluctuates to the eye;
     Dark hollows seem to glide along and chase
15   The sunny ridges. Breezes of the South!
     Who toss the golden and the flame-like flowers,
     And pass the prairie-hawk that, poised on high,
     Flaps his broad wings, yet moves not—ye have played
     Among the palms of Mexico and vines
20   Of Texas, and have crisped the limpid brooks
     That from the fountains of Sonora[1] glide
     Into the calm Pacific—have ye fanned
     A nobler or a lovelier scene than this?
     Man hath no part in all this glorious work:
25   The hand that built the firmament hath heaved
     And smoothed these verdant swells, and sown their slopes
     With herbage, planted them with island-groves,
     And hedged them round with forests. Fitting floor
     For this magnificent temple of the sky—
30   With flowers whose glory and whose multitude

---

[1]The name of a state in Mexico.

Rival the constellations! The great heavens
Seem to stoop down upon the scene in love,—
A nearer vault, and of a tenderer blue,
Than that which bends above our Eastern hills.

35   As o'er the verdant waste I guide my steed,
Among the high rank grass that sweeps his sides
The hollow beating of his footstep seems
A sacrilegious sound. I think of those
Upon whose rest he tramples. Are they here—
40   The dead of other days?—and did the dust
Of these fair solitudes once stir with life
And burn with passion? Let the mighty mounds
That overlook the rivers, or that rise
In the dim forest crowded with old oaks,
45   Answer. A race, that long has passed away,
Built them; a disciplined and populous race
Heaped, with long toil, the earth, while yet the Greek
Was hewing the Pentelicus[2] to forms
Of symmetry, and rearing on its rock
50   The glittering Parthenon. These ample fields
Nourished their harvests, here their herds were fed,
When haply by their stalls the bison lowed,
And bowed his maned shoulder to the yoke.
All day this desert murmured with their toils,
55   Till twilight blushed, and lovers walked, and wooed
In a forgotten language, and old tunes,
From instruments of unremembered form,
Gave the soft winds a voice. The red-man came—
The roaming hunter-tribes, warlike and fierce,
60   And the mound-builders vanished from the earth.
The solitude of centuries untold
Has settled where they dwelt. The prairie-wolf
Hunts in their meadows, and his fresh-dug den
Yawns by my path. The gopher mines the ground
65   Where stood their swarming cities. All is gone;
All—save the piles of earth that hold their bones,
The platforms where they worshipped unknown gods,
The barriers which they builded from the soil
To keep the foe at bay—till o'er the walls
70   The wild beleaguerers broke, and, one by one,
The strongholds of the plain were forced, and heaped

[2]The mountain from which the Greeks quarried the stone for the Parthenon.

With corpses. The brown vultures of the wood
Flocked to those vast uncovered sepulchres,
And sat, unscared and silent, at their feast.
75 Haply some solitary fugitive,
Lurking in marsh and forest, till the sense
Of desolation and of fear became
Bitterer than death, yielded himself to die.
Man's better nature triumphed then. Kind words
80 Welcomed and soothed him; the rude conquerors
Seated the captive with their chiefs; he chose
A bride among their maidens, and at length
Seemed to forget—yet ne'er forgot—the wife
Of his first love, and her sweet little ones.
85 Butchered, amid their shrieks, with all his race.

Thus change the forms of being. Thus arise
Races of living things, glorious in strength,
And perish, as the quickening breath of God
Fills them, or is withdrawn. The red-man, too,
90 Has left the blooming wilds he ranged so long,
And, nearer to the Rocky Mountains, sought
A wilder hunting-ground. The beaver builds
No longer by these streams, but far away,
On waters whose blue surface ne'er gave back
95 The white man's face—among Missouri's springs,
And pools whose issues swell the Oregon—
He rears his little Venice. In these plains
The bison feeds no more. Twice twenty leagues
Beyond remotest smoke of hunter's camp,
100 Roams the majestic brute, in herds that shake
The earth with thundering steps—yet here I meet
His ancient footprints stamped beside the pool.

Still this great solitude is quick with life.
Myriads of insects, gaudy as the flowers
105 They flutter over, gentle quadrupeds,
And birds, that scarce have learned the fear of man,
Are here, and sliding reptiles of the ground,
Startlingly beautiful. The graceful deer
Bounds to the wood at my approach. The bee,
110 A more adventurous colonist than man,
With whom he came across the eastern deep,
Fills the savannas with his murmurings,
And hides his sweets, as in the golden age,

Within the hollow oak. I listen long
115   To his domestic hum, and think I hear
The sound of that advancing multitude
Which soon shall fill these deserts. From the ground
Comes up the laugh of children, the soft voice
Of maidens, and the sweet and solemn hymn
120   Of Sabbath worshippers. The low of herds
Blends with the rustling of the heavy grain
Over the dark brown furrows. All at once
A fresher wind sweeps by, and breaks my dream,
And I am in the wilderness alone.

Ralph Waldo Emerson (1803–1882)

Son of the liberal pastor of the First Unitarian Church of Boston, Emerson became pastor of the Second Church in 1829 after graduating from Harvard College (1821) and the Harvard Divinity School. In 1831 his consumptive wife of seventeen months, Ellen Tucker, died; in the following year he resigned from his pulpit because he no longer accepted the main tenets of Christianity. In 1833 he went to Europe to recover from his grief and to think about his life's vocation. There he met Landor, Wordsworth, Coleridge, and Carlyle, who encouraged him to study the German Idealist philosophers.

On his return Emerson moved to Concord; from the "Old Manse" came his manifesto, *Nature* (1836). With "The American Scholar" (1837) and "The Divinity School Address" (1838), he began a long career as lecturer and essayist on matters philosophical, ethical, and aesthetic. A group of Transcendentalists gathered about him in Concord, and they became a revolutionary force not just in philosophy, theology, and poetry but in education, social experimentation, and women's rights.

Emerson's conviction that Nature is symbol of Spirit led him to conceive of the poet as a seer, open to the Oversoul as it worked through material forms, and expressing his intuitive insights in verse whose organic form grew out of the experience. He was aware of his limitations in verse and said that much of his best poetry was in his essays. Yet his ideas about the poet and the poetic process, as well as his experiments with a freer technique, mark the beginning of a distinctive American poetry. With Margaret Fuller he edited *The Dial* from 1840 to 1844; this publication became the organ for Transcendentalists like Thoreau and

---

TEXT

Emerson, Ralph Waldo. *The Complete Works of Ralph Waldo Emerson,* Centenary Edition. Ed. Edward Waldo Emerson. Boston: Houghton Mifflin, 1903–1904.

REFERENCE

Ralph Waldo Emerson: A Collection of Critical Essays. Ed. Milton R. Konvitz and Stephen E. Whicher. Englewood Cliffs, N.J.: Prentice-Hall, 1962.

Hopkins, Vivian C. *Spires of Form: A Study of Emerson's Aesthetic Theory.* New York: Russell and Russell, 1951, 1965.

Matthiessen, F. O. *American Renaissance.* London and New York: Oxford University Press, 1941.

Paul, Sherman. *Emerson's Angle of Vision.* Cambridge, Mass.: Harvard University Press, 1952.

Porte, Joel. *Emerson and Thoreau: Transcendentalists in Conflict.* Middletown, Conn.: Wesleyan University Press, 1966.

Rusk, Ralph L. *The Life of Ralph Waldo Emerson.* New York: Scribner, 1949.

Whicher, Stephen E. *Freedom and Fate: An Inner Life of Ralph Waldo Emerson.* Philadelphia: University of Pennsylvania Press, 1953.

Theodore Parker. By 1860 the man who had been denounced for preaching "the latest form of infidelity" was the revered "Sage of Concord," and a favorite lecturer on the Lyceum circuit. Except for the death of his son Waldo in 1842 and the burning of his house in 1872, Emerson lived a long and serene life, assimilating neo-Platonism, German Idealism and Eastern mysticism into his conviction that each man, if he were self-reliant enough, would discover his harmony with Nature and the Oversoul. His volumes of verse are *Poems* (1847) and *May-Day* (1867); other major volumes of prose are *Essays* (1841 and 1844), *Representative Men* (1850), and *The Conduct of Life* (1860).

EACH AND ALL

Little thinks, in the field, yon red-cloaked clown[1]
Of thee from the hill-top looking down;
The heifer that lows in the upland farm,
Far-heard, lows not thine ear to charm;
5 The sexton, tolling his bell at noon,
Deems not that great Napoleon
Stops his horse, and lists with delight,
Whilst his files sweep round yon Alpine height;
Nor knowest thou what argument
10 Thy life to thy neighbor's creed has lent.
All are needed by each one;
Nothing is fair or good alone.
I thought the sparrow's note from heaven,
Singing at dawn on the alder bough;
15 I brought him home, in his nest, at even;
He sings the song, but it cheers not now,
For I did not bring home the river and sky;—
He sang to my ear,—they sang to my eye.
The delicate shells lay on the shore;
20 The bubbles of the latest wave
Fresh pearls to their enamel gave,
And the bellowing of the savage sea
Greeted their safe escape to me.
I wiped away the weeds and foam,
25 I fetched my sea-born treasures home;
But the poor, unsightly, noisome things
Had left their beauty on the shore
With the sun and the sand and the wild uproar.
The lover watched his graceful maid,
30 As 'mid the virgin train she strayed,
Nor knew her beauty's best attire
Was woven still by the snow-white choir.
At last she came to his hermitage,
Like the bird from the woodlands to the cage;—
35 The gay enchantment was undone,
A gentle wife, but fairy none.
Then I said, 'I covet truth;
Beauty is unripe childhood's cheat;
I leave it behind with the games of youth:'—

[1]Peasant.

40 As I spoke, beneath my feet
    The ground-pine curled its pretty wreath,
    Running over the club-moss burrs;
    I inhaled the violet's breath;
    Around me stood the oaks and firs;
45 Pine-cones and acorns lay on the ground;
    Over me soared the eternal sky,
    Full of light and of deity;
    Again I saw, again I heard,
    The rolling river, the morning bird;—
50 Beauty through my senses stole;
    I yielded myself to the perfect whole.

URIEL[1]

It fell in the ancient periods
    Which the brooding soul surveys,
Or ever the wild Time coined itself
    Into calendar months and days.

5   This was the lapse of Uriel,
    Which in Paradise befell.
    Once, among the Pleiads[2] walking
    Seyd[3] overheard the young gods talking;
    And the treason, too long pent,
10 To his ears was evident.
    The young deities discussed
    Laws of form, and metre just,
    Orb, quintessence, and sunbeams,
    What subsisteth, and what seems.
15 One, with low tones that decide,
    And doubt and reverend use defied,
    With a look that solved the sphere,

[1]In Milton's *Paradise Lost* Uriel is Archangel of the Sun and is one of the seven angels standing near the throne of God. Emerson wrote this poem after his "Divinity School Address," delivered in 1838 at the Harvard Divinity School, had brought vehement condemnation from orthodox theologians as "the latest form of infidelity."
[2]A group of stars in the constellation Taurus.
[3]Possibly Sadi, a thirteenth-century Persian poet, about whom Emerson wrote a poem; here, the figure of the poet overhearing and recording the words of the gods.

And stirred the devils everywhere,
Gave his sentiment divine
20 Against the being of a line.
'Line in nature is not found;
Unit and universe are round;
In vain produced, all rays return;
Evil will bless, and ice will burn.'
25 As Uriel spoke with piercing eye,
A shudder ran around the sky;
The stern old war-gods shook their heads,
The seraphs frowned from myrtle-beds;
Seemed to the holy festival
30 The rash word boded ill to all;
The balance-beam of Fate was bent;
The bounds of good and ill were rent;
Strong Hades could not keep his own,
But all slid to confusion.

35 A sad self-knowledge, withering, fell
On the beauty of Uriel;
In heaven once eminent, the god
Withdrew, that hour, into his cloud;
Whether doomed to long gyration
40 In the sea of generation,[4]
Or by knowledge grown too bright
To hit the nerve of feebler sight.
Straightway, a forgetting wind
Stole over the celestial kind,
45 And their lips the secret kept,
If in ashes the fire-seed slept.
But now and then, truth-speaking things
Shamed the angels' veiling wings;
And, shrilling from the solar course,
50 Or from fruit of chemic force,
Procession of a soul in matter,
Or the speeding change of water,
Or out of the good of evil born,
Came Uriel's voice of cherub scorn,
55 And a blush tinged the upper sky,
And the gods shook, they knew not why.

---

[4]The Pythagorean doctrine of metempsychosis, or transmigration of souls from one corporeal form to another in successive life cycles.

HAMATREYA[1]

Bulkeley, Hunt, Willard, Hosmer, Meriam, Flint,[2]
Possessed the land which rendered to their toil
Hay, corn, roots, hemp, flax, apples, wool and wood.
Each of these landlords walked amidst his farm,
5 Saying, ' 'Tis mine, my children's and my name's.
How sweet the west wind sounds in my own trees!
How graceful climb those shadows on my hill!
I fancy these pure waters and the flags
Know me, as does my dog: we sympathize;
10 And, I affirm, my actions smack of the soil.'

Where are these men? Asleep beneath their grounds:
And strangers, fond as they, their furrows plough.
Earth laughs in flowers, to see her boastful boys
Earth-proud, proud of the earth which is not theirs;
15 Who steer the plough, but cannot steer their feet
Clear of the grave.
They added ridge to valley, brook to pond,
And sighed for all that bounded their domain;
'This suits me for a pasture; that's my park;
20 We must have clay, lime, gravel, granite-ledge,
And misty lowland, where to go for peat.
The land is well,—lies fairly to the south.
'Tis good, when you have crossed the sea and back,
To find the sitfast acres where you left them.'
25 Ah! the hot owner sees not Death, who adds
Him to his land, a lump of mould the more.
Hear what the Earth says:—

EARTH-SONG

'Mine and yours;
Mine, not yours.
30 Earth endures;
Stars abide—
Shine down in the old sea;

---

[1]The poem adapts a passage from the fourth book of the *Vishnu Purana*, one of the sacred texts of the Hindus. Hamatreya is Emerson's version of Maitreya, one name of a Hindu god meaning "The Loved One" and mentioned in the passage in the *Vishnu Purana*.

[2]Bulkeley is a seventeenth-century settler; Willard bought land from the Indians and founded Concord; the rest are also early settlers.

Old are the shores;
But where are old men?
35　I who have seen much,
Such have I never seen.

'The lawyer's deed
Ran sure,
In tail,[3]
40　To them, and to their heirs
Who shall succeed,
Without fail,
Forevermore.

'Here is the land,
45　Shaggy with wood,
With its old valley,
Mound and flood.
But the heritors?—
Fled like the flood's foam.
50　The lawyer, and the laws,
And the kingdom,
Clean swept herefrom.

'They called me theirs,
Who so controlled me;
55　Yet every one
Wished to stay, and is gone,
How am I theirs,
If they cannot hold me,
But I hold them?'

60　When I heard the Earth-song
I was no longer brave;
My avarice cooled
Like lust in the chill of the grave.

[3]Restricted to inheritance by immediate bodily heirs of the owner.

THE RHODORA:

On Being Asked, Whence Is the Flower?

In May, when sea-winds pierced our solitudes,
I found the fresh Rhodora in the woods,
Spreading its leafless blooms in a damp nook,
To please the desert and the sluggish brook.
5 The purple petals, fallen in the pool,
Made the black water with their beauty gay;
Here might the red-bird come his plumes to cool,
And court the flower that cheapens his array.
Rhodora! if the sages ask thee why
10 This charm is wasted on the earth and sky,
Tell them, dear, that if eyes were made for seeing,
Then Beauty is its own excuse for being:
Why thou wert there, O rival of the rose!
I never thought to ask, I never knew:
15 But, in my simple ignorance, suppose
The self-same Power that brought me there brought you.

THE SNOW-STORM

Announced by all the trumpets of the sky,
Arrives the snow, and, driving o'er the fields,
Seems nowhere to alight: the whited air
Hides hills and woods, the river, and the heaven,
5 And veils the farm-house at the garden's end.
The sled and traveller stopped, the courier's feet
Delayed, all friends shut out, the housemates sit
Around the radiant fireplace, enclosed
In a tumultuous privacy of storm.

10   Come see the north wind's masonry.
Out of an unseen quarry evermore
Furnished with tile, the fierce artificer
Curves his white bastions with projected roof
Round every windward stake, or tree, or door.
15 Speeding, the myriad-handed, his wild work
So fanciful, so savage, nought cares he
For number or proportion. Mockingly,

On coop or kennel he hangs Parian[1] wreaths;
A swan-like form invests the hidden thorn;
20 Fills up the farmer's lane from wall to wall,
Maugre[2] the farmer's sighs; and at the gate
A tapering turret overtops the work.
And when his hours are numbered, and the world
Is all his own, retiring, as he were not,
25 Leaves, when the sun appears, astonished Art
To mimic in slow structures, stone by stone,
Built in an age, the mad wind's night-work,
The frolic architecture of the snow.

FABLE

The mountain and the squirrel
Had a quarrel,
And the former called the latter 'Little Prig;'
Bun replied,
5 'You are doubtless very big;
But all sorts of things and weather
Must be taken in together,
To make up a year
And a sphere.
10 And I think it no disgrace
To occupy my place.
If I'm not so large as you,
You are not so small as I,
And not half so spry.
15 I'll not deny you make
A very pretty squirrel track;
Talents differ; all is well and wisely put;
If I cannot carry forests on my back,
Neither can you crack a nut.'

[1]Paros is a Greek island noted for its marble.
[2]Despite.

ODE

Inscribed to W. H. Channing[1]

Though loath to grieve
The evil time's sole patriot,
I cannot leave
My honied thought
5   For the priest's cant,
Or statesman's rant.

If I refuse
My study for their politique,
Which at the best is trick,
10   The angry Muse
Puts confusion in my brain.

But who is he that prates
Of the culture of mankind,
Of better arts and life?
15   Go, blindworm, go,
Behold the famous States
Harrying Mexico[2]
With rifle and with knife!

Or who, with accent bolder,
20   Dare praise the freedom-loving mountaineer?
I found by thee, O rushing Contoocook![3]
And in thy valleys, Agiochook![4]
The jackals of the negro-holder.[5]

The God who made New Hampshire
25   Taunted the lofty land

[1]William Henry Channing (1810–1884), the nephew of the great Unitarian minister William Ellery Channing (1780–1842), was a Unitarian clergyman as well as a Transcendentalist poet and friend of Emerson. Channing had urged Emerson to commit himself more actively to social and political issues, and, particularly to take action, beyond his previous verbal endorsement and moral support, in the Abolitionists' fight against slavery. The "Ode" is Emerson's response.

[2]The War with Mexico (1846–1848) was widely condemned in New England as an imperialistic attack on a weaker nation in order to expand national boundaries.

[3]A river in New Hampshire.

[4]The Indian name for the White Mountains.

[5]Dogs used to hunt down slaves under the Fugitive Slave Act.

With little men;—
Small blat and wren
House in the oak:—
If earth-fire cleave
30 The upheaved land, and bury the folk,
The southern crocodile would grieve.
Virtue palters; Right is hence;
Freedom praised, but hid;
Funeral eloquence
35 Rattles the coffin-lid.

What boots thy zeal,
O glowing friend,
That would indignant rend
The northland from the south?
40 Wherefore? to what good end?
Boston Bay and Bunker Hill
Would serve things still;—
Things are of the snake.

The horseman serves the horse,
45 The neatherd serves the neat,[6]
The merchant serves the purse,
The eater serves his meat;
'Tis the day of the chattel,
Web to weave, and corn to grind;
50 Things are in the saddle,
And ride mankind.

There are two laws discrete,[7]
Not reconciled,—
Law for man, and law for thing;
55 The last builds town and fleet,
But it runs wild,
And doth the man unking.

'Tis fit the forest fall,
The steep be graded,
60 The mountain tunnelled,
The sand shaded,
The orchard planted,

[6]Cattle.
[7]Distinct.

The glebe[8] tilled,
The prairie granted,
65 The steamer built.

Let man serve law for man;
Live for friendship, live for love,
For truth's and harmony's behoof;
The state may follow how it can,
70 As Olympus follows Jove.

Yet do not I implore
The wrinkled shopman to my sounding woods,
Nor bid the unwilling senator
Ask votes of thrushes in the solitudes.
75 Every one to his chosen work;—
Foolish hands may mix and mar;
Wise and sure the issues are.
Round they roll till dark is light,
Sex to sex, and even to odd;—
80 The over-god
Who marries Right to Might,
Who peoples, unpeoples,—
He who exterminates
Races by stronger races,
85 Black by white faces,—
Knows to bring honey
Out of the lion;[9]
Grafts gentlest scion
On pirate and Turk.[10]

90 The Cossack eats Poland,[11]
Like stolen fruit;
Her last noble is ruined,
Her last poet mute:
Straight, into double band
95 The victors divide;
Half for freedom strike and stand;—
The astonished Muse finds thousands at her side.

[8]Field.
[9]In Judges 14, Samson finds a honeycomb in the body of a lion he has slain.
[10]Both notable for their ferocity.
[11]The Russians had successively taken over Polish territory in a series of "partitions" in the late eighteenth century and had quelled a Polish revolution against Russian rule in 1830.

MERLIN[1]

I

Thy trivial harp will never please
Or fill my craving ear;
Its chords should ring as blows the breeze,
Free, peremptory, clear.
5 No jingling serenader's art,[2]
Nor tinkle of piano strings,
Can make the wild blood start
In its mystic springs.
The kingly bard
10 Must smite the chords rudely and hard,
As with hammer or with mace;
That they may render back
Artful thunder, which conveys
Secrets of the solar track,
15 Sparks of the supersolar blaze.
Merlin's blows are strokes of fate,
Chiming with the forest tone,
When boughs buffet boughs in the wood;
Chiming with the gasp and moan
20 Of the ice-imprisoned flood;
With the pulse of manly hearts;
With the voice of orators;
With the din of city arts;
With the cannonade of wars;
25 With the marches of the brave;
And prayers of might from martyrs' cave.

Great is the art,
Great be the manners, of the bard.
He shall not his brain encumber
30 With the coil of rhythm and number;
But, leaving rule and pale forethought,
He shall aye climb
For his rhyme.

[1]Merlin, the magician of Arthurian legend, is here the type of the prophetic bard. Emerson saw in Norse and Welsh sagas the kind of poetry he was calling for in America and associated such poetry with Merlin.
[2]Emerson is almost surely referring here to Poe, the skilled craftsman of artifice, whom he called "the jingle man," as the type of the opposite kind of poetry from Merlin.

'Pass in, pass in,' the angels say,
35 'In to the upper doors,
Nor count compartments of the floors,
But mount to paradise
By the stairway of surprise.'

Blameless master of the games,
40 King of sport that never shames,
He shall daily joy dispense
Hid in song's sweet influence.
Forms more cheerly live and go,
What time the subtle mind
45 Sings aloud the tune whereto
Their pulses beat,
And march their feet,
And their members are combined.

By Sybarites[3] beguiled,
50 He shall no task decline;
Merlin's mighty line[4]
Extremes of nature reconciled,—
Bereaved a tyrant of his will,
And made the lion mild.
55 Songs can the tempest still,
Scattered on the stormy air,
Mould the year to fair increase,
And bring in poetic peace.

He shall not seek to weave,
60 In weak, unhappy times,
Efficacious rhymes;
Wait his returning strength.
Bird that from the nadir's floor
To the zenith's top can soar,—
65 The soaring orbit of the muse exceeds that
journey's length.
Nor profane affect to hit
Or compass that, by meddling wit,[5]
Which only the propitious mind

[3]The people of a Greek city in Italy known for their luxuriation in epicurean pleasure.
[4]In "To the Memory of My Beloved Master William Shakespeare," Ben Jonson coined the phrase "Marlowe's mighty line."
[5]Wordsworth spoke of "meddling intellect."

Publishes when 'tis inclined.
70 There are open hours
When the God's will sallies free,
And the dull idiot might see
The flowing fortunes of a thousand years;—
Sudden, at unawares,
75 Self-moved, fly-to the doors,
Nor sword of angels could reveal
What they conceal.

II

The rhyme of the poet
Modulates the king's affairs;
80 Balance-loving Nature
Made all things in pairs.
To every foot its antipode;
Each color with its counter glowed;
To every tone beat answering tones,
85 Higher or graver;
Flavor gladly blends with flavor;
Leaf answers leaf upon the bough;
And match the paired cotyledons.[6]
Hands to hands, and feet to feet,
90 In one body grooms and brides;
Eldest rite, two married sides
In every mortal meet.
Light's far furnace shines,
Smelting balls and bars,
95 Forging double stars,
Glittering twins and trines.
The animals are sick with love,
Lovesick with rhyme;
Each with all propitious Time
100 Into chorus wove.

Like the dancers' ordered band,
Thoughts come also hand in hand;
In equal couples mated,
Or else alternated;
105 Adding by their mutual gage,
One to other, health and age.

[6]The leaf of a plant embryo, the first to appear from a sprouting seed.

Solitary fancies go
Short-lived wandering to and fro,
Most like to bachelors,
110   Or an ungiven maid,
Not ancestors,
With no posterity to make the lie afraid,
Or keep truth undecayed.
Perfect-paired as eagle's wings,
115   Justice is the rhyme of things;
Trade and counting use
The self-same tuneful muse;
And Nemesis,[7]
Who with even matches odd,
120   Who athwart space redresses
The partial wrong,
Fills the just period,
And finishes the song.

Subtle rhymes, with ruin rife,
125   Murmur in the house of life,
Sung by the Sisters[8] as they spin;
In perfect time and measure they
Build and unbuild our echoing clay,
As the two twilights of the day
130   Fold us music-drunken in.

BACCHUS[1]

Bring me wine, but wine which never grew
In the belly of the grape,
Or grew on vine whose tap-roots, reaching through
Under the Andes to the Cape,
5   Suffer no savor of the earth to scape.

[7]The goddess of justice and retribution.
[8]The Fates, who spin, measure, and cut the thread of each life.

[1]The god of wine. In his own copy of *Poems* Emerson wrote as epigraph to "Bacchus" the following citation from Plato: "The man who is his own master knocks in vain at the doors of poetry." Here, as in "Merlin," Emerson favors the seer over the craftsman.

Let its grapes the morn salute
From a nocturnal root,
Which feels the acrid juice
Of Styx and Erebus;[2]
10 And turns the woe of Night,
By its own craft, to a more rich delight.

We buy ashes for bread;
We buy diluted wine;
Give me of the true,—
15 Whose ample leaves and tendrils curled
Among the silver hills of heaven
Draw everlasting dew;
Wine of Wine,
Blood of the world,
20 Form of forms,[3] and mould of statures,
That I intoxicated,
And by the draught assimilated,
May float at pleasure through all natures;
The bird-language rightly spell,
25 And that which roses say so well.

Wine that is shed
Like the torrents of the sun
Up the horizon walls,
Or like the Atlantic streams, which run
30 When the South Sea calls.

Water and bread,
Food which needs no transmuting,
Rainbow-flowering, wisdom-fruiting,
Wine which is already man,
35 Food which teach and reason can.

Wine which Music[4] is,—
Music and wine are one,—
That I, drinking this,
Shall hear far Chaos[5] talk with me;

---

[2]Erebus is the region beneath the earth that the dead must pass to reach Hades;
the river Styx is the boundary they must cross into Hades, the land of the dead.
[3]This phrase is meant to suggest the Platonic doctrine of forms behind the
phenomenological world, and the final unity of all forms.
[4]The harmony that orders the universe, as in Plato's music of the spheres.
[5]The original chaos from which cosmos, an ordered universe, emerged.

40 Kings unborn shall walk with me;
    And the poor grass shall plot and plan
    What it will do when it is man.
    Quickened so, will I unlock
    Every crypt of every rock.

45 I thank the joyful juice
    For all I know;—
    Winds of remembering
    Of the ancient being blow,
    And seeming-solid walls of use
50 Open and flow.

    Pour, Bacchus! the remembering wine;[6]
    Retrieve the loss of me and mine!
    Vine for vine be antidote,
    And the grape requite the lote![7]
55 Haste to cure the old despair,—
    Reason in Nature's lotus drenched,
    The memory of ages quenched;
    Give them again to shine;
    Let wine repair what this undid;
60 And where the infection slid,
    A dazzling memory revive;
    Refresh the faded tints,
    Recut the aged prints,
    And write my old adventures with the pen
65 Which on the first day drew,
    Upon the tablets blue,
    The dancing Pleiads[8] and eternal men.

[6]The phrase suggests Jung's theory of the archetypes of the collective uncon-
scious as well as Plato's notion of a recollected pre-existence. C. G. Jung
(1875–1961), the psychologist.
[7]The lotus, associated with forgetfulness.
[8]A group of stars, mythologically personified as maidens, in the constellation
Taurus.

THE DAY'S RATION

When I was born,
From all the seas of strength Fate filled a chalice,
Saying, 'This be thy portion, child; this chalice,
Less than a lily's, thou shalt daily draw
5 From my great arteries,—nor less, nor more.'
All substances the cunning chemist Time
Melts down into that liquor of my life,—
Friends, foes, joys, fortunes, beauty and disgust.
And whether I am angry or content,
10 Indebted or insulted, loved or hurt,
All he distils into sidereal[1] wine
And brims my little cup; heedless, alas!
Of all he sheds how little it will hold,
How much runs over on the desert sands.
15 If a new Muse draw me with splendid ray,
And I uplift myself into its heaven,
The needs of the first sight absorb my blood,
And all the following hours of the day
Drag a ridiculous age.
20 To-day, when friends approach, and every hour
Brings book, or starbright scroll of genius,
The little cup will hold not a bead more,
And all the costly liquor runs to waste;
Nor gives the jealous lord one diamond drop
25 So to be husbanded for poorer days.
Why need I volumes, if one word suffice?
Why need I galleries, when a pupil's draught
After the master's sketch fills and o'erfills
My apprehension? Why seek Italy,
30 Who cannot circumnavigate the sea
Of thoughts and things at home, but still adjourn
The nearest matters for a thousand days?

[1]Measured or determined by the stars.

BLIGHT[1]

Give me truths;
For I am weary of the surfaces,
And die of inanition. If I knew
Only the herbs and simples of the wood,
5   Rue, cinquefoil, gill, vervain and agrimony,
Blue-vetch and trillium, hawkweed, sassafras,
Milkweeds and murky brakes, quaint pipes and sundew,
And rare and virtuous roots, which in these woods
Draw untold juices from the common earth,
10   Untold, unknown, and I could surely spell
Their fragrance, and their chemistry apply
By sweet affinities to human flesh,
Driving the foe and stablishing the friend,—
O, that were much, and I could be a part
15   Of the round day, related to the sun
And planted world, and full executor
Of their imperfect functions.
But these young scholars, who invade our hills,
Bold as the engineer who fells the wood,
20   And travelling often in the cut he makes,
Love not the flower they pluck, and know it not,
And all their botany is Latin names.
The old men studied magic in the flowers,
And human fortunes in astronomy,
25   And an omnipotence in chemistry,[2]
Preferring things to names, for these were men,
Were unitarians of the united world,
And, wheresoever their clear eye-beams fell,
They caught the footsteps of the SAME. Our eyes
30   Are armed, but we are strangers to the stars,
And strangers to the mystic beast and bird,
And strangers to the plant and to the mine.
The injured elements say, 'Not in us;'
And night and day, ocean and continent,
35   Fire, plant and mineral say, 'Not in us;'
And haughtily return us stare for stare.
For we invade them impiously for gain;
We devastate them unreligiously,

[1]First published with the title "The Times."
[2]Emerson is here referring to such pre-scientific sciences as distilling potions from herbs, astrology, and alchemy.

And coldly ask their pottage, not their love.
40 Therefore they shove us from them, yield to us
Only what to our griping toil is due;
But the sweet affluence of love and song,
The rich results of the divine consents
Of man and earth, of world beloved and lover,
45 The nectar and ambrosia, are withheld;
And in the midst of spoils and slaves, we thieves
And pirates of the universe, shut out
Daily to a more thin and outward rind,
Turn pale and starve. Therefore, to our sick eyes,
50 The stunted trees look sick, the summer short,
Clouds shade the sun, which will not tan our hay,
And nothing thrives to reach its natural term;
And life, shorn of its venerable length,
Even at its greatest space is a defeat,
55 And dies in anger that it was a dupe;
And, in its highest noon and wantonness,
Is early frugal, like a beggar's child;
Even in the hot pursuit of the best aims
And prizes of ambition, checks its hand,
60 Like Alpine cataracts frozen as they leaped,
Chilled with a miserly comparison
Of the toy's purchase with the length of life.

BRAHMA[1]

If the red slayer think he slays,
  Or if the slain think he is slain,
They know not well the subtle ways
  I keep, and pass, and turn again.

5 Far or forgot to me is near;
  Shadow and sunlight are the same;
The vanished gods to me appear;
  And one to me are shame and fame.

---

[1]In Sanskrit "brahman" means "universal soul." Brahma is the person of the
Hindu trinity that is divinity in its creative aspect. In the journals this poem
appears with the title "The Song of the Soul"; the poem shows Emerson's
reading of the *Vishnu Purana* and the *Bhagavat-Gita* and the notebook entries
are filled with extracts from Hindu Scriptures.

They reckon ill who leave me out;
10   When me they fly, I am the wings;
I am the doubter and the doubt,
And I the hymn the Brahmin sings.

The strong gods pine for my abode,
And pine in vain the sacred Seven;[2]
15   But thou, meek lover of the good!
Find me, and turn thy back on heaven.

DAYS

Daughters of Time, the hypocritic Days,
Muffled and dumb like barefoot dervishes,[1]
And marching single in an endless file,
Bring diadems and fagots[2] in their hands.
5   To each they offer gifts after his will,
Bread, kingdoms, stars, and sky that holds them all.
I, in my pleached[3] garden, watched the pomp,
Forgot my morning wishes, hastily
Took a few herbs and apples, and the Day
10   Turned and departed silent. I, too late,
Under her solemn fillet[4] saw the scorn.

THE TITMOUSE[1]

You shall not be overbold
When you deal with arctic cold,
As late I found my lukewarm blood
Chilled wading in the snow-choked wood.
5   How should I fight? my foeman fine

[2]Edward Emerson's note in the Centenary Edition: "The 'Strong Gods' of the fourth verse are Indra, god of sky and wielder of the thunderbolt; Agni, the god of fire; and Yama, the god of death and judgment. These shall finally be absorbed into Brahma. The 'Sacred Seven' are the Maharshis or highest saints."

[1]An order of Muslim ascetics, some of whom sought to achieve ecstasy through whirling dances.
[2]Sticks.
[3]Bordered with interlacing vines or branches.
[4]A band or ribbon, here worn around the hair.

[1]A small, crested, gray-feathered bird of North America.

Has million arms to one of mine:
East, west, for aid I looked in vain,
East, west, north, south, are his domain.
Miles off, three dangerous miles, is home;
10 Must borrow his winds who there would come.
Up and away for life! be fleet!—
The frost-king ties my fumbling feet,
Sings in my ears, my hands are stones,
Curdles the blood to the marble bones,
15 Tugs at the heart-strings, numbs the sense,
And hems in life with narrowing fence.
Well, in this broad bed lie and sleep,—
The punctual stars will vigil keep,—
Embalmed by purifying cold;
20 The winds shall sing their dead-march old,
The snow is no ignoble shroud,
The moon thy mourner, and the cloud.

Softly,—but this way fate was pointing,
'Twas coming fast to such anointing,
25 When piped a tiny voice hard by,
Gay and polite, a cheerful cry,
Chic-chíc-a-dee-dee saucy note
Out of sound heart and merry throat,
As if it said, 'Good day, good sir!
30 Fine afternoon, old passenger!
Happy to meet you in these places,
Where January brings few faces.'

This poet, though he live apart,
Moved by his hospitable heart,
35 Sped, when I passed his sylvan fort,
To do the honors of his court,
As fits a feathered lord of land;
Flew near, with soft wing grazed my hand,
Hopped on the bough, then, darting low,
40 Prints his small impress on the snow,
Shows feats of his gymnastic play,
Head downward, clinging to the spray.

Here was this atom in full breath,
Hurling defiance at vast death;
45 This scrap of valor just for play
Fronts the north-wind in waistcoat gray,

As if to shame my weak behavior;
I greeted loud my little savior,
You pet! what dost here? and what for?
50 In these woods, thy small Labrador,
At this pinch, wee San Salvador!
What fire burns in that little chest
So frolic, stout and self-possest?
Henceforth I wear no stripe but thine;
55 Ashes and jet all hues outshine.
Why are not diamonds black and gray,
To ape thy dare-devil array?
And I affirm, the spacious North
Exists to draw thy virtue forth.
60 I think no virtue goes with size;
The reason of all cowardice
Is, that men are overgrown,
And, to be valiant, must come down
To the titmouse dimension.'

65   'Tis good-will makes intelligence,
And I began to catch the sense
Of my bird's song: 'Live out of doors
In the great woods, on prairie floors.
I dine in the sun; when he sinks in the sea,
70 I too have a hole in a hollow tree;
And I like less when Summer beats
With stifling beams on these retreats,
Than noontide twilights which snow makes
With tempest of the blinding flakes.
75 For well the soul, if stout within,
Can arm impregnably the skin;
And polar frost my frame defied,
Made of the air that blows outside.'

With glad remembrance of my debt,
80 I homeward turn; farewell, my pet!
When here again thy pilgrim comes,
He shall bring store of seeds and crumbs.
Doubt not, so long as earth has bread,
Thou first and foremost shalt be fed;
85 The Providence that is most large
Takes hearts like thine in special charge,
Helps who for their own need are strong,
And the sky doats on cheerful song.

Henceforth I prize thy wiry chant
90   O'er all that mass and minster vaunt;
For men mis-hear thy call in Spring,
As 'twould accost some frivolous wing,
Crying out of the hazel copse, *Phe-be!*
And, in winter, *Chic-a-dee-dee!*
95   I think old Caesar must have heard
In northern Gaul my dauntless bird,
And, echoed in some frosty wold,
Borrowed thy battle-numbers bold.
And I will write our annals new,
100   And thank thee for a better clew,
I, who dreamed not when I came here
To find the antidote of fear,
Now hear thee say in Roman key,
Paean! Veni, vidi, vici.[2]

TERMINUS[1]

It is time to be old,
To take in sail:—
The god of bounds,
Who sets to seas a shore,
5   Came to me in his fatal rounds,
And said: 'No more!
No farther shoot
Thy broad ambitious branches, and thy root.
Fancy departs: no more invent;
10   Contract thy firmament
To compass of a tent.
There's not enough for this and that,
Make thy option which of two;
Economize the failing river,
15   Not the less revere the Giver,
Leave the many and hold the few.
Timely wise accept the terms,
Soften the fall with wary foot;
A little while

[2]Caesar's remark about his Gallic campaign: "I came, I saw, I conquered." Besides meaning "song of praise," *paean* means, in its Greek root, "war cry."

[1]The Roman god of boundaries and landmarks.

20 Still plan and smile,
And,—fault of novel germs,—[2]
Mature the unfallen fruit.
Curse, if thou wilt, thy sires,
Bad husbands of their fires,
25 Who, when they gave thee breath,
Failed to bequeath
The needful sinew stark as once,
The Baresark[3] marrow to thy bones,
But left a legacy of ebbing veins,
30 Inconstant heat and nerveless reins,—
Amid the Muses, left thee deaf and dumb,
Amid the gladiators, halt and numb.'

As the bird trims her to the gale,
I trim myself to the storm of time,
35 I man the rudder, reef the sail,
Obey the voice at eve obeyed at prime:
'Lowly faithful, banish fear,
Right onward drive unharmed;
The port, well worth the cruise, is near,
40 And every wave is charmed.'

PAN

O what are heroes, prophets, men,
But pipes through which the breath of Pan[1] doth blow
A momentary music. Being's tide
Swells hitherward, and myriads of forms
5 Live, robed with beauty, painted by the sun;
Their dust, pervaded by the nerves of God,
Throbs with an overmastering energy
Knowing and doing. Ebbs the tide, they lie
White hollow shells upon the desert shore.
10 But not the less the eternal wave rolls on
To animate new millions, and exhale
Races and planets, its enchanted foam.

[2]For lack of new germs.
[3]Literally: "bare-shirt." Baresark—or Berserk or Berserker—is a ferocious Norse warrior. Here, strong as a Berserker.

[1]The nature diety.

Henry Wadsworth Longfellow (1807–1882)

Born in Portland, Maine, of long and distinguished lineage on both sides, Henry Wadsworth Longfellow graduated from Bowdoin College in 1825 in the same class as Hawthorne. Already he was showing the poetic talents he inherited from his mother, and he traveled in Europe from 1826 to 1829, gathering impressions for his poetry and preparing for a professorship of modern languages at Bowdoin. He married Mary Storer Potter in 1831, accepted a chair at Harvard, and went abroad again to study especially German and Scandinavian literature. During the trip his wife died suddenly.

Returning to the United States, Longfellow moved to Cambridge, Massachusetts, and began to publish his first books: *Hyperion,* a Germanic prose romance, and *Voices of Night,* his initial book of verse, both in 1839; *Poems on Slavery* (1842); *The Poets and Poetry of Europe* (1843), an anthology important in bringing continental literature to America. This same year he married Frances Elizabeth Appleton. His absorption in his writing prompted him to resign from Harvard in 1854, but the years of fame and honors, here and abroad, were marred by the accidental death by fire of his second wife in 1861.

The most important titles of Longfellow's later years are: *Evangeline* (1847), *Kavanagh: A Tale* (1849), *The Song of Hiawatha* (1855), *The Courtship of Miles Standish* (1858), *Tales of a Wayside Inn* (1863, 1872, 1873), a translation of *The Divine Comedy* (1865–1867), and two long dramatic poems: *Christus: A Mystery* (1872), in three parts, *The Divine Tragedy, The Golden Legend,* and *The New England Tragedies;* and the uncompleted *Michael Angelo* (1883). Unquestionably the most popular poet of his century among readers of every class and station, Longfellow voiced a kind of Victorian didacticism, at once melancholy and upbeat. Most modern readers find poems like "A Psalm of Life" facile and platitudinous and find the long narratives boring despite their effort to make myth of American history. The chief poetic interest of Longfellow today, besides his historical importance, resides in some of the shorter lyrics.

TEXT

Longfellow, Henry Wadsworth. *The Poetical Works of Henry Wadsworth Longfellow.* Boston: Houghton Mifflin, 1887–1888.

REFERENCE

Arvin, Newton. *Longfellow: His Life and Work.* Boston: Little, Brown, 1963.

A PSALM OF LIFE[1]

What the Heart of the Young Man Said to the Psalmist

Tell me not, in mournful numbers,
    Life is but an empty dream!—
For the soul is dead that slumbers,
    And things are not what they seem.

5 Life is real! Life is earnest!
    And the grave is not its goal;
Dust thou art, to dust returnest,
    Was not spoken of the soul.

Not enjoyment, and not sorrow,
10   Is our destined end or way;
But to act, that each to-morrow
    Find us farther than to-day.

Art is long, and Time is fleeting,
    And our hearts, though stout and brave,
15 Still, like muffled drums, are beating
    Funeral marches to the grave.

In the world's broad field of battle,
    In the bivouac of Life,
Be not like dumb, driven cattle!
20   Be a hero in the strife!

Trust no Future, howe'er pleasant!
    Let the dead Past bury its dead!
Act,—act in the living Present!
    Heart within, and God o'erhead!

25 Lives of great men all remind us
    We can make our lives sublime,
And, departing, leave behind us
    Footprints on the sands of time;

[1]Longfellow remarked about this poem: "I kept it some time in manuscript, unwilling to show it to anyone, it being a voice from my inmost heart, at a time when I was rallying from the depression of disappointment." It first appeared with an epigraph from the metaphysical poet Richard Crashaw:
  Life that shall send
  A challenge to its end,
  And when it comes say, Welcome, friend.

Footprints, that perhaps another,
30   Sailing o'er life's solemn main,
A forlorn and shipwrecked brother,
      Seeing, shall take heart again.

Let us, then, be up and doing,
      With a heart for any fate;
35   Still achieving, still pursuing,
      Learn to labor and to wait.

THE WARNING

Beware! The Israelite of old,[1] who tore
    The lion in his path,—when, poor and blind,
He saw the blessed light of heaven no more,
    Shorn of his noble strength and forced to grind
5 In prison, and at last led forth to be
A pander to Philistine revelry,—

Upon the pillars of the temple laid
    His desperate hands, and in its overthrow
Destroyed himself, and with him those who made
10   A cruel mockery of his sightless woe;
The poor, blind Slave, the scoff and jest of all,
Expired, and thousands perished in the fall!

There is a poor, blind Samson in this land,
    Shorn of his strength and bound in bonds of steel,
15 Who may, in some grim revel, raise his hand,
    And shake the pillars of this Commonweal,
Till the vast Temple of our liberties
A shapeless mass of wreck and rubbish lies.

---

[1]The story of Samson—his strength, his heroism in the struggle of his people with the Philistines, his betrayal and enslaved labor for the Philistines as a blind captive, his destruction of his enemies by shaking the pillars of the temple and bringing the walls down on all their heads—is told in Judges 13–16.

THE FIRE OF DRIFT WOOD

Devereux Farm, Near Marblehead[1]

We sat within the farm-house old,
  Whose windows, looking o'er the bay,
Gave to the sea-breeze, damp and cold
  An easy entrance, night and day.

5 Not far away we saw the port,
  The strange, old-fashioned, silent town,
The lighthouse, the dismantled fort,
  The wooden houses, quaint and brown.

We sat and talked until the night,
10 Descending, filled the little room;
Our faces faded from the sight,
  Our voices only broke the gloom.

We spake of many a vanished scene,
  Of what we once had thought and said,
15 Of what had been, and might have been,
  And who was changed, and who was dead;

And all that fills the hearts of friends,
  When first they feel, with secret pain,
Their lives thenceforth have separate ends,
20 And never can be one again;

The first slight swerving of the heart,
  That words are powerless to express,
And leave it still unsaid in part,
  Or say it in too great excess.

25 The very tones in which we spake
  Had something strange, I could but mark;
The leaves of memory seemed to make
  A mournful rustling in the dark.

Oft died the words upon our lips,
30 As suddenly, from out the fire

---

[1]An old harbor town in Massachusetts, near Boston.

Built of the wreck of stranded ships,
   The flames would leap and then expire.

And, as their splendor flashed and failed,
   We thought of wrecks upon the main,
35 Of ships dismasted, that were hailed
   And sent no answer back again.

The windows, rattling in their frames,
   The ocean, roaring up the beach,
The gusty blast, the bickering flames,
40   All mingled vaguely in our speech;

Until they made themselves a part
   Of fancies floating through the brain,
The long-lost ventures of the heart,
   That send no answers back again.

45 O flames that glowed! O hearts that yearned!
   They were indeed too much akin,
The drift-wood fire without that burned,
   The thoughts that burned and glowed within.

THE SONG OF HIAWATHA[1]

Introduction

Should you ask me, whence these stories?
Whence these legends and traditions,
With the odors of the forest,
With the dew and damp of meadows,
5 With the curling smoke of wigwams,
With the rushing of great rivers,
With their frequent repetitions,
And their wild reverberations,
As of thunder in the mountains?

[1]In his diary entry for June 22, 1854, Longfellow wrote: "I have at length hit upon a plan for a poem on the American Indians, which seems to me the right one and the only. It is to weave together their beautiful traditions into a whole. I have hit upon a measure, too, which I think the right and only one for such a theme." The meter was adapted from the Finnish epic *Kalevala*, and Longfellow wrote his epic rapidly in high excitement. It was published the next year, 1855, the same year as the first edition of *Leaves of Grass*.

10   I should answer, I should tell you,
        "From the forests and the prairies,
        From the great lakes of the Northland,
        From the land of the Ojibways,
        From the land of the Dacotahs,
15   From the mountains, moors, and fen-lands
        Where the heron, the Shuh-shuh-gah,
        Feeds among the reeds and rushes.
        I repeat them as I heard them
        From the lips of Nawadaha,
20   The musician, the sweet singer."
            Should you ask where Nawadaha
        Found these songs so wild and wayward,
        Found these legends and traditions,
        I should answer, I should tell you,
25   "In the bird's-nests of the forest,
        In the lodges of the beaver,
        In the hoof-prints of the bison,
        In the eyry of the eagle!
            "All the wild-fowl sang them to him,
30   In the moorlands and the fen-lands,
        In the melancholy marshes;
        Chetowaik, the plover, sang them,
        Mahng, the loon, the wild-goose, Wawa,
        The blue heron, the Shuh-shuh-gah,
35   And the grouse, the Mushkodasa!"
            If still further you should ask me,
        Saying, "Who was Nawadaha?
        Tell us of this Nawadaha,"
        I should answer your inquiries
40   Straightway in such words as follow.
            "In the vale of Tawasentha,
        In the green and silent valley,
        By the pleasant water-courses,
        Dwelt the singer Nawadaha.
45   Round about the Indian village
        Spread the meadows and the corn-fields,
        And beyond them stood the forest,
        Stood the groves of singing pine-trees,
        Green in Summer, white in Winter,
50   Ever sighing, ever singing.
            "And the pleasant water-courses,
        You could trace them through the valley,
        By the rushing in the Spring-time,

By the alders in the Summer,
55 By the white fog in the Autumn,
By the black line in the Winter;
And beside them dwelt the singer,
In the vale of Tawasentha,
In the green and silent valley.
60   "There he sang of Hiawatha,
Sang the Song of Hiawatha,
Sang his wondrous birth and being,
How he prayed and how he fasted,
How he lived, and toiled, and suffered,
65 That the tribes of men might prosper,
That he might advance his people!"
    Ye who love the haunts of Nature,
Love the sunshine of the meadow,
Love the shadow of the forest,
70 Love the wind among the branches,
And the rain-shower and the snow-storm,
And the rushing of great rivers
Through their palisades of pine-trees,
And the thunder in the mountains,
75 Whose innumerable echoes
Flap like eagles in their eyries;—
Listen to these wild traditions,
To this Song of Hiawatha!
    Ye who love a nation's legends,
80 Love the ballads of a people,
That like voices from afar off
Call to us to pause and listen,
Speak in tones so plain and childlike,
Scarcely can the ear distinguish
85 Whether they are sung or spoken;—
Listen to this Indian Legend,
To this Song of Hiawatha!
    Ye whose hearts are fresh and simple,
Who have faith in God and Nature,
90 Who believe that in all ages
Every human heart is human,
That in even savage bosoms
There are longings, yearnings, strivings
For the good they comprehend not,
95 That the feeble hands and helpless,
Groping blindly in the darkness,
Touch God's right hand in that darkness

And are lifted up and strengthened;—
Listen to this simple story,
100   To this Song of Hiawatha!
        Ye, who sometimes, in your rambles
Through the green lanes of the country,
Where the tangled barberry-bushes
Hang their tufts of crimson berries
105   Over stone walls gray with mosses,
Pause by some neglected graveyard,
For a while to muse, and ponder
On a half-effaced inscription,
Written with little skill of song-craft,
110   Homely phrases, but each letter
Full of hope and yet of heart-break,
Full of all the tender pathos
Of the Here and the Hereafter;—
Stay and read this rude inscription,
115   Read this Song of Hiawatha!

THE JEWISH CEMETERY AT NEWPORT

How strange it seems! These Hebrews in their graves,
    Close by the street of this fair seaport town,
Silent beside the never-silent waves,
    At rest in all this moving up and down!

5   The trees are white with dust, that o'er their sleep
        Wave their broad curtains in the southwind's breath,
While underneath these leafy tents they keep
        The long, mysterious Exodus of Death.[1]

And these sepulchral stones, so old and brown,
10   That pave with level flags their burial-place,
Seem like the tablets of the Law, thrown down
        And broken by Moses at the mountain's base.

The very names recorded here are strange,
        Of foreign accent, and of different climes;

---

[1]For this and next stanza, see Exodus 32.

15   Alvares and Rivera² interchange
      With Abraham and Jacob of old times.

"Blessed be God, for he created Death!"
      The mourners said, "and Death is rest and peace;"
Then added, in the certainty of faith,
20   "And giveth Life that nevermore shall cease."

Closed are the portals of their Synagogue,
      No Psalms of David now the silence break,
No Rabbi reads the ancient Decalogue
      In the grand dialect the Prophets spake.

25   Gone are the living, but the dead remain,
      And not neglected; for a hand unseen,
Scattering its bounty, like a summer rain,
      Still keeps their graves and their remembrance green.

How came they here? What burst of Christian hate,
30   What persecution, merciless and blind,
Drove o'er the sea—that desert desolate—
      These Ishmaels and Hagars³ of mankind?

They lived in narrow streets and lanes obscure,
      Ghetto and Judenstrass,⁴ in mirk and mire;
35   Taught in the school of patience to endure
      The life of anguish and the death of fire.

All their lives long, with the unleavened bread
      And bitter herbs of exile and its fears,
The wasting famine of the heart they fed,
40   And slaked its thirst with marah⁵ of their tears.

Anathema maranatha!⁶ was the cry
      That rang from town to town, from street to street:

---

²These were Spanish Jews.
³In Genesis 16–17, Ishmael is the son of Abraham by Hagar, his childless wife's slave. But after the birth of Isaac, the legitimate son, Hagar and Ishmael are driven out into exile.
⁴German for "Jews' Street."
⁵Literally "bitter" in Hebrew. Also a reference to the brackish spring of Marah during the desert wanderings of the Israelites in Exodus 15.
⁶A curse; literally "Let him be cursed; the Lord has come." See I Corinthians 16:22.

At every gate the accursed Mordecai[7]
  Was mocked and jeered, and spurned by Christian feet.

45 Pride and humiliation hand in hand
  Walked with them through the world where'er they went;
  Trampled and beaten were they as the sand,
  And yet unshaken as the continent.

For in the background figures vague and vast
50   Of patriarchs and of prophets rose sublime,
  And all the great traditions of the Past
  They saw reflected in the coming time.

And thus forever with reverted look
  The mystic volume of the world they read,
55 Spelling it backward, like a Hebrew book,
  Till life became a Legend of the Dead.

But ah! what once has been shall be no more!
  The groaning earth in travail and in pain
Brings forth its races, but does not restore,
60   And the dead nations never rise again.

THE ROPEWALK

In that building, long and low,
With its windows all a-row,
  Like the port-holes of a hulk,
Human spiders spin and spin,
5 Backward down their threads so thin
  Dropping, each a hempen bulk.[1]

At the end, an open door;
Squares of sunshine on the floor
  Light the long and dusky lane;
10 And the whirring of a wheel,
Dull and drowsy, makes me feel
  All its spokes are in my brain.

---

[7]See the Book of Esther, in which Mordecai represents the Jew devoted to his people's welfare.

[1]This stanza is a description in metaphorical terms of a mill factory in one of the mill towns of New England.

As the spinners to the end
Downward go and reascend,
15   Gleam the long threads in the sun;
While within this brain of mine
Cobwebs brighter and more fine
    By the busy wheel are spun.

Two fair maidens in a swing,
20   Like white doves upon the wing,
    First before my vision pass;
Laughing, as their gentle hands
Closely clasp the twisted strands,
    At their shadow on the grass.

25 Then a booth of mountebanks,
With its smell of tan and planks,
    And a girl poised high in air
On a cord, in spangled dress,
With a faded loveliness,
30   And a weary look of care.

Then a homestead among farms,
And a woman with bare arms
    Drawing water from a well;
As the bucket mounts apace,
35 With it mounts her own fair face,
    As at some magician's spell.

Then an old man in a tower,
Ringing loud the noontide hour,
    While the rope coils round and round
40 Like a serpent at his feet,
And again, in swift retreat,
    Nearly lifts him from the ground.

Then within a prison-yard,
Faces fixed, and stern, and hard,
45   Laughter and indecent mirth;
Ah! it is the gallows-tree!
Breath of Christian charity,
    Blow, and sweep it from the earth!

Then a school-boy, with his kite
50 Gleaming in a sky of light,

And an eager, upward look;
Steeds pursued through lane and field;
Fowlers with their snares concealed;
And an angler by a brook.

55 Ships rejoicing in the breeze,
Wrecks that float o'er unknown seas,
    Anchors dragged through faithless sand;
Sea-fog drifting overhead,
And, with lessening line and lead,
60   Sailors feeling for the land.

All these scenes do I behold,
These, and many left untold,
    In that building long and low;
While the wheel goes round and round,
65 With a drowsy, dreamy sound,
    And the spinners backward go.

THE CHALLENGE

I have a vague remembrance
    Of a story, that is told
In some ancient Spanish legend
    Or chronicle of old.

5 It was when brave King Sanchez
    Was before Zamora slain,
And his great besieging army
    Lay encamped upon the plain.

Don Diego de Ordoñez
10   Sallied forth in front of all,
And shouted loud his challenge
    To the warders on the wall.

All the people of Zamora,
    Both the born and the unborn,
15 As traitors did he challenge
    With taunting words of scorn.

The living, in their houses,
  And in their graves, the dead!
And the waters of their rivers,
20   And their wine, and oil, and bread!

There is a greater army,
  That besets us round with strife,
A starving, numberless army,
  At all the gates of life.

25 The poverty-stricken millions
  Who challenge our wine and bread,
And impeach us all as traitors,
  Both the living and the dead.

And whenever I sit at the banquet,
30   Where the feast and song are high,
Amid the mirth and the music
  I can hear that fearful cry.

And hollow and haggard faces
  Look into the lighted hall,
35 And wasted hands are extended
  To catch the crumbs that fall.

For within there is light and plenty,
  And odors fill the air;
But without there is cold and darkness,
40   And hunger and despair.

And there in the camp of famine
  In wind and cold and rain,
Christ, the great Lord of the army,
  Lies dead upon the plain!

AFTERMATH

When the summer fields are mown,
When the birds are fledged and flown,
  And the dry leaves strew the path:
With the falling of the snow,
5 With the cawing of the crow,

Once again the fields we mow
And gather in the aftermath.

Not the sweet, new grass with flowers
Is this harvesting of ours;
10   Not the upland clover bloom;
But the rowen mixed with weeds,
Tangled tufts from marsh and meads,
Where the poppy drops its seeds
In the silence and the gloom.

THE CROSS OF SNOW

In the long, sleepless watches of the night
A gentle face—the face of one long dead—[1]
Looks at me from the wall, where round its head
The night-lamp casts a halo of pale light.
5   Here in this room she died; and soul more white
Never through martyrdom of fire was led
To its repose; nor can in books be read
The legend of a life more benedight.[2]
There is a mountain in the distant West
10   That, sun-defying, in its deep ravines
Displays a cross of snow upon its side.
Such is the cross I wear upon my breast
These eighteen years, through all the changing scenes
And seasons, changeless since the day she died.

THE TIDE RISES, THE TIDE FALLS

The tide rises, the tide falls,
The twilight darkens, the curlew calls;
Along the sea-sands damp and brown
The traveller hastens toward the town,
5   And the tide rises, the tide falls.

[1]Frances Appleton, Longfellow's second wife, who died of burns in 1861.
[2]Blessed.

Darkness settles on roofs and walls,
But the sea, the sea in the darkness calls;
The little waves, with their soft, white hands,
Efface the footprints in the sands,
10   And the tide rises, the tide falls.

The morning breaks; the steeds in their stalls
Stamp and neigh, as the hostler calls;
The day returns, but nevermore
Returns the traveller to the shore,
15   And the tide rises, the tide falls.

CHIMES

Sweet chimes! that in the loneliness of night
   Salute the passing hour, and in the dark
   And silent chambers of the household mark
   The movements of the myriad orbs of light!
5 Through my closed eyelids, by the inner sight,
   I see the constellations in the arc
   Of their great circles moving on, and hark!
   I almost hear them singing in their flight.
Better than sleep it is to lie awake,
10   O'er-canopied by the vast starry dome
   Of the immeasurable sky; to feel
The slumbering world sink under us, and make
   Hardly an eddy,—a mere rush of foam
   On the great sea beneath a sinking keel.

John Greenleaf Whittier (1807–1892)

Whittier came from a line of Quaker farmers. Born in East Haverhill, Massachusetts, he was a genuine yeoman-poet whose education did not go beyond twelve months at Haverhill Academy. Introduced by a teacher to the poetry of Burns, he began to versify his intense religious zeal. His first piece was published in the Newburyport *Free Press,* edited by Abolitionist William Lloyd Garrison. Under Garrison's encouragement Whittier edited newspapers in Boston and then in Hartford, and was associated with *The Atlantic Monthly* from 1857 till his death. In 1831 he brought out *Legends of New England in Prose and Verse,* and the next year he returned to Haverhill, later moving to nearby Amesbury. Until the end of the Civil War Whittier was unceasingly active in the Abolitionist cause and helped form the Republican Party, but he took a conservative line on other social and economic issues.

Volumes of verse, lyrical and polemical, had made him famous even before *Snow-Bound* (1866) and *The Tent on the Beach* (1867). Most of his popular successes are spoiled for us today: anti-slavery poems like "Massachusetts to Virginia," by a preachiness that nonetheless had its contemporary effect; "Barbara Frietchie," by its flag-waving patriotism; "The Barefoot Boy," "Maud Mullen," and "Telling the Bees," by their indulgence in maudlin sentimentality. But *Snow-Bound,* for all its length, re-creates rural New England through vividly remembered details, and "The Cable Hymn" has analogues in Whitman's "Passage to India" and Crane's "Cape Hatteras" as attempts to spiritualize American technological progress.

TEXT

Whittier, John Greenleaf. *The Complete Poems of John Greenleaf Whittier.* Ed. Horace E. Scudder. Boston: Houghton, Mifflin, 1894.

REFERENCE

Leary, Lewis. *John Greenleaf Whittier.* New York: Twayne, 1962.

THE CABLE HYMN[1]

O lonely bay of Trinity,
  O dreary shores, give ear!
Lean down unto the white-lipped sea
  The voice of God to hear!

5 From world to world His couriers fly,
    Thought-winged and shod with fire;
The angel of His stormy sky
  Rides down the sunken wire.

What saith the herald of the Lord?
10   "The world's long strife is done;
Close wedded by that mystic cord,
  Its continents are one.

"And one in heart, as one in blood,
  Shall all her peoples be;
15 The hands of human brotherhood
  Are clasped beneath the sea.

"Through Orient seas, o'er Afric's plain
  And Asian mountains borne,
The vigor of the Northern brain
20   Shall nerve the world outworn.

"From clime to clime, from shore to shore,
  Shall thrill the magic thread;
The new Prometheus steals once more
  The fire that wakes the dead."[2]

25 Throb on, strong pulse of thunder! beat
    From answering beach to beach;
Fuse nations in thy kindly heat,
  And melt the chains of each!

Wild terror of the sky above,
30   Glide tamed and dumb below!
Bear gently, Ocean's carrier-dove,
  Thy errands to and fro.

[1]The Atlantic cable was laid in 1866.
[2]The titan Prometheus stole the gods' immortal fire for the benefit of earthly creatures.

Weave on, swift shuttle of the Lord,
   Beneath the deep so far,
35 The bridal robe of earth's accord,
   The funeral shroud of war!

For lo! the fall of Ocean's wall
   Space mocked and time outrun;
And round the world the thought of all
40   Is as the thought of one!

The poles unite, the zones agree,
   The tongues of striving cease;
As on the Sea of Galilee
   The Christ is whispering, Peace!

SNOW-BOUND

A Winter Idyl

TO THE MEMORY OF THE HOUSEHOLD IT DESCRIBES
THIS POEM IS DEDICATED BY THE AUTHOR

*"As the Spirits of Darkness be
stronger in the dark, so Good
Spirits, which be Angels of Light,
are augmented not only by the
Divine light of the Sun, but also by
our common Wood Fire: and as
the Celestial Fire drives away dark
spirits, so also this our Fire of
Wood doth the same." —
Cor. Agrippa. Occult Philosophy, Book I ch. v.*[1]

*"Announced by all the trumpets of the sky,
Arrives the snow, and, driving o'er the fields
Seems nowhere to alight: the whited air
Hides hills and woods, the river
   and the heaven,
And veils the farm-house at the
   garden's end.
The sled and traveller stopped, the
   courier's feet
Delayed, all friends shut out, the
   housemates sit
Around the radiant fireplace, enclosed
In a tumultuous privacy of storm."*

                    Emerson.   The Snow Storm.

[1]Henry Cornelius Agrippa's *Three Books of Occult Philosophy* (1651); he was
for a time a Massachusetts resident.

The sun that brief December day
Rose cheerless over hills of gray,
And, darkly circled, gave at noon
A sadder light than waning moon.
5 Slow tracing down the thickening sky
Its mute and ominous prophecy,
A portent seeming less than threat,
It sank from sight before it set.
A chill no coat, however stout,
10 Of homespun stuff could quite shut out,
A hard, dull bitterness of cold,
That checked, mid-vein, the circling race
Of life-blood in the sharpened face,
The coming of the snow-storm told.
15 The wind blew east; we heard the roar
Of Ocean on his wintry shore,
And felt the strong pulse throbbing there
Beat with low rhythm our inland air.

Meanwhile we did our nightly chores,—
20 Brought in the wood from out of doors,
Littered the stalls, and from the mows
Raked down the herd's-grass for the cows;
Heard the horse whinnying for his corn;
And, sharply clashing horn on horn,
25 Impatient down the stanchion rows
The cattle shake their walnut bows;[2]
While, peering from his early perch
Upon the scaffold's pole of birch,
The cock his crested helmet bent
30 And down his querulous challenge sent.

Unwarmed by any sunset light
The gray day darkened into night,
A night made hoary with the swarm
And whirl-dance of the blinding storm,
35 As zigzag, wavering to and fro,
Crossed and recrossed the wingèd snow:
And ere the early bedtime came
The white drift piled the window-frame,
And through the glass the clothes-line posts
40 Looked in like tall and sheeted ghosts.

[2]Yokes.

So all night long the storm roared on:
The morning broke without a sun;
In tiny spherule traced with lines
Of Nature's geometric signs,
45   In starry flake, and pellicle,
All day the hoary meteor fell;
And, when the second morning shone,
We looked upon a world unknown,
On nothing we could call our own.
50   Around the glistening wonder bent
The blue walls of the firmament,
No cloud above, no earth below,—
A universe of sky and snow!
The old familiar sights of ours
55   Took marvellous shapes; strange domes and towers
Rose up where sty or corn-crib stood,
Or garden-wall, or belt of wood;
A smooth white mound the brush-pile showed,
A fenceless drift what once was road;
60   The bridle-post an old man sat
With loose-flung coat and high cocked hat;
The well-curb had a Chinese roof;
And even the long sweep, high aloof,
In its slant splendor, seemed to tell
65   Of Pisa's leaning miracle.

A prompt, decisive man, no breath
Our father wasted: "Boys, a path!"
Well pleased, (for when did farmer boy
Count such a summons less than joy?)
70   Our buskins on our feet we drew;
With mittened hands, and caps drawn low,
To guard our necks and ears from snow,
We cut the solid whiteness through.
And, where the drift was deepest, made
75   A tunnel walled and overlaid
With dazzling crystal: we had read
Of rare Aladdin's wondrous cave,
And to our own his name we gave,
With many a wish the luck were ours
80   To test his lamp's supernal powers.
We reached the barn with merry din,
And roused the prisoned brutes within.
The old horse thrust his long head out,

And grave with wonder grazed about;
85   The cock his lusty greeting said,
And forth his speckled harem led;
The oxen lashed their tails, and hooked,
And mild reproach of hunger looked;
The hornëd patriarch of the sheep,
90   Like Egypt's Amun[3] roused from sleep,
Shook his sage head with gesture mute,
And emphasized with stamp of foot.

All day the gusty north-wind bore
The loosening drift its breath before;
95   Low circling round its southern zone,
The sun through dazzling snow-mist shone.
No church-bell lent its Christian tone
To the savage air, no social smoke
Curled over woods of snow-hung oak.
100   A solitude made more intense
By dreary-voicëd elements,
The shrieking of the mindless wind,
The moaning tree-boughs swaying blind,
And on the glass the unmeaning beat
105   Of ghostly finger-tips of sleet.
Beyond the circle of our hearth
No welcome sound of toil or mirth
Unbound the spell, and testified
Of human life and thought outside.
110   We minded that the sharpest ear
The buried brooklet could not hear,
The music of whose liquid lip
Had been to us companionship,
And, in our lonely life, had grown
115   To have an almost human tone.

As night drew on, and, from the crest
Of wooded knolls that ridged the west,
The sun, a snow-blown traveller, sank
From sight beneath the smothering bank,
120   We piled, with care, our nightly stack
Of wood against the chimney-back,—
The oaken log, green, huge, and thick,
And on its top the stout back-stick;

---

[3] Ammon, the Egyptian god of the life cycle, had the head of a ram.

The knotty forestick laid apart,
125   And filled between with curious art
The ragged brush; then, hovering near,
We watched the first red blaze appear,
Heard the sharp crackle, caught the gleam
On whitewashed wall and sagging beam,
130   Until the old, rude-furnished room
Burst, flower-like, into rosy bloom;
While radiant with a mimic flame
Outside the sparkling drift became,
And through the bare-boughed lilac-tree
135   Our own warm hearth seemed blazing free.
The crane and pendent trammels showed,
The Turks' heads on the andirons glowed;
While childish fancy, prompt to tell
The meaning of the miracle,
140   Whispered the old rhyme: "*Under the tree,*
When fire outdoors burns merrily,
There the witches are making tea."

The moon above the eastern wood
Shone at its full; the hill-range stood
145   Transfigured in the silver flood,
Its blown snows flashing cold and keen,
Dead white, save where some sharp ravine
Took shadow, or the sombre green
Of hemlocks turned to pitchy black
150   Against the whiteness at their back.
For such a world and such a night
Most fitting that unwarming light,
Which only seemed where'er it fell
To make the coldness visible.

155   Shut in from all the world without,
We sat the clean-winged hearth about,
Content to let the north-wind roar
In baffled rage at pane and door,
While the red logs before us beat
160   The frost-line back with tropic heat;
And ever, when a louder blast
Shook beam and rafter as it passed,
The merrier up its roaring draught
The great throat of the chimney laughed;
165   The house-dog on his paws outspread

Laid to the fire his drowsy head,
The cat's dark silhouette on the wall
A couchant tiger's seemed to fall;
And, for the winter fireside meet,
170 Between the andirons' straddling feet,
The mug of cider simmered slow,
The apples sputtered in a row,
And, close at hand, the basket stood
With nuts from brown October's wood.

175 What matter how the night behaved?
What matter how the north-wind raved?
Blow high, blow low, not all its snow
Could quench our hearth-fire's ruddy glow.
O Time and Change!—with hair as gray
180 As was my sire's that winter day,
How strange it seems, with so much gone
Of life and love, to still live on!
Ah, brother! only I and thou
Are left of all that circle now,—
185 The dear home faces whereupon
That fitful firelight paled and shone.
Henceforward, listen as we will,
The voices of that hearth are still;
Look where we may, the wide earth o'er
190 Those lighted faces smile no more.
We tread the paths their feet have worn,
    We sit beneath their orchard trees,
    We hear, like them, the hum of bees
And rustle of the bladed corn;
195 We turn the pages that they read,
    Their written words we linger o'er,
But in the sun they cast no shade,
No voice is heard, no sign is made,
    No step is on the conscious floor!
200 Yet Love will dream, and Faith will trust,
(Since He who knows our need is just,)
That somehow, somewhere, meet we must.
Alas for him who never sees
The stars shine through his cypress-trees!
205 Who, hopeless, lays his dead away,
Nor looks to see the breaking day
Across the mournful marbles play!
Who hath not learned, in hours of faith,

The truth to flesh and sense unknown,
210   That Life is ever lord of Death,
And Love can never lose its own!

We sped the time with stories old,
Wrought puzzles out, and riddles told,
Or stammered from our school-book lore
215   "The Chief of Gambia's golden shore."[4]
How often since, when all the land
Was clay in Slavery's shaping hand,
As if a far-blown trumpet stirred
The languorous sin-sick air, I heard:
220   *"Does not the voice of reason cry,*
Claim the first right which Nature gave,
From the red scourge of bondage fly,
Nor deign to live a burdened slave!"
Our father rode again his ride
225   On Memphremagog's wooded side;
Sat down again to moose and samp[5]
In trappers hut and Indian camp;
Lived o'er the old idyllic ease
Beneath St. François' hemlock-trees;
230   Again for him the moonlight shone
On Norman cap and bodiced zone;
Again he heard the violin play
Which led the village dance away.
And mingled in its merry whirl
235   The grandam and the laughing girl.
Or, nearer home, our steps he led
Where Salisbury's[6] level marshes spread
Mile-wide as flies the laden bee;
Where merry mowers, hale and strong,
240   Swept, scythe on scythe, their swaths along
The low green prairies of the sea.
We shared the fishing off Boar's Head,
And round the rocky Isles of Shoals
The hake-broil[7] on the drift-wood coals;
245   The chowder on the sand-beach made,

[4]Here and below the lines are from "The African Chief" by the Abolitionist poet Sarah Wentworth Morton.
[5]A porridge made from hominy.
[6]A neighboring town in Massachusetts, near which are Boar's Head and the Isles of Shoals, mentioned below.
[7]Hake is a fish related to cod.

Dipped by the hungry, steaming hot,
With spoons of clam-shell from the pot.
We heard the tales of witchcraft old,
And dream and sign and marvel told
250 To sleepy listeners as they lay
Stretched idly on the salted hay,
Adrift along the winding shores,
When favoring breezes deigned to blow
The square sail of the gundelow[8]
255 And idle lay the useless oars.

Our mother, while she turned her wheel
Or run the new-knit stocking-heel,
Told how the Indian hordes came down
At midnight on Cocheco town,[9]
260 And how her own great-uncle bore
His cruel scalp-mark to fourscore.
Recalling, in her fitting phrase,
So rich and picturesque and free,
(The common unrhymed poetry
265 Of simple life and country ways,)
The story of her early days,—
She made us welcome to her home;
Old hearths grew wide to give us room;
We stole with her a frightened look
270 At the gray wizard's conjuring-book,[10]
The fame whereof went far and wide
Through all the simple country side;
We heard the hawks at twilight play,
The boat-horn on Piscataqua,
275 The loon's weird laughter far away;
We fished her little trout-brook, knew
What flowers in wood and meadow grew,
What sunny hillsides autumn-brown
She climbed to shake the ripe nuts down,
280 Saw where in sheltered cove and bay
The ducks' black squadron anchored lay,
And heard the wild-geese calling loud
Beneath the gray November cloud.

[8] A flat-bottomed boat, like a scow.
[9] A nearby town in New Hampshire.
[10] Agrippa's *Three Books of Occult Philosophy*, from which one of the epigraphs for the poem was taken.

Then, haply, with a look more grave,
285   And soberer tone, some tale she gave
From painful Sewel's ancient tome,[11]
Beloved in every Quaker home,
Of faith fire-winged by martyrdom,
Or Chalkley's Journal, old and quaint,—[12]
290   Gentlest of skippers, rare sea-saint!—
Who, when the dreary calms prevailed,
And water-butt and bread-cask failed,
And cruel, hungry eyes pursued
His portly presence mad for food,
295   With dark hints muttered under breath
Of casting lots for life or death,
Offered, if Heaven withheld supplies,
To be himself the sacrifice.
Then, suddenly, as if to save
300   The good man from his living grave,
A ripple on the water grew,
A school of porpoise flashed in view.
"Take, eat," he said, "and be content;
These fishes in my stead are sent
305   By Him who gave the tangled ram
To spare the child of Abraham."[13]

Our uncle, innocent of books,
Was rich in lore of fields and brooks,
The ancient teachers never dumb
310   Of Nature's unhoused lyceum.
In moons and tides and weather wise,
He read the clouds as prophecies,
And foul or fair could well divine,
By many an occult hint and sign,
315   Holding the cunning-warded[14] keys
To all the woodcraft mysteries;
Himself to Nature's heart so near
That all her voices in his ear
Of beast or bird had meanings clear,
320   Like Apollonius of old,[15]

---

[11]William Sewel's *History of the Quakers* (1717, 1725).
[12]Thomas Chalkley's *Journal* (1747).
[13]In Genesis 22, God put Abraham to the test by directing him to sacrifice his
    son Isaac; but, when He saw Abraham's faithful obedience, he spared Isaac
    and Abraham sacrificed instead a ram who had his horns caught in a bush.
[14]Skillfully cut.
[15]Apollonius of Tyana, a first-century Greek mystic and philosopher.

Who knew the tales the sparrows told,
Or Hermes who interpreted
What the sage cranes of Nilus said;[16]
A simple, guileless, childlike man,
325 Content to live where life began;
Strong only on his native grounds,
The little world of sights and sounds
Whose girdle was the parish bounds,
Whereof his fondly partial pride
330 The common features magnified,
As Surrey hills to mountains grew
In White of Selborne's loving view,—
He told how teal and loon he shot,
And how the eagle's eggs he got,
335 The feats on pond and river done,
The prodigies of rod and gun;
Till, warming with the tales he told,
Forgotten was the outside cold,
The bitter wind unheeded blew,
340 From ripening corn the pigeons flew,
The partridge drummed i' the wood, the mink
Went fishing down the river-brink.
In fields with bean or clover gay,
The woodchuck, like a hermit gray,
345   Peered from the doorway of his cell;
The muskrat plied the mason's trade,
And tier by tier his mud-walls laid;
And from the shagbark overhead
    The grizzled squirrel dropped his shell.

350 Next, the dear aunt, whose smile of cheer
And voice in dreams I see and hear –
The sweetest woman ever Fate
Perverse denied a household mate,
Who, lonely, homeless, not the less
355 Found peace in love's unselfishness,
And welcome wheresoe'er she went,
A calm and gracious element,
Whose presence seemed the sweet income
And womanly atmosphere of home,—
360 Called up her girlhood memories,

[16]Hermes Trismegistus (the thrice-greatest), the founder of occult science and alchemy.

The huskings and the apple-bees,
The sleigh-rides and the summer sails,
Weaving through all the poor details
And homespun warp of circumstance
365 A golden woof-thread of romance.
For well she kept her genial mood
And simple faith of maidenhood;
Before her still a cloud-land lay,
The mirage loomed across her way;
370 The morning dew, that dries so soon
With others, glistened at her noon;
Through years of toil and soil and care,
From glossy tress to thin gray hair,
All unprofaned she held apart
375 The virgin fancies of the heart.
Be shame to him of woman born
Who hath for such but thought of scorn.

There, too, our elder sister plied
Her evening task the stand beside;
380 A full, rich nature, free to trust,
Truthful and almost sternly just,
Impulsive, earnest, prompt to act,
And make her generous thought a fact,
Keeping with many a light disguise
385 The secret of self-sacrifice.
O heart sore-tried! thou hast the best
That Heaven itself could give thee,—rest,
Rest from all bitter thoughts and things!
    How many a poor one's blessing went
390   With thee beneath the low green tent
Whose curtain never outward swings!

As one who held herself a part
Of all she saw, and let her heart
    Against the household bosom lean,
395 Upon the motley-braided mat
Our youngest and our dearest sat,
Lifting her large, sweet, asking eyes,
    Now bathed in the unfading green
And holy peace of Paradise.
400 Oh, looking from some heavenly hill,
    Or from the shade of saintly palms,
    Or silver reach of river calms,

Do those large eyes behold me still?
With me one little year ago:—

405 The chill weight of the winter snow
       For months upon her grave has lain;
   And now, when summer south-winds blow
       And brier and harebell bloom again,
   I tread the pleasant paths we trod,

410 I see the violet-sprinkled sod
   Whereon she leaned, too frail and weak
   The hillside flowers she loved to seek,
   Yet following me where'er I went
   With dark eyes full of love's content.

415 The birds are glad; the brier-rose fills
   The air with sweetness; all the hills
   Stretch green to June's unclouded sky;
   But still I wait with ear and eye
   For something gone which should be nigh,

420 A loss in all familiar things,
   In flower that blooms, and bird that sings.
   And yet, dear heart! remembering thee,
       Am I not richer than of old?
   Safe in thy immortality,

425   What change can reach the wealth I hold?
       What chance can mar the pearl and gold
   Thy love hath left in trust with me?
   And while in life's late afternoon,
       Where cool and long the shadows grow,

430 I walk to meet the night that soon
       Shall shape and shadow overflow,
   I cannot feel that thou art far,
   Since near at need the angels are;
   And when the sunset gates unbar,

435   Shall I not see thee waiting stand,
   And, white against the evening star,
       The welcome of thy beckoning hand?

   Brisk wielder of the birch and rule,
   The master of the district school

440 Held at the fire his favored place,
   Its warm glow lit a laughing face
   Fresh-hued and fair, where scarce appeared
   The uncertain prophecy of beard.
   He teased the mitten-blinded cat,

445 Played cross-pins on my uncle's hat,

Sang songs, and told us what befalls
In classic Dartmouth's college halls.
Born the wild Northern hills among,
From whence his yeoman father wrung
450 By patient toil subsistence scant,
Not competence and yet not want,
He early gained the power to pay
His cheerful, self-reliant way;
Could doff at ease his scholar's gown
455 To peddle wares from town to town;
Or through the long vacation's reach
In lonely lowland districts teach,
Where all the droll experience found
At stranger hearths in boarding round,
460 The moonlit skater's keen delight,
The sleigh-drive through the frosty night,
The rustic-party, with its rough
Accompaniment of blind-man's-buff,
And whirling-plate, and forfeits paid,
465 His winter task a pastime made.
Happy the snow-locked homes wherein
He tuned his merry violin,
Or played the athlete in the barn,
Or held the good dame's winding-yarn,
470 Or mirth-provoking versions told
Of classic legends rare and old,
Wherein the scenes of Greece and Rome
Had all the commonplace of home,
And little seemed at best the odds
475 'Twixt Yankee pedlers and old gods;
Where Pindus-born Arachthus[17] took
The guise of any grist-mill brook,
And dread Olympus at his will
Became a huckleberry hill.

480 A careless boy that night he seemed;
    But at his desk he had the look
And air of one who wisely schemed,
    And hostage from the future took
    In trainéd thought and lore of book.
485 Large-brained, clear-eyed, of such as he
Shall Freedom's young apostles be,

[17]A river in Greece whose source is in the Pindus Mountains.

Who, following in War's bloody trail,[18]
Shall every lingering wrong assail;
All chains from limb and spirit strike,
490 Uplift the black and white alike;
Scatter before their swift advance
The darkness and the ignorance,
The pride, the lust, the squalid sloth,
Which nurtured Treason's monstrous growth,
495 Made murder pastime, and the hell
Of prison-torture possible;
The cruel lie of caste refute,
Old forms remould, and substitute
For Slavery's lash the freeman's will,
500 For blind routine, wise-handed skill;
A school-house plant on every hill,
Stretching in radiate nerve-lines thence
The quick wires of intelligence;
Till North and South together brought
505 Shall own the same electric thought,
In peace a common flag salute,
And, side by side in labor's free
And unresentful rivalry,
Harvest the fields wherein they fought.

510 Another guest[19] that winter night
Flashed back from lustrous eyes the light.
Unmarked by time, and yet not young,
The honeyed music of her tongue
And words of meekness scarcely told
515 A nature passionate and bold,
Strong, self-concentred, spurning guide,
Its milder features dwarfed beside
Her unbent will's majestic pride.
She sat among us, at the best,
520 A not unfeared, half-welcome guest,
Rebuking with her cultured phrase
Our homeliness of words and ways.
A certain pard-like, treacherous grace
Swayed the lithe limbs and dropped the lash,
525 Lent the white teeth their dazzling flash;
And under low brows, black with night,

---

[18]*Snow-Bound* was published in 1866.
[19]Harriet Livermore (1788–1867), a religious zealot who spent many years in the Near East awaiting the Second Coming.

Rayed out at times a dangerous light;
The sharp heat-lightnings of her face
Presaging ill to him whom Fate
530 Condemned to share her love or hate.
A woman tropical, intense
In thought and act, in soul and sense,
She blended in a like degree
The vixen and the devotee,
535 Revealing with each freak or feint
The temper of Petruchio's Kate,[20]
The raptures of Siena's saint.[21]
Her tapering hand and rounded wrist
Had facile power to form a fist;
540 The warm, dark languish of her eyes
Was never safe from wrath's surprise.
Brows saintly calm and lips devout
Knew every change of scowl and pout;
And the sweet voice had notes more high
545 And shrill for social battle-cry.

Since then what old cathedral town
Has missed her pilgrim staff and gown,
What convent-gate has held its lock
Against the challenge of her knock!
550 Through Smyrna's plague-hushed thoroughfares,
Up sea-set Malta's rocky stairs,
Gray olive slopes of hills that hem
Thy tombs and shrines, Jerusalem,
Or startling on her desert throne
555 The crazy Queen of Lebanon[22]
With claims fantastic as her own,
Her tireless feet have held their way;
And still, unrestful, bowed, and gray,
She watches under Eastern skies,
560 With hope each day renewed and fresh,
The Lord's quick coming in the flesh,
Whereof she dreams and prophesies!

[20]The main characters in Shakespeare's *Taming of the Shrew*.
[21]St. Catherine of Siena (1347–1380).
[22]Lady Hester Stanhope, with whom Harriet Livermore lived for years in various places, including Lebanon, and with whom she shared her religious fanaticism.

Where'er her troubled path may be,
   The Lord's sweet pity with her go!
565 The outward wayward life we see,
   The hidden springs we may not know.
Nor is it given us to discern
   What threads the fatal sisters[23] spun,
   Through what ancestral years has run
570 The sorrow with the woman born,
What forged her cruel chain of moods,
What set her feet in solitudes,
   And held the love within her mute,
What mingled madness in the blood,
575   A life-long discord and annoy,
   Water of tears with oil of joy,
And hid within the folded bud
   Perversities of flower and fruit.
It is not ours to separate
580   The tangled skein of will and fate,
To show what metes and bound should stand
Upon the soul's debatable land,
And between choice and Providence
Divide the circle of events;
585 But He who knows our frame is just,
Merciful and compassionate,
And full of sweet assurances
And hope for all the language is,
That He remembereth we are dust!

590 At last the great logs, crumbling low,
Sent out a dull and duller glow,
The bull's-eye watch that hung in view,
Ticking its weary circuit through,
Pointed with mutely warning sign
595 Its black hand to the hour of nine.
That sign the pleasant circle broke:
My uncle ceased his pipe to smoke,
Knocked from its bowl the refuse gray,
And laid it tenderly away;
600 Then roused himself to safely cover
The dull red brands with ashes over.
And while, with care, our mother laid
The work aside, her steps she stayed

---

[23]The Fates who spin, measure, and cut the thread of human life.

One moment, seeking to express
605 Her grateful sense of happiness
For food and shelter, warmth and health,
And love's contentment more than wealth,
With simple wishes (not the weak,
Vain prayers which no fulfilment seek,
610 But such as warm the generous heart,
O'er-prompt to do with Heaven its part)
That none might lack, that bitter night,
For bread and clothing, warmth and light.

Within our beds awhile we heard
615 The wind that round the gables roared,
With now and then a ruder shock,
Which made our very bedsteads rock.
We heard the loosened clapboards tost,
The board-nails snapping in the frost;
620 And on us, through the unplastered wall,
Felt the light sifted snow-flakes fall.
But sleep stole on, as sleep will do
When hearts are light and life is new;
Faint and more faint the murmurs grew,
625 Till in the summer-land of dreams
They softened to the sound of streams,
Low stir of leaves, and dip of oars,
And lapsing waves on quiet shores.

Next morn we wakened with the shout
630 Of merry voices high and clear;
And saw the teamsters drawing near
To break the drifted highways out.
Down the long hillside treading slow
We saw the half-buried oxen go,
635 Shaking the snow from heads uptost,
Their straining nostrils white with frost.
Before our door the straggling train
Drew up, an added team to gain.
The elders threshed their hands a-cold,
640   Passed, with the cider-mug, their jokes
From lip to lip; the younger folks
Down the loose snow-banks, wrestling, rolled,
Then toiled again the cavalcade
O'er windy hill, through clogged ravine,
645   And woodland paths that wound between

Low drooping pine-boughs winter-weighed.
From every barn a team afoot,
At every house a new recruit,
Where, drawn by Nature's subtlest law,
650   Haply the watchful young men saw
Sweet doorway pictures of the curls
And curious eyes of merry girls,
Lifting their hands in mock defence
Against the snow-ball's compliments,
655   And reading in each missive tost
The charm with Eden never lost.

We heard once more the sleigh-bells' sound;
    And, following where the teamsters led,
The wise old Doctor went his round,
660   Just pausing at our door to say,
In the brief autocratic way
Of one who, prompt at Duty's call,
Was free to urge her claim on all,
    That some poor neighbor sick abed
665   At night our mother's aid would need.
For, one in generous thought and deed,
    What mattered in the sufferer's sight
    The Quaker matron's inward light,
The Doctor's mail of Calvin's creed?
670   All hearts confess the saints elect
    Who, twain in faith, in love agree,
And melt not in an acid sect
    The Christian pearl of charity!

So days went on: a week had passed
675   Since the great world was heard from last.
The Almanac we studied o'er,
Read and reread our little store
Of books and pamphlets, scarce a score;
One harmless novel, mostly hid
680   From younger eyes, a book forbid,
And poetry, (or good or bad,
A single book was all we had,)
Where Ellwood's[24] meek, drab-skirted Muse,
    A stranger to the heathen Nine,
685   Sang, with a somewhat nasal whine,

[24]Thomas Ellwood (1639–1714) wrote a Biblical epic called *Davideis*.

The wars of David and the Jews.
At last the floundering carrier bore
The village paper to our door.
Lo! broadening outward as we read,
690 To warmer zones the horizon spread
In panoramic length unrolled
We saw the marvels that it told.
Before us passed the painted Creeks,[25]
    And daft McGregor on his raids
695   In Costa Rica's everglades.[26]
And up Taygetos winding slow
Rode Ypsilanti's Mainote Greeks,
A Turk's head at each saddle-bow![27]
Welcome to us its week-old news,
700 Its corner for the rustic Muse,
    Its monthly gauge of snow and rain,
Its record, mingling in a breath
The wedding bell and dirge of death:
Jest, anecdote, and love-lorn tale,
705 The latest culprit sent to jail;
Its hue and cry of stolen and lost,
Its vendue sales and goods at cost,
    And traffic calling loud for gain.
We felt the stir of hall and street,
710 The pulse of life that round us beat;
The chill embargo of the snow
Was melted in the genial glow;
Wide swung again our ice-locked door,
And all the world was ours once more!

715 Clasp, Angel of the backward look
    And folded wings of ashen gray
    And voice of echoes far away,
The brazen covers of thy book;
The weird palimpsest[28] old and vast,
720 Wherein thou hid'st the spectral past;
Where, closely mingling, pale and glow

[25]Indians inhabiting the southern Atlantic states.
[26]Sir Gregor MacGregor made a vain attempt in 1819 to colonize Costa Rica.
[27]In 1820 there was a battle at Mount Taygetos near the town of Maina in the Greek war against the Turks.
[28]A document, written on several times, with vestiges of the previous writing imperfectly erased and still visible; often important as a source of information of ancient civilizations.

The characters of joy and woe;
The monographs of outlived years,
Or smile-illumed or dim with tears,
725   Green hills of life that slope to death,
And haunts of home, whose vistaed trees
Shade off to mournful cypresses
    With the white amaranths underneath.
Even while I look, I can but heed
730   The restless sands' incessant fall,
Importunate hours that hours succeed,
Each clamorous with its own sharp need,
    And duty keeping pace with all.
Shut down and clasp the heavy lids;
735 I hear again the voice that bids
The dreamer leave his dream midway
For larger hopes and graver fears:
Life greatens in these later years,
The century's aloe flowers to-day!

740 Yet, haply, in some lull of life,
Some Truce of God which breaks its strife,
The worldling's eyes shall gather dew,
    Dreaming in throngful city ways
Of winter joys his boyhood knew;
745 And dear and early friends—the few
Who yet remain—shall pause to view
    These Flemish pictures of old days;[29]
Sit with me by the homestead hearth,
And stretch the hands of memory forth
750   To warm them at the wood-fire's blaze!
And thanks untraced to lips unknown
Shall greet me like the odors blown
From unseen meadows newly mown,
Or lilies floating in some pond,
755 Wood-fringed, the wayside gaze beyond;
The traveller owns the grateful sense
Of sweetness near, he knows not whence,
And, pausing, takes with forehead bare
The benediction of the air.

---

[29]Especially domestic scenes of everyday life, such as Brueghel painted.

Edgar Allan Poe (1809–1849)

Born in Boston of theatrical parents and orphaned before the age of three, Poe was raised by John Allan of Richmond, Virginia. When Poe was in his teens, a rift developed between the hard-headed, wealthy merchant and the sensitive young genius. After a term at the University of Virginia, Poe made his way to Boston and there published *Tamerlane and Other Poems* (1827) before he was twenty. He attended West Point for a year during a temporary reconciliation with Allan, but a final break with his foster father left him in severe need. *Al Aaraaf, Tamerlane,* and *Minor Poems* (1829), and *Poems* (1831) provided no income.

Poe's aunt, Mrs. Maria Clemm, took him into her Baltimore home in 1831. Five years later, Poe married Mrs. Clemm's ailing thirteen-year-old daughter Virginia. Meanwhile he had written some of his best Gothic tales and detective stories, worked on several magazines (including the *Southern Literary Messenger*), and made a name for himself as editor, critic, and fiction writer. However, *Tales of the Grotesque and Arabesque* (1840) and *The Raven and Other Poems* (1845) were financial failures, and Poe, always highly susceptible to alcohol, increasingly sought escape in drink from the sickness, poverty, and depression that plagued him. Virginia died after a long illness in 1847, and throughout several stormy courtships Poe's own life was rapidly disintegrating. Nonetheless, he was doing some of his most interesting writing: poems and the long prose-poem *Eureka,* a last effort to distance disaster by inventing an imaginative and pseudo-scientific cosmology. Found dying in Baltimore, he lingered for several days in a Washington hospital without regaining consciousness.

Essays like "The Philosophy of Composition" and "The Poetic Principle" argue against Emerson and the Transcendentalists for a consciously crafted art in which selection and revision achieve the preconceived effect and thereby a self-sufficient entity. "The Rationale of Verse" argues for a prosody based on an assumed analogy between verse and music. The intricate artifice of Poe's poems represents an at-

---

TEXT

Poe, Edgar Allan. *The Poems of Edgar Allan Poe.* Ed. Floyd Stovall. Charlottesville: University of Virginia Press, 1965.

REFERENCE

Davidson, Edward H. *Poe: A Critical Study.* Cambridge, Mass.: Harvard University Press, 1957.

Poe: A Collection of Critical Essays. Ed. Robert Regan. Englewood Cliffs, N.J.: Prentice-Hall, 1967.

Poe, Edgar Allan. *The Letters of Edgar Allan Poe.* Ed. John Ward Ostrom. Cambridge, Mass.: Harvard University Press, 1948.

Quinn, Arthur H. *Edgar Allan Poe: A Critical Biography.* New York: D. Appleton-Century, 1941.

Wagenknecht, Edward. *Edgar Allan Poe: The Man Behind the Legend.* New York: Oxford University Press, 1963.

tempt to supply through the musical creations of the imagination the harmony and beauty that life lacks. The woman doomed to die for the purity of her beauty is the recurrent symbol for the failure of life and nature to live up to the poet's imagined ideal. Poe is the most dramatic figure in nineteenth-century American poetry: the Romantic genius doomed by the height of his aspirations.

A DREAM WITHIN A DREAM

Take this kiss upon the brow!
And, in parting from you now,
Thus much let me avow—
You are not wrong, who deem
5   That my days have been a dream;
Yet if Hope has flown away
In a night, or in a day,
In a vision, or in none,
Is it therefore the less *gone?*
10   *All* that we see or seem
Is but a dream within a dream.

I stand amid the roar
Of a surf-tormented shore,
And I hold within my hand
15   Grains of the golden sand—
How few! yet how they creep
Through my fingers to the deep,
While I weep—while I weep!
O God! can I not grasp
20   Them with a tighter clasp?
O God! can I not save
One from the pitiless wave?
Is *all* that we see or seem
But a dream within a dream?

SONNET—TO SCIENCE

Science! true daughter of Old Time thou art!
    Who alterest all things with thy peering eyes.
Why preyest thou thus upon the poet's heart,
    Vulture, whose wings are dull realities?
5   How should he love thee? or how deem thee wise,
    Who wouldst not leave him in his wandering
To seek for treasure in the jewelled skies,
    Albeit he soared with an undaunted wing?
Hast thou not dragged Diana from her car?[1]

[1]The moon-goddess riding across the skies.

10   And driven the Hamadryad[2] from the wood
To seek a shelter in some happier star?
Hast thou not torn the Naiad[3] from her flood,
The Elfin[4] from the green grass, and from me
The summer dream beneath the tamarind tree?

TO HELEN[1]

Helen, thy beauty is to me
  Like those Nicéan[2] barks of yore,
That gently, o'er a perfumed sea,
  The weary, way-worn wanderer[3] bore
5   To his own native shore.

On desperate seas long wont to roam,
  Thy hyacinth hair, thy classic face,
Thy Naiad[4] airs have brought me home
  To the glory that was Greece,
10   And the grandeur that was Rome.

Lo! in yon brilliant window-niche
  How statue-like I see thee stand,
The agate lamp within thy hand!
Ah, Psyche,[5] from the regions which
15   Are Holy-Land!

[2]A wood nymph who is the spirit of the tree in which she lives.
[3]Water nymph.
[4]In German myth, small people with magical powers.

---

[1]Mrs. Jane Stith Stanard, whom Poe adored in his Richmond boyhood and apostrophizes here as the famous beauty of antiquity over whom the Greeks and Trojans fought.
[2]Referring to Nicaea, a city in ancient Bithynia in Asia Minor, and perhaps connecting Nicaea with westward-going ships.
[3]Ulysses returning home to Greece after the ten years of the Trojan War.
[4]Water nymph.
[5]Maiden loved by Eros, or Cupid; the word literally means "soul" or "spirit."

ISRAFEL

*And the angel Israel, whose heart-
strings are a lute, and who has the
sweetest voice of all God's creatures.*
—Koran.[1]

In Heaven a spirit doth dwell
   "Whose heart-strings are a lute;"
None sing so wildly well
As the angel Israfel,
5 And the giddy stars (so legends tell)
Ceasing their hymns, attend the spell
   Of his voice, all mute.

Tottering above
   In her highest noon,
10   The enamoured moon
Blushes with love,
   While, to listen, the red levin
   (With the rapid Pleiads,[2] even,
   Which were seven,)
15   Pauses in Heaven.

And they say (the starry choir
   And the other listening things)
That Israfeli's fire
Is owing to that lyre
20   By which he sits and sings—
The trembling living wire
   Of those unusual strings.

But the skies that angel trod,
   Where deep thoughts are a duty—
25 Where Love's a grown-up God—[3]
   Where the Houri[4] glances are
Imbued with all the beauty
   Which we worship in a star.

[1]Poe has added to the quotation from the Koran the phrase "whose heart-
strings are a lute," adapted from a line from Béranger which is part of the
epigraph to "The Fall of the House of Usher": *"Son coeur est un luth sus-
pendu"* (His heart is a suspended lute).
[2]A group of stars that form part of the constellation Taurus.
[3]As opposed to Cupid.
[4]The beautiful virgins in the Koran's depiction of paradise.

Therefore, thou art not wrong,
30   Israfeli, who despisest
An unimpassioned song;
To thee the laurels belong,
    Best bard, because the wisest!
Merrily live, and long!

35   The ecstasies above
    With thy burning measures suit—
Thy grief, thy joy, thy hate, thy love,
    With the fervour of thy lute—
    Well may the stars be mute!

40   Yes, Heaven is thine; but this
    Is a world of sweets and sours;
    Our flowers are merely—flowers,
And the shadow of thy perfect bliss
    Is the sunshine of ours.

45   If I could dwell
Where Israfel
    Hath dwelt, and he where I,
He might not sing so wildly well
    A mortal melody,
50   While a bolder note than this might swell
    From my lyre within the sky.

THE CITY IN THE SEA

Lo! Death has reared himself a throne
In a strange city lying alone
Far down within the dim West,
Where the good and the bad and the worst and the best
5   Have gone to their eternal rest.
There shrines and palaces and towers
(Time-eaten towers that tremble not!)
Resemble nothing that is ours.
Around, by lifting winds forgot,
10   Resignedly beneath the sky
The melancholy waters lie.

No rays from the holy heaven come down
On the long night-time of that town;
But light from out the lurid sea
15 Streams up the turrets silently—
Gleams up the pinnacles far and free—
Up domes—up spires—up kingly halls—
Up fanes[1]—up Babylon-like walls—
Up shadowy long-forgotten bowers
20 Of sculptured ivy and stone flowers—
Up many and many a marvellous shrine
Whose wreathéd friezes intertwine
The viol, the violet, and the vine.

Resignedly beneath the sky
25 The melancholy waters lie.
So blend the turrets and shadows there
That all seem pendulous in air,
While from a proud tower in the town
Death looks gigantically down.

30 There open fanes and gaping graves
Yawn level with the luminous waves;
But not the riches there that lie
In each idol's diamond eye—
Not the gaily-jewelled dead
35 Tempt the waters from their bed;
For no ripples curl, alas!
Along that wilderness of glass—
No swellings tell that winds may be
Upon some far-off happier sea—
40 No heavings hint that winds have been
On seas less hideously serene.

But lo, a stir is in the air!
The wave—there is a movement there!
As if the towers had thrust aside,
45 In slightly sinking, the dull tide—
As if their tops had feebly given
A void within the filmy Heaven.
The waves have now a redder glow—
The hours are breathing faint and low—

[1]Temples.

50   And when, amid no earthly moans,
   Down, down that town shall settle hence,
   Hell, rising from a thousand thrones,
   Shall do it reverence.

ALONE

From childhood's hour I have not been
As others were—I have not seen
As others saw—I could not bring
My passions from a common spring—
5   From the same source I have not taken
My sorrow—I could not awaken
My heart to joy at the same tone—
And all I lov'd—*I* lov'd alone—
Then—in my childhood, in the dawn
10   Of a most stormy life—was drawn
From ev'ry depth of good and ill
The mystery which binds me still—
From the torrent, or the fountain—
From the red cliff of the mountain—
15   From the sun that round me roll'd
In its autumn tint of gold—
From the lightning in the sky
As it pass'd me flying by—
From the thunder, and the storm—
20   And the cloud that took the form
(When the rest of Heaven was blue)
Of a demon in my view.—

TO ONE IN PARADISE

Thou wast that all to me, love,
   For which my soul did pine—
A green isle in the sea, love,
   A fountain and a shrine,
5   All wreathed with fairy fruits and flowers,
   And all the flowers were mine.

Ah, dream too bright to last!
    Ah, starry Hope! that didst arise
But to be overcast!
10   A voice from out the Future cries,
"On! on!"—but o'er the Past
    (Dim gulf!) my spirit hovering lies
Mute, motionless, aghast!

For, alas! alas! with me
15   The light of Life is o'er!
No more—no more—no more—
(Such language holds the solemn sea
    To the sands upon the shore)
Shall bloom the thunder-blasted tree,
20   Or the stricken eagle soar!

And all my days are trances,
    And all my nightly dreams
Are where thy grey eye glances,
    And where thy footstep gleams—
25 In what ethereal dances,
    By what eternal streams.

THE HAUNTED PALACE

In the greenest of our valleys
    By good angels tenanted,
Once a fair and stately palace—
    Radiant palace—reared its head.
5 In the monarch Thought's dominion—
    It stood there!
Never seraph spread a pinion
    Over fabric half so fair!

Banners yellow, glorious, golden,
10   On its roof did float and flow,
(This—all this—was in the olden
    Time long ago,)
And every gentle air that dallied,
    In that sweet day,
15 Along the ramparts plumed and pallid,
    A wingéd odor went away.

Wanderers in that happy valley,
   Through two luminous windows, saw
Spirits moving musically,
20   To a lute's well-tunéd law,
Round about a throne where, sitting,
   Porphyrogene![1]
In state his glory well befitting,
   The ruler of the realm was seen.

25 And all with pearl and ruby glowing
   Was the fair palace door,
Through which came flowing, flowing, flowing,
   And sparkling evermore,
A troop of Echoes, whose sweet duty
30   Was but to sing,
In voices of surpassing beauty,
   The wit and wisdom of their king.

But evil things, in robes of sorrow,
   Assailed the monarch's high estate.
35 (Ah, let us mourn!—for never morrow
   Shall dawn upon him desolate!)
And round about his home the glory
   That blushed and bloomed,
Is but a dim-remembered story
40   Of the old time entombed.

And travellers, now, within that valley,
   Through the red-litten windows see
Vast forms, that move fantastically
   To a discordant melody,
45 While, like a ghastly rapid river,
   Through the pale door
A hideous throng rush out forever
   And laugh—but smile no more.

---

[1]Literally, "born to the purple"; the rightful king.

SONNET—SILENCE

There are some qualities—some incorporate things,
   That have a double life, which thus is made
A type of that twin entity which springs
   From matter and light, evinced in solid and shade.
5 There is a two-fold *Silence*—sea and shore—
   Body and soul. One dwells in lonely places,
   Newly with grass o'ergrown; some solemn graces,
Some human memories and tearful lore,
Render him terrorless: his name's "No More."
10 He is the corporate Silence: dread him not!
   No power hath he of evil in himself;
But should some urgent fate (untimely lot!)
   Bring thee to meet his shadow (nameless elf,
That haunteth the lone regions where hath trod
15 No foot of man,) commend thyself to God!

THE CONQUEROR WORM

Lo! 'tis a gala night
   Within the lonesome latter years!
An angel throng, bewinged, bedight[1]
   In veils, and drowned in tears,
5 Sit in a theatre, to see
   A play of hopes and fears,
While the orchestra breathes fitfully
   The music of the spheres.

Mimes, in the form of God on high,
10   Mutter and mumble low,
And hither and thither fly—
   Mere puppets they, who come and go
At bidding of vast formless things
   That shift the scenery to and fro,
15 Flapping from out their Condor wings
   Invisible Wo!

[1]Bedecked.

That motley drama—oh, be sure
   It shall not be forgot!
With its Phantom chased for evermore,
20   By crowd that seize it not,
Through a circle that ever returneth in
   To the self-same spot,
And much of Madness, and more of Sin,
   And Horror the soul of the plot.

25 But see, amid the mimic rout
   A crawling shape intrude!
A blood-red thing that writhes from out
   The scenic solitude!
It writhes!—it writhes!—with mortal pangs
30   The mimes become its food,
And seraphs sob at vermin fangs
   In human gore imbued.

Out—out are the lights—out all!
   And, over each quivering form,
35 The curtain, a funeral pall,
   Comes down with the rush of a storm,
While the angels, all pallid and wan,
   Uprising, unveiling, affirm
That the play is the tragedy, "Man,"
40   And its hero the Conqueror Worm.

THE RAVEN[1]

Once upon a midnight dreary, while I pondered, weak and weary,
Over many a quaint and curious volume of forgotten lore—
While I nodded, nearly napping, suddenly there came a tapping,
As of some one gently rapping, rapping at my chamber door.
5 " 'Tis some visiter," I muttered, "tapping at my chamber door—
              Only this and nothing more."

Ah, distinctly I remember it was in the bleak December;
And each separate dying ember wrought its ghost upon the floor.
Eagerly I wished the morrow;—vainly I had sought to borrow

---

[1]Poe has provided his own explanation of his poem in "The Philosophy of Composition."

10 From my books surcease of sorrow—sorrow for the lost Lenore—
For the rare and radiant maiden whom the angels name Lenore—
      Nameless *here* for evermore.

And the silken, sad, uncertain rustling of each purple curtain
Thrilled me—filled me with fantastic terrors never felt before;
15 So that now, to still the beating of my heart, I stood repeating
" 'Tis some visiter entreating entrance at my chamber door—
Some late visiter entreating entrance at my chamber door;—
      This it is and nothing more."

Presently my soul grew stronger; hesitating then no longer,
20 "Sir," said I, "or Madam, truly your forgiveness I implore;
But the fact is I was napping, and so gently you came rapping,
And so faintly you came tapping, tapping at my chamber door,
That I scarce was sure I heard you"—here I opened wide the door:—
      Darkness there and nothing more.

25 Deep into that darkness peering, long I stood there wondering,
  fearing,
Doubting, dreaming dreams no mortal ever dared to dream before;
But the silence was unbroken, and the stillness gave no token,
And the only word there spoken was the whispered word, "Lenore?"
      Merely this and nothing more.

30 Back into the chamber turning, all my soul within me burning,
Soon again I heard a tapping somewhat louder than before.
"Surely," said I, "surely that is something at my window lattice;
Let me see, then, what thereat is, and this mystery explore—
Let my heart be still a moment and this mystery explore;—
35   'Tis the wind and nothing more!"

Open here I flung the shutter, when, with many a flirt and flutter
In there stepped a stately Raven of the saintly days of yore;
Not the least obeisance made he; not a minute stopped or stayed he;
But, with mien of lord or lady, perched above my chamber door—
40 Perched upon a bust of Pallas[2] just above my chamber door—
      Perched, and sat, and nothing more.

Then this ebony bird beguiling my sad fancy into smiling,
By the grave and stern decorum of the countenance it wore,

[2]Greek goddess of wisdom and the arts; Minerva is the Roman equivalent.

"Though thy crest be shorn and shaven, thou," I said, "art sure
     no craven,
Ghastly grim and ancient Raven wandering from the Nightly shore—
Tell me what thy lordly name is on the Night's Plutonian shore!"[3]
                 Quoth the Raven "Nevermore."

Much I marvelled this ungainly fowl to hear discourse so plainly,
Though its answer little meaning—little relevancy bore;
For we cannot help agreeing that no living human being
Ever yet was blessed with seeing bird above his chamber door—
Bird or beast upon the sculptured bust above his chamber door,
               With such name as "Nevermore."

But the Raven, sitting lonely on the placid bust, spoke only
That one word, as if his soul in that one word he did outpour.
Nothing farther then he uttered—not a feather then he fluttered—
Till I scarcely more than muttered "Other friends have flown
     before–
On the morrow *he* will leave me, as my Hopes have flown before."
              Then the bird said "Nevermore."

Startled at the stillness broken by reply so aptly spoken,
"Doubtless," said I, "what it utters is its only stock and store
Caught from some unhappy master whom unmerciful Disaster
Followed fast and followed faster till his songs one burden bore—
Till the dirges of his Hope that melancholy burden bore
               Of 'Never—nevermore.' "

But the Raven still beguiling all my fancy into smiling,
Straight I wheeled a cushioned seat in front of bird, and bust and
     door;
Then, upon the velvet sinking, I betook myself to linking
Fancy unto fancy, thinking what this ominous bird of yore—
What this grim, ungainly, ghastly, gaunt, and ominous bird of yore
             Meant in croaking "Nevermore."

This I sat engaged in guessing, but no syllable expressing
To the fowl whose fiery eyes now burned into my bosom's core;
This and more I sat divining, with my head at ease reclining
On the cushion's velvet lining that the lamp light gloated o'er,
But whose velvet-violet lining with the lamp-light gloating o'er,
            She shall press, ah, nevermore!

[3]Pluto is lord of the underworld.

Then, methought, the air grew denser, perfumed from an unseen
    censer
Swung by Seraphim whose foot-falls tinkled on the tufted floor.
80 "Wretch," I cried, "thy God hath lent thee—by these angels he hath
    sent thee
Respite—respite and nepenthe[4] from thy memories of Lenore;
Quaff, oh quaff this kind nepenthe and forget this lost Lenore!"
                      Quoth the Raven "Nevermore."

"Prophet!" said I, "thing of evil!—prophet still, if bird or devil!—
85 Whether Tempter sent, or whether tempest tossed thee here ashore,
Desolate yet all undaunted, on this desert land enchanted—
On this home by Horror haunted—tell me truly, I implore—
Is there—*is* there balm in Gilead?[5]—tell me—tell me, I implore!"
                      Quoth the Raven "Nevermore."

90 "Prophet!" said I, "thing of evil!—prophet still, if bird or devil!
By that Heaven that bends above us—by that God we both adore!—
Tell this soul with sorrow laden if, within the distant Aidenn,[6]
It shall clasp a sainted maiden whom the angels name Lenore—
Clasp a rare and radiant maiden whom the angels name Lenore."
95   Quoth the Raven "Nevermore."

"Be that word our sign of parting, bird or fiend!" I shrieked,
    upstarting—
"Get thee back into the tempest and the Night's Plutonian shore!
Leave no black plume as a token of that lie thy soul hath spoken!
Leave my loneliness unbroken!—quit the bust above my door!
100 Take thy beak from out my heart, and take thy form from off my
    door!"
                      Quoth the Raven "Nevermore."

And the Raven, never flitting, still is sitting, *still* is sitting
On the pallid bust of Pallas just above my chamber door;
And his eyes have all the seeming of a demon's that is dreaming,
105 And the lamp-light o'er him streaming throws his shadow on the
    floor;
And my soul from out that shadow that lies floating on the floor
                  Shall be lifted—nevermore!

---

[4]A drug, mentioned in *The Odyssey* as a remedy for grief.
[5]See Jeremiah 8:22: "Is there no balm in Gilead?" Gilead is a region east of
the Jordan River. Balm is an evergreen tree used as a soothing medicine.
[6]Eden.

ULALUME—A BALLAD

The skies they were ashen and sober;
   The leaves they were crispéd and sere—
   The leaves they were withering and sere;
It was night, in the lonesome October
5   Of my most immemorial year;
It was hard by the dim lake of Auber,[1]
   In the misty mid region of Weir:—
It was down by the dank tarn of Auber,
   In the ghoul-haunted woodland of Weir.

10 Here once, through an alley Titanic,
   Of cypress,[2] I roamed with my Soul—
   Of cypress, with Psyche, my Soul.
These were days when my heart was volcanic
   As the scoriac[3] rivers that roll—
15   As the lavas that restlessly roll
Their sulphurous currents down Yaanek,
   In the ultimate climes of the Pole—
That groan as they roll down Mount Yaanek,
   In the realms of the Boreal Pole.[4]

20 Our talk had been serious and sober,
   But our thoughts they were palsied and sere—
   Our memories were treacherous and sere;
For we knew not the month was October,
   And we marked not the night of the year—
25   (Ah, night of all nights in the year!)—
We noted not the dim lake of Auber
   (Though once we had journeyed down here)—
We remembered not the dank tarn of Auber,
   Nor the ghoul-haunted woodland of Weir.

30 And now, as the night was senescent,
   And star-dials pointed to morn—
   As the star-dials hinted of morn—
At the end of our path a liquescent
   And nebulous lustre was born,

[1]The geographical names are Poe's inventions.
[2]That is, an alley of gigantic (Titan-like) cypresses.
[3]Volcanic.
[4]The North Pole, with its northern lights, or aurora borealis.

35 Out of which a miraculous crescent
  Arose with a duplicate horn—
Astarte's bediamonded crescent,
  Distinct with its duplicate horn.

  And I said—"She is warmer than Dian:[5]
40 She rolls through an ether of sighs—
  She revels in a region of sighs:
She has seen that the tears are not dry on
  These cheeks where the worm never dies,
And has come past the stars of the Lion,[6]
45 To point us the path to the skies—
  To the Lethean[7] peace of the skies—
Come up, in despite of the Lion,
  To shine on us with her bright eyes—
Come up, through the lair of the Lion,
50 With Love in her luminous eyes."

  But Psyche, uplifting her finger,
  Said—"Sadly this star I mistrust—
  Her pallor I strangely mistrust:
Ah, hasten!—ah, let us not linger!
55 Ah, fly!—let us fly!—for we must."
In terror she spoke; letting sink her
  Wings till they trailed in the dust—
In agony sobbed; letting sink her
  Plumes till they trailed in the dust—
60 Till they sorrowfully trailed in the dust.

  I replied—"This is nothing but dreaming.
  Let us on, by this tremulous light!
  Let us bathe in this crystalline light!
Its Sybillic[8] splendor is beaming
65 With Hope and in Beauty to-night:
  See!—it flickers up the sky through the night!
Ah, we safely may trust to its gleaming,
  And be sure it will lead us aright—
We surely may trust to a gleaming,
70 That cannot but guide us aright,
  Since it flickers up to Heaven through the night."

[5]Diana, goddess of chastity and of the moon.
[6]The constellation Leo.
[7]Lethe, a river in the underworld, brought forgetfulness.
[8]Prophetic. The Sibyl was a Greek oracle.

Thus I pacified Psyche and kissed her,
　　And tempted her out of her gloom—
　　And conquered her scruples and gloom:
75　And we passed to the end of the vista,
　　But were stopped by the door of a tomb—
　　By the door of a legended tomb:—
　　And I said—"What is written, sweet sister,
　　On the door of this legended tomb?"
80　　She replied—"Ulalume—Ulalume!—
　　'Tis the vault of thy lost Ulalume!"

Then my heart it grew ashen and sober
　　As the leaves that were crispéd and sere—
　　As the leaves that were withering and sere;
85　And I cried—"It was surely October
　　On *this* very night of last year
　　That I journeyed—I journeyed down here!—
　　That I brought a dread burden down here—
　　On this night of all nights in the year,
90　　Ah, what demon hath tempted me here?
　　Well I know, now, this dim lake of Auber—
　　This misty mid region of Weir:—
　　Well I know, now, this dank tarn of Auber—
　　This ghoul-haunted woodland of Weir."

ELDORADO

　　Gaily bedight,[1]
　　A gallant knight,
　In sunshine and in shadow,
　　Had journeyed long,
5　　Singing a song,
　In search of Eldorado.[2]

　　But he grew old—
　　This knight so bold—
　And o'er his heart a shadow

---

[1]Bedecked.
[2]The legendary kingdom in Latin America, rich in gold and jewels, sought by explorers. Literally "the golden place."

10   Fell as he found
No spot of ground
That looked like Eldorado.

And, as his strength
Failed him at length,
15   He met a pilgrim shadow—
"Shadow," said he,
"Where can it be—
This land of Eldorado?"

"Over the Mountains
20   Of the Moon,
Down the Valley of the Shadow,
Ride, boldly ride,"
The shade replied,—
"If you seek for Eldorado!"

FOR ANNIE[1]

Thank Heaven! the crisis—
The danger is past,
And the lingering illness
Is over at last—
5   And the fever called "Living"
Is conquered at last.

Sadly, I know
I am shorn of my strength,
And no muscle I move
10   As I lie at full length—
But no matter!—I feel
I am better at length.

And I rest so composedly,
Now, in my bed,
15   That any beholder
Might fancy me dead—

---

[1]Mrs. Annie Richmond of Lowell, Massachusetts, with whom Poe was infatuated and on whom he depended emotionally during his last years.

Might start at beholding me,
  Thinking me dead.

The moaning and groaning,
20   The sighing and sobbing,
Are quieted now,
  With that horrible throbbing
At heart:—ah, that horrible,
  Horrible throbbing!

25 The sickness—the nausea—
    The pitiless pain—
Have ceased, with the fever
  That maddened my brain—
With the fever called "Living"
30   That burned in my brain.

And oh! of all tortures
  That torture the worst
Has abated—the terrible
  Torture of thirst
35 For the naphthaline river
    Of Passion accurst:—
I have drank of a water
  That quenches all thirst:—

Of a water that flows,
40   With a lullaby sound,
From a spring but a very few
  Feet under ground—
From a cavern not very far
  Down under ground.

45 And ah! let it never
    Be foolishly said
That my room it is gloomy
  And narrow my bed;
For man never slept
50   In a different bed—
And, to *sleep,* you must slumber
  In just such a bed.

My tantalized spirit
  Here blandly reposes,

55　Forgetting, or never
　　　Regretting, its roses—
　　Its old agitations
　　　Of myrtles and roses:

　　For now, while so quietly
60　　Lying, it fancies
　　A holier odor
　　　About it, of pansies—
　　A rosemary odor,
　　　Commingled with pansies—
65　With rue and the beautiful
　　　Puritan pansies.

　　And so it lies happily,
　　　Bathing in many
　　A dream of the truth
70　　And the beauty of Annie—
　　Drowned in a bath
　　　Of the tresses of Annie.

　　She tenderly kissed me,
　　　She fondly caressed,
75　And then I fell gently
　　　To sleep on her breast—
　　Deeply to sleep
　　　From the heaven of her breast.

　　When the light was extinguished,
80　　She covered me warm,
　　And she prayed to the angels
　　　To keep me from harm—
　　To the queen of the angels
　　　To shield me from harm.

85　And I lie so composedly,
　　　Now, in my bed,
　　(Knowing her love)
　　　That you fancy me dead—
　　And I rest so contentedly,
90　　Now, in my bed,
　　(With her love at my breast)
　　　That you fancy me dead—

That you shudder to look at me,
    Thinking me dead:—

95 But my heart it is brighter
    Than all of the many
Stars in the sky,
    For it sparkles with Annie—
It glows with the light
100   Of the love of my Annie—
With the thought of the light
    Of the eyes of my Annie.

ANNABEL LEE[1]

It was many and many a year ago,
    In a kingdom by the sea,
That a maiden there lived whom you may know
    By the name of Annabel Lee;—
5 And this maiden she lived with no other thought
    Than to love and be loved by me.

She was a child and *I* was a child,
    In this kingdom by the sea,
But we loved with a love that was more than love—
10   I and my Annabel Lee—
With a love that the wingéd seraphs of Heaven
    Coveted her and me.

And this was the reason that, long ago,
    In this kingdom by the sea,
15 A wind blew out of a cloud by night
    Chilling my Annabel Lee;
So that her high-born kinsmen came
    And bore her away from me,
To shut her up in a sepulchre
20   In this kingdom by the sea.

---

[1]Generally taken to refer to Poe's dead wife Virginia, though perhaps it is a tribute to Mrs. Sarah Whitman, with whom Poe was infatuated after Virginia's death.

The angels, not half so happy in Heaven,
      Went envying her and me—
Yes!—that was the reason (as all men know,
      In this kingdom by the sea)
25   That the wind came out of the cloud chilling
      And killing my Annabel Lee.

But our love it was stronger by far than the love
   Of those who were older than we—
   Of many far wiser than we—
30   And neither the angels in Heaven above,
   Nor the demons down under the sea,
Can ever dissever my soul from the soul
   Of the beautiful Annabel Lee:—

For the moon never beams without bringing me dreams
35   Of the beautiful Annabel Lee;
And the stars never rise but I see the bright eyes
   Of the beautiful Annabel Lee;
And so, all the night-tide, I lie down by the side
Of my darling, my darling, my life and my bride,
40   In her sepulchre there by the sea—
   In her tomb by the side of the sea.

Oliver Wendell Holmes (1809–1894)

Born in Cambridge, Massachusetts, of a long line of clergymen and successful merchants, Holmes came to reject the Calvinism of his minister father in favor of humane culture and the more liberal Unitarianism of King's Chapel. After graduating from Harvard with the class of 1829 (for whose annual reunions he wrote a poem each year for almost forty years), he studied medicine in Boston and abroad and received his M.D. from Harvard in 1836, the year of his first *Poems*. He was already famous as the author of "Old Ironsides," which had helped save the frigate *Constitution* from destruction.

Holmes also pursued medical research and writing, including a pioneering paper on puerperal fever, and was a popular professor of anatomy at Harvard for decades. In 1840 he married Amelia Lee Jackson, and one of their children was the Supreme Court Justice. With Lowell he was a leading conversationalist in the exclusive Saturday Club, but he would not join Lowell in espousing abolition and other social reforms. To the new *Atlantic Monthly*, edited by Lowell, Holmes contributed the witty and worldy-wise papers of *The Autocrat of the Breakfast Table,* as comfortably personal as they were comfortably cultivated. Published as a collection in 1858, they were followed by *The Professor at the Breakfast Table (1860)* and *The Poet at the Breakfast Table* (1872).

Holmes wrote three novels exploring neurotic states of mind, the best of which is *Elsie Venner* (1861). Other volumes include personal essays, medical essays, travel, poetry, and a biography of Emerson. Some of Holmes's sharp remarks shocked his contemporaries, but today he seems the quintessential nineteenth-century Boston Brahmin, so secure in his social position as an educated gentleman that he could address himself to local anecdotes and to classics with equal ease and zest.

TEXT

Holmes, Oliver Wendell. *The Complete Poetical Works of Oliver Wendell Holmes.* Cambridge Edition. Ed. Horace E. Scudder. Boston: Houghton Mifflin, 1895.

THE LAST LEAF[1]

I saw him once before,
As he passed by the door,
   And again
The pavement stones resound,
5 As he totters o'er the ground
   With his cane.

They say that in his prime,
Ere the pruning-knife of Time
   Cut him down,
10 Not a better man was found
By the Crier on his round
   Through the town.

But now he walks the streets,
And he looks at all he meets
15   Sad and wan,
And he shakes his feeble head,
That it seems as if he said,
   "They are gone."

The mossy marbles rest
20 On the lips that he has prest
   In their bloom,
And the names he loved to hear
Have been carved for many a year
   On the tomb.

25 My grandmamma has said—
Poor old Lady, she is dead
   Long ago—
That he had a Roman nose,
And his cheek was like a rose
30   In the snow;

But now his nose is thin,
And it rests upon his chin
   Like a staff,

[1]Holmes's note: "The poem was suggested by the sight of a figure well known to Bostonians, that of Major Thomas Melville, 'the last of the cocked hats,' as he was sometimes called."

And a crook is in his back,
35   And a melancholy crack
In his laugh.

I know it is a sin
For me to sit and grin
At him here;
40   But the old three-cornered hat,
And the breeches, and all that,
Are so queer!

And if I should live to be
The last leaf upon the tree,
45   In the spring,
Let them smile, as I do now,
At the old forsaken bough
Where I cling.

THE CHAMBERED NAUTILUS

This is the ship of pearl, which, poets feign,
Sails the unshadowed main,—
The venturous bark that flings
On the sweet summer wind its purpled wings
5   In gulfs enchanted, where the Siren sings,[1]
And coral reefs lie bare,
Where the cold sea-maids rise to sun their streaming hair.

Its webs of living gauze no more unfurl;
Wrecked is the ship of pearl!
10   And every chambered cell,
Where its dim dreaming life was wont to dwell,
As the frail tenant shaped his growing shell,
Before thee lies revealed,—
Its irised ceiling rent, its sunless crypt unsealed!

15   Year after year beheld the silent toil
That spread his lustrous coil;
Still, as the spiral grew,

[1]In legend, the singing of sea nymphs lured sailors to destruction on the rocks around their island.

He left the past year's dwelling for the new,
Stole with soft step its shining archway through,
20   Built up its idle door,
Stretched in his last-found home, and knew the old no more.

Thanks for the heavenly message brought by thee,
    Child of the wandering sea,
    Cast from her lap, forlorn!
25 From thy dead lips a clearer note is born
Than ever Triton² blew from wreathèd horn!
    While on mine ear it rings,
Through the deep caves of thought I hear a voice that sings:—

Build thee more stately mansions, O my soul,
30   As the swift seasons roll!
    Leave thy low-vaulted past!
Let each new temple, nobler than the last,
Shut thee from heaven with a dome more vast,
    Till thou at length art free,
35 Leaving thine outgrown shell by life's unresting sea!

THE DEACON'S MASTERPIECE

or, The Wonderful "One-Hoss Shay"
A Logical Story

Have you heard of the wonderful one-hoss shay,
That was built in such a logical way
It ran a hundred years to a day,
And then, of a sudden, it—ah, but stay,
5 I'll tell you what happened without delay,
Scaring the parson into fits,
Frightening people out of their wits,—
Have you ever heard of that, I say?

Seventeen hundred and fifty-five.
10 *Georgius Secundus* was then alive,—
Snuffy old drone from the German hive.¹

---

²A sea god.

---

¹The Georges who came to the throne of England in the eighteenth century
were German and established the House of Hanover.

That was the year when Lisbon-town
Saw the earth open and gulp her down,
And Braddock's army was done so brown,
15   Left without a scalp to its crown.[2]
It was on the terrible Earthquake-day
That the Deacon finished the one-hoss shay.

Now in building of chaises, I tell you what,
There is always *somewhere* a weakest spot,—
20   In hub, tire, felloe, in spring or thill,
In panel, or crossbar, or floor, or sill,
In screw, bolt, thoroughbrace,—lurking still,
Find it somewhere you must and will,—
Above or below, or within or without,—
25   And that's the reason, beyond a doubt,
That a chaise *breaks down,* but doesn't *wear out.*

But the Deacon swore (as Deacons do,
With an "I dew vum," or an "I tell *yeou*")
He would build one shay to beat the taown
30   'N' the keounty 'n' all the kentry raoun';
It should be so built that it *could n'* break daown:
"Fur," said the Deacon, "'t's mighty plain
Thut the weakes' places mus' stan' the strain;
'N' the way t' fix it, uz I maintain,
35   Is only jest
T' make that place uz strong uz the rest."

So the Deacon inquired of the village folk
Where he could find the strongest oak,
That couldn't be split nor bent nor broke,—
40   That was for spokes and floor and sills;
He sent for lancewood to make the thills;
The crossbars were ash, from the straightest trees,
The panels of white-wood, that cuts like cheese,
But lasts like iron for things like these;
45   The hubs of logs from the "Settler's ellum[3],"—
Last of its timber,—they couldn't sell 'em.
Never an axe had seen their chips,
And the wedges flew from between their lips,
Their blunt ends frizzled like celery-tips;

[2]Edward Braddock was British commander-in-chief during the French and
Indian War and met defeat by the Indians.
[3]Elm.

50 Step and prop-iron, bolt and screw,
Spring, tire, axle, and linchpin too,
Steel of the finest, bright and blue;
Thoroughbrace bison-skin, thick and wide;
Boot, top, dasher, from tough old hide
55 Found in the pit when the tanner died.
That was the way he "put her through."
"There!" said the Deacon, "naow she'll dew!"

Do! I tell you, I rather guess
She was a wonder, and nothing less!
60 Colts grew horses, beards turned gray,
Deacon and deaconess dropped away,
Children and grandchildren—where were they?
But there stood the stout old one-hoss shay
As fresh as on Lisbon-earthquake-day!

65 EIGHTEEN HUNDRED;—it came and found
The Deacon's masterpiece strong and sound.
Eighteen hundred increased by ten;—
"Hahnsum kerridge" they called it then.
Eighteen hundred and twenty came;—
70 Running as usual; much the same.
Thirty and forty at last arrive,
And then come fifty, and FIFTY-FIVE.

Little of all we value here
Wakes on the morn of its hundredth year
75 Without both feeling and looking queer.
In fact, there's nothing that keeps its youth,
So far as I know, but a tree and truth.
(This is a moral that runs at large;
Take it.—You're welcome.—No extra charge.)

80 FIRST OF NOVEMBER,—the Earthquake-day,—
There are traces of age in the one-hoss shay,
A general flavor of mild decay,
But nothing local, as one may say.
There couldn't be,—for the Deacon's art
85 Had made it so like in every part
That there wasn't a chance for one to start.
For the wheels were just as strong as the thills,
And the floor was just as strong as the sills,
And the panels just as strong as the floor,

90 And the whipple-tree neither less nor more,
And the back crossbar as strong as the fore,
And spring and axle and hub *encore.*
And yet, *as a whole,* it is past a doubt
In another hour it will be *worn out!*

95 First of November, 'Fifty-five!
This morning the parson takes a drive.
Now, small boys, get out of the way!
Here comes the wonderful one-hoss shay,
Drawn by a rat-tailed, ewe-necked bay.
100 "Huddup!" said the parson.—Off went they.
The parson was working his Sunday's text,—
Had got to *fifthly,* and stopped perplexed
At what the—Moses—was coming next.
All at once the horse stood still,
105 Close by the meet'n'-house on the hill.
First a shiver, and then a thrill,
Then something decidedly like a spill,—
And the parson was sitting upon a rock,
At half past nine by the meet'n'-house clock,—
110 Just the hour of the Earthquake shock!
What do you think the parson found,
When he got up and stared around?
The poor old chaise in a heap or mound,
As if it had been to the mill and ground!
115 You see, of course, if you're not a dunce,
How it went to pieces all at once,—
All at once, and nothing first,—
Just as bubbles do when they burst.

End of the wonderful one-hoss shay.
120 Logic is logic. That's all I say.

DOROTHY Q.[1]

A Family Portrait

Grandmother's mother: her age, I guess,
Thirteen summers, or something less;
Girlish bust, but womanly air;
Smooth, square forehead with uprolled hair;
5   Lips that lover has never kissed;
Taper fingers and slender wrist;
Hanging sleeves of stiff brocade;
So they painted the little maid.

On her hand a parrot green
10 Sits unmoving and broods serene.
Hold up the canvas full in view,—
Look! there's a rent the light shines through,
Dark with a century's fringe of dust,—
That was a Red-Coat's rapier-thrust!
15 Such is the tale the lady old,
Dorothy's daughter's daughter, told.

Who the painter was none may tell,—
One whose best was not over well;
Hard and dry, it must be confessed,
20 Flat as a rose that has long been pressed;
Yet in her cheek the hues are bright,
Dainty colors of red and white,
And in her slender shape are seen
Hint and promise of stately mien.

25 Look not on her with eyes of scorn,—
Dorothy Q. was a lady born!
Ay! since the galloping Normans came,
England's annals have known her name;
And still to the three-hilled rebel town
30 Dear is that ancient name's renown,
For many a civic wreath they won,
The youthful sire and the gray-haired son.

O Damsel Dorothy! Dorothy Q.!
Strange is the gift that I owe to you;
35 Such a gift as never a king

[1]Dorothy Quincy.

Save to daughter or son might bring,—
All my tenure of heart and hand,
All my title to house and land;
Mother and sister and child and wife
40 And joy and sorrow and death and life!

What if a hundred years ago
Those close-shut lips had answered No,
When forth the tremulous question came
That cost the maiden her Norman name,
45 And under the folds that look so still
The bodice swelled with the bosom's thrill?
Should I be I, or would it be
One tenth another, to nine tenths me?

Soft is the breath of a maiden's YES:
50 Not the light gossamer stirs with less;
But never a cable that holds so fast
Through all the battles of wave and blast,
And never an echo of speech or song
That lives in the babbling air so long!
55 There were tones in the voice that whispered then
You may hear to-day in a hundred men.

O lady and lover, how faint and far
Your images hover,—and here we are,
Solid and stirring in flesh and bone,—
60 Edward's and Dorothy's—all their own,—
A goodly record for Time to show
Of a syllable spoken so long ago!—
Shall I bless you, Dorothy, or forgive
For the tender whisper that bade me live?

65 It shall be a blessing, my little maid!
I will heal the stab of the Red-Coat's blade,[2]
And freshen the gold of the tarnished frame,
And gild with a rhyme your household name;
So you shall smile on us brave and bright
70 As first you greeted the morning's light,
And live untroubled by woes and fears
Through a second youth of a hundred years.

[2]Holmes's note: "The canvas of the painting was so much decayed that it had to be replaced by a new one, in doing which the rapier thrust was of course filled up."

NEARING THE SNOW-LINE

1870

Slow toiling upward from the misty vale,
   I leave the bright enamelled zones below;
   No more for me their beauteous bloom shall glow,
Their lingering sweetness load the morning gale;
5 Few are the slender flowerets, scentless, pale,
   That on their ice-clad stems all trembling blow
   Along the margin of unmelting snow;
Yet with unsaddened voice thy verge I hail,
   White realm of peace above the flowering line;
10 Welcome thy frozen domes, thy rocky spires!
   O'er thee undimmed the moon-girt planets shine,
On thy majestic altars fade the fires
That filled the air with smoke of vain desires,
   And all the unclouded blue of heaven is thine!

Jones Very (1813–1880)

The son of a sea captain from Salem, Massachusetts, Very accompanied his father on several voyages. Upon graduation from Harvard College in 1836, the year of Emerson's *Nature*, he entered the Harvard Divinity School and about this time began to receive religious visions and revelations. So intense were these mystical experiences that Very spent a month in 1838 at the McLean Asylum outside Boston. Emerson, however, found him "profoundly sane" and made the selections for *Essays and Poems* (1839). Soon Very's visions subsided and after several stints as pastor he retired to Salem to live in virtual seclusion with his sisters. There were two posthumous volumes: *Poems* (1883) and *Poems and Essays* (1886). Despite Very's connections with the Transcendentalists, his spirit was more orthodox, and his technique more traditional. He and Tuckerman, another New England recluse, are the best American sonneteers of the nineteenth century.

REFERENCE

Gittleman, Edwin. *Jones Very: The Effective Years, 1833–1840*. New York: Columbia University Press, 1967.

THE HAND AND FOOT

The hand and foot that stir not, they shall find
Sooner than all the rightful place to go:
Now in their motion free as roving wind,
Though first no snail so limited and slow;
5   I mark them full of labor all the day,
Each active motion made in perfect rest;
They cannot from their path mistaken stray,
Though 'tis not theirs, yet in it they are blest;
The bird has not their hidden track found out,
10 The cunning fox though full of art he be;
It is the way unseen, the certain route,
Where ever bound, yet thou art ever free;
The path of Him, whose perfect law of love
Bids spheres and atoms in just order move.

THE NEW BIRTH

'Tis a new life;—thoughts move not as they did,
With slow uncertain steps across my mind;
In thronging haste fast pressing on they bid
The portals open to the viewless wind,
5   That comes not save when in the dust is laid
The crown of pride that gilds each mortal brow,
And from before man's vision melting fade
The heavens and earth;—their walls are falling now.
Fast crowding on, each thought asks utterance strong;
10 Storm-lifted waves swift rushing to the shore,
On from the sea they send their shouts along,
Back through the cave-worn rocks their thunders roar;
And I, a child of God by Christ made free,
Start from death's slumbers to eternity.

THE GARDEN

I saw the spot where our first parents dwelt;[1]
And yet it wore to me no face of change,
For while amid its fields and groves, I felt
As if I had not sinned, nor thought it strange;
5 My eye seemed but a part of every sight,
My ear heard music in each sound that rose;
Each sense forever found a new delight,
Such as the spirit's vision only knows;
Each act some new and ever-varying joy
10 Did by my Father's love for me prepare;
To dress the spot my ever fresh employ,
And in the glorious whole with Him to share;
No more without the flaming gate to stray,
No more for sin's dark stain the debt of death to pay.

THE CREATED

There is naught for thee by thy haste to gain;
'Tis not the swift with Me that win the race;
Through long endurance of delaying pain,
Thine opened eye shall see thy Father's face;
5 Nor here nor there, where now thy feet would turn,
Thou wilt find Him who ever seeks for thee;
But let obedience quench desires that burn,
And where thou art, thy Father, too, will be.
Behold! as day by day the spirit grows,
10 Thou see'st by inward light things hid before;
Till what God is, thyself, his image shows;
And thou dost wear the robe that first thou wore,
When bright with radiance from his forming hand,
He saw thee Lord of all his creatures stand.

[1]Eden.

THE MORNING WATCH

'Tis near the morning watch: the dim lamp burns,
But scarcely shows how dark the slumbering street;
No sound of life the silent mart returns;
No friends from house to house their neighbors greet.
5   It is the sleep of death,—a deeper sleep
Than e'er before on mortal eyelids fell;
No stars above the gloom their places keep;
No faithful watchmen of the morning tell;
Yet still they slumber on, though rising day
10 Hath through their windows poured the awakening light;
Or, turning in their sluggard trances, say,—
"There yet are many hours to fill the night."
They rise not yet; while on the Bridegroom[1] goes
Till He the day's bright gates forever on them close.

THE LOST

The fairest day that ever yet has shone,
Will be when thou the day within shalt see;
The fairest rose that ever yet has blown,
When thou the flower thou lookest on shalt be.
5   But thou art far away among Time's toys;
Thyself the day thou lookest for in them,
Thyself the flower that now thine eye enjoys,
But wilted now thou hang'st upon thy stem.
The bird thou hearest on the budding tree,
10 Thou hast made sing with thy forgotten voice;
But when it swells again to melody,
The song is thine in which thou wilt rejoice;
And thou new risen 'midst these wonders live,
That now to them dost all thy substance give.

---

[1]In scriptural imagery, especially in the Gospels and Epistles, the Messiah and specifically Jesus are depicted as a bridegroom.

THE COLUMBINE

Still, still my eye will gaze long fixed on thee,
Till I forget that I am called a man,
And at thy side fast-rooted seem to be,
And the breeze comes my cheek with thine to fan.
5 Upon this craggy hill our life shall pass,—
A life of summer days and summer joys,—
Nodding our honey-bells mid pliant grass
In which the bee, half-hid, his time employs;
And here we'll drink with thirsty pores the rain,
10 And turn dew-sprinkled to the rising sun,
And look when in the flaming west again
His orb across the heaven its path has run;
Here left in darkness on the rocky steep,
My weary eyes shall close like folding flowers in sleep.

Henry David Thoreau (1817–1862)

Born in Concord, Massachusetts, Thoreau graduated from Harvard in 1837, taught school unsuccessfully, and worked in his father's pencil factory, where he devised a graphite flotation process for better pencils. Through the Transcendentalist Orestes Brownson he learned about German literature and thought to supplement his thorough knowledge of the classics. After meeting Emerson in 1837 he came into the group of writers and seers gathered in Concord; the Transcendentalist journal *The Dial* published some of his prose and verse.

On Emerson's advice Thoreau began to keep his voluminous journals, filled with nature descriptions and philosophical reflections, all carefully revised. The journals furnished the materials for his two published books: *A Week on the Concord and Merrimack Rivers* (1849), an account of a trip made ten years earlier with his brother John and recounted now with discourses on Transcendentalist themes; and *Walden, or, Life in the Woods* (1854), an intricately worked condensation of a two-year sojourn in a cabin on Walden Pond into a celebration—at once naturalistic and mythic, personal and epic—of his participation in the natural cycle.

Thoreau liked lecturing on the Lyceum circuit but was never as effective and popular as Emerson. He was an Abolitionist and an advocate of John Brown; he spent a night in jail for refusing to pay taxes in protest against slavery and the Mexican War. After his death from tuberculosis, several volumes of selections from the journals were published, as well as a collection of essays called *Excursions* (1863). His best essays are "Walking" and "Civil Disobedience," and his poems, though overshadowed by his prose, display at their best the use of graphically observed detail for suggestive effect, Thoreau's characteristic kind of perception.

TEXT

Thoreau, Henry David. *Collected Poems of Henry Thoreau.* Ed. Carl Bode. Chicago: Packard and Co., 1943.

REFERENCE

A Collection of Critical Essays. Ed. Sherman Paul. Englewood Cliffs, N. J.: Prentice-Hall, 1962.

Harding, Walter R. *Thoreau, Man of Concord.* New York: Holt, Rinehart and Winston, 1960.

Krutch, Joseph Wood. *Henry David Thoreau.* New York: W. Sloane Associates, 1948.

Miller, Perry. *Consciousness in Concord.* Boston: Houghton Mifflin, 1957.

Porte, Joel. *Emerson and Thoreau: Transcendentalists in Conflict.* Middletown, Conn.: Wesleyan University Press, 1966.

Thoreau, Henry David. *Correspondence of Henry David Thoreau.* Ed. Walter R. Harding and Carl Bode. New York: New York University Press, 1958.

WITHIN THE CIRCUIT OF THIS PLODDING LIFE

Within the circuit of this plodding life
There enter moments of an azure hue,
Untarnished fair as is the violet
Or anemone, when the spring strews them
5   By some meandering rivulet, which make
The best philosophy untrue that aims
But to console man for his grievances.
I have remembered, when the winter came,
High in my chamber in the frosty nights,
10   When in the still light of the cheerful moon,
On every twig and rail and jutting spout,
The icy spears were adding to their length
Against the arrows of the coming sun,
How in the shimmering noon of summer past
15   Some unrecorded beam slanted across
The upland pastures where the Johnswort grew;
Or heard, amid the verdure of my mind,
The bee's long smothered hum, on the blue flag
Loitering amidst the mead; or busy rill,
20   Which now through all its course stands still and dumb
Its own memorial,—purling at its play
Along the slopes, and through the meadows next,
Until its youthful sound was hushed at last
In the staid current of the lowland stream;
25   Or seen the furrows shine but late upturned,
And where the fieldfare[1] followed in the rear,
When all the fields around lay bound and hoar
Beneath a thick integument of snow.
So by God's cheap economy made rich
30   To go upon my winter's task again.

GREAT GOD! I ASK THEE FOR NO MEANER PELF

Great God! I ask thee for no meaner pelf
Than that I may not disappoint myself;
That in my action I may soar as high,
As I can now discern with this clear eye;

[1]A kind of thrush.

5 And next in value, which thy kindness lends,
That I may greatly disappoint my friends,
Howe'er they think or hope that it may be,
They may not dream how thou'st distinguished me;

That my weak hand may equal my firm faith,
10 And my life practice more than my tongue saith;
That my low conduct may not show,
Nor my relenting lines,
That I thy purpose did not know,
Or overrated thy designs.

CONSCIENCE IS INSTINCT BRED IN THE HOUSE

Conscience is instinct bred in the house.
Feeling and Thinking propagate the sin
By an unnatural breeding in and in.
I say, Turn it outdoors
5 Into the moors.
I love a life whose plot is simple,
And does not thicken with every pimple,
A soul so sound no sickly conscience binds it,
That makes the universe no worse than 't finds it.
10 I love an earnest soul,
Whose mighty joy and sorrow
Are not drowned in a bowl,
And brought to life to-morrow;
That lives one tragedy,
15 And not seventy;
A conscience worth keeping,
Laughing not weeping;
A conscience wise and steady,
And forever ready;
20 Not changing with events,
Dealing in compliments;
A conscience exercised about
Large things, where one *may* doubt.
I love a soul not all of wood,
25 Predestinated to be good,
But true to the backbone
Unto itself alone,

And false to none;
Born to its own affairs,
30 Its own joys and own cares;
By whom the work which God begun
Is finished, and not undone;
Taken up where he left off,
Whether to worship or to scoff;
35 If not good, why then evil,
If not good god, good devil.
Goodness!—you hypocrite, come out of that,
Live your life, do your work, then take your hat.
I have no patience towards
40 Such conscientious cowards.
Give me simple laboring folk,
Who love their work,
Whose virtue is a song
To cheer God along.

HAZE

Woof of the sun, ethereal gauze,
Woven of Nature's richest stuffs,
Visible heat, air-water, and dry sea,
Last conquest of the eye;
5 Toil of the day displayed, sun-dust,
Aerial surf upon the shores of earth,
Ethereal estuary, frith[1] of light,
Breakers of air, billows of heat,
Fine summer spray on inland seas;
10 Bird of the sun, transparent-winged
Owlet of noon, soft-pinioned,
From heath or stubble rising without song;
Establish thy serenity o'er the fields.

---

[1]An estuary, where the river flows into the sea and its currents meet the tides.

MY LOVE MUST BE AS FREE

My love must be as free
   As is the eagle's wing,
Hovering o'er land and sea
   And everything.

5 I must not dim my eye
   In thy saloon,
I must not leave my sky
   And nightly moon.

Be not the fowler's net
10   Which stays my flight,
And craftily is set
   T' allure the sight.

But be the favoring gale
   That bears me on,
15 And still doth fill my sail
   When thou art gone.

I cannot leave my sky
   For thy caprice,
True love would soar as high
20   As heaven is.

The eagle would not brook
   Her mate thus won,
Who trained his eye to look
   Beneath the sun.

THE INWARD MORNING

Packed in my mind lie all the clothes
   Which outward nature wears,
And in its fashion's hourly change
   It all things else repairs.

5 In vain I look for change abroad,
   And can no difference find,

Till some new ray of peace uncalled
   Illumes my inmost mind.

What is it gilds the trees and clouds,
10   And paints the heavens so gay,
But yonder fast-abiding light
   With its unchanging ray?

Lo, when the sun streams through the wood,
   Upon a winter's morn,
15 Where'er his silent beams intrude
   The murky night is gone.

How could the patient pine have known
   The morning breeze would come,
Or humble flowers anticipate
20   The insect's noonday hum,—

Till the new light with morning cheer
   From far streamed through the aisles,
And nimbly told the forest trees
   For many stretching miles?

25 I've heard within my inmost soul
   Such cheerful morning news,
In the horizon of my mind
   Have seen such orient hues.

As in the twilight of the dawn,
30   When the first birds awake,
Are heard within some silent wood,
   Where they the small twigs break,

Or in the eastern skies are seen,
   Before the sun appears,
35 The harbingers of summer heats
   Which from afar he bears.

James Russell Lowell (1819-1891)

Lowell was born and died in the family mansion, Elmwood, in Cambridge, Massachusetts. The son of a Unitarian clergyman and an exquisitely sensitive mother, he graduated from Harvard in 1838 and launched his career with *Poems* (1844). In the single year 1848 he published many of his most famous works: *Poems: Second Series; A Fable for Critics,* a good-humored satire of the literary pantheon lined out in rollicking couplets and laced with outrageous puns and rhymes; the first series of *The Biglow Papers,* which adopt a Yankee dialect to pronounce on contemporary issues; and *The Vision of Sir Launfal,* a sentimental and moralizing extension of the Grail legend.

Lowell followed Longfellow in the chair of modern languages at Harvard in 1855, became the first editor of the *Atlantic Monthly* (1857–1861), and worked with Charles Eliot Norton on the *North American Review* for some years after 1864. Through his journalism Lowell emerged as an important liberal voice on political and social as well as on religious matters. The "Ode," largely written in one night and read the next day at the Harvard commemoration for the war dead, is generally recognized as his noblest poem. Lowell served as ambassador to Spain and to England, and upon the death of his second wife, returned to Elmwood, writing to the end. Other titles in poetry are: *The Biglow Papers, Second Series* (1867), *The Cathedral* (1870), *Heartsease and Rue* (1888); in literary criticism, *Among My Books* (1870, 1876); in politics, *Democracy and Other Essays* (1887), *Political Essays* (1888). Too didactic to be a great poet, as he himself knew, Lowell was a man of letters whose writings in several areas had a wide impact.

TEXT

Lowell, James Russell. *The Complete Writings of James Russell Lowell.* Elmwood Edition. Boston: Houghton Mifflin, 1904.

from **The Biglow Papers: First Series, No. VI**

THE PIOUS EDITOR'S CREED

I du believe in Freedom's cause,
 Ez fur away ez Payris is;
I love to see her stick her claws
 In them infarnal Phayrisees;[1]
5 It's wal enough agin a king
  To dror resolves an' triggers,—
But libbaty's a kind o' thing
 Thet don't agree with niggers.

I du believe the people want
10 A tax on teas an' coffees,
Thet nothin' aint extravygunt,—
 Purvidin' I'm in office;
Fer I hev loved my country sence
 My eye-teeth filled their sockets,
15 An' Uncle Sam I reverence,
  Partic'larly his pockets.

I du believe in *any* plan
 O' levying' the texes,
Ez long ez, like a lumberman,
20 I git jest wut I axes;
I go free-trade thru thick an' thin,
 Because it kind o' rouses
The folks to vote,—an' keeps us in
 Our quiet custom-houses.

25 I du believe it's wise an' good
  To sen' out furrin missions,
Thet is, on sartin understood
 An' orthydox conditions;—
I mean nine thousan' dolls. per ann.,[2]
30 Nine thousan' more fer outfit,
An' me to recommend a man
 The place 'ould jest about fit.

---

[1]Reference to the French Revolution of 1848. "Pharisees," besides securing the
humorous rhyme, is used loosely here to call the French hypocrites—ironically,
since the speaker defends freedom there, but not in the United States.
[2]Dollars per annum.

I du believe in special ways
    O' prayin' an' convartin';
35   The bread comes back in many days,
    An' buttered, tu, fer sartin;

I mean in preyin' till one busts
    On wut the party chooses,
An' in convartin' public trusts
40   To very privit uses.

I du believe hard coin[3] the stuff
    Fer 'lectioneers to spout on;
The people's ollers soft enough
    To make hard money out on;
45   Dear Uncle Sam pervides fer his,
    An' gives a good-sized junk to all,—
I don't care *how* hard money is,
    Ez long ez mine's paid punctooal.

I du believe with all my soul
50   In the gret Press's freedom,
To pint the people to the goal
    An' in the traces lead 'em;
Palsied the arm thet forges yokes
    At my fat contracts squintin',
55   An' withered be the nose thet pokes
    Inter the gov'ment printin'!

I du believe thet I should give
    Wut's his'n unto Cæsar,[4]
Fer it's by him I move an' live,
60   Frum him my bread an' cheese air;
I du believe thet all o' me
    Doth bear his superscription,—
Will, conscience, honor, honesty,
    An' things o' thet description.

65   I du believe in prayer an' praise
    To him thet hez the grantin'
O' jobs,—in every thin' thet pays,
    But most of all in Cantin';[5]

[3]As opposed to paper currency.
[4]See Matthew 22:15–22.
[5]Intoning a prayer.

This doth my cup with marcies fill,
70   This lays all thought o' sin to rest,—
I *don't* believe in princerple,
     But oh, I *du* in interest.

I du believe in bein' this
     Or thet, ez it may happen
75   One way or t' other hendiest is
     To ketch the people nappin';
It aint by princerples nor men
     My preudunt course is steadied,—
I scent wich pays the best, an' then
80   Go into it baldheaded.

I du believe thet holdin' slaves
     Comes nat'ral to a Presidunt,
Let 'lone the rowdedow it saves
     To hev a wal-broke precedunt;
85   Fer any office, small or gret,
     I couldn't ax with no face,
'uthout I'd ben, thru dry an' wet,
     Th' unrizzest[6] kind o' doughface.

I du believe wutever trash
90   'll keep the people in blindness,—
Thet we the Mexicuns[7] can thrash
     Right inter brotherly kindness,
Thet bombshells, grape, an' powder 'n' ball
     air good-will's strongest magnets,
95   Thet peace, to make it stick at all,
     Must be druv in with bagnets.[8]

In short, I firmly du believe
     In Humbug generally,
Fer it's a thing thet I perceive
100   To hev a solid vally;
This heth my faithful shepherd ben,
     In pasturs sweet heth led me,[9]
An' this'll keep the people green
     To feed ez they hev fed me.

[6]Unrisingest; a pun on dough rising and elevation to public office.
[7]The Mexican War, 1846–1848.
[8]Bayonets.
[9]See Psalms 23.

from **The Biglow Papers: First Series, No. VII**

A LETTER
FROM A CANDIDATE FOR THE PRESIDENCY[1]
IN ANSWER TO SUTTIN QUESTIONS PROPOSED
BY MR. HOSEA BIGLOW

DEAR SIR,—You wish to know my notions
    On sartin pints thet rile the land;
There's nothin' thet my natur so shuns
    Ez being' mum or underhand;
5 I'm a straight-spoken kind o' creetur
    Thet blurts right out wut's in his head,
An' ef I've one pecooler feetur,
    It is a nose thet wunt be led.

So, to begin at the beginnin'
10   An' come direcly to the pint,
I think the country's underpinnin'
    Is some consid'ble out o' jint;
I aint agoin' to try your patience
    By tellin' who done this or thet,
15 I don't make no insinooations,
    I jest let on I smell a rat.

Thet is, I mean, it seems to me so,
    But, ef the public think I'm wrong,
I wunt deny but wut I be so,—
20   An', fact, it don't smell very strong;
My mind's tu fair to lose its balance
    An' say wich party hez most sense;
There may be folks o' greater talence
    Thet can't set stiddier on the fence.

25 I'm an eclectic; ez to choosin'
    'Twixt this an' thet, I'm plaguy lawth;
I leave a side thet looks like losin',
    But (wile there's doubt) I stick to both;
I stan' upon the Constitution,
30   Ez preudunt statesmun say, who've planned

---

[1]The satire is a parody of the vacillating political views of Zachary Taylor, the Whig candidate for President in 1848, whose fame as a general and hero of the Mexican War helped him defeat the Democratic candidate, Lewis Cass.

A way to git the most profusion
   O' chances ez to *ware* they'll stand.

Ez fer the war, I go agin it.—
   I mean to say I kind o' du,
35 Thet is, I mean thet, bein' in it,
   The best way wuz to fight it thru;
Not but wut abstract war is horrid,
   I sign to thet with all my heart,—
But civylzation *doos* git forrid
40 Sometimes upon a powder-cart.

About thet darned Proviso[2] matter
   I never hed a grain o' doubt,
Nor I aint one my sense to scatter
   So 'st no one couldn't pick it out;
45 My love fer North an' South is equil,[3]
   So I'll jest answer plump an' frank,
No matter wut may be the sequil,—
   Yes, Sir, I *am* agin a Bank.[4]

Ez to the answerin' o' questions,
50 I'm an off ox at bein' druv,
Though I aint one thet ary test shuns
   'll give our folks a helpin' shove;
Kind o' permiscoous I go it
   Fer the holl country, an' the ground
55 I take, ez nigh ez I can show it,
   Is pooty gen'ally all round.

I don't appruve o' givin' pledges;
   You'd ough' to leave a feller free,
An' not go knockin' out the wedges
60 To ketch his fingers in the tree;
Pledges air awfle breachy cattle
   Thet preudunt farmers don't turn out,—

[2]The Wilmot Proviso (1846) sought to prohibit slavery in any territory acquired by the United States from Mexico as part of a peace settlement of the Mexican War. It was twice passed by the House, but never by the Senate, and so was never adopted.
[3]Taylor was a Louisianian and a slave owner, but appealed to the North as well because of his military glory.
[4]The Democrats, since Andrew Jackson, had generally opposed a national bank. Jackson's presidential veto in 1836 had killed the Second Bank of the United States by not extending its charter.

Ez long 'z the people git their rattle,
    Wut is there fer 'm to grout about?

65 Ez to the slaves, there's no confusion
        In *my* idees consarnin' them,—
    I think they air an Institution,
        A sort of—yes, jest so,—ahem:
    Do *I* own any? Of my merit
70   On thet pint you yourself may jedge;
    All is, I never drink no sperit,
        Nor I haint never signed no pledge.

    Ez to my princerples, I glory
        In hevin' nothing' o' the sort;
75 I aint a Wig, I aint a Tory,
        I'm jest a canderdate, in short;
    Thet's fair an' square an' parpendicler,
        But, ef the Public cares a fig
    To hev me an' thin' in particler,
80   Why, I'm a kind o' peri-Wig.[5]

P.S.

    Ez we're a sort o' privateerin',
        O' course, you know, it's sheer an' sheer,
    An' there is sutthin' wuth your hearin'
        I'll mention in *your* privit ear;
85 Ef you git *me* inside the White House,
        Your head with ile I'll kin' o' 'nint[6]
    By gettin' *you* inside the Light-house
        Down to the eend o' Jaalam Pint.

    An' ez the North hez took to brustlin'
90   At bein' scrouged frum off the roost,
    I'll tell ye wut 'll save all tusslin'
        An' give our side a harnsome boost,—
    Tell 'em thet on the Slavery question
        I'm RIGHT, although to speak I'm lawth;
95 This gives you a safe pint to rest on,
        An' leaves me frontin' South by North.

[5]Taylor indicated his political affiliations by saying in 1847 that he was a Whig "but not an ultra Whig." "Peri" means "around" in Greek; here, an all-around Whig with no central position, in addition to the pun on "periwig."
[6]Psalms 23:5: "You anoint my head with oil, my cup brims over." The anointing of the head was a sign of hospitality.

ODE RECITED AT THE HARVARD COMMEMORATION[1]

July 21, 1865

I

Weak-winged is song,
Nor aims at that clear-ethered height
Whither the brave deed climbs for light:
   We seem to do them wrong,
5 Bringing our robin's-leaf to deck their hearse
Who in warm life-blood wrote their nobler verse,
Our trivial song to honor those who come
With ears attuned to strenuous trump and drum,
And shaped in squadron-strophes their desire,
10 Live battle-odes whose lines were steel and fire:
   Yet sometimes feathered words are strong,
A gracious memory to buoy up and save
From Lethe's[2] dreamless ooze, the common grave
   Of the unventurous throng.

II

15 To-day our Reverend Mother welcomes back
   Her wisest Scholars, those who understood
The deeper teaching of her mystic tome,
   And offered their fresh lives to make it good:
     No lore of Greece or Rome,
20 No science peddling with the names of things,
Or reading stars to find inglorious fates,
   Can lift our life with wings
Far from Death's idle gulf that for the many waits,
   And lengthen out our dates
25 With that clear fame whose memory sings
In manly hearts to come, and nerves them and dilates:

[1]The commemoration was a tribute to the Harvard men who had served in the Civil War. Lowell was deeply concerned about the consequences of the war, and deeply concerned with Harvard as an alumnus and a faculty member. Of the irregular form of the "Ode," he noted that "my problem was to contrive a measure which should not be tedious by uniformity, but which should vary with varying moods, in which the transitions . . . should be managed without a jar."

[2]The river of forgetfulness in the underworld.

Nor such thy teaching, Mother of us all!
    Not such the trumpet-call
    Of thy diviner mood,
30   That could thy sons entice
From happy homes and toils, the fruitful nest
Of those half-virtues which the world calls best,
    Into War's tumult rude;
    But rather far that stern device
35 The sponsors chose that round thy cradle stood
    In the dim, unventured wood,
    The VERITAS[3] that lurks beneath
    The letter's unprolific sheath,
Life of whate'er makes life worth living,
40 Seed-grain of high emprise, immortal food,
    One heavenly thing whereof earth hath the giving.

III

Many loved Truth, and lavished life's best oil
    Amid the dust of books to find her,
Content at last, for guerdon of their toil,
45   With the cast mantle she hath left behind her.
    Many in sad faith sought for her,
    Many with crossed hands sighed for her;
    But these, our brothers, fought for her;
    At life's dear peril wrought for her,
50   So loved her that they died for her,
    Tasting the raptured fleetness
    Of her divine completeness:
    Their higher instinct knew
Those love her best who to themselves are true,
55 And what they dare to dream of, dare to do;
    They followed her and found her
    Where all may hope to find,
Not in the ashes of the burnt-out mind,
But beautiful, with danger's sweetness round her.
60   Where faith made whole with deed
    Breathes its awakening breath
    Into the lifeless creed,
    They saw her plumed and mailed,
    With sweet, stern face unveiled,
65 And all-repaying eyes, look proud on them in death.

---

[3]Latin for "Truth"; the motto of Harvard, inscribed in its seal.

IV

Our slender life runs rippling by, and glides
　　Into the silent hollow of the past;
　　　　What is there that abides
　　To make the next age better for the last?
70　　　　　Is earth too poor to give us
　　Something to live for here that shall outlive us?
　　　　Some more substantial boon
Than such as flows and ebbs with Fortune's fickle moon?
　　　　The little that we see
75　　　　From doubt is never free;
　　　　The little that we do
　　　　Is but half-nobly true;
　　　　With our laborious hiving
What men call treasure, and the gods call dross,
80　　Life seems a jest of Fate's contriving,
　　Only secure in every one's conniving,
A long account of nothings paid with loss,
Where we poor puppets, jerked by unseen wires,
　　After our little hour of strut and rave,
85　With all our pasteboard passions and desires,
Loves, hates, ambitions, and immortal fires,
　　Are tossed pell-mell together in the grave.
　　But stay! no age was e'er degenerate,
　　Unless men held it at too cheap a rate,
90　For in our likeness still we shape our fate.
　　　　Ah, there is something here
　　Unfathomed by the cynic's sneer,
　　Something that gives our feeble light
　　A high immunity from Night,
95　Something that leaps life's narrow bars
To claim its birthright with the hosts of heaven;
　　A seed of sunshine that can leaven
　　Our earthy dulness with the beams of stars,
　　　　And glorify our clay
100　With light from fountains elder than the Day;
　　　A conscience more divine than we,
　　　A gladness fed with secret tears,
　　　A vexing, forward-reaching sense
　　　Of some more noble permanence;
105　　　A light across the sea,
　Which haunts the soul and will not let it be,
Still beaconing from the heights of undegenerate years.

V

Whither leads the path
To ampler fates that leads?
110   Not down through flowery meads,
To reap an aftermath
Of youth's vainglorious weeds,
But up the steep, amid the wrath
And shock of deadly-hostile creeds,
115   Where the world's best hope and stay
By battle's flashes gropes a desperate way,
And every turf the fierce foot clings to bleeds.
Peace hath her not ignoble wreath,
Ere yet the sharp, decisive word
120 Light the black lips of cannon, and the sword
Dreams in its easeful sheath;
But some day the live coal behind the thought,
Whether from Baäl's stone obscene,[4]
Or from the shrine serene
125   Of God's pure altar brought,
Bursts up in flame; the war of tongue and pen
Learns with what deadly purpose it was fraught,
And, helpless in the fiery passion caught,
Shakes all the pillared state with shock of men:
130 Some day the soft Ideal that we wooed
Confronts us fiercely, foe-beset, pursued,
And cries reproachful: "Was it, then, my praise,
And not myself was loved? Prove now thy truth;
I claim of thee the promise of thy youth;
135 Give me thy life, or cower in empty phrase,
The victim of thy genius, not its mate!"
Life may be given in many ways,
And loyalty to Truth be sealed
As bravely in the closet as the field,
140   So bountiful is Fate;
But then to stand beside her,
When craven churls deride her,
To front a lie in arms and not to yield,
This shows, methinks, God's plan
145   And measure of a stalwart man,

[4]Baal was a nature god considered by the Hebrews to be a false god and therefore a blasphemous idol.

> Limbed like the old heroic breeds,
> Who stands self-poised on manhood's solid earth,
> Not forced to frame excuses for his birth,
> Fed from within with all the strength he needs.

VI

150 Such was he, our Martyr-Chief,[5]
> Whom late the Nation he had led,
> With ashes on her head,
> Wept with the passion of an angry grief:
> Forgive me, if from present things I turn
155 To speak what in my heart will beat and burn,
> And hang my wreath on his world-honored urn.
>> Nature, they say, doth dote,
>> And cannot make a man
>> Save on some worn-out plan,
160 >> Repeating us by rote:
> For him her Old-World moulds aside she threw,
>> And, choosing sweet clay from the breast
>> Of the unexhausted West,
> With stuff untainted shaped a hero new,
165 Wise, steadfast in the strength of God, and true.
>> How beautiful to see
> Once more a shepherd of mankind indeed,
> Who loved his charge, but never loved to lead;
> One whose meek flock the people joyed to be,
170 >> Not lured by any cheat of birth,
>> But by his clear-grained human worth,
> And brave old wisdom of sincerity!
>> They knew that outward grace is dust;
>> They could not choose but trust
175 In that sure-footed mind's unfaltering skill,
>> And supple-tempered will
> That bent like perfect steel to spring again and thrust.
>> His was no lonely mountain-peak of mind,
>> Thrusting to thin air o'er our cloudy bars,
180 >> A sea-mark now, now lost in vapors blind;
>> Broad prairie rather, genial, level-lined,
>> Fruitful and friendly for all human kind,
> Yet also nigh to heaven and loved of loftiest stars.
>> Nothing of Europe here,

[5]The slain Lincoln. Section VI was added after the recital of the "Ode" at the public ceremonies.

185 Or, then, of Europe fronting mornward still,
   Ere any names of Serf and Peer
   Could Nature's equal scheme deface
   And thwart her genial[6] will;
   Here was a type of the true elder race,
190 And one of Plutarch's men[7] talked with us face to face.
   I praise him not; it were too late;
  And some innative weakness there must be
  In him who condescends to victory
  Such as the Present gives, and cannot wait,
195   Safe in himself as in a fate.
   So always firmly he:
   He knew to bide his time,
   And can his fame abide,
 Still patient in his simple faith sublime,
200   Till the wise years decide.
  Great captains, with their guns and drums,
   Disturb our judgment for the hour,
   But at last silence comes;
  These all are gone, and, standing like a tower,
205 Our children shall behold his fame,
   The kindly-earnest, brave, foreseeing man,
 Sagacious, patient, dreading praise, not blame,
  New birth of our new soil, the first American.

VII

  Long as man's hope insatiate can discern
210   Or only guess some more inspiring goal
   Outside of Self, enduring as the pole,
  Along whose course the flying axles burn
  Of spirits bravely-pitched, earth's manlier brood;
   Long as below we cannot find
215 The meed that stills the inexorable mind;
  So long this faith to some ideal Good,
  Under whatever mortal names it masks,
  Freedom, Law, Country, this ethereal mood
 That thanks the Fates for their severer tasks,
220   Feeling its challenged pulses leap,
   While others skulk in subterfuges cheap,
 And, set in Danger's van, has all the boon it asks,
   Shall win man's praise and woman's love,

---

[6]Not just "kindly," but also denoting genius.
[7]Plutarch's *Lives* gave biographies of classical heroes.

Shall be a wisdom that we set above
225   All other skills and gifts to culture dear,
     A virtue round whose forehead we inwreathe
     Laurels that with a living passion breathe
When other crowns grow, while we twine them, sear.
     What brings us thronging these high rites to pay,
230   And seal these hours the noblest of our year,
     Save that our brothers found this better way?

VIII

     We sit here in the Promised Land.[8]
     That flows with Freedom's honey and milk:
     But 't was they won it, sword in hand,
235   Making the nettle danger soft for us as silk.
     We welcome back our bravest and our best;—
     Ah me! not all! some come not with the rest,
Who went forth brave and bright as any here!
I strive to mix some gladness with my strain,
240   But the sad strings complain,
        And will not please the ear:
I sweep them for a pæan, but they wane
        Again and yet again
Into a dirge, and die away, in pain.
245   In these brave ranks I only see the gaps,
     Thinking of dear ones whom the dumb turf wraps,
     Dark to the triumph which they died to gain:
        Fitlier may others greet the living,
        For me the past is unforgiving;
250   I with uncovered head
        Salute the sacred dead,
Who went, and who return not—Say not so!
'Tis not the grapes of Canaan that repay,
But the high faith that failed not by the way;
255   Virtue treads paths that end not in the grave;
No ban of endless night exiles the brave;
        And to the saner mind
We rather seem the dead that stayed behind.
Blow, trumpets, all your exultations blow!
260   For never shall their aureoled presence lack:

[8]Canaan (mentioned below) was the Promised Land, the section of Palestine between the Jordan River and the Mediterranean, and promised to the Israelites as part of God's covenant with them. Here America is linked, as it often was and is, with the Promised Land flowing with milk and honey as the Scripture promised.

I see them muster in a gleaming row,
With ever-youthful brows that nobler show;
We find in our dull road their shining track;
    In every nobler mood
265 We feel the orient of their spirit glow,
Part of our life's unalterable good,
Of all our saintlier aspiration;
    They come transfigured back,
Secure from change in their high-hearted ways,
270 Beautiful evermore, and with the rays
Of morn on their white Shields of Expectation!

IX

    But is there hope to save
Even this ethereal essence from the grave?
What ever 'scaped Oblivion's subtle wrong
275 Save a few clarion names, or golden threads of song?
    Before my musing eye
    The mighty ones of old sweep by,
Disvoicëd now and insubstantial things,
As noisy once as we; poor ghosts of kings,
280 Shadows of empire wholly gone to dust,
And many races, nameless long ago,
To darkness driven by that imperious gust
Of ever-rushing Time that here doth blow:
O visionary world, condition strange,
285 Where naught abiding is but only Change,
Where the deep-bolted stars themselves still shift and range!
    Shall we to more continuance make pretence?
Renown builds tombs; a life-estate is Wit;
    And, bit by bit,
290 The cunning years steal all from us but woe;
Leaves are we, whose decays no harvest sow.
    But, when we vanish hence,
Shall they lie forceless in the dark below,
Save to make green their little length of sods,
295 Or deepen pansies for a year or two,
Who now to us are shining-sweet as gods?
Was dying all they had the skill to do?
That were not fruitless; but the Soul resents
Such short-lived service, as if blind events
300 Ruled without her, or earth could so endure;

She claims a more divine investiture
Of longer tenure than Fame's airy rents;
Whate'er she touches doth her nature share;
Her inspiration haunts the ennobled air,
305   Gives eyes to mountains blind,
Ears to the deaf earth, voices to the wind,
And her clear trump sings succor everywhere
By lonely bivouacs to the wakeful mind;
For soul inherits all that soul could dare:
310   Yea, Manhood hath a wider span
And larger privilege of life than man.
The single deed, the private sacrifice,
So radiant now through proudly-hidden tears,
Is covered up erelong from mortal eyes
315 With thoughtless drift of the deciduous years;
But that high privilege that makes all men peers,
That leap of heart whereby a people rise
        Up to a noble anger's height,
And, flamed on by the Fates, not shrink, but grow more bright,
320   That swift validity in noble veins,
Of choosing danger and disdaining shame,
        Of being set on flame
By the pure fire that flies all contact base,
But wraps its chosen with angelic might,
325   There are imperishable gains,
Sure as the sun, medicinal as light,
These hold great futures in their lusty reins
And certify to earth a new imperial race.

X

        Who now shall sneer?
330   Who dare again to say we trace
Our lines to a plebeian race?
        Roundhead and Cavalier![9]
Dumb are those names erewhile in battle loud;
Dream-footed as the shadow of a cloud,
335   They flit across the ear:
That is best blood that hath most iron in 't.
To edge resolve with, pouring without stint
        For what makes manhood dear.
        Tell us not of Plantagenets,

[9]The Puritans and the Royalists, the contending sides in the English Civil War
of the 1640's.

340 Hapsburgs, and Guelfs,[10] whose thin bloods crawl
     Down from some victor in a border-brawl!
        How poor their outworn coronets,
     Matched with one leaf of that plain civic wreath
     Our brave for honor's blazon shall bequeath,
345   Through whose desert a rescued Nation sets
     Her heel on treason, and the trumpet hears
     Shout victory, tingling Europe's sullen ears
        With vain resentments and more vain regrets!

XI

        Not in anger, not in pride,
350   Pure from passion's mixture rude
        Ever to base earth allied,
        But with far-heard gratitude,
        Still with heart and voice renewed,
     To heroes living and dear martyrs dead,
355 The strain should close that consecrates our brave.
        Lift the heart and lift the head!
        Lofty be its mood and grave,
        Not without a martial ring,
        Not without a prouder tread
360   And a peal of exultation:
        Little right has he to sing
        Through whose heart in such an hour
        Beats no march of conscious power,
        Sweeps no tumult of elation!
365   'T is no Man we celebrate,
        By his country's victories great,
     A hero half, and half the whim of Fate,
        But the pith and marrow of a Nation
        Drawing force from all her men,
370   Highest, humblest, weakest, all,
        For her time of need, and then
        Pulsing it again through them,
     Till the basest can no longer cower,
     Feeling his soul spring up divinely tall,
375 Touched but in passing by her mantle-hem.
        Come back, then, noble pride, for 't is her dower!
        How could poet ever tower,

[10]The Plantagenets were an English royal family; the Hapsburgs, the royal family of the Holy Roman Empire; the Guelphs, a ruling family in medieval Italy.

If his passions, hopes, and fears,
If his triumphs and his tears,
    Kept not measure with his people?
380 Boom, cannon, boom to all the winds and waves!
Clash out, glad bells, from every rocking steeple!
Banners, adance with triumph, bend your staves!
    And from every mountain-peak
385   Let beacon-fire to answering beacon speak,
    Katahdin tell Monadnock, Whiteface he,[11]
And so leap on in light from sea to sea,
    Till the glad news be sent
    Across a kindling continent,
390 Making earth feel more firm and air breathe braver:
"Be proud! for she is saved, and all have helped to save her!
    She that lifts up the manhood of the poor,
    She of the open soul and open door,
    With room about her hearth for all mankind!
395   The fire is dreadful in her eyes no more;
    From her bold front the helm she doth unbind,
    Sends all her handmaid armies back to spin,
    And bids her navies, that so lately hurled
    Their crashing battle, hold their thunders in,
400   Swimming like birds of calm along the unharmful shore.
    No challenge sends she to the elder world,
    That looked askance and hated; a light scorn
    Plays o'er her mouth, as round her mighty knees
    She calls her children back, and waits the morn
405 Of nobler day, enthroned between her subject seas."

XII

Bow down, dear Land, for thou hast found release!
    Thy God, in these distempered days,
    Hath taught thee the sure wisdom of His ways,
And through thine enemies hath wrought thy peace!
410   Bow down in prayer and praise!
No poorest in thy borders but may now
Lift to the juster skies a man's enfranchised brow.
O Beautiful! my Country! ours once more!
Smoothing thy gold of war-dishevelled hair
415 O'er such sweet brows as never other wore,
    And letting thy set lips,
    Freed from wrath's pale eclipse,

[11]Famous mountains in Maine, New Hampshire, and New York.

The rosy edges of their smile lay bare,
What words divine of love or of poet
420   Could tell our love and make thee know it,
Among the Nations bright beyond compare?
        What were our lives without thee?
        What all our lives to save thee?
        We reck not what we gave thee;
425   We will not dare to doubt thee,
But ask whatever else, and we will dare!

Herman Melville (1819–1891)

Born in New York City, Melville grew up in Albany, where his father died in 1832, leaving the family in debt and dependent on relatives. In 1839 Melville made his first ocean voyage, to Liverpool, fictionalized later in *Redburn* (1849). In 1841 he sailed aboard the whaler *Acushnet* to the South Seas, where he jumped ship and lived briefly among the headhunters before making his way home aboard the frigate *United States*. These adventures were the materials from which he wrote his romances: *Typee* (1846), *Omoo* (1847), *Mardi* (1849), *White Jacket* (1850), and *Moby-Dick* (1851).

Meanwhile Melville had married Elizabeth Shaw, the daughter of a prominent Massachusetts judge, and had come to know Hawthorne as a neighbor in the Berkshire Mountains of Western Massachusetts during the seminal period in which he was reworking *Moby-Dick*. Bitterly disappointed at being accepted only as an adventure writer and increasingly preoccupied with the metaphysical uncertainty darkening man's doom, Melville poured out his frustrations into *Pierre: or the Ambiguities* (1852) and went abroad to recover his balance, traveling in Europe and the Holy Land.

After *Israel Potter* (1855), *The Piazza Tales* (1856), and *The Confidence Man* (1857), he stopped writing prose and lived in retirement, supporting his family as Inspector of Customs in New York. Meanwhile he was publishing books of verse that received little notice: *Battle Pieces and Aspects of the War* (1866), *John Marr and Other Sailors* (1888), and *Timoleon* (1891), as well as the long episodic narrative in rhymed verse, *Clarel* (1876), based on his trip to the Holy Land. More poems and *Billy Budd* were left in manuscript when he died in obscurity. Melville's great achievement is his best prose, but in many of the poems he finds the images and rhythms to express his stoic reflections on man's threatened situation and unresolved destiny.

TEXT

Melville, Herman. *Collected Poems of Herman Melville*. Ed. Howard P. Vincent. Chicago: Packard and Co., 1947.

REFERENCE

Arvin, Newton. *Herman Melville*. New York: Sloan Associates, 1950.

Sedgwick, William Ellery. *Herman Melville: The Tragedy of Mind*. Cambridge, Mass.: Harvard University Press, 1944.

Howard, Leon. *Herman Meville: A Biography*. Berkeley: University of California Press, 1951.

Matthiessen, F. O. *American Renaissance*. London and New York: Oxford University Press, 1941.

Melville: A Collection of Critical Essays. Ed. Richard Chase. Englewood Cliffs, N. J.: Prentice-Hall, 1962.

Olson, Charles. *Call Me Ishmael*. New York: Reynal and Hitchcock, 1947.

MISGIVINGS

(1860)

When ocean-clouds over inland hills
Sweep storming in late autumn brown,
And horror the sodden valley fills,
    And the spire falls crashing in the town,
5   I muse upon my country's ills—
The tempest bursting from the waste of Time
On the world's fairest hope linked with man's foulest crime.

Nature's dark side is heeded now—
    (Ah! optimist-cheer disheartened flown)—
10   A child may read the moody brow
        Of yon black mountain lone.
With shouts the torrents down the gorges go,
And storms are formed behind the storm we feel:
The hemlock shakes in the rafter, the oak in the driving keel.

THE MARCH INTO VIRGINIA

Ending in the First Manassas[1]
(July, 1861)

Did all the lets and bars[2] appear
    To every just or larger end,
Whence should come the trust and cheer?
    Youth must its ignorant impulse lend—
5   Age finds place in the rear.
        All wars are boyish, and are fought by boys,
    The champions and enthusiasts of the state:
        Turbid ardors and vain joys
            Not barrenly abate—
10   Stimulants to the power mature,
        Preparatives of fate.

---

[1]A town in Virginia near which two battles were fought during the Civil War in 1861 and 1862. Also called the battles of Bull Run.
[2]Impediments and hindrances.

Who here forecasteth the event?
What heart but spurns at precedent
And warnings of the wise,
15 Contemned foreclosures of surprise?
The banners play, the bugles call,
The air is blue and prodigal.
    No berrying party, pleasure-wooed,
No picnic party in the May,
20 Ever went less loth than they
    Into that leafy neighborhood.
In Bacchic³ glee they file toward Fate,
Moloch's⁴ uninitiate;
Expectancy, and glad surmise
25 Of battle's unknown mysteries.

All they feel is this: 'tis glory,
A rapture sharp, though transitory,
Yet lasting in belaureled story.
So they gayly go to fight,
30 Chatting left and laughing right.

But some who this blithe mood present,
    As on in lightsome files they fare,
Shall die experienced ere three days be spent—
    Perish, enlightened by the vollied glare;
35 Or shame survive, and, like to adamant,
    Thy after shock, Manassas, share.⁵

THE MALDIVE SHARK

About the Shark, phlegmatical one,
Pale sot of the Maldive sea,¹
The sleek little pilot-fish, azure and slim,
How alert in attendance be.
5 From his saw-pit of mouth, from his charnel of maw

---

³Bacchus was the god of wine and revelry.
⁴A pagan idol to whom children were sacrificed; in Milton's *Paradise Lost*, he was one of the devils.
⁵"After-shock" would normally be hyphenated. Here, as above, the verbs and objects are inverted from normal order.

---

¹The Maldive Islands in the Indian Ocean.

They have nothing of harm to dread,
But liquidly glide on his ghastly flank
Or before his Gorgonian[2] head;
Or lurk in the port of serrated teeth
10   In white triple tiers of glittering gates,
And there find a haven when peril's abroad,
An asylum in jaws of the Fates!
They are friends; and friendly they guide him to prey,
Yet never partake of the treat—
15   Eyes and brains to the dotard lethargic and dull,
Pale ravener of horrible meat.

THE BERG

(A Dream)

I saw a ship of martial build
(Her standards set, her brave apparel on)
Directed as by madness mere
Against a stolid iceberg steer,
5   Nor budge it, though the infatuate[1] ship went down.
The impact made huge ice-cubes fall
Sullen, in tons that crashed the deck;
But that one avalanche was all—
No other movement save the foundering wreck.

10   Along the spurs of ridges pale,
Not any slenderest shaft and frail,
A prism over glass-green gorges lone,
Toppled; or lace of traceries fine,
Nor pendant drops in grot or mine
15   Were jarred, when the stunned ship went down.
Nor sole[2] the gulls in cloud that wheeled
Circling one snow-flanked peak afar,
But nearer fowl the floes that skimmed
And crystal beaches, felt no jar.
20   No thrill transmitted stirred the lock
Of jack-straw needle-ice at base;

---

[2]In Greek mythology the Gorgons are three monstrous sisters.

---

[1]Infatuated; possessed by an unreasoning or foolish attraction.
[2]Not only.

Towers undermined by waves—the block
Atilt impending—kept their place.
Seals, dozing sleek on sliddery[3] ledges
25   Slipt never, when by loftier edges
Through very inertia overthrown,
The impetuous ship in bafflement went down.

Hard Berg (methought), so cold, so vast,
With mortal damps self-overcast;
30   Exhaling still thy dankish breath—
Adrift dissolving, bound for death;
Though lumpish thou, a lumbering one—
A lumbering lubbard[4] loitering slow,
Impingers rue thee and go down,
35   Sounding thy precipice below,
Nor stir the slimy slug that sprawls
Along thy dead indifference of walls.

THE NIGHT-MARCH

With banners furled, and clarions mute,
    An army passes in the night;
And beaming spears and helms salute
    The dark with bright.

5   In silence deep the legions stream,
    With open ranks, in order true;
Over boundless plains they stream and gleam—
    No chief in view!

Afar, in twinkling distance lost,
10   (So legends tell) he lonely wends
And back through all that shining host
    His mandate sends.

[3]Slippery.
[4]Lubber: a clumsy person; an inexperienced sailor.

THE RAVAGED VILLA

In shards the sylvan vases lie,
  Their links of dance undone,
And brambles wither by thy brim,
  Choked fountain of the sun!
5   The spider in the laurel spins,
  The weed exiles the flower:
And, flung to kiln, Apollo's[1] bust
  Makes lime for Mammon's[2] tower.

BUDDHA

*"For what is your life? It is even
a vapor that appeareth for a little
time and then vanisheth away."*[1]

Swooning swim to less and less,
  Aspirant to nothingness!
Sobs of the worlds, and dole of kinds
  That dumb endurers be—
5   Nirvana![2] absorb us in your skies,
  Annul us into thee.

IN THE DESERT

Never Pharaoh's Night,
Whereof the Hebrew wizards croon,[1]
Did so the Theban flamens[2] try
As me this veritable Noon.

---

[1]The god of poetry.
[2]The false god of riches and worldly goods. See Matthew 6:24.

---

[1]From James 4:14.
[2]In Buddhist and Hindu philosophy, the state of absolute blessedness, characterized by release from the cycle of bodily reincarnations and by the loss of individual existence in the All which is Nothing.

---

[1]During the long exile when the Israelites were held in captivity in Egypt.
[2]Thebes was the ancient religious and political capital of upper Egypt. Flamen: priest; here also punning on the burning intensity of the desert noon.

5   Like blank ocean in blue calm
Undulates the ethereal frame;
In one flowing oriflamme[3]
God flings his fiery standard out.

Battling with the Emirs[4] fierce
10   Napoleon a great victory won,
Through and through his sword did pierce;
But, bayonetted by this sun
His gunners drop beneath the gun.

Holy, holy, holy Light!
15   Immaterial incandescence,
Of God the effluence of the essence,
Shekinah[5] intolerably bright!

A BATTLE PICTURE

Three mounted buglers laced in gold,
   Sidelong veering, light in seat,
High on the crest of battle rolled
   Ere yet the surge is downward beat,
5   The pennoned trumpets lightly hold—
   Mark how they snatch the swift occasion
   To thrill their rearward invocation—
While the sabres, never coy,
   Ring responses as they ride;
10   And, like breakers of the tide,
   All the mad plumes dance for joy!

---

[3]The red and orange flag used as a standard by the early kings of France; hence any symbolic standard. Literally: gold flame, continuing the pun on flaming noon.
[4]Arabic for "princes, commanders." The Egyptian adversaries whom Napoleon conquered on his Egyptian campaign.
[5]In Jewish theology, the visible manifestation of the divine presence. Melville is recalling here his experience of the desert on his journey to the Near East in the 1850's.

Walt Whitman (1819–1892)

Born into a large and oddly sorted family with an unreliable father and a strong mother, Whitman grew up in Brooklyn and came to know Manhattan early. Printer and journalist, he became editor of two Brooklyn papers, the *Daily Eagle* and the *Freeman*. A brief but traumatic sojourn in New Orleans in 1848 has made biographers speculate about the possibility of a disturbing sexual experience, either with a woman or with a man, but there is no clear evidence.

Whitman was reading Emerson during the early fifties, while writing the poems in the first *Leaves of Grass* (1855), printed by the author with a long Preface as manifesto. He expanded the volume the next year and added a laudatory letter from Emerson and his own excited reply. Boldly linking the life force with the sexual urge and asserting sexuality as the key to the identity of body and soul, Whitman as Bard assumed an androgynous role, adding the "Children of Adam" and "Calamus" sections in 1860 to celebrate the love between the sexes and between manly comrades. Emerson objected to the eroticism of the former, but not to what seems to us today the homosexual overtones of "Calamus."

Whitman went to Virginia to look for his brother George in the Union Army in 1862, spent some time with the troops, and remained in Washington, as a volunteer nurse in army hospitals throughout the war, and for years afterwards while working in government offices. He was fired by the Secretary of the Interior for the scurrilousness of *Leaves of Grass* but was granted another post by the Attorney General. *Drum*

TEXT

Whitman, Walt. *Leaves of Grass,* Ed. Harold W. Blodgett and Sculley Bradley. New York: New York University Press, 1965.

REFERENCE

Allen, Gay Wilson. *The Solitary Singer: A Critical Biography*. New York: New York University Press, 1967.

Allen, Gay Wilson. *Walt Whitman Handbook*. New York: Hendricks House, 1957.

Asselineau, Roger. *The Evolution of Walt Whitman*. 2 vols. Cambridge, Mass.: Harvard University Press, 1960, 1962.

Chase, Richard. *Walt Whitman Reconsidered*. New York: Sloane Associates, 1955.

Hindus, Milton, (Ed.). *Leaves of Grass One Hundred Years After*. Stanford: Stanford University Press, 1955.

Matthiessen, F. O. *American Renaissance*. London and New York: Oxford University Press, 1941.

Whitman: A Collection of Critical Essays. Ed. Roy Harvey Pearce. Englewood Cliffs, N. J.: Prentice-Hall, 1962.

Whitman, Walt. *The Correspondence (1842–1885)*. Ed. Edwin H. Miller. New York: New York University Press, 1961, 1964, 1969.

Whitman, Walt. *Prose Works 1892*. Ed. Floyd Stovall. New York: New York University Press, 1963, 1964.

Taps and Sequel (1865) contained the war poems, many of them terse and sharply observed, and the Lincoln elegy, "When Lilacs Last in the Dooryard Bloom'd." Subsequent editions of *Leaves of Grass* followed, always with revisions and additions, ending in the "Deathbed Edition" of 1891–1892. In 1873 Whitman was partially paralyzed by a stroke from which he never recovered; he moved to Camden, New Jersey, where he lived out the rest of his life amid a growing group of disciples. *Prose Works* (1892) contained *Democratic Vistas* (1871) and *Specimen Days and Collect* (1882).

As the national bard for whom Emerson and others had been calling, Whitman celebrated himself as the mythic American epitomizing and synthesizing the variety of his land and the energy of his polyglot people; he envisioned an ideal America in which love and comradeship created an open, free society. The sources of Whitman's self-reliance and self-apotheosis were his mother's Quaker faith and Emerson's Transcendentalism, confirmed later by his readings in Hegel and the Germans and in Eastern mysticism. His affirmations are the more convincing because they are earned, tested by self-questioning and self-doubt. As a result, his prophetic presence and his experiments in free verse and organic form have changed the shape of American—and indeed of all—modern poetry. In Ezra Pound's words, "Whitman is to my fatherland . . . what Dante is to Italy": the creator of the poetic speech and metric of his people.

SONG OF MYSELF

1

I celebrate myself, and sing myself,[1]
And what I assume you shall assume,
For every atom belonging to me as good belongs to you.

I loafe and invite my soul,
5 I lean and loafe at my ease observing a spear of summer grass.

My tongue, every atom of my blood, form'd from this soil, this air,
Born here of parents born here from parents the same, and their
    parents the same,
I, now thirty-seven years old in perfect health begin,
Hoping to cease not till death.

10 Creeds and schools in abeyance,
Retiring back a while sufficed at what they are, but never forgotten,
I harbor for good or bad, I permit to speak at every hazard,
Nature without check with original energy.

2

Houses and rooms are full of perfumes, the shelves are crowded
    with perfumes,
15 I breathe the fragrance myself and know it and like it,
The distillation would intoxicate me also, but I shall not let it.

The atmosphere is not a perfume, it has no taste of the distillation,
    it is odorless,
It is for my mouth forever, I am in love with it,
I will go to the bank by the wood and become undisguised and
    naked,
20 I am mad for it to be in contact with me.

The smoke of my own breath,
Echoes, ripples, buzz'd whispers, love-root, silk-thread, crotch and
    vine,
My respiration and inspiration, the beating of my heart, the passing
    of blood and air through my lungs,

---

[1]The first line indicates the epic intention of the poem by rephrasing the first
line of *Vergil's* Aeneid: "I sing of arms and the man," which begins an account
of the Trojan War and of the hero Aeneas.

The sniff of green leaves and dry leaves, and of the shore and dark-
color'd sea-rocks, and of hay in the barn,
The sound of the belch'd words of my voice loos'd to the eddies of
the wind,
A few light kisses, a few embraces, a reaching around of arms,
The play of shine and shade on the trees as the supple boughs wag,
The delight alone or in the rush of the streets, or along the fields
and hill-sides,
The feeling of health, the full-noon trill, the song of me rising from
bed and meeting the sun.

Have you reckon'd a thousand acres much? have you reckon'd the
earth much?
Have you practis'd so long to learn to read?
Have you felt so proud to get at the meaning of poems?

Stop this day and night with me and you shall possess the origin of
all poems,
You shall possess the good of the earth and sun, (there are millions
of sun left,)
You shall no longer take things at second or third hand, nor look
through the eyes of the dead, nor feed on the spectres in books,
You shall not look through my eyes either, nor take things from me,
You shall listen to all sides and filter them from your self.

3

I have heard what the talkers were talking, the talk of the beginning
and the end,
But I do not talk of the beginning or the end.

There was never any more inception than there is now,
Nor any more youth or age than there is now,
And will never be any more perfection than there is now,
Nor any more heaven or hell than there is now.

Urge and urge and urge,
Always the procreant urge of the world.
Out of the dimness opposite equals advance, always substance and
increase, always sex,
Always a knit of identity, always distinction, always a breed of life.

To elaborate is no avail, learn'd and unlearn'd feel that it is so.

Sure as the most certain sure, plumb in the uprights, well entretied,[2]
    braced in the beams,
50   Stout as a horse, affectionate, haughty, electrical,
I and this mystery here we stand.

Clear and sweet is my soul, and clear and sweet is all that is not my
    soul.

Lack one lacks both, and the unseen is proved by the seen,
Till that becomes unseen and receives proof in its turn.

55   Showing the best and dividing it from the worst age vexes age,
Knowing the perfect fitness and equanimity of things, while they
    discuss I am silent, and go bathe and admire myself.

Welcome is every organ and attribute of me, and of any man hearty
    and clean,
Not an inch nor a particle of an inch is vile, and none shall be less
    familiar than the rest.

I am satisfied—I see, dance, laugh, sing;
60   As the hugging and loving bed-fellow sleeps at my side through the
    night;[3] and withdraws at the peep of the day with stealthy
    tread,
Leaving me baskets cover'd with white towels swelling the house
    with their plenty,
Shall I postpone my acceptation and realization and scream at my
    eyes,
That they turn from gazing after and down the road,
And forthwith cipher and show me to a cent,
65   Exactly the value of one and exactly the value of two, and which is
    ahead?

4

Trippers and askers surround me,
People I meet, the effect upon me of my early life or the ward and
    city I live in, or the nation,
The latest dates, discoveries, inventions, societies, authors old and
    new,
My dinner, dress, associates, looks, compliments, dues,
70   The real or fancied indifference of some man or woman I love,

---

[2]Tied together, braced.
[3]The line in the 1855 edition reads: "As God comes a loving bedfellow and
sleeps at my side all night . . ."

The sickness of one of my folks or of myself, or ill-doing or loss or
    lack of money, or depressions or exaltations,
Battles, the horrors of fratricidal war, the fever of doubtful news,
    the fitful events;
These come to me days and nights and go from me again,
But they are not the Me myself.

Apart from the pulling and hauling stands what I am,
Stands amused, complacent, compassionate, idle, unitary,
Looks down, is erect, or bends an arm on an impalpable certain rest,
Looking with side-curved head curious what will come next,
Both in and out of the game and watching and wondering at it.

Backward I see in my own days where I sweated through fog with
    linguists and contenders,
I have no mockings or arguments, I witness and wait.

5

I believe in you my soul, the other I am must not abase itself to you,
And you must not be abased to the other.

Loafe with me on the grass, loose the stop from your throat,
Not words, not music or rhyme I want, not custom or lecture, not
    even the best,
Only the lull I like, the hum of your valvèd voice.

I mind how once we lay such a transparent summer morning,
How you settled your head athwart my hips and gently turn'd over
    upon me,
And parted the shirt from my bosom-bone, and plunged your
    tongue to my bare-stript heart,
And reach'd till you felt my beard, and reach'd till you held my feet.

Swiftly arose and spread around me the peace and knowledge that
    pass all the argument of the earth,
And I know that the hand of God is the promise of my own,
And I know that the spirit of God is the brother of my own,
And that all the men ever born are also my brothers, and the women
    my sisters and lovers,
And that a kelson of the creation is love,
And limitless are leaves stiff or drooping in the fields,
And brown ants in the little wells beneath them,
And mossy scabs of the worm fence, heap'd stones, elder, mullein
    and poke-weed.

6

A child said *What is the grass?* fetching it to me with full hands;
How could I answer the child? I do not know what it is any more
    than he.

I guess it must be the flag of my disposition, out of hopeful green
    stuff woven.

Or I guess it is the handkerchief of the Lord,
A scented gift and remembrancer designedly dropt,
Bearing the owner's name someway in the corners, that we may see
    and remark, and say *Whose?*

Or I guess the grass is itself a child, the produced babe of the
    vegetation.

Or I guess it is a uniform hieroglyphic,
And it means, Sprouting alike in broad zones and narrow zones,
Growing among black folks as among white,
Kanuck, Tuckahoe, Congressman, Cuff,[4] I give them the same, I
    receive them the same.

And now it seems to me the beautiful uncut hair of graves.

Tenderly will I use you curling grass,
It may be you transpire from the breasts of young men,
It may be if I had known them I would have loved them,
It may be you are from old people, or from offspring taken soon out
    of their mothers' laps,
And here you are the mothers' laps.

This grass is very dark to be from the white heads of old mothers,
Darker than the colorless beards of old men,
Dark to come from under the faint red roofs of mouths.

O I perceive after all so many uttering tongues,
And I perceive they do not come from the roofs of mouths for
    nothing.

[4]Kanuck: a French-Canadian; Tuckahoe: a Virginian who farmed the poor
lands and supposedly lived off an underground fungus called tuckahoe; Cuff:
a negro.

I wish I could translate the hints about the dead young men and
    women,
And the hints about old men and mothers, and the offspring taken
    soon out of their laps.

What do you think has become of the young and old men?
And what do you think has become of the women and children?

They are alive and well somewhere,
The smallest sprout shows there is really no death,
And if ever there was it led forward life, and does not wait at the
    end to arrest it,
And ceas'd the moment life appear'd.

All goes onward and outward, nothing collapses,
And to die is different from what any one supposed, and luckier.

7

Has any one supposed it lucky to be born?
I hasten to inform him or her it is just as lucky to die, and I know it.

I pass death with the dying and birth with the new-wash'd babe,
    and am not contain'd between my hat and boots,
And peruse manifold objects, no two alike and every one good,
The earth good and the stars good, and their adjuncts all good.

I am not an earth nor an adjunct of an earth,
I am the mate and companion of people, all just as immortal and
    fathomless as myself,
(They do not know how immortal, but I know.)

Every kind for itself and its own, for me mine male and female,
For me those that have been boys and that love women,
For me the man that is proud and feels how it stings to be slighted,
For me the sweet-heart and the old maid, for me mothers and the
    mothers of mothers,
For me lips that have smiled, eyes that have shed tears,
For me children and the begetters of children.

Undrape! you are not guilty to me, nor stale nor discarded,
I see through the broadcloth and gingham whether or no,
And am around, tenacious, acquisitive, tireless, and cannot be shaken
    away.

8

The little one sleeps in its cradle,
I lift the gauze and look a long time, and silently brush away flies
with my hand.

150   The youngster and the red-faced girl turn aside up the bushy hill,
I peeringly view them from the top.

The suicide sprawls on the bloody floor of the bedroom,
I witness the corpse with its dabbled hair, I note where the pistol has
fallen.

The blab of the pave, tires of carts, sluff of boot-soles, talk of the
promenaders,
155   The heavy omnibus, the driver with his interrogating thumb, the
clank of the shod horses on the granite floor,
The snow-sleighs, clinking, shouted jokes, pelts of snow-balls,
The hurrahs for popular favorites, the fury of rous'd mobs,
The flap of the curtain'd litter, a sick man inside borne to the hospital,
The meeting of enemies, the sudden oath, the blows and fall,
160   The excited crowd, the policeman with his star quickly working his
passage to the centre of the crowd,
The impassive stones that receive and return so many echoes,
What groans of over-fed or half-starv'd who fall sunstruck or in fits,
What exclamations of women taken suddenly who hurry home and
give birth to babes,
What living and buried speech is always vibrating here, what howls
restrain'd by decorum,
165   Arrests of criminals, slights, adulterous offers made, acceptances,
rejections with convex lips,
I mind them or the show or resonance of them—I come and I depart.

9

The big doors of the country barn stand open and ready,
The dried grass of the harvest-time loads the slow-drawn wagon,
The clear light plays on the brown gray and green intertinged,
170   The armfuls are pack'd to the sagging mow.

I am there, I help, I came stretch'd atop of the load,
I felt its soft jolts, one leg reclined on the other,
I jump from the cross-beams and seize the clover and timothy,
And roll head over heels and tangle my hair full of wisps.

10

Alone far in the wilds and mountains I hunt,
Wandering amazed at my own lightness and glee,
In the late afternoon choosing a safe spot to pass the night,
Kindling a fire and broiling the fresh-kill'd game,
Falling asleep on the gather'd leaves with my dog and gun by my
     side.

The Yankee clipper is under her sky-sails, she cuts the sparkle and
     scud,
My eyes settle the land, I bend at her prow or shout joyously from
     the deck.

The boatmen and clam-diggers arose early and stopt for me,
I tuck'd my trowser-ends in my boots and went and had a good
     time;
You should have been with us that day round the chowder-kettle.

I saw the marriage of the trapper in the open air in the far west, the
     bride was a red girl,
Her father and his friends sat near cross-legged and dumbly smok-
     ing, they had moccasins to their feet and large thick blankets
     hanging from their shoulders,
On a bank lounged the trapper, he was drest mostly in skins, his
     luxuriant beard and curls protected his neck, he held his bride
     by the hand,
She had long eyelashes, her head was bare, her coarse straight locks
     descended upon her voluptuous limbs and reach'd to her feet.

The runaway slave came to my house and stopt outside,
I heard his motions crackling the twigs of the woodpile,
Through the swung half-door of the kitchen I saw him limpsy and
     weak,
And went where he sat on a log and led him in and assured him,
And brought water and fill'd a tub for his sweated body and bruis'd
     feet,
And gave him a room that enter'd from my own, and gave him some
     coarse clean clothes,
And remember perfectly well his revolving eyes and his awkward-
     ness,
And remember putting plasters on the galls of his neck and ankles;
He staid with me a week before he was recuperated and pass'd
     north,
I had him sit next me at table, my fire-lock lean'd in the corner.

11

Twenty-eight young men bathe by the shore,
200 Twenty-eight young men and all so friendly;
Twenty-eight years of womanly life and all so lonesome.

She owns the fine house by the rise of the bank,
She hides handsome and richly drest aft the blinds of the window.

Which of the young men does she like the best?
205 Ah the homeliest of them is beautiful to her.

Where are you off to, lady? for I see you,
You splash in the water there, yet stay stock still in your room.

Dancing and laughing along the beach came the twenty-ninth bather,
The rest did not see her, but she saw them and loved them.

210 The beards of the young men glisten'd with we, it ran from their
         long hair,
Little streams pass'd all over their bodies.

An unseen hand also pass'd over their bodies,
It descended tremblingly from their temples and ribs.

The young men float on their backs, their white bellies bulge to the
         sun, they do not ask who seizes fast to them,
215 They do not know who puffs and declines with pendant and bending
         arch,
They do not think whom they souse with spray.

12

The butcher-boy puts off his killing-clothes, or sharpens his knife
         at the stall in the market,
I loiter enjoying his repartee and his shuffle and break-down.

Blacksmiths with grimed and hairy chests environ the anvil,
220 Each has his main-sledge, they are all out, there is a great heat in the
         fire.

From the cinder-strew'd threshold I follow their movements,
The lithe sheer[5] of their waists plays even with their massive arms,

[5]Curving line.

Overhand the hammers swing, overhand so slow, overhand so sure,
They do not hasten, each man hits in his place.

13

The negro holds firmly the reins of his four horses, the block swags
    underneath on its tied-over chain,
The negro that drives the long dray of the stone-yard, steady and
    tall he stands pois'd on one leg on the string-piece,
His blue shirt exposes his ample neck and breast and loosens over
    his hip-band,
His glance is calm and commanding, he tosses the slouch of his hat
    away from his forehead,
The sun falls on his crispy hair and mustache, falls on the black of
    his polish'd and perfect limbs.

I behold the picturesque giant and love him, and I do not stop there,
I go with the team also.

In me the caresser of life wherever moving, backward as well as
    forward sluing,[6]
To niches aside and junior bending, not a person or object missing,
Absorbing all to myself and for this song.

Oxen that rattle the yoke and chain or halt in the leafy shade, what
    is that you express in your eyes?
It seems to me more than all the print I have read in my life.

My tread scares the wood-drake and wood-duck on my distant and
    day-long ramble,
They rise together, they slowly circle around.

I believe in those wing'd purposes,
And acknowledge red, yellow, white, playing within me,
And consider green and violet and the tufted crown intentional,
And do not call the tortoise unworthy because she is not something
    else,
And the jay in the woods never studied the gamut,[7] yet trills pretty
    well to me,
And the look of the bay mare shames silliness out of me.

[6]Turning.
[7]The complete musical scale.

14

245   The wild gander leads his flock through the cool night,
     Ya-honk he says, and sounds it down to me like an invitation,
     The pert may suppose it meaningless, but I listening close,
     Find its purpose and place up there toward the wintry sky.

     The sharp-hoof'd moose of the north, the cat on the house-sill, the
        chickadee, the prairie-dog,
250   The litter of the grunting sow as they tug at her teats,
     The brood of the turkey-hen and she with her half-spread wings,
     I see in them and myself the same old law.

     The press of my foot to the earth springs a hundred affections,
     They scorn the best I can do to relate them.

255   I am enamour'd of growing out-doors,
     Of men that live among cattle or taste of the ocean or woods,
     Of the builders and steerers of ships and the wielders of axes and
        mauls, and the drivers of horses,
     I can eat and sleep with them week in and week out.

     What is commonest, cheapest, nearest, easiest, is Me,
260   Me going in for my chances, spending for vast returns,
     Adorning myself to bestow myself on the first that will take me,
     Not asking the sky to come down to my good will,
     Scattering it freely forever.

15

     The pure contralto sings in the organ loft,
265   The carpenter dresses his plank, the tongue of his foreplane whistles
        its wild ascending lisp,
     The married and unmarried children ride home to their Thanks-
        giving dinner,
     The pilot seizes the king-pin, he heaves down with a strong arm,
     The mate stands braced in the whale-boat, lance and harpoon are
        ready,
     The duck-shooter walks by silent and cautious stretches,
270   The deacons are ordain'd with cross'd hands at the altar,
     The spinning-girl retreats and advances to the hum of the big wheel,
     The farmer stops by the bars[8] as he walks on a First-day[9] loafe and
        looks at the oats and rye,

[8]Railings.
[9]The Quaker name for Sunday.

The lunatic is carried at last to the asylum a confirm'd case,
(He will never sleep any more as he did in the cot in his mother's
    bed-room;)
The jour[10] printer with gray head and gaunt jaws works at his case,
He turns his quid of tobacco while his eyes blurr with the manu-
    script;
The malform'd limbs are tied to the surgeon's table,
What is removed drops horribly in a pail;
The quadroon girl is sold at the auction-stand, the drunkard nods by
    the bar-room stove,
The machinist rolls up his sleeves, the policeman travels his beat,
    the gate-keeper marks who pass,
The young fellow drives the express-wagon, (I love him though
    I do not know him;)
The half-breed straps on his light boots to compete in the race,
The western turkey-shooting draws old and young, some lean on
    their rifles, some sit on logs,
Out from the crowd steps the marksman, takes his position, levels
    his piece;
The groups of newly-come immigrants cover the wharf or levee,
As the wooley-pates hoe in the sugar-field, the overseer views them
    from his saddle,
The bugle calls in the ball-room, the gentlemen run for their part-
    ners, the dancers bow to each other,
The youth lies awake in the cedar-roof'd garret and harks to the
    musical rain,
The Wolverine[11] sets traps on the creek that helps fill the Huron,
The squaw wrapt in her yellow-hemm'd cloth is offering moccasins
    and bead-bags for sale,
The connoisseur peers along the exhibition-gallery with half-shut
    eyes bent sideways,
As the deck-hands make fast the steamboat the plank is thrown for
    the shore-going passengers,
The young sister holds out the skein while the elder sister winds it
    off in a ball, and stops now and then for the knots,
The one-year wife is recovering and happy having a week ago borne
    her first child,
The clean-hair'd Yankee girl works with her sewing-machine or in
    the factory or mill,

---

[10]Journeyman—that is, the artisan or mechanic who has completed apprentice-
ship and is a practitioner of his trade.
[11]An inhabitant of Michigan.

The paving-man leans on his two-handed rammer, the reporter's
    lead flies swiftly over the note-book, the sign-painter is letter-
    ing with blue and gold,

The canal boy trots on the tow-path, the book-keeper counts at his
    desk, the shoemaker waxes his thread,

The conductor beats time for the band and all the performers follow
    him,

The child is baptized, the convert is making his first professions,

300 The regatta is spread on the bay, the race is begun, (how the white
    sails sparkle!)

The drover watching his drove sings out to them that would stray,

The pedler sweats with his pack on his back, (the purchaser hig-
    gling[12] about the odd cent;)

The bride unrumples her white dress, the minute-hand of the clock
    moves slowly,

The opium-eater reclines with rigid head and just-open'd lips,

305 The prostitute draggles her shawl, her bonnet bobs on her tipsy and
    pimpled neck,

The crowd laugh at her blackguard oaths, the men jeer and wink to
    each other,

(Miserable! I do not laugh at your oaths nor jeer you;)

The President holding a cabinet council is surrounded by the great
    Secretaries,

On the piazza walk three matrons stately and friendly with twined
    arms,

310 The crew of the fish-smack pack repeated layers of halibut in the
    hold,

The Missourian crosses the plains toting his wares and his cattle,

As the fare-collector goes through the train he gives notice by the
    jingling of loose change,

The floor-men are laying the floor, the tinners are tinning the roof,
    the masons are calling for mortar,

In single file each shouldering his hod pass onward the laborers;

315 Seasons pursuing each other the indescribable crowd is gather'd, it is
    the fourth of Seventh-month,[13] (what salutes of cannon and
    small arms!)

Seasons pursuing each other the plougher ploughs, the mower
    mows, and the winter-grain falls in the ground;

Off on the lakes the pike-fisher watches and waits by the hole in the
    frozen surface,

---

[12]Haggling.
[13]The Quaker name for July.

The stumps stand thick round the clearing, the squatter strikes deep
with his axe,

Flatboatmen make fast towards dusk near the cotton-wood or pecan-
trees,

20 Coon-seekers go through the regions of the Red river[14] or through
those drain'd by the Tennessee, or through those of the Ar-
kansas,

Torches shine in the dark that hangs on the Chattahooche or Altam-
ahaw,

Patriarchs sit at supper with sons and grandsons and great-grand-
sons around them,

In walls of adobie, in canvas tents, rest hunters and trappers after
their day's sport,

The city sleeps and the country sleeps,

325 The living sleep for their time, the dead sleep for their time,

The old husband sleeps by his wife and the young husband sleeps by
his wife;

And these tend inward to me, and I tend outward to them,

And such as it is to be of these more or less I am,

And of these one and all I weave the song of myself.

16

330 I am of old and young, of the foolish as much as the wise,

Regardless of others, ever regardful of others,

Maternal as well as paternal, a child as well as a man,

Stuff'd with the stuff that is coarse and stuff'd with the stuff that is
fine,

One of the Nation of many nations, the smallest the same and the
largest the same,

335 A Southerner soon as a Northerner, a planter nonchalant and hos-
pitable down by the Oconee[15] I live,

A Yankee bound my own way ready for trade, my joints the limber-
est joints on earth and the sternest joints on earth,

A Kentuckian walking the vale of the Elkhorn in my deer-skin leg-
gings, a Louisianian or Georgian,

A boatman over lakes or bays or along coasts, a Hoosier, Badger,
Buckeye;[16]

At home on Kanadian snow-shoes or up in the bush, or with fisher-
men off Newfoundland,

[14]The Red River along the Texas-Oklahoma border; below, the Chattahoochee
and the Altamaha, rivers in Georgia.
[15]A river in Georgia.
[16]An inhabitant of Indiana, Wisconsin, and Ohio, respectively.

340 At home in the fleet of ice-boats, sailing with the rest and tacking,
At home on the hills of Vermont or in the woods of Maine, or the
    Texas ranch,
Comrade of Californians, comrade of free North-Westerners, (loving
    their big proportions,)
Comrade of raftsmen and coalmen, comrade of all who shake hands
    and welcome to drink and meat,
A learner with the simplest, a teacher of the thoughtfullest,
345 A novice beginning yet experient of myriads of seasons,
Of every hue and caste am I, of every rank and religion,
A farmer, mechanic, artist, gentleman, sailor, quaker,
Prisoner, fancy-man, rowdy, lawyer, physician, priest.

I resist any thing better than my own diversity,
350 Breathe the air but leave plenty after me,
And am not stuck up, and am in my place.

(The moth and the fish-eggs are in their place,
The bright suns I see and the dark suns I cannot see are in their
    place,
The palpable is in its place and the impalpable is in its place.)

17

355 These are really the thoughts of all men in all ages and lands, they
    are not original with me,
If they are not yours as much as mine they are nothing, or next to
    nothing,
If they are not the riddle and the untying of the riddle they are
    nothing,
If they are not just as close as they are distant they are nothing.

This is the grass that grows wherever the land is and the water is,
360 This the common air that bathes the globe.

18

With music strong I come, with my cornets and my drums,
I play not marches for accepted victors only, I play marches for
    conquer'd and slain persons.

Have you heard that it was good to gain the day?
I also say it is good to fall, battles are lost in the same spirit in which
    they are won.

I beat and pound for the dead,
I blow through my embouchures my loudest and gayest for them.

Vivas to those who have fail'd!
And to those whose war-vessels sank in the sea!
And to those themselves who sank in the sea!
And to all generals that lost engagements, and all overcome heroes!
And the numberless unknown heroes equal to the greatest heroes
    known!

19

This is the meal equally set, this the meat for natural hunger,
It is for the wicked just the same as the righteous, I make appoint-
    ments with all,
I will not have a single person slighted or left away,
The kept-woman, sponger, thief, are hereby invited,
The heavy-lipp'd slave is invited, the venerealee is invited;
There shall be no difference between them and the rest.

This is the press of a bashful hand, this the float and odor of hair,
This the touch of my lips to yours, this the murmur of yearning,
This the far-off depth and height reflecting my own face,
This the thoughtful merge[17] of myself, and the outlet again.

Do you guess I have some intricate purpose?
Well I have, for the Fourth-month[18] showers have, and the mica on
    the side of a rock has.

Do you take it I would astonish?
Does the daylight astonish? does the early redstart twittering through
    the woods?
Do I astonish more than they?

This hour I tell things in confidence,
I might not tell everybody, but I will tell you.

20

Who goes there? hankering, gross, mystical, nude;
How is it I extract strength from the beef I eat?

What is a man anyhow? what am I? what are you?

[17]Convergence, synthesis.
[18]The Quaker name for April.

All I mark as my own you shall offset it with your own,
Else it were time lost listening to me.

I do not snivel that snivel the world over,
395   That months are vacuums and the ground but wallow and filth.

Whimpering and truckling fold with powders for invalids, con-
    formity goes to the fourth-remov'd,
I wear my hat as I please indoors or out.

Why should I pray? why should I venerate and be ceremonious?

Having pried through the strata, analyzed to a hair, counsel'd with
    doctors and calculated close,
400   I find no sweeter fat than sticks to my own bones.

In all people I see myself, none more and not one a barley-corn less,
And the good or bad I say of myself I say of them.

I know I am solid and sound,
To me the converging objects of the universe perpetually flow,
405   All are written to me, and I must get what the writing means.

I know I am deathless,
I know this orbit of mine cannot be swept by a carpenter's compass,
I know I shall not pass like a child's carlacue[19] cut with a burnt stick
    at night.

I know I am august,
410   I do not trouble my spirit to vindicate itself or be understood,
I see that the elementary laws never apologize,
(I reckon I behave no prouder than the level I plant my house by,
    after all.)

I exist as I am, that is enough,
If no other in the world be aware I sit content,
415   And if each and all be aware I sit content.

One world is aware and by far the largest to me, and that is myself,
And whether I come to my own to-day or in ten thousand or ten
    million years,
I can cheerfully take it now, or with equal cheerfulness I can wait.

[19]A curved or curled toy or ornament.

My foothold is tenon'd and mortis'd in granite,
I laugh at what you call dissolution,
And I know the amplitude of time.

21

I am the poet of the Body and I am the poet of the Soul,
The pleasures of heaven are with me and the pains of hell are with
　　me,
The first I graft and increase upon myself, the latter I translate into
　　a new tongue.

I am the poet of the woman the same as the man,
And I say it is as great to be a woman as to be a man,
And I say there is nothing greater than the mother of men.

I chant the chant of dilation or pride,
We have had ducking and deprecating about enough,
I show that size is only development.

Have you outstript the rest? are you the President?
It is a trifle, they will more than arrive there every one, and still pass
　　on.

I am he that walks with the tender and growing night,
I call to the earth and sea half-held by the night.

Press close bare-bosom'd night—press close magnetic nourishing
　　night!
Night of south winds—night of the large few stars!
Still nodding night—mad naked summer night.

Smile, O voluptuous cool-breath'd earth!
Earth of the slumbering and liquid trees!
Earth of departed sunset—earth of the mountains misty-topt!
Earth of the vitreous[20] pour of the full moon just tinged with blue!
Earth of shine and dark mottling the tide of the river!
Earth of the limpid gray of clouds brighter and clearer for my sake!
Far-swooping elbow'd earth—rich apple-blossom'd earth!
Smile, for your lover comes.

Prodigal, you have given me love—therefore I to you give love!
O unspeakable passionate love.

[20]Glassy; glass-like.

22

You sea! I resign myself to you also—I guess what you mean,
I behold from the beach your crooked inviting fingers,
450   I believe you refuse to go back without feeling of me,
We must have a turn together, I undress, hurry me out of sight of
the land,
Cushion me soft, rock me in billowy drowse,
Dash me with amorous wet, I can repay you.

Sea of stretch'd ground-swells,
455   Sea breathing broad and convulsive breaths,
Sea of the brine of life and of unshovell'd yet always-ready graves,
Howler and scooper of storms, capricious and dainty sea,
I am integral with you, I too am of one phase and of all phases.

Partaker of influx and efflux I, extoller of hate and conciliation,
460   Extoller of amies and those that sleep in each others' arms.

I am he attesting sympathy,
(Shall I make my list of things in the house and skip the house that
supports them?)

I am not the poet of goodness only, I do not decline to be the poet of
wickedness also.

What blurt is this about virtue and about vice?
465   Evil propels me and reform of evil propels me, I stand indifferent,
My gait is no fault-finder's or rejecter's gait,
I moisten the roots of all that has grown.

Did you fear some scrofula out of the unflagging pregnancy?
Did you guess the celestial laws are yet to be work'd over and recti-
fied?

470   I find one side a balance and the antipodal side a balance,
Soft doctrine as steady help as stable doctrine,
Thoughts and deeds of the present our rouse and early start.

This minute that comes to me over the past decillions,[21]
There is no better than it and now.

---

[21]A decillion is the number 1 followed by 33 zeros.

What behaved well in the past or behaves well to-day is not such a
  wonder,
The wonder is always and always how there can be a mean man or
  an infidel.

23

Endless unfolding of words of ages!
And mine a word of the modern, the word En-Masse.[22]

A word of the faith that never balks,
Here or henceforward it is all the same to me, I accept Time abso-
  lutely.

It alone is without flaw, it alone rounds and completes all,
That mystic baffling wonder alone completes all.

I accept Reality and dare not question it,
Materialism first and last imbuing.

Hurrah for positive science! long live exact demonstration!
Fetch stonecrop[23] mixt with cedar and branches of lilac,
This is the lexicographer, this the chemist, this made a grammar of
  the old cartouches,[24]
These mariners put the ship through dangerous unknown seas,
This is the geologist, this works with the scalpel, and this is a
  mathematician.

Gentlemen, to you the first honors always!
Your facts are useful, and yet they are not my dwelling,
I but enter by them to an area of my dwelling.

Less the reminders of properties told my words,
And more the reminders they of life untold, and of freedom and
  extrication,
And make short account of neuters and geldings, and favor men and
  women fully equipt,
And beat the gong of revolt, and stop with fugitives and them that
  plot and conspire.

---

[22]French for "in a group collectively, all together."
[23]A kind of wild flower.
[24]In Egyptian hieroglyphics, an oval or oblong figure enclosing characters ex-
  pressing the name or titles of a royal or divine personage.

24

Walt Whitman, a kosmos, of Manhattan the son,
Turbulent, fleshy, sensual, eating, drinking and breeding,
No sentimentalist, no stander above men and women or apart from
them,
500   No more modest than immodest.

Unscrew the locks from the doors!
Unscrew the doors themselves from their jambs!

Whoever degrades another degrades me,
And whatever is done or said returns at last to me.

505   Through me the afflatus surging and surging, through me the cur-
rent and index.

I speak the pass-word primeval, I give the sign of democracy,
By God! I will accept nothing which all cannot have their counter-
part of on the same terms.

Through me many long dumb voices,
Voices of the interminable generations of prisoners and slaves,
510   Voices of the diseas'd and despairing and of thieves and dwarfs,
Voices of cycles of preparation and accretion,
And of the threads that connect the stars, and of wombs and of the
father-stuff,[25]
And of the rights of them the others are down upon,
Of the deform'd, trivial, flat, foolish, despised,
515   Fog in the air, beetles rolling balls of dung.

Through me forbidden voices,
Voices of sexes and lusts, voices veil'd and I remove the veil,
Voices indecent by me clarified and transfigur'd.

I do not press my fingers across my mouth,
520   I keep as delicate around the bowels as around the head and heart,
Copulation is no more rank to me than death is.

I believe in the flesh and the appetites,
Seeing, hearing, feeling, are miracles, and each part and tag of me is
a miracle.

[25]Semen.

Divine am I inside and out, and I make holy whatever I touch or am
    touch'd from,
The scent of these arm-pits aroma finer than prayer,
This head more than churches, bibles, and all the creeds.

If I worship one thing more than another it shall be the spread of my
    own body, or any part of it,
Translucent mould of me it shall be you!
Shaded ledges and rests it shall be you!
Firm masculine colter[26] it shall be you!
Whatever goes to the tilth[27] of me it shall be you!
You my rich blood! your milky stream pale strippings of my life!
Breast that presses against other breasts it shall be you!
My brain it shall be your occult convolutions!
Root of wash'd sweet-flag![28] timorous pond-snipe! nest of guarded
    duplicate eggs! it shall be you!
Mix'd tussled hay of head, beard, brawn, it shall be you!
Trickling sap of maple, fibre of manly wheat, it shall be you!
Sun so generous it shall be you!
Vapors lighting and shading my face it shall be you!
You sweaty brooks and dews it shall be you!
Winds whose soft-tickling genitals rub against me it shall be you!
Broad muscular fields, branches of live oak, loving lounger in my
    winding paths, it shall be you!
Hands I have taken, face I have kiss'd, mortal I have ever touch'd,
    it shall be you.

I dote on myself, there is that lot of me and all so luscious,
Each moment and whatever happens thrills me with joy,
I cannot tell how my ankles bend, nor whence the cause of my
    faintest wish,
Nor the cause of the friendship I emit, nor the cause of the friend-
    ship I take again.

That I walk up my stoop, I pause to consider if it really be,
A morning glory at my window satisfies me more than the meta-
    physics of books.

To behold the day-break!
The little light fades the immense and diaphanous shadows,
The air tastes good to my palate.

[26]The blade of a plow.
[27]Tilled earth.
[28]A wild flower, also called calamus.

Hefts of the moving world at innocent gambols silently rising
    freshly exuding,
Scooting obliquely high and low.

555 Something I cannot see puts upward libidinous prongs,
Seas of bright juice suffuse heaven.

The earth by the sky staid with, the daily close of their junction,
The heav'd challenge from the east that moment over my head,
The mocking taunt, See then whether you shall be master!

25

560 Dazzling and tremendous how quick the sun-rise would kill me,
If I could not now and always send sun-rise out of me.

We also ascend dazzling and tremendous as the sun,
We found our own O my soul in the calm and cool of the day-break.

My voice goes after what my eyes cannot reach,
565 With the twirl of my tongue I encompass worlds and volumes of
    worlds.

Speech is the twin of my vision, it is unequal to measure itself,
It provokes me forever, it says sarcastically,
Walt you contain enough, why don't you let it out then?

Come now I will not be tantalized, you conceive too much of
    articulation,
570 Do you not know O speech how the buds beneath you are folded?
Waiting in gloom, protected by frost,
The dirt receding before my prophetical screams,
I underlying causes to balance them at last,
My knowledge my live parts, it keeping tally with the meaning of all
    things,
575 Happiness, (which whoever hears me let him or her set out in search
    of this day.)

My final merit I refuse you, I refuse putting from me what I really
    am,
Encompass worlds, but never try to encompass me,
I crowd your sleekest and best by simply looking toward you.

Writing and talk do not prove me,

I carry the plenum[29] of proof and every thing else in my face,
With the hush of my lips I wholly confound the skeptic.

26

Now I will do nothing but listen,
To accrue what I hear into this song, to let sounds contribute toward
   it.

I hear bravuras of birds, bustle of growing wheat, gossip of flames,
   clack of sticks cooking my meals,
I hear the sound I love, the sound of the human voice,
I hear all sounds running together, combined, fused or following,
Sounds of the city and sounds out of the city, sounds of the day and
   night,
Talkative young ones to those that like them, the loud laugh of
   work-people at their meals,
The angry base of disjointed friendship, the faint tones of the sick,
The judge with hands tight to the desk, his pallid lips pronouncing
   a death-sentence,
The heave'e'yo of stevedores unlading ships by the wharves, the
   refrain of the anchor-lifters,
The ring of alarm-bells, the cry of fire, the whirr of swift-streaking
   engines and hose-carts with premonitory tinkles and color'd
   lights,
The steam-whistle, the solid roll of the train of approaching cars,
The slow march play'd at the head of the association marching two
   and two,
(They go to guard some corpse, the flag-tops are draped with black
   muslin.)

I hear the violoncello, ('tis the young man's heart's complaint,)
I hear the key'd cornet, it glides quickly in through my ears,
It shakes mad-sweet pangs through my belly and breast.

I hear the chorus, it is a grand opera,
Ah this indeed is music—this suits me.

A tenor large and fresh as the creation fills me,
The orbic flex of his mouth is pouring and filling me full.

I hear the train'd soprano (what work with hers is this?)
The orchestra whirls me wider than Uranus flies,

[29]Fullness.

605 It wrenches such ardors from me I did not know I possess'd them,
It sails me, I dab with bare feet, they are lick'd by the indolent
waves,
I am cut by bitter and angry hail, I lose my breath,
Steep'd amid honey'd morphine, my windpipe throttled in fakes[30] of
death,
At length let up again to feel the puzzle of puzzles,
610 And that we call Being.

27

To be in any form, what is that?
(Round and round we go, all of us, and ever come back thither,)
If nothing lay more develop'd the quahaug[31] in its callous shell were
enough.

Mine is no callous shell,
615 I have instant conductors all over me whether I pass or stop,
They seize every object and lead it harmlessly through me.

I merely stir, press, feel with my fingers, and am happy,
To touch my person to some one else's is about as much as I can
stand.

28

Is this then a touch? quivering me to a new identity,
620 Flames and ether making a rush for my veins,
Treacherous tip of me reaching and crowding to help them,
My flesh and blood playing out lightning to strike what is hardly
different from myself,
On all sides prurient provokers stiffening my limbs,
Straining the udder of my heart for its withheld drip,
625 Behaving licentious toward me, taking no denial,
Depriving me of my best as for a purpose,
Unbuttoning my clothes, holding me by the bare waist,
Deluding my confusion with the calm of the sunlight and pasture-
fields,
Immodestly sliding the fellow-senses away,
630 They bribed to swap off with touch and go and graze at the edges of
me,
No consideration, no regard for my draining strength or my anger,

[30]Coils.
[31]A kind of Atlantic coast clam.

Fetching the rest of the herd around to enjoy them a while,
Then all uniting to stand on a headland and worry me.

The sentries desert every other part of me,
They have left me helpless to a red marauder,
They all come to the headland to witness and assist against me.

I am given up by traitors,
I talk wildly, I have lost my wits, I and nobody else am the greatest
    traitor,
I went myself first to the headland, my own hands carried me there.

You villain touch! what are you doing? my breath is tight in its
    throat,
Unclench your floodgates, you are too much for me.

29

Blind loving wrestling touch, sheath'd hooded sharp-tooth'd touch!
Did it make you ache so, leaving me?

Parting track'd by arriving, perpetual payment of perpetual loan,
Rich showering rain, and recompense richer afterward.

Sprouts take and accumulate, stand by the curb prolific and vital,
Landscapes projected masculine, full-sized and golden.

30

All truths wait in all things,
They neither hasten their own delivery nor resist it,
They do not need the obstetric forceps of the surgeon,
The insignificant is as big to me as any,
(What is less or more than a touch?)

Logic and sermons never convince,
The damp of the night drives deeper into my soul.

(Only what proves itself to every man and woman is so,
Only what nobody denies is so.)

A minute and a drop of me settle my brain,
I believe the soggy clods shall become lovers and lamps,
And a compend of compends[32] is the meat of a man or woman,

[32]Compendium—that is, a complete summary in brief.

660 And a summit and flower there is the feeling they have for each
         other,
     And they are to branch boundlessly out of that lesson until it be-
         comes omnific,[33]
     And until one and all shall delight us, and we them.

31

     I believe a leaf of grass is no less than the journey-work of the stars,
     And the pismire is equally perfect, and a grain of sand, and the egg
         of the wren,
665 And the tree-toad is a chef-d'œuvre[34] for the highest,
     And the running blackberry would adorn the parlors of heaven,
     And the narrowest hinge in my hand puts to scorn all machinery,
     And the cow crunching with depress'd head surpasses any statue,
     And a mouse is miracle enough to stagger sextillions[35] of infidels.

670 I find I incorporate gneiss, coal, long-threaded moss, fruits, grains,
         esculent roots,
     And am stucco'd with quadrupeds and birds all over,
     And have distanced what is behind me for good reasons,
     But call any thing back again when I desire it.

     In vain the speeding or shyness,
675 In vain the plutonic rocks send their old heat against my approach,
     In vain the mastodon retreats beneath its own powder'd bones,
     In vain objects stand leagues off and assume manifold shapes,
     In vain the ocean settling in hollows and the great monsters lying
         low,
     In vain the buzzard houses herself with the sky,
680 In vain the snake slides through the creepers and logs,
     In vain the elk takes to the inner passes of the woods,
     In vain the razor-bill'd auk sails far north to Labrador,
     I follow quickly, I ascend to the nest in the fissure of the cliff.

32

     I think I could turn and live with animals, they are so placid and self-
         contain'd,
685 I stand and look at them long and long.

     They do not sweat and whine about their condition,

---

[33]Whitman's coinage: made into all, making into all, all-inclusive.
[34]Masterpiece.
[35]Sextillion: the number 1 followed by 21 zeros.

They do not lie awake in the dark and weep for their sins,
They do not make me sick discussing their duty to God,
Not one is dissatisfied, not one is demented with the mania of own-
    ing things,
Not one kneels to another, nor to his kind that lived thousands of
    years ago,
Not one is respectable or unhappy over the whole earth.

So they show their relations to me and I accept them,
They bring me tokens of myself, they evince them plainly in their
    possession.

I wonder where they get those tokens,
Did I pass that way huge times ago and negligently drop them?
Myself moving forward then and now and forever,
Gathering and showing more always and with velocity,
Infinite and omnigenous,[36] and the like of these among them,
Not too exclusive toward the reachers of my remembrancers,
Picking out here one that I love, and now go with him on brotherly
    terms.

A gigantic beauty of a stallion, fresh and responsive to my caresses,
Head high in the forehead, wide between the ears,
Limbs glossy and supple, tail dusting the ground,
Eyes full of sparkling wickedness, ears finely cut, flexibly moving.

His nostrils dilate as my heels embrace him,
His well-built limbs tremble with pleasure as we race around and
    return.

I but use you a minute, then I resign you, stallion,
Why do I need your paces when I myself out-gallop them?
Even as I stand or sit passing faster than you.

33

Space and Time! now I see it is true, what I guess'd at,
What I guess'd when I loaf'd on the grass,
What I guess'd while I lay alone in my bed,
And again as I walk'd the beach under the paling stars of the
    morning.

---

[36]Whitman's coinage: generating all things.

My ties and ballasts leave me, my elbows rest in sea-gaps,
715   I skirt sierras, my palms cover continents,
I am afoot with my vision.

By the city's quadrangular houses—in log huts, camping with lum-
bermen,
Along the ruts of the turnpike, along the dry gulch and rivulet bed,
Weeding my onion-patch or hoeing rows of carrots and parsnips,
crossing savannas,[37] trailing in forests,
720   Prospecting, gold-digging, girdling the trees of a new purchase,
Scorch'd ankle-deep by the hot sand, hauling my boat down the
shallow river,
Where the panther walks to and fro on a limb overhead, where the
buck turns furiously at the hunter,
Where the rattlesnake suns his flabby length on a rock, where the
otter is feeding on fish,
Where the alligator in his tough pimples sleeps by the bayou,
725   Where the black bear is searching for roots or honey, where the
beaver pats the mud with his paddle-shaped tail;
Over the growing sugar, over the yellow-flower'd cotton plant, over
the rice in its low moist field,
Over the sharp-peak'd farm house, with its scallop'd scum and
slender shoots from the gutters,
Over the western persimmon, over the long-leav'd corn, over the
delicate blue-flower flax,
Over the white and brown buckwheat, a hummer and buzzer there
with the rest,
730   Over the dusky green of the rye as it ripples and shades in the
breeze;
Scaling mountains, pulling myself cautiously up, holding on by low
scragged limbs,
Walking the path worn in the grass and beat through the leaves of
the brush,
Where the quail is whistling betwixt the woods and the wheat-lot,
Where the bat flies in the Seventh-month eve, where the great gold-
bug drops through the dark,
735   Where the brook puts out of the roots of the old tree and flows to
the meadow,
Where cattle stand and shake away flies with the tremulous shud-
dering of their hides,
Where the cheese-cloth hangs in the kitchen, where andirons

---

[37]Flat grass lands.

straddle the hearth-slab, where cobwebs fall in festoons from
the rafters;
Where trip-hammers crash, where the press is whirling its cylinders,
Wherever the human heart beats with terrible throes under its ribs,
Where the pear-shaped balloon is floating aloft, (floating in it my-
self and looking composedly down,)
Where the life-car is drawn on the slip-noose, where the heat
hatches pale-green eggs in the dented sand,
Where the she-whale swims with her calf and never forsakes it,
Where the steam-ship trails hind-ways its long pennant of smoke,
Where the fin of the shark cuts like a black chip out of the water,
Where the half-burn'd brig is riding on unknown currents,
Where shells grow to her slimy deck, where the dead are corrupting
below;
Where the dense-starr'd flag is borne at the head of the regiments,
Approaching Manhattan up by the long-stretching island,
Under Niagara, the cataract falling like a veil over my countenance,
Upon a door-step, upon the horse-block of hard wood outside,
Upon the race-course, or enjoying picnics or jigs or a good game of
base-ball,
At he-festivals, with blackguard gibes, ironical license, bull-dances,
drinking, laughter,
At the cider-mill tasting the sweets of the brown mash, sucking the
juice through a straw,
At apple-peelings wanting kisses for all the red fruit I find,
At musters, beach-parties, friendly bees, huskings, house-raisings;
Where the mocking-bird sounds his delicious gurgles, cackles,
screams, weeps,
Where the hay-rick stands in the barn-yard, where the dry-stalks
are scatter'd, where the brood-cow waits in the hovel,
Where the bull advances to do his masculine work, where the stud
to the mare, where the cock is treading the hen,
Where the heifers browse, where geese nip their food with short
jerks,
Where sun-down shadows lengthen over the limitless and lonesome
prairie,
Where herds of buffalo make a crawling spread of the square miles
far and near,
Where the humming-bird shimmers, where the neck of the long-
lived swan is curving and winding,
Where the laughing-gull scoots by the shore, where she laughs her
near-human laugh,
Where bee-hives range on a gray bench in the garden half hid by the
high weeds,

765   Where band-neck'd partridges roost in a ring on the ground with
          their heads out,
       Where burial coaches enter the arch'd gates of a cemetery,
       Where winter wolves bark amid wastes of snow and icicled trees,
       Where the yellow-crown'd heron comes to the edge of the marsh at
          night and feeds upon small crabs,
       Where the splash of swimmers and divers cools the warm noon,
770   Where the katy-did works her chromatic reed on the walnut-tree
          over the well,
       Through patches of citrons[38] and cucumbers with silver-wired
          leaves,
       Through the salt-lick or orange glade, or under conical firs,
       Through the gymnasium, through the curtain'd saloon, through the
          office or public hall;
       Pleas'd with the native and pleas'd with the foreign, pleas'd with the
          new and old,
775   Pleas'd with the homely woman as well as the handsome,
       Pleas'd with the quakeress as she puts off her bonnet and talks
          melodiously,
       Pleas'd with the tune of the choir of the whitewash'd church,
       Pleas'd with the earnest words of the sweating Methodist preacher,
          impress'd seriously at the camp-meeting;
       Looking in at the shop-windows of Broadway the whole forenoon,
          flatting the flesh of my nose on the thick plate glass,
780   Wandering the same afternoon with my face turn'd up to the clouds,
          or down a lane or along the beach,
       My right and left arms round the sides of two friends, and I in the
          middle;
       Coming home with the silent and dark-cheek'd bush-boy, (behind
          me he rides at the drape of the day,)
       Far from the settlements studying the print of animals' feet, or the
          moccasin print,
       By the cot in the hospital reaching lemonade to a feverish patient,
785   Nigh the coffin'd corpse when all is still, examining with a candle;
       Voyaging to every port to dicker and adventure,
       Hurrying with the modern crowd as eager and fickle as any,
       Hot toward one I hate, ready in my madness to knife him,
       Solitary at midnight in my back yard, my thoughts gone from me a
          long while,
790   Walking the old hills of Judæa with the beautiful gentle God by my
          side,

---

[38]A kind of watermelon.

Speeding through space, speeding through heaven and the stars,
Speeding amid the seven satellites and the broad ring, and the
     diameter of eighty thousand miles,
Speeding with tail'd meteors, throwing fire-balls like the rest,
Carrying the crescent child that carries its own full mother in its
     belly,
Storming, enjoying, planning, loving, cautioning,
Backing and filling, appearing and disappearing,
I tread day and night such roads.

I visit the orchards of spheres and look at the product,
And look at quintillions ripen'd and look at quintillions[39] green.

I fly those flights of a fluid and swallowing soul,
My course runs below the soundings of plummets.

I help myself to material and immaterial,
No guard can shut me off, no law prevent me.

I anchor my ship for a little while only,
My messengers continually cruise away or bring their returns to me.

I go hunting polar furs and the seal, leaping chasms with a pike-
     pointed staff, clinging to topples of brittle and blue.

I ascend to the foretruck,
I take my place late at night in the crow's-nest,
We sail the arctic sea, it is plenty light enough,
Through the clear atmosphere I stretch around on the wonderful
     beauty,
The enormous masses of ice pass me and I pass them, the scenery is
     plain in all directions,
The white-topt mountains show in the distance, I fling out my
     fancies toward them,
We are approaching some great battle-field in which we are soon to
     be engaged,
We pass the colossal outposts of the encampment, we pass with still
     feet and caution,
Or we are entering by the suburbs some vast and ruin'd city,
The blocks and fallen architecture more than all the living cities of
     the globe.

---

[39]The number represented by 1 followed by 18 zeros.

I am a free companion, I bivouac by invading watchfires,
I turn the bridegroom out of bed and stay with the bride myself,
I tighten her all night to my thighs and lips.

820 My voice is the wife's voice, the screech by the rail of the stairs,
They fetch my man's body up dripping and drown'd.

I understand the large hearts of heroes,
The courage of present times and all times,
How the skipper saw the crowded and rudderless wreck of the
steam-ship, and Death chasing it up and down the storm,
825 How he knuckled tight and gave not back an inch, and was faithful
of days and faithful of nights,
And chalk'd in large letters on a board, *Be of good cheer, we will
not desert you;*
How he follow'd with them and tack'd them three days and would
not give it up,
How he saved the drifting company at last,
How the lank loose-gown'd women look'd when boated from the
side of their prepared graves,
830 How the silent old-faced infants and the lifted sick, and the sharp-
lipp'd unshaved men;
All this I swallow, it tastes good, I like it well, it becomes mine,
I am the man, I suffer'd, I was there.

The disdain and calmness of martyrs,
The mother of old, condemn'd for a witch, burnt with dry wood, her
children gazing on,
835 The hounded slave that flags in the race, leans by the fence, blow-
ing, cover'd with sweat,
The twinges that sting like needles his legs and neck, the murderous
buckshot and the bullets,
All these I feel or am.

I am the hounded slave, I wince at the bite of the dogs,
Hell and despair are upon me, crack and again crack the marksmen,
840 I clutch the rails of the fence, my gore dribs, thinn'd with the ooze
of my skin,
I fall on the weeds and stones,
The riders spur their unwilling horses, haul close,
Taunt my dizzy ears and beat me violently over the head with
whip-stocks.

Agonies are one of my changes of garments,
I do not ask the wounded person how he feels, I myself become the
    wounded person,
My hurts turn livid upon me as I lean on a cane and observe.

I am the mash'd fireman with breast-bone broken,
Tumbling walls buried me in their debris,
Heat and smoke I inspired, I heard the yelling shouts of my com-
    rades,
I heard the distant click of their picks and shovels,
They have clear'd the beams away, they tenderly lift me forth.

I lie in the night air in my red shirt, the pervading hush is for my
    sake,
Painless after all I lie exhausted but not so unhappy,
White and beautiful are the faces around me, the heads are bared of
    their fire-caps,
The kneeling crowd fades with the light of the torches.

Distant and dead resuscitate,
They show as the dial or move as the hands of me, I am the clock
    myself.

I am an old artillerist, I tell of my fort's bombardment,
I am there again.

Again the long roll of the drummers,
Again the attacking cannon, mortars,
Again to my listening ears the cannon responsive.

I take part, I see and hear the whole,
The cries, curses, roar, the plaudits for well-aim'd shots,
The ambulanza[40] slowly passing trailing its red drip,
Workmen searching after damages, making indispensable repairs,
The fall of grenades through the rent roof, the fan-shaped explo-
    sion,
The whizz of limbs, heads, stone, wood, iron, high in the air.

Again gurgles the mouth of my dying general, he furiously waves
    with his hand,
He gasps through the clot *Mind not me—mind—the entrenchments.*

---

[40]Ambulance.

34

Now I tell what I knew in Texas in my early youth,
(I tell not the fall of Alamo,
Not one escaped to tell the fall of Alamo,
The hundred and fifty are dumb yet at Alamo,)
875   'Tis the tale of the murder in cold blood of four hundred and twelve
        young men.[41]

Retreating they had form'd in a hollow square with their baggage
        for breastworks,
Nine hundred lives out of the surrounding enemy's, nine times
        their number, was the price they took in advance,
Their colonel was wounded and their ammunition gone,
They treated for an honorable capitulation, receiv'd writing and
        seal, gave up their arms and march'd back prisoners of war.

880   They were the glory of the race of rangers,
Matchless with horse, rifle, song, supper, courtship,
Large, turbulent, generous, handsome, proud, and affectionate,
Bearded, sunburnt, drest in the free costume of hunters,
Not a single one over thirty years of age.

885   The second First-day morning they were brought out in squads and
        massacred, it was beautiful early summer,
The work commenced about five o'clock and was over by eight.

None obey'd the command to kneel,
Some made a mad and helpless rush, some stood stark and straight,
A few fell at once, shot in the temple or heart, the living and dead
        lay together,
890   The maim'd and mangled dug in the dirt, the new-comers saw them
        there,
Some half-kill'd attempted to crawl away,
These were despatch'd with bayonets or batter'd with the blunts of
        muskets,
A youth not seventeen years old seiz'd his assassin till two more
        came to release him,
The three were all torn and cover'd with the boy's blood.

[41]The episode is not something Whitman witnessed, as the first line may sug-
gest, but something he read about. On March 11, 1846, he had printed in the
Brooklyn *Eagle* an article called "Fannin's Men, or the Massacre at Goliad,"
which he excerpted from a piece in *Blackwood's Magazine*. Captain Fannin
and his company were slaughtered by the Mexicans after their surrender at
Goliad, Texas, in March 1836.

At eleven o'clock began the burning of the bodies;
That is the tale of the murder of the four hundred and twelve young
    men.

35

Would you hear of an old-time sea-fight?[42]
Would you learn who won by the light of the moon and stars?
List to the yarn, as my grandmother's father the sailor told it to me.

Our foe was no skulk in his ship I tell you, (said he,)
His was the surly English pluck, and there is no tougher or truer,
    and never was, and never will be;
Along the lower'd eve he came horribly raking us.

We closed with him, the yards entangled, the cannon touch'd,
My captain lash'd fast with his own hands.

We had receiv'd some eighteen pound shots under the water,
On our lower-gun-deck two large pieces had burst at the first fire,
    killing all around and blowing up overhead.

Fighting at sun-down, fighting at dark,
Ten o'clock at night, the full moon well up, our leaks on the gain,
    and five feet of water reported,
The master-at-arms loosing the prisoners confined in the after-hold
    to give them a chance for themselves.

The transit to and from the magazine is now stopt by the sentinels,
They see so many strange faces they do not know whom to trust.

Our frigate takes fire,
The other asks if we demand quarter?
If our colors are struck and the fighting done?

Now I laugh content, for I hear the voice of my little captain,
We have not struck, he composedly cries, *we have just begun our
    part of the fighting.*

Only three guns are in use,
One is directed by the captain himself against the enemy's main-
    mast,

[42]The famous sea battle in 1779 between the *Bon Homme Richard* under John
Paul Jones and the British ship *Serapis.*

Two well serv'd with grape and canister[43] silence his musketry and
   clear his decks.

920   The tops alone second the fire of this little battery, especially the
          main-top,
       They hold out bravely during the whole of the action.

Not a moment's cease,
The leaks gain fast on the pumps, the fire eats toward the powder-
   magazine.
One of the pumps has been shot away, it is generally thought we are
   sinking.

925   Serene stands the little captain,
       He is not hurried, his voice is neither high nor low,
       His eyes give more light to us than our battle-lanterns.

Toward twelve there in the beams of the moon they surrender to us.

36

Stretch'd and still lies the midnight,
930   Two great hulls motionless on the breast of the darkness,
       Our vessel riddled and slowly sinking, preparations to pass to the
          one we have conquer'd,
       The captain on the quarter-deck coldly giving his orders through a
          countenance white as a sheet,
       Near by the corpse of the child that serv'd in the cabin,
       The dead face of an old salt with long white hair and carefully
          curl'd whiskers,
935   The flames spite of all that can be done flickering aloft and below,
       The husky voices of the two or three officers yet fit for duty,
       Formless stacks of bodies and bodies by themselves, dabs of flesh
          upon the masts and spars,
       Cut of cordage, dangle of rigging, slight shock of the soothe of
          waves,
       Black and impassive guns, litter of powder-parcels, strong scent,
940   A few large stars overhead, silent and mournful shining,
       Delicate sniffs of sea-breeze, smells of sedgy grass and fields by the
          shore, death-messages given in charge to survivors,
       The hiss of the surgeon's knife, the gnawing teeth of his saw,

---

[43]A cylinder that is fired from a gun and bursts, scattering the iron "grape-
shot" inside.

Wheeze, cluck, swash of falling blood, short wild scream, and long,
    dull, tapering groan,
These so, these irretrievable.

37

You laggards there on guard! look to your arms!
In at the conquer'd doors they crowd! I am possess'd!
Embody all presences outlaw'd or suffering,
See myself in prison shaped like another man,
And feel the dull unintermitted pain.

For me the keepers of convicts shoulder their carbines and keep
    watch,
It is I let out in the morning and barr'd at night.

Not a mutineer walks handcuff'd to jail but I am handcuff'd to him
    and walk by his side,
(I am less the jolly one there, and more the silent one with sweat on
    my twitching lips.)

Not a youngster is taken for larceny but I go up too, and am tried
    and sentenced.

Not a cholera patient lies at the last gasp but I also lie at the last
    gasp,
My face is ash-color'd, my sinews gnarl, away from me people
    retreat.

Askers embody themselves in me and I am embodied in them,
I project my hat, sit shame-faced, and beg.

38

Enough! enough! enough!
Somehow I have been stunn'd. Stand back!
Give me a little time beyond my cuff'd head, slumbers, dreams,
    gaping,
I discover myself on the verge of a usual mistake.

That I could forget the mockers and insults!
That I could forget the trickling tears and the blows of the bludg-
    eons and hammers!
That I could look with a separate look on my own crucifixion and
    bloody crowning.

I remember now,
I resume the overstaid fraction,
The grave of rock multiplies what has been confided to it, or to any
        graves,
Corpses rise, gashes heal, fastenings roll from me.

970 I troop forth replenish'd with supreme power, one of an average
        unending procession,
Inland and sea-coast we go, and pass all boundary lines,
Our swift ordinances on their way over the whole earth,
The blossoms we wear in our hats the growth of thousands of years.

Eleves,[44] I salute you! come forward!
975 Continue your annotations, continue your questionings.

39

The friendly and flowing savage, who is he?
Is he waiting for civilization, or past it and mastering it?

Is he some Southwesterner rais'd out-doors? is he Kanadian?
Is he from the Mississippi country? Iowa, Oregon, California?
980 The mountains? prairie-life, bush-life? or sailor from the sea?

Wherever he goes men and women accept and desire him,
They desire he should like them, touch them, speak to them, stay
        with them.

Behavior lawless as snow-flakes, words simple as grass, uncomb'd
        head, laughter, and naiveté,
Slow-stepping feet, common features, common modes and emana-
        tions,
985 They descend in new forms from the tips of his fingers,
They are wafted with the odor of his body or breath, they fly out of
        the glance of his eyes.

40

Flaunt of the sunshine I need not your bask—lie over!
You light surfaces only, I force surfaces and depths also.

Earth! you seem to look for something at my hands,
990 Say, old top-knot, what do you want?

[44]French for "students" or "pupils."

Man or woman, I might tell how I like you, but cannot,
And might tell what it is in me and what it is in you, but cannot,
And might tell that pining I have, that pulse of my nights and days.

Behold, I do not give lectures or a little charity,
When I give I give myself.

You there, impotent, loose in the knees,
Open your scarf'd[45] chops till I blow grit within you,
Spread your palms and lift the flaps of your pockets,
I am not to be denied, I compel, I have stores plenty and to spare,
And any thing I have I bestow.

I do not ask who you are, that is not important to me,
You can do nothing and be nothing but what I will infold you.

To cotton-field drudge or cleaner of privies I lean,
On his right cheek I put the family kiss,
And in my soul I swear I never will deny him.

On women fit for conception I start bigger and nimbler babes,
(This day I am jetting the stuff of far more arrogant republics.)

To any one dying, thither I speed and twist the knob of the door,
Turn the bed-clothes toward the foot of the bed,
Let the physician and the priest go home.

I seize the descending man and raise him with resistless will,
O despairer, here is my neck,
By God, you shall not go down! hang your whole weight upon me.

I dilate you with tremendous breath, I buoy you up,
Every room of the house do I fill with an arm'd force,
Lovers of me, bafflers of graves.

Sleep—I and they keep guard all night,
Not doubt, not decease shall dare to lay finger upon you,
I have embraced you, and henceforth possess you to myself,
And when you rise in the morning you will find what I tell you is so.

---

[45]Notched and jointed together.

41

I am he bringing help for the sick as they pant on their backs,
And for strong upright men I bring yet more needed help.

I heard what was said of the universe,
Heard it and heard it of several thousand years;
1025   It is middling well as far as it goes—but is that all?

Magnifying and applying come I,
Outbidding at the start the old cautious hucksters,
Taking myself the exact dimensions of Jehovah,[46]
Lithographing Kronos, Zeus his son, and Hercules his grandson,[47]
1030   Buying drafts of Osiris, Isis, Belus, Brahma, Buddha,[48]
In my portfolio placing Manito loose, Allah on a leaf, the crucifix
        engraved,[49]
With Odin and the hideous-faced Mexitli[50] and every idol and
        image,
Taking them all for what they are worth and not a cent more,
Admitting they were alive and did the work of their days,
1035   (They bore mites as for unfledg'd birds who have now to rise and
        fly and sing for themselves,)
Accepting the rough deific[51] sketches to fill out better in myself,
        bestowing them freely on each man and woman I see,
Discovering as much or more in a framer framing a house,
Putting higher claims for him there with his roll'd-up sleeves driv-
        ing the mallet and chisel,
Not objecting to special revelations, considering a curl of smoke or a
        hair on the back of my hand just as curious as any revelation,
1040   Lads ahold of fire-engines and hook-and-ladder ropes no less to me
        than the gods of the antique wars,
Minding their voices peal through the crash of destruction,
Their brawny limbs passing safe over charr'd laths, their white fore-
        heads whole and unhurt out of the flames;
By the mechanic's wife with her babe at her nipple interceding for
        every person born,

[46]The God of the Old Testament.
[47]Generations of Greek gods.
[48]Osiris: an Egyptian fertility god; Isis: his sister and wife; Belus: the Greek
        name for the Phoenician god Baal; Brahma: one of the triad of the Hindu
        deity; Buddha: Gautama Siddhartha, a philosopher and visionary who became
        the Buddha or the Awakened One.
[49]Manito: the spirit of nature for the Algonquin Indians; Allah: the supreme
        deity for the Mohammedans; the crucified Jesus of Christianity.
[50]Odin: the supreme Norse deity and creator; Mexitli: chief deity of the Aztecs.
[51]Divine.

Three scythes at harvest whizzing in a row from three lusty angels
    with shirts bagg'd out at their waists,
The snag-tooth'd hostler[52] with red hair redeeming sins past and to
    come,
Selling all he possesses, traveling on foot to fee lawyers for his
    brother and sit by him while he is tried for forgery;
What was strewn in the amplest strewing the square rod about me,
    and not filling the square rod then,
The bull and the bug never worshipp'd half enough,
Dung and dirt more admirable than was dream'd,
The supernatural of no account, myself waiting my time to be one of
    the supremes,
The day getting ready for me when I shall do as much good as the
    best, and be as prodigious;
By my life-lumps![53] becoming already a creator,
Putting myself here and now to the ambush'd womb of the shadows.

42

A call in the midst of the crowd,
My own voice, orotund sweeping and final.

Come my children,
Come my boys and girls, my women, household and intimates,
Now the performer launches his nerve, he has pass'd his prelude on
    the reeds within.

Easily written loose-finger'd chords—I feel the thrum of your climax
    and close.

My head slues round on my neck,
Music rolls, but not from the organ,
Folks are around me, but they are no household of mine.

Ever the hard unsunk ground,
Ever the eaters and drinkers, ever the upward and downward sun,
    ever the air and the ceaseless tides,
Ever myself and my neighbors, refreshing, wicked, real,
Ever the old inexplicable query, ever that thorn'd thumb, that
    breath of itches and thirsts,
Ever the vexer's *hoot! hoot!* till we find where the sly one hides and
    bring him forth,

[52]Stablekeeper.
[53]Testicles.

Ever love, ever the sobbing liquid of life,
Ever the bandage under the chin, ever the trestles of death.

1070 Here and there with dimes on the eyes walking,
To feed the greed of the belly the brains liberally spooning,
Tickets buying, taking, selling, but in to the feast never once going,
Many sweating, ploughing, thrashing, and then the chaff for payment receiving,
A few idly owning, and they the wheat continually claiming.

1075 This is the city and I am one of the citizens,
Whatever interests the rest interests me, politics, wars, markets, newspapers, schools,
The mayor and councils, banks, tariffs, steamships, factories, stocks, stores, real estate and personal estate.

The little plentiful manikins skipping around in collars and tail'd coats,
I am aware who they are, (they are positively not worms or fleas,)
1080 I acknowledge the duplicates of myself, the weakest and shallowest is deathless with me,
What I do and say the same waits for them,
Every thought that flounders in me the same flounders in them.

I know perfectly well my own egotism,
Know my omnivorous lines and must not write any less,
1085 And would fetch you whoever you are flush with myself.

Not words of routine this song of mine,
But abruptly to question, to leap beyond yet nearer bring;
This printed and bound book—but the printer and the printing-office boy?
The well-taken photographs—but your wife or friend close and solid in your arms?
1090 The black ship mail'd with iron, her mighty guns in her turrets—but the pluck of the captain and engineers?
In the houses the dishes and fare and furniture—but the host and hostess, and the look out of their eyes?
The sky up there—yet here or next door, or across the way?
The saints and sages in history—but you yourself?
Sermons, creeds, theology—but the fathomless human brain,
1095 And what is reason? and what is love? and what is life?

43

I do not despise you priests, all time, the world over,
My faith is the greatest of faiths and the least of faiths,
Enclosing worship ancient and modern and all between ancient and
    modern,
Believing I shall come again upon the earth after five thousand
    years,
Waiting responses from oracles, honoring the gods, saluting the
    sun,
Making a fetich of the first rock or stump, powowing with sticks in
    the circle of obis,[54]
Helping the llama or brahmin[55] as he trims the lamps of the idols,
Dancing yet through the streets in a phallic procession, rapt and
    austere in the woods a gymnosophist,[56]
Drinking mead from the skull-cup, to Shastas and Vedas admirant,
    minding the Koran,[57]
Walking the teokallis,[58] spotted with gore from the stone and knife,
    beating the serpent-skin drum,
Accepting the Gospels, accepting him that was crucified, knowing
    assuredly that he is divine,
To the mass kneeling or the puritan's prayer rising, or sitting pa-
    tiently in a pew,
Ranting and frothing in my insane crisis, or waiting dead-like till
    my spirit arouses me,
Looking forth on pavement and land, or outside of pavement and
    land,
Belonging to the winders of the circuit of circuits.

One of that centripetal and centrifugal gang I turn and talk like a
    man leaving charges before a journey.

Down-hearted doubters dull and excluded,
Frivolous, sullen, moping, angry, affected, dishearten'd, atheistical,
I know every one of you, I know the sea of torment, doubt, despair
    and unbelief.

[54]Obi, or obeah: a West Indian form of witchcraft or voodoo in which fetishes
are used. Fetich: fetish.
[55]Lama: a Buddhist monk of Tibet or Mongolia; brahmin: the Hindu priestly
caste.
[56]A member of an ancient Hindu ascetic sect.
[57]Mead: an alcoholic beverage made from fermented honey and water and
drunk by the Anglo-Saxons; shasters (or shastri) and Vedas: Hindu sacred
writings; the Koran: the sacred book of the Mohammedans.
[58]Teocalli: a temple of ancient Mexico and Central America, usually built upon
a mount of a truncated pyramidal shape.

1115 How the flukes[59] splash!
How they contort rapid as lightning, with spasms and spouts of blood!

Be at peace bloody flukes of doubters and sullen mopers,
I take my place among you as much as among any,
The past is the push of you, me, all, precisely the same,
1120 And what is yet untried and afterward is for you, me, all, precisely the same.

I do not know what is untried and afterward,
But I know it will in its turn prove sufficient, and cannot fail.

Each who passes is consider'd, each who stops is consider'd, not a single one can it fail.

It cannot fail the young man who died and was buried,
1125 Nor the young woman who died and was put by his side,
Nor the little child that peep'd in at the door, and then drew back and was never seen again,
Nor the old man who has lived without purpose, and feels it with bitterness worse than gall,
Nor him in the poor house tubercled by rum and the bad disorder,
Nor the numberless slaughter'd and wreck'd, nor the brutish koboo[60] call'd the ordure of humanity,
1130 Nor the sacs merely floating with open mouths for food to slip in,
Nor any thing in the earth, or down in the oldest graves of the earth,
Nor any thing in the myriads of spheres, nor the myriads of myriads that inhabit them,
Nor the present, nor the least wisp that is known.

44

It is time to explain myself—let us stand up.

1135 What is known I strip away,
I launch all men and women forward with me into the Unknown.

The clock indicates the moment—but what does eternity indicate?

We have thus far exhausted trillions of winters and summers,
There are trillions ahead, and trillions ahead of them.

[59]The tail of a whale.
[60]A native of the east coast of Sumatra.

Births have brought us richness and variety,
And other births will bring us richness and variety.

I do not call one greater and one smaller,
That which fills its period and place is equal to any.

Were mankind murderous or jealous upon you, my brother, my
  sister?
I am sorry for you, they are not murderous or jealous upon me,
All has been gentle with me, I keep no account with lamentation,
(What have I to do with lamentation?)

I am an acme of things accomplish'd, and I an encloser of things to be.

My feet strike an apex of the apices[61] of the stairs,
On every step bunches of ages, and larger bunches between the
  steps,
All below duly travel'd, and still I mount and mount.

Rise after rise bow the phantoms behind me,
Afar down I see the huge first Nothing, I know I was even there,
I waited unseen and always, and slept through the lethargic mist,
And took my time, and took no hurt from the fetid carbon.

Long I was hugg'd close—long and long.

Immense have been the preparations for me,
Faithful and friendly the arms that have help'd me.

Cycles ferried my cradle, rowing and rowing like cheerful boatmen,
For room to me stars kept aside in their own rings,
They sent influences to look after what was to hold me.

Before I was born out of my mother generations guided me,
My embryo has never been torpid, nothing could overlay it.

For it the nebula cohered to an orb,
The long slow strata piled to rest it on,
Vast vegetables gave it sustenance,
Monstrous sauroids[62] transported it in their mouths and deposited
  it with care.

[61]Plural of apex.
[62]Giant lizards, such as dinosaurs.

All forces have been steadily employ'd to complete and delight me,
Now on this spot I stand with my robust soul.

45

1170 O span of youth! ever-push'd elasticity!
O manhood, balanced, florid and full.

My lovers suffocate me,
Crowding my lips, thick in the pores of my skin,
Jostling me through streets and public halls, coming naked to me at
    night,
1175 Crying by day *Ahoy!* from the rocks of the river, swinging and
    chirping over my head,
Calling my name from flower-beds, vines, tangled underbrush,
Lighting on every moment of my life,
Bussing my body with soft balsamic[63] busses,
Noiselessly passing handfuls out of their hearts and giving them to
    be mine.

1180 Old age superbly rising! O welcome, ineffable grace of dying days!

Every condition promulges[64] not only itself, it promulges what
    grows after and out of itself,
And the dark hush promulges as much as any.

I open my scuttle at night and see the far-sprinkled systems,
And all I see multiplied as high as I can cipher edge but the rim of
    the farther systems.

1185 Wider and wider they spread, expanding, always expanding,
Outward and outward and forever outward.

My sun has his sun and round him obediently wheels,
He joins with his partners a group of superior circuit,
And greater sets follow, making specks of the greatest inside them.

1190 There is no stoppage and never can be stoppage,
If I, you, and the worlds, and all beneath or upon their surfaces,
    were this moment reduced back to a pallid float, it would not
    avail in the long run,

[63]Fragrant and soothing as the ointment balsam.
[64]Whitman's variant for "promulgates" in the sense of "puts into effect, gen-
erates."

We should surely bring up again where we now stand,
And surely go as much farther, and then farther and farther.

A few quadrillions of eras, a few octillions[65] of cubic leagues, do
    not hazard the span or make it impatient,
They are but parts, any thing is but a part.

See ever so far, there is limitless space outside of that,
Count ever so much, there is limitless time around that.

My rendezvous is appointed, it is certain,
The Lord will be there and wait till I come on perfect terms,
The great Camerado,[66] the lover true for whom I pine will be there.

46

I know I have the best of time and space, and was never measured
    and never will be measured.

I tramp a perpetual journey, (come listen all!)
My signs are a rain-proof coat, good shoes, and a staff cut from the
    woods,
No friend of mine takes his ease in my chair,
I have no chair, no church, no philosophy,
I lead no man to a dinner-table, library, exchange,
But each man and each woman of you I lead upon a knoll,
My left hand hooking you round the waist,
My right hand pointing to landscapes of continents and the public
    road.

Not I, not any one else can travel that road for you,
You must travel it for yourself.

It is not far, it is within reach,
Perhaps you have been on it since you were born and did not know,
Perhaps it is everywhere on water and on land.

Shoulder your duds dear son, and I will mine, and let us hasten
    forth,
Wonderful cities and free nations we shall fetch as we go.

If you tire, give me both burdens, and rest the chuff of your hand
    on my hip,

---

[65] A number 1 followed by 27 zeros.
[66] Comrade (in Spanish).

And in due time you shall repay the same service to me,
For after we start we never lie by again.

1220 This day before dawn I ascended a hill and look'd at the crowded
heaven,
And I said to my spirit *When we become the enfolders of those orbs,
and the pleasure and knowledge of every thing in them, shall
we be fill'd and satisfied then?*
And my spirit said *No, we but level that lift to pass and continue
beyond.*

You are also asking me questions and I hear you,
I answer that I cannot answer, you must find out for yourself.

1225 Sit a while dear son,
Here are biscuits to eat and here is milk to drink,
But as soon as you sleep and renew yourself in sweet clothes, I kiss
you with a good-by kiss and open the gate for your egress
hence.

Long enough have you dream'd contemptible dreams,
Now I wash the gum from your eyes,
1230 You must habit yourself to the dazzle of the light and of every mo-
ment of your life.

Long have you timidly waded holding a plank by the shore,
Now I will you to be a bold swimmer,
To jump off in the midst of the sea, rise again, nod to me, shout,
and laughingly dash with your hair.

47

I am the teacher of athletes,
1235 He that by me spreads a wider breast than my own proves the
width of my own,
He most honors my style who learns under it to destroy the teacher.

The boy I love, the same becomes a man not through derived
power, but in his own right,
Wicked rather than virtuous out of conformity or fear,
Fond of his sweetheart, relishing well his steak,
1240 Unrequited love or a slight cutting him worse than sharp steel cuts,
First-rate to ride, to fight, to hit the bull's-eye, to sail a skiff, to
sing a song or play on the banjo,

Preferring scars and the beard and faces pitted with small-pox over
    all latherers,
And those well-tann'd to those that keep out of the sun.

I teach straying from me, yet who can stray from me?
I follow you whoever you are from the present hour,
My words itch at your ears till you understand them.

I do not say these things for a dollar or to fill up the time while I
    wait for a boat,
(It is you talking just as much as myself, I act as the tongue of you,
Tied in your mouth, in mine it begins to be loosen'd.)

I swear I will never again mention love or death inside a house,
And I swear I will never translate myself at all, only to him or her
    who privately stays with me in the open air.

If you would understand me go to the heights or water-shore,
The nearest gnat is an explanation, and a drop or motion of waves
    a key,
The maul, the oar, the hand-saw, second my words.

No shutter'd room or school can commune with me,
But roughs and little children better than they.

The young mechanic is closest to me, he knows me well,
The woodman that takes his axe and jug with him shall take me
    with him all day,
The farm-boy ploughing in the field feels good at the sound of
    my voice,
In vessels that sail my words sail, I go with fishermen and seamen
    and love them.

The soldier camp'd or upon the march is mine,
On the night ere the pending battle many seek me, and I do not
    fail them,
On that solemn night (it may be their last) those that know me
    seek me.

My face rubs to the hunter's face when he lies down alone in his
    blanket,
The driver thinking of me does not mind the jolt of his wagon,
The young mother and old mother comprehend me,

The girl and the wife rest the needle a moment and forget where
they are,
They and all would resume what I have told them.

48

I have said that the soul is not more than the body,
1270 And I have said that the body is not more than the soul,
And nothing, not God, is greater to one than one's self is,
And whoever walks a furlong without sympathy walks to his own
funeral drest in his shroud,
And I or you pocketless of a dime may purchase the pick of the
earth,
And to glance with an eye or show a bean in its pod confounds the
learning of all times,
1275 And there is no trade or employment but the young man following
it may become a hero,
And there is no object so soft but it makes a hub for the wheel'd
universe,
And I say to any man or woman, Let your soul stand cool and com-
posed before a million universes.

And I say to mankind, Be not curious about God,
For I who am curious about each am not curious about God,
1280 (No array of terms can say how much I am at peace about God and
about death.)

I hear and behold God in every object, yet understand God not in
the least,
Nor do I understand who there can be more wonderful than myself.

Why should I wish to see God better than this day?
I see something of God each hour of the twenty-four, and each
moment then,
1285 In the faces of men and women I see God, and in my own face in
the glass,
I find letters from God dropt in the street, and every one is sign'd
by God's name,
And I leave them where they are, for I know that wheresoe'er I go,
Others will punctually come for ever and ever.

49

And as to you Death, and you bitter hug of mortality, it is idle to try
to alarm me.

To his work without flinching the accoucheur[67] comes,
I see the elder-hand pressing receiving supporting,
I recline by the sills of the exquisite flexible doors,
And mark the outlet, and mark the relief and escape.

And as to you Corpse I think you are good manure, but that does
    not offend me,
I smell the white roses sweet-scented and growing,
I reach to the leafy lips, I reach to the polish'd breasts of melons.

And as to you Life I reckon you are the leavings of many deaths,
(No doubt I have died myself ten thousand times before.)

I hear you whispering there O stars of heaven,
O suns—O grass of graves—O perpetual transfers and promotions,
If you do not say any thing how can I say any thing?

Of the turbid pool that lies in the autumn forest,
Of the moon that descends the steeps of the soughing twilight,
Toss, sparkles of day and dusk—toss on the black stems that decay
    in the muck,
Toss to the moaning gibberish of the dry limbs.

I ascend from the moon, I ascend from the night,
I perceive that the ghastly glimmer is noonday sunbeams reflected,
And debouch[68] to the steady and central from the offspring great or
    small.

50

There is that in me—I do not know what it is—but I know it is in
    me.

Wrench'd and sweaty—calm and cool then my body becomes,
I sleep—I sleep long.

I do not know it—it is without name—it is a word unsaid,
It is not in any dictionary, utterance, symbol.

Something it swings on more than the earth I swing on,
To it the creation is the friend whose embracing awakes me.

---

[67]Maternity doctor.
[68]Emerge into the open.

Perhaps I might tell more. Outlines! I plead for my brothers and
   sisters.

Do you see O my brothers and sisters?
It is not chaos or death—it is form, union, plan—it is eternal life—it
   is Happiness.

51

The past and present wilt—I have fill'd them, emptied them,
1320   And proceed to fill my next fold of the future.

Listener up there! what have you to confide to me?
Look in my face while I snuff the sidle[69] of evening,
(Talk honestly, no one else hears you, and I stay only a minute
   longer.)

Do I contradict myself?
1325   Very well then I contradict myself,
(I am large, I contain multitudes.)

I concentrate toward them that are nigh, I wait on the door-slab.

Who has done his day's work? who will soonest be through with
   his supper?
Who wishes to walk with me?

1330   Will you speak before I am gone? will you prove already too late?

52

The spotted hawk swoops by and accuses me, he complains of my
   gab and my loitering.

I too am not a bit tamed, I too am untranslatable,
I sound my barbaric yawp over the roofs of the world.

The last scud[70] of day holds back for me,
1335   It flings my likeness after the rest and true as any on the shadow'd
   wilds,
It coaxes me to the vapor and the dusk.

[69]Fading light.
[70]Wind-blown clouds.

I depart as air, I shake my white locks at the runaway sun,
I effuse my flesh in eddies, and drift it in lacy jags.

I bequeath myself to the dirt to grow from the grass I love,
If you want me again look for me under your boot-soles.

You will hardly know who I am or what I mean,
But I shall be good health to you nevertheless,
And filter and fibre your blood.

Failing to fetch me at first keep encouraged,
Missing me one place search another,
I stop somewhere waiting for you.

CROSSING BROOKLYN FERRY

1

Flood-tide below me! I see you face to face!
Clouds of the west—sun there half an hour high—I see you also face
    to face.

Crowds of men and women attired in the usual costumes, how curi-
    ous you are to me!
On the ferry-boats the hundreds and hundreds that cross, returning
    home, are more curious to me than you suppose,
And you that shall cross from shore to shore years hence are more
    to me, and more in my meditations, than you might suppose.

2

The impalpable sustenance of me from all things at all hours of the
    day,
The simple, compact, well-join'd scheme, myself disintegrated,
    every one disintegrated yet part of the scheme,
The similitudes of the past and those of the future,
The glories strung like beads on my smallest sights and hearings, on
    the walk in the street and the passage over the river,
The current rushing so swiftly and swimming with me far away,
The others that are to follow me, the ties between me and them,
The certainty of others, the life, love, sight, hearing of others.

Others will enter the gates of the ferry and cross from shore to
    shore,
Others will watch the run of the flood-tide,
15 Others will see the shipping of Manhattan north and west, and the
    heights of Brooklyn to the south and east,
Others will see the islands large and small;
Fifty years hence, others will see them as they cross, the sun half an
    hour high,
A hundred years hence, or ever so many hundred years hence,
    others will see them,
Will enjoy the sunset, the pouring-in of the flood-tide, the falling-
    back to the sea of the ebb-tide.

3

20 It avails not, time nor place—distance avails not,
I am with you, you men and women of a generation, or ever so many
    generations hence,
Just as you feel when you look on the river and sky, so I felt,
Just as any of you is one of a living crowd, I was one of a crowd,
Just as you are refresh'd by the gladness of the river and the bright
    flow, I was refresh'd,
25 Just as you stand and lean on the rail, yet hurry with the swift cur-
    rent, I stood yet was hurried,
Just as you look on the numberless masts of ships and the thick-
    stemm'd pipes of steamboats, I look'd.

I too many and many a time cross'd the river of old,
Watched the Twelfth-month[1] sea-gulls, saw them high in the air
    floating with motionless wings, oscillating their bodies,
Saw how the glistening yellow lit up parts of their bodies and left
    the rest in strong shadow,
30 Saw the slow-wheeling circles and the gradual edging toward the
    south,
Saw the reflection of the summer sky in the water,
Had my eyes dazzled by the shimmering track of beams,
Look'd at the fine centrifugal spokes of light round the shape of my
    head in the sunlit water,
Look'd on the haze on the hills southward and south-westward,
35 Look'd on the vapor as it flew in fleeces tinged with violet,
Look'd toward the lower bay to notice the vessels arriving,
Saw their approach, saw aboard those that were near me,
Saw the white sails of schooners and sloops, saw the ships at anchor,

[1]The Quaker name for December.

The sailors at work in the rigging or out astride the spars,
The round masts, the swinging motion of the hulls, the slender ser-
    pentine pennants,
The large and small steamers in motion, the pilots in their pilot-
    houses,
The white wake left by the passage, the quick tremulous whirl of
    the wheels,
The flags of all nations, the falling of them at sunset,
The scallop-edged waves in the twilight, the ladled cups, the frolic-
    some crests and glistening,
The stretch afar growing dimmer and dimmer, the gray walls of the
    granite storehouses by the docks,
On the river the shadowy group, the big steam-tug closely flank'd
    on each side by the barges, the hay-boat, the belated lighter,
On the neighboring shore the fires from the foundry chimneys
    burning high and glaringly into the night,
Casting their flicker of black contrasted with wild red and yellow
    light over the tops of houses, and down into the clefts of streets.

4

These and all else were to me the same as they are to you,
I loved well those cities, loved well the stately and rapid river,
The men and women I saw were all near to me,
Others the same—others who look back on me because I look'd for-
    ward to them,
(The time will come, though I stop here to-day and to-night.)

5

What is it then between us?
What is the count of the scores or hundreds of years between us?

Whatever it is, it avails not—distance avails not, and place avails not,
I too lived, Brooklyn of ample hills was mine,
I too walk'd the streets of Manhattan island, and bathed in the
    waters around it,
I too felt the curious abrupt questionings stir within me,
In the day among crowds of people sometimes they came upon me,
In my walks home late at night or as I lay in my bed they came
    upon me,
I too had been struck from the float forever held in solution,
I too had receiv'd identity by my body,
That I was I knew was of my body, and what I should be I knew I
    should be of my body.

6

65 It is not upon you alone the dark patches fall,
The dark threw its patches down upon me also,
The best I had done seem'd to me blank and suspicious,
My great thoughts as I supposed them, were they not in reality meagre?
Nor is it you alone who know what it is to be evil,
70 I am he who knew what it was to be evil,
I too knitted the old knot of contrariety,
Blabb'd, blush'd, resented, lied, stole, grudg'd,
Had guile, anger, lust, hot wishes I dared not speak,
Was wayward, vain, greedy, shallow, sly, cowardly, malignant,
75 The wolf, the snake, the hog, not wanting in me,
The cheating look, the frivolous word, the adulterous wish, not wanting,
Refusals, hates, postponements, meanness, laziness, none of these wanting,
Was one with the rest, the days and haps of the rest,
Was call'd by my nighest name by clear loud voices of young men as they saw me approaching or passing,
80 Felt their arms on my neck as I stood, or the negligent leaning of their flesh against me as I sat,
Saw many I loved in the street or ferry-boat or public assembly, yet never told them a word,
Lived the same life with the rest, the same old laughing, gnawing, sleeping,
Play'd the part that still looks back on the actor or actress,
The same old role, the role that is what we make it, as great as we like,
85 Or as small as we like, or both great and small.

7

Closer yet I approach you,
What thoughts you have of me now, I had as much of you—I laid in my stores in advance,
I consider'd long and seriously of you before you were born.

Who was to know what should come home to me?
90 Who knows but I am enjoying this?
Who knows, for all the distance, but I am as good as looking at you now, for all you cannot see me?

8

Ah, what can ever be more stately and admirable to me than mast-
    hemm'd Manhattan?
River and sunset and scallop-edg'd waves of flood-tide?
The sea-gulls oscillating their bodies, the hay-boat in the twilight,
    and the belated lighter?

What gods can exceed these that clasp me by the hand, and with
    voices I love call me promptly and loudly by my nighest name
    as I approach?
What is more subtle than this which ties me to the woman or man
    that looks in my face?
Which fuses me into you now, and pours my meaning into you?

We understand then do we not?
What I promis'd without mentioning it, have you not accepted?
What the study could not teach—what the preaching could not ac-
    complish is accomplish'd, is it not?

9

Flow on, river! flow with the flood-tide, and ebb with the ebb-tide!
Frolic on, crested and scallop-edg'd waves!
Gorgeous clouds of the sunset! drench with your splendor me, or
    the men and women generations after me!
Cross from shore to shore, countless crowds of passengers!
Stand up, tall masts of Mannahatta! stand up, beautiful hills of
    Brooklyn!
Throb, baffled and curious brain! throw out questions and answers!
Suspend here and everywhere, eternal float of solution!
Gaze, loving and thirsting eyes, in the house or street or public
    assembly!
Sound out, voices of young men! loudly and musically call me by
    my nighest name!
Live, old life! play the part that looks back on the actor or actress!
Play the old role, the role that is great or small according as one
    makes it!
Consider, you who peruse me, whether I may not in unknown ways
    be looking upon you;
Be firm, rail over the river, to support those who lean idly, yet haste
    with the hasting current;
Fly on, sea-birds! fly sideways, or wheel in large circles high in the
    air;

115   Receive the summer sky, you water, and faithfully hold it till all
       downcast eyes have time to take it from you!
       Diverge, fine spokes of light, from the shape of my head, or any
       one's head, in the sunlit water!
       Come on, ships from the lower bay! pass up or down, white-sail'd
       schooners, sloops, lighters!
       Flaunt away, flags of all nations! be duly lower'd at sunset!
       Burn high your fires, foundry chimneys! cast black shadows at
       nightfall! cast red and yellow light over the tops of the houses!
120   Appearances, now or henceforth, indicate what you are,
       You necessary film, continue to envelop the soul,
       About my body for me, and your body for you, be hung our divinest
       aromas,
       Thrive, cities—bring you freight, bring your shows, ample and
       sufficient rivers,
       Expand, being than which none else is perhaps more spiritual,
125   Keep your places, objects than which none else is more lasting.

       You have waited, you always wait, you dumb, beautiful ministers,
       We receive you with free sense at last, and are insatiate hence for-
       ward,
       Not you any more shall be able to foil us, or withhold yourselves
       from us,
       We use you, and do not cast you aside—we plant you permanently
       within us,
130   We fathom you not—we love you—there is perfection in you also,
       You furnish your parts toward eternity,
       Great or small, you furnish your parts toward the soul.

OUT OF THE CRADLE ENDLESSLY ROCKING

       Out of the cradle endlessly rocking,
       Out of the mocking-bird's throat, the musical shuttle,
       Out of the Ninth-month[1] midnight,
       Over the sterile sands and the fields beyond, where the child leaving
       his bed wander'd alone, bareheaded, barefoot,
5   Down from the shower'd halo,
       Up from the mystic play of shadows twining and twisting as if they
       were alive,
       Out from the patches of briers and blackberries,

[1]The Quaker name for September.

From the memories of the bird that chanted to me,
From your memories sad brother, from the fitful risings and fallings
  I heard,
From under that yellow half-moon late-risen and swollen as if with
  tears,
From those beginning notes of yearning and love there in the mist,
From the thousand responses of my heart never to cease,
From the myriad thence-arous'd words,
From the word stronger and more delicious than any,
From such as now they start the scene revisiting,
As a flock, twittering, rising, or overhead passing,
Borne hither, ere all eludes me, hurriedly,
A man, yet by these tears a little boy again,
Throwing myself on the sand, confronting the waves,
I, chanter of pains and joys, uniter of here and hereafter,
Taking all hints to use them, but swiftly leaping beyond them,
A reminiscence sing.

One Paumanok,[2]
When the lilac-scent was in the air and Fifth-month[3] grass was
  growing,
Up this seashore in some briers,
Two feather'd guests from Alabama, two together,
And their nest, and four light-green eggs spotted with brown,
And every day the he-bird to and fro near at hand,
And every day the she-bird crouch'd on her nest, silent, with bright
  eyes,
And every day I, a curious boy, never too close, never disturbing
  them,
Cautiously peering, absorbing, translating.

Shine! shine! shine!
Pour down your warmth, great sun!
While we bask, we two together.

Two together!
Winds blow south, or winds blow north,
Day come white, or night come black,
Home, or rivers and mountains from home,
Singing all time, minding no time,
While we two keep together.

[2]Indian name for Long Island.
[3]The Quaker name for May.

Till of a sudden,
May-be kill'd, unknown to her mate,
One forenoon the she-bird crouch'd not on the nest,
Nor return'd that afternoon, nor the next,
45 Nor ever appear'd again.

And thenceforward all summer in the sound of the sea,
And at night under the full of the moon in calmer weather,
Over the hoarse surging of the sea,
Or flitting from brier to brier by day,
50 I saw, I heard at intervals the remaining one, the he-bird,
The solitary guest from Alabama.

Blow! blow! blow!
Blow up sea-winds along Paumanok's shore;
I wait and I wait till you blow my mate to me.

55 Yes, when the stars glisten'd,
All night long on the prong of a moss-scallop'd stake,
Down almost amid the slapping waves,
Sat the lone singer wonderful causing tears.

He call'd on his mate,
60 He pour'd forth the meanings which I of all men know.

Yes my brother I know,
The rest might not, but I have treasur'd every note,
For more than once dimly down to the beach gliding,
Silent, avoiding the moonbeams, blending myself with the shadows,
65 Recalling now the obscure shapes, the echoes, the sounds and sights
         after their sorts,
The white arms out in the breakers tirelessly tossing,
I, with bare feet, a child, the wind wafting my hair,
Listen'd long and long.

Listen'd to keep, to sing, now translating the notes,
70 Following you my brother.

Soothe! soothe! soothe!
Close on its wave soothes the wave behind,
And again another behind embracing and lapping, every one close,
But my love soothes not me, not me.

Low hangs the moon, it rose late,
It is lagging—O I think it is heavy with love, with love.

O madly the sea pushes upon the land,
With love, with love.

O night! do I not see my love fluttering out among the breakers?
What is that little black thing I see there in the white?

Loud! loud! loud!
Loud I call to you, my love!
High and clear I shoot my voice over the waves,
Surely you must know who is here, is here,
You must know who I am, my love.

Low-hanging moon!
What is that dusky spot in your brown yellow?
O it is the shape, the shape of my mate!
O moon do not keep her from me any longer.

Land! land! O land!
Whichever way I turn, O I think you could give me my mate back
        again if you only would,
For I am almost sure I see her dimly whichever way I look.

O rising stars!
Perhaps the one I want so much will rise, will rise with some of you.

O throat! O trembling throat!
Sound clearer through the atmosphere!
Pierce the woods, the earth,
Somewhere listening to catch you must be the one I want.

Shake out carols!
Solitary here, the night's carols!
Carols of lonesome love! death's carols!
Carols under that lagging, yellow, waning moon!
O under that moon where she droops almost down into the sea!
O reckless despairing carols.

But soft! sink low!
Soft! let me just murmur,
And do you wait a moment you husky-nois'd sea,
For somewhere I believe I heard my mate responding to me,

So faint, I must be still, be still to listen,
110 But not altogether still, for then she might not come immediately
        to me.

Hither my love!
Here I am! here!
With this just-sustain'd note I announce myself to you,
This gentle call is for you my love, for you.

115 Do not be decoy'd elsewhere,
That is the whistle of the wind, it is not my voice,
That is the fluttering, the fluttering of the spray,
Those are the shadows of leaves.

O darkness! O in vain!
120 O I am very sick and sorrowful.

O brown halo in the sky near the moon, drooping upon the sea!
O troubled reflection in the sea!
O throat! O throbbing heart!
And I singing uselessly, uselessly all the night.

125 O past! O happy life! O songs of joy!
In the air, in the woods, over fields,
Loved! loved! loved! loved! loved!
But my mate no more, no more with me!
We two together no more.

130 The aria sinking,
All else continuing, the stars shining,
The winds blowing, the notes of the bird continuous echoing,
With angry moans the fierce old mother incessantly moaning,
On the sands of Paumanok's shore gray and rustling,
135 The yellow half-moon enlarged, sagging down, drooping, the face
        of the sea almost touching,
The boy ecstatic, with his bare feet the waves, with his hair the
        atmosphere dallying,
The love in the heart long pent, now loose, now at last tumultuously
        bursting,
The aria's meaning, the ears, the soul, swiftly depositing,
The strange tears down the cheeks coursing,
140 The colloquy there, the trio, each uttering,
The undertone, the savage old mother incessantly crying,

To the boy's soul's questions sullenly timing, some drown'd secret
    hissing,
To the outsetting bard.

Demon[4] or bird! (said the boy's soul,)
Is it indeed toward your mate you sing? or is it really to me?
For I, that was a child, my tongue's use sleeping, now I have heard
    you,
Now in a moment I know what I am for, I awake,
And already a thousand singers, a thousand songs, clearer, louder
    and more sorrowful than yours,
A thousand warbling echoes have started to life within me, never
    to die.

O you singer solitary, singing by yourself, projecting me,
O solitary me listening, never more shall I cease perpetuating you,
Never more shall I escape, never more the reverberations,
Never more the cries of unsatisfied love be absent from me,
Never again leave me to be the peaceful child I was before what
    there in the night,
By the sea under the yellow and sagging moon,
The messenger there arous'd, the fire, the sweet hell within,
The unknown want, the destiny of me.

O give me the clew! (it lurks in the night here somewhere,)
O if I am to have so much, let me have more!

A word then, (for I will conquer it,)
The word final, superior to all,
Subtle, sent up—what is it?—I listen;
Are you whispering it, and have been all the time, you sea-waves?
Is that it from your liquid rims and wet sands?

Whereto answering, the sea,
Delaying not, hurrying not,
Whisper'd me through the night, and very plainly before daybreak,
Lisp'd to me the low and delicious word death,
And again death, death, death, death,
Hissing melodious, neither like the bird nor like my arous'd child's
    heart,
But edging near as privately for me rustling at my feet,

---

[4]Daimon: an attendant spirit or genius.

Creeping thence steadily up to my ears and laving me softly all
    over,
Death, death, death, death, death.

Which I do not forget,
175   But fuse the song of my dusky demon and brother,
That he sang to me in the moonlight on Paumanok's gray beach,
With the thousand responsive songs at random,
My own songs awaked from that hour,
And with them the key, the word up from the waves,
180   The word of the sweetest song and all songs,
That strong and delicious word which, creeping to my feet,
(Or like some old crone rocking the cradle, swathed in sweet gar-
    ments, bending aside,)
The sea whisper'd me.

A NOISELESS PATIENT SPIDER

A noiseless patient spider,
I mark'd where on a little promontory it stood isolated,
Mark'd how to explore the vacant vast surrounding,
It launch'd forth filament, filament, filament, out of itself,
5   Ever unreeling down, ever tirelessly speeding them.

And you O my soul where you stand,
Surrounded, detached, in measureless oceans of space,
Ceaselessly musing, venturing, throwing, seeking the spheres to
    connect them,
Till the bridge you will need be form'd, till the ductile anchor hold,
10   Till the gossamer thread you fling catch somewhere, O my soul.

CAVALRY CROSSING A FORD

A line in long array where they wind betwixt green islands,
They take a serpentine course, their arms flash in the sun—hark to
    the musical clank,
Behold the silvery river, in it the splashing horses loitering stop to
    drink,

Behold the brown-faced men, each group, each person a picture, the
    negligent rest on the saddles,
Some emerge on the opposite bank, others are just entering the ford
    —while,
Scarlet and blue and snowy white,
The guidon flags[1] flutter gayly in the wind.

BIVOUAC ON A MOUNTAIN SIDE

I see before me now a traveling army halting,
Below a fertile valley spread, with barns and the orchards of sum-
    mer,
Behind, the terraced sides of a mountain, abrupt, in places rising
    high,
Broken, with rocks, with clinging cedars, with tall shapes dingily
    seen,
The numerous camp-fires scatter'd near and far, some away up on
    the mountain,
The shadowy forms of men and horses, looming, large-sized, flick-
    ering,
And over all the sky—the sky! far, far out of reach, studded, break-
    ing out, the eternal stars.

AN ARMY CORPS ON THE MARCH

With its cloud of skirmishers in advance,
With now the sound of a single shot snapping like a whip, and now
    an irregular volley,
The swarming ranks press on and on, the dense brigades press on,
Glittering dimly, toiling under the sun—the duct-cover'd men,
In columns rise and fall to the undulations of the ground,
With artillery interspers'd—the wheels rumble, the horses sweat,
As the army corps advances.

[1]The flag or pennant that is the standard of the military unit.

WHEN LILACS LAST
IN THE DOORYARD BLOOM'D

1

When lilacs last in the dooryard bloom'd,
And the great star early droop'd in the western sky in the night,
I mourn'd, and yet shall mourn with ever-returning spring.

Ever-returning spring, trinity sure to me you bring,
5   Lilac blooming perennial and drooping star in the west,
And thought of him I love.

2

O powerful western fallen star!
O shades of night—O moody, tearful night!
O great star disappear'd—O the black murk that hides the star!
10   O cruel hands that hold me powerless—O helpless soul of me!
O harsh surrounding cloud that will not free my soul.

3

In the dooryard fronting an old farm-house near the white-wash'd
    palings,
Stands the lilac-bush tall-growing with heart-shaped leaves of rich
    green,
With many a pointed blossom rising delicate, with the perfume
    strong I love,
15   With every leaf a miracle—and from this bush in the dooryard,
With delicate-color'd blossoms and heart-shaped leaves of rich
    green,
A sprig with its flower I break.

4

In the swamp in secluded recesses,
A shy and hidden bird is warbling a song.

20   Solitary the thrush,
The hermit withdrawn to himself, avoiding the settlements,
Sings by himself a song.

Song of the bleeding throat,
Death's outlet song of life, (for well dear brother I know,
25   If thou wast not granted to sing thou woulds't surely die.)

5

Over the breast of the spring, the land, amid cities,
Amid lanes and through old woods, where lately the violets peep'd
    from the ground, spotting the gray debris,
Amid the grass in the fields each side of the lanes, passing the
    endless grass,
Passing the yellow-spear'd wheat, every grain from its shroud in the
    dark-brown fields uprisen,
Passing the apple-tree blows of white and pink in the orchards,
Carrying a corpse to where it shall rest in the grave,
Night and day journeys a coffin.[1]

6

Coffin that passes through lanes and streets,
Through day and night with the great cloud darkening the land,
With the pomp of the inloop'd flags with the cities draped in black,
With the show of the States themselves as of crape-veil'd women
    standing,
With processions long and winding and the flambeaus of the night,
With the countless torches lit, with the silent sea of faces and the
    unbared heads,
With the waiting depot, the arriving coffin, and the sombre faces,
With dirges through the night, with the thousand voices rising
    strong and solemn,
With all the mournful voices of the dirges pour'd around the coffin,
The dim-lit churches and the shuddering organs—where amid these
    you journey,
With the tolling tolling bells' perpetual clang,
Here, coffin that slowly passes,
I give you my sprig of lilac.

7

(Nor for you, for one alone,
Blossoms and branches green to coffins all I bring,
For fresh as the morning, thus would I chant a song for you O sane
    and sacred death.

All over bouquets of roses,
O death, I cover you over with roses and early lilies,
But mostly and now the lilac that blooms the first,

[1]The funeral train that carried Lincoln's body back to Illinois for burial, which
  thousands all along the route came in mourning to see pass.

Copious I break, I break the sprigs from the bushes,
With loaded arms I come, pouring for you,
For you and the coffins all of you O death.)[2]

8

55 O western orb sailing the heaven,
    Now I know what you must have meant as a month since I walk'd,
    As I walk'd in silence the transparent shadowy night,
    As I saw you had something to tell as you bent to me night after
        night,
    As you droop'd from the sky low down as if to my side, (while the
        other stars all look'd on,)
60 As we wander'd together the solemn night, (for something I know
        not what kept me from sleep,)
    As the night advanced, and I saw on the rim of the west how full
        you were of woe,
    As I stood on the rising ground in the breeze in the cool transparent
        night,
    As I watch'd where you pass'd and was lost in the netherward black
        of the night,
    As my soul in its trouble dissatisfied sank, as where you sad orb,
65 Concluded, dropt in the night, and was gone.

9

    Sing on there in the swamp,
    O singer bashful and tender, I hear your notes, I hear your call,
    I hear, I come presently, I understand you,
    But a moment I linger, for the lustrous star has detain'd me,
70 The star my departing comrade holds and detains me.

10

    O how shall I warble myself for the dead one there I loved?
    And how shall I deck my song for the large sweet soul that has gone?
    And what shall my perfume be for the grave of him I love?

    Sea-winds blown from east and west,
75 Blown from the Eastern sea and blown from the Western sea, till
        there on the prairies meeting,
    These and with these and the breath of my chant,
    I'll perfume the grave of him I love.

[2]Flower offerings for the corpse are a convention in classical elegies.

11

O what shall I hang on the chamber walls?
And what shall the pictures be that I hang on the walls,
To adorn the burial-house of him I love?

Pictures of growing spring and farms and homes,
With the Fourth-month[3] eve at sundown, and the gray smoke lucid
     and bright,
With floods of the yellow gold of the gorgeous, indolent, sinking
     sun, burning, expanding the air,
With the fresh sweet herbage under foot, and the pale green leaves
     of the trees prolific,
In the distance the flowing glaze, the breast of the river, with a wind-
     dapple here and there,
With ranging hills on the banks, with many a line against the sky,
     and shadows,
And the city at hand with dwellings so dense, and stacks of chim-
     neys,
And all the scenes of life and the workshops, and the workmen
     homeward returning.

12

Lo, body and soul—this land,
My own Manhattan with spires, and the sparkling and hurrying
     tides, and the ships,
The varied and ample land, the South and the North in the light,
     Ohio's shores and flashing Missouri,
And ever the far-spreading prairies cover'd with grass and corn.

Lo, the most excellent sun so calm and haughty,
The violet and purple morn with just-felt breezes,
The gentle soft-born measureless light,
The miracle spreading bathing all, the fulfill'd noon,
The coming eve delicious, the welcome night and the stars,
Over my cities shining all, enveloping man and land.

13

Sing on, sing on you gray-brown bird,
Sing from the swamps, the recesses, pour your chant from the
     bushes,
Limitless out of the dusk, out of the cedars and pines.

[3]The Quaker name for April.

Sing on dearest brother, warble your reedy song,
Loud human song, with voice of uttermost woe.

O liquid and free and tender!
105   O wild and loose to my soul—O wondrous singer!
You only I hear—yet the star holds me, (but will soon depart,)
Yet the lilac with mastering odor holds me.

14

Now while I sat in the day and look'd forth,
In the close of the day with its light and the fields of spring, and the
    farmers preparing their crops,
110   In the large unconscious scenery of my land with its lakes and
    forests,
In the heavenly aerial beauty, (after the perturb'd winds and the
    storms,)
Under the arching heavens of the afternoon swift passing, and the
    voices of children and women,
The many-moving sea-tides, and I saw the ships how they sail'd,
And the summer approaching with richness, and the fields all busy
    with labor,
115   And the infinite separate houses, how they all went on, each with its
    meals and minutia of daily usages,
And the streets how their throbbings throbb'd, and the cities pent—
    lo, then and there,
Falling upon them all and among them all, enveloping me with the
    rest,
Appear'd the cloud, appear'd the long black trail,
And I knew death, its thought, and the sacred knowledge of death.

120   Then with the knowledge of death as walking one side of me,
And the thought of death close-walking the other side of me,
And I in the middle as with companions, and as holding the hands of
    companions,
I fled forth to the hiding receiving night that talks not,
Down to the shores of the water, the path by the swamp in the dim-
    ness,
125   To the solemn shadowy cedars and ghostly pines so still.

And the singer so shy to the rest receiv'd me,
The gray-brown bird I know receiv'd us comrades three,
And he sang the carol of death, and a verse for him I love.

From deep secluded recesses,
From the fragrant cedars and the ghostly pines so still,
Came the carol of the bird.

And the charm of the carol rapt me,
As I held as if by their hands my comrades in the night,
And the voice of my spirit tallied the song of the bird.

Come lovely and soothing death,
Undulate round the world, serenely arriving, arriving,
In the day, in the night, to all, to each,
Sooner or later delicate death.

Prais'd be the fathomless universe,
For life and joy, and for objects and knowledge curious,
And for love, sweet love—but praise! praise! praise!
For the sure-enwinding arms of cool-enfolding death.

Dark mother always gliding near with soft feet,
Have none chanted for thee a chant of fullest welcome?
Then I chant it for thee, I glorify thee above all,
I bring thee a song that when thou must indeed come, come unfal-
teringly.

Approach strong deliveress,
When it is so, when thou hast taken them I joyously sing the dead,
Lost in the loving floating ocean of thee,
Laved in the flood of thy bliss O death.

From me to thee glad serenades,
Dances for thee I propose saluting thee, adornments and feastings
for thee,
And the sights of the open landscape and the high-spread sky are
fitting,
And life and the fields, and the huge and thoughtful night.

The night in silence under many a star,
The ocean shore and the husky whispering wave whose voice I
know,
And the soul turning to thee O vast and well-veil'd death,
And the body gratefully nestling close to thee.

Over the tree-tops I float thee a song,

160 *Over the rising and sinking waves, over the myriad fields and the*
*   prairies wide,*
Over the dense-pack'd cities all and the teeming wharves and ways,
I float this carol with joy, with joy to thee O death.

15

To the tally of my soul,
Loud and strong kept up the gray-brown bird,
165   With pure deliberate notes spreading filling the night.

Loud in the pines and cedars dim,
Clear in the freshness moist and the swamp-perfume,
And I with my comrades there in the night.

While my sight that was bound in my eyes unclosed,
170   As to long panoramas of visions.

And I saw askant the armies,
I saw as in noiseless dreams hundreds of battle-flags,
Borne through the smoke of the battles and pierc'd with missiles I
    saw them,
And carried hither and yon through the smoke, and torn and bloody,
175   And at last but a few shreds left on the staffs, (and all in silence,)
And the staffs all splinter'd and broken.

I saw battle-corpses, myriads of them,
And the white skeletons of young men, I saw them,
I saw the debris and debris of all the slain soldiers of the war,
180   But I saw they were not as was thought,
They themselves were fully at rest, they suffer'd not,
The living remain'd and suffer'd, the mother suffer'd,
And the wife and the child and the musing comrade suffer'd,
And the armies that remain'd suffer'd.

16

185   Passing the visions, passing the night,
Passing, unloosing the hold of my comrades' hands,
Passing the song of the hermit bird and the tallying song of my soul,
Victorious song, death's outlet song, yet varying ever-altering song,
As low and wailing, yet clear the notes, rising and falling, flooding
    the night,

Sadly sinking and fainting, as warning and warning, and yet again
    bursting with joy,
Covering the earth and filling the spread of the heaven,
As that powerful psalm in the night I heard from recesses,
Passing, I leave thee lilac with heart-shaped leaves,
I leave thee there in the door-yard, blooming, returning with spring.

I cease from my song for thee,
From my gaze on thee in the west, fronting the west, communing
    with thee,
O comrade lustrous with silver face in the night.[4]

Yet each to keep and all, retrievements out of the night,
The song, the wondrous chant of the gray-brown bird,
And the tallying chant, the echo arous'd in my soul,
With the lustrous and drooping star with the countenance full of
    woe,
With the holders holding my hand nearing the call of the bird,
Comrades mine and I in the midst, and their memory ever to keep,
    for the dead I loved so well,
For the sweetest, wisest soul of all my days and lands—and this for
    his dear sake,
Lilac and star and bird twined with the chant of my soul,
There in the fragrant pines and the cedars dusk and dim.

THE DALLIANCE OF THE EAGLES

Skirting the river road, (my forenoon walk, my rest,)
Skyward in air a sudden muffled sound, the dalliance[1] of the eagles,
The rushing amorous contact high in space together,
The clinching interlocking claws, a living, fierce, gyrating wheel,
Four beating wings, two beaks, a swirling mass tight grappling,
In tumbling turning clustering loops, straight downward falling,
Till o'er the river pois'd, the twain yet one, a moment's lull,
A motionless still balance in the air, then parting, talons loosing,
Upward again on slow-firm pinions slanting, their separate diverse
    flight,
She hers, he his, pursuing.

[4]In classical elegies the dead one's immortality through identification with na-
ture is often expressed by identifying him with a star in the heavens.

[1]Amorous play, flirtation, with overtones of courtly love.

A PRAIRIE SUNSET

Shot gold, maroon and violet, dazzling silver, emerald, fawn,
The earth's whole amplitude and Nature's multiform power consign'd for once to colors;
The light, the general air possess'd by them—colors till now unknown,

No limit, confine—not the Western sky alone—the high meridian—North, South, all,
5 Pure luminous color fighting the silent shadows to the last.

Frederick Goddard Tuckerman (1821–1873)

Youngest son of a successful businessman from an eminent Boston family, Tuckerman graduated from Harvard Law School in 1842, but gave up the law and moved into seclusion near Greenfield, Massachusetts, after his marriage in 1847. There he devoted himself to studying botany and astronomy and to writing verse. On a trip abroad he stayed with Tennyson and became a close friend. His wife Hannah died in 1857 after the birth of their third child, a loss that intensified Tuckerman's melancholy.

His verse appeared in such magazines as *Atlantic Monthly* and *Putnam's,* and was collected in *Poems* (1860). Recognized as an authority on New England flora, Tuckerman was relatively unknown as a poet, despite praise from Emerson, Longfellow, and Lowell, until Witter Bynner published his verse in the 1930's. The bulk of his work is five series of sonnets, notable for experiments with the sonnet form and for their ability to concentrate emotion in an image so sharply observed and felt that it imprints itself on the mind. Yvor Winters has called Tuckerman's longest poem, "The Cricket," "the greatest poem in English of the century."

TEXT

Tuckerman, Frederick Goddard. *The Complete Poems of Frederick Goddard Tuckerman.* Ed. N. Scott Momaday. New York: Oxford University Press, 1965.

REFERENCE

Golden, Samuel. *Frederick Goddard Tuckerman.* New York: Twayne, 1966.

from **Sonnets: First Series**

X

An upper chamber in a darkened house,
Where, ere his footsteps reached ripe manhood's brink,
Terror and anguish were his lot to drink;
I cannot rid the thought nor hold it close
5   But dimly dream upon that man alone:
Now though the autumn clouds most softly pass,
The cricket chides beneath the doorstep stone
And greener than the season grows the grass.
Nor can I drop my lids nor shade my brows,
10   But there he stands beside the lifted sash;
And with a swooning of the heart, I think
Where the black shingles slope to meet the boughs
And, shattered on the roof like smallest snows,
The tiny petals of the mountain ash.

XXVI

For Nature daily through her grand design
Breathes contradiction where she seems most clear,
For I have held of her the gift to hear
And felt indeed endowed of sense divine
5   When I have found by guarded insight fine,
Cold April flowers in the green end of June,
And thought myself possessed of Nature's ear
When by the lonely mill-brook into mine,
Seated on slab or trunk asunder sawn,
10   The night-hawk blew his horn at summer noon;
And in the rainy midnight I have heard
The ground sparrow's long twitter from the pine,
And the catbird's silver song, the wakeful bird
That to the lighted window sings for dawn.

XXVIII

Not the round natural world, not the deep mind,
The reconcilement holds: the blue abyss
Collects it not; our arrows sink amiss
And but in Him may we our import find.
5 The agony to know, the grief, the bliss
Of toil, is vain and vain: clots of the sod
Gathered in heat and haste and flung behind
To blind ourselves and others, what but this
Still grasping dust and sowing toward the wind?
10 No more thy meaning seek, thine anguish plead,
But leaving straining thought and stammering word,
Across the barren azure pass to God:
Shooting the void in silence like a bird,
A bird that shuts his wings for better speed.

from **Sonnets: Second Series**

XVI

Under the mountain, as when first I knew
Its low dark roof and chimney creeper-twined,
The red house stands; and yet my footsteps find,
Vague in the walks, waste balm and feverfew.[1]
5 But they are gone: no soft-eyed sisters[2] trip
Across the porch or lintels; where, behind,
The mother sat, sat knitting with pursed lip.
The house stands vacant in its green recess,
Absent of beauty as a broken heart.
10 The wild rain enters, and the sunset wind
Sighs in the chambers of their loveliness
Or shakes the pane—and in the silent noons
The glass falls from the window, part by part,
And ringeth faintly in the grassy stones.

[1]Balm: a medicinal herb of the mint family; feverfew: an herb of the aster family.
[2]Several of Tuckerman's sonnets concern Gertrude and Gulielma, two sisters whom he had known as neighbors. Both had died.

XVII

Roll on, sad world! not Mercury or Mars[1]
Could swifter speed, or slower, round the sun
Than in this year of variance thou hast done
To me: yet pain, fear, heart-break, woes and wars
5   Have natural limit; from his dread eclipse
The swift sun hastens, and the night debars
The day but to bring in the day more bright.
The flowers renew their odorous fellowships;
The moon runs round and round, the slow earth dips,
10   True to her poise, and lifts; the planet-stars
Roll and return from circle to ellipse;
The day is dull and soft, the eavetrough drops,
And yet I know the splendor of the light
Will break anon. Look! where the gray is white!

XVIII

And change with hurried hand has swept these scenes:
The woods have fallen, across the meadow-lot
The hunter's trail and trap-path is forgot,
And fire has drunk the swamps of evergreens;
5   Yet for a moment let my fancy plant
These autumn hills again: the wild dove's haunt,
The wild deer's walk. In golden umbrage shut,
The Indian river runs, Quonecktacut!
Here, but a lifetime back, where falls tonight
10   Behind the curtained pane a sheltered light
On buds of rose or vase of violet
Aloft upon the marble mantel set,
Here in the forest-heart, hung blackening
The wolfbait on the bush beside the spring.

[1]Planets nearer to the sun than earth is. The identification of Mercury as the swift-footed messenger and of Mars as the god of war and conflict suit the theme of the sonnet.

XXXIII

One still dark night I sat alone and wrote:
So still it was that distant Chanticleer
Seemed to cry out his warning at my ear,
Save for the brooding echo in his throat.
5 Sullen I sat, when like the nightwind's note
A voice said, "Wherefore doth he weep and fear?
Doth he not know no cry to God is dumb?"
Another spoke: "His heart is dimmed and drowned
With grief." I knew the shape that bended then[1]
10 To kiss me, when suddenly I once again
Across the watches of the starless gloom
Heard the cock scream and pause: the morning bell
Into the gulfs of night dropped One! The vision fell
And left me listening to the sinking sound.

from **Sonnets, Third Series**

X

Sometimes I walk where the deep water dips
Against the land. Or on where fancy drives
I walk and muse aloud, like one who strives
To tell his half-shaped thought with stumbling lips,
5 And view the ocean sea, the ocean ships,
With joyless heart: still but myself I find
And restless phantoms of my restless mind:
Only the moaning of my wandering words,
Only the wailing of the wheeling plover,
10 And this high rock beneath whose base the sea
Has wormed long caverns, like my tears in me:
And hard like this I stand, and beaten and blind,
This desolate rock with lichens rusted over,
Hoar with salt-sleet and chalkings of the birds.

[1]Tuckerman's wife Hannah died in 1857, days after their third child was **born.**

from **Sonnets: Fifth Series**

IV

But man finds means, grant him but place and room,
To gauge the depths and views a wonder dawn,
Sees all the worlds in utmost space withdrawn
In shape and structure like a honeycomb,
5   Locates his sun and grasps the universe
Or to their bearings bids the orbs disperse;
Now seems to stand like that great angel girt
With moon and stars: now, sick for shelter even,
Craves but a roof to turn the thunder-rain—
10   Or finds his vaunted reach and wisdom vain,
Lost in the myriad meaning of a word,
Or starts at its bare import, panic-stirred:
For earth is earth or hearth or dearth or dirt,
The sky heaved over our faint heads is heaven.

THE CRICKET

I

The humming bee purrs softly o'er his flower;
    From lawn and thicket
The dogday locust singeth in the sun
    From hour to hour:
5   Each has his bard, and thou, ere day be done,
    Shalt have no wrong.
So bright that murmur mid the insect crowd,
Muffled and lost in bottom-grass, or loud
    By pale and picket:
10   Shall I not take to help me in my song
    A little cooling cricket?

II

The afternoon is sleepy; let us lie
Beneath these branches whilst the burdened brook,
Muttering and moaning to himself, goes by;
15   And mark our minstrel's carol whilst we look

Toward the faint horizon swooning blue.
   Or in a garden bower,
Trellised and trammeled with deep drapery
   Of hanging green,
20   Light glimmering through—
There let the dull hop be
Let bloom, with poppy's dark refreshing flower:
Let the dead fragrance round our temples beat,
Stunning the sense to slumber, whilst between
25 The falling water and fluttering wind
    Mingle and meet,
    Murmur and mix,
No few faint pipings from the glades behind,
   Or alder-thicks:
30 But louder as the day declines,
From tingling tassel, blade, and sheath,
Rising from nets of river vines,
    Winrows and ricks,
    Above, beneath,
35   At every breath,
At hand, around, illimitably
Rising and falling like the sea,
    Acres of cricks!

III

Dear to the child who hears thy rustling voice
40 Cease at his footstep, though he hears thee still,
Cease and resume with vibrance crisp and shrill,
Thou sittest in the sunshine to rejoice.
Night lover too; bringer of all things dark
And rest and silence; yet thou bringest to me
45 Always that burthen of the unresting Sea,
The moaning cliffs, the low rocks blackly stark;
These upland inland fields no more I view,
But the long flat seaside beach, the wild seamew,
    And the overturning wave!
50 Thou bringest too, dim accents from the grave
To him who walketh when the day is dim,
Dreaming of those who dream no more of him,
With edged remembrances of joy and pain;
And heyday looks and laughter come again:
55 Forms that in happy sunshine lie and leap,
With faces where but now a gap must be,

Renunciations, and partitions deep
And perfect tears, and crowning vacancy!
And to thy poet at the twilight's hush,
60 No chirping touch of lips with laugh and blush,
But wringing arms, hearts wild with love and woe,
Closed eyes, and kisses that would not let go!

IV

So wert thou loved in that old graceful time
When Greece was fair,
65 While god and hero hearkened to thy chime;
Softly astir
Where the long grasses fringed Cayster's[1] lip;
Long-drawn, with shimmering sails of swan and ship,
And ship and swan;
70 Or where
Reedy Eurotas[2] ran.
Did that low warble teach thy tender flute
Xenaphyle?[3]
Its breathings mild? say! did the grasshopper
75 Sit golden in thy purple hair
O Psammathe?[4]
Or wert thou mute,
Grieving for Pan amid the alders there?
And by the water and along the hill
80 That thirsty tinkle in the herbage still,
Though the lost forest wailed to horns of Arcady?[5]

V

Like the Enchanter old—
Who sought mid the dead water's weeds and scum
For evil growths beneath the moonbeam cold,
85 Or mandrake or dorcynium;
And touched the leaf that opened both his ears,
So that articulate voices now he hears
In cry of beast, or bird, or insect's hum,—

[1]A river in Asia Minor; the ruins of Ephesus are near its mouth.
[2]A river in Laconia in Greece; the modern name is Iris.
[3]Possibly Xenophilos, a Pythagorean philosopher who wrote a treatise on music and was therefore called the musician.
[4]Calliope, who bore Apollo's son, the poet-musician Linus.
[5]A rustic mountain region of Greece that has been used poetically to stand for pastoral harmony.

Might I but find thy knowledge in thy song!
90   That twittering tongue,
Ancient as light, returning like the years.
   So might I be,
Unwise to sing, thy true interpreter
Through denser stillness and in sounder dark,
95 Than ere thy notes have pierced to harrow me.
   So might I stir
   The world to hark
   To thee my lord and lawgiver,
   And cease my quest:
100 Content to bring thy wisdom to the world;
Content to gain at last some low applause,
   Now low, now lost
Like thine from mossy stone, amid the stems and straws,
   Or garden gravemound tricked and dressed—
105   Powdered and pearled
   By stealing frost—
In dusky rainbow beauty of euphorbias!
For larger would be less indeed, and like
The ceaseless simmer in the summer grass
110 To him who toileth in the windy field.
   Or where the sunbeams strike,
Naught in innumerable numerousness.
   So might I much possess,
   So much must yield;
115 But failing this, the dell and grassy dike,
The water and the waste shall still be dear,
And all the pleasant plots and places
   Where thou hast sung, and I have hung
   To ignorantly hear.
120 Then Cricket, sing thy song! or answer mine!
Thine whispers blame, but mine has naught but praises.
It matters not. Behold! the autumn goes,
   The shadow grows,
The moments take hold of eternity;
125 Even while we stop to wrangle or repine
   Our lives are gone—
   Like thinnest mist,
Like yon escaping color in the tree;
Rejoice! rejoice! whilst yet the hours exist—
130 Rejoice or mourn, and let the world swing on
Unmoved by cricket song of thee or me.

Emily Dickinson (1830–1886)

Emily Dickinson was the middle of three children in an Amherst, Massachusetts family dominated by Edward Dickinson, the stern father, who was lawyer, college treasurer, civic leader, and legislator. Neither Emily nor her younger sister Lavinia wed; her much-loved brother Austin merely moved next door upon marriage. A year at Mount Holyoke Female Seminary under the tutelage of the evangelical Mary Lyons proved so great a strain that Emily did not return. One by one her family made a profession of faith and joined the church, but Emily never did so. Instead she was reading Emerson and finding her vocation as a poet.

The late fifties and early sixties were years of terrible stress and turmoil for Emily Dickinson. Part of the difficulty seems to have been a hopeless love, perhaps for the Reverend Charles Wadsworth, perhaps for family friend and newspaper editor Samuel Bowles. The evidence is inconclusive, but by this time Emily was a complete recluse. Living in the closed circle of the family and working around the house and garden, she wrote almost 1800 poems, only seven of which appeared in print during her lifetime. Through letters she cultivated many friendships, including a long correspondence with the popular critic and essayist Thomas Wentworth Higginson. Her last decades were marked by a series of deaths—of her father suddenly, of her mother after a lingering illness, of friends—and relieved by the love she shared with Judge Otis Lord, an old friend of her father.

In the 1890's her poems began to be published and to establish her as one of the best and most original of American poets. So compact as

TEXT

Dickinson, Emily. *The Poems of Emily Dickinson.* Ed. Thomas H. Johnson. Cambridge, Mass.: Harvard University Press, 1955.

REFERENCE

Anderson, Charles R. *Emily Dickinson's Poetry: Stairway of Surprise.* New York: Holt, Rinehart and Winston, 1960.

Dickinson, Emily. *The Letters of Emily Dickinson.* Ed. Thomas H. Johnson and Theodora Ward. Cambridge, Mass.: Harvard University Press, 1958.

Dickinson, Emily. *The Years and Hours of Emily Dickinson.* Ed. Jay Leyda. New Haven: Yale University Press, 1960.

Gelpi, Albert J. *Emily Dickinson: The Mind of The Poet.* Cambridge, Mass.: Harvard University Press, 1965.

Griffith, Clark. *The Long Shadow: Emily Dickinson's Tragic Poetry.* Princeton: Princeton University Press, 1964.

Johnson, Thomas H. *Emily Dickinson: An Interpretive Biography.* Cambridge, Mass.: Harvard University Press, 1955.

The Recognition of Emily Dickinson: Selected Criticism Since 1890. Ed. C. R. Blake and Carlton F. Wells. Ann Arbor: University of Michigan Press, 1964.

Whicher, George Frisbie. *This Was a Poet: A Critical Biography.* New York: Scribner, 1939.

to charge each word and phrase with resonance, they piece out a woman at once bold and withdrawn, devoted with a fierce honesty to face out the contradictions she finds in nature and in her psyche. Her concerns were basic—love, death, immortality, poetry, but refracted through her sensibility, her responses were various and ambivalent. Her supreme experiences came with the momentary manifestation of a transcendent power in nature; but so unsure was she of life and afterlife that she came finally to depend on the power of the poet's mind to concentrate and fix the moment in the forms of language; poetry became the vehicle of consciousness to preserve, comprehend, control—and thereby to wring immortality from—the temporary flux.

19

A sepal,[1] petal, and a thorn
Upon a common summer's morn—
A flask of Dew—A Bee or two—
A Breeze—a caper in the trees—
5   And I'm a Rose!

49

I never lost as much but twice,
And that was in the sod.
Twice have I stood a beggar
Before the door of God!

5   Angels—twice descending
Reimbursed my store—
Burglar! Banker—Father!
I am poor once more!

61

Papa above!
Regard a Mouse
O'erpowered by the Cat!
Reserve within thy kingdom
5   A "Mansion"[1] for the Rat!

Snug in seraphic Cupboards
To nibble all the day,
While unsuspecting Cycles
Wheel solemnly away!

---

[1]One of the modified leaves making up the green calyx of the flower.

[1]John 14:2: Jesus' words that "In My Father's house there are many mansions."

130

These are the days when Birds come back—
A very few—a Bird or two—
To take a backward look.

These are the days when skies resume
5   The old—old sophistries of June—
A blue and gold mistake.

Oh fraud that cannot cheat the Bee—
Almost thy plausibility
Induces my belief.

10   Till ranks of seeds their witness bear—
And softly thro' the altered air
Hurries a timid leaf.

Oh Sacrament of summer days,
Oh Last Communion in the Haze—
15   Permit a child to join.

Thy sacred emblems to partake—
Thy consecrated bread to take
And thine immortal wine!

185

"Faith" is a fine invention
When Gentlemen can *see*—
But *Microscopes* are prudent
In an Emergency.

199

I'm "wife"—I've finished that—
That other state—
I'm Czar—I'm "Woman" now—
It's safer so—

5 How odd the Girl's life looks
Behind this soft Eclipse—
I think that Earth feels so
To folks in Heaven—now—

This being comfort—then
10 That other kind—was pain—
But why compare?
I'm "Wife"! Stop there!

213

Did the Harebell[1] loose her girdle
To the lover Bee
Would the Bee the Harebell *hallow*
Much as formerly?

5 Did the "Paradise"—persuaded—
Yield her moat of pearl—
Would the Eden *be* an Eden,
Or the Earl—an *Earl?*

214

I taste a liquor never brewed—
From Tankards scooped in Pearl—
Not all the Frankfort Berries[1]
Yield such an Alcohol!

5 Inebriate of Air—am I—
And Debauchee of Dew—
Reeling—thro endless summer days
From inns of Molten Blue—

---

[1]An herb, also called "blue bell."

---

[1]Variant line in manuscript:
    Not all the Vats upon the Rhine;
in either case, the reference is to Rhine wine.

When "Landlords" turn the drunken Bee
10 Out of the Foxglove's door—
When Butterflies—renounce their "drams"—
I shall but drink the more!

Till Seraphs swing their snowy Hats—
And Saints—to windows run—
15 To see the little Tippler
From Manzanilla come!²

216

Safe in their Alabaster Chambers—
Untouched by Morning—
And untouched by Noon—
Lie the meek members of the Resurrection—
5 Rafter of Satin—and Roof of Stone!

Grand go the Years—in the Crescent—above them—
Worlds scoop their Arcs—
And Firmaments—row—
Diadems—drop—and Doges¹—surrender—
10 Soundless as dots—on a Disc of Snow—

249

Wild Nights—Wild Nights!
Were I with thee
Wild Nights should be
Our luxury!

5 Futile—the Winds—
To a Heart in port—

---

²Manzanilla in Spain produces sherry; variant line:
    Leaning against the—Sun—

---

¹The Doge was the chief magistrate of the Venetian republic from the seventh
through the eighteenth centuries.

Done with the Compass—
Done with the Chart!

Rowing in Eden—
10　Ah, the Sea!
Might I but moor—Tonight—
In Thee!

258

There's a certain Slant of light,
Winter Afternoons—
That oppresses, like the Heft[1]
Of Cathedral Tunes—

5　Heavenly Hurt, it gives us—
We can find no scar,
But internal difference,
Where the Meanings, are—

None may teach it—Any—
10　'Tis the Seal Despair—
An imperial affliction
Sent us of the Air—

When it comes, the Landscape listens—
Shadows—hold their breath—
15　When it goes, 'tis like the Distance
On the look of Death—

280

I felt a Funeral, in my Brain,
And Mourners to and fro
Kept treading—treading—till it seemed
That Sense was breaking through—

[1]Variant in manuscript: weight.

₅ And when they all were seated,
A Service, like a Drum—
Kept beating—beating—till I thought
My Mind was going numb—

And then I heard them lift a Box
₁₀ And creak across my Soul
With those same Boots of Lead, again,
Then Space—began to toll,

As all the Heavens were a Bell,
And Being, but an Ear,
₁₅ And I, and Silence, some strange Race
Wrecked, solitary, here—

And then a Plank in Reason, broke,
And I dropped down, and down—
And hit a World, at every plunge,
₂₀ And Finished knowing—then—

322

There came a Day at Summer's full,
Entirely for me—
I thought that such were for the Saints,
Where Resurrections—be—

₅ The Sun, as common, went abroad,
The flowers, accustomed, blew,
As if no soul the solstice passed
That maketh all things new—[1]

The time was scarce profaned, by speech—
₁₀ The symbol of a word
Was needless, as at Sacrament,
The Wardrobe—of our Lord—

Each was to each The Sealed Church,
Permitted to commune this—time—

---

[1]Revelations 21:5: "Behold, I make all things new!"

15 Lest we too awkward show
     At Supper of the Lamb.

The Hours slid fast—as Hours will,
Clutched tight, by greedy hands—
So faces on two Decks, look back,
20 Bound to opposing lands—

And so when all the time had leaked,
Without external sound
Each bound the Other's Crucifix—
We gave no other Bond—

25 Sufficient troth, that we shall rise—
     Deposed—at length, the Grave—
     To that new Marriage,[2]
     Justified[3]—through Calvaries of Love—

324

Some keep the Sabbath going to Church—
I keep it, staying at Home—
With a Bobolink for a Chorister—
And an Orchard, for a Dome—

5 Some keep the Sabbath in Surplice—
    I just wear my Wings—
    And instead of tolling the Bell, for Church,
    Our little Sexton—sings.

God preaches, a noted Clergyman—
10 And the sermon is never long,
     So instead of getting to Heaven, at last—
     I'm going, all along.

[2]In the imagery of the Gospels and Epistles, Jesus was sometimes depicted as the Bridegroom.
[3]In Puritan theology justification indicates the individual's election by God, the conferring of grace that is a sign of his salvation.

338

I know that He exists.
Somewhere—in Silence—
He has hid his rare[1] life
From our gross eyes.

5   'Tis an instant's play.
'Tis a fond Ambush—
Just to make Bliss
Earn her own surprise!

But—should the play
10 Prove piercing earnest—
Should the glee—glaze—
In Death's—stiff—stare—

Would not the fun
Look too expensive!
15 Would not the jest—
Have crawled too far!

341

After great pain, a formal feeling comes—
The Nerves sit ceremonious, like Tombs—
The stiff Heart questions was it He, that bore,
And Yesterday, or Centuries before?—

5 The Feet, mechanical, go round—
Of Ground, or Air, or Ought—
A Wooden way
Regardless grown,
A Quartz contentment, like a stone—

10 This is the Hour of Lead—
Remembered, if outlived,
As Freezing persons, recollect the Snow—
First—Chill—then Stupor—then the letting go—

[1]Not just "unusual" or "precious," but "spiritual, rarefied," as opposed to "gross" in the next line.

370

Heaven is so far of the Mind
That were the Mind dissolved—
The Site—of it—by Architect
Could not again be proved—

5   'Tis vast—as our Capacity—
As fair—as our idea—
To Him of adequate desire
No further 'tis, than Here—

378

I saw no Way—The Heavens were stitched—
I felt the Columns[1] close[2]—
The Earth reversed[3] her Hemispheres—
I touched the Universe—

5   And back it slid—and I alone—
A Speck upon a Ball—
Went out upon Circumference—
Beyond the Dip of Bell—

420

You'll know it—as you know 'tis Noon—
By Glory—
As you do the Sun—
As you will in Heaven—
5   Know God the Father—and the Son.

By intuition, Mightiest Things
Assert themselves—and not by terms—

---

[1]Columns of air or cloud; or, air or clouds depicted metaphorically as columns.
[2]Both "shut" and "near."
[3]Turned inside out; or turned upside down.

"I'm Midnight"—need the Midnight say—
"I'm Sunrise"—Need the Majesty?

10 Omnipotence—had not a Tongue—
His lisp—is Lightning—and the Sun—
His Conversation—with the Sea—
"How shall you know"?
Consult your Eye!

435

Much Madness is divinest Sense—
To a discerning Eye—
Much Sense—the starkest Madness—
'Tis the Majority
5 In this, as All, prevail—
Assent—and you are sane—
Demur—you're straightway dangerous—
And handled with a Chain—

465

I heard a Fly buzz—when I died—
The Stillness in the Room
Was like the Stillness in the Air—
Between the Heaves of Storm—

5 The Eyes around—had wrung them dry—
And Breaths were gathering firm
For that last Onset—when the King
Be witnessed—in the Room—

I willed my Keepsakes—Signed away
10 What portion of me be
Assignable—and then it was
There interposed a Fly—

With Blue—uncertain stumbling Buzz—
Between the light—and me—
15   And then the Windows failed—and then
I could not see to see—

505

I would not paint—a picture—
I'd rather be the One
It's bright impossibility
To dwell—delicious—on—
5   And wonder how the fingers feel
Whose rare—celestial—stir—
Evokes so sweet a Torment—
Such sumptuous—Despair—

I would not talk, like Cornets—
10   I'd rather be the One
Raised softly to the Ceilings—
And out, and easy on—
Through Villages of Ether—
Myself endued Balloon
15   By but a lip of Metal—
The pier to my Pontoon—

Nor would I be a Poet—
It's finer—own the Ear—
Enamored—impotent—content—
20   The License to revere,
A privilege so awful
What would the Dower be,
Had I the Art to stun myself
With Bolts of Melody!

508

I'm ceded—I've stopped being Theirs—
The name They dropped upon my face
With water, in the country church
Is finished using, now,
5   And They can put it with my Dolls,

My childhood, and the string of spools,
I've finished threading—too—

Baptized, before, without the choice,
But this time, consciously, of Grace—
10 Unto supremest name—
Called to my Full—The Crescent dropped—
Existence's whole Arc,[1] filled up,
With one small Diadem.

My second Rank—too small the first—
15 Crowned—Crowing[2]—on my Father's breast—
A half unconscious [3] Queen—
But this time—Adequate—Erect,
With Will[4] to choose, or to reject,
And I choose, just a Crown—

512

The Soul has Bandaged moments—
When too appalled to stir—
She feels some ghastly Fright come up
And stop to look at her—

5 Salute her—with long fingers—
Caress her freezing hair—
Sip, Goblin, from the very lips
The Lover—hovered—o'er—
Unworthy, that a thought so mean
10 Accost a Theme—so—fair—

The soul has moments of Escape
When bursting all the doors—
She dances like a Bomb, abroad,
And swings upon the Hours,

[1]Variants in manuscript: eye, rim (both crossed out).
[2]Variants: whimpering, dangling.
[3]Variants: too unconscious, insufficient.
[4]Variant: power.

15 As do[1] the Bee—delirious borne—
Long Dungeoned from his Rose—
Touch Liberty—then know no more,
But Noon, and Paradise—

The Soul's retaken moments—
20 When, Felon led along,
With shackles on the plumed feet,
With staples,[2] in the Song,

The Horror welcomes her, again,
These, are not brayed of Tongue—

515

No Crowd that has occurred
Exhibit[1]—I suppose
That General Attendance
That Resurrection—does—

5 Circumference be full—
The long restricted Grave
Assert her Vital Privilege—
The Dust—connect—and live—

On Atoms—features place—
10 All Multitudes that were
Efface in the Comparison—
As Suns—dissolve a star—

Solemnity—prevail—
It's Individual Doom
15 Possess each separate Consciousness—
August—Absorbed—Numb—

[1]Emily Dickinson often avoids the third person singular form of the present tense and uses "do," for example, where the normal usage would be "does."
[2]A metal fastener driven into something to hold it in place. Variant: rivets.

[1]Again, the more usual form here and throughout the poem would be the third person singular form of the verb, "exhibits."

What Duplicate—exist—
What Parallel can be—
Of the Significance of This—
20   To Universe—and Me?

569

I reckon—when I count at all—
First—Poets—Then the Sun—
Then Summer—Then the Heaven of God—
And then—the List is done—

5   But, looking back—the First so seems
To Comprehend the Whole—
The Others look a needless Show—
So I write—Poets—all—

Their Summer—lasts a Solid Year—
10   They can afford a Sun
The East—would deem extravagant—
And if the Further Heaven—

Be Beautiful as they prepare
For Those who worship Them—
15   It is too difficult a Grace—
To justify the Dream—

605

The Spider holds a Silver Ball
In unperceived Hands—
And dancing softly to Himself
His Yarn of Pearl—unwinds—

5   He plies from Nought to Nought—
In unsubstantial Trade—
Supplants our Tapestries with His—
In half the period—

An Hour to rear supreme
10   His Continents[1] of Light—
Then dangle from the Housewife's Broom—
His Boundaries[2]—forgot—

633

When Bells stop ringing—Church—begins—
The Positive[1]—of Bells—
When Cogs—stop—that's Circumference—
The Ultimate—of Wheels.

640

I cannot live with You—
It would be Life—
And Life is over there—
Behind the Shelf

5   The Sexton keeps the Key to—
Putting up
Our Life—His Porcelain—
Like a Cup—

Discarded of the Housewife—
10   Quaint—or Broke—
A newer Sevres[1] pleases—
Old Ones crack—

I could not die—with You—
For One must wait
15   To shut the Other's Gaze down—
You—could not—

---

[1]Variant in manuscript: theories.
[2]Variant: sophistries.

---

[1]Variant in manuscript: transitive.

---

[1]A porcelain made in Sèvres in France.

And I—Could I stand by
And see You—freeze—
Without my Right of Frost—
20 Death's privilege?

Nor could I rise—with You—
Because Your Face
Would put out Jesus'—
That New Grace

25 Glow plain—and foreign
On my homesick Eye—
Except that You than He
Shone closer by—

They'd judge Us—How—
30 For You—served Heaven—You know,
Or sought to—
I could not—

Because You saturated Sight—
And I had no more Eyes
35 For sordid excellence²
As Paradise

And were You lost, I would be—
Though My Name
Rang loudest
40 On the Heavenly fame—

And were You—saved—
And I—condemned to be
Where You were not—
That self—were Hell to Me—

45 So We must meet apart—
You there—I—here—
With just the Door ajar
That Oceans are—and Prayer—
And that White Sustenance—
50 Despair—

²For such sordid excellence as Paradise.

670

One need not be a Chamber—to be Haunted—
One need not be a House—
The Brain has Corridors—surpassing
Material Place—

5   Far safer, of a Midnight Meeting
External Ghost
Than it's interior Confronting—
That Cooler Host.

Far safer, through an Abbey gallop,
10   The Stones a'chase—
Than Unarmed, one's a'self[1] encounter—
In lonesome Place—

Ourself behind ourself, concealed—
Should startle most—
15   Assassin hid in our Apartment
Be Horror's least.

The Body—borrows a Revolver—
He bolts the Door—
O'erlooking a superior spectre—
20   Or More—

675

Essential Oils—are wrung—
The Attar from the Rose
Be not expressed by Suns—alone—
It is the gift of Screws—

5   The General Rose—decay—
But this—in Lady's Drawer
Make Summer—When the Lady lie
In Ceaseless Rosemary—

[1]One's own self.

677

To be alive—is Power—
Existence—in itself—
Without a further function—
Omnipotence—Enough—

5   To be alive—and Will!
'Tis able as a God—
The Maker—of Ourselves—be what—
Such being Finitude!

679

Conscious am I in my Chamber,
Of a shapeless friend—
He doth not attest by Posture—
Nor Confirm—by Word—

5   Neither Place—need I present Him—
Fitter Courtesy
Hospitable intuition
Of His Company—

Presence—is His furthest license—
10 Neither He to Me
Nor Myself to Him—by Accent—
Forfeit Probity—

Weariness of Him, were quainter
Than Monotony
15 Knew a Particle—of Space's
Vast Society—[1]

Neither if He visit Other—
Do He dwell—or Nay—know I—
But Instinct esteem Him
20 Immortality—

[1]Paraphrase: Quainter than if a particle knew monotony in the vast society of space.

712

Because I could not stop for Death—
He kindly stopped for me—
The Carriage held but just Ourselves—
And Immortality.

5   We slowly drove—He knew no haste
And I had put away
My labor and my leisure too,
For His Civility—

We passed the School, where Children strove
10   At Recess—in the Ring—
We passed the Fields of Gazing Grain—
We passed the Setting Sun—

Or rather—He passed Us—
The Dews drew quivering and chill—
15   For only Gossamer, my Gown—
My Tippet—only Tulle—[1]

We paused before a House that seemed
A Swelling of the Ground—
The Roof was scarcely visible—
20   The Cornice—in the Ground—[2]

Since then—'tis Centuries—and yet
Feels shorter than the Day
I first surmised the Horses' Heads
Were toward Eternity—

745

Renunciation—is a piercing Virtue—
The letting go
A Presence—for an Expectation—
Not now—
5   The putting out of Eyes—

[1] A tippet is a long covering for the shoulders, like a stole; tulle is a net veil.
[2] Variant in the manuscript: but a mound.

Just Sunrise—[1]
Lest Day—
Day's Great Progenitor—
Outvie[2]
10 Renunciation—is the Choosing
Against itself—
Itself to justify
Unto itself—
When larger function—
15 Make that appear—
Smaller—that Covered[3] Vision—Here—

754

My Life had stood—a Loaded Gun—
In Corners—till a Day
The Owner passed—identified—
And carried Me away—

5 And now We roam in Sovereign Woods—
And now We hunt the Doe—
And every time I speak for Him—
The Mountains straight reply—

And do I smile, such cordial light
10 Upon the Valley glow—
It is as a Vesuvian face[1]
Had let its pleasure through—

And when at Night—Our good Day done—
I guard My Master's Head—
15 'Tis better than the Eider-Duck's
Deep Pillow—to have shared—

To foe of His—I'm deadly foe—
None stir the second time—

[1]Just at sunrise.
[2]Variants in manuscript: outshow, outglow.
[3]Variants: flooded, sated.

[1]Mount Vesuvius is a volcano near Naples, Italy.

On whom I lay a Yellow Eye—
20　Or an emphatic Thumb—

Though I than He—may longer live
He longer must—than I—
For I have but the power to kill,
Without—the power[2] to die—

798

She staked her Feathers—Gained an Arc—
Debated—Rose again—
This time—beyond the estimate
Of Envy, or of Men—

5　And now, among Circumference—
Her steady Boat be seen—
At home—among the Billows—As
The Bough where she was born—

802

Time feels so vast that were it not
For an Eternity—
I fear me this Circumference
Engross my Finity—

5　To His exclusion, who prepare
By Processes[1] of Size
For the Stupendous Vision[2]
Of His diameters—

[2]Variant: Art.

---

[1]Variants: Rudiments, Prefaces.
[2]Variant: Volume.

865

He outstripped Time with but a Bout,
He outstripped Stars and Sun
And then, unjaded, challenged God
In presence of the Throne.

5 And He and He in mighty List
Unto this present, run,
The larger Glory for the less
A just sufficient Ring.

883

The Poets light but Lamps—
Themselves—go out—
The Wicks they stimulate—
If vital Light

5 Inhere as do the Suns—
Each Age a Lens
Disseminating their
Circumference—

889

Crisis is a Hair
Toward which the forces creep
Past which forces retrograde
If it come in sleep

5 To suspend the Breath
Is the most we can
Ignorant is it Life or Death
Nicely balancing.

Let an instant push
10 Or an Atom press

Or a Circle hesitate
In Circumference

It—may jolt the Hand
That adjusts the Hair
15 That secures Eternity
From presenting—Here—

967

Pain—expands the Time—
Ages coil within
The minute Circumference
Of a single Brain—

5   Pain contracts—the Time—
Occupied with Shot
Gammuts[1] of Eternities
Are as they were not—

986

A narrow Fellow in the Grass
Occasionally rides—
You may have met Him—did you not
His notice sudden is—

5   The Grass divides as with a Comb—
A spotted shaft is seen—
And then it closes at your feet
And opens further on—

He likes a Boggy Acre
10 A Floor too cool for Corn—
Yet when a Boy, and Barefoot—
I more than once at Noon
Have passed, I thought, a Whip lash
Unbraiding in the Sun

[1]Gamuts.

15 When stooping to secure it
It wrinkled, and was gone—

Several of Nature's People
I know, and they know me—
I feel for them a transport
20 Of cordiality—

But never met this Fellow
Attended, or alone
Without a tighter breathing
And Zero at the Bone—

1072

Title divine—is mine!
The Wife—without the Sign!
Acute Degree—conferred on me—
Empress of Calvary!
5 Royal—all but the Crown!
Betrothed—without the swoon
God sends us Women—
When you—hold—Garnet to Garnet—
Gold—to Gold—
10 Born—Bridalled—Shrouded
In a Day—
Tri Victory—
"My Husband"—women say—
Stroking the Melody—
15 Is *this*—the way?

1090

I am afraid to own a Body—
I am afraid to own a Soul—
Profound—precarious Property—
Possession, not optional—

5   Double Estate—entailed[1] at pleasure
Upon an unsuspecting Heir—
Duke in a moment of Deathlessness
And God, for a Frontier.

1129

Tell all the Truth but tell it slant—
Success in Circuit lies
Too bright for our infirm Delight
The Truth's superb surprise
5   As Lightning to the Children eased
With explanation kind
The Truth must dazzle gradually
Or every man be blind—

1138

A Spider sewed at Night
Without a Light
Upon an Arc of White.

If Ruff it was of Dame
5   Or Shroud of Gnome
Himself himself inform.[1]

Of Immortality
His Strategy
Was Physiognomy.

---

[1]Inherited through a specified line of succession.

---

[1]Informs, in the sense of "gives information to," and also of "gives form to,"
"is the formative and life-giving principle of."

1224

Like Trains of Cars on Tracks of Plush
I hear the level Bee—
A Jar across the Flowers goes[1]
Their Velvet Masonry

5 Withstands until the sweet Assault
Their Chivalry consumes—
While He, victorious tilts away
To vanquish other Blooms.

1275

The Spider as an Artist
Has never been employed—
Though his surpassing Merit
Is freely certified

5 By every Broom and Bridget
Throughout a Christian Land—
Neglected Son of Genius
I take thee by the Hand—

1343

A single Clover Plank
Was all that saved a Bee
A Bee I personally knew
From sinking in the sky—

5 'Twixt Firmament above
And Firmament below
The Billows of Circumference
Were sweeping him away—

[1]There would normally be a period here.

The idly swaying Plank
10 Responsible to nought
A sudden Freight of Wind assumed
And Bumble Bee was not—

This harrowing event
Transpiring in the Grass
15 Did not so much as wring from him
A wandering "Alas"—

1433

How brittle are the Piers
On which our Faith doth tread—
No Bridge below doth totter so—
Yet none hath such a Crowd.

5 It is as old as God—
Indeed—'twas built by him—
He sent his Son to test the Plank,
And he pronounced it firm.

1461

"Heavenly Father"—take to thee
The supreme iniquity
Fashioned by thy candid Hand
In a moment contraband—
5 Though to trust us—seem to us
More respectful—"We Are Dust"—
We apologize to thee
For thine own Duplicity—

1620

Circumference thou Bride of Awe
Possessing thou shalt be
Possessed by every hallowed Knight
That dares to covet thee[1]

1651

A Word made Flesh is seldom
And tremblingly partook
Nor then perhaps reported
But have I not mistook
5   Each one of us has tasted
With ecstasies of stealth
The very food debated
To our specific strength—

A Word that breathes distinctly
10   Has not the power to die
Cohesive as the Spirit
It may expire if He—
"Made Flesh and dwelt among us[1]
Could condescension be
15   Like this consent of Language
This loved Philology

[1]Variant line: That bends a Knee to thee.

[1]The description of the Incarnation of the Word of God into the body of Jesus in John 1:14. Here the closing quotation marks are omitted.

Sidney Lanier (1842–1881)

Born in Macon, Georgia, of good Virginia stock (and further back of royal musicians in the Stuart courts), Lanier thought ambitiously of a career in both music and literature when he graduated from now extinct Oglethorpe College in 1860. The next year he enlisted to fight for the Confederacy, fought in several battles, and was captured as captain of a blockade-running vessel in 1864. Four months in prison—the basis for his novel *Tiger Lilies* (1867)—made him the more susceptible to the consumption that ran in both sides of the family and killed his mother; in fact, the rest of his life was a strenuous attempt to stave off death. He married Mary Day in 1867, supported his growing family by a series of jobs, and moved to Baltimore in search of a more healthful climate.

Lanier played many instruments and studied music theory, just as he studied English poetry for his own verses. In 1873 he became first flutist of the Peabody Symphony in Baltimore and in 1879 was appointed lecturer at Johns Hopkins University. "Corn" and "The Symphony" established his fame when they appeared in 1875; both attacked the corruptive force of commerce and money in favor of an agrarian-chivalric ideal. Lanier admired the verse of his fellow-Southerner Poe and worked out Poe's correlation of poetry and music, "The Rationale of Verse," to its final extreme in *The Science of English Verse* (1880), which set up rigorous rules for prosody on the assumption that verse and music were both melodic lines made up of bars (feet) controlled not only by stress but by duration of note (syllable). The pieces written after *Poems* (1877) try to implement the theory fully in rhythm and tone-color. Sometimes Lanier's poems sound like Poe, Tennyson, and Swinburne compounded (or confounded), and the self-intoxicated straining for the diffuse effect tend to fuzz over meaning and dislocate sound from sense. However, Lanier's conviction of his genius was matched by contemporary admiration; Thomas Wentworth Higginson hailed him as "the Sir Galahad among our American poets." And his very excesses indicate his effort to make language express the inexpressible rhapsody of his religious passion.

TEXT

Lanier, Sidney. *The Centennial Edition of the Works of Sidney Lanier.* Ed. Charles R. Anderson *et al.* Baltimore: Johns Hopkins Press, 1945.

THE MARSHES OF GLYNN[1]

Glooms of the live-oaks, beautiful-braided and woven
With intricate shades of the vines that myriad-cloven
    Clamber the forks of the multiform boughs,—
        Emerald twilights,—
        Virginal shy lights,
Wrought of the leaves to allure to the whisper of vows,
When lovers pace timidly down through the green colonnades
Of the dim sweet woods, of the dear dark woods,
    Of the heavenly woods and glades,
That run to the radiant marginal sand-beach within
      The wide sea-marshes of Glynn;—

Beautiful glooms, soft dusks in the noon-day fire,—
Wildwood privacies, closets of lone desire,
Chamber from chamber parted with wavering arras of leaves,—
Cells for the passionate pleasure of prayer to the soul that grieves,
Pure with a sense of the passing of saints through the wood,
Cool for the dutiful weighing of ill with good;—

O braided dusks of the oak and woven shades of the vine,
While the riotous noon-day sun of the June-day long did shine
Ye held me fast in your heart and I held you fast in mine;
But now when the noon is no more, and riot is rest,
And the sun is a-wait at the ponderous gate of the West,
And the slant yellow beam down the wood-aisle doth seem
Like a lane into heaven that leads from a dream,—
Ay, now, when my soul all day hath drunken the soul of the oak,
And my heart is at ease from men, and the wearisome sound of the
       stroke
    Of the scythe of time and the trowel of trade is low,
     And belief overmasters doubt, and I know that I know,
    And my spirit is grown to a lordly great compass within,
That the length and the breadth and the sweep of the marshes of
       Glynn
Will work me no fear like the fear they have wrought me of yore
When length was fatigue, and when breadth was but bitterness sore,
And when terror and shrinking and dreary unnamable pain
Drew over me out of the merciless miles of the plain,—

[1]Glynn County on the coast of Georgia.

35 Oh, now, unafraid, I am fain to face
　　The vast sweet visage of space.
　To the edge of the wood I am drawn, I am drawn,
　Where the gray beach glimmering runs, as a belt of the dawn,
　　For a mete and a mark
40　　　To the forest-dark:—
　　　　　So:
　Affable live-oak, leaning low,—
　Thus—with your favor—soft, with a reverent hand,
　(Not lightly touching your person, Lord of the land!)
45 Bending your beauty aside, with a step I stand
　On the firm-packed sand,
　　　　Free
　By a world of marsh that borders a world of sea.
　　Sinuous southward and sinuous northward the shimmering band
50　　Of the sand-beach fastens the fringe of the marsh to the folds of
　　　the land.
　Inward and outward to northward and southward the beach-lines
　　　linger and curl
　As a silver-wrought garment that clings to and follows the firm
　　　sweet limbs of a girl.
　Vanishing, swerving, evermore curving again into sight,
　Softly the sand-beach wavers away to a dim gray looping of light.
55 And what if behind me to westward the wall of the woods stands
　　　high?
　The world lies east: how ample, the marsh and the sea and the sky!
　A league and a league of marsh-grass, waist-high, broad in the blade,
　Green, and all of a height, and unflecked with a light or a shade,
　Stretch leisurely off, in a pleasant plain,
60 To the terminal blue of the main.

　Oh, what is abroad in the marsh and the terminal sea?
　　Somehow my soul seems suddenly free
　From the weighing of fate and the sad discussion of sin,
　By the length and the breadth and the sweep of the marshes of
　　　Glynn.

65 Ye marshes, how candid and simple and nothing-withholding and
　　　free
　Ye publish yourselves to the sky and offer yourselves to the sea!
　Tolerant plains, that suffer the sea and the rains and the sun,
　Ye spread and span like the catholic man who hath mightily won
　God out of knowledge and good out of infinite pain
70 And sight out of blindness and purity out of a stain.

As the marsh-hen secretly builds on the watery sod,
Behold I will build me a nest on the greatness of God:
I will fly in the greatness of God as the marsh-hen flies
In the freedom that fills all the space 'twixt the marsh and the skies:
By so many roots as the marsh-grass sends in the sod
I will heartily lay me a-hold on the greatness of God:
Oh, like to the greatness of God is the greatness within
The range of the marshes, the liberal marshes of Glynn.

And the sea lends large, as the marsh: lo, out of his plenty the sea
Pours fast: full soon the time of the flood-tide must be:
Look how the grace of the sea doth go
About and about through the intricate channels that flow
     Here and there,
         Everywhere,
Till his waters have flooded the uttermost creeks and the low-lying
    lanes,
And the marsh is meshed with a million veins,
That like as with rosy and silvery essences flow
  In the rose-and-silver evening glow.
       Farewell, my lord Sun!
The creeks overflow: a thousand rivulets run
'Twixt the roots of the sod; the blades of the marsh-grass stir;
Passeth a hurrying sound of wings that westward whirr;
Passeth, and all is still; and the currents cease to run;
And the sea and the marsh are one.

How still the plains of the waters be!
The tide is in his ecstasy.
The tide is at his highest height:
     And it is night.

And now from the Vast of the Lord will the waters of sleep
Roll in on the souls of men,
But who will reveal to our waking ken
The forms that swim and the shapes that creep
     Under the waters of sleep?
And I would I could know what swimmeth below when the tide
    comes in
On the length and the breadth of the marvellous marshes of Glynn.

SUNRISE[1]

In my sleep I was fain of their fellowship, fain
   Of the live-oak, the marsh, and the main.
The little green leaves would not let me alone in my sleep;
Up-breathed from the marshes, a message of range and of sweep,
5   Interwoven with waftures of wild sea-liberties, drifting,
     Came through the lapped leaves sifting, sifting,
       Came to the gates of sleep.
Then my thoughts, in the dark of the dungeon-keep
Of the Castle of Captives hid in the City of Sleep,
10   Upstarted, by twos and by threes assembling:
     The gates of sleep fell a-trembling
Like as the lips of a lady that forth falter *yes*,
     Shaken with happiness:
     The gates of sleep stood wide.

15   I have waked, I have come, my beloved! I might not abide:
I have come ere the dawn, O beloved, my live-oaks, to hide
     In your gospelling glooms,—to be
As a lover in heaven, the marsh my marsh and the sea my sea.

Tell me, sweet burly-bark'd, man-bodied Tree
20   That mine arms in the dark are embracing, dost know
From what fount are these tears at thy feet which flow?
They rise not from reason, but deeper inconsequent deeps.
     Reason's not one that weeps.
     What logic of greeting lies
25   Betwixt dear over-beautiful trees and the rain of the eyes?

O cunning green leaves, little masters! like as ye gloss
All the dull-tissued dark with your luminous darks that emboss
The vague blackness of night into pattern and plan,
     So,
30   (But would I could know, but would I could know,)
With your question embroid'ring the dark of the question of man,—
So, with your silences purfling[2] this silence of man
While his cry to the dead for some knowledge is under the ban,
     Under the ban,—
35   So, ye have wrought me

---

[1]Lanier's last completed poem, written in extreme weakness with a fever of 104°.
[2]Decorating the edge.

Designs on the night of our knowledge,—yea, ye have taught me,
     So,
That haply we know somewhat more than we know.

    Ye lispers, whisperers, singers in storms,
40   Ye consciences murmuring faiths under forms,
    Ye ministers meet for each passion that grieves,
    Friendly, sisterly, sweetheart leaves,
Oh, rain me down from your darks that contain me
Wisdoms ye winnow from winds that pain me,—
45 Sift down tremors of sweet-within-sweet
That advise me of more than they bring,—repeat
Me the woods-smell that swiftly but now brought breath
From the heaven-side bank of the river of death,—
    Teach me the terms of silence,—preach me
50   The passion of patience,—sift me,—impeach me,—
      And there, oh there
As you hang with your myriad palms upturned in the air,
      Pray me a myriad prayer.

    My gossip, the owl,—is it thou
55 That out of the leaves of the low-hanging bough,
    As I pass to the beach, art stirred?
     Dumb woods, have ye uttered a bird?

        •

Reverend Marsh, low-couched along the sea,
    Old chemist, rapt in alchemy,[3]
60   Distilling silence,—lo,
That which our father-age had died to know—
    The menstruum[4] that dissolves all matter—thou
Hast found it: for this silence, filling now
The globéd clarity of receiving space,
65 This solves us all: man, matter, doubt, disgrace,
Death, love, sin, sanity,
Must in yon silence' clear solution lie.
Too clear! that crystal nothing who'll peruse?
The blackest night could bring us brighter news.
70 Yet precious qualities of silence haunt
Round these vast margins, ministrant.

---

[3]Science or pseudo-science, part chemistry and part magic, that sought to turn
baser metals into gold and to distill material substances into spiritual.
[4]A solvent, originally connected with the alchemical solvent, that would trans-
mute or spiritualize lower substances into higher.

Oh, if thy soul's at latter gasp for space,
With trying to breathe no bigger than thy race
Just to be fellow'd, when that thou hast found
75   No man with room, or grace enough of bound
To entertain that New thou tell'st, thou art,—
'Tis here, 'tis here thou canst unhand thy heart
And breathe it free, and breathe it free,
By rangy marsh, in lone sea-liberty.

80   The tide's at full: the marsh with flooded streams
Glimmers, a limpid labyrinth of dreams.
Each winding creek in grave entrancement lies
A rhapsody of morning-stars. The skies
Shine scant with one forked galaxy,—
85   The marsh brags ten: looped on his breast they lie.

Oh, what if a sound should be made!
Oh, what if a bound should be laid
To this bow-and-string tension of beauty and silence a-spring,—
To the bend of beauty the bow, or the hold of silence the string!
90   I fear me, I fear me yon dome of diaphanous gleam
Will break as a bubble o'er-blown in a dream,—
Yon dome of too-tenuous tissues of space and of night,
Over-weighted with stars, over-freighted with light,
Over-sated with beauty and silence, will seem
95   But a bubble that broke in a dream,
If a bound of degree to this grace be laid,
    Or a sound or a motion made.

But no: it is made: list![5] somewhere,—mystery, where?
          In the leaves? in the air?
100   In my heart? is a motion made:
'Tis a motion of dawn, like a flicker of shade on shade.
In the leaves 'tis palpable: low multitudinous stirring
Upwinds through the woods; the little ones, softly conferring,
Have settled my lord's to be looked for; so; they are still;
105   But the air and my heart and the earth are a-thrill,—
And look where the wild duck sails round the bend of the river,—
    And look where a passionate shiver
    Expectant is bending the blades
Of the marsh-grass in serial shimmers and shades,—
110   And invisible wings, fast fleeting, fast fleeting,
          Are beating

[5]Listen.

The dark overhead as my heart beats,— and steady and free
Is the ebb-tide flowing from marsh to sea—
     (Run home, little streams,
     With your lapfulls of stars and dreams),—
And a sailor unseen is hoisting a-peak,
For list, down the inshore curve of the creek
     How merrily flutters the sail,—
And lo, in the East! Will the East unveil?
The East is unveiled, the East hath confessed
A flush: 'tis dead; 'tis alive; 'tis dead, ere the West
Was aware of it: nay, 'tis abiding, 'tis unwithdrawn:
     Have a care, sweet Heaven! 'Tis Dawn.

Now a dream of a flame through that dream of a flush is up-rolled:
     To the zenith ascending, a dome of undazzling gold
Is builded, in shape as a bee-hive, from out of the sea:
The hive is of gold undazzling, but oh, the Bee,
     The star-fed Bee, the build-fire Bee,
     Of dazzling gold is the great Sun-Bee
That shall flash from the hive-hole over the sea.

     Yet now the dew-drop, now the morning gray,
     Shall live their little lucid sober day
     Ere with the sun their souls exhale away.
Now in each pettiest personal sphere of dew
The summ'd morn shines complete as in the blue
Big dew-drop of all heaven: with these lit shrines
O 'er-silvered to the farthest sea-confines,
The sacramental marsh one pious plain
Of worship lies. Peace to the ante-reign[6]
Of Mary Morning, blissful mother mild,
Minded of nought but peace, and of a child.

Not slower than Majesty moves, for a mean and a measure
Of motion,—not faster than dateless Olympian[7] leisure
Might pace with unblown ample garments from pleasure to
     pleasure,—
The wave-serrate[8] sea-rim sinks unjarring, unreeling,
     Forever revealing, revealing, revealing,
Edgewise, bladewise, halfwise, wholewise,—'tis done!
     Good-morrow, lord Sun!

[6]The sunrise is a foreshadowing of the reign of the Madonna and the Christ
Child.
[7]The Greek gods lived on Mount Olympus.
[8]Notched, like teeth, with waves.

With several voice, with ascription one,
150   The woods and the marsh and the sea and my soul
Unto thee, whence the glittering stream of all morrows doth roll,
Cry good and past-good and most heavenly morrow, lord Sun.

O Artisan born in the purple,—Workman Heat,—
Parter of passionate atoms that travail to meet
155   And be mixed in the death-cold oneness,—innermost Guest
At the marriage of elements,—fellow of publicans,—blest
King in the blouse of flame, that loiterest o'er
The idle skies yet laborest fast evermore,—
Thou, in the fine forge-thunder, thou, in the beat
160   Of the heart of a man, thou Motive,—Laborer Heat:
Yea, Artist, thou, of whose art yon sea's all news,
With his inshore greens and manifold mid-sea blues,
Pearl-glint, shell-tint, ancientest perfectest hues
Ever shaming the maidens,—lily and rose
165   Confess thee, and each mild flame that glows
In the clarified virginal bosoms of stones that shine,
                    It is thine, it is thine:

Thou chemist of storms, whether driving the winds a-swirl
Or a-flicker the subtiler essences polar that whirl
170   In the magnet earth,[9]—yea, thou with a storm for a heart,
Rent with debate, many-spotted with question, part
From part oft sundered, yet ever a globéd light,
Yet ever the artist, ever more large and bright
That the eye of a man may avail of:—manifold One,
175   I must pass from thy face, I must pass from the face of the Sun:
Old Want is awake and agog, every wrinkle a-frown;
The worker must pass to his work in the terrible town:
But I fear not, nay, and I fear not the things to be done;
        I am strong with the strength of my lord the Sun:
180   How dark, how dark soever the race that must needs be run,
                    I am lit with the Sun.

Oh, never the mast-high run of the seas
            Of traffic shall hide thee,
Never the hell-colored smoke of the factories
185   Hide thee,

---

[9]The sun is seen as an alchemist controlling the motions of the winds and the rarefied essences in the earth's center, whose oppositions create the "magnetic" field and set the earth turning.

Never the reck of the time's fen-politics
        Hide thee,
And ever my heart through the night shall with knowledge abide
    thee,
And ever by day shall my spirit, as one that hath tried thee,
190   Labor, at leisure, in art,—till yonder beside thee
        My soul shall float, friend Sun,
        The day being done.

Stephen Crane (1871–1900)

The son of a Methodist minister in Newark, New Jersey, Crane early came to scorn his father's religion as based on fear and intimidation. He attended various colleges without graduating. Working as a journalist in New York, Crane wrote *The Red Badge of Courage* (1895), an imaginary re-creation of a young soldier's experience in the Civil War. The book was so successful that it brought the republication of the previously privately printed *Maggie: A Girl of the Streets*, a realistic account of life in the Bowery. It is said that Crane wrote the poems in *The Black Riders* (1895) after hearing Howells read from the newly published verses of Emily Dickinson.

On newspaper assignments Crane went to the West, Mexico, Cuba, Greece, and finally settled in England with his wife in a fourteenth-century Sussex manor house called Brede Place. When death by consumption brought his short life to a close, many of the leading literary figures on both sides of the Atlantic recognized that in those few years he had made exciting technical experiments in fiction and verse. Besides other novels, stories, and sketches, he published a second book of poems, *War Is Kind* (1899). His terse, economical manner of expressing an ironic view of man's hard lot in an indifferent universe does not hide the vulnerability, even sentimentality, of his tender heart.

TEXT

Crane, Stephen. *The Work of Stephen Crane.* Ed. Wilson Follett. New York: Russell and Russell, 1963.

REFERENCE

Beer, Thomas. *Stephen Crane: A Study in American Letters.* London: Heinemann, 1924.

Berryman, John. *Stephen Crane.* Cleveland: World Publishing Co., 1950, 1962.

Hoffman, Daniel. *The Poetry of Stephen Crane.* New York: Columbia University Press, 1957.

Stallman, R. W. *Stephen Crane: A Biography.* New York: G. Braziller, 1968.

In the desert
I saw a creature, naked, bestial,
Who, squatting upon the ground,
Held his heart in his hands,
5   And ate of it.
I said, "Is it good, friend?"
"It is bitter—bitter," he answered;
"But I like it
Because it is bitter,
10   And because it is my heart."

There was, before me,
Mile upon mile
Of snow, ice, burning sand.
And yet I could look beyond all this,
5   To a place of infinite beauty;
And I could see the loveliness of her
Who walked in the shade of the trees.
When I gazed,
All was lost
10   But this place of beauty and her.
When I gazed,
And in my gazing, desired,
Then came again
Mile upon mile
15   Of snow, ice, burning sand.

I saw a man pursuing the horizon;
Round and round they sped.
I was disturbed at this;
I accosted the man.
5   "It is futile," I said,
"You can never——"

"You lie," he cried,
And ran on.

A youth in apparel that glittered
Went to walk in a grim forest.
There he met an assassin
Attired all in garb of old days;
5 He, scowling through the thickets,
And dagger poised quivering,
Rushed upon the youth.
"Sir," said this latter,
"I am enchanted, believe me,
10 To die, thus,
In this medieval fashion,
According to the best legends;
Ah, what joy!"
Then took he the wound, smiling,
15 And died, content.

A man saw a ball of gold in the sky;
He climbed for it,
And eventually he achieved it—
It was clay.

5 Now this is the strange part:
When the man went to the earth
And looked again,
Lo, there was the ball of gold.
Now this is the strange part:
10 It was a ball of gold.
Ay, by the heavens, it was a ball of gold.

Many red devils ran from my heart
And out upon the page.
They were so tiny
The pen could mash them.
5 And many struggled in the ink.
It was strange
To write in this red muck
Of things from my heart.

Once, I knew a fine song
—It is true, believe me—
It was all of birds,
And I held them in a basket;
5　When I opened the wicket,
Heavens! they all flew away.
I cried, "Come back, little thoughts!"
But they only laughed.
They flew on
10　Until they were as sand
Thrown between me and the sky.

God lay dead in heaven;
Angels sang the hymn of the end;
Purple winds went moaning,
Their wings drip-dripping
5　With blood
That fell upon the earth.
It, groaning thing,
Turned black and sank.
Then from the far caverns
10　Of dead sins
Came monsters, livid with desire.
They fought,
Wrangled over the world,
A morsel.
15　But of all sadness this was sad—
A woman's arms tried to shield
The head of a sleeping man
From the jaws of the final beast.

WAR IS KIND

Do not weep, maiden, for war is kind.
Because your lover threw wild hands toward the sky
And the affrighted steed ran on alone,
Do not weep.
5 War is kind.

Hoarse, booming drums of the regiment,
Little souls who thirst for fight,
These men were born to drill and die.
The unexplained glory flies above them,
10 Great is the battle-god, great, and his kingdom—
A field where a thousand corpses lie.

Do not weep, babe, for war is kind.
Because your father tumbled in the yellow trenches,
Raged at his breast, gulped and died,
15 Do not weep.
War is kind.

Swift blazing flag of the regiment,
Eagle with crest of red and gold,
These men were born to drill and die.
20 Point for them the virtue of slaughter,
Make plain to them the excellence of killing
And a field where a thousand corpses lie.

Mother whose heart hung humble as a button
On the bright splendid shroud of your son,
25 Do not weep.
War is kind.

Fast rode the knight
With spurs, hot and reeking,
Ever waving an eager sword,
"To save my lady!"
5 Fast rode the knight,
And leaped from saddle to war.

Men of steel flickered and gleamed
Like riot of silver lights,
And the gold of the knight's good banner
10   Still waved on a castle wall.

●

A horse,
Blowing, staggering, bloody thing,
Forgotten at foot of castle wall.
A horse
15   Dead at foot of castle wall.

The wayfarer,
Perceiving the pathway to truth,
Was struck with astonishment.
It was thickly grown with weeds.
5   "Ha," he said,
"I see that none has passed here
In a long time."
Later he saw that each weed
Was a singular knife.
10   "Well," he mumbled at last,
"Doubtless there are other roads."

A slant of sun on dull brown walls,
A forgotten sky of bashful blue.

Toward God a mighty hymn,
A song of collisions and cries,
5   Rumbling wheels, hoof-beats, bells,
Welcomes, farewells, love-calls, final moans,
Voices of joy, idiocy, warning, despair,
The unknown appeals of brutes,
The chanting of flowers,
10   The screams of cut trees,
The senseless babble of hens and wise men—
A cluttered incoherency that says at the stars:
"O God, save us!"

There was a man with tongue of wood
Who essayed to sing,
And in truth it was lamentable.
But there was one who heard
5   The clip-clapper of his tongue of wood
And knew what the man
Wished to sing,
And with that the singer was content.

The impact of a dollar upon the heart
Smiles warm red light,
Sweeping from the hearth rosily upon the white table,
With the hanging cool velvet shadows
5   Moving softly upon the door.

The impact of a million dollars
Is a crash of flunkeys,
And yawning emblems of Persia
Cheeked against oak, France and a sabre,
10   The outcry of old beauty
Whored by pimping merchants
To submission before wine and chatter.
Silly rich peasants stamp the carpets of men,
Dead men who dreamed fragrance and light
15   Into their woof, their lives;
The rug of an honest bear
Under the feet of a cryptic slave
Who speaks always of baubles,
Forgetting state, multitude, work, and state,
20   Champing and mouthing of hats,
Making ratful squeak of hats,
Hats.

A man said to the universe:
"Sir, I exist!"
"However," replied the universe,
"The fact has not created in me
5 A sense of obligation."

"Incantation," oil painting, 1946, by Charles Sheeler (1883–1965). (Courtesy of the Collections of The Brooklyn Museum, Ella C. and John B. Woodward Memorial Funds)

Part Three

THE AMERICAN POETIC RENAISSANCE

During the years just before and after World War I, the following poets published their first volumes of verse: Vachel Lindsay, Robert Frost, Ezra Pound, T. S. Eliot, William Carlos Williams, Carl Sandburg, Edgar Lee Masters, H. D. (Hilda Doolittle), Amy Lowell, Robinson Jeffers, Marianne Moore, John Crowe Ransom, Conrad Aiken, Edna St. Vincent Millay, Archibald MacLeish, E. E. Cummings, Yvor Winters; by the end of the twenties Hart Crane and Allen Tate had published books as well. What makes this an astonishing manifestation of imaginative energy is not just the quantity, but the unmistakable originality of their writing. Moreover, poetry was not confined to the Atlantic seaboard in New York and Boston; it had spanned the continent at last, and most regions found poetic expression: New England in Edwin Arlington Robinson, Frost, and the early Eliot; the metropolitan East in Williams, Cummings, and Hart Crane; the Midwest in Sandburg, Lindsay, and Masters; the Pacific West in Jeffers and Winters; the South in Ransom and Tate.

There was no single program or movement, but a host of poets with strong notions about their practice. The New Englanders and the Southerners were, as might be expected, the most traditional. Frost said that he and Robinson "stayed content with the old-fashioned way to be new," avoiding faddish unintelligibility and revitalizing the tested resources of language with modern rhythms, locutions, themes, and attitudes. The skill lay in making the intonations of the individual voice shape the metered line without violating it; Frost liked to compare free verse to playing tennis without a net. After study at Harvard and the Sorbonne, Eliot made a more intellectual argument for tradition, insisting that only a recovery of the past provided the ground for growth and that the individual talent could mature only within the living tradition that it augmented and modified. So conservative was the group around Ransom at Vanderbilt that Tate's advocacy of Eliot during the early twenties seemed at first too "modern."

Meanwhile Sandburg, Lindsay, and Masters had extended Whitman's spirit to the Midwest, and their popularity, along with Harriet Monroe's *Poetry* magazine, marked the American heartland on the literary map. Whitman was a touchstone for all these new poets: the image of the American poet to be followed or resisted. Expounding the sources of Pound's experiments in 1917, Eliot indicated the Latin and French poets and declared pointedly: "Whitman is certainly not an influence; there is not a trace of him anywhere; Whitman and Mr. Pound are antipodean to each other." Eliot was at pains to contend that *vers libre*, such as he and Pound were writing, was not to be confused with free verse; *vers libre* was as painstakingly written as meter, and its interest lay in the tension between the underlying metrical pattern and the deliberate departures from it. For Eliot, as for others in Pound's London circle, poetry had to be hard, dry, and objective in order to wipe out the last vestiges of the fuzziness and stickiness that made the Romantics "palpitating Narcissi."

In Pound's mind, too, Whitman was the rub: "his crudity is an exceeding great stench," yet like Chaucer and Dante he was "the first great man to write in the language of his people." The American poet was, like it or not, a descendant of Whitman, but Pound took it as his mission "to drive Whitman into the old world . . . and to scourge America with all the old beauty" in order to make way for a cultivated "American Renaissance." His imitation of European and Chinese poetry was his training and education, and he expunged the late-Romantic tone of his own first verses by defining his goals as Imagism: "1. Direct treatment of the 'thing' whether subjective or objective. 2. To use absolutely no word that does not contribute to the presentation. 3. As regarding rhythm: to compose in the sequence of the musical phrase, not in the sequence of a metronome." There were developments parallel to Imagism: Eliot's symbolism; Williams' "objectivism"; Marianne Moore's visual imagination and intricate syllabics; H. D.'s chiseled verse. Pound himself found Imagism static and constricting almost as soon as he defined it; an Image "presents an intellectual and emotional complex in an instant of time," and poetry needed movement and action. Consequently Pound found his way to *The Cantos* through Wyndham Lewis' "Vorticism," which viewed art as the expression of intellectual and emotional energy, and through the ideogrammic language of the Chinese, which depicted ideas in concrete action-pictures.

In retrospect we can see that, despite the close association between Eliot and Pound just before and after 1920, they were really moving in different directions. The differences between *Four Quartets* and *The Cantos* make the point dramatically, and Pound admitted it when he said after Eliot's death: "His was the true Dantescan voice." Pound remained more indomitably American: *The Chinese Written Character as a Medium for Poetry* reads like a reformulation of the "Language" chapter of Emerson's *Nature*, and *The Cantos*, for all the Greek and Chinese and for all the experiments in theme and technique, is the closest analogue to *Leaves of Grass* in twentieth-century poetry, exemplifying the organicism it envisions.

This connection of *The Cantos* with *Leaves of Grass* links Pound more closely with Whitman than Pound publicly admitted or recognized. As Pound and Williams sparred with each other over the years about the commitments of the American poet, Pound saw Williams as electing the Whitmanian position, and it is true that Williams' allegiances are to America as it is rather than as it might be. Williams placed himself in his home town and made poems of those realities, working out a "variable foot" for the rhythms of American speech and projecting in *Paterson* a localized epic in open form. Williams called *Leaves of Grass* "a book as important as we are likely to see in the next thousand years," and his work, as Robert Lowell observed, represents "Whitman's America, grown pathetic and tragic, brutalized by inequality, disorganized by industrial chaos, and faced with annihilation"—but also sustained finally, as Lowell does not say, by Williams' underlying sense of ongoing process.

The reaction against organic form during this century centered in Eliot's and Wallace Stevens' different brands of aestheticism: both poets were adumbrated by Poe and the French *symbolistes*, and both tended to conceive of the art object as detached from the flux and suspended in its own immutability. Eliot's attitudes underwent substantial revision during his career: he began by speaking of the art object as "autotelic," its own end, and by postulating an "ideal order" among works of art; he ended by saying that while the formal precision of art was one way to grasp the pattern of time, in the long run "the poetry does not matter" in itself when one has gone beyond time into eternity. But, early and late, Eliot saw the possibility of form in some dimension beyond nature, apprehensible only in scattered incarnations as works of art or moments of revelation. Stevens was naturalistic where Eliot was religious: he conceived of the imagination as inventing the fictions necessary to transcend the violence of reality, and at times he assumed a total disjunction between the world and the "mundo" made by the imagination in the poem. Archibald MacLeish's "Ars Poetica" summed up the aesthetic temper of the twenties with the dictum that "a poem should not mean/ but be"; detached from "truth," it is not a gloss on something else but is itself, hypostatized in its own sealed perfection. Even poets who resisted the tendency to separate art from life had difficulty finding their way back to a mode of correspondence with nature. Frost rejected aestheticism like Stevens' for a struggle with the ambiguous question that nature proposes, but to that end he depended on form as "a momentary stay against confusion." In *The Bridge* Hart Crane joined hands with Whitman to defeat the pessimism of Eliot's *The Waste Land*, but the ecstatic sections of the poem suggest the *sym-*

boliste technique of Rimbaud and Baudelaire more than they resemble *Leaves of Grass.*

The New Criticism provided the most trenchant exposition of the poem as an encapsulated and self-contained entity, and demonstrated a methodology for textual analysis based on that premise. The term "New Criticism" was John Crowe Ransom's, but he was only promulgating the principles shared with a close group of associates at Vanderbilt, which came to include Allen Tate and Robert Penn Warren. They opposed Romantic subjectivity and idealism and insisted that poetry was, in Ransom's words, "the act of an adult mind" to contrive poems whose structure distanced and contained the tensions and divisions of a fallen and fractured existence. The poem registered its meaning as poem on its own terms and could not be reduced to sociology or politics or scholarship or paraphrase; the critic who recognized the irreducible integrity of the poem scrutinized the techniques and devices that made this design of words work. Tate carried the point about as far as it could go: "We know the particular poem, not what it says that we can restate. In a manner of speaking, the poem is its own knower, neither poet nor reader knowing anything that the poem says apart from the words of the poem." Ransom cited I. A. Richards, Eliot, and Winters as approximations of the kind of critic he was calling for, but the New Criticism made its greatest impact through Ransom's circle and their students and disciples. They taught at many colleges and universities; wrote textbooks used on hundreds of other campuses; founded and edited journals such as the *Sewanee Review, The Kenyon Review* and *The Southern Review*; wrote essays and reviews for these and other journals, whose pages were filled with poems and stories reinforcing the premises of the New Criticism.

The result was to widen the opposition, always present in American poetry, between the formalists and the open-form poets. One group became increasingly identified with universities, and the other group became increasingly testy about the academic poet-critics who promulgated a canon that ignored them. This continuing dualism in American poetry is epitomized in the two poetic presences who dominated the poetic scene in California during the period. In the twenties Yvor Winters decided to abandon imagistic free verse and take his models from the English Renaissance. Thereafter he used his critical writing and his classes at Stanford to denounce the Romanticism whose pernicious effects, moral and aesthetic, blighted predecessors like Emerson and Whitman and most of his contemporaries. His own criterion was clear: "A poem is a statement in language about human experience; since language is conceptual in its nature, this statement will be more or less rational or at least apprehensible in rational terms, or else the medium will be violated and the poem weakened." Meanwhile, a short way down the coast, Robinson Jeffers was writing narratives to trace out the irrational impulses and the archetypal urges that sway man's behavior, and was celebrating in verse the inhuman mystery of creation into which man should submerge himself. The miles that separated the two poets were virtually absolute. Winters' *In Defense of Reason* contains a scathing attack on Jeffers because his writing was "loose, turgid, and careless" and because he was an anti-intellectual who "relies on his feelings alone and has no standard of criticism for them outside of themselves." From Jeffers there came no response, no mention of Winters in his letters; outside of and heedless of the academic community he continued to translate the rhythms of the unconscious and of nature into long free-verse lines. In this characteristic polarization the poets who emerged during the forties and after would find a major challenge and impetus.

Edwin Arlington Robinson (1869–1935)

Robinson was born in Head Tide, Maine, but grew up in Gardiner, the model for his Tilbury Town. After having to leave Harvard upon his father's death in 1893, Robinson remained in Gardiner until he moved to New York after his mother's death in 1896. He was a hermit in the metropolis, holding various jobs only long enough to allow him to go on writing poetry. After the first two volumes were published at Robinson's own expense, President Theodore Roosevelt helped get him a publisher and a job as customs inspector, which he left after a few years to devote himself wholly to poetry. He regularly spent his summers in the MacDowell colony in Peterboro, New Hampshire.

Some of Robinson's twenty-nine volumes are: *The Children of the Night* (1897), *The Man Against the Sky* (1916), *Merlin* (1917), *Launcelot* (1920), *The Man Who Died Twice* (1924), *Tristram* (1927), and *Talifer* (1933). He won his third Pulitzer Prize and some financial security with *Tristram*, which completed the Arthurian trilogy, but he was beset by loneliness, depression and a sense of failure. In his later years he wrote mostly long narratives in a strong blank verse, but he made his most lasting impression with the shorter lyric and dramatic poems in which melancholy is controlled by irony and wit. Robert Frost wrote in his introduction to the posthumous *King Jasper* (1935): "His theme was unhappiness, but his skill was as happy as it was playful . . . . We mourn, but with the qualification that, after all, his life was a revel in the felicities of language."

TEXT

Robinson, Edwin Arlington. *Collected Poems of Edwin Arlington Robinson*. New York: Macmillan, 1945.

REFERENCE

Barnard, Ellsworth. *Edwin Arlington Robinson: A Critical Study*. New York: Macmillan, 1952.

Hagedorn, Hermann. *Edwin Arlington Robinson: A Biography*. New York: Macmillan, 1938.

Neff, Emery. *Edwin Arlington Robinson*. New York: W. Sloane Associates, 1948.

Robinson, Edwin Arlington. *Selected Letters*. New York: Macmillan, 1940.

Winters, Yvor. *Edwin Arlington Robinson*. New York: New Directions, 1946, 1971.

LUKE HAVERGAL

Go to the western gate, Luke Havergal,
There where the vines cling crimson on the wall,
And in the twilight wait for what will come.
The leaves will whisper there of her, and some,
5   Like flying words, will strike you as they fall;
But go, and if you listen she will call.
Go the western gate, Luke Havergal—
Luke Havergal.

No, there is not a dawn in eastern skies
10 To rift the fiery night that's in your eyes;
But there, where western glooms are gathering,
The dark will end the dark, if anything;
God slays Himself with every leaf that flies,
And hell is more than half of paradise.
15 No, there is not a dawn in eastern skies—
In eastern skies.

Out of a grave I come to tell you this,
Out of a grave I come to quench the kiss
That flames upon your forehead with a glow
20 That blinds you to the way that you must go.
Yes, there is yet one way to where she is,
Bitter, but one that faith may never miss.
Out of a grave I come to tell you this—
To tell you this.

25 There is the western gate, Luke Havergal,
There are the crimson leaves upon the wall.
Go, for the winds are tearing them away,—
Nor think to riddle the dead words they say,
Nor any more to feel them as they fall;
30 But go, and if you trust her she will call.
There is the western gate, Luke Havergal—
Luke Havergal.

CLIFF KLINGENHAGEN

Cliff Klingenhagen had me in to dine
With him one day; and after soup and meat,
And all the other things there were to eat,
Cliff took two glasses and filled one with wine
5 And one with wormwood. Then, without a sign
For me to choose at all, he took the draught
Of bitterness himself, and lightly quaffed
It off, and said the other one was mine.

And when I asked him what the deuce he meant
10 By doing that, he only looked at me
And smiled, and said it was a way of his.
And though I know the fellow, I have spent
Long time a-wondering when I shall be
As happy as Cliff Klingenhagen is.

THE CLERKS

I did not think that I should find them there
When I came back again; but there they stood,
As in the days they dreamed of when young blood
Was in their cheeks and women called them fair.
5 Be sure, they met me with an ancient air,—
And yes, there was a shop-worn brotherhood
About them; but the men were just as good,
And just as human as they ever were.

And you that ache so much to be sublime,
10 And you that feed yourselves with your descent,
What comes of all your visions and your fears?
Poets and kings are but the clerks of Time,
Tiering[1] the same dull webs of discontent,
Clipping the same sad alnage[2] of the years.

[1] Arranging in rows.
[2] Measurement of length by the ell.

CREDO

I cannot find my way: there is no star
In all the shrouded heavens anywhere;
And there is not a whisper in the air
Of any living voice but one so far
5   That I can hear it only as a bar
Of lost, imperial music, played when fair
And angel fingers wove, and unaware,
Dead leaves to garlands where no roses are.

No, there is not a glimmer, nor a call,
10 For one that welcomes, welcomes when he fears,
The black and awful chaos of the night;
For through it all—above, beyond it all—
I know the far-sent message of the years,
I feel the coming glory of the Light.

MINIVER CHEEVY

Miniver Cheevy, child of scorn,
    Grew lean while he assailed the seasons;
He wept that he was ever born,
    And he had reasons.

5   Miniver loved the days of old
    When swords were bright and steeds were prancing;
The vision of a warrior bold
    Would set him dancing.

Miniver sighed for what was not,
10   And dreamed, and rested from his labors;
He dreamed of Thebes and Camelot,
    And Priam's neighbors.[1]

Miniver mourned the ripe renown
    That made so many a name so fragrant;
15 He mourned Romance, now on the town,
    And Art, a vagrant.

[1]The royal house of Cadmus in the Grecian city of Thebes; the court of King
Arthur at Camelot; King Priam of Troy.

Miniver loved the Medici,[2]
   Albeit he had never seen one;
He would have sinned incessantly
20   Could he have been one.

Miniver cursed the commonplace
   And eyed a khaki suit with loathing;
He missed the mediæval grace
   Of iron clothing.

25 Miniver scorned the gold he sought,
   But sore annoyed was he without it;
Miniver thought, and thought, and thought,
   And thought about it.

Miniver Cheevy, born too late,
30   Scratched his head and kept on thinking;
Miniver coughed, and called it fate,
   And kept on drinking.

FOR A DEAD LADY

No more with overflowing light
Shall fill the eyes that now are faded,
Nor shall another's fringe with night
Their woman-hidden world as they did.
5 No more shall quiver down the days
The flowing wonder of her ways,
Whereof no language may requite
The shifting and the many-shaded.

The grace, divine, definitive,
10 Clings only as a faint forestalling;
The laugh that love could not forgive
Is hushed, and answers to no calling;
The forehead and the little ears
Have gone where Saturn keeps the years;
15 The breast where roses could not live
Has done with rising and with falling.

[2]The dynastic family that dominated Florence through the Italian Renaissance.

The beauty, shattered by the laws
That have creation in their keeping,
No longer trembles at applause,
20   Or over children that are sleeping;
And we who delve in beauty's lore
Know all that we have known before
Of what inexorable cause
Makes Time so vicious in his reaping.

EROS TURANNOS[1]

She fears him, and will always ask
    What fated her to choose him;
She meets in his engaging mask
    All reasons to refuse him;
5   But what she meets and what she fears
Are less than are the downward years,
Drawn slowly to the foamless weirs[2]
    Of age, were she to lose him.

Between a blurred sagacity
10   That once had power to sound him,
And Love, that will not let him be
    The Judas[3] that she found him,
Her pride assuages her almost,
As if it were alone the cost.—
15 He sees that he will not be lost,
    And waits and looks around him.

A sense of ocean and old trees
    Envelops and allures him;
Tradition, touching all he sees,
20   Beguiles and reassures him;
And all her doubts of what he says
Are dimmed with what she knows of days—
Till even prejudice delays
    And fades, and she secures him.

---

[1]Eros the Tyrant; Eros (the Latin equivalent of Cupid) is the god of love.
[2]A dam or fence placed in a stream or river to raise the water level or to catch fish.
[3]Judas as the type of betrayer, because of his betrayal of Jesus.

25 The falling leaf inaugurates
        The reign of her confusion;
    The pounding wave reverberates
        The dirge of her illusion;
    And home, where passion lived and died,
30 Becomes a place where she can hide,
    While all the town and harbor side
        Vibrate with her seclusion.

    We tell you, tapping on our brows,
        The story as it should be,—
35 As if the story of a house
        Were told, or ever could be;
    We'll have no kindly veil between
    Her visions and those we have seen,—
    As if we guessed what hers have been,
40   Or what they are or would be.

    Meanwhile we do no harm; for they
        That with a god have striven,
    Not hearing much of what we say,
        Take what the god has given;
45 Though like waves breaking it may be,
    Or like a changed familiar tree,
    Or like a stairway to the sea
        Where down the blind are driven.

VETERAN SIRENS

    The ghost of Ninon[1] would be sorry now
    To laugh at them, were she to see them here,
    So brave and so alert for learning how
    To fence with reason for another year.

5   Age offers a far comelier diadem
    Than theirs; but anguish has no eye for grace,
    When time's malicious mercy cautions them
    To think a while of number and of space.

---

[1]Ninon de Lenclos (1620–1705): a famous Parisian beauty who had affairs with some of the most illustrious men of her time.

The burning hope, the worn expectancy,
10   The martyred humor, and the maimed allure,
Cry out for time to end his levity,
And age to soften its investiture;

But they, though others fade and are still fair,
Defy their fairness and are unsubdued;
15   Although they suffer, they may not forswear
The patient ardor of the unpursued.

Poor flesh, to fight the calendar so long;
Poor vanity, so quaint and yet so brave;
Poor folly, so deceived and yet so strong,
20   So far from Ninon and so near the grave.

THE FLYING DUTCHMAN[1]

Unyielding in the pride of his defiance,
    Afloat with none to serve or to command,
Lord of himself at last, and all by Science,
    He seeks the Vanished Land.

5   Alone, by the one light of his one thought,
    He steers to find the shore from which we came,
Fearless of in what coil he may be caught
    On seas that have no name.

Into the night he sails; and after night
10   There is a dawning, though there be no sun;
Wherefore, with nothing but himself in sight,
    Unsighted, he sails on.

At last there is a lifting of the cloud
    Between the flood before him and the sky;
15   And then—though he may curse the Power aloud
    That has no power to die—

He steers himself away from what is haunted
    By the old ghost of what has been before,—
Abandoning, as always, and undaunted,
20   One fog-walled island more.

[1]The legendary mariner doomed to sail the seas in endless quest.

MR. FLOOD'S PARTY

Old Eben Flood, climbing alone one night
Over the hill between the town below
And the forsaken upland hermitage
That held as much as he should ever know
5   On earth again of home, paused warily.
The road was his with not a native near;
And Eben, having leisure, said aloud,
For no man else in Tilbury Town[1] to hear:

"Well, Mr. Flood, we have the harvest moon
10   Again, and we may not have many more;
The bird is on the wing, the poet says,[2]
And you and I have said it here before.
Drink to the bird." He raised up to the light
The jug that he had gone so far to fill,
15   And answered huskily: "Well, Mr. Flood,
Since you propose it, I believe I will."

Alone, as if enduring to the end
A valiant armor of scarred hopes outworn,
He stood there in the middle of the road
20   Like Roland's ghost winding a silent horn.[3]
Below him, in the town among the trees,
Where friends of other days had honored him,
A phantom salutation of the dead
Rang thinly till old Eben's eyes were dim.

25   Then, as a mother lays her sleeping child
Down tenderly, fearing it may awake,
He set the jug down slowly at his feet
With trembling care, knowing that most things break;
And only when assured that on firm earth
30   It stood, as the uncertain lives of men
Assuredly did not, he paced away,
And with his hand extended paused again:

[1]The imaginary New England small town that Robinson invented and peopled with the characters of many of his poems.
[2]From a lyric by Robert Browning in *Pippa Passes:* "The Lark's on the wing."
[3]The legendary French hero slain at Roncesvalles fighting the Saracens. Roland refused to sound his horn to summon help from his uncle Charlemagne. Finally, surrounded, he blew the horn so mightily that he burst an artery and died of the effort.

"Well, Mr. Flood, we have not met like this
In a long time; and many a change has come
35   To both of us, I fear, since last it was
We had a drop together. Welcome home!"
Convivially returning with himself,
Again he raised the jug up to the light;
And with an acquiescent quaver said:
40   "Well, Mr. Flood, if you insist, I might.

"Only a very little, Mr. Flood—
For auld lang syne.[4] No more, sir; that will do."
So, for the time, apparently it did,
And Eben evidently thought so too;
45   For soon amid the silver loneliness
Of night he lifted up his voice and sang,
Secure, with only two moons listening,
Until the whole harmonious landscape rang—

"For auld lang syne." The weary throat gave out,
50   The last word wavered, and the song was done.
He raised again the jug regretfully
And shook his head, and was again alone.
There was not much that was ahead of him,
And there was nothing in the town below—
55   Where strangers would have shut the many doors
That many friends had opened long ago.

LOST ANCHORS

Like a dry fish flung inland far from shore,
There lived a sailor, warped and ocean-browned.
Who told of an old vessel, harbor-drowned
And out of mind a century before,
5   Where divers, on descending to explore
A legend that had lived its way around
The world of ships, in the dark hulk had found
Anchors, which had been seized and seen no more.

[4]Scottish for "for old times' sake," "for the old long ago," from Robert Burns'
famous song.

Improving a dry leisure to invest
10   Their misadventure with a manifest
Analogy that he may read who runs,
The sailor made it old as ocean grass—
Telling of much that once had come to pass
With him, whose mother should have had no sons.

MANY ARE CALLED[1]

The Lord Apollo,[2] who has never died,
Still holds alone his immemorial reign,
Supreme in an impregnable domain
That with his magic he has fortified;
5   And though melodious multitudes have tried
In ecstasy, in anguish, and in vain,
With invocation sacred and profane
To lure him, even the loudest are outside.

Only at unconjectured intervals,
10   By will of him on whom no man may gaze,
By word of him whose law no man has read,
A questing light may rift the sullen walls,
To cling where mostly its infrequent rays
Fall golden on the patience of the dead.

THE SHEAVES

Where long the shadows of the wind had rolled,
Green wheat was yielding to the change assigned;
And as by some vast magic undivined
The world was turning slowly into gold.
5   Like nothing that was ever bought or sold
It waited there, the body and the mind;
And with a mighty meaning of a kind
That tells the more the more it is not told.

---

[1]Matthew 22:14: "Many are called, but few are chosen."
[2]The god of poetry.

So in a land where all days are not fair,
10   Fair days went on till on another day
A thousand golden sheaves were lying there,
Shining and still, but not for long to stay—
As if a thousand girls with golden hair
Might rise from where they slept and go away.

KARMA[1]

Christmas was in the air and all was well
With him, but for a few confusing flaws
In divers of God's images. Because
A friend of his would neither buy nor sell,
5   Was he to answer for the axe that fell?
He pondered; and the reason for it was,
Partly, a slowly freezing Santa Claus
Upon the corner, with his beard and bell.

Acknowledging an improvident surprise,
10   He magnified a fancy that he wished
The friend whom he had wrecked were here again.
Not sure of that, he found a compromise;
And from the fulness of his heart he fished
A dime for Jesus who had died for men.

MAYA[1]

Through an ascending emptiness of night,
Leaving the flesh and the complacent mind
Together in their sufficiency behind,
The soul of man went up to a far height;
5   And where those others would have had no sight
Or sense of else than terror for the blind,
Soul met the Will, and was again consigned
To the supreme illusion which is right.

---

[1]In Hinduism and Buddhism, the total consequences of one's actions, which determine one's fate or destiny.

---

[1]In Hinduism and Buddhism, the illusory appearance of the world.

"And what goes on up there," the Mind inquired,
10   "That I know not already to be true?"—
"More than enough, but not enough for you,"
Said the descending Soul: "Here in the dark,
Where you are least revealed when most admired,
You may still be the bellows and the spark."

NEW ENGLAND

Here where the wind is always north-north-east
And children learn to walk on frozen toes,
Wonder begets an envy of all those
Who boil elsewhere with such a lyric yeast
5   Of love that you will hear them at a feast
Where demons would appeal for some repose,
Still clamoring where the chalice overflows
And crying wildest who have drunk the least.

Passion is here a soilure of the wits,
10   We're told, and Love a cross for them to bear;
Joy shivers in the corner where she knits
And Conscience always has the rocking-chair,
Cheerful as when she tortured into fits
The first cat that was ever killed by Care.

Robert Frost (1874–1963)

Frost was born in San Francisco after his parents had moved west, but his mother took him back to Lawrence, Massachusetts, after his father's death in 1885. After trying college at Dartmouth and then at Harvard, Frost devoted himself to writing poetry. He had married Elinor White in 1895, and in order to support his growing family he accepted a farm near Derry, New Hampshire, from his grandfather, who imposed the stipulation that he had to stick to it for ten years. He did so, and then took his family to England in 1912.

A Boy's Will and North of Boston came out in the next two years, and Pound took Frost as an instance of the refusal of America to honor its artists. But Frost was indomitably American and returned in 1915 to find himself already recognized. Frost lived in Vermont and in New Hampshire; and in later years, after his wife's death in 1938, he had houses in Cambridge, Massachusetts, and in Miami, Florida, and spent part of the year at Amherst College. He was a very popular reader and poet-in-residence at campuses, and he was so revered a figure that John Kennedy asked Frost to participate in his inauguration as President.

Other volumes of poetry are: Mountain Interval (1916), New Hampshire (1923), West-Running Brook (1928), A Further Range (1936), A Witness Tree (1942), Steeple Bush (1947), Complete Poems (1949), and In the Clearing (1962), plus the two verse dramas The Masque of Reason (1945) and The Masque of Mercy (1947). He scorned free verse and insisted that the skill lay in making the dramatic tones and quality of the speaking voice emerge through the pattern of meter and rhyme. He argued that poetry was not raw confession, and that the poet needed the aesthetic distance of form and the psychological distance of irony to keep him from being too exposed. His audiences enjoyed in him the wit of the Yankee philosopher, but the poems show again and again the shrewd scepticism that wanted to keep both faith and disbelief in play. For Frost the associativeness that made for metaphors and the concentration that made for form allowed the poem to be a "momentary stay against confusion." Receiving the Emerson-Thoreau medal in 1958, he said that from Emerson he had learned to write sentences so realized in their simplicity that they bleed when cut, but he took Emerson's monism to task for being oblivious to the evil that made for an irreconcilable dualism. The recipient of four Pulitzer Prizes and many honorary degrees in the United States and in England, Frost achieved his high ambition of becoming at once both a public figure and a major poet of the twentieth century.

TEXT

Frost, Robert. The Complete Poems of Robert Frost. Ed. Edward Connery Lathem. New York: Holt, Rinehart and Winston, 1969.

REFERENCES

Brower, Reuben A. *The Poetry of Robert Frost: Constellations of Intention.*
New York: Oxford University Press, 1963.

Frost, Robert. *Selected Letters.* Ed. Lawrance Thompson. New York: Holt,
Rinehart and Winston, 1964.

Frost, Robert. *Selected Prose.* Ed. Hyde Cox and Edward Connery Lathem.
New York: Holt, Rinehart and Winston, 1966.

Robert Frost: A Collection of Critical Essays. Ed. James M. Cox. Engle-
wood Cliffs, N.J.: Prentice-Hall, 1962.

Sergeant, Elizabeth Shepley. *Robert Frost: The Trial by Existence.* New
York: Holt, Rinehart and Winston, 1960.

Thompson, Lawrance. *Fire and Ice: The Art and Thought of Robert Frost.*
New York: Holt, 1942.

Thompson, Lawrance. *Robert Frost.* New York: Holt, Rinehart and Win-
ston, 1966, 1970.

MENDING WALL

Something there is that doesn't love a wall,
That sends the frozen-ground-swell under it
And spills the upper boulders in the sun,
And makes gaps even two can pass abreast.
5 The work of hunters is another thing:
I have come after them and made repair
Where they have left not one stone on a stone,
But they would have the rabbit out of hiding,
To please the yelping dogs. The gaps I mean,
10 No one has seen them made or heard them made,
But at spring mending-time we find them there.
I let my neighbor know beyond the hill;
And on a day we meet to walk the line
And set the wall between us once again.
15 We keep the wall between us as we go.
To each the boulders that have fallen to each.
And some are loaves and some so nearly balls
We have to use a spell to make them balance:
"Stay where you are until our backs are turned!"
20 We wear our fingers rough with handling them.
Oh, just another kind of outdoor game,
One on a side. It comes to little more:
There where it is we do not need the wall:
He is all pine and I am apple orchard.
25 My apple trees will never get across
And eat the cones under his pines, I tell him.
He only says, "Good fences make good neighbors."
Spring is the mischief in me, and I wonder
If I could put a notion in his head:
30 "*Why* do they make good neighbors? Isn't it
Where there are cows? But here there are no cows.
Before I built a wall I'd ask to know
What I was walling in or walling out,
And to whom I was like to give offense.
35 Something there is that doesn't love a wall,
That wants it down." I could say "Elves" to him,
But it's not elves exactly, and I'd rather
He said it for himself. I see him there,
Bringing a stone grasped firmly by the top
40 In each hand, like an old-stone savage armed.
He moves in darkness as it seems to me,

Not of woods only and the shade of trees.
He will not go behind his father's saying,
And he likes having thought of it so well
45   He says again, "Good fences make good neighbors."

HOME BURIAL

He saw her from the bottom of the stairs
Before she saw him. She was starting down,
Looking back over her shoulder at some fear.
She took a doubtful step and then undid it
5   To raise herself and look again. He spoke
Advancing toward her: "What is it you see
From up there always?—for I want to know."
She turned and sank upon her skirts at that,
And her face changed from terrified to dull.
10   He said to gain time: "What is it you see?"
Mounting until she cowered under him.
"I will find out now—you must tell me, dear."
She, in her place, refused him any help,
With the least stiffening of her neck and silence.
15   She let him look, sure that he wouldn't see,
Blind creature; and awhile he didn't see.
But at last he murmured, "Oh," and again, "Oh."

"What is it—what?" she said.

                                "Just that I see."

20   "You don't," she challenged. "Tell me what it is."

"The wonder is I didn't see at once.
I never noticed it from here before.
I must be wonted[1] to it—that's the reason.
The little graveyard where my people are!
25   So small the window frames the whole of it.
Not so much larger than a bedroom, is it?
There are three stones of slate and one of marble,
Broad-shouldered little slabs there in the sunlight
On the sidehill. We haven't to mind *those*.

[1]Accustomed.

30 But I understand: it is not the stones,
But the child's mound—

"Don't, don't, don't, don't," she cried.

She withdrew, shrinking from beneath his arm
That rested on the banister, and slid downstairs;
35 And turned on him with such a daunting look,
He said twice over before he knew himself:
"Can't a man speak of his own child he's lost?"

"Not you!—Oh, where's my hat? Oh, I don't need it!
I must get out of here. I must get air.—
40 I don't know rightly whether any man can."

"Amy! Don't go to someone else this time.
Listen to me. I won't come down the stairs."
He sat and fixed his chin between his fists.
"There's something I should like to ask you, dear."

45 "You don't know how to ask it."

"Help me, then."

Her fingers moved the latch for all reply.

"My words are nearly always an offense.
I don't know how to speak of anything
50 So as to please you. But I might be taught,
I should suppose. I can't say I see how.
A man must partly give up being a man
With womenfolk. We could have some arrangement
By which I'd bind myself to keep hands off
55 Anything special you're a-mind to name.
Though I don't like such things 'twixt those that love.
Two that don't love can't live together without them.
But two that do can't live together with them."
She moved the latch a little. "Don't—don't go.
60 Don't carry it to someone else this time.
Tell me about it if it's something human.
Let me into your grief. I'm not so much
Unlike other folks as your standing there
Apart would make me out. Give me my chance.
65 I do think, though, you overdo it a little.

What was it brought you up to think it the thing
To take your mother-loss of a first child
So inconsolably—in the face of love.
You'd think his memory might be satisfied—"

70   "There you go sneering now!"

"I'm not, I'm not!
You make me angry. I'll come down to you.
God, what a woman! And it's come to this,
A man can't speak of his own child that's dead."

75   "You can't because you don't know how to speak.
If you had any feelings, you that dug
With your own hand—how could you?—his little grave;
I saw you from that very window there,
Making the gravel leap and leap in air,
80   Leap up, like that, like that, and land so lightly
And roll back down the mound beside the hole.
I thought, Who is that man? I didn't know you.
And I crept down the stairs and up the stairs
To look again, and still your spade kept lifting.
85   Then you came in. I heard your rumbling voice
Out in the kitchen, and I don't know why,
But I went near to see with my own eyes.
You could sit there with the stains on your shoes
Of the fresh earth from your own baby's grave
90   And talk about your everyday concerns.
You had stood the spade up against the wall
Outside there in the entry, for I saw it."

"I shall laugh the worst laugh I ever laughed.
I'm cursed. God, if I don't believe I'm cursed."

95   "I can repeat the very words you were saying:
'Three foggy mornings and one rainy day
Will rot the best birch fence a man can build.'
Think of it, talk like that at such a time!
What had how long it takes a birch to rot
100   To do with what was in the darkened parlor?
You *couldn't* care! The nearest friends can go
With anyone to death, comes so far short
They might as well not try to go at all.
No, from the time when one is sick to death,

105   One is alone, and he dies more alone.
      Friends make pretense of following to the grave,
      But before one is in it, their minds are turned
      And making the best of their way back to life
      And living people, and things they understand.
110   But the world's evil. I won't have grief so
      If I can change it. Oh, I won't, I won't!"

      "There, you have said it all and you feel better.
      You won't go now. You're crying. Close the door.
      The heart's gone out of it: why keep it up?
115   Amy! There's someone coming down the road!"

      "You—oh, you think the talk is all. I must go—
      Somewhere out of this house. How can I make you—"

      "If—you—do!" She was opening the door wider.
      "Where do you mean to go? First tell me that.
120   I'll follow and bring you back by force. I *will!*—"

AN OLD MAN'S WINTER NIGHT

      All out-of-doors looked darkly in at him
      Through the thin frost, almost in separate stars,
      That gathers on the pane in empty rooms.
      What kept his eyes from giving back the gaze
5   Was the lamp tilted near them in his hand.
      What kept him from remembering what it was
      That brought him to that creaking room was age.
      He stood with barrels round him—at a loss.
      And having scared the cellar under him
10   In clomping here, he scared it once again
      In clomping off—and scared the outer night,
      Which has its sounds, familiar, like the roar
      Of trees and crack of branches, common things,
      But nothing so like beating on a box.
15   A light he was to no one but himself
      Where now he sat, concerned with he knew what,
      A quiet light, and then not even that.
      He consigned to the moon—such as she was,
      So late-arising—to the broken moon,

20   As better than the sun in any case
     For such a charge, his snow upon the roof,
     His icicles along the wall to keep;
     And slept. The log that shifted with a jolt
     Once in the stove, disturbed him and he shifted,
25   And eased his heavy breathing, but still slept.
     One aged man—one man—can't keep a house,
     A farm, a countryside, or if he can,
     It's thus he does it of a winter night.

THE OVEN BIRD[1]

There is a singer everyone has heard,
Loud, a mid-summer and a mid-winter bird,
Who makes the solid tree trunks sound again.
He says that leaves are old and that for flowers
5   Mid-summer is spring as one to ten.
He says the early petal-fall is past,
When pear and cherry bloom went down in showers
On sunny days a moment overcast;
And comes that other fall we name the fall.[2]
10   He says the highway dust is over all.
The bird would cease and be as other birds
But that he knows in singing not to sing.
The question that he frames in all but words
Is what to make of a diminished thing.

---

[1] A thrush-like bird that builds oven-shaped nests, noted for its shrill call.
[2] The petal-fall and the season of fall are meant to recall the original fall of man into mortality.

"OUT, OUT—"[1]

The buzz saw snarled and rattled in the yard
And made dust and dropped stove-length sticks of wood,
Sweet-scented stuff when the breeze drew across it.
And from there those that lifted eyes could count
5   Five mountain ranges one behind the other
Under the sunset far into Vermont.
And the saw snarled and rattled, snarled and rattled,
As it ran light, or had to bear a load.
And nothing happened: day was all but done.
10 Call it a day, I wish they might have said
To please the boy by giving him the half hour
That a boy counts so much when saved from work.
His sister stood beside them in her apron
To tell them "Supper." At the word, the saw,
15 As if to prove saws knew what supper meant,
Leaped out at the boy's hand, or seemed to leap—
He must have given the hand. However it was,
Neither refused the meeting. But the hand!
The boy's first outcry was a rueful laugh,
20 As he swung toward them holding up the hand,
Half in appeal, but half as if to keep
The life from spilling. Then the boy saw all—
Since he was old enough to know, big boy
Doing a man's work, though a child at heart—
25 He saw all spoiled. "Don't let him cut my hand off—
The doctor, when he comes. Don't let him, sister!"
So. But the hand was gone already.
The doctor put him in the dark of ether.
He lay and puffed his lips out with his breath.
30 And then—the watcher at his pulse took fright.
No one believed. They listened at his heart.
Little—less—nothing!—and that ended it.
No more to build on there. And they, since they
Were not the one dead, turned to their affairs.

[1]The title suggests Macbeth's lines in Act V,:
          Out, out brief candle!
  Life's but a walking shadow; a poor player
  That struts and frets his hour upon the stage,
  And then is heard no more: it is a tale
  told by an idiot; full of sound and fury,
    signifying nothing.
Also the words of Lady Macbeth, maddened and rubbing the imagined blood
from her hands in Act V,: "out, damned spot! Out, I say!"

STOPPING BY WOODS
ON A SNOWY EVENING

Whose woods these are I think I know.
His house is in the village, though;
He will not see me stopping here
To watch his woods fill up with snow.

5   My little horse must think it queer
To stop without a farmhouse near
Between the woods and frozen lake
The darkest evening of the year.

He gives his harness bells a shake
10 To ask if there is some mistake.
The only other sound's the sweep
Of easy wind and downy flake.

The woods are lovely, dark, and deep,
But I have promises to keep,
15 And miles to go before I sleep,
And miles to go before I sleep.

FOR ONCE, THEN, SOMETHING

Others taunt me with having knelt at well-curbs
Always wrong to the light, so never seeing
Deeper down in the well than where the water
Gives me back in a shining surface picture
5   Me myself in the summer heaven, godlike,
Looking out of a wreath of fern and cloud puffs.
Once, when trying with chin against a well-curb,
I discerned, as I thought, beyond the picture,
Through the picture, a something white, uncertain,
10 Something more of the depths—and then I lost it.
Water came to rebuke the too clear water.
One drop fell from a fern, and lo, a ripple
Shook whatever it was lay there at bottom,
Blurred it, blotted it out. What was that whiteness?
15 Truth? A pebble of quartz? For once, then, something.

THE NEED OF BEING VERSED IN COUNTRY THINGS

The house had gone to bring again
To the midnight sky a sunset glow.
Now the chimney was all of the house that stood,
Like a pistil[1] after the petals go.

5   The barn opposed across the way,
That would have joined the house in flame
Had it been the will of the wind, was left
To bear forsaken the place's name.

No more it opened with all one end
10   For teams that came by the stony road
To drum on the floor with scurrying hoofs
And brush the mow with the summer load.

The birds that came to it through the air
At broken windows flew out and in,
15   Their murmur more like the sigh we sigh
From too much dwelling on what has been.

Yet for them the lilac renewed its leaf,
And the aged elm, though touched with fire;
And the dry pump flung up an awkward arm;
20   And the fence post carried a strand of wire.

For them there was really nothing sad.
But though they rejoiced in the nest they kept,
One had to be versed in country things
Not to believe the phoebes wept.

SPRING POOLS

These pools that, though in forests, still reflect
The total sky almost without defect,
And like the flowers beside them, chill and shiver,
Will like the flowers beside them soon be gone,
5   And yet not out by any brook or river,
But up by roots to bring dark foliage on.

[1]The long seed-bearing organ of the flower.

The trees that have it in their pent-up buds
To darken nature and be summer woods—
Let them think twice before they use their powers
10   To blot out and drink up and sweep away
These flowery waters and these watery flowers
From snow that melted only yesterday.

ONCE BY THE PACIFIC

The shattered water made a misty din.
Great waves looked over others coming in,
And thought of doing something to the shore
That water never did to land before.
5   The clouds were low and hairy in the skies,
Like locks blown forward in the gleam of eyes.
You could not tell, and yet it looked as if
The shore was lucky in being backed by cliff,
The cliff in being backed by continent;
10   It looked as if a night of dark intent
Was coming, and not only a night, an age.
Someone had better be prepared for rage.
There would be more than ocean-water broken
Before God's last *Put out the Light*[1] was spoken.

WEST-RUNNING BROOK

"Fred, where is north?"

"North? North's there, my love.

The brook runs west."

"West-Running Brook then call it."[1]
5   (West-Running Brook men call it to this day.)
"What does it think it's doing running west
When all the other country brooks flow east
To reach the ocean? It must be the brook

[1]The de-creative act that is the opposite of God's creative fiat: "Let there be light" (Genesis 1:3).

[1]Like Adam and Eve naming things in Eden.

Can trust itself to go by contraries
10 The way I can with you—and you with me—
Because we're—we're—I don't know what we are.
What are we?"

   "Young or new?"

          "We must be something.
15 We've said we two. Let's change that to we three.
As you and I are married to each other,
We'll both be married to the brook. We'll build
Our bridge across it, and the bridge shall be
Our arm thrown over it asleep beside it.
20 Look, look, it's waving to us with a wave
To let us know it hears me."

        "Why, my dear,
That wave's been standing off this jut of shore—"
(The black stream, catching on a sunken rock,
25 Flung backward on itself in one white wave,
And the white water rode the black forever,
Not gaining but not losing, like a bird
White feathers from the struggle of whose breast
Flecked the dark stream and flecked the darker pool
30 Below the point, and were at last driven wrinkled
In a white scarf against the far-shore alders.)
"That wave's been standing off this jut of shore
Ever since rivers, I was going to say,
Were made in heaven. It wasn't waved to us."

35 "It wasn't, yet it was. If not to you,
It was to me—in an annunciation."

"Oh, if you take it off to lady-land,
As't were the country of the Amazons[2]
We men must see you to the confines of
40 And leave you there, ourselves forbid to enter—
It is your brook! I have no more to say."

"Yes, you have, too. Go on. You thought of something."

"Speaking of contraries, see how the brook
In that white wave runs counter to itself.

[2]A nation of female warriors reputed to have lived in Scythia near the Black Sea.

45 It is from that in water we were from
    Long, long before we were from any creature.
    Here we, in our impatience of the steps,
    Get back to the beginning of beginnings,
    The stream of everything that runs away.
50 Some say existence like a Pirouot
    And Pirouette,[3] forever in one place,
    Stands still and dances, but it runs away;
    It seriously, sadly, runs away
    To fill the abyss's void with emptiness.
55 It flows beside us in this water brook,
    But it flows over us. It flows between us
    To separate us for a panic moment.
    It flows between us, over us, and *with* us.
    And it is time, strength, tone, light, life, and love—
60 And even substance lapsing unsubstantial;
    The universal cataract of death
    That spends to nothingness—and unresisted,
    Save by some strange resistance in itself,
    Not just a swerving, but a throwing back,
65 As if regret were in it and were sacred.
    It has this throwing backward on itself
    So that the fall of most of it is always
    Raising a little, sending up a little.
    Our life runs down in sending up the clock.
70 The brook runs down in sending up our life.
    The sun runs down in sending up the brook.
    And there is something sending up the sun.
    It is this backward motion toward the source,
    Against the stream, that most we see ourselves in,
75 The tribute of the current to the source.
    It is from this in nature we are from.
    It is most us."

            "Today will be the day

    You said so."

80   "No, today will be the day
    You said the brook was called West-Running Brook."

    "Today will be the day of what we both said."

[3]Frost's combination of "Pierrot" and "Pierrette," from French pantomime,
with "pirouette," the ballet step that is a full turn of the body on the toe.

DESERT PLACES

Snow falling and night falling fast, oh, fast
In a field I looked into going past,
And the ground almost covered smooth in snow,
But a few weeds and stubble showing last.

5   The woods around it have it—it is theirs.
All animals are smothered in their lairs.
I am too absent-spirited to count;
The loneliness includes me unawares.

And lonely as it is, that loneliness
10   Will be more lonely ere it will be less—
A blanker whiteness of benighted snow
With no expression, nothing to express.

They cannot scare me with their empty spaces
Between stars—on stars where no human race is.
15   I have it in me so much nearer home
To scare myself with my own desert places.

DESIGN

I found a dimpled spider, fat and white,
On a white heal-all,[1] holding up a moth
Like a white piece of rigid satin cloth—
Assorted characters of death and blight
5   Mixed ready to begin the morning right,
Like the ingredients of a witches' broth—
A snow-drop spider, a flower like a froth,
And dead wings carried like a paper kite.

What had that flower to do with being white,
10   The wayside blue and innocent heal-all?
What brought the kindred spider to that height,
Then steered the white moth thither in the night?
What but design of darkness to appall?—
If design govern in a thing so small.

[1]A plant with violet-blue flowers, reputed to have healing powers; also called
"self-heal."

THE SILKEN TENT

She is as in a field a silken tent
At midday when a sunny summer breeze
Has dried the dew and all its ropes relent,
So that in guys it gently sways at ease,
5   And its supporting central cedar pole,
That is its pinnacle to heavenward
And signifies the sureness of the soul,
Seems to owe naught to any single cord,
But strictly held by none, is loosely bound
10   By countless silken ties of love and thought
To everything on earth the compass round,
And only by one's going slightly taut
In the capriciousness of summer air
Is of the slightest bondage made aware.

ALL REVELATION

A head thrusts in as for the view,
But where it is it thrusts in from
Or what it is it thrusts into
By that Cyb'laean[1] avenue,
5   And what can of its coming come,

And whither it will be withdrawn,
And what take hence or leave behind,
These things the mind has pondered on
A moment and still asking gone.
10   Strange apparition of the mind!

But the impervious geode[2]
Was entered, and its inner crust
Of crystals with a ray cathode[3]
At every point and facet glowed
15   In answer to the mental thrust.

---

[1]Cybele was the earth goddess of the Phrygians, loved by the fertility god Attis.
[2]A small spheroidal rock lined with crystals inside; the literal meaning of the word is "earth-like."
[3]A stream of electrons emitted by the cathode, or negative electrode, in an electrical discharge tube.

Eyes seeking the response of eyes
Bring out the stars, bring out the flowers,
Thus concentrating earth and skies
So none need be afraid of size.
20   All revelation has been ours.

THE MOST OF IT

He thought he kept the universe alone;
For all the voice in answer he could wake
Was but the mocking echo of his own
From some tree-hidden cliff across the lake.
5   Some morning from the boulder-broken beach
He would cry out on life, that what it wants
Is not its own love back in copy speech,
But counter-love, original response.
And nothing ever came of what he cried
10   Unless it was the embodiment that crashed
In the cliff's talus[1] on the other side,
And then in the far-distant water splashed,
But after a time allowed for it to swim,
Instead of proving human when it neared
15   And someone else additional to him,
As a great buck it powerfully appeared,
Pushing the crumpled water up ahead,
And landed pouring like a waterfall,
And stumbled through the rocks with horny tread,
20   And forced the underbrush—and that was all.

DIRECTIVE

Back out of all this now too much for us,
Back in a time made simple by the loss
Of detail, burned, dissolved, and broken off
Like graveyard marble sculpture in the weather,
5   There is a house that is no more a house
Upon a farm that is no more a farm

[1]A sloping mass of debris at the base of a cliff.

And in a town that is no more a town.
The road there, if you'll let a guide direct you
Who only has at heart your getting lost,
10 May seem as if it should have been a quarry—
Great monolithic knees the former town
Long since gave up pretense of keeping covered.
And there's a story in a book about it:
Besides the wear of iron wagon wheels
15 The ledges show lines ruled southeast-northwest,
The chisel work of an enormous Glacier
That braced his feet against the Arctic Pole.
You must not mind a certain coolness from him
Still said to haunt this side of Panther Mountain.
20 Nor need you mind the serial ordeal
Of being watched from forty cellar holes
As if by eye pairs out of forty firkins.[1]
As for the woods' excitement over you
That sends light rustle rushes to their leaves,
25 Charge that to upstart inexperience.
Where were they all not twenty years ago?
They think too much of having shaded out
A few old pecker-fretted apple trees.
Make yourself up a cheering song of how
30 Someone's road home from work this once was,
Who may be just ahead of you on foot
Or creaking with a buggy load of grain.
The height of the adventure is the height
Of country where two village cultures faded
35 Into each other. Both of them are lost.
And if you're lost enough to find yourself
By now, pull in your ladder road behind you
And put a sign up CLOSED to all but me.
Then make yourself at home. The only field
40 Now left's no bigger than a harness gall.[2]
First there's the children's house of make-believe,
Some shattered dishes underneath a pine,
The playthings in the playhouse of the children.
Weep for what little things could make them glad.
45 Then for the house that is no more a house,
But only a belilaced cellar hole,
Now slowly closing like a dent in dough.

[1]Small wooden barrels.
[2]Sore made by the friction of the harness.

This was no playhouse but a house in earnest.
Your destination and your destiny's
50 A brook that was the water of the house,
Cold as a spring as yet so near its source,
Too lofty and original to rage.
(We know the valley streams that when aroused
Will leave their tatters hung on barb and thorn.)
55 I have kept hidden in the instep arch
Of an old cedar at the waterside
A broken drinking goblet like the Grail[3]
Under a spell so the wrong ones can't find it,
So can't get saved, as Saint Mark says they mustn't.
60 (I stole the goblet from the children's playhouse.)
Here are your waters and your watering place.
Drink and be whole again beyond confusion.

A CABIN IN THE CLEARING

For Alfred Edwards

MIST.   I don't believe the sleepers in this house
Know where they are.

SMOKE.   They've been here long enough
To push the woods back from around the house
5 And part them in the middle with a path.

MIST.   And still I doubt if they know where they are.
And I begin to fear they never will.
All they maintain the path for is the comfort
Of visiting with the equally bewildered.
10 Nearer in plight their neighbors are than distance.

SMOKE.   I am the guardian wraith of starlit smoke
That leans out this and that way from their chimney.
I will not have their happiness despaired of.

MIST.   No one—not I—would give them up for lost
15 Simply because they don't know where they are.

[3] In medieval legend, the cup used by Jesus at the Last Supper in the institution
of the Eucharist; sought after by many knights on quests.

I am the damper counterpart of smoke,
That gives off from a garden ground at night
But lifts no higher than a garden grows.
I cotton to their landscape. That's who I am.
20   I am no further from their fate than you are.

SMOKE.   They must by now have learned the native tongue.
Why don't they ask the Red Man where they are?

MIST.   They often do, and none the wiser for it.
So do they also ask philosophers
25   Who come to look in on them from the pulpit.
They will ask anyone there is to ask—
In the fond faith accumulated fact
Will of itself take fire and light the world up.
Learning has been a part of their religion.

30   SMOKE.   If the day ever comes when they know who
They are, they may know better where they are.
But who they are is too much to believe—
Either for them or the onlooking world.
They are too sudden to be credible.

35   MIST.   Listen, they murmur talking in the dark
On what should be their daylong theme continued.
Putting the lamp out has not put their thought out.
Let us pretend the dewdrops from the eaves
Are you and I eavesdropping on their unrest—
40   A mist and smoke eavesdropping on a haze—
And see if we can tell the bass from the soprano.

Than smoke and mist who better could appraise
The kindred spirit of an inner haze?

THE DRAFT HORSE

With a lantern that wouldn't burn
In too frail a buggy we drove
Behind too heavy a horse
Through a pitch-dark limitless grove.

5 And a man came out of the trees
And took our horse by the head
And reaching back to his ribs
Deliberately stabbed him dead.

The ponderous beast went down
10 With a crack of a broken shaft.
And the night drew through the trees
In one long invidious draft.

The most unquestioning pair
That ever accepted fate
15 And the least disposed to ascribe
Any more than we had to to hate,

We assumed that the man himself
Or someone he had to obey
Wanted us to get down
20 And walk the rest of the way.

IN WINTER IN THE WOODS ALONE

In winter in the woods alone
Against the trees I go.
I mark a maple for my own
And lay the maple low.

5 At four o'clock I shoulder ax,
And in the afterglow
I link a line of shadowy tracks
Across the tinted snow.

I see for Nature no defeat
10 In one tree's overthrow
Or for myself in my retreat
For yet another blow.

Carl Sandburg (1878–1967)

Born in Galesburg, Illinois, of Swedish immigrants, Sandburg knocked about before entering Lombard College in his home town. He left college without graduating and he began newspaper work in Milwaukee; there he married Lillian Steichen, sister of the photographer Edward Steichen. He moved to Chicago to work on the *Daily News*, began publishing in Harriet Monroe's new magazine *Poetry*, and was part of the Chicago literary scene. *Chicago Poems* (1916), *Cornhuskers* (1918), *Smoke and Steel* (1920), and *Slabs of the Sunburnt West* (1922) established him as the poet of the Midwest, singing the raw energies of the industrial metropolis and the beautiful stretches of prairieland in a Whitmanesque free verse rough and tender, slangy and lyrical in turn. *The People, Yes* (1936) absorbed folk-sayings and anecdotes into a book-length hymn to the ongoing human spirit.

Sandburg's other books include: *The Chicago Race Riots* (1919); an immense, Pulitzer-Prize-winning biography of Lincoln (1926, 1939); *Rootabaga Stories* (1922) for children; a sprawling novel, *Remembrance Rock* (1948); collections of folk songs, *The American Songbag* (1927, 1950); and autobiography, *Always the Young Strangers* (1952). *Complete Poems* (1950) won another Pulitzer Prize and was followed by a final volume, *Honey and Salt* (1963). During his last years Sandburg lived in Flat Rock, North Carolina. By the time of his death he was acclaimed and honored as a national bard who rendered his country, fact and ideal, into prose, verse, and song.

TEXT

Sandburg, Carl. *Complete Poems*. New York: Harcourt Brace Jovanovich, 1970.

REFERENCE

Callahan, North. *Carl Sandburg: Lincoln of Our Literature*. New York: New York University Press, 1970.

Crowder, Richard. *Carl Sandburg*. New York: Twayne, 1969.

Sandburg, Carl. *Letters*. Ed. Herbert Mitgang. New York: Harcourt Brace and World, 1968.

CHICAGO

Hog Butcher for the World,
Tool Maker, Stacker of Wheat,
Player with Railroads and the Nation's Freight Handler;
Stormy, husky, brawling,
City of the Big Shoulders:

They tell me you are wicked and I believe them, for I have seen your
    painted women under the gas lamps luring the farm boys.
And they tell me you are crooked and I answer: Yes, it is true I have
    seen the gunman kill and go free to kill again.
And they tell me you are brutal and my reply is: On the faces of
    women and children I have seen the marks of wanton hunger.
And having answered so I turn once more to those who sneer at this
    my city, and I give them back the sneer and say to them:
Come and show me another city with lifted head singing so proud to
    be alive and coarse and strong and cunning.
Flinging magnetic curses amid the toil of piling job on job, here is a
    tall bold slugger set vivid against the little soft cities;
Fierce as a dog with tongue lapping for action, cunning as a savage
    pitted against the wilderness,
    Bareheaded,
    Shoveling,
    Wrecking,
    Planning,
    Building, breaking, rebuilding,
Under the smoke, dust all over his mouth, laughing with white teeth,
Under the terrible burden of destiny laughing as a young man
    laughs,
Laughing even as an ignorant fighter laughs who has never lost a
    battle,
Bragging and laughing that under his wrist is the pulse, and under
    his ribs the heart of the people,
            Laughing!
Laughing the stormy, husky, brawling laughter of Youth, half-
    naked, sweating, proud to be Hog Butcher, Tool Maker,
    Stacker of Wheat, Player with Railroads and Freight Handler
    to the Nation.

CHILD OF THE ROMANS

The dago[1] shovelman sits by the railroad track
Eating a noon meal of bread and bologna.
    A train whirls by, and men and women at tables
    Alive with red roses and yellow jonquils,
5   Eat steaks running with brown gravy,
    Strawberries and cream, eclairs and coffee.
The dago shovelman finishes the dry bread and bologna,
Washes it down with a dipper from the water-boy,
And goes back to the second half of a ten-hour day's work
10 Keeping the road-bed so the roses and jonquils
Shake hardly at all in the cut glass vases
Standing slender on the tables in the dining cars.

FOG

The fog comes
on little cat feet.

It sits looking
over harbor and city
5 on silent haunches
and then moves on.

WILDERNESS

There is a wolf in me . . . fangs pointed for tearing gashes . . . a red
tongue for raw meat . . . and the hot lapping of blood—I keep
this wolf because the wilderness gave it to me and the wilderness
will not let it go.

There is a fox in me . . . a silver-gray fox . . . I sniff and guess . . . I
pick things out of the wind and air . . . I nose in the dark night
and take sleepers and eat them and hide the feathers . . . I circle
and loop and double-cross.

[1]Slang term for an Italian, sometimes used derisively and here used by Sandburg to show the prejudice which the workmen labored under.

There is a hog in me ... a snout and a belly ... a machinery for
   eating and grunting ... a machinery for sleeping satisfied in the
   sun—I got this too from the wilderness and the wilderness will
   not let it go.

There is a fish in me ... I know I came from salt-blue water-gates ...
   I scurried with shoals of herring ... I blew waterspouts with
   porpoises ... before land was ... before the water went down
   ... before Noah[1] ... before the first chapter of Genesis.[2]

5   There is a baboon in me ... clambering-clawed ... dog-faced ...
   yawping a galoot's hunger ... hairy under the armpits ... here
   are the hawk-eyed hankering men ... here are the blonde and
   blue-eyed women ... here they hide curled asleep waiting ...
   ready to snarl and kill ... ready to sing and give milk ...
   waiting—I keep the baboon because the wilderness says so.

There is an eagle in me and a mockingbird ... and the eagle flies
   among the Rocky Mountains of my dreams and fights among
   the Sierra crags of what I want ... and the mockingbird warbles
   in the early forenoon before the dew is gone, warbles in the
   underbrush of my Chattanoogas of hope, gushes over the blue
   Ozark foothills of my wishes—And I got the eagle and the
   mockingbird from the wilderness.

O, I got a zoo, I got a menagerie, inside my ribs, under my bony head,
   under my red-valve heart—and I got something else: it is a
   man-child heart, a woman-child heart: it is a father and mother
   and lover: it came from God-Knows-Where: it is going to
   God-Knows-Where—For I am the keeper of the zoo: I say yes
   and no: I sing and kill and work: I am a pal of the world: I
   came from the wilderness.

[1]The story of Noah and the flood is told in Genesis 6–9.
[2]In which the dry land is separated from the waters.

BILBEA

(From tablet writing, Babylonian excavations of 4th millennium B.C.)

Bilbea, I was in Babylon on Saturday night.
I saw nothing of you anywhere.
I was at the old place and the other girls were there, but no Bilbea.

Have you gone to another house? or city?
5 Why don't you write?
I was sorry. I walked home half-sick.

Tell me how it goes.
Send me some kind of a letter.
And take care of yourself.

COOL TOMBS

When Abraham Lincoln was shoveled into the tombs, he forgot
    the copperheads[1] and the assassin[2] . . . in the dust, in the cool
    tombs.

And Ulysses Grant lost all thought of con men and Wall Street, cash
    and collateral turned ashes . . . in the dust, in the cool tombs.

Pocahontas'[3] body, lovely as a poplar, sweet as a red haw[4] in No-
    vember or a pawpaw[5] in May, did she wonder? does she re-
    member? . . . in the dust, in the cool tombs?

Take any streetful of people buying clothes and groceries, cheering
    a hero or throwing confetti and blowing tin horns . . . tell me if
    the lovers are losers . . . tell me if any get more than the lovers
    . . . in the dust . . . in the cool tombs.

[1] A Northerner who sympathized with the Confederacy during the Civil War.
[2] John Wilkes Booth.
[3] Indian princess who allegedly saved Captain John Smith's life.
[4] Hawthorn.
[5] Papaya.

GRASS

Pile the bodies high at Austerlitz and Waterloo.[1]
Shovel them under and let me work—
> I am the grass; I cover all.

And pile them high at Gettysburg
5 And pile them high at Ypres and Verdun.[2]
Shovel them under and let me work.
Two years, ten years, and passengers ask the conductor:
> What place is this?
> Where are we now?

10   I am the grass.
> Let me work.

FOUR PRELUDES ON PLAYTHINGS OF THE WIND

"The past is a bucket of ashes."

1

The woman named Tomorrow
sits with a hairpin in her teeth
and takes her time
and does her hair the way she wants it
5 and fastens at last the last braid and coil
and puts the hairpin where it belongs
and turns and drawls: Well, what of it?
My grandmother, Yesterday, is gone.
What of it? Let the dead be dead.

2

10 The doors were cedar
and the panels strips of gold
and the girls were golden girls
and the panels read and the girls chanted:
> We are the greatest city,

---

[1]Napoleon was victorious at Austerlitz and defeated at Waterloo.
[2]Battles in World War I.

15   the greatest nation:
        nothing like us ever was.
     The doors are twisted on broken hinges.
     Sheets of rain swish through on the wind
             where the golden girls ran and the panels read:
20   We are the greatest city,
             the greatest nation,
             nothing like us ever was.

                              3

     It has happened before.
     Strong men put up a city and got
25   a nation together,
     And paid singers to sing and women
             to warble: We are the greatest city,
                 the greatest nation,
                 nothing like us ever was.

30   And while the singers sang
     and the strong men listened
     and paid the singers well
     and felt good about it all,
             there were rats and lizards who listened
35   . . . and the only listeners left now
             . . . are . . . the rats . . . and the lizards.

     And there are black crows
     crying, "Caw, caw,"
     bringing mud and sticks
40   building a nest
     over the words carved
     on the doors where the panels were cedar
     and the strips on the panels were gold
     and the golden girls came singing:
45   We are the greatest city,
             the greatest nation:
             nothing like us ever was.

   The only singers now are crows crying, "Caw, caw,"
   And the sheets of rain whine in the wind and doorways.
50 And the only listeners now are . . . the rats . . . and the lizards.

4

The feet of the rats
scribble on the doorsills;
the hieroglyphs of the rat footprints
chatter the pedigrees of the rats
55   and babble of the blood
and gabble of the breed
of the grandfathers and the great-grandfathers
of the rats.

And the wind shifts
60   and the dust on a doorsill shifts
and even the writing of the rat footprints
tells us nothing, nothing at all
about the greatest city, the greatest nation
where the strong men listened
65   and the women warbled: Nothing like us ever was.

UPSTREAM

The strong men keep coming on.
They go down shot, hanged, sick, broken.
They live on fighting, singing, lucky as plungers.
The strong mothers pulling them on . . .
5   The strong mothers pulling them from a dark sea, a great prairie, a
       long mountain.
Call hallelujah, call amen, call deep thanks.
The strong men keep coming on.

THE PEOPLE WILL LIVE ON[1]

The people will live on.
The learning and blundering people will live on.
They will be tricked and sold and again sold
And go back to the nourishing earth for rootholds,
5   The people so peculiar in renewal and comeback,
You can't laugh off their capacity to take it.
The mammoth rests between his cyclonic[2] dramas.

[1]This poem is section 107 of the long, loose sequence *The People, Yes.*
[2]Like a cyclone.

The people so often sleepy, weary, enigmatic,
is a vast huddle with many units saying:
10   "I earn my living.
I make enough to get by
and it takes all my time.
If I had more time
I could do more for myself
15   and maybe for others.
I could read and study
and talk things over
and find out about things.
It takes time.
20   I wish I had the time."

The people is a tragic and comic two-face:
hero and hoodlum: phantom and gorilla twist-
ing to moan with a gargoyle mouth: "They
buy me and sell me . . . it's a game . . .
25   sometime I'll break loose . . ."

          Once having marched
Over the margins of animal necessity,
Over the grim line of sheer subsistence
          Then man came
30   To the deeper rituals of his bones,
To the lights lighter than any bones,
To the time for thinking things over,
To the dance, the song, the story,
Or the hours given over to dreaming,
35   Once having so marched.

Between the finite limitations of the five senses
and the endless yearnings of man for the beyond
the people hold to the humdrum bidding of work and food
while reaching out when it comes their way
40   for lights beyond the prism of the five senses,
for keepsakes lasting beyond any hunger or death.
          This reaching is alive.
The panderers and liars have violated and smutted it.
          Yet this reaching is alive yet
45   for lights and keepsakes.

The people know the salt of the sea
and the strength of the winds
lashing the corners of the earth.
The people take the earth
50   as a tomb of rest and a cradle of hope.
Who else speaks for the Family of Man?
They are in tune and step
with constellations of universal law.

The people is a polychrome,
55   a spectrum and a prism
held in a moving monolith,
a console organ of changing themes,
a clavilux[2] of color poems
wherein the sea offers fog
60   and the fog moves off in rain
and the labrador sunset shortens
to a nocturne of clear stars
serene over the shot spray
of northern lights.

65   The steel mill sky is alive.
The fire breaks white and zigzag
shot on a gun-metal gloaming.
Man is a long time coming.
Man will yet win.
70   Brother may yet line up with brother:

This old anvil laughs at many broken hammers.
There are men who can't be bought.
The fireborn are at home in fire.
The stars make no noise.
75   You can't hinder the wind from blowing.
Time is a great teacher.
Who can live without hope?

In the darkness with a great bundle of grief
the people march.
80   In the night, and overhead a shovel of stars for
keeps, the people march:
                  "Where to? what next?"

[2]A projector that throws changing patterns of light and color on a screen; also
called a "color organ."

EARLY COPPER

A slim and singing copper girl,
They lived next to the earth for her sake
And the yellow corn was in their faces
And the copper curve of prairie sunset.

5   In her April eyes bringing
Corn tassels shining from Duluth and Itasca,
From La Crosse to Keokuk and St. Louis,[1] to the Big Muddy,
The yellow-hoofed Big Muddy meeting the Father of Waters,[2]
In her eyes corn rows running to the prairie ends,
10   In her eyes copper men living next to the earth for her sake.

CHEAP RENT

The laws of the bronze gods
are irrevocable.

And yet—in the statue of
General Grant astride a horse
5   on rolling prairie, on little
hills looking from Lincoln
Park at Lake Michigan—[1]
here the sparrows have a nest
in General Grant's spy glass—
10   here the sparrows have rented
a flat in General Grant's
right stirrup—

It is true? The laws of the
bronze gods are irrevocable?

[1]Cities down the Mississippi Valley: Duluth and Itasca, Minnesota; LaCrosse, Wisconsin; Keokuk, Iowa; St. Louis, Missouri.
[2]The Missouri (the Big Muddy) flows into the Mississippi (named by the Indians the Father of Waters) just above St. Louis.

[1]On the lakefront in Chicago.

ELM BUDS

Elm buds are out.
Yesterday morning, last night,
   they crept out.
They are the mice of early
   spring air.

To the north is the gray sky.
5 Winter hung it gray for the gray
   elm to stand dark against.
Now the branches all end with the
   yellow and gold mice of early
   spring air.
They are moving mice creeping out
   with leaf and leaf.

SKYSCRAPERS STAND PROUD

The skyscrapers stand proud.
They seem to say they have
   sought the absolute
   and made it their own.
Yet they are blameless, innocent
   as dumb steel and the dumber
   concrete of their bastions.
"Man made us," they murmur. "We are
   proud only as man is proud and we
   have no more found the absolute
   than has man."

Wallace Stevens (1879–1955)

Stevens was born in Reading, Pennsylvania, and attended Harvard as a special student from 1897 to 1900. From New York Law School he was admitted to the bar in 1904. He married a home-town girl, Elsie Kachel Moll, in 1909, and joined the legal staff of the Hartford (Connecticut) Accident and Indemnity Company, where he worked his way up to vice president by 1934. But the events of Stevens' external life afford few clues to the rich internal life that made for his poems.

Harmonium (1923) brought together poems that had been appearing in magazines for some years, and it was followed by *Ideas of Order* (1936), *The Man with the Blue Guitar* (1937), *Parts of a World* (1942), *Transport to Summer* (1947), *The Auroras of Autumn* (1950), and *Collected Poems* (1954) which Stevens at one point wanted to call *The Whole of Harmonium*. Most of his poems are about the poetic act: its materials, methods, and ends. Obsessed by a "rage for order" and nostalgia for a belief in the harmonious correspondence between the individual and his world, Stevens began with the sense of dislocation and sought ways to achieve or to suggest consonance. To this end the imagination composes elements abstracted from the flux of reality into an artificial structure (Stevens called it the "mundo" of the imagination, as opposed to the actual world), and the aesthetic object relates back to reality either by serving as a means of comprehending the flux, or by erecting a fiction that reflects a notion of a possible pattern on the flux.

Charged with escapist hedonism by critics as different as Yvor Winters and the Marxists of the thirties, Stevens insisted that the poet fulfilled his role in society by affecting the sensibilities of the people and thus changing their notions of the terms on which life is lived. The early poems use extravagant wit and exotic effects of sound and color to dramatize the discords within and without, but during the forties and fifties the poems increasingly took on a meditative calm as the mind revolved on the intersection of imagination and reality in stately and lovely discriminations.

TEXT

Stevens, Wallace. *Collected Poems.* New York: Knopf, 1954.
Stevens, Wallace. *Opus Posthumous.* Ed. Samuel French Morse. New York: Knopf, 1957.

REFERENCE

Morse, Samuel French. *Wallace Stevens: Poetry As Life*. New York: Pegasus, 1970.

Riddel, Joseph N. *The Clairvoyant Eye: The Poetry and Poetics of Wallace Stevens*. Baton Rouge: Louisiana State University Press, 1965.

Stevens, Wallace. *Letters*. Ed. Holly Stevens. New York: Knopf, 1966.

Stevens, Wallace. *The Necessary Angel: Essays on Reality and the Imagination*. New York: Knopf, 1951.

Sukenick, Ronald. *Wallace Stevens: Musing the Obscure*. New York: New York University Press, 1967.

The Act of the Mind: Essays on the Poetry of Wallace Stevens. Ed. Roy Harvey Pearce and J. Hillis Miller. Baltimore: Johns Hopkins Press, 1965.

DOMINATION OF BLACK

At night, by the fire,
The colors of the bushes
And of the fallen leaves,
Repeating themselves,
5 Turned in the room,
Like the leaves themselves
Turning in the wind.
Yes: but the color of the heavy hemlocks
Came striding.
10 And I remembered the cry of the peacocks.

The colors of their tails
Were like the leaves themselves
Turning in the wind,
In the twilight wind.
15 They swept over the room,
Just as they flew from the boughs of the hemlocks

Down to the ground.
I heard them cry—the peacocks.
Was it a cry against the twilight
20 Or against the leaves themselves
Turning in the wind,
Turning as the flames
Turned in the fire,
Turning as the tails of the peacocks
25 Turned in the loud fire,
Loud as the hemlocks
Full of the cry of the peacocks?
Or was it a cry against the hemlocks?

Out of the window,
30 I saw how the planets gathered
Like the leaves themselves
Turning in the wind.
I saw how the night came,
Came striding like the color of the heavy hemlocks.
35 I felt afraid.
And I remembered the cry of the peacocks.

THE SNOW MAN

One must have a mind of winter
To regard the frost and the boughs
Of the pine-trees crusted with snow;

And have been cold a long time
5   To behold the junipers shagged with ice,
The spruces rough in the distant glitter

Of the January sun; and not to think
Of any misery in the sound of the wind,
In the sound of a few leaves,

10   Which is the sound of the land
Full of the same wind
That is blowing in the same bare place

For the listener, who listens in the snow,
And, nothing himself, beholds
15   Nothing that is not there and the nothing that is.

A HIGH-TONED OLD CHRISTIAN WOMAN

Poetry is the supreme fiction, madame.
Take the moral law and make a nave of it
And from the nave[1] build haunted heaven. Thus,
The conscience is converted into palms,[2]
5   Like windy citherns[3] hankering for hymns.
We agree in principle. That's clear. But take
The opposing law and make a peristyle,[4]
And from the peristyle project a masque[5]
Beyond the planets. Thus, our bawdiness,
10   Unpurged by epitaph, indulged at last,
Is equally converted into palms,
Squiggling like saxophones. And palm for palm,

[1] The central part of the church flanked by the aisles.
[2] The emblem of victory.
[3] The sixteenth-century guitar with a pear-shaped body.
[4] Colonnade surrounding a temple.
[5] In contrast to the Mass celebrated in church.

Madame, we are where we began. Allow,
Therefore, that in the planetary scene
15 Your disaffected flagellants, well-stuffed,
Smacking their muzzy[6] bellies in parade,
Proud of such novelties of the sublime,
Such tink and tank and tunk-a-tunk-tunk,
May, merely may, madame, whip from themselves
20 A jovial hullabaloo among the spheres.
This will make widows wince. But fictive things
Wink as they will. Wink most when widows wince.

THE EMPEROR OF ICE-CREAM

Call the roller of big cigars,
The muscular one, and bid him whip
In kitchen cups concupiscent[1] curds.
Let the wenches dawdle in such dress
5 As they are used to wear, and let the boys
Bring flowers in last month's newspapers.
Let be be finale of seem.
The only emperor is the emperor[2] of ice-cream.

Take from the dresser of deal,[3]
10 Lacking the three glass knobs, that sheet
On which she embroidered fantails once
And spread it so as to cover her face.
If her horny feet protrude, they come
To show how cold she is, and dumb.
15 Let the lamp affix its beam.
The only emperor is the emperor of ice-cream.

---

[6]Muddled.

---

[1]Lustful, sexual.
[2]Perhaps Stevens is demonstrating the debased vulgarity of the modern world by punning on "emperor" and the Greek *"emporos,"* which means "merchant" and is the root of "emporium."
[3]Fir or pine wood.

SUNDAY MORNING

I

Complacencies of the peignoir,[1] and late
Coffee and oranges in a sunny chair,
And the green freedom of a cockatoo
Upon a rug mingle to dissipate
5   The holy hush of ancient sacrifice.[2]
She dreams a little, and she feels the dark
Encroachment of that old catastrophe,
As a calm darkens among water-lights.
The pungent oranges and bright, green wings
10   Seem things in some procession of the dead,
Winding across wide water, without sound.
The day is like wide water, without sound,
Stilled for the passing of her dreaming feet
Over the seas, to silent Palestine,
15   Dominion of the blood and sepulchre.

II

Why should she give her bounty to the dead?
What is divinity if it can come
Only in silent shadows and in dreams?
Shall she not find in comforts of the sun,
20   In pungent fruit and bright, green wings, or else
In any balm or beauty of the earth,
Things to be cherished like the thought of heaven?
Divinity must live within herself:
Passions of rain, or moods in falling snow;
25   Grievings in loneliness, or unsubdued
Elations when the forest blooms; gusty
Emotions on wet roads on autumn nights;
All pleasures and all pains, remembering
The bough of summer and the winter branch.
30   These are the measures destined for her soul.

---

[1]A woman's dressing gown.
[2]The "ancient sacrifice" and "old catastrophe" are, as later lines indicate, Jesus'
crucifixion and death.

III

Jove[3] in the clouds had his inhuman birth.
No mother suckled him, no sweet land gave
Large-mannered motions to his mythy mind
He moved among us, as a muttering king,
35   Magnificent, would move among his hinds[4]
Until our blood, commingling, virginal,
With heaven, brought such requital to desire
The very hinds discerned it, in a star.
Shall our blood fail? Or shall it come to be
40   The blood of paradise? And shall the earth
Seem all of paradise that we shall know?
The sky will be much friendlier then than now,
A part of labor and a part of pain,
And next in glory to enduring love,
45   Not this dividing and indifferent blue.

IV

She says, "I am content when wakened birds,
Before they fly, test the reality
Of misty fields, by their sweet questionings;
But when the birds are gone, and their warm fields
50   Return no more, where, then, is paradise?"
There is not any haunt of prophecy,
Nor any old chimera[5] of the grave,
Neither the golden underground,[6] nor isle
Melodious, where spirits gat them home,
55   Nor visionary south, nor cloudy palm
Remote on heaven's hill, that has endured
As April's green endures; or will endure
Like her remembrance of awakened birds,
Or her desire for June and evening, tipped
60   By the consummation of the swallow's wings.

V

She says, "But in contentment I still feel
The need of some imperishable bliss."
Death is the mother of beauty; hence from her,

[3]Or Jupiter, the supreme god in Roman mythology; the equivalent of Zeus for the Greeks.
[4]Female deer.
[5]Imaginative fancy; originally a grotesque she-monster.
[6]The next few lines give different images for an imagined paradise.

Alone, shall come fulfilment to our dreams
65 And our desires. Although she strews the leaves
Of sure obliteration on our paths,
The path sick sorrow took, the many paths
Where triumph rang its brassy phrase, or love
Whispered a little out of tenderness,
70 She makes the willow shiver in the sun
For maidens who were wont to sit and gaze
Upon the grass, relinquished to their feet.
She causes boys to pile new plums and pears
On disregarded plate. The maidens taste
75 And stray impassioned in the littering leaves.

VI

Is there no change of death in paradise?
Does ripe fruit never fall? Or do the boughs
Hang always heavy in that perfect sky,
Unchanging, yet so like our perishing earth,
80 With rivers like our own that seek for seas
They never find, the same receding shores
That never touch with inarticulate pang?
Why set the pear upon those river-banks
Or spice the shores with odors of the plum?
85 Alas, that they should wear our colors there,
The silken weavings of our afternoons,
And pick the strings of our insipid lutes!
Death is the mother of beauty, mystical,
Within whose burning bosom we devise
90 Our earthly mothers waiting, sleeplessly.

VII

Supple and turbulent, a ring of men
Shall chant in orgy on a summer morn
Their boisterous devotion to the sun,
Not as a god, but as a god might be,
95 Naked among them, like a savage source.
Their chant shall be a chant of paradise,
Out of their blood, returning to the sky;
And in their chant shall enter, voice by voice,
The windy lake wherein their lord delights,
100 The trees, like serafin,[7] and echoing hills,
That choir among themselves long afterward.

[7]One of the orders of angels.

They shall know well the heavenly fellowship
Of men that perish and of summer morn.
And whence they came and whither they shall go
105   The dew upon their feet shall manifest.

VIII

She hears, upon that water without sound,
A voice that cries, "The tomb in Palestine
Is not the porch of spirits lingering.
It is the grave of Jesus, where he lay."
110   We live in an old chaos of the sun,
Or old dependency of day and night,
Or island solitude, unsponsored, free,
Of that wide water, inescapable.
Deer walk upon our mountains, and the quail
115   Whistle about us their spontaneous cries;
Sweet berries ripen in the wilderness;
And, in the isolation of the sky,
At evening, casual flocks of pigeons make
Ambiguous undulations as they sink,
120   Downward to darkness, on extended wings.

THE MAN WHOSE PHARYNX WAS BAD

The time of year has grown indifferent.
Mildew of summer and the deepening snow
Are both alike in the routine I know.
I am too dumbly in my being pent.

5   The wind attendant on the solstices[1]
Blows on the shutters of the metropoles,
Stirring no poet in his sleep, and tolls
The grand ideas of the villages.

The malady of the quotidian.[2]. . .
10   Perhaps, if winter once could penetrate
Through all its purples to the final slate,
Persisting bleakly in an icy haze,

[1]The turning of the seasons, about June 22 and December 22.
[2]Daily, everyday routine.

One might in turn become less diffident,
Out of such mildew plucking neater[3] mould
15 And spouting new orations of the cold.
One might. One might. But time will not relent.

THE IDEA OF ORDER AT KEY WEST

She sang beyond the genius of the sea.
The water never formed to mind or voice,
Like a body wholly body, fluttering
Its empty sleeves and; yet its mimic motion
5 Made constant cry, caused constantly a cry,
That was not ours although we understood,
Inhuman, of the veritable ocean.

The sea was not a mask. No more was she.
The song and water were not medleyed sound
10 Even if what she sang was what she heard,
Since what she sang was uttered word by word.
It may be that in all her phrases stirred
The grinding water and the gasping wind;
But it was she and not the sea we heard.

15 For she was the maker of the song she sang.
The ever-hooded, tragic-gestured sea
Was merely a place by which she walked to sing.
Whose spirit is this? we said, because we knew
It was the spirit that we sought and knew
20 That we should ask this often as she sang.

If it was only the dark voice of the sea
That rose, or even colored by many waves;
If it was only the outer voice of sky
And cloud, of the sunken coral water-walled,
25 However clear, it would have been deep air,
The heaving speech of air, a summer sound
Repeated in a summer without end
And sound alone. But it was more than that,
More even than her voice, and ours, among

[3]More precise or exact.

30 The meaningless plungings of water and the wind,
Theatrical distances, bronze shadows heaped
On high horizons, mountainous atmospheres
Of sky and sea.

It was her voice that made
35 The sky acutest at its vanishing.
She measured to the hour its solitude.
She was the single artificer of the world
In which she sang. And when she sang, the sea,
Whatever self it had, became the self
40 That was her song, for she was the maker. Then we,
As we beheld her striding there alone,
Knew that there never was a world for her
Except the one she sang and, singing, made.

Ramon Fernandez,[1] tell me, if you know,
45 Why, when the singing ended and we turned
Toward the town, tell why the glassy lights,
The lights in the fishing boats at anchor there,
As the night descended, tilting in the air,
Mastered the night and portioned out the sea,
50 Fixing emblazoned zones and fiery poles,
Arranging, deepening, enchanting night.

Oh! Blessed rage for order, pale Ramon,
The maker's rage to order words of the sea,
Words of the fragrant portals, dimly-starred,
55 And of ourselves and of our origins,
In ghostlier demarcations, keener sounds.

MRS. ALFRED URUGUAY

So what said the others and the sun went down
And, in the brown blues of evening, the lady said,
In the donkey's ear, "I fear that elegance
Must struggle like the rest." She climbed until
5 The moonlight in her lap, mewing[1] her velvet,

---

[1]A French literary critic (1894–1944).

---

[1]Mixing with.

And her dress were one and she said, "I have said no
To everything, in order to get at myself.
I have wiped away moonlight like mud. Your innocent ear
And I, if I rode naked, are what remain."

10 The moonlight crumbled to degenerate forms,
While she approached the real, upon her mountain,
With lofty darkness. The donkey was there to ride,
To hold by the ear, even though it wished for a bell,
Wished faithfully for a falsifying bell.
15 Neither the moonlight could change it. And for her,
To be, regardless of velvet, could never be more
Than to be, she could never differently be,
Her no and no made yes impossible.

Who was it passed her there on a horse all will,
20 What figure of capable imagination?
Whose horse clattered on the road on which she rose,
As it descended, blind to her and
The moonlight? Was it a rider intent on the sun,
A youth, a lover with phosphorescent hair,
25 Dressed poorly, arrogant of his streaming forces,
Lost in an integration of the martyrs' bones,
Rushing from what was real; and capable?

The villages slept as the capable man went down,
Time swished on the village clocks and dreams were alive,
30 The enormous gongs gave edges to their sounds,
As the rider, no chevalere[2] and poorly dressed.
Impatient of the bells and midnight forms,
Rode over the picket rocks, rode down the road,
And, capable, created in his mind,
35 Eventual victor, out of the martyrs' bones,
The ultimate elegance: the imagined land.

[2]Chevalier, or knight.

THIS SOLITUDE OF CATARACTS

He never felt twice the same about the flecked river,
Which kept flowing and never the same way twice, flowing

Through many places, as if it stood still in one,
Fixed like a lake on which the wild ducks fluttered,

5   Ruffling its common reflections, thought-like Monadnocks.[1]
There seemed to be an apostrophe that was not spoken.

There was so much that was real that was not real at all.
He wanted to feel the same way over and over.

He wanted the river to go on flowing the same way,
10   To keep on flowing. He wanted to walk beside it,

Under the buttonwoods, beneath a moon nailed fast.
He wanted his heart to stop beating and his mind to rest

In a permanent realization, without any wild ducks
Or mountains that were not mountains, just to know how it
        would be,

15   Just to know how it would feel, released from destruction,
To be a bronze man breathing under archaic lapis,[2]

Without the oscillations of planetary pass-pass,
Breathing his bronzen breath at the azury centre of time.

THE POEM THAT TOOK
THE PLACE OF A MOUNTAIN

There it was, word for word,
The poem that took the place of a mountain.

He breathed its oxygen,
Even when the book lay turned in the dust of his table.

[1]Mountain in New Hampshire.
[2]Latin for "stone."

5 It reminded him how he had needed
A place to go to in his own direction,

How he had recomposed the pines,
Shifted the rocks and picked his way among clouds,

For the outlook that would be right,
10 Where he would be complete in an unexplained completion:

The exact rock where his inexactnesses
Would discover, at last, the view toward which they had edged,

Where he could lie and, gazing down at the sea,
Recognize his unique and solitary home.

THE WORLD AS MEDITATION

*J'ai passé trop de temps à travailler mon violon, à voyager. Mais
l'exercice essentiel du compositeur—la méditation—rien ne l'a jamais
suspendu en moi . . . Je vis un rêve permanent, qui ne s'arrête ni nuit
ni jour.*[1]   Georges Enesco

Is it Ulysses that approaches from the east,
The interminable adventurer? The trees are mended.
That winter is washed away. Someone is moving

On the horizon and lifting himself up above it.
A form of fire approaches the cretonnes[2] of Penelope,[3]
Whose mere savage presence awakens the world in which she dwells.

She has composed, so long, a self with which to welcome him,
Companion to his self for her, which she imagined,
Two in a deep-founded sheltering, friend and dear friend.

The trees had been mended, as an essential exercise
In an inhuman meditation, larger than her own.
No winds like dogs watched over her at night.

[1]"I have spent too much time working on my violin, traveling. But the essential
work of the composer—meditation—nothing has ever suspended that in me
. . . I live a permanent dream that does not cease night or day." Georges
Enesco (1881–1955), Rumanian composer and musician.
[2]A heavy fabric used for draperies or covers.
[3]Ulysses' wife, who waited years for her wandering husband's return from Troy.

She wanted nothing he could not bring her by coming alone.
She wanted no fetchings. His arms would be her necklace
15 And her belt, the final fortune of their desire.

But was it Ulysses? Or was it only the warmth of the sun
On her pillow? The thought kept beating in her like her heart.
The two kept beating together. It was only day.

It was Ulysses and it was not. Yet they had met,
20 Friend and dear friend and a planet's encouragement.
The barbarous strength within her would never fail.

She would talk a little to herself as she combed her hair,
Repeating his name with its patient syllables,
Never forgetting him that kept coming constantly so near.

FINAL SOLILOQUY OF THE INTERIOR PARAMOUR

Light the first light of evening, as in a room
In which we rest and, for small reason, think
The world imagined is the ultimate good.

This is, therefore, the intensest rendezvous.
5 It is in that thought that we collect ourselves,
Out of all the indifferences, into one thing:

Within a single thing, a single shawl
Wrapped tightly round us, since we are poor, a warmth,
A light, a power, the miraculous influence.

10 Here, now, we forget each other and ourselves.
We feel the obscurity of an order, a whole,
A knowledge, that which arranged the rendezvous.

Within its vital boundary, in the mind.
We say God and the imagination are one . . .
15 How high that highest candle lights the dark.

Out of this same light, out of the central mind,
We make a dwelling in the evening air,
In which being there together is enough.

William Carlos Williams (1883–1963)   Like

Wallace Stevens, Williams had a long, successful, double career. He earned his medical degree at the University of Pennsylvania in 1906; there too he was already writing and had become a close friend of Ezra Pound and Hilda Doolittle (H.D.). He published *Poems* in 1909. Settling back into his birthplace, Rutherford, New Jersey, he married Florence Herman in 1912 and moved the next year to 9 Ridge Road, their home thereafter; he had a private medical practice and a position at the Passaic General Hospital.

Williams was included in Pound's anthology *Des Imagistes* and from the first was a source of energy and inspiration for contemporaries and younger poets. In his letters and friendships, in the little magazines he edited and wrote for, in his poetic practice and theory, he expressed an objectivist approach that countered intellectual abstraction and romantic subjectivity with the motto "no ideas but in things." Technically he strove for an idiom and rhythm for American poetry in vehement opposition to expatriates like Eliot who had succumbed to the traditions of the Old World. The many volumes of poetry published through 1939 (including *Spring and All,* 1922) were gathered in *The Collected Earlier Poems* (1951), which received the National Book Award; *The Collected Later Poems* (1950) actually contains only the shorter pieces of the forties. *Paterson,* published in five books between 1946 and 1958, creates, in the identification of the poet with his city, a free-form epic affirming life in the face of its ugliness and pain. The last collections, written often in triadic lines that Williams called "the variable foot," are: *The Desert Music* (1954); *Journey to Love* (1955); and *Pictures from Breughel* (1962), which brought Williams the Pulitzer Prize.

Besides verse, Williams wrote stories, novels, plays, and a book of poetic essays re-creating figures from American history, *In the American Grain* (1925). A series of strokes forced him to give up medical practice in the fifties and restricted his writing. The Bollingen Prize of 1953 and the Pulitzer Prize posthumously in 1963 were a recognition of his pervasive presence in the poetic scene, influencing poets as different as Robert Lowell and Allen Ginsberg, Charles Olson and Adrienne Rich. His power was his integrity, sourcing his art in the immediacies and asserting their validity in poems open and joyous.

REFERENCE

Miller, J. Hillis. *Poets of Reality.* Cambridge, Mass.: Harvard University Press, 1965.

Wagner, Linda W. *The Poems of William Carlos Williams.* Middletown, Conn.: Wesleyan University Press, 1964.

Wagner, Linda W. *The Prose of William Carlos Williams.* Middletown, Conn.: Wesleyan University Press, 1970.

Weaver, Mike. *William Carlos Williams: The American Background.* New York: Cambridge University Press, 1971.

William Carlos Williams: A Collection of Critical Essays. Ed. J. Hillis Miller. Englewood Cliffs, N. J.: Prentice-Hall, 1966.

Williams, William Carlos. *The Autobiography.* New York: New Directions, 1951.

Williams, William Carlos. *Selected Essays.* New York: Random House, 1954.

Williams, William Carlos. *Selected Letters.* Ed. John C. Thirlwall. New York: McDowell, Obolenky, 1957.

THE LOCUST TREE IN FLOWER

Among
of
green

stiff
5 old
bright

broken
branch
come

10 white
sweet
May

again

PROLETARIAN PORTRAIT

A big young bareheaded woman
in an apron

Her hair slicked back standing
on the street

5 One stockinged foot toeing
the sidewalk

Her shoe in her hand. Looking
intently into it

She pulls out the paper insole
10 to find the nail

That has been hurting her

THE YACHTS

contend in a sea which the land partly encloses
shielding them from the too-heavy blows
of an ungoverned ocean which when it chooses

tortures the biggest hulls, the best man knows
5 to pit against its beatings, and sinks them pitilessly.
Mothlike in mists, scintillant in the minute

brilliance of cloudless days, with broad bellying sails
they glide to the wind tossing green water
from their sharp prows while over them the crew crawls

10 ant-like, solicitously grooming them, releasing,
making fast as they turn, lean far over and having
caught the wind again, side by side, head for the mark.

In a well guarded arena of open water surrounded by
lesser and greater craft which, sycophant, lumbering
15 and flittering follow them, they appear youthful, rare

as the light of a happy eye, live with the grace
of all that in the mind is fleckless, free and
naturally to be desired. Now the sea which holds them

is moody, lapping their glossy sides, as if feeling
20 for some slightest flaw but fails completely.
Today no race. Then the wind comes again. The yachts

move, jockeying for a start, the signal is set and they
are off. Now the waves strike at them but they are too
well made, they slip through, though they take in canvas.

25 Arms with hands grasping seek to clutch at the prows.
Bodies thrown recklessly in the way are cut aside.
It is a sea of faces about them in agony, in despair

until the horror of the race dawns staggering the mind;
the whole sea become an entanglement of watery bodies
30 lost to the world bearing what they cannot hold. Broken,

beaten, desolate, reaching from the dead to be taken up
they cry out, failing, failing! their cries rising
in waves still as the skillful yachts pass over.

THE YOUNG HOUSEWIFE

At ten A.M. the young housewife
moves about in negligee behind
the wooden walls of her husband's house.
I pass solitary in my car.

5   Then again she comes to the curb
to call the ice-man, fish-man, and stands
shy, uncorseted, tucking in
stray ends of hair, and I compare her
to a fallen leaf.

10 The noiseless wheels of my car
rush with a crackling sound over
dried leaves as I bow and pass smiling.

PATERSON¹

Before the grass is out the people are out
and bare twigs still whip the wind—
when there is nothing, in the pause between
snow and grass in the parks and at the street ends
5   —Say it, no ideas but in things—
nothing but the blank faces of the houses
and cylindrical trees
bent, forked by preconception and accident
split, furrowed, creased, mottled, stained
10 secret—into the body of the light—
These are the ideas, savage and tender
somewhat of the music, et cetera
of Paterson, that great philosopher—

From above, higher than the spires, higher
15 even than the office towers, from oozy fields
abandoned to grey beds of dead grass
black sumac, withered weed stalks

---

¹Written in 1926, twenty years before the publication of Book One of the long
poem *Paterson*. But this poem does make the link between the city and the
man Paterson, and between Paterson and the poet. Some lines survive in the
later poem.

mud and thickets cluttered with dead leaves—
the river comes pouring in above the city
20   and crashes from the edge of the gorge
in a recoil of spray and rainbow mists—
—Say it, no ideas but in things—
and factories crystallized from its force,
like ice from spray upon the chimney rocks

•

25   Say it! No ideas but in things. Mr.
Paterson has gone away
to rest and write. Inside the bus one sees
his thoughts sitting and standing. His thoughts
alight and scatter—

30   Who are these people (how complex
this mathematic) among whom I see myself
in the regularly ordered plateglass of
his thoughts, glimmering before shoes and bicycles—?
They walk incommunicado, the
35   equation is beyond solution, yet
its sense is clear—that they may live
his thought is listed in the Telephone
Directory—

and there's young Alex Shorn
40   whose dad the boot-black bought a house
and painted it inside
with seascapes of a pale green monochrome—
the infant Dionysus springing from
Apollo's arm—the floors oakgrained in
45   Balkan fashion—Hermes' nose, the body
of a gourmand, the lips of Cupid, the eyes
the black eyes of Venus' sister—[2]

But who! who are these people? It is
his flesh making the traffic, cranking the car
50   buying the meat—
Defeated in achieving the solution they
fall back among cheap pictures, furniture
filled silk, cardboard shoes, bad dentistry

[2]Dionysus, the god of wine and fertility; Apollo, the god of the sun and the lyre; Hermes, the god of commerce and invention; Venus, the love goddess with her offspring Cupid.

windows that will not open, poisonous gin
55 scurvy, toothache—

●

But never, in despair and anxiety
forget to drive wit in, in till it
discover that his thoughts are decorous and simple
and never forget that though his thoughts are decorous
60 and simple, the despair and anxiety
the grace and detail of
a dynamo—

Divine thought! Jacob fell backwards off the press
and broke his spine. What pathos, what mercy
65 of nurses (who keep birthday books)
and doctors who can't speak proper english—
is here correctly on a spotless bed
painless to the Nth power—the two legs
perfect without movement or sensation

70 Twice a month Paterson receives letters
from the Pope, his works are translated
into French, the clerks in the post office
ungum the rare stamps from his packages
and steal them for their children's albums

75 So in his high decorum he is wise

●

What wind and sun of children stamping the snow
stamping the snow and screaming drunkenly
The actual, florid detail of cheap carpet
amazingly upon the floor and paid for
80 as no portrait ever was—Canary singing
and geraniums in tin cans spreading their leaves
reflecting red upon the frost—
They are the divisions and imbalances
of his whole concept, made small by pity
85 and desire, they are—no ideas beside the facts—

SPRING AND ALL

By the road to the contagious hospital
under the surge of the blue
mottled clouds driven from the
northeast—a cold wind. Beyond, the
5   waste of broad, muddy fields
brown with dried weeds, standing and fallen

patches of standing water
the scattering of tall trees

All along the road the reddish
10   purplish, forked, upstanding, twiggy
stuff of bushes and small trees
with dead, brown leaves under them
leafless vines—

Lifeless in appearance, sluggish
15   dazed spring approaches—

They enter the new world naked,
cold, uncertain of all
save that they enter. All about them
the cold, familiar wind—

20   Now the grass, tomorrow
the stiff curl of wildcarrot leaf
One by one objects are defined—
It quickens: clarity, outline of leaf

But now the stark dignity of
25   entrance—Still, the profound change
has come upon them: rooted, they
grip down and begin to awaken

THE POT OF FLOWERS

Pink confused with white
flowers and flowers reversed
take and spill the shaded flame
darting it back
5 into the lamp's horn

petals aslant darkened with mauve

red where in whorls
petal lays its glow upon petal
round flamegreen throats

10 petals radiant with transpiercing light
contending
            above
the leaves
reaching up their modest green
15 from the pot's rim

and there, wholly dark, the pot
gay with rough moss.

THE RED WHEELBARROW

so much depends
upon

a red wheel
barrow

5 glazed with rain
water

beside the white
chickens.

POEM

As the cat
climbed over
the top of

the jamcloset
5 first the right
forefoot

carefully
then the hind
stepped down

10 into the pit of
the empty
flowerpot

THIS IS JUST TO SAY

I have eaten
the plums
that were in
the icebox

5 and which
you were probably
saving
for breakfast

Forgive me
10 they were delicious
so sweet
and so cold

BURNING THE CHRISTMAS GREENS

Their time past, pulled down
cracked and flung to the fire
—go up in a roar

All recognition lost, burnt clean
5   clean in the flame, the green
dispersed, a living red,
flame red, red as blood wakes
on the ash—

and ebbs to a steady burning
10   the rekindled bed become
a landscape of flame

At the winter's midnight
we went to the trees, the coarse
holly, the balsam and
15   the hemlock for their green

At the thick of the dark
the moment of the cold's
deepest plunge we brought branches
cut from the green trees

20   to fill our need, and over
doorways, about paper Christmas
bells covered with tinfoil
and fastened by red ribbons

we stuck the green prongs
25   in the windows hung
woven wreaths and above pictures
the living green. On the

mantle we built a green forest
and among those hemlock
30   sprays put a herd of small
white deer as if they

were walking there. All this!
and it seemed gentle and good

    to us. Their time past,
35 relief! The room bare. We

    stuffed the dead grate
    with them upon the half burnt out
    log's smoldering eye, opening
    red and closing under them

40 and we stood there looking down.
    Green is a solace
    a promise of peace, a fort
    against the cold (though we

    did not say so) a challenge
45 above the snow's
    hard shell. Green (we might
    have said) that, where

    small birds hide and dodge
    and lift their plaintive
50 rallying cries, blocks for them
    and knocks down

    the unseeing bullets of
    the storm. Green spruce boughs
    pulled down by a weight of
55 snow—Transformed!

    Violence leaped and appeared.
    Recreant! roared to life
    as the flame rose through and
    our eyes recoiled from it.

60 In the jagged flames green
    to red, instant and alive. Green!
    those sure abutments . . . Gone!
    lost to mind

    and quick in the contracting
65 tunnel of the grate
    appeared a world! Black
    mountains, black and red—as

yet uncolored—and ash white,
an infant landscape of shimmering
70   ash and flame and we, in
that instant, lost,

breathless to be witnesses,
as if we stood
ourselves refreshed among
75   the shining fauna of that fire.

THE DANCE

In Breughel's great picture, The Kermess,[1]
the dancers go round, they go round and
around, the squeal and the blare and the
tweedle of bagpipes, a bugle and fiddles
5   tipping their bellies (round as the thick-
sided glasses whose wash they impound)
their hips and their bellies off balance
to turn them. Kicking and rolling about
the Fair Grounds, swinging their butts, those
10   shanks must be sound to bear up under such
rollicking measures, prance as they dance
in Breughel's great picture, The Kermess.

THE DESCENT

The descent beckons
            as the ascent beckoned.
                        Memory is a kind
of accomplishment,
5   a sort of renewal
                        even
an initiation, since the spaces it opens are new places
            inhabited by hordes
                        heretofore unrealized,

[1]Peter Breughel (or Brueghel) (1525?–1569), Flemish painter. "Kermess" means
"fair."

10 of new kinds—
                    since their movements
                                are toward new objectives
            (even though formerly they were abandoned).

      No defeat is made up entirely of defeat—since
15   the world it opens is always a place
                        formerly
                                unsuspected. A
            world lost,
                    a world unsuspected,
20   beckons to new places
            and no whiteness (lost) is so white as the memory
            of whiteness   .

      With evening, love wakens
                        though its shadows
25   which are alive by reason
            of the sun shining—
                        grow sleepy now and drop away
                                from desire   .

      Love without shadows stirs now
30   beginning to awaken
                                    as night
            advances.

      The descent
                    made up of despairs
35   and without accomplishment
            realizes a new awakening:
                            which is a reversal
            of despair.
                        For what we cannot accomplish, what
40   is denied to love,
                    what we have lost in the anticipation—
                            a descent follows,
            endless and indestructible   .

THE YELLOW FLOWER

What shall I say, because talk I must?
        That I have found a cure
                for the sick?
I have found no cure
5   for the sick   .
                but this crooked flower
which only to look upon
        all men
                are cured. This
10 is that flower
        for which all men
                sing secretly their hymns
of praise. This
        is that sacred
15   flower!

Can this be so?
        A flower so crooked
                and obscure? It is
a mustard flower
20   and not a mustard flower,
                a single spray
topping the deformed stem
        of fleshy leaves
                in this freezing weather
25 under glass.

An ungainly flower and
        an unnatural one,
                in this climate; what
can be the reason
30   that it has picked me out
                to hold me, openmouthed,
rooted before this window
        in the cold,
                my will
35 drained from me
        so that I have only eyes
                for these yellow,
twisted petals   . ?

That the sight,
40   though strange to me,
                must be a common one,
is clear: there are such flowers
       with such leaves
             native to some climate
45 which they can call
       their own.

But why the torture
       and the escape through
             the flower? It is
50 as if Michelangelo
       had conceived the subject
             of his *Slaves*[1] from this
—or might have done so.
       And did he not make
55   the marble bloom? I
am sad
       as he was sad
             in his heroic mood.
But also
60   I have eyes
             that are made to see and if
they see ruin for myself
       and all that I hold
             dear, they see
65 also
       through the eyes
             and through the lips
and tongue the power
       to free myself
70   and speak of it, as
Michelangelo through his hands
       had the same, if greater,
             power.

Which leaves, to account for,
75   the tortured bodies
             of
the slaves themselves

---

[1]Unfinished sculptures of Michelangelo Buonarroti (1475–1564), in which the rough forms are embedded in the stone from which they are being carved.

and

the tortured body of my flower

80 which is not a mustard flower at all

but some unrecognized

and unearthly flower

for me to naturalize

and acclimate

85 and choose it for my own.

THE MENTAL HOSPITAL GARDEN

It is far to Assisi,[1]

but not too far:

Over this garden,

brooding over this garden,

5 there is a kindly spirit,

brother to the poor

and who is poorer than he

who is in love

when birds are nesting

10 in the spring of the year?

They came

to eat from his hand

who had nothing,

and yet

15 from his plenty

he fed them all.

All mankind

grew to be his debtors,

a simple story.

20 Love is in season.

At such a time,

hyacinth time

in

the hospital garden,

25 the time

of the coral-flowered

---

[1] Italian hill town associated with St. Francis (1182?–1226), the mystic known for his spirit of love and humility and poverty.

and early salmon-pink
clusters, it is
the time also of
30   abandoned birds' nests
before
the sparrows start
to tear them apart
against the advent of that bounty
35   from which
they will build anew.

All about them
on the lawns
the young couples
40   embrace   .
as in a tale
by Boccaccio.[2]
They are careless
under license of the disease
45   which has restricted them
to these grounds.
St. Francis forgive them
and all lovers
whoever they may be.
50   They have seen
a great light, it
springs from their own bawdy foreheads.
The light
is sequestered there
55   by these enclosing walls.
They are divided
from their fellows.
It is a bounty
from a last year's bird's nest.
60   St. Francis,
who befriended the wild birds,
by their aid,
those who
have nothing
65   and live
by the Holy light of love

---

[2]Giovanni Boccaccio (1313–1375), known for his tales of love and sexual passion.

that rules,
> blocking despair,
>> over this garden.

70 Times passes.
> The pace has slackened
>> But with the falling off
of the pace
> the scene has altered.
75 >> The lovers raise their heads,
at that which has come over them.
> It is summer now.
>> The broad sun
shines!
80 > Blinded by the light
>> they walk bewildered,
seeking
> between the leaves
>> for a vantage
85 from which to view
> the advancing season.
>> They are incredulous
of their own cure
> and half minded
90 >> to escape
into the dark again.
> The scene
>> indeed has changed.
By St. Francis
95 > the whole scene
>> has changed.
They glimpse
> a surrounding sky
>> and the whole countryside.
100 Filled with terror
> they seek
>> a familiar flower
at which to warm themselves,
> but the whole field
105 >> accosts them.
They hide their eyes
> ashamed
>> before that bounty,
peering through their fingers

110   timidly.
                              The saint is watching,
            his eyes filled with pity.

        The year is still young
                      but not so young
115   as they
            who face the fears
                      with which
                              they are confronted.
            Reawakened
120   after love's first folly
                              they resemble children
            roused from a long sleep.
                      Summer is here,
                              right enough.
125   The saint
                  has tactfully withdrawn.
                              One
            emboldened,
                      parting the leaves before her,
130   stands in the full sunlight,
            alone
                      shading her eyes
                              as her heart
            beats wildly
135   and her mind
                              drinks up
            the full meaning
                      of it
                              all!

THE SPARROW

TO MY FATHER

        This sparrow
                  who comes to sit at my window
                              is a poetic truth
            more than a natural one.
5   His voice,
                              his movements,

his habits—
>   how he loves to
>   flutter his wings
10 in the dust—
>   all attest it;
>   granted, he does it
to rid himself of lice
>   but the relief he feels
15   makes him
cry out lustily—
>   which is a trait
>   more related to music
than otherwise.
20   Wherever he finds himself
>   in early spring,
on back streets
>   or beside palaces,
>   he carries on
25 unaffectedly
>   his amours.
>   It begins in the egg,
his sex genders it:
>   What is more pretentiously
30   useless
or about which
>   we more pride ourselves?
>   It leads as often as not
to our undoing.
35   The cockerel, the crow
>   with their challenging voices
cannot surpass
>   the insistence
>   of his cheep!
40 Once
>   at El Paso
>   toward evening,
I saw—and heard!—
>   ten thousand sparrows
45   who had come in from
the desert
>   to roost. They filled the trees
>   of a small park. Men fled
(with ears ringing!)
50   from their droppings,
>   leaving the premises

          to the alligators
                    who inhabit
                              the fountain. His image
55   is familiar
                    as that of the aristocratic
                              unicorn, a pity
          there are not more oats eaten
                    nowadays
60   to make living easier
          for him.
                    At that,
                              his small size,
          keen eyes,
65   serviceable beak
                              and general truculence
          assure his survival—
                    to say nothing
                              of his innumerable
70   brood.
                    Even the Japanese
                              know him
          and have painted him
                    sympathetically,
75   with profound insight
          into his minor
                    characteristics.
                              Nothing even remotely
          subtle
80   about his lovemaking.
                              He crouches
          before the female,
                    drags his wings,
                              waltzing,
85   throws back his head
                    and simply—
                              yells! The din
          is terrific.
                    The way he swipes his bill
90   across a plank
          to clean it,
                    is decisive.
                              So with everything
          he does. His coppery
95   eyebrows

                    give him the air
of being always
            a winner—and yet
                    I saw once,
100   the female of his species
            clinging determinedly
                    to the edge of
a water pipe,
            catch him
105   by his crown-feathers
to hold him
            silent,
                    subdued,
hanging above the city streets
110   until
                    she was through with him.
What was the use
            of that?
                    She hung there
115   herself,
            puzzled at her success.
                    I laughed heartily.
Practical to the end,
            it is the poem
120   of his existence
that triumphed
            finally;
                    a wisp of feathers
flattened to the pavement,
125   wings spread symmetrically
                    as if in flight,
the head gone,
            the black escutcheon of the breast
                    undecipherable,
130   an effigy of a sparrow,
            a dried wafer only,
                    left to say
and it says it
            without offense,
135   beautifully;
This was I,
            a sparrow.
                    I did my best;
farewell.

Ezra Pound (1885–1972)

Although born in mining country in Hailey, Idaho, Pound grew up in Wyncote, Pennsylvania. After graduating from Hamilton College, he got an M. A. in Romanics at the University of Pennsylvania, where he became a close friend of William Carlos Williams and Hilda Doolittle (H.D.). In 1908 he went to Venice, where his first book, *A Lume Spento,* was published. Then he settled in England, became companion and secretary to W. B. Yeats, and soon was the center of the American expatriate group in London. Through his reviews, his connection with little magazines, his zestful enthusiasm, even his financial assistance when he himself had little money, Pound did more than any other individual for the promotion of modern letters, sponsoring among others Frost, Eliot, and Joyce. He drew up the axioms of Imagism in *Poetry* magazine in 1913 and edited an anthology, *Des Imagistes,* the next year.

To escape the static limitations of Imagist technique Pound embraced Vorticism with Wyndham Lewis, because Vorticism asserted the dynamism of art and saw particular cities and cultures as centers for a creative outburst in art and society, poetry and politics. In fact, for all his loathing of American materialism the expatriate's energy was bent on arousing an American renaissance.

Pound's numerous volumes of shorter poems were collected, along with *Homage to Sextus Propertius* (1919) and *Hugh Selwyn Mauberley* (1920), into *Personae* (1926). But by 1917 the first versions of three cantos had appeared in *Poetry,* and Pound was launched on his life's work: a personal and historical epic whose form was organic to his developing perceptions and intuitions, and whose sources ranged from Greek myth to Renaissance chronicles to Confucian ethics to newspaper headlines to the poet's unconscious. Pound had become fascinated with the Chinese ideogrammic method, largely through editing Ernest Fenellosa's manuscript into "The Chinese Written Character as a Medium for Poetry." *The Cantos* are an extended effort to fashion in the juxtaposition of phrases and images some English equivalent to the pictograph that presents ideas in concrete actions.

In 1914 Pound had married Dorothy Shakespear; they moved to Paris in 1920 and to Italy in 1924, settling in Rapallo. His economic concerns had brought him to denounce the capitalist profit-motive as the unnatural perversion of man's relation to nature and to society, and now he saw in Social Credit an equitable method for the distribution of goods and in Mussolini's brand of Fascism the modern counterpart of Jeffersonian social ideals. During World War II he made vehement, anti-Semitic radio broadcasts from Rome blaming the war on the money interests and urging his countrymen to refuse to fight for usurers. Arrested in 1944, Pound was kept by the American forces in solitary confinement in a detention camp near Pisa, until he was brought back to stand trial for treason. Found mentally unfit for trial, he was kept in St. Elizabeth's Hospital near Washington, where friends and disciples gathered about him until his release in 1958. Upon his return to Italy he lived in Merano and Venice, where he died. His last years were spent in silent meditation.

The principal segments of *The Cantos* (1970) are: *A Draft of XXX Cantos* (1930), *Eleven New Cantos* (1934), *Fifth Decade of Cantos* (1937), *Cantos LII–LXXI* (1940), *The Pisan Cantos* (1948), *Section Rock-Drill* (1955), *Thrones* (1959), and *Drafts and Fragments of Cantos CX–CXVII* (1968). Pound pursued his ideas in his prose as well: *An ABC of Economics* (1933), *An ABC of Reading* (1934), *Guide to Kulchur* (1938), *Literary Essays* (1954), *Impact* (1960). Not only is Pound supremely important as an emanating influence in twentieth-century poetry; *The Cantos* is one of the monumental works of the American imagination and the most ambitious experiment in organic form since *Leaves of Grass*.

REFERENCE

Davie, Donald. *Ezra Pound: Poet As Sculptor*. New York: Oxford University Press, 1964.

Edwards, John and William Vasse. *An Annotated Index to the Cantos of Ezra Pound*. Berkeley: University of California Press, 1958.

Emery, Clark. *Ideas into Action: A Study of Pound's Cantos*. Miami: University of Miami Press, 1957.

Ezra Pound: A Collection of Critical Essays. Ed. Walter Sutton. Englewood Cliffs, N.J.: Prentice-Hall, 1963.

Kenner, Hugh. *The Poetry of Ezra Pound*. London: Faber and Faber, 1951.

Kenner, Hugh. *The Pound Era*. Berkeley: University of California Press, 1971.

Pearlman, Daniel. *The Barb of Time: On the Unity of Ezra Pound's Cantos*. New York: Oxford University Press, 1969.

Pound, Ezra. *The Letters of Ezra Pound, 1907–1941*. Ed. D. D. Paige. New York: Harcourt, Brace, 1950.

Stock, Noel. *The Life of Ezra Pound*. New York: Pantheon, 1970.

Witemeyer, Hugh. *The Poetry of Ezra Pound: Forms and Renewal, 1908–1920*. Berkeley: University of California Press, 1969.

THE TREE

I stood still and was a tree amid the wood,
Knowing the truth of things unseen before;
Of Daphne[1] and the laurel bow
And that god-feasting couple[2] old
5   That grew elm-oak amid the wold.[3]
'Twas not until the gods had been
Kindly entreated, and been brought within
Unto the hearth of their heart's home
That they might do this wonder thing;
10   Nathless[4] I have been a tree amid the wood
And many a new thing understood
That was rank folly to my head before.

PARACELSUS IN EXCELSIS[1]

"Being no longer human, why should I
Pretend humanity or don the frail attire?
Men have I known and men, but never one
Was grown so free an essence, or become
5   So simply element as what I am.
The mist goes from the mirror and I see.
Behold! the world of forms is swept beneath—
Turmoil grown visible beneath our peace,
And we that are grown formless, rise above—
10   Fluids intangible that have been men,
We seem as statues round whose high-risen base
Some overflowing river is run mad,
In us alone the element of calm."

[1]A nymph who was metamorphosed into a laurel tree to escape the advances of Apollo.
[2]As recounted by Ovid in *Metamorphoses*, an aged couple named Philemon and Baucis were rewarded for their generous hospitality to Zeus and Hermes, wandering in human form, so that they were permitted after a long and loving life to die at the same time and be changed into intertwining trees.
[3]Plain.
[4]Nevertheless.

[1]"Paracelsus on High" in Latin; Paracelsus, whose real name was Theophrastus Bombastus von Hohenheim (1493–1541), was a Swiss alchemist who probed the mysteries of life, nature, and eternity.

THE GARDEN

En robe de parade.
Samain[1]

Like a skein of loose silk blown against a wall
She walks by the railing of a path in Kensington Gardens,[2]
And she is dying piece-meal
    of a sort of emotional anæmia.

And round about there is a rabble
5 Of the filthy, sturdy, unkillable infants of the very poor.
They shall inherit the earth.[3]

In her is the end of breeding.
Her boredom is exquisite and excessive.
She would like some one to speak to her,
10 And is almost afraid that I
    will commit that indiscretion.

SALUTATION

O generation of the thoroughly smug
    and thoroughly uncomfortable,
I have seen fishermen picnicking in the sun,
I have seen them with untidy families,
I have seen their smiles full of teeth
    and heard ungainly laughter.
5 And I am happier than you are,
And they were happier than I am;
And the fish swim in the lake
    and do not even own clothing.

---

[1]In parade uniform; Albert Samain (1858–1900) was a French Parnassian poet.
[2]In London.
[3]One of Jesus' Beatitudes: "Blessed are the humble, for they shall inherit the earth" (Matthew 5:4).

A PACT

I make a pact with you, Walt Whitman—
I have detested you long enough.
I come to you as a grown child
Who has had a pig-headed father;
5   I am old enough now to make friends.
It was you that broke the new wood,
Now is a time for carving.
We have one sap and one root—
Let there be commerce between us.

IN A STATION OF THE METRO[1]

The apparition of these faces in the crowd;
Petals on a wet, black bough.

ALBA[1]

As cool as the pale wet leaves
                              of lily-of-the-valley
She lay beside me in the dawn.

[1]The Paris subway system.

[1]Feminine of Latin adjective for "white"; hence, white girl.

THE JEWEL STAIRS' GRIEVANCE

The jewelled steps are already quite white with dew,
It is so late that the dew soaks my gauze stockings,
And I let down the crystal curtain
And watch the moon through the clear autumn.[1]

By Rihaku[2]

LAMENT OF THE FRONTIER GUARD

By the North Gate, the wind blows full of sand,
Lonely from the beginning of time until now!
Trees fall, the grass goes yellow with autumn,
I climb the towers and towers
    to watch out the barbarous land:
5   Desolate castle, the sky, the wide desert.
There is no wall left to this village.
Bones white with a thousand frosts,
High heaps, covered with trees and grass;
Who brought this to pass?
10 Who has brought the flaming imperial anger?
Who has brought the army with drums and with kettle-drums?
Barbarous kings.
A gracious spring, turned to blood-ravenous autumn,
A turmoil of wars-men, spread over the middle kingdom,
15 Three hundred and sixty thousand,
And sorrow, sorrow like rain.
Sorrow to go, and sorrow, sorrow returning.
Desolate, desolate fields,
And no children of warfare upon them,
20   No longer the men for offence and defence.
Ah, how shall you know the dreary sorrow at the North Gate,
With Rihoku's name forgotten,
And we guardsmen fed to the tigers.

By Rihaku

[1]Pound's note: "Jewel stairs, therefore a palace. Grievance, therefore there is
something to complain of. Gauze stockings, therefore a court lady, not a ser-
vant who complains. Clear autumn, therefore he has no excuse on account of
weather. Also she has come early, for the dew has not merely whitened the
stairs, but has soaked her stockings. The poem is especially prized because she
utters no direct reproach."
[2]Rihaku or Rihoku or Li Po (c. 700–762): Chinese poet, several of whose poems
Pound translated and adapted.

from **Hugh Selwyn Mauberley**

I

E. P. ODE POUR L'ÉLECTION DE SON SÉPULCHRE[1]

For three years, out of key with his time,
He strove to resuscitate the dead art
Of poetry; to maintain "the sublime"
In the old sense. Wrong from the start—

5   No, hardly, but seeing he had been born
In a half savage country, out of date;
Bent resolutely on wringing lilies from the acorn;
Capaneus;[2] trout for factitious bait;

Ἴδμεν γάρ τοι πάνθ', 'ὅσ' 'ενὶ Τροίῃ[3]
10   Caught in the unstopped ear;
Giving the rocks small lee-way
The chopped seas held him, therefore, that year.

His true Penelope was Flaubert,[4]
He fished by obstinate isles;
15   Observed the elegance of Circe's[5] hair
Rather than the mottoes on sun-dials.

Unaffected by "the march of events,"
He passed from men's memory in *l'an trentiesme
De son eage*;[6] the case presents
20   No adjunct to the Muses'[7] diadem.

---

[1]"Ode for the Choice of His Tomb." Pierre de Ronsard (1524–1585) wrote a poem entitled "De l'Élection de son Sépulchre." The initials "E. P." identify Pound as the subject, but he is seen from the outside—in part ironically by the world in which he has been a failure, in part heroically as a modern wanderer like Odysseus.

[2]One of the seven warrior-leaders who fought against Eteocles of Thebes on behalf of Eteocles' brother Polynices. Capaneus was struck down from the city walls by Zeus' lightning for his impiety.

[3]Odyssey, XII, 189: "For we know all the things that are in Troy." A phrase from the song of the Sirens, sea nymphs whose voices lured sailors to death on the rocks. Odysseus escaped death by tying himself to the mast while he listened to their song.

[4]Penelope: Odysseus' wife who waited years for his return in Troy; Gustave Flaubert (1821–1880): French novelist whose style Pound admired.

[5]The enchantress who held Odysseus and his men captive for a time.

[6]"The thirtieth year of his age"; from *Le Testament* of François Villon (1431–1463).

[7]Nine sisters who presided over the arts.

II

The age demanded an image
Of its accelerated grimace,
Something for the modern stage,
Not, at any rate, an Attic[1] grace;

5   Not, not certainly, the obscure reveries
Of the inward gaze;
Better mendacities
Than the classics in paraphrase!

The "age demanded" chiefly a mould in plaster,
10 Made with no loss of time,
A prose kinema,[2] not, not assuredly, alabaster
Or the "sculpture" of rhyme.

IV

These fought in any case,
and some believing,
          pro domo,[1] in any case . . .

Some quick to arm,
5   some for adventure,
some from fear of weakness,
some from fear of censure,
some for love of slaughter, in imagination,
learning later . . .
10 some in fear, learning love of slaughter;

Died some, pro patria,
         non "dulce" non "et decor" . . .[2]
walked eye-deep in hell
believing in old men's lies, then unbelieving
15 came home, home to a lie,

[1]Athens was in Attica in ancient Greece.
[2]Cinema.

---

[1]Latin for "for home"; Cicero's *Pro Domo Sua (For His Home).*
[2]Horace, *Carmina,* III, ii, 13: "Dulce et decorum est pro patria mori." (It is sweet and fitting to die for the country.)

home to many deceits,
home to old lies and new infamy;
usury age-old and age-thick
and liars in public places.

20   Daring as never before, wastage as never before.
Young blood and high blood,
fair cheeks, and fine bodies;

fortitude as never before

frankness as never before,
25   disillusions as never told in the old days,
hysterias, trench confessions,
laughter out of dead bellies.

V

There died a myriad,
And of the best, among them,
For an old bitch gone in the teeth,
For a botched civilization,

5   Charm, smiling at the good mouth,
Quick eyes gone under earth's lid,

For two gross of broken statues,
For a few thousand battered books.

CANTO II

Hang it all, Robert Browning,[1]
there can be but the one "Sordello."
But Sordello, and my Sordello?
Lo Sordels si fo di Mantovana.
5   So-shu[2] churned in the sea.
Seal sports in the spray-whited circles of cliff-wash,
Sleek head, daughter of Lir,[3]
           eyes of Picasso[4]
Under black fur-hood, lithe daughter of Ocean;
10   And the wave runs in the beach-groove:[5]
"Eleanor, ἑλέναυς and ἑλέπτοις!"[6]
           And poor old Homer blind, blind, as a bat,
Ear, ear for the sea-surge, murmur of old men's voices:
"Let her go back to the ships,
15   Back among Grecian faces, lest evil come on our own,
Evil and further evil, and a curse cursed on our children,
Moves, yes she moves like a goddess
And has the face of a god
           and the voice of Schoeney's daughters.[7]
20   And doom goes with her in walking,
Let her go back to the ships,
           back among Grecian voices."
And by the beach-run, Tyro,[8]
           Twisted arms of the sea-god,
25   Lithe sinews of water, gripping her, cross-hold,
And the blue-gray glass of the wave tents them,
Glare azure of water, cold-welter, close cover.

[1]Pound is declaring that in *The Cantos* he cannot continue to imitate the dramatic monologues of Robert Browning (1812–1889), as he had done in earlier poems. There can be only one poem like Browning's "Sordello." But what about the historical man Sordello and the poet's image of him? The answer in Italian is fact: "The Sordello come from Mantua." Instead of a straightforward dramatic monologue, the Canto constructs an extended and intricate ideogram.
[2]The Japanese name of the Chinese poet Li Po.
[3]A Celtic sea god. The Canto is a series of images and episodes of the sea.
[4]Pablo Picasso, the Spanish artist (1881–   ); the woman's eyes like those in Picasso's paintings.
[5]An imitation of a line from Homer, leading into the subsequent episode from the third book of *The Iliad.*
[6]Helen (Eleanor) is the type of woman whose beauty is a powerful and dangerous force. The Greek epithets mean: "Destroyer of ships, destroyer of men."
[7]Atalanta was Schoeneus' daughter, famous for her beauty and swiftness of foot.
[8]The daughter of Salmoneus, loved by Poseidon, the god of the sea.

Quiet sun-tawny sand-stretch,
The gulls broad out their wings,
30   nipping between the splay feathers;
Snipe come for their bath,
       bend out their wing-joints,
Spread wet wings to the sun-film,
And by Scios,[9]
35   to left of the Naxos[10] passage,
Naviform rock overgrown,
       algæ cling to its edge,
There is a wine-red glow in the shallows,
       a tin flash in the sun-dazzle.

40 The ship landed in Scios,
       men wanting spring water,
And by the rock-pool a young boy loggy with vine-must,[11]
       To Naxos? Yes, we'll take you to Naxos,
Cum' along lad." "Not that way!"
45 "Aye, that way is Naxos."
       And I said: "It's a straight ship."
And an ex-convict out of Italy
       knocked me into the fore-stays,
(He was wanted for manslaughter in Tuscany)[12]
50   And the whole twenty against me,
Mad for a little slave money.
       And they took her out of Scios
And off her course . . .
       And the boy came to, again, with the racket,
55 And looked out over the bows,
       and to eastward, and to the Naxos passage.
God-sleight then, god-sleight:[13]
       Ship stock fast in sea-swirl,

---

[9]This extended episode is adapted from Ovid's *Metmorphoses* and presented as Acoetes' words to King Pentheus of Thebes. Acoetes was captain of a ship that picked up Dionysus in the form of a boy. Dionysus is the god of fertility as symbolized in the vine. The crew defied the captain and seized the boy to sell him into slavery. Dionysus manifested his power, stopping the ship in place, twining it with his vines, materializing his lynxes and leopards out of thin air, and turning the sailors into fish and dolphins. The irony is that Acoetes' warning of the god's power went unheeded by Pentheus. Later when he tried to suppress Dionysian rites in Thebes, he was torn to pieces by the maddened worshippers. The Canto is a series of manifestations and metamorphoses of the divine in human form. Scios: a Greek island.

[10]An island sacred to Dionysus. In next line, naviform: shaped like a ship.

[11]Dionysus.

[12]A district of Italy.

[13]Sleight: trick, manifestation.

Ivy upon the oars, King Pentheus,
60   grapes with no seed but sea-foam,
Ivy in scupper-hole.
Aye, I, Accœtes, stood there,
        and the god stood by me,
Water cutting under the keel,
65 Sea-break from stern forrards,
            wake running off from the bow,
And where was gunwale, there now was vine-trunk,
And tenthril where cordage had been,
            grape-leaves on the rowlocks,
70 Heavy vine on the oarshafts,
And, out of nothing, a breathing,
        hot breath on my ankles,
Beasts like shadows in glass,
        a furred tail upon nothingness.
75 Lynx-purr, and heathery smell of beasts,
            where tar smell had been,
Sniff and pad-foot of beasts,
            eye-glitter out of black air.
The sky overshot, dry, with no tempest,
80 Sniff and pad-foot of beasts,
            fur brushing my knee-skin,
Rustle of airy sheaths,
            dry forms in the *æther*.[14]
And the ship like a keel in ship-yard,
85   slung like an ox in smith's sling,
Ribs stuck fast in the ways,
            grape-cluster over pin-rack,
            void air taking pelt.
Lifeless air become sinewed,
90   feline leisure of panthers,
Leopards sniffing the grape shoots by scupper-hole,
Crouched panthers by fore-hatch,
And the sea blue-deep about us,
            green-ruddy in shadows,
95 And Lyæus:[15] "From now, Accœtes, my altars,
Fearing no bondage,
            fearing no cat of the wood,
Safe with my lynxes,
            feeding grapes to my leopards,

[14]The atmosphere beyond earth's atmosphere; the heavens.
[15]A name for Dionysus.

100   Olibanum[16] is my incense,
                the vines grow in my homage."

        The back-swell now smooth in the rudder-chains,
        Black snout of a porpoise
                where Lycabs had been,
105   Fish-scales on the oarsmen:
                And I worship.
        I have seen what I have seen.
                When they brought the boy I said:
        "He has a god in him,
110   though I do not know which god."
        And they kicked me into the fore-stays.
        I have seen what I have seen:
                Medon's face like the face of a dory,
        Arms shrunk into fins. And you, Pentheus,
115   Had as well listen to Tiresias, and to Cadmus,[17]
                or your luck will go out of you.
        Fish-scales over groin muscles,
                lynx-purr amid sea . . .
        And of a later year,
120   pale in the wine-red algæ,
        If you will lean over the rock,
                the coral face under wave-tinge,
        Rose-paleness under water-shift,
                Ileuthyeria, fair Dafne of sea-bords,[18]
125   The swimmer's arms turned to branches,
        Who will say in what year,
                fleeing what band of tritons,[19]
        The smooth brows, seen, and half seen,
                now ivory stillness.

130   And So-shu churned in the sea, So-shu also,
                using the long moon for a churn-stick . . .
        Lithe turning of water,
                sinews of Poseidon,

---

[16]Frankincense.

[17]Tiresias: the prophet and seer; Cadmus: the ancestor of Theban aristocracy, whose actions after a prophecy of the Delphic oracle led to a number of castrophes for the family.

[18]Ileuthyeria: probably an invention of Pound's to be the sea-equivalent of Daphne. As Daphne was metamorphosed into a laurel to escape Apollo, so Ileuthyeria was changed into coral to escape the tritons.

[19]Lesser sea gods.

Black azure and hyaline,
135   glass wave over Tyro,
Close cover, unstillness,
          bright welter of wave-cords,
Then quiet water,
          quiet in the buff sands,
140   Sea-fowl stretching wing-joints,
          splashing in rock-hollows and sand-hollows
In the wave-runs by the half-dune;
Glass-glint of wave in the tide-rips against sunlight,
          pallor of Hesperus,[20]
145   Grey peak of the wave,
          wave, colour of grape's pulp,

Olive grey in the near,
          far, smoke grey of the rock-slide
Salmon-pink wings of the fish hawk
150   cast grey shadows in water,
The tower like a one-eyed great goose
          cranes up out of the olive-grove,

And we have heard the fauns chiding Proteus[21]
          in the smell of hay under the olive-trees,
155   And the frogs singing against the fauns
          in the half-light.
And . . .

CANTO XIII

Kung[1] walked
          by the dynastic temple
and into the cedar grove,
          and then out by the lower river,
5   And with him Khieu, Tchi
          and Tian the low speaking

[20]The evening star; also the father of the Hesperides, nymphs who guarded the
golden apples in the Isles of the Blest.
[21]A sea god who could change his shape at will.

[1]Kung Fu-tseu, or Confucius (551–479 B.C.): Chinese philosopher whose
thought emphasized order, right thinking, rational control, and practical action
on all levels from the individual through the family to the state. Confucian
ideas about ethical standards and social structure are basic to The Cantos and
balance the sexual and eruptive life-energy of Dionysus.

And "we are unknown," said Kung,
"You will take up charioteering?
　　　　Then you will become known?
10 "Or perhaps I should take up charioteering, or archery?
"Or the practice of public speaking?"
And Tseu-lou said, "I would put the defences in order,"
And Khieu said, "If I were lord of a province
I would put it in better order than this is."
15 And Tchi said, "I would prefer a small mountain temple,
"With order in the observances,
　　　　with a suitable performance of the ritual,"
And Tian said, with his hand on the strings of his lute
The low sounds continuing
20 　　　　after his hand left the strings,
And the sound went up like smoke, under the leaves,
And he looked after the sound:
　　　　"The old swimming hole,
"And the boys flopping off the planks,
25 "Or sitting in the underbrush playing mandolins."
　　　　And Kung smiled upon all of them equally.
And Thseng-sie desired to know:
　　　　"Which had answered correctly?"
And Kung said, "They have all answered correctly,
30 "That is to say, each in his nature."
And Kung raised his cane against Yuan Jang,
　　　　Yuan Jang being his elder,
For Yuan Jang sat by the roadside pretending to
　　　　be receiving wisdom.
35 And Kung said
　　　　"You old fool, come out of it,
Get up and do something useful."
　　　　And Kung said
"Respect a child's faculties
40 "From the moment it inhales the clear air,
"But a man of fifty who knows nothing
　　　　Is worthy of no respect."
And "When the prince has gathered about him
"All the savants and artists, his riches will be fully employed."
45 And Kung said, and wrote on the bo² leaves:
　　　　If a man have not order within him
He can not spread order about him;
And if a man have not order within him

²A kind of Chinese tea.

His family will not act with due order;
50   And if the prince have not order within him
He can not put order in his dominions.
And Kung gave the words "order"
and "brotherly deference"
And said nothing of the "life after death."
55 And he said
        "Anyone can run to excesses,
It is easy to shoot past the mark,
It is hard to stand firm in the middle."

And they said: If a man commit murder
60   Should his father protect him, and hide him?
And Kung said:
        He should hide him.

And Kung gave his daughter to Kong-Tch 'ang
        Although Kong-Tch 'ang was in prison.
65 And he gave his niece to Nan-Young
        although Nan-Young was out of office.

And Kung said "Wan ruled with moderation,
        In his day the State was well kept,
And even I can remember
70 A day when the historians left blanks in their writings,
I mean for things they didn't know,
But that time seems to be passing."
And Kung said, "Without character you will
        be unable to play on that instrument
75 Or to execute the music fit for the Odes.
The blossoms of the apricot
        blow from the east to the west,
And I have tried to keep them from falling."

CANTO XLV

With *Usura*[1]
With usura hath no man a house of good stone
each block cut smooth and well fitting
that design might cover their face,
5   with usura
hath no man a painted paradise on his church wall
harpes et luthes[2]
or where virgin receiveth message
and halo projects from incision,
10   with usura
seeth no man Gonzaga[3] his heirs and his concubines
no picture is made to endure nor to live with
but it is made to sell and sell quickly
with usura, sin against nature,
15   is thy bread ever more of stale rags
is thy bread dry as paper,
with no mountain wheat, no strong flour
with usura the line grows thick
with usura is no clear demarcation
20   and no man can find site for his dwelling.
Stone cutter is kept from his stone
weaver is kept from his loom
WITH USURA
wool comes not to market
25   sheep bringeth no gain with usura
Usura is a murrain, usura
blunteth the needle in the maid's hand
and stoppeth the spinner's cunning. Pietro Lombardo[4]
came not by usura
30   Duccio came not by usura
nor Pier della Francesca; Zuan Bellin' not by usura
nor was 'La Calunnia' painted.
Came not by usura Angelico; came not Ambrogio Praedis,

[1]Usury is here explicitly identified with the mentality and morality that allows the acquisition of money and the proliferation of wealth to triumph over the quality of art, life, and civilization.
[2]French: harps and lutes. The image is from Villon's"Prayer for His Mother."
[3]Ercole Gonzaga, Duke of Mantua (1505–1563).
[4]The names and references in the following lines are to Italian Renaissance artists: Pietro Lombardo (1435–1515); Agostino di Duccio (1418–1481); Piero della Francesca (1420–1498); Giovanni Bellini (1426–1516); Sandro Botticelli (1444–1510), who painted "La Calunnia"; Fra Angelico (1387–1455); Ambrogio de Predis (1455–1506).

Came no church of cut stone signed: *Adamo me fecit,*[5]
35 Not by usura St Trophime[6]
Not by usura Saint Hilaire,
Usura rusteth the chisel
It rusteth the craft and the craftsman
It gnaweth the thread in the loom
40 None learneth to weave gold in her pattern;
Azure[7] hath a canker by usura; cramoisi[8] is unbroidered[9]
Emerald findeth no Memling[10]
Usura slayeth the child in the womb
It stayeth the young man's courting
45 It hath brought palsey to bed, lyeth
between the young bride and her bridegroom
          CONTRA NATURAM
They have brought whores for Eleusis[11]
Corpses are set to banquet
50 at behest of usura.[12]

CANTO XLVII

Who even dead, yet hath his mind entire![1]
This sound came in the dark[2]
First must thou go the road
              to hell
5 And to the bower of Ceres' daughter Proserpine,[3]
Through overhanging dark, to see Tiresias,
Eyeless that was, a shade, that is in hell

[5]"Adamo made me"; Adam was a Renaissance sculptor and architect.
[6]St. Trophime and St. Hilaire: famous French Romanesque churches in Arles and Poitiers respectively.
[7]Either the blue stone lapis lazuli or cloth dyed azure blue.
[8]French: crimson cloth.
[9]Unembroidered.
[10]Hans Memling (1430–1495): Flemish painter.
[11]Greek town where the mysteries of Demeter and Persephone were celebrated.
[12]Pound's note: "Usury: A charge for the use of purchasing power, levied without regard to production, often without regard to the possibilities of production."

[1]As subsequent lines make clear, this line refers to the prophet Tiresias in the underworld.
[2]Here Circe is speaking to Odysseus in the dark, instructing him that he must descend to the underworld to consult Tiresias about the long voyage back home to Greece.
[3]Proserpine: the Latin form of Persephone, daughter of Ceres (or Demeter): stolen by Pluto to be his queen in Hades for half of each year and thus associated with the mystery of death and rebirth.

So full of knowing that the beefy men know less than he,
Ere thou come to thy road's end.

10   Knowledge the shade of a shade,
Yet must thou sail after knowledge
Knowing less than drugged beasts, *phtheggometha
thasson*[4]

Ψθεγγωμεθα θᾶσσον

15   The small lamps drift in the bay
And the sea's claw gathers them.
Neptunus drinks after neap-tide.[5]
Tamuz! Tamuz!![6]
The red flame going seaward.

20   By this gate art thou measured.
From the long boats they have set lights in the water,
The sea's claw gathers them outward.
Scilla's[7] dogs snarl at the cliff's base,
The white teeth gnaw in under the crag,

25   But in the pale night the small lamps float seaward

                        Τυ Διώνα
                        TU DIONA

Καὶ Μοῖραι' Ἄδονιν[8]
KAI MOIRAI' ADONIN

30   The sea is streaked red with Adonis,
The lights flicker red in small jars.
Wheat shoots rise new by the altar,
              flower from the swift seed.
Two span, two span to a woman,[9]

35   Beyond that she believes not. Nothing is of any importance.
To that is she bent, her intention
To that art thou called ever turning intention,
Whether by night the owl-call, whether by sap in shoot,
Never idle, by no means by no wiles intermittent

---

[4]*Odyssey* X, 228: "Let us raise our voices right away." Reproduced in Greek below.

[5]Neptune: the Roman name for Poseidon, the god of the sea. Neap-tide: low tide.

[6]A Babylonian fertility god, here linked with the Greek Adonis, both worshiped in spring rituals of death and rebirth. One such ritual—floating the lights out to sea—is described in these lines.

[7]Scilla: a sea monster who barks like a dog, here depicted as having dogs metamorphically in the waves. Also Seylla.

[8]From Bion's *Lament for Adonis:* "You, Diona [Aphrodite's mother] . . . and the Fates [weep for] Adonis." Bion: Greek poet of the second century B.C.

[9]The Canto returns here to Odysseus and to Tiresias' prophetic words that carry him from Circe's captivity home to harmony with the natural rhythm in Penelope's bed and in the plowing of his lands.

40 Moth is called over mountain
The bull runs blind on the sword, *naturans*[10]
To the cave art thou called, Odysseus,
By Molü[11] hast thou respite for a little,
By Molü art thou freed from the one bed
45   that thou may'st return to another
The stars are not in her counting,
        To her they are but wandering holes.
Begin thy plowing
When the Pleiades[12] go down to their rest,
50 Begin thy plowing
40 days are they under seabord,
Thus do in fields by seabord
And in valleys winding down toward the sea.
When the cranes fly high
55   think of plowing.
By this gate art thou measured
Thy day is between a door and a door
Two oxen are yoked for plowing
Or six in the hill field
60 White bulk under olives, a score for drawing down stone,
Here the mules are gabled with slate on the hill road.
Thus was it in time.
And the small stars now fall from the olive branch,
Forked shadow falls dark on the terrace
65 More black than the floating martin[13]
        that has no care for your presence,
His wing-print is black on the roof tiles
And the print is gone with his cry.
So light is thy weight on Tellus[14]
70 Thy notch no deeper indented
Thy weight less than the shadow
Yet hast thou gnawed through the mountain,
        Scylla's white teeth less sharp.
Hast thou found a nest softer than cunnus[15]
75 Or hast thou found better rest
Hast'ou a deeper planting, doth thy death year

[10]Latin: acting in accord with nature's plan. The passage suggests Hesiod's *Works and Days*, a Greek work of the eighth century B.C.
[11]Molü or moly: the magic herb that Hermes gave Odysseus so that he would not become utterly enslaved by Circe and turned into a swine.
[12]A group of stars, personified as sisters, in the constellation Taurus.
[13]A bird related to the swallow.
[14]Earth, as goddess.
[15]Latin: sexual organs of a woman.

Bring swifter shoot?
Hast thou entered more deeply the mountain?

The light has entered the cave. Io! Io![16]
80   The light has gone down into the cave,
Splendour on splendour!
By prong have I entered these hills:
That the grass grow from my body,
That I hear the roots speaking together,
85   The air is new on my leaf,
The forked boughs shake with the wind.
Is Zephyrus more light on the bough, Apeliota[17]
more light on the almond branch?
By this door have I entered the hill.
90   Falleth,
Adonis falleth.
Fruit cometh after. The small lights drift out with the tide,
sea's claw has gathered them outward,
Four banners to every flower
95   The sea's claw draws the lamps outward.
Think thus of thy plowing
When the seven stars go down to their rest
Forty days for their rest, by seabord
And in valleys that wind down toward the sea
100   Καὶ Μοῖραῑ᾽ Ἄδονιν
                  Kαι moirai' adonin
When the almond bough puts forth its flame,
When the new shoots are brought to the altar,
               Τυ Διώνα, Καὶ Μοῖραι
105   TU DIONA, KAI MOIRAI
Καὶ Μοῖραῑ᾽ Ἄδονιν
Kαι moirai' adonin
        that hath the gift of healing,
that hath the power over wild beasts.

[16]Greek exclamation of invocation. Here the perspective of the Canto shifts from Tiresias as speaker to Odysseus as speaker.
[17]Zephyrus and Apeliota: the west and east wind respectively.

H. D. (1886–1961)

Born in Bethlehem, Pennsylvania, Hilda Doolittle came to know both Pound and Williams at the University of Pennsylvania. In London in 1912, she, Pound, and the British poet Richard Aldington, whom she married the next year, formulated the principles of Imagism, which more than any other single movement, helped to strip away nineteenth-century mannerisms and to advance a "modern" way to conceive of poems and poetic style. In hard-edged, classical imagery and in still clarity of diction, like air humming with resonance, her lines continued to exemplify Imagist tenets more strictly than the work of any of her cohorts. She lived abroad, and her writing is filled with the light and pungency of the Mediterranean, especially of Greece. Her volumes of poetry include: *Sea Garden* (1916), *Hymen* (1921), *Heliodora and Other Poems* (1924), *Collected Poems* (1925, 1940), and *The Walls Do Not Fall* (1944). She also wrote two verse plays, *Hippolytus Tempories* (1927) and *The Flowering of the Rod* (1946); *Tribute to Freud* (1956), telling of her psychoanalysis by Freud; and fiction: *Palimpsest* (1926), *Hedylus* (1928) and *Bid Me Live* (1960), the last an autobiographical novel of literary London during World War I depicting some of her contemporaries. *Selected Poems* (1957) is the most readily available collection. The poet Robert Duncan has been working on a critical study centering on H. D.'s work, especially in the mystic and mystical aspects of her later work, for which *Helen in Egypt* (1961) and *Hermetic Definition* (1972) stand as final statements.

REFERENCE

Quinn, Vincent. *Hilda Doolittle (H. D.)*. New York: Twayne, 1968.

Swann, Thomas B. *The Classical World of H. D.* Lincoln: University of Nebraska Press, 1962.

SEA POPPIES

Amber husk,
fluted with gold,
fruit on the sand,
marked with a rich grain,

5   treasure,
spilled near the shrub-pines
to bleach on the boulders:

your stalk has caught root
among wet pebbles
10   and drift flung by the sea
and grated shells
and split conch-shells.

Beautiful, wide-spread,
fire upon leaf,
15   what meadow yields
so fragrant a leaf
as your bright leaf?

HEAT

O wind, rend open the heat,
cut apart the heat,
rend it to tatters.

Fruit cannot drop
5   through this thick air—
fruit cannot fall into heat
that presses up and blunts
the points of pears
and rounds the grapes.

10   Cut the heat—
plough through it,
turning it on either side
of your path.

OREAD[1]

Whirl up, sea—
whirl your pointed pines,
splash your great pines
on our rocks,
5   hurl your green over us,
cover us with your pools of fir.

FRAGMENT 113[1]

"Neither honey nor bee for me."
           —Sappho.

Not honey,
not the plunder of the bee
from meadow or sand-flower
or mountain-bush,
5   from winter-flower or shoot,
born of the later heat;
not honey, not the sweet
stain on the lips and teeth;
not honey, not the deep
10   plunge of soft belly
and the clinging of the gold-edged,
pollen-dusted feet;

Not so—
though rapture blind my eyes,
15   and hunger crisp,
dark and inert, my mouth;
not honey, not the south,
not the tall stalk
of red twin-lilies,
20   nor light branch of fruit-tree,
caught in flexible light branch;

[1]Mountain nymph.

---

[1]This fragment of Sappho, the greatest woman poet of antiquity, who lived in the sixth century B.C., consists completely of a single Greek phrase translated just below. H.D. expands it into this poem. The numbering of the fragment follows Henry T. Wharton's edition of *Sappho* (1885).

Not honey, not the south;
ah, flower of purple iris,
flower of white,
25   or of the iris, withering the grass—
for fleck of the sun's fire,
gathers such heat and power,
that shadow-print is light,
cast through the petals
30   of the yellow iris-flower;

Not iris—old desire—old passion—
old forgetfulness—old pain—
not this, nor any flower,
but if you turn again,
35   seek strength of arm and throat,
touch as the god;
neglect the lyre-note;
knowing that you shall feel,
about the frame,
40   no trembling of the string,
but heat, more passionate
of bone and the white shell
and fiery tempered steel.

LETHE[1]

Nor skin nor hide nor fleece
shall cover you,
nor curtain of crimson nor fine
shelter of cedar-wood be over you,
5   nor the fir-tree
nor the pine.

Nor sight of whin nor gorse
nor river-yew,
nor fragrance of flowering bush,
10   nor wailing of reed-bird to waken you,
nor of linnet,
nor of thrush.

[1]The river crossed over for entry into the classical underword; associated with forgetfulness.

Nor word nor touch nor sight
    of lover, you
15 shall long through the night but for this:
the roll of the full tide to cover you
    without question,
    without kiss.

CALLYPSO SPEAKS

Callypso[1]

  O you clouds,
  here is my song;
  man is clumsy and evil
  a devil.

5 O you sand,
  this is my command,
  drown all men in slow breathless suffocation—
  then they may understand.

  O you winds,
10 beat his sails flat,
  shift a wave sideways
  that he suffocate.

  O you waves
  run counter to his oars,
15 waft him to blistering shores,
  where he may die of thirst.

  O you skies,
  send rain
  to wash salt from my eyes,

20 and witness, all earth and heaven,
  it was of my heart-blood
  his sails were woven;

[1]A nymph, daughter of Atlas, who lived on the island of Ogygia. Odysseus reached the island after shipwreck had destroyed all his crew. Callypso loved Odysseus and promised him eternal youth if he remained with her. But he longed for Penelope and home, and after seven years sailed off on a hand-made raft for Ithaca.

witness, river and sea and land;
you, you must hear me—
25   man is a devil,
man will not understand.

Odysseus (on the sea)

She gave me fresh water in an earth-jar,
strange fruits
to quench thirst,
30   a golden zither
to work magic on the water;

she gave me wine in a cup
and white wine in a crystal shell;
she gave me water and salt,
35   wrapped in a palm-leaf,
and palm-dates:

she gave me wool and a pelt of fur,
she gave me a pelt of silver-fox,
and a brown soft skin of a bear,

40   she gave me an ivory comb for my hair,
she washed brine and mud from my body,
and cool hands
held balm
for a rust-wound;

45   she gave me water
and fruit in a basket,
and shallow
baskets of pulse[1] and grain, and a ball
of hemp
50   for mending the sail;

she gave me a willow-basket
for letting into the shallows
for eels;

she gave me peace in her cave

[1]Peas and beans.

Callypso (from land)

55   He has gone,
     he has forgotten;
     he took my lute and my shell of crystal—
     he never looked back—

Odysseus (on the sea)

     She gave me a wooden flute
60   and a mantle,
     she wove this wool—

Callypso (from land)

     For man is a brute and a fool.

Robinson Jeffers (1887–1962)

Born in Pittsburgh, where his minister-father was teaching at a Presbyterian seminary, Jeffers received his education largely at home. The family moved to Long Beach, California, in 1903, and Jeffers graduated from Occidental College in 1905. He did graduate study in English, in medicine, and in forestry before devoting himself single-mindedly to his poetry. After his marriage to Una Call Kuster in 1913, they moved to Carmel, and Jeffers began in 1919 to build, by his own hands with stones from the beach, a house and tower fronting the Pacific. Except for a few trips abroad this was his place, and the rugged coast was his subject. As the world moved from war to depression to war, Jeffers pondered the "brute beauty of things" and the disruptive violence that was man's mark. He insisted that his "inhumanism" was not pessimistic in its anticipation of the extinction of the human species, because it proceeded from a pantheistic recognition of the majestic wholeness and power of creation.

Jeffers' narrative poems act out archetypally the dislocations that turn man against himself and his kind. At land's edge Jeffers stood as Whitman's shadow: an apocalyptic prophet as Calvinist as his father, shunning society, denouncing America, seeking the peace of things free of consciousness. Some main titles are: *Tamar* (1924), *Roan Stallion* (1925), *The Women at Point Sur* (1927), *Cawdor* (1928), *Give Your Heart to the Hawks* (1933), *Such Counsels You Gave Me* (1937), *Medea* (1946, written for Judith Anderson and successful on Broadway), *The Double Axe* (1948), *Hungerfield* (1954), and the posthumous *The Beginning and the End* (1963).

REFERENCE

Brother Antoninus (Williams Everson). *Robinson Jeffers: Fragments of an Older Fury*. Berkeley: Oyez, 1968.

Bennett, Melba Berry. *The Stone Mason of Tor House: The Life and Work of Robinson Jeffers*. Los Angeles: W. Ritchie Press, 1966.

Selected Letters of Robinson Jeffers, 1897–1962. Ed. Ann N. Ridgway. Baltimore: Johns Hopkins Press, 1968.

Squires, Radcliffe. *The Loyalties of Robinson Jeffers*. Ann Arbor: University of Michigan Press, 1956.

DIVINELY SUPERFLUOUS BEAUTY

The storm-dances of gulls, the barking game of seals,
Over and under the ocean . . .
Divinely superfluous beauty
Rules the games, presides over destinies, makes trees grow
5   And hills tower, waves fall.
The incredible beauty of joy
Stars with fire the joining of lips, O let our loves too
Be joined, there is not a maiden
Burns and thirsts for love
10   More than my blood for you, by the shore of seals while the wings
Weave like a web in the air
Divinely superfluous beauty.

TO THE STONE-CUTTERS

Stone-cutters fighting time with marble, you foredefeated
Challengers of oblivion
Eat cynical earnings, knowing rock splits, records fall down,
The square-limbed Roman letters
5   Scale in the thaws, wear in the rain. The poet as well
Builds his monument mockingly;
For man will be blotted out, the blithe earth die, the brave sun
Die blind and blacken to the heart:
Yet stones have stood for a thousand years, and pained thoughts
    found
10   The honey of peace in old poems.

SHINE, PERISHING REPUBLIC

While this America settles in the mould of its vulgarity, heavily
    thickening to empire,
And protest, only a bubble in the molten mass, pops and sighs out,
    and the mass hardens,

I sadly smiling remember that the flower fades to make fruit, the
    fruit rots to make earth.

Out of the mother; and through the spring exultances, ripeness and
    decadence; and home to the mother.

5   You making haste haste on decay: not blameworthy; life is good, be
    it stubbornly long or suddenly
A mortal splendor: meteors are not needed less than mountains:
    shine, perishing republic.

But for my children, I would have them keep their distance from
    the thickening center; corruption
Never has been compulsory, when the cities lie at the monster's
    feet there are left the mountains.

And boys, be in nothing so moderate as in love of man, a clever
    servant, insufferable master.
10 There is the trap that catches noblest spirits, that caught—they say
    —God, when he walked on earth.

POST MORTEM

Happy people die whole, they are all dissolved in a moment, they
    have had what they wanted,
No hard gifts; the unhappy
Linger a space, but pain is a thing that is glad to be forgotten; but
    one who has given
His heart to a cause or a country,
5   His ghost may spaniel[1] it a while, disconsolate to watch it. I was
    wondering how long the spirit
That sheds this verse will remain
When the nostrils are nipped, when the brain rots in its vault or
    bubbles in the violence of fire
To be ash in metal. I was thinking
Some stalks of the wood whose roots I married to the earth of this
    place will stand five centuries;
10 I held the roots in my hand,
The stems of the trees between two fingers: how many remote
    generations of women
Will drink joy from men's loins,
And dragged from between the thighs of what mothers will giggle
    at my ghost when it curses the axemen,

---

[1]Remain like a loyal and loving spaniel.

Gray impotent voice on the sea-wind,
15 When the last trunk falls? The women's abundance will have built
    roofs over all this foreland;
Will have buried the rock foundations
I laid here: the women's exuberance will canker and fail in its time
    and like clouds the houses
Unframe, the granite of the prime
Stand from the heaps: come storm and wash clean: the plaster is all
    run to the sea and the steel
20 All rusted; the foreland resumes
The form we loved when we saw it. Though one at the end of the
    age and far off from this place
Should meet my presence in a poem,
The ghost would not care but be here, long sunset shadow in the
    seams of the granite, and forgotten
The flesh, a spirit for the stone.

HURT HAWKS

I

The broken pillar of the wing jags from the clotted shoulder,
The wing trails like a banner in defeat,
No more to use the sky forever but live with famine
And pain a few days: cat nor coyote
5 Will shorten the week of waiting for death, there is game without
    talons.
He stands under the oak-bush and waits
The lame feet of salvation; at night he remembers freedom
And flies in a dream, the dawns ruin it.
He is strong and pain is worse to the strong, incapacity is worse.
10 The curs of the day come and torment him
At distance, no one but death the redeemer will humble that head,
The intrepid readiness, the terrible eyes.
The wild God of the world is sometimes merciful to those
That ask mercy, not often to the arrogant.
15 You do not know him, you communal people, or you have for-
    gotten him;
Intemperate and savage, the hawk remembers him;
Beautiful and wild, the hawks, and men that are dying, remember
    him.

II

I'd sooner, except the penalties, kill a man than a hawk; but the great
    redtail[1]
Had nothing left but unable misery
20 From the bone too shattered for mending, the wing that trailed
    under his talons when he moved.
We had fed him six weeks, I gave him freedom,
He wandered over the foreland hill and returned in the evening,
    asking for death,
Not like a begger, still eyed with the old
Implacable arrogance. I gave him the lead gift in the twilight. What
    fell was relaxed,
25 Owl-downy, soft feminine feathers; but what
Soared: the fierce rush: the night-herons by the flooded river cried
    fear at its rising
Before it was quite unsheathed from reality.

THE BED BY THE WINDOW

I chose the bed downstairs by the sea-window for a good deathbed
When we built the house; it is ready waiting,
Unused unless by some guest in a twelvemonth, who hardly
    suspects
Its latter purpose. I often regard it,
5 With neither dislike nor desire; rather with both, so equalled
That they kill each other and a crystalline interest
Remains alone. We are safe to finish what we have to finish;
And then it will sound rather like music
When the patient daemon[1] behind the screen of sea-rock and sky
10 Thumps with his staff, and calls thrice: "Come, Jeffers."

[1]A kind of hawk.

[1]Spirit.

LOVE THE WILD SWAN

"I hate my verses, every line, every word.
Oh pale and brittle pencils ever to try
One grass-blade's curve, or the throat of one bird
That clings to twig, ruffled against white sky.
5 Oh cracked and twilight mirrors ever to catch
One color, one glinting flash, of the splendor of things.
Unlucky hunter, Oh bullets of wax,
The lion beauty, the wild-swan wings, the storm of the wings."
—This wild swan of a world is no hunter's game.
10 Better bullets than yours would miss the white breast,
Better mirrors than yours would crack in the flame.
Does it matter whether you hate your . . . self? At least
Love your eyes that can see, your mind that can
Hear the music, the thunder of the wings. Love the wild swan.

NIGHT WITHOUT SLEEP

The world's as the world is; the nations rearm and prepare to
change; the age of tyrants returns;
The greatest civilization that has ever existed builds itself higher
towers on breaking foundations.
Recurrent episodes; they were determined when the ape's children
first ran in packs, chipped flint to an edge.

I lie and hear
5   dark rain beat the roof, and the blind wind.

In the morning perhaps
I shall find strength again
To value the immense beauty of this time of the world, the flowers
of decay their pitiful loveliness, the fever-dream
Tapestries that back the drama and are called the future. This ebb
of vitality feels the ignoble and cruel
10 Incidents, not the vast abstract order.

I lie and hear dark rain beat
the roof, and the night-blind wind.

In the Ventana country darkness and rain and the roar of waters fill
    the deep mountain-throats.
The creekside shelf of sand where we lay last August under a slip
    of stars,

15 And firelight played on the leaning gorge-walls, is drowned and
    lost. The deer of the country huddle on a ridge
In a close herd under madrone-trees; they tremble when a rock-
    slide goes down, they open great darkness-
Drinking eyes and press closer.
                        Cataracts of rock
Rain down the mountain from cliff to cliff and torment the stream-
    bed. The stream deals with them. The laurels are wounded,

20 Redwoods go down with their earth and lie thwart the gorge. I hear
    the torrent boulders battering each other,
I feel the flesh of the mountain move on its bones in the wet
    darkness.

                Is this more beautiful
Than man's disasters? These wounds will heal in their time; so will
    humanity's. This is more beautiful . . . at night . . .

CASSANDRA[1]

The mad girl with the staring eyes and long white fingers
Hooked in the stones of the wall,
The storm-wrack hair and the screeching mouth: does it matter,
    Cassandra,
Whether the people believe

5 Your bitter fountain? Truly men hate the truth; they'd liefer
Meet a tiger on the road.
Therefore the poets honey their truth with lying; but religion-
Venders and political men
Pour from the barrel, new lies on the old, and are praised for kindly

10 Wisdom. Poor bitch, be wise.
No: you'll still mumble in a corner a crust of truth, to men
And gods disgusting.—You and I, Cassandra.

---

[1]The daughter of King Priam of Troy, gifted with prophecy but doomed never
to be believed, even by her countrymen during the Trojan War, as Jeffers'
condemnation of the impending World War II went unheeded.

THE EYE

The Atlantic is a stormy moat; and the Mediterranean,
The blue pool in the old garden,
More than five thousand years has drunk sacrifice
Of ships and blood, and shines in the sun; but here the Pacific—
5 Our ships, planes, wars are perfectly irrelevant.
Neither our present blood-feud with the brave dwarfs
Nor any future world-quarrel of westering
And eastering man, the bloody migrations, greed of power, clash of
      faiths—
Is a speck of dust on the great scale-pan.
10 Here from this mountain shore, headland beyond stormy headland
      plunging like dolphins through the blue sea-smoke
Into pale sea—look west at the hill of water: it is half the planet:
      this dome, this half-globe, this bulging
Eyeball of water, arched over to Asia,
Australia and white Antarctica: those are the eyelids that never
      close; this is the staring unsleeping
Eye of the earth; and what it watches is not our wars.

ORIGINAL SIN

The man-brained and man-handed ground-ape, physically
The most repulsive of all hot-blooded animals
Up to that time of the world: they had dug a pitfall
And caught a mammoth, but how could their sticks and stones
5 Reach the life in that hide? They danced around the pit, shrieking
With ape excitement, flinging sharp flints in vain, and the stench of
      their bodies
Stained the white air of dawn; but presently one of them
Remembered the yellow dancer, wood-eating fire
That guards the cave-mouth: he ran and fetched him, and others
10 Gathered sticks at the wood's edge; they made a blaze
And pushed it into the pit, and they fed it high, around the mired
      sides
Of their huge prey. They watched the long hairy trunk
Waver over the stifle-trumpeting pain,
And they were happy.
                    Meanwhile the intense color and nobility of
      sunrise,

Rose and gold and amber, flowed up the sky. Wet rocks were
    shining, a little wind
Stirred the leaves of the forest and the marsh flag-flowers; the soft
    valley between the low hills
Became as beautiful as the sky; while in its midst, hour after hour,
    the happy hunters
20 Roasted their living meat slowly to death.
                                 These are the people.
This is the human dawn. As for me, I would rather
Be a worm in a wild apple than a son of man.
But we are what we are, and we might remember
25 Not to hate any person, for all are vicious;
And not be astonished at any evil, all are deserved;
And not fear death; it is the only way to be cleansed.

CARMEL POINT

The extraordinary patience of things!
This beautiful place defaced with a crop of suburban houses—
How beautiful when we first beheld it,
Unbroken field of poppy and lupin walled with clean cliffs;
5 No intrusion but two or three horses pasturing,
Or a few milch cows rubbing their flanks on the outcrop rock-heads—
Now the spoiler has come: does it care?
Not faintly. It has all time. It knows the people are a tide
That swells and in time will ebb, and all
10 Their works dissolve. Meanwhile the image of the pristine beauty
Lives in the very grain of the granite,
Safe as the endless ocean that climbs our cliff.—As for us:
We must uncenter our minds from ourselves;
We must unhumanize our views a little, and become confident
15 As the rock and ocean that we were made from.

THE DEER LAY DOWN THEIR BONES

I followed the narrow cliffside trail half way up the mountain
Above the deep river-canyon. There was a little cataract crossed the
    path, flinging itself
Over tree roots and rocks, shaking the jeweled fern-fronds, bright
    bubbling water

Pure from the mountain, but a bad smell came up. Wondering at it
　　I clambered down the steep stream

Some forty feet, and found in the midst of bush-oak and laurel,

Hung like a bird's nest on the precipice brink a small hidden
　　clearing,

Grass and a shallow pool. But all about there were bones lying in
　　the grass, clean bones and stinking bones,

Antlers and bones: I understood that the place was a refuge for
　　wounded deer; there are so many

Hurt ones escape the hunters and limp away to lie hidden; here they
　　have water for the awful thirst

And peace to die in; dense green laurel and grim cliff

Make sanctuary, and a sweet wind blows upward from the deep
　　gorge.—I wish my bones were with theirs.

But that's a foolish thing to confess, and a little cowardly. We know
　　that life

Is on the whole quite equally good and bad, mostly gray neutral,
　　and can be endured

To the dim end, no matter what magic of grass, water and precipice,
　　and pain of wounds,

Makes death look dear. We have been given life and have used it—
　　not a great gift perhaps—but in honesty

Should use it all. Mine's empty since my love[1] died—Empty? The
　　flame-haired grandchild with great blue eyes

That look like hers?—What can I do for the child? I gaze at her and
　　wonder what sort of man

In the fall of the world . . . I am growing old, that is the trouble. My
　　children and little grandchildren

Will find their way, and why should I wait ten years yet, having
　　lived sixty-seven, ten years more or less,

Before I crawl out on a ledge of rock and die snapping, like a wolf

Who has lost his mate?—I am bound by my own thirty-year-old
　　decision: who drinks the wine

Should take the dregs; even in the bitter lees and sediment

New discovery may lie. The deer in that beautiful place lay down
　　their bones: I must wear mine.

[1]Jeffers' wife Una.

VULTURE

I had walked since dawn and lay down to rest on a bare hillside
Above the ocean. I saw through half-shut eyelids a vulture
   wheeling high up in heaven,
And presently it passed again, but lower and nearer, its orbit
   narrowing, I understood then
That I was under inspection. I lay death-still and heard the flight-
   feathers
5   Whistle above me and make their circle and come nearer.
I could see the naked red head between the great wings
Bear downward staring. I said, "My dear bird, we are wasting time
   here.
These old bones will still work; they are not for you." But how
   beautiful he looked, gliding down
On those great sails; how beautiful he looked, veering away in the
   sea-light over the precipice. I tell you solemnly
10   That I was sorry to have disappointed him. To be eaten by that beak
   and become part of him, to share those wings and those eyes—
What a sublime end of one's body, what an enskyment; what a life
   after death.

BIRDS AND FISHES

Every October millions of little fish come along the shore,
Coasting this granite edge of the continent
On their lawful occasions: but what a festival for the sea-fowl.
What a witches' sabbath[1] of wings
5   Hides the dark water. The heavy pelicans shout "Haw!" like Job's
   friend's warhorse
And dive from the high air, the cormorants[2]
Slip their long black bodies under the water and hunt like wolves
Through the green half-light. Screaming, the gulls watch,
Wild with envy and malice, cursing and snatching. What hysterical
   greed!
10   What a filling of pouches! the mob
Hysteria is nearly human—these decent birds!—as if they were
   finding

[1]An orgy of witches and demons.
[2]An aquatic bird with dark plumage.

Gold in the street. It is better than gold,
It can be eaten: and which one in all this fury of wild-fowl pities the
     fish?
No one certainly. Justice and mercy
Are human dreams, they do not concern the birds nor the fish nor
     eternal God.
However—look again before you go.
The wings and the wild hungers, the wave-worn skerries, the
     bright quick minnows
Living in terror to die in torment—
Man's fate and theirs—and the island rocks and immense ocean
     beyond, and Lobos[3]
Darkening above the bay: they are beautiful?
That is their quality: not mercy, not mind, not goodness, but the
     beauty of God.

[3]Point Lobos just below Carmel on the California coast.

Marianne Moore (1887–1972)

Miss Moore was born in St. Louis into a Presbyterian family close-knit in faith and love. After graduating from Bryn Mawr in 1909 and teaching in an Indian school in Carlisle, Pennsylvania, she lived with her minister-brother in Philadelphia for a couple of years before moving to New York to work in the Public Library and settling in Brooklyn. By this time Pound, Eliot, and Williams were all admirers of the bright, hard imagery of her syllabic verse, and she exerted a wide influence as editor of *The Dial* from 1926 to 1929. *Collected Poems* (1951) brought together *Observations* (1924), *Selected Poems* (1935), *What Are Years* (1941), and *Nevertheless* (1944). These were followed by *Like a Bulwark* (1956), *O To Be a Dragon* (1959), *Tell Me, Tell Me* (1966), and *Complete Poems* (1967).

Miss Moore was a deliberately anti-"poetic" poet. She used the imagination to make the analogies that associate the eye's observations with the mind's perceptions; the results are at once descriptive and metaphorical because Miss Moore found in the animal realm the emblems of human weakness and virtue. So it is not surprising that she made a witty translation of La Fontaine's *Fables (1954)*. Her verse displays the characteristics she most admired not just in animals but in artists and sports figures: honesty, modesty, discipline, grace, quiet strength—all developed qualities that deliver us from ego to moral integrity. In 1951 she received all three major American poetry awards: the Bollingen Prize, the Pulitzer Prize, and the National Book Award.

REFERENCE

A Collection of Critical Essays. Ed. Charles Tomlinson. Englewood Cliffs, N. J.: Prentice-Hall, 1969.

Garrigue, Jean. *Marianne Moore.* Minneapolis: University of Minnesota Press, 1965.

Hall, Donald. *Marianne Moore: The Cage and the Animal.* New York: Pegasus, 1970.

Moore, Marianne. *Predilections: Literary Essays.* New York: Viking, 1955.

Weatherhead, Andrew K. *The Edge of the Image: Marianne Moore, William Carlos Williams, and Some Other Poets.* Seattle: University of Washington Press, 1967.

THE FISH

wade[1]
through black jade.
   Of the crow-blue mussel shells, one keeps
   adjusting the ash heaps;
5   opening and shutting itself like

an
injured fan.
   The barnacles which encrust the side
   of the wave, cannot hide
10   there for the submerged shafts of the

sun,
split like spun
   glass, move themselves with spotlight swiftness
   into the crevices—
15   in and out, illuminating

the
turquoise sea
   of bodies. The water drives a wedge
   of iron through the iron edge
20   of the cliff; whereupon the stars,

pink
rice-grains, ink-
   bespattered jellyfish, crabs like green
   lilies, and submarine
25   toadstools, slide each on the other.

All
external
   marks of abuse are present on this
   defiant edifice—
30   all the physical features of

[1]Like many of Miss Moore's poems, this one is written in syllabics; that is, the length of the line in each stanza is governed not by stresses or metrical feet but by the numbers of syllables, which establish the pattern of the stanza.

ac-
cident—lack
   of cornice, dynamite grooves, burns, and
   hatchet strokes, these things stand
35   out on it; the chasm side is

dead.
Repeated
   evidence has proved that it can live
   on what can not revive
40   its youth. The sea grows old in it.

POETRY

I, too, dislike it: there are things that are important beyond
   all this fiddle.
  Reading it, however, with a perfect contempt for it, one
   discovers in
5 it after all, a place for the genuine.[1]
    Hands that can grasp, eyes
    that can dilate, hair that can rise
      if it must, these things are important not because a

high-sounding interpretation can be put upon them but be-
10   cause they are
useful. When they become so derivative as to become
   unintelligible,
  the same thing may be said for all of us, that we
   do not admire what
15   we cannot understand: the bat
     holding on upside down or in quest of something to

eat, elephants pushing, a wild horse taking a roll, a tireless
   wolf under
  a tree, the immovable critic twitching his skin like a horse
20   that feels a flea, the base-
  ball fan, the statistician—
    nor is it valid
     to discriminate against "business documents and

[1]Miss Moore ends the poem here in *Complete Poems* with the comment: "Omissions are not accidents."

school-books";[1] all these phenomena are important. One

25 　　　　　must make a distinction

however: when dragged into prominence by half poets,

　　　　the result is not poetry,

nor till the poets among us can be

　　　"literalists of

30 　　　the imagination"[2]—above

　　　　　insolence and triviality and can present

for inspection, "imaginary gardens with real toads in them,"[3]

　　　　shall we have

it. In the meantime, if you demand on the one hand,

35 　　the raw material of poetry in

　　　　all its rawness and

　　　that which is on the other hand

　　　　　genuine, you are interested in poetry.

IN THE DAYS OF PRISMATIC COLOR

not in the days of Adam and Eve, but when Adam

　　　was alone; when there was no smoke and color was

fine, not with the refinement

　　　of early civilization art, but because

5 　of its originality; with nothing to modify it but the

mist that went up, obliqueness was a variation

　　　of the perpendicular, plain to see and

to account for: it is no

　　　longer that; nor did the blue-red-yellow band

10 　of incandescence that was color keep its stripe: it also is one of

those things into which much that is peculiar can be

　　　read; complexity is not a crime, but carry

it to the point of murkiness

　　　and nothing is plain. Complexity,

15 　moreover, that has been committed to darkness, instead of

[1]Miss Moore's note indicates Tolstoy's Diary: "poetry is everything with the exception of business documents and school books."
[2]The phrase is adapted from W. B. Yeats' *Ideas of Good and Evil.*
[3]No source has been identified, and the suggestion has been made that Miss Moore sometimes uses quotation marks for rhetorical emphasis as well as for quotation. This phrase is almost surely her own.

granting itself to be the pestilence that it is, moves all a-
   bout as if to bewilder us with the dismal
fallacy that insistence
   is the measure of achievement and that all
20 truth must be dark. Principally throat, sophistication is as it al-

ways has been—at the antipodes from the init-
   ial great truths. "Part of it was crawling, part of it
was about to crawl, the rest
   was torpid in its lair."[1] In the short-legged, fit-
25 ful advance, the gurgling and all the minutiae—we have the
                                        classic

multitude of feet. To what purpose! Truth is no Apollo
   Belvedere,[2] no formal thing. The wave may go over it if it likes.
Know that it will be there when it says,
   "I shall be there when the wave has gone by."

AN EGYPTIAN PULLED
GLASS BOTTLE IN THE SHAPE OF A FISH

Here we have thirst
   and patience, from the first,
      and art, as in a wave held up for us to see
      in its essential perpendicularity;

5 not brittle but
   intense—the spectrum, that
      spectacular and nimble animal the fish,
      whose scales turn aside the sun's sword by their polish.

---

[1]Miss Moore's note: "Nestor: *Greek Anthology* (Loeb Classical Library), Vol. III, p. 129." Sophistication is a complicated monster, like a great mythological beast.
[2]A statue of the god of poetry in the Vatican Museum.

TO A SNAIL

If "compression is the first grace of style,"[1]
you have it. Contractility is a virtue
as modesty is a virtue.
It is not the acquisition of any one thing
5   that is able to adorn,
or the incidental quality that occurs
as a concomitant of something well said,
that we value in style,
but the principle that is hid:
10 in the absence of feet, "a method of conclusions";
"a knowledge of principles,"
in the curious phenomenon of your occipital horn.

SILENCE

My father used to say,[1]
"Superior people never make long visits,
have to be shown Longfellow's grave[2]
or the glass flowers at Harvard.[3]
5 Self-reliant like the cat—
that takes its prey to privacy,
the mouse's limp tail hanging like a shoelace from its mouth—
they sometimes enjoy solitude,
and can be robbed of speech
10 by speech which has delighted them.
The deepest feeling always shows itself in silence;
not in silence, but restraint."
Nor was he insincere in saying, "Make my house your inn."[4]
Inns are not residences.

[1]Often Miss Moore's quotations are not allusions that require the source for comprehension; generally the words are thoroughly incorporated into the text and find their meaning there. In these notes the sources will be indicated only where it is pertinent to the sense of the line; otherwise, the quotation marks can be taken, for our purposes as readers, to indicate principally the accuracy of Miss Moore's acknowledgments of phrases from her reading.

[1]Miss Moore's note indicates that she is not quoting her father but quoting someone else, Miss A. M. Homans, about her own father.
[2]In Cambridge, Massachusetts, in the Mount Auburn Cemetery.
[3]A famous collection of flowers made out of glass and remarkable for their delicacy and botanical accuracy; on display at the Peabody Museum at Harvard University, Cambridge, Massachusetts.
[4]A quotation from the English statesman Edmund Burke (1729–1797).

WHAT ARE YEARS?

What is our innocence,
what is our guilt? All are
   naked, none is safe. And whence
is courage: the unanswered question,
5 the resolute doubt—
dumbly calling, deafly listening—that
in misfortune, even death,
    encourages others
    and in its defeat, stirs

10   the soul to be strong? He
sees deep and is glad, who
   accedes to mortality
and in his imprisonment rises
upon himself as
15 the sea in a chasm, struggling to be
free and unable to be,
    in its surrendering
    finds its continuing.

So he who strongly feels,
20 behaves. The very bird,
   grown taller as he sings, steels
his form straight up. Though he is captive,
his mighty singing
says, satisfaction is a lowly
25 thing, how pure a thing is joy.
    This is mortality,
    this is eternity.

THE WOOD WEASEL

emerges daintily, the skunk—
don't laugh—in sylvan black and white chipmunk
regalia. The inky thing
adaptively whited with glistening
5 goat fur, is wood-warden. In his
ermined well-cuttlefish-inked wool, he is
determination's totem. Out-

lawed? His sweet face and powerful feet go about
in chieftain's coat of Chilcat cloth.

10   He is his own protection from the moth,

noble little warrior. That
otter-skin on it, the living polecat,[1]
smothers anything that stings. Well,
this same weasel's playful and his weasel

15   associates are too. Only
wood-weasels shall associate with me.

THE MIND IS AN ENCHANTING THING

is an enchanted thing
         like the glaze on a
katydid-wing
                 subdivided by sun
5   till the nettings are legion.
Like Gieseking playing Scarlatti;[1]

like the apteryx-awl[2]
         as a beak, or the
kiwi's rain-shawl
10   of haired feathers, the mind
                 feeling its way as though blind,
walks along with its eyes on the ground.

It has memory's ear
         that can hear without
15   having to hear.
                 Like the gyroscope's[3] fall,
                 truly unequivocal
because trued by regnant certainty,

---

[1]Again, the skunk, generically related to the weasel, therefore called, as the poem indicates, a wood-weasel.

[1]Walter Gieseking (1875–1956): German pianist; Domenico Scarlatti (1659–1725): the Baroque composer.

[2]The apteryx (wingless) or kiwi has only vestigial wings and a long pointed bill. Awl: a tool for punching holes.

[3]Gyroscope: a navigational instrument whose movement, in relation to the earth's rotation, makes it possible to steer a stable and true direction.

it is a power of
20   strong enchantment. It
is like the dove-
               neck animated by
               sun; it is memory's eye;
it's conscientious inconsistency.

25   It tears off the veil; tears
          the temptation, the
mist the heart wears,
               from its eyes—if the heart
               has a face; it takes apart
30   dejection. It's fire in the dove-neck's

iridescence; in the
          inconsistencies
of Scarlatti.
               Unconfusion submits
35   its confusion to proof; it's
not a Herod's oath[4] that cannot change.

A FACE

"I am not treacherous, callous, jealous, superstitious,
supercilious, venomous, or absolutely hideous":
          studying and studying its expression,
          exasperated desperation
5   though at no real impasse,
               would gladly break the glass;

when love of order, ardor, uncircuitous simplicity
with an expression of inquiry, are all one needs to be!
          Certain faces, a few, one or two—or one
10   face photographed by recollection—
               to my mind, to my sight,
               must remain a delight.

---

[4]King Herod of Judea, who ordered the murder of the Holy Innocents (Matthew 2); his son, Herod Antipas, executed St. John the Baptist and turned Jesus over to Pilate for punishment (Luke 23: 7–12). Both were known for violent and irrational commands.

LIKE A BULWARK

Affirmed. Pent by power that holds it fast—
a paradox. Pent. Hard pressed,
     you take the blame and are inviolate.
        Abased at last?
5   Not the tempest-tossed.
Compressed; firmed by the thrust of the blast
     till compact, like a bulwark against fate;
       lead-saluted,
       saluted by lead?
10 As though flying Old Glory full mast.

MELCHIOR VULPIUS

c. 1560–1615

a contrapuntalist—
        composer of chorales
and wedding-hymns to Latin words
but best of all an anthem:
5   "God be praised for conquering faith
   which feareth neither pain nor death."

We have to trust this art—
      this mastery which none
can understand. Yet someone has
10 acquired it and is able to
    direct it. Mouse-skin-bellows'-breath
    expanding into rapture saith

"Hallelujah." Almost
       utmost absolutist
15 and fugue-ist, Amen; slowly building
from miniature thunder,
    crescendos antidoting death—
    love's signature cementing faith.

GRANITE AND STEEL

Enfranchising cable, silvered by the sea,
   of woven wire, grayed by the mist,
   and Liberty dominate the Bay—[1]
   her feet as one on shattered chains,
5   once whole links wrought by Tyranny.

Caged Circe[2] of steel and stone,
   her parent German ingenuity.[3]
   "O catenary curve" from tower to pier,
   implacable enemy of the mind's deformity,
10   of man's uncompunctious greed,
   his crass love of crass priority
     just recently
   obstructing acquiescent feet
   about to step ashore when darkness fell
15   without a cause,
   as if probity had not joined our cities
    in the sea.

"O path amid the stars
   crossed by the seagull's wing!"
20   "O radiance that doth inherit me!"
   —affirming inter-acting harmony!

Untried expedient, untried; then tried;
   way out; way in; romantic passageway
   first seen by the eye of the mind,
25   then by the eye. O steel! O stone!
   Climactic ornament, double rainbow,
   as if inverted by French perspicacity,
    John Roebling's monument,
    German tenacity's also;
30   composite span—an actuality.

---

[1]The Brooklyn Bridge and the statue of Liberty in the New York harbor.
[2]The enchantress in *The Odyssey* who enticed Odysseus and his men and held them captive. The bridge is called a Circe, according to Miss Moore's note, because of the young reporter in the 1870's who was so drawn by the bridge that he climbed to the top of one of its towers and was trapped there for hours until he was rescued.
[3]John Roebling (1806–1869), a German immigrant, was the architect of the Brooklyn Bridge. He personally supervised construction till his death, at which point his son took charge.

ARTHUR MITCHELL[1]

Slim dragonfly
too rapid for the eye
   to cage—
contagious gem of virtuosity—
5 make visible, mentality.
Your jewels of mobility

    reveal
      and veil
        a peacock-tail.

SUN

Hope and Fear accost him

"No man may him hyde
From Deth holow-eyed";
  For us, this inconvenient truth does not suffice.
You are not male or female, but a plan
5 deep-set within the heart of man.
Splendid with splendor hid you come, from your Arab abode,
a fiery topaz smothered in the hand of a great prince who rode
  before you, Sun—whom you outran,
  piercing his caravan.

10 O Sun, you shall stay
    with us; holiday,
    consuming wrath, be wound in a device
of Moorish gorgeousness, round glasses spun
to flame as hemispheres of one
15 great hour-glass dwindling to a stem. Consume hostility;
employ your weapon in this meeting-place of surging enmity!
  Insurgent feet shall not outrun
  multiplied flames, O Sun.

[1]A ballet dancer who danced Puck in the New York City Center production of
A Midsummer Night's Dream.

John Crowe Ransom (1888–   ) From Pulaski,

Tennessee, where his father was a minister, Ransom went to Vanderbilt University, graduated in 1909, and earned another B.A. from Oxford as a Rhodes Scholar. After military service in France during World War I, he taught at Vanderbilt until 1937. Ransom became the center for an extraordinary group of poets, literary critics, and social critics that included Allen Tate, Robert Penn Warren, and Donald Davidson, and they came to be known as The Fugitive Group because they put out a magazine called *The Fugitive* from 1922 to 1925. In 1930 they issued a collection of essays, *I'll Take My Stand,* in opposition to the dehumanizing forces of urban life, technology, and materialistic communism, and in support of a decentralized agrarian economy in which all classes accept their place in a community close to the native soil.

By this time most of Ransom's poetry was published: *Poems About God* (1919), *Chills and Fever* (1924), and *Two Gentlemen in Bonds* (1927). The diminutiveness of the poems, the courtly formality, the irony and paradox and witty understatement are Ransom's devices to control and objectify his disillusionment. His is a fallen world in which death is an omnipresent fact, transcendence is only an idea, and the divisions of head from heart make love almost impossible. The tenets of the New Criticism proceeded from such assumptions about the inadequacy of the natural order; in *The World's Body* (1938) and *The New Criticism* (1941), Ransom argued for the self-contained integrity of the achieved work of art and for an "ontological" criticism that would avoid reducing the aesthetic object to subjective response or paraphrase or politics or morality, and would examine in a quasi-scientific way the technical and structural properties of the text.

From 1937 to 1958 Ransom was at Kenyon College, where his teaching and editorship of *The Kenyon Review* made him one of the most influential figures in American poetry during the forties and fifties. *Selected Poems* (1945) was enlarged in 1963 and in 1965 with revisions of some poems and the addition of a few substantially new ones. *Beating the Bushes* (1972) is a selection of essays since 1941.

REFERENCE

Buffington, Robert. *The Equilibrist: A Study of John Crowe Ransom's Poems, 1916–1963.* Nashville: Vanderbilt University Press, 1969.

Cowan, Louise. *The Fugitive Group: A Literary History.* Baton Rouge: Louisiana State University Press, 1959.

Stewart, John L. *The Burden of Time: The Fugitives and Agrarians.* Princeton: Princeton University Press, 1965.

Williams, Miller. *The Poetry of John Crowe Ransom.* New Brunswick, N. J.: Rutgers University Press, 1972.

DEAD BOY

The little cousin is dead, by foul subtraction,[1]
A green bough from Virginia's aged tree,
And none of the county kin like the transaction,[2]
Nor some of the world of outer dark, like me.

5   A boy not beautiful, nor good, nor clever,
A black cloud full of storms too hot for keeping,
A sword beneath his mother's heart[3]—yet never
Woman bewept her babe as this is weeping.

A pig with a pasty face, so I had said,
10 Squealing for cookies, kinned by poor pretense
With a noble house. But the little man quite dead,
I see the forbears' antique lineaments.

The elder men have strode by the box of death
To the wide flag porch, and muttering low send round
15 The bruit of the day. O friendly waste of breath!
Their hearts are hurt with a deep dynastic wound.

He was pale and little, the foolish neighbors say;
The first-fruits,[4] saith the Preacher, the Lord hath taken;
But this was the old tree's late branch wrenched away,
20 Grieving the sapless limbs, the shorn and shaken.

SPECTRAL LOVERS

By night they haunted a thicket of April mist,
Out of that black ground suddenly come to birth,
Else angels lost in each other and fallen on earth.
Lovers they knew they were, but why unclasped, unkissed?
5 Why should two lovers be frozen apart in fear?
And yet they were, they were.

[1]Pun: the Latin roots mean "drawn down or under."
[2]Pun: the Latin roots mean "done or driven across."
[3]Luke 2:35: "and a sword shall pierce your heart too." Simeon's prophecy to
Mary in anticipation of Jesus' death.
[4]The first fruits in the Bible are associated with the first born as especially
sacred to God and so to man.

Over the shredding of an April blossom
Scarcely her fingers touched him, quick with care,
Yet of evasions even she made a snare.
10   The heart was bold that clanged within her bosom,
The moment perfect, the time stopped for them,
Still her face turned from him.

Strong were the batteries of the April night
And the stealthy emanations of the field;
15   Should the walls of her prison undefended yield
And open her treasure to the first clamorous knight?
"This is the mad moon, and shall I surrender all?
If he but ask it I shall."

And gesturing largely to the moon of Easter,
20   Mincing his steps and swishing the jubilant grass,
Beheading some field-flowers that had come to pass,
He had reduced his tributaries faster
Had not considerations pinched his heart
Unfitly for his art.

25   "Do I reel with the sap of April like a drunkard?
Blessed is he that taketh this richest of cities:
But it is so stainless the sack were a thousand pities.
This is that marble fortress not to be conquered,
Lest its white peace in the black flame turn to tinder
30   And an unutterable cinder."

They passed me once in April, in the mist,
No other season is it when one walks and discovers
Two tall and wandering, like spectral lovers,
White in the season's moon-gold and amethyst,
35   Who touch quick fingers fluttering like a bird
Whose songs shall never be heard.

NECROLOGICAL[1]

The friar had said his paternosters[2] duly
And scourged his limbs, and afterwards would have slept;
But with much riddling his head became unruly,
He arose, from the quiet monastery he crept.

5   Dawn lightened the place where the battle had been won.
The people were dead—it is easy he thought to die—
These dead remained, but the living all were gone,
Gone with the wailing trumps of victory.

The dead men wore no raiment against the air,
10 Bartholomew's men had spoiled them where they fell;
In defeat the heroes' bodies were whitely bare,
The field was white like meads[3] of asphodel.

Not all were white; some gory and fabulous
Whom the sword had pierced and then the gray wolf eaten;
15 But the brother reasoned that heroes' flesh was thus;
Flesh fails, and the postured bones lie weather-beaten.

The lords of chivalry lay prone and shattered,
The gentle and the bodyguard of yeomen;
Bartholomew's stroke went home—but little it mattered,
20 Bartholomew went to be stricken of other foemen.

Beneath the blue ogive[4] of the firmament
Was a dead warrior, clutching whose mighty knees
Was a leman,[5] who with her flame had warmed his tent,
For him enduring all men's pleasantries.

25 Close by the sable stream that purged the plain
Lay the white stallion and his rider thrown,
The great beast had spilled there his little brain,
And the little groin of the knight was spilled by a stone.

[1]Concerned with a record of the dead.
[2]Latin for "Our Fathers," that is, the Lord's Prayer.
[3]Meadows.
[4]Arch, as in a Gothic cathedral.
[5]Paramour, mistress.

The youth possessed him then of a crooked blade
30 Deep in the belly of a lugubrious wight;[6]
He fingered it well, and it was cunningly made;
But strange apparatus was it for a Carmelite.[7]

He sat upon a hill and bowed his dead
As under a riddle, and in a deep surmise
35 So still that he likened himself unto those dead
Whom the kites[8] of Heaven solicited with sweet cries.

BELLS FOR JOHN WHITESIDE'S DAUGHTER

There was such speed in her little body,
And such lightness in her footfall,
It is no wonder her brown study[1]
Astonishes us all.

5   Her wars were bruited[2] in our high window.
We looked among orchard trees and beyond
Where she took arms against her shadow,
Or harried unto the pond

The lazy geese, like a snow cloud
10 Dripping their snow on the green grass,
Tricking and stopping, sleepy and proud,
Who cried in goose, Alas,

For the tireless heart within the little
Lady with rod that made them rise
15 From their noon apple-dreams and scuttle
Goose-fashion under the skies!

But now go the bells, and we are ready,
In one house we are sternly stopped
To say we are vexed at her brown study,
20 Lying so primly propped.

[6]A human being, person.
[7]Monastic order.
[8]Predatory bird.

[1]Melancholy reverie.
[2]Rumored.

JUDITH OF BETHULIA[1]

Beautiful as the flying legend of some leopard
She had not chosen yet her captain, nor Prince
Depositary to her flesh, and our defense;
A wandering beauty is a blade out of its scabbard.
5   You know how dangerous, gentlemen of threescore?
May you know it yet ten more.

Nor by process of veiling she grew less fabulous.
Grey or blue veils, we were desperate to study
The invincible emanations of her white body,
10   And the winds at her ordered raiment were ominous.
Might she walk in the market, sit in the council of soldiers?
Only of the extreme elders.

But a rare chance was the girl's then, when the Invader
Trumpeted from the South, and rumbled from the North,
15   Beleaguered the city from four quarters of the earth,
Our soldiery too craven and sick to aid her—
Where were the arms could countervail this horde?
Her beauty was the sword.

She sat with the elders, and proved on their blear visage
20   How bright was the weapon unrusted in her keeping,
While he lay surfeiting on their harvest heaping
Wasting the husbandry[2] of their rarest vintage—
And dreaming of the broad-breasted dames for concubine?
These floated on his wine.

25   He was lapped with bay-leaves, and grass and fumiter weed,
And from under the wine-film encountered his mortal[3] vision,
For even within his tent she accomplished his derision,
Loosing one veil and another, she stood unafraid;
So he perished. Nor brushed her with even so much as a daisy?
30   She found his destruction easy.

---

[1]See the book of Judith in the Old Testament. Judith became a heroine of her people by saving them from the Assyrian invaders under Holofernes who were besieging the town of Bethulia. She went to Holofernes' tent, got him drunk, decapitated him and brought his head home as her trophy.
[2]Pun: refers to the vines, and continues the sustained sexual references throughout the poem.
[3]Pun: human, and death-dealing.

The heathen have all perished. The victory was furnished.
We smote them hiding in vineyards, barns, annexes,
And now their white bones clutter the holes of foxes,
And the chieftain's head, with grinning sockets, and varnished—
35 Is it hung on the sky with a hideous epitaphy?
No, the woman keeps the trophy.

May God send unto our virtuous lady her Prince!
It is stated she went reluctant to that orgy,
Yet a madness fevers our young men, and not the clergy
40 Nor the elders have turned them unto modesty since.
Inflamed by the thought of her nakedness with desire?
Yes, and chilled with fear and despair.

PIAZZA PIECE

—I am a gentleman in a dustcoat trying
To make you hear. Your ears are soft and small
And listen to an old man not at all,
They want the young men's whispering and sighing.
5 But see the roses on your trellis dying
And hear the spectral singing of the moon;
For I must have my lovely lady soon,
I am a gentleman in a dustcoat trying.

—I am a lady young in beauty waiting
10 Until my truelove comes, and then we kiss.
But what grey man among the vines is this
Whose words are dry and faint as in a dream?
Back from my trellis, Sir, before I scream!
I am a lady young in beauty waiting.

JANET WAKING

Beautifully Janet slept
Till it was deeply morning.[1] She woke then
And thought about her dainty-feathered hen,
To see how it had kept.

5   One kiss she gave her mother.
Only a small one gave she to her daddy
Who would have kissed each curl of his shining baby;
No kiss at all for her brother.

"Old Chucky, old Chucky!" she cried,
10 Running across the world upon the grass
To Chucky's house, and listening. But alas,
Her Chucky had died.

It was a transmogrifying[2] bee
Came droning down on Chucky's old bald head
15 And sat and put the poison. It scarcely bled,
But how exceedingly

And purply did the knot
Swell with the venom and communicate
Its rigor![3] Now the poor comb stood up straight
20 But Chucky did not.

So there was Janet
Kneeling on the wet grass, crying her brown hen
(Translated[4] far beyond the daughters of men)
To rise and walk upon it.

25 And weeping fast as she had breath
Janet implored us, "Wake her from her sleep!"
And would not be instructed in how deep
Was the forgetful kingdom of death.

[1]Pun: Morning, and mourning.
[2]Transforming.
[3]Pun: strength, and rigor mortis.
[4]Pun: Latin roots mean "carried across."

PERSISTENT EXPLORER

The noise of water teased his literal ear
Which heard the distant drumming, and so scored:
"Water is falling—it fell—therefore it roared.
Yet something else is there: is it cheer or fear?"

5   He strode much faster, till on the dizzy brink
His eye confirmed with vision what he'd heard:
"A simple physical water." Again he demurred:
"More than a roaring flashing water, I think."

But listen as he might, look fast or slow,
10   It was common water, millions of tons of it
Gouging its gorge deeper, and every bit
Was water, the insipid chemical H_2O.

Its thunder smote[1] him somewhat as the loud
Words of the god that rang around a man
15   Walking by the Mediterranean.
Its cloud of froth was whiter than the cloud

That clothed the goddess sliding down the air
Unto a mountain shepherd, white as she
That issued from the smoke refulgently.[2]
20   The cloud was, but the goddess was not there.

Deafening was the sound, but never a voice
That talked with him; spacious the spectacle
But it spelled nothing; there was not any spell
Whether to bid him cower or rejoice.

25   What would he have it spell? He scarcely knew;
Only that water and nothing but water filled
His eyes and ears; only water that spilled;
And if the smoke and rattle of water drew

From the deep thickets of his mind the train,[3]
30   The fierce fauns and the timid tenants there

[1]Struck.
[2]Shining brilliantly.
[3]Procession.

That burst their bonds and rushed upon the air,
Why, he must turn and beat them down again.

So be it. And no unreasonable outcry
The pilgrim made; only a rueful grin
35 Spread over his lips until he drew them in;
He would not sit upon a rock and die.

Many are the ways of dying; witness, if he
Commit himself to the water, and descend
Wrapped in the water, turn water at the end,
40 Part of a water rolling to the sea.

But there were many ways of living, too,
And let his enemies gibe, but let them say
That he would throw this continent away
And seek another country—as he would do.

PAINTED HEAD

By dark severance the apparition head[1]
Smiles from the air a capital[2] on no
Column or a Platonic perhaps head[3]
On a canvas sky depending[4] from nothing;

5 Stirs up an old illusion of grandeur
By tickling the instinct of heads to be
Absolute and to try decapitation
And to play truant from the body bush;

But too happy and beautiful for those sorts
10 Of head (homekeeping heads are happiest)
Discovers[5] maybe thirty unwidowed years
Of not dishonoring the faithful stem;

---

[1]Ransom is describing a portrait of a head, detached from a body on a dark background. Pun on "apparition": appearance, specter, sudden or unusual sight.
[2]The top of a column; the Latin word for "head." The first of many puns throughout the poem on "head."
[3]That is, the Platonic idea or form of head.
[4]Hanging from.
[5]Reveals.

Is nameless and has authored for the evil
Historian headhunters neither book
15 Nor state and is therefore distinct from tart
Heads with crowns and guilty gallery heads;

Wherefore the extravagant device of art
Unhousing by abstraction this once head
Was capital[6] irony by a loving hand
20 That knew the no treason of a head like this;

Makes repentance in an unlovely head
For having vinegarly traduced the flesh
Till, the hurt flesh recusing, the hard egg[7]
Is shrunken to its own deathlike surface;

25 And an image thus. The body bears[8] the head
(So hardly one they terribly are two)
Feeds and obeys and unto please what end?
Not to the glory of tyrant head but to

The estate of body. Beauty is of body.
30 The flesh contouring shallowly on a head[9]
Is a rock-garden needing body's love
And best bodiness to colorify

The big blue birds sitting and sea-shell flats[10]
And caves, and on the iron acropolis
35 To spread the hyacinthine[11] hair and rear
The olive garden for the nightingales.

---

[6]First-rate; again a pun on "head."

[7]The head, abstracted from body by art, is thereby killed into an egg-head. Perhaps also an indirect reference to tempera, a painting medium in which the pigment is mixed with and fixed by egg, as above "vinegarly," besides meaning sourly may refer to vinegar as a solvent for dye to color eggs, for example at Easter.

[8]Pun: carries, gives birth to.

[9]That is, the thin layers of flesh on the skull.

[10]The features of the face described as a rock garden.

[11]Hyacinth: a plant that grows from a bulb into clusters of fragrant flowers. In Greek mythology Hyacinth was a youth from whose blood, when he was slain, flowers sprang.

T. S. Eliot (1888–1965)

Thomas Stearns Eliot was born in St. Louis of New England stock and went East to study philosophy at Harvard, receiving his A.B. in 1909 and his M.A. in 1910, and writing a dissertation for the Ph.D. on the English philosopher F. H. Bradley. He was already at work on the poems that showed his reading of the metaphysical poets and of the French *symbolistes* and that would comprise much of *Prufrock and Other Observations* (1917). After graduate study at the Sorbonne and at Oxford, he settled in London in 1914. He married Vivien Haigh-Wood, whose frail health made her increasingly an invalid till her death in 1947. After working for Lloyd's Bank, Eliot joined the publishing firm of Faber and Gwynn (later Faber and Faber) in 1925 and remained there till his death.

Meanwhile he had begun editing *The Criterion*. His early essays argued for a historical sense, for a tradition within which the individual worked, for an impersonal art that avoided the romantic trap of narcissistic isolation by finding the "objective correlative" of the precise emotion in the exactitudes of language. His early poems—the Prufrock volume, *Poems* (1920), *The Waste Land* (1922), *The Hollow Men* (1925)— expressed the disillusionment of the sophisticated intellectual who could analyze the individual and social failure of feeling and spirit but could not break out into love or faith. *The Waste Land*, dedicated to Pound who had become his sponsor and had helped in the editing of the manuscript, builds a panoramic view of the modern world on the brink of collapse in a series of dramatic vignettes whose different styles and voices employ myth and literary allusion for maximum concentration and intensity of effect.

In 1927 Eliot became an Anglican and a British subject. His conversion and his new commitments to theological, ecclesiastical, and social structures inform his later poems, *Ash Wednesday* (1930) and *Four Quartets* (1943), as well as such prose works as *The Idea of a Christian Society (1939)* and *Notes Towards the Definition of Culture* (1948). *Four Quartets* is the culmination of his poetic work: a sequence of meditations whose psychological, social, historical, aesthetic, and religious dimensions are unified by the poet's own voice seeking to construe within the possibilities of language those transfiguring moments when time and eternity cross and when he sees that "only through time time is conquered." The *Quartets* are personal and universal, formal and exploratory; Allen Tate has called them the finest achievement of English poetry in this century.

Eliot was Charles Eliot Norton Professor at Harvard in the early thirties and returned to the United States regularly in his later years. His best literary essays are gathered into *Selected Essays* (1932), *On Poets and Poetry* (1957), and *To Criticise the Critic* (1965). Always interested in the theater, he became increasingly concerned with finding a poetic idiom for the modern stage, and several of his plays dramatizing the struggle for salvation were popular successes, notably *Murder in the Cathedral* (1935), *The Cocktail Party* (1950), and *The Confidential Clerk* (1954). His numerous degrees and awards, including the Nobel Prize and the Order of Merit, took official note of the fact that Eliot is the most honored and influential poet-critic of the century. When pressed to declare himself either an English or an American poet, Eliot once remarked that probably his American origins and experience were deeper. Among American poets he is perhaps the supreme example of one who could come to himself only by recovering the orthodoxies of the Western tradition. His verse is gathered into the *Collected Poems* (1963) and *Complete Plays* (1967).

REFERENCE

Drew, Elizabeth. *T. S. Eliot: The Design of His Poetry*. New York: Scribner, 1949.

T. S. Eliot: A Collection of Critical Essays. Ed. Hugh Kenner. Englewood Cliffs, N. J.: Prentice-Hall, 1962.

T. S. Eliot: The Man and His Work. Ed. Allen Tate. New York: Delacorte Press, 1966.

T. S. Eliot: A Selected Critique. Ed. Leonard Unger. New York: Rinehart, 1948.

Gardner, Helen. *The Art of T. S. Eliot*. London: Cresset Press, 1949.

Kenner, Hugh. *The Invisible Poet: T. S. Eliot*. New York: McDowell, Obolensky, 1959.

Matthiessen, F. O. *The Achievement of T. S. Eliot,* with a chapter on Eliot's later work by C. L. Barber. N. Y.: Oxford University Press, 1958.

Sencourt, Robert. *T. S. Eliot: A Memoir*. New York: Dodd, Mead, 1971.

Smith, Grover. *T. S. Eliot's Poetry and Plays: A Study in Sources and Meaning*. Chicago: University of Chicago Press, 1956.

Williamson, George. *A Reader's Guide to T. S. Eliot*. New York: Noonday Press, 1953.

MORNING AT THE WINDOW

They are rattling breakfast plates in basement kitchens,
And along the trampled edges of the street
I am aware of the damp souls of housemaids
Sprouting despondently at area gates.[1]

5   The brown waves of fog toss up to me
Twisted faces from the bottom of the street,
And tear from a passer-by with muddy skirts
An aimless smile that hovers in the air
And vanishes along the level of the roofs.

LA FIGLIA CHE PIANGE[1]

O quam te memorem virgo . . .[2]

Stand on the highest pavement of the stair—
Lean on a garden urn—
Weave, weave the sunlight in your hair—
Clasp your flowers to you with a pained surprise—
5 Fling them to the ground and turn
With a fugitive resentment in your eyes:
But weave, weave the sunlight in your hair.

    So I would have had him leave,
So I would have had her stand and grieve,
10 So he would have left
As the soul leaves the body torn and bruised,
As the mind deserts the body it has used.
I should find
Some way incomparably light and deft,
15 Some way we both should understand,
Simple and faithless as a smile and shake of the hand.

---

[1]Gates of the areaways of houses.

---

[1]Italian: the girl who weeps.
[2]Aeneas' words to Venus in disguise: "O maiden how shall I recall you?"
(*Aeneid*, I, 327).

She turned away, but with the autumn weather
Compelled my imagination many days,
Many days and many hours:
20   Her hair over her arms and her arms full of flowers.
And I wonder how they should have been together!
I should have lost a gesture and a pose.
Sometimes these cogitations still amaze
The troubled midnight and the noon's repose.

THE WASTE LAND

"*Nam Sibyllam quidem Cumis ego ipse oculis meis vidi
in ampulla pendere, et cum illi pueri dicerent: Σίβυλλα
τί θέλεις: respondebat illa: ἀποθάνειν θέλω.*"[1]

FOR EZRA POUND
il miglior fabbro.[2]

I. THE BURIAL OF THE DEAD[3]

April is the cruellest month, breeding
Lilacs out of the dead land, mixing
Memory and desire, stirring
Dull roots with spring rain.
5   Winter kept us warm, covering

[1]From the *Satyricon* of Petronius, a satire written in the first century A.D. on the corruption and sexual excesses of Rome: "I myself once saw with my own eyes the Sibyl of Cumae suspended in a bottle; and when the boys asked her, 'Sibyl, what is the matter?' she replied, 'I want to die.' " The epigraph, therefore, strikes a prophetic note of decline and impending death.

[2]"The better craftsman": Dante's epithet for Arnaut Daniel, the Provencal poet, in *Purgatorio* 26, 117. Pound had advised Eliot in his revisions of the poem and urged the excision of three long passages as well as smaller changes.

[3]Eliot's notes indicate indebtedness to anthropological studies: Jessie Weston's *From Ritual to Romance* and Sir James Frazer's *The Golden Bough*, particularly the sections on Adonis, Attis and Osiris. The former is a study of the myth of the Holy Grail (the cup used by Jesus at the Supper) as it developed from pagan fertility rites to chivalric legend. The Grail is in the safekeeping of the Fisher King; it is stolen and he is wounded: incapacitated and sexually maimed. As a result the land and people are blighted. With the king impotent, knight after knight goes out on quest for the Grail, and here the legend becomes associated with the Arthurian myth. The sections of *The Golden Bough* tell of various fertility gods and spring vegetation rituals to enact the cyclical mystery of death and rebirth.

Earth in forgetful snow, feeding
A little life with dried tubers.
Summer surprised us, coming over the Starnbergersee[4]
With a shower of rain; we stopped in the colonnade,
10 And went on in sunlight, into the Hofgarten,[5]
And drank coffee, and talked for an hour.
Bin gar keine Russin, stamm' aus Litauen, echt deutsch.[6]
And when we were children, staying at the archduke's,
My cousin's, he took me out on a sled,
15 And I was frightened. He said, Marie,
Marie, hold on tight. And down we went.
In the mountains, there you feel free.
I read, much of the night, and go south in the winter.

What are the roots that clutch, what branches grow
20 Out of this stony rubbish? Son of man,[7]
You cannot say, or guess, for you know only
A heap of broken images, where the sun beats,
And the dead tree gives no shelter, the cricket no relief,[8]
And the dry stone no sound of water. Only
25 There is shadow under this red rock,
(Come in under the shadow of this red rock),
And I will show you something different from either
Your shadow at morning striding behind you
Or your shadow at evening rising to meet you;
30 I will show you fear in a handful of dust.
                    Frisch weht der Wind
                    Der Heimat zu

[4]The first of the dramatic, as distinguished from the lyric, or meditative, episodes that make up the collage of the poem. One of Eliot's innovations was the attempt to structure without transitions or explicit connectives through the rapid shifts and juxtapositions. George L. K. Morris has shown that the source of this passage is *My Past* (1916) by Austrian Countess Marie Larisch, who did live on the Starnberger Lake.
[5]Literally, "court garden"; here, a public garden with a cafe.
[6]"I am not Russian, I am from Lithuania, pure German."
[7]Ezekiel 2:1 ff. "And he said unto me, Son of man, stand up; I am going to speak to you. . . . I am sending you to the Israelites, to the rebels who have turned against me. . . ." Eliot alludes throughout the poem to other writings for economy and intensity, in order to bring the meaning of the work alluded to into his poem for re-enforcement or contrast.
[8]Ecclesiastes 12:1, 5, 7–8. "And remember your creator in the days of your youth, before the evil days come and the years approach when you say, 'These give me no pleasure.' . . . Yet the almond tree is in flower, the grasshopper is heavy with food and the caper bush bears its fruit, while man goes to his everlasting home. And the mourners are already walking to and fro in the street . . . before the dust returns to the earth as it once came from it, and the breath to God who gave it. Vanity of vanities, says the preacher, all is vanity."

Mein Irisch Kind,
Wo weilest du?[9]

35   "You gave me hyacinths first a year ago;
"They called me the hyacinth girl."
—Yet when we came back, late, from the Hyacinth[10] garden,
Your arms full, and your hair wet, I could not
Speak, and my eyes failed, I was neither

40   Living nor dead, and I knew nothing,
Looking into the heart of light, the silence.
Oed' und leer das Meer.[11]

Madame Sosostris, famous clairvoyante,
Had a bad cold, nevertheless

45   Is known to be the wisest woman in Europe,
With a wicked pack of cards.[12] Here, said she,
Is your card, the drowned Phoenician Sailor,
(Those are pearls that were his eyes. Look!)[13]
Here is Belladonna, the Lady of the Rocks,[14]

50   The lady of situations.
Here is the man with three staves, and here the Wheel,[15]
And here is the one-eyed merchant, and this card,
Which is blank, is something he carries on his back,
Which I am forbidden to see. I do not find

[9]Richard Wagner (1813–1883), *Tristan and Isolde* I, 5–8: "Fresh blows the breeze from off the bow; my Irish maid, where do you linger?" Tristan, the Arthurian knight, is expressing his grand and doomed passion for the Irish princess Isolde, betrothed to King Mark of Cornwall.

[10]One of the fertility gods worshiped in spring rituals was Hyacinth.

[11]*Tristan and Isolde* III, 24: "Wide and empty the sea."

[12]Eliot's note: "I am not familiar with the exact constitution of the Tarot pack of cards, from which I have obviously departed to suit my own convenience. The Hanged Man, a member of the traditional pack, fits my purpose in two ways: because he is associated in my mind with the Hanged God of Frazer, and because I associate him with the hooded figure in the passage of the disciples to Emmaus in Part V. The Phoenician Sailor and the Merchant appear later; also the 'crowds of people,' and Death by Water is executed in Part IV. The Man with Three Staves (an authentic member of the Tarot pack) I associate, quite arbitrarily, with the Fisher King himself."
The tarot pack was used in ancient Egypt to forecast the rise and fall of the Nile.

[13]Shakespeare's *The Tempest* I, ii: Ariel's song to the shipwrecked Ferdinand about his father, presumed falsely to have drowned: "Full fathom five thy father lies;/Of his bones are coral made;/Those are pearls that were his eyes. . . ."

[14]Belladonna: lovely lady (in Italian); also nightshade, deadly poison. The Lady of the Rock: suggests a Siren, or Da Vinci's "Mona Lisa" or his "Madonna of the Rocks."

[15]Staves: poles, as in fishing poles; also verses, as in the three verses of the last section, "What the Thunder said." The Wheel: fortune, life, cyclical change.

55 The Hanged Man. Fear death by water.
    I see crowds of people, walking round in a ring.
    Thank you. If you see dear Mrs. Equitone,
    Tell her I bring the horoscope myself:
    One must be so careful these days.

60 Unreal City,[16]
    Under the brown fog of a winter dawn,
    A crowd flowed over London Bridge, so many,
    I had not thought death had undone so many.[17]
    Sighs, short and infrequent, were exhaled,[18]
65 And each man fixed his eyes before his feet.
    Flowed up the hill and down King William Street,
    To where Saint Mary Woolnoth[19] kept the hours
    With a dead sound on the final stroke of nine.
    There I saw one I knew, and stopped him, crying: "Stetson!
70 "You who were with me in the ships of Mylae![20]
    "That corpse you planted last year in your garden,
    "Has it begun to sprout? Will it bloom this year?
    "Or has the sudden frost disturbed its bed?
    "Oh keep the Dog far hence, that's friend to men,[21]
75 "Or with his nails he'll dig it up again!
    "You! hypocrite lecteur!—mon semblable,—mon frère!"[22]

II. A GAME OF CHESS[23]

The Chair she sat in, like a burnished throne,[24]
Glowed on the marble, where the glass

[16]An allusion to the famous phrase "fourmillante cité" (ant-heap city), which Charles Baudelaire (1821–1867), the symbolist poet, used in his poem "Les Sept Viellards" ("The Seven Old Men").

[17]Translated from Dante's *Inferno* III, 55–57.

[18]*Inferno* IV, 25–27.

[19]A London church, as King William is a London Street.

[20]The battle of Mylae between the Romans and Carthaginians in the Punic War.

[21]John Webster, *The White Devil* (1612) V, iv:

                call unto his funeral dole
            The ant, the fieldmouse, and the mole,
        To rear him hillocks that shall keep him warm,
        And (when gay tombs are robb'd) sustain no harm;
        But keep the wolf far thence, that's foe to men;
        For with his nails he'll dig it up again.

[22]"You! hypocrite reader! one like me, my brother!": the last line of Baudelaire's poem "Au Lecteur" ("To the Reader") in *Les Fleurs du Mal* (*The Flowers of Evil*).

[23]Eliot's note calls attention to Thomas Middleton's *Women Beware Women* (1621), in which a game of chess is part of the sexual intrigue of the plot.

[24]Enobarbus' description of Cleopatra in Shakespeare's *Antony & Cleopatra* II, ii: "The barge she sat in, like a burnished throne,/Burned on the water. . . ."

Held up by standards wrought with fruited vines
80 From which a golden Cupidon peeped out
(Another hid his eyes behind his wing)
Doubled the flames of sevenbranched candelabra
Reflecting light upon the table as
The glitter of her jewels rose to meet it,
85 From satin cases poured in rich profusion;
In vials of ivory and coloured glass
Unstoppered, lurked her strange synthetic perfumes,
Unguent, powdered, or liquid—troubled, confused
And drowned the sense in odours; stirred by the air
90 That freshened from the window, these ascended
In fattening the prolonged candle-flames,
Flung their smoke into the laquearia,[25]
Stirring the pattern on the coffered ceiling.
Huge sea-wood fed with copper
95 Burned green and orange, framed by the coloured stone,
In which sad light a carvèd dolphin swam.
Above the antique mantel was displayed
As though a window gave upon the sylvan scene[26]
The change of Philomel,[27] by the barbarous king
100 So rudely forced; yet there the nightingale
Filled all the desert with inviolable voice
And still she cried, and still the world pursues,
"Jug Jug" to dirty ears.
And other withered stumps of time
105 Were told upon the walls; staring forms
Leaned out, leaning, hushing the room enclosed.
Footseps shuffled on the stair.
Under the firelight, under the brush, her hair
Spread out in fiery points
110 Glowed into words, then would be savagely still.

"My nerves are bad to-night. Yes, bad. Stay with me.
"Speak to me. Why do you never speak. Speak.

---

[25]Ceiling. Eliot's note indicates that he is alluding to Vergil's *Aeneid* I, 726, a description of the banquet given by Dido, Queen of Carthage, for Aeneas.

[26]Eliot's note indicates that the phrase is an allusion to *Paradise Lost* IV, 140, from Milton's description of Eden as Satan approaches it to tempt Adam and Eve.

[27]Philomela was raped by the Thracian prince Tereus, husband of her sister Procne. Tereus cut out her tongue so that she could not tell, but Philomela and Procne avenged themselves by cooking Itys, Terus' son by Procne, and serving him to Tereus to eat. Tereus tried to kill the sisters, but they were changed into birds (a swallow and a nightingale) and escaped.

"What are you thinking of? What thinking? What?
"I never know what you are thinking. Think."

115 I think we are in rats' alley
Where the dead men lost their bones.

"What is that noise?"
                    The wind under the door.
"What is that noise now? What is the wind doing?"
120   Nothing again nothing.
                              "Do
"You know nothing? Do you see nothing? Do you remember
"Nothing?"

     I remember
125 Those are pearls that were his eyes.
"Are you alive, or not? Is there nothing in your head?"

O O O O that Shakespeherian Rag—   But
It's so elegant
130 So intelligent
"What shall I do now? What shall I do?"
"I shall rush out as I am, and walk the street
"With my hair down, so. What shall we do to-morrow?
"What shall we ever do?"
135   The hot water at ten.
And if it rains, a closed car at four.
And we shall play a game of chess,
Pressing lidless eyes and waiting for a knock upon the door.

When Lil's husband got demobbed,[28] I said—
140 I didn't mince my words, I said to her myself,
HURRY UP PLEASE ITS TIME[29]
Now Albert's coming back, make yourself a bit smart.
He'll want to know what you done with that money he gave you
To get yourself some teeth. He did, I was there.
145 You have them all out, Lil, and get a nice set,
He said, I swear, I can't bear to look at you.
And no more can't I, I said, and think of poor Albert,
He's been in the army four years, he wants a good time,

[28]Demobilized (from the army).
[29]The bartender in the lower-class pub, announcing closing time. "The Game of Chess" juxtaposes the scene in the lady's boudoir with the pub-scene that begins two lines above this line.

And if you don't give it him, there's others will, I said.
150 Oh is there, she said. Something o' that, I said.
Then I'll know who to thank, she said, and give me a straight look.
HURRY UP PLEASE ITS TIME
If you don't like it you can get on with it, I said.
Others can pick and choose if you can't.
155 But if Albert makes off, it won't be for lack of telling.
You ought to be ashamed, I said, to look so antique.
(And her only thirty-one.)
I can't help it, she said, pulling a long face,
It's them pills I took, to bring it off, she said.
160 (She's had five already, and nearly died of young George.)
The chemist[30] said it would be all right, but I've never
been the same.
You *are* a proper fool, I said.
Well, if Albert won't leave you alone, there it is, I
said,
What you get married for if you don't want children?
165 HURRY UP PLEASE ITS TIME
Well, that Sunday Albert was home, they had a
hot gammon,[31]
And they asked me in to dinner, to get the beauty
of it hot—
HURRY UP PLEASE ITS TIME
HURRY UP PLEASE ITS TIME
170 Goonight Bill. Goonight Lou. Goonight May. Goonight.
Ta ta. Goonight. Goonight.
Good night, ladies, good night, sweet ladies, good night, good
night.[32]

III. THE FIRE SERMON[33]

The river's tent is broken: the last fingers of leaf
Clutch and sink into the wet bank. The wind
175 Crosses the brown land, unheard. The nymphs are departed.
Sweet Thames, run softly, till I end my song.[34]
The river bears no empty bottles, sandwich papers,

---

[30]Druggist.
[31]Ham or bacon.
[32]*Hamlet* IV, v, 72: the mad Ophelia's last line as she goes out to her death by drowning.
[33]A famous sermon preached by the Buddha against lust and carnal passions.
[34]The *Prothalamion* of Edmund Spenser (1554–1586): this is the refrain of the poem, also set on the Thames.

Silk handkerchiefs, cardboard boxes, cigarette ends
Or other testimony of summer nights. The nymphs are departed.
180 And their friends, the loitering heirs of city directors;
Departed, have left no addresses.
By the waters of Leman I sat down and wept . . .[35]
Sweet Thames, run softly till I end my song,
Sweet Thames, run softly, for I speak not loud or long.
185 But at my back in a cold blast I hear[36]
The rattle of the bones, and chuckle spread from ear to ear.
A rat crept softly through the vegetation
Dragging its slimy belly on the bank
While I was fishing in the dull canal
190 On a winter evening round behind the gashouse
Musing upon the king my brother's wreck
And on the king my father's death before him.[37]
White bodies naked on the low damp ground
And bones cast in a little low dry garret,
195 Rattled by the rat's foot only, year to year.
But at my back from time to time I hear
The sound of horns and motors, which shall bring
Sweeney to Mrs. Porter in the spring.[38]
O the moon shone bright on Mrs. Porter
200 And on her daughter
They wash their feet in soda water[39]
Et O ces voix d'enfants, chantant dans la coupole![40]

Twit twit twit
Jug jug jug jug jug jug

[35]Psalm 137: a lament of the Israelites exiled from their homeland in Babylonian captivity: "By the waters of Babylon we sat down and wept when we remembered Zion." Leman: an Archiac word for "mistress"; also Lake Leman, or Lake Geneva, near which Eliot was staying in a sanatorium while writing much of *The Waste Land.*

[36]Andrew Marvell (1621–1678); "To his coy mistress": "But at my back I always hear/Time's winged chariot hurrying near."

[37]*The Tempest* I, ii: Just before Ariel's song cited in the first two sections Ferdinand speaks of "sitting on a bank,/weeping again the King my father's wrack."

[38]Eliot's note indicates lines from *Parliament of Bees*, by John Day (1574–1640): "When of the Sudden, listening, you shall hear,/A noise of horns and hunting, which shall bring/Actaeon to Diana in the spring. . . ." Actaeon saw Diana naked and was punished by being changed into a stag and hunted to death by his hounds.

[39]Lines from a bawdy song popular among Australian troops during World War I.

[40]From "Parsifal" by Paul Verlaine (1844–1896): "And O those children's voices singing in the dome." Parsifal was a chaste knight searching for the Holy Grail.

205   So rudely forc'd.
       Tereu

       Unreal City
       Under the brown fog of a winter noon
       Mr. Eugenides, the Smyrna merchant[41]
210   Unshaven, with a pocket full of currants
       C.i.f. London: documents at sight,[42]
       Asked me in demotic[43] French
       To luncheon at the Cannon Street Hotel[44]
       Followed by a weekend at the Metropole.[45]

215   At the violet hour, when the eyes and back
       Turn upward from the desk, when the human engine waits
       Like a taxi throbbing waiting,
       I Tiresias,[46] though blind, throbbing between two lives,
       Old man with wrinkled female breasts, can see
220   At the violet hour, the evening hour that strives
       Homeward, and brings the sailor home from sea,[47]
       The typist home at teatime, clears her breakfast, lights
       Her stove, and lays out food in tins.
       Out of the window perilously spread
225   Her drying combinations[48] touched by the sun's last rays,
       On the divan are piled (at night her bed)
       Stockings, slippers, camisoles, and stays.[49]

---

[41]Eugenides: literally, from the Greek, "well-born"; Smyrna: a Turkish port.

[42]Eliot's note: "The currants were quoted at a price 'carriage and insurance free to London'; and the Bill of Lading etc. were to be handed to the buyer upon payment of the sight draft."

[43]Vulgar, lower-class.

[44]Near the railroad terminal in London.

[45]A Brighton resort hotel.

[46]The blind prophet of Thebes who for a time had been changed into a woman. All the prophets of the poem—Sibyl, Ezekiel, Dante, Buddha, St. Augustine, the voice of the Upanishads—constellate around Tiresias at the center of the poem. Eliot's note says:

> Tiresias, although a mere spectator and not indeed a "character," is yet the most important personage in the poem, uniting all the rest. Just as the one-eyed merchant, seller of currants, melts into the Phoenician Sailor, and the latter is not wholly distinct from Ferdinand Prince of Naples, so all the women are one woman, and the two sexes meet in Tiresias. What Tiresias sees, in fact, is the substance of the poem.

[47]Recalls Sappho's lines to Hesperus, the evening star, and "Requiem" by Robert Louis Stevenson (1850–1894): "Home is the sailor, home from the sea,/And the hunter home from the hill."

[48]Combination: a one-piece undergarment.

[49]Camisole: a short negligee; stays: a corset braced with bone.

I Tiresias, old man with wrinkled dugs
Perceived the scene, and foretold the rest—
230   I too awaited the expected guest.
He, the young man carbuncular,[50] arrives,
A small house agent's clerk, with one bold stare,
One of the low on whom assurance sits
As a silk hat on a Bradford[51] millionaire.
235   The time is now propitious, as he guesses,
The meal is ended, she is bored and tired,
Endeavours to engage her in caresses
Which still are unreproved, if undesired.
Flushed and decided, he assaults at once;
240   Exploring hands encounter no defence;
His vanity requires no response,
And makes a welcome of indifference.
(And I Tiresias have foresuffered all
Enacted on this same divan or bed;
245   I who have sat by Thebes below the wall
And walked among the lowest of the dead.)[52]
Bestows one final patronising kiss,
And gropes his way, finding the stairs unlit . . .

She turns and looks a moment in the glass,
250   Hardly aware of her departed lover;
Her brain allows one half-formed thought to pass:
"Well now that's done: and I'm glad it's over."
When lovely woman stoops to folly and[53]
Paces about her room again, alone,
255   She smoothes her hair with automatic hand,
And puts a record on the gramophone.

"This music crept by me upon the waters"[54]

---

[50]Pimply.

[51]A Yorkshire town where *nouveau-riche* fortunes were made in woolens during World War I.

[52]Tiresias had foreseen Oedipus' downfall and the struggle between his sons that brought havoc to Thebes. Odysseus later sought out Tiresias in Hades.

[53]Oliver Goldsmith's *The Vicar of Wakefield* (1766): Olivia, one of the daughters of the Rev. Mr. Primrose, is seduced and sings this song, which begins: "When lovely woman stoops to folly,/And finds too late that men betray;/What charm can soothe her melancholy?/What art can wash her guilt away?"—The song ends saying that all she can do is die.

[54]This line is quoted from the speech of Ferdinand, quoted above from *The Tempest* I, ii: "This music crept by me upon the waters,/Allaying both their fury and my passion,/With its sweet airs: thence I have followed it,/Or it hath drawn me rather. . . ."

And along the Strand, up Queen Victoria Street.[55]
O City city, I can sometimes hear
260   Beside a public bar in Lower Thames Street,
The pleasant whining of a mandoline
And a clatter and a chatter from within
Where fishmen lounge at noon: where the walls
Of Magnus Martyr[56] hold
265   Inexplicable splendour of Ionian white and gold.[57]

The river sweats[58]
Oil and tar
The barges drift
With the turning tide
270   Red sails
Wide
To leeward,[59] swing on the heavy spar.
The barges wash
Drifting logs
275   Down Greenwich reach
Past the Isle of Dogs.[60]
Weialala leia[61]
Wallala leialala

Elizabeth and Leicester[62]
280   Beating oars
The stern was formed
A gilded shell
Red and gold
The brisk swell

[55]These are all London streets.
[56]Eliot's note: "The interior of St. Magnus Martyr [church in London] is to my mind one of the finest among Wren's interiors." Sir Christopher Wren (1623–1723): one of England's best architects, famous for the restrained elegance of his designs.
[57]A scrolled Ionic column, white decorated with gold or gilt.
[58]Eliot's note indicates that the Song of the Thames-daughters begins here. They sing two verses together, and then each of the three sings of her seduction separately. Eliot has in mind the Rhine-maidens in Wagner's opera *Die Götterdämmerung (The Twilight of the Gods)*. They are guardians of the Rhinegold; they are seduced and the gold stolen, so that they are left to lament their ruin and the river's.
[59]Moving toward the side toward which the wind is blowing.
[60]Greenwich: a borough of London historically associated with shipping and sea commerce, opposite which is the Isle of Dogs peninsula in the Thames.
[61]The refrain from Wagner's opera.
[62]Queen Elizabeth I in a royal barge with her lover, the Earl of Leicester.

285 Rippled both shores
Southwest wind
Carried down stream
The peal of bells
White towers
290   Weialala leia
         Wallala leialala

"Trams[63] and dusty trees.
Highbury bore me. Richmond and Kew[64]
Undid me. By Richmond I raised my knees
295 Supine on the floor of a narrow canoe."

"My feet are at Moorgate,[65] and my heart
Under my feet. After the event
He wept. He promised 'a new start.'
I made no comment. What should I resent?"

300 "On Margate Sands.[66]
I can connect
Nothing with nothing.
The broken fingernails of dirty hands.
My people humble people who expect
305 Nothing."
         la la

To Carthage then I came[67]

Burning burning burning burning[68]
O Lord Thou pluckest me out[69]
310 O Lord Thou pluckest

burning

---

[63]Streetcars or cablecars.
[64]Suburbs of London on the Thames.
[65]A London slum area.
[66]A seaside resort on the Thames estuary.
[67]Eliot's note indicates St. Augustine's *Confessions*: "To Carthage then I came, where a cauldron of unholy loves sang all about mine ears."
[68]Eliot's note comments that the Buddha's Fire Sermon "corresponds in importance to the Sermon on the Mount" of Jesus. He added that he intended to bring together "these two representatives of eastern and western asceticism, as the culmination of this part of the poem."
[69]St. Augustine's *Confessions*: "I entangle my steps with these outward beauties, but Thou pluckest me out, O Lord."

IV. DEATH BY WATER

Phlebas the Phoenician, a fortnight dead,
Forgot the cry of gulls, and the deep sea swell
And the profit and loss.

315   A current under sea
Picked his bones in whispers. As he rose and fell
He passed the stages of his age and youth
Entering the whirlpool.

                                Gentile or Jew

320   O you who turn the wheel and look to windward,
Consider Phlebas, who was once handsome and tall as you.

V. WHAT THE THUNDER SAID

After the torchlight red on sweaty faces[70]
After the frosty silence in the gardens[71]
After the agony in stony places

325   The shouting and the crying
Prison and palace and reverberation
Of thunder of spring over distant mountains
He who was living is now dead
We who were living are now dying

330   With a little patience

Here is no water but only rock[72]
Rock and no water and the sandy road
The road winding above among the mountains
Which are mountains of rock without water

335   If there were water we should stop and drink
Amongst the rock one cannot stop or think
Sweat is dry and feet are in the sand
If there were only water amongst the rock
Dead mountain mouth of carious[73] teeth that cannot spit

340   Here one can neither stand nor lie nor sit

---

[70]Eliot's note indicates that the first part of this section—that is, up to the thunder's speaking—develops three themes: "the journey to Emmaus, the approach to the Chapel Perilous (see Miss Weston's book) and the present decay of Eastern Europe."

[71]Here Jesus' agony in the garden of Gethsemane, the betrayal by Judas, and the trial and crucifixion are all suggested. Jesus' death and resurrection in spring recall the fertility gods alluded to earlier.

[72]This passage suggests the difficulties of the knight on quest for the Holy Grail through the Waste Land; the end of the quest is the Chapel Perilous, where he should find the Grail that will restore the Fisher King and the Waste Land to health.

[73]Decayed.

There is not even silence in the mountains
But dry sterile thunder without rain
There is not even solitude in the mountains
But red sullen faces sneer and snarl
345 From doors of mudcracked houses
                              If there were water
          And no rock
          If there were rock
          And also water
350   And water
          A spring
          A pool among the rock
          If there were the sound of water only
          Not the cicada
355   And dry grass singing
          But sound of water over a rock
          Where the hermit-thrush sings in the pine trees
          Drip drop drip drop drop drop drop[74]
          But there is no water

360 Who is the third who walks always beside you?[75]
When I count, there are only you and I together
But when I look ahead up the white road
There is always another one walking beside you
Gliding wrapt in a brown mantle, hooded
365 I do not know whether a man or a woman
—But who is that on the other side of you?

          What is that sound high in the air
          Murmur of maternal lamentation
          Who are those hooded hordes swarming
370   Over endless plains, stumbling in cracked earth
          Ringed by the flat horizon only
          What is the city over the mountain
          Cracks and reforms and bursts in the violet air
          Falling towers

[74]Eliot comments that the "water-dripping song" of the hermit-thrush is "justly celebrated."
[75]Luke 24 tells the episode after Christ's death and resurrection of his appearance to two disciples journeying to Emmaus. They did not recognize him until he revealed himself at the end of the journey. Eliot's notes indicate that his passage is also based on a story about an Antarctic expedition on which "the party of explorers, at the extremity of their strength, had the constant delusion that there was one more member than could actually be counted."

375 Jerusalem Athens Alexandria
Vienna London
Unreal[76]

A woman drew her long black hair out tight
And fiddled whisper music on those strings
380 And bats with baby faces in the violet light
Whistled, and beat their wings
And crawled head downward down a blackened wall
And upside down in air were towers
Tolling reminiscent bells, that kept the hours
385 And voices singing out of empty cisterns and exhausted wells.

In this decayed hole among the mountains
In the faint moonlight, the grass is singing
Over the tumbled graves, about the chapel[77]
There is the empty chapel, only the wind's home.
390 It has no windows, and the door swings,
Dry bones harm no one.
Only a cock stood on the rooftree
Co co rico co co rico
In a flash of lightning. Then a damp gust
395 Bringing rain

Ganga[78] was sunken, and the limp leaves
Waited for rain, while the black clouds
Gathered far distant, over Himavant.[79]
The jungle crouched, humped in silence.
400 Then spoke the thunder
DA
Datta:[80] what have we given?
My friend, blood shaking my heart

[76]Eliot's note cites a pasage from *Blick ins Chaos* (*Glimpse into Chaos*) by Herman Hesse (1877–1962), which translates from the German: "Already half of Europe, at least half of eastern Europe, is already on the way to chaos, drives drunk in holy fascination along the edge of the abyss, singing drunkenly, as though singing a hymn, like Dmitri Karamazov [in Feodor Dostoyevski's novel *The Brothers Karamazov*]. The offended bourgeois laughs at these songs, the saint and the prophet hear them with tears."
[77]The knight's arrival at the Chapel Perilous.
[78]The Indian river Ganges.
[79]A mountain in the Himalayas.
[80]Eliot's note: " 'Datta, dayadhvam, damyata' (Give, sympathize, control). The fable of the meaning of the Thunder is found in the *Brihadaranyaka— Upanishad*, 5, 1"—one of the Hindu sacred texts. In the context "damyata" seems to signify here something closer to "surrender to control."

The awful daring of a moment's surrender
405　Which an age of prudence can never retract
By this, and this only, we have existed
Which is not to be found in our obituaries
Or in memories draped by the beneficent spider
Or under seals broken by the lean solicitor
410　In our empty rooms
DA
Dayadhvam: I have heard the key[81]
Turn in the door once and turn once only
We think of the key, each in his prison
415　Thinking of the key, each confirms a prison
Only at nightfall, aethereal rumours
Revive for a moment a broken Coriolanus[82]
DA
Damyata: The boat responded
420　Gaily, to the hand expert with sail and oar
The sea was calm, your heart would have responded
Gaily, when invited, beating obedient
To controlling hands

I sat upon the shore
425　Fishing,[83] with the arid plain behind me
Shall I at least set my lands in order?
London Bridge is falling down falling down falling down[84]
Poi s'ascose nel foco che gli affina[85]
Quando fiam uti chelidon[86]—O swallow swallow
430　*Le Prince d' Aquitaine à la tour abolie*[87]

[81]Dante's *Inferno* XXXIII, 46ff: Ugolino imprisoned in a tower with his children, where they died: "And I heard down below the door of the horrible tower being locked shut."

[82]The Roman whose sense of proud integrity brought him to tragedy through leading an enemy force against his own people. See Shakespeare's *Coriolanus*.

[83]The identification of the "I" with the Fisher King. Fishing: fishing around, seeking; also "fish" as sign of the Christian, as in Jesus' assurance to his Apostles, "Hence forth you shall be fishers of men."

[84]The nursery rhyme.

[85]*Purgatorio* XXVI, 145–148: the words of Arnaut Daniel, the Provençal poet, to Dante: " 'Now I pray you, by that virtue that leads you to the top of the stairway, remember in time my pain.' He hid himself in the fire that refines them." The last is the line quoted here.

[86]From *Pervigilium Veneris* (*Vigil of Venus*), an anonymous late Latin poem, here rehearsing the story of Philomela, Procne, and Tereus: Philomela with her tongue cut out (here identified with the swallow instead of the nightingale) saying "When shall I be like the swallow so that I may break out of silence?"

[87]Gérard de Nerval (1808–1855), "El Desdichado" ("The Disinherited"): "The Prince of Aquitaine at the ruined tower."

> These fragments I have shored against my ruins
> Why then Ile fit you. Hieronymo's mad againe.[88]
> Datta. Dayadhvam. Damyata.
>   Shantih   shantih   shantih[89]

MARINA[1]

Quis hic locus, quae regio, quae mundi plaga?[2]

What seas what shores what grey rocks and what islands
What water lapping the bow
And scent of pine and the woodthrush singing through the fog
What images return
5   O my daughter.

     Those who sharpen the tooth of the dog, meaning
Death
Those who glitter with the glory of the humming-bird, meaning
Death
10   Those who sit in the stye of contentment, meaning
Death
Those who suffer the ecstasy of the animals, meaning
Death

     Are become unsubstantial, reduced by a wind,
15   A breath of pine, and the woodsong fog
By this grace dissolved in place

     What is this face, less clear and clearer
The pulse in the arm, less strong and stronger—
Given or lent? more distant than stars and nearer than the eye

[88]Thomas Kyd's *Spanish Tragedy* (1594), subtitled "Hieronymo's Mad Againe." Hieronymo, maddened by his son's murder, is asked to write a play; he says "Why then I'll fit [accommodate] you!" and works the performance so that the murderers are killed.

[89]Hindu for "the Peace which passes understanding"; "a formal ending to an Upanishad" (Eliot's note).

[1]Pericles' daugther, lost at sea and recovered from the sea. Cf. Shakespeare's *Pericles.*

[2]From Seneca's first-century Latin tragedy, *Hercules Furens:* "What is this place, what region, what shore of the world?" Pericles' first words here echo Hercules', but his situation is the opposite. Hercules is awakening to find that, cursed by a spell from Juno, he has murdered his family.

20 Whispers and small laughter between leaves and hurrying feet
Under sleep, where all the waters meet.

Bowsprit[3] cracked with ice and paint cracked with heat.
I made this, I have forgotten
And remember.
25 The rigging weak and the canvas rotten
Between one June and another September.
Made this unknowing, half conscious, unknown, my own.
The garboard strake[4] leaks, the seams need caulking.
This form, this face, this life
30 Living to live in a world of time beyond me; let me
Resign my life for this life, my speech for that unspoken,
The awakened, lips parted, the hope, the new ships.

What seas what shores what granite islands towards my timbers
And woodthrush calling through the fog
35 My daughter.

THE DRY SALVAGES

(The Dry Salvages—presumably les trois sauvages—is a small group of rocks with a beacon, off the N.E. coast of Cape Ann, Massachusetts. Salvages is pronounced to rhyme with assuages. Groaner: a whistling buoy.)

I

I do not know much about gods; but I think that the river[1]
Is a strong brown god—sullen, untamed and intractable,
Patient to some degree, at first recognised as a frontier;
Useful, untrustworthy, as a conveyor of commerce;
5 Then only a problem confronting the builder of bridges.
The problem once solved, the brown god is almost forgotten
By the dwellers in cities—ever, however, implacable,
Keeping his seasons and rages, destroyer, reminder
Of what men choose to forget. Unhonoured, unpropitiated

---

[3]A spar extending out from prow of a ship.
[4]The first planks next to the ship's keel.

[1]The Mississippi. This the third of the *Four Quartets* (1943). The individual poems are "Burnt Norton" (1935), "East Coker" (1940), "The Dry Salvages" (1941), and "Little Gidding" (1942).

10   By worshippers of the machine, but waiting, watching and waiting.
His rhythm was present in the nursery bedroom,
In the rank ailanthus of the April dooryard,
In the smell of grapes on the autumn table,
And the evening circle in the winter gaslight.

15   The river is within us, the sea is all about us;
The sea is the land's edge also, the granite
Into which it reaches, the beaches where it tosses
Its hints of earlier and other creation:
The starfish, the hermit crab, the whale's backbone;
20   The pools where it offers to our curiosity
The more delicate algae and the sea anemone.
It tosses up our losses, the torn seine,
The shattered lobsterpot, the broken oar
And the gear of foreign dead men. The sea has many voices,
25   Many gods and many voices.
                              The salt is on the briar rose,
The fog is in the fir trees.
                              The sea howl
And the sea yelp, are different voices
30   Often together heard; the whine in the rigging,
The menace and caress of wave that breaks on water,
The distant rote[2] in the granite teeth,
And the wailing warning from the approaching headland
Are all sea voices, and the heaving groaner
35   Rounded homewards, and the seagull:
And under the oppression of the silent fog
The tolling bell
Measures time not our time, rung by the unhurried
Ground swell, a time
40   Older than the time of chronometers, older
Than time counted by anxious worried women
Lying awake, calculating the future,
Trying to unweave, unwind, unravel
And piece together the past and the future,
45   Between midnight and dawn, when the past is all deception,
The future futureless, before the morning watch
When time stops and time is never ending;
And the ground swell, that is and was from the beginning,
Clangs
50   The bell.

[2]The sound of breaking surf.

II

Where is there an end of it, the soundless wailing,
The silent withering of autumn flowers
Dropping their petals and remaining motionless;
Where is there an end to the drifting wreckage,
55 The prayer of the bone on the beach, the unprayable
Prayer at the calamitous annunciation?

There is no end, but addition: the trailing
Consequence of further days and hours,
While emotion takes to itself the emotionless
60 Years of living among the breakage
Of what was believed in as the most reliable—
And therefore the fittest for renunciation.

There is the final addition, the failing
Pride or resentment at failing powers,
65 The unattached devotion which might pass for devotionless,
In a drifting boat with a slow leakage,
The silent listening to the undeniable
Clamour of the bell of the last annunciation.

Where is the end of them, the fishermen sailing
70 Into the wind's tail, where the fog cowers?
We cannot think of a time that is oceanless
Or of an ocean not littered with wastage
Or of a future that is not liable
Like the past, to have no destination.

75 We have to think of them as forever bailing,
Setting and hauling, while the North East lowers
Over shallow banks unchanging and erosionless
Or drawing their money, drying sails at dockage;
Not as making a trip that will be unpayable
80 For a haul that will not bear examination.

There is no end of it, the voiceless wailing,
No end to the withering of withered flowers,
To the movement of pain that is painless and motionless,
To the drift of the sea and the drifting wreckage,

85 The bone's prayer to Death its God. Only the hardly, barely prayable
Prayer of the one Annunciation.[3]

It seems, as one becomes older,
That the past has another pattern, and ceases to be a mere sequence—
Or even development: the latter a partial fallacy,
90 Encouraged by superficial notions of evolution,
Which becomes, in the popular mind, a means of disowning the past.
The moments of happiness—not the sense of well-being.
Fruition, fulfilment, security or affection,
Or even a very good dinner, but the sudden illumination—
95 We had the experience but missed the meaning,
And approach to the meaning restores the experience
In a different form, beyond any meaning
We can assign to happiness. I have said before
That the past experience revived in the meaning
100 Is not the experience of one life only
But of many generations—not forgetting
Something that is probably quite ineffable:
The backward look behind the assurance
Of recorded history, the backward half-look
105 Over the shoulder, towards the primitive terror.
Now, we come to discover that the moments of agony
(Whether, or not, due to misunderstanding,
Having hoped for the wrong things or dreaded the wrong things,
Is not in question) are likewise permanent
110 With such permanence as time has. We appreciate this better
In the agony of others, nearly experienced,
Involving ourselves, than in our own.
For our own past is covered by the currents of action,
But the torment of others remains an experience
115 Unqualified, unworn by subsequent attrition.
People change, and smile: but the agony abides.
Time the destroyer is time the preserver,
Like the river with its cargo of dead Negroes, cows and chicken
    coops,
The bitter apple and the bite in the apple.
120 And the ragged rock in the restless waters,
Waves wash over it, fogs conceal it;
On a halcyon day it is merely a monument,
In navigable weather it is always a seamark
To lay a course by: but in the sombre season
125 Or the sudden fury, is what it always was.

[3]When the angel announced to Mary that she would bear the Son of God, she
said: "I am the handmaiden of the Lord; let what you said be done to me."

III

I sometimes wonder if that is what Krishna meant—[4]
Among other things—or one way of putting the same thing:
That the future is a faded song, a Royal Rose[5] or a lavender spray
Of wistful regret for those who are not yet here to regret,
Pressed between yellow leaves of a book that has never been opened.
And the way up is the way down, the way forward is the way back.[6]
You cannot face it steadily, but this thing is sure,
That time is no healer: the patient is no longer here.
When the train starts, and the passengers are settled
To fruit, periodicals and business letters
(And those who saw them off have left the platform)
Their faces relax from grief into relief,
To the sleepy rhythm of a hundred hours.
Fare forward, travellers! not escaping from the past
Into different lives, or into any future;
You are not the same people who left that station
Or who will arrive at any terminus,
While the narrowing rails slide together behind you;
And on the deck of the drumming liner
Watching the furrow that widens behind you,
You shall not think "the past is finished"
Or "the future is before us."
At nightfall, in the rigging and the aerial,
Is a voice descanting (though not to the ear,
The murmuring shell of time, and not in any language)
"Fare forward, you who think that you are voyaging;
You are not those who saw the harbour
Receding, or those who will disembark.
Here between the hither and the farther shore
While time is withdrawn, consider the future
And the past with an equal mind.
At the moment which is not of action or inaction
You can receive this: 'on whatever sphere of being
The mind of a man may be intent
At the time of death'—that is the one action

---

[4]In the Hindu scripture *Bhagavad Gita*, when Prince Arjuna on the battlefield questions whether it was moral to enter the fray, Krishna reveals himself as the God who transcends time and urges Arjuna to fight because time is the pattern through which He works and destines all things.
[5]The War of the Roses (1455–1485) between two English noble houses, York (white rose) and Lancaster (red rose).
[6]This motto from the Greek philosopher Heraclitus (sixth century B.C.) is an epigraph to *Four Quartets*.

(And the time of death is every moment)
Which shall fructify in the lives of others:
And do not think of the fruit of action.
Fare forward.

165   O voyagers, O seamen,
You who come to port, and you whose bodies
Will suffer the trial and judgement of the sea,
Or whatever event, this is your real destination."
So Krishna, as when he admonished Arjuna

170   On the field of battle.
                                Not fare well,
But fare forward, voyagers.

IV

Lady, whose shrine stands on the promontory,
Pray for all those who are in ships, those

175   Whose business has to do with fish,[7] and
Those concerned with every lawful traffic
And those who conduct them.

    Repeat a prayer also on behalf of
Women who have seen their sons or husbands

180   Setting forth, and not returning:
Figlia del tuo figlio,[8]
Queen of Heaven.

    Also pray for those who were in ships, and
Ended their voyage on the sand, in the sea's lips

185   Or in the dark throat which will not reject them
Or wherever cannot reach them the sound of the sea bell's
Perpetual angelus.[9]

V

To communicate with Mars,[10] converse with spirits,
To report the behaviour of the sea monster,

190   Describe the horoscope, haruspicate or scry,[11]

---

[7]Fish as a Christian symbol: most of Apostles were fishermen and Jesus charged them with being fishers of men.
[8]Italian: "daughter of your son."
[9]A prayer beginning "Angelus dei" ("The angel of the Lord"), to commemorate the Annunciation, often recited at morning, noon, and evening when the church bell is rung as a call to prayer.
[10]One of the planets, which are powerful astrological influences.
[11]Haruspicate: prophesy by reading the entrails of birds or animals; scry: prophesy by gazing into a crystal ball.

Observe disease in signatures, evoke
Biography from the wrinkles of the palm
And tragedy from fingers; release omens
By sortilege,[12] or tea leaves, riddle the inevitable
195 With playing cards, fiddle with pentagrams[13]
Or barbituric acids, or dissect
The recurrent image into pre-conscious terrors—
To explore the womb, or tomb, or dreams; all these are usual
Pastimes and drugs, and features of the press:
And always will be, some of them especially
200 When there is distress of nations and perplexity
Whether on the shores of Asia, or in the Edgware Road.[14]
Men's curiosity searches past and future
And clings to that dimension. But to apprehend
The point of intersection of the timeless
205 With time, is an occupation for the saint—
No occupation either, but something given
And taken, in a lifetime's death in love,
Ardour and selflessness and self-surrender.
For most of us, there is only the unattended
210 Moment, the moment in and out of time,
The distraction fit, lost in a shaft of sunlight,
The wild thyme unseen, or the winter lightning
Or the waterfall, or music heard so deeply
That it is not heard at all, but you are the music
215 While the music lasts. These are only hints and guesses,
Hints followed by guesses; and the rest
Is prayer, observance, discipline, thought and action.
The hint half guessed, the gift half understood, is Incarnation.[15]
Here the impossible union
220 Of spheres of existence is actual,
Here the past and future
Are conquered, and reconciled,
Where action were otherwise movement
Of that which is only moved
225 And has in it no source of movement—
Driven by daemonic, chthonic
Powers.[16] And right action is freedom

---

[12]Drawing lots.
[13]A Pentagram: a five-pointed star, a figure in occult symbolism and a suit in the Tarot cards.
[14]In London.
[15]The central mystery of Christianity, through which God became man as Jesus in order to redeem mankind.
[16]Powers that come from an earth spirit.

From past and future also.
For most of us, this is the aim
230 Never here to be realised;
Who are only undefeated
Because we have gone on trying;
We, content at the last
If our temporal reversion nourish
235 (Not too far from the yew-tree)[17]
The life of significant soil.

[17]Associated with mourning.

Archibald MacLeish (1892–   )

MacLeish went from Glencoe, Illinois, to graduate from Yale in 1915 and from Harvard Law School in 1919. While in school he married Ada Hitchcock. After service in France during the First World War, MacLeish practiced law but decided quickly in favor of a poetic career. After living in France during the twenties, where he knew such other expatriates as Hemingway and Pound, he returned to America and settled into a successful career. He worked for *Fortune* magazine for several years, was Librarian of Congress from 1939 to 1944, and held various political posts during Franklin Roosevelt's administration, including Assistant Secretary of State and chief American delegate to UNESCO, which he helped to organize.

As a writer MacLeish moved from intense subjectivity and aesthetic symbolism in the twenties to social commitment in the thirties to public-spirited concern in the forties to brooding over the human dilemma in the fifties. He has been a mirror and an index of a rapidly changing era by joining together poet and public man. Some of his longer poems are: *The Pot of Earth* (1925), *The Hamlet of A. MacLeish* (1928), *Conquistador* (1932; winner of the Pulitzer Prize), *Elpenor* (1933), *America Was Promises* (1939), and *Actfive* (1948). But in retrospect MacLeish seems more lyric poet than philosopher or politician. In his verse he expresses his acute awareness of his times in haunting images and in a fine sense of rhythm and sound. When his *Collected Poems* came out in 1952, it received the Pulitzer Prize, the Bollingen Prize, and the National Book Award. Since then he has published *Songs for Eve* (1954) and *"The Wild Wicked Old Man"* (1968). His verse plays include: *Panic* (1935), *The Fall of the City* (1937), and *J.B.* (1958), an immensely successful version of the story of Job. In 1949 he became Boylston Professor at Harvard, and since his retirement has lived with his wife at North Conway, New Hampshire.

REFERENCE
Falk, Signi. *Archibald MacLeish*. New York: Twayne, 1965.

THE END OF THE WORLD

Quite unexpectedly as Vasserot
The armless ambidextrian was lighting
A match between his great and second toe
And Ralph the lion was engaged in biting
5   The neck of Madame Sossman while the drum
Pointed, and Teeny was about to cough
In waltz-time swinging Jocko by the thumb—
Quite unexpectedly the top blew off:

And there, there overhead, there, there, hung over
10   Those thousands of white faces, those dazed eyes,
There in the starless dark the poise, the hover,
There with vast wings across the canceled skies,
There in the sudden blackness the black pall
Of nothing, nothing, nothing—nothing at all.

ARS POETICA

A poem should be palpable and mute
As a globed fruit,

Dumb
As old medallions to the thumb,

5   Silent as the sleeve-worn stone
Of casement ledges where the moss has grown—

A poem should be wordless
As the flight of birds.

          ●

A poem should be motionless in time
10   As the moon climbs,

Leaving, as the moon releases
Twig by twig the night-entangled trees,

Leaving, as the moon behind the winter leaves,
Memory by memory the mind—

15 A poem should be motionless in time
    As the moon climbs.

                    •

    A poem should be equal to:
    Not true.

    For all the history of grief
20 An empty doorway and a maple leaf.

    For love
    The leaning grasses and two lights above the sea—

    A poem should not mean
    But be.

YOU, ANDREW MARVELL[1]

    And here face down beneath the sun
    And here upon earth's noonward height
    To feel the always coming on
    The always rising of the night:

5   To feel creep up the curving east
    The earthy chill of dusk and slow
    Upon those under lands the vast
    And ever climbing shadow grow

    And strange at Ecbatan[2] the trees
10 Take leaf by leaf the evening strange
    The flooding dark about their knees
    The mountains over Persia change

    And now at Kermanshah[3] the gate
    Dark empty and the withered grass
15 And through the twilight now the late
    Few travelers in the westward pass

    And Baghdad darken and the bridge
    Across the silent river gone

[1]The English metaphysical poet (1621–1678).
[2]Ancient name for the city of Hamadan in western Iran.
[3]City in Iran.

And through Arabia the edge
20   Of evening widen and steal on

And deepen on Palmyra's[4] street
The wheel rut in the ruined stone
And Lebanon fade out and Crete
High through the clouds and overblown

25   And over Sicily the air
Still flashing with the landward gulls
And loom and slowly disappear
The sails above the shadowy hulls

And Spain go under and the shore
30   Of Africa the gilded sand
And evening vanish and no more
The low pale light across that land

Nor now the long light on the sea:

And here face downward in the sun
35   To feel how swift how secretly
The shadow of the night comes on . . .

CALYPSO'S ISLAND[1]

I know very well, goddess, she is not beautiful
As you are: could not be. She is a woman,
Mortal, subject to the chances: duty of

Childbed, sorrow that changes cheeks, the tomb—
5   For unlike you she will grow grey, grow older,
Grey and older, sleep in that small room.

She is not beautiful as you, O golden!

---

[4]City in Syria.

[1]Orygia, where the nymph Calypso dwelt. Odysseus after shipwreck came
to her island, and she promised him immortality if he wed her. However, he
spurned her attractions because he longed for Penelope and home, and after
seven years on the island he was released by the gods and permitted to con-
tinue on his journey to Ithaca.

You are immortal and will never change
And can make me immortal also, fold

10   Your garment round me, make me whole and strange
As those who live forever, not the while
That we live, keep me from those dogging dangers—

Ships and the wars—in this green, far-off island,
Silent of all but sea's eternal sound
15   Or sea-pine's when the lull of surf is silent.

Goddess, I know how excellent this ground,
What charmed contentment of the removed heart
The bees make in the lavender where pounding

Surf sounds far off and the bird that darts
20   Darts through its own eternity of light,
Motionless in motion, and the startled

Hare is startled into stone, the fly
Forever golden in the flickering glance
Of leafy sunlight that still holds it. I

25   Know you, goddess, and your caves that answer
Ocean's confused voices with a voice:
Your poplars where the storms are turned to dances;

Arms where the heart is turned. You give the choice
To hold forever what forever passes,
30   To hide from what will pass, forever. Moist,

Moist are your well-stones, goddess, cool your grasses!
And she—she is a woman with that fault
Of change that will be death in her at last!

Nevertheless I long for the cold, salt,
35   Restless, contending sea and for the island
Where the grass dies and the seasons alter:

Where that one wears the sunlight for a while.

WHAT ANY LOVER LEARNS

Water is heavy silver over stone.
Water is heavy silver over stone's
Refusal. It does not fall. It fills. It flows
Every crevice, every fault of the stone,
5   Every hollow. River does not run.
River presses its heavy silver self
Down into stone and stone refuses.

What runs,
Swirling and leaping into sun, is stone's
10   Refusal of the river, not the river.

THE OLD MAN TO THE LIZARD

Lizard, lover of heat, of high
Noon, of the hot stone, the golden
Sun in your unblinking eye—
And they say you are old, lizard, older than

5   Rocks you run on with those delicate
Fishbone fingers, skittering over
Ovens even cricket in his shell
Could never sing in—tell me, lover of

Sun, lover of noon, lizard,
10   Is it because the sun is gold with
Flame you love it so? Or is
Your love because your blood is cold?

REASONS FOR MUSIC

FOR WALLACE STEVENS

Why do we labor at the poem
Age after Age—even an age like
This one, when the living rock
No longer lives and the cut stone perishes?—

5   Hölderlin's[1] question. Why be poet
Now when the meanings do not mean?—
When the stone shape is shaped stone?—
Dürftiger Zeit?[2]—time without inwardness?

Why lie upon our beds at night
10   Holding a mouthful of words, exhausted
Most by the absence of the adversary?

Why be poet? Why be man!

Far out in the uttermost Andes
Mortised enormous stones are piled.
15   What is a man? Who founds a poem
In the rubble of wild world—wilderness.

The acropolis of eternity that crumbles
Time and again is mine—my task.
The heart's necessity compels me:
20   Man I am: poet must be.

The labor of order has no rest:
To impose on the confused, fortuitous
Flowing away of the world, From—
Still, cool, clean, obdurate,

25   Lasting forever, or at least
Lasting: a precarious monument
Promising immortality, for the wing
Moves and in the moving balances.

[1]Johann Christian Friedrich Hölderlin (1770–1843): German Romantic poet.
[2]Lifeless time.

Why do we labor at the poem?
30   Out of the turbulence of the sea,
Flower by brittle flower, rises
The coral reef that calms the water.

Generations of the dying
Fix the sea's dissolving salts
35   In stone, still trees, their branches immovable,
Meaning
      the movement of the sea.

E. E. Cummings (1894–1962)

Cummings' father began as a teacher of English at Harvard and became a Unitarian minister in Boston. Edward Estlin Cummings was born in Cambridge, Massachusetts, and got his bachelor's and master's degrees at Harvard before World War I. He served as an ambulance driver and as a soldier during the war, and the months spent in a French prison on a minor (and false) charge provided the material for the novel *The Enormous Room* (1922). During the twenties and thirties he divided the years between New York and Paris, later settling into Patchin Place, in Greenwich Village, and his New Hampshire farm.

Cummings drew, painted, and wrote in various modes: the novel already mentioned; *Tom* (1935), a ballet based on *Uncle Tom's Cabin;* allegorical plays, *Him* (1927) and *Santa Claus* (1946); a travel diary of the Soviet Union, *Eimi* (1933); and the outpouring of poems that are his chief achievement. He could adopt a realist's manner—tough, satirical, shocking—but he is one of the most unabashedly romantic of modern lyric poets. His theme is the sacred supremacy of the individual person, and his transcendence of limits in love and in the harmony of the natural order. Cummings' invective proceeds from outrage at the violation of the individual by mass society and its collective institutions. His techniques seem bizarre at first: the punctuation, the typography, the dislocation of syntax, the interchange of parts of speech. But they are efforts to reclaim traditional themes, metaphors, and forms (such as the ballad and sonnet) into a language as unique and immediate as the individual experience.

The main titles are: *Tulips and Chimneys* (1923), *&* (1925), *is 5* (1926), *Viva* (1931), *No Thanks* (1935), *1 x 1* (1944), *XAIPΣ* (1950), *95 Poems* (1958), and the posthumous *73 Poems* (1963). A *Collected Poems* (1938) was followed by *Poems 1923–1954* (1954), which brought a National Book Award citation and later the Bollingen Prize. Through his father Cummings' roots are deep in New England Transcendentalism, and his religious sense of life became explicit in some of the later poems; his iconoclasm was as conservative as it was radical and experimental.

TEXT

Cummings, E. E. *Complete Poems.* New York: Harcourt Brace Jovanovich, 1972.

REFERENCE

Cummings, E. E. *I: six non-lectures.* Cambridge, Mass.: Harvard University Press, 1953.

Cummings, E. E. *Selected Letters of E. E. Cummings.* Ed. F. W. Dupee and George Stade. New York: Harcourt Brace and World, 1969.

Friedman, Norman. *E. E. Cummings: The Art of His Poetry.* Baltimore: Johns Hopkins Press, 1960.

Norman, Charles. *E. E. Cummings: The Magic Maker.* New York: Duell, Sloane and Pearce, 1964.

in Just-
spring   when the world is mud-
luscious the little
lame balloonman

5   whistles   far   and wee

and eddieandbill come
running from marbles and
piracies and it's
spring

10   when the world is puddle-wonderful

the queer
old balloonman whistles
far   and   wee
and bettyandisbel come dancing

15   from hop-scotch and jump-rope and

it's
spring
and
        the

20   goat-footed[1]

balloonMan   whistles
far
and
wee

Buffalo Bill's
defunct
        who used to
        ride a watersmooth-silver
5   stallion

[1]Pan, the nature deity, associated with the awakening of spring and of
sexuality.

and break onetwothreefourfive pigeonsjustlikethat
                                                    Jesus

he was a handsome man
                          and what i want to know is
10   how do you like your blueeyed boy
     Mister Death

Spring is like a perhaps hand
(which comes carefully
out of Nowhere)arranging
a window,into which people look(while
5   people stare
arranging and changing placing
carefully there a strange
thing and a known thing here)and

changing everything carefully

10   spring is like a perhaps
Hand in a window
(carefully to
and fro moving New and
Old things,while
15   people stare carefully
moving a perhaps
fraction of flower here placing
an inch of air there)and

without breaking anything.

POEM, OR BEAUTY HURTS MR. VINAL

take it from me kiddo
believe me
my country, 'tis of

you, land of the Cluett
5   Shirt Boston Garter and Spearmint

Girl With The Wrigley Eyes(of you
land of the Arrow Ide
and Earl &
Wilson
10   Collars) of you i
sing:land of Abraham Lincoln and Lydia E. Pinkham,[1]
land above all of Just Add Hot Water And Serve—
from every B. V. D.

let freedom ring

15   amen. i do however protest, anent[2] the un
-spontaneous and otherwise scented merde[3] which
greets one (Everywhere Why) as divine poesy per
that and this radically defunct periodical. i would
suggest that certain ideas gestures
20   rhymes, like Gillette Razor Blades
having been used and reused
to the mystical moment of dullness emphatically are
Not To Be Resharpened.   (Case in point

if we are to believe these gently O sweetly
25   melancholy trillers amid the thrillers
these crepuscular violinists among my and your
skyscrapers—Helen & Cleopatra[4] were Just Too Lovely,
The Snail's On The Thorn enter Morn and God's
In His andsoforth[5]

30   do you get me?)according
to such supposedly indigenous
throstles Art is O World O Life[6]
a formula:example, Turn Your Shirttails Into
Drawers and If It Isn't An Eastman It Isn't A
35   Kodak therefore my friends let

---

[1]A patent medicine used for menstrual pain.
[2]Concerning.
[3]Excrement.
[4]Helen: the wife of Greek king Menelaus, carried off to Troy by the Trojan prince Paris, and thus the cause of the Trojan War; Cleopatra: Queen of Egypt.
[5]A parody of the lyric from Robert Browning's *Pippa Passes*; it begins: "the year's at the spring/ and day's at the morn" and concludes "The snail's on the thorn:/ God's in his heaven—/All's right with the world!"
[6]Percy Shelley's overwrought Romantic lyric "A Lament," which begins "O world! O life! O time!"

us now sing each and all fortissimo A-
mer
i

ca, I
40   love,
You.   And there're a
hun-dred-mil-lion-oth-ers, like
all of you successfully if
delicately gelded(or spaded)
45   gentlemen(and ladies)—pretty

littleliverpill-[7]
hearted-Nujolneeding-[8]There's-A-Reason
americans(who tensetendoned and with
upward vacant eyes, painfully
50   perpetually crouched, quivering, upon the
sternly allotted sandpile
—how silently
emit a tiny violetflavoured nuisance:Odor?

ono.[9]
55   comes out like a ribbon lies flat on the brush

a man who had fallen among thieves
lay by the roadside on his back
dressed in fifteenthrate ideas
wearing a round jeer for a hat

5   fate per a somewhat more than less
emancipated evening
had in return for consciousness
endowed him with a changeless grin

whereon a dozen staunch and leal[1]
10   citizens did graze at pause

---

[7]Carter's Little Liver Pills, a patent medicine.
[8]Nujol: a mineral oil used as a laxative.
[9]Odorono, a deodorant.

---

[1]Scottish dialect and archaic: loyal, honest, true.

then fired by hypercivic zeal
sought newer pastures or because

swaddled with a frozen brook
of pinkest vomit out of eyes
15   which noticed nobody he looked
as if he did not care to rise

one hand did nothing on the vest
its wideflung friend clenched weakly dirt
while the mute trouserfly confessed
20   a button solemnly inert.

Brushing from whom the stiffened puke
i put him all into my arms
and staggered banged with terror through
a million billion trillion stars

if there are any heavens my mother will(all by herself)have
one.   It will not be a pansy heaven nor
a fragile heaven of lilies-of the-valley but
it will be a heaven of blackred roses

5   my father will be(deep like a rose
tall like a rose)

standing near my

swaying over her
silent)
10   with eyes which are really petals and see

nothing with the face of a poet really which
is a flower and not a face with
hands
which whisper
15   This is my beloved my

                    (suddenly in sunlight
he will bow,

  & the whole garden will bow)

                                    r-p-o-p-h-e-s-s-a-g-r
                        who
        a)s w(e loo)k
        upnowgath
5   PPEGORHRASS
                                    eringint(o-
        aThe):l
                eA
                    !p:
10   S
                                                a
                            (r
        rIvInG   .gRrEaPsPhOs)
                                                to
15   rea(be)rran(com)gi(e)ngly
        ,grasshopper;

            this little bride & groom are
            standing)in a kind
            of crown he dressed
            in black candy she

5   veiled with candy white
            carrying a bouquet of
            pretend flowers this
            candy crown with this candy

            little bride & little
10   groom in it kind of stands on
            a thin ring which stands on a much
            less thin very much more

            big & kinder of ring & which
            kinder of stands on a
15   much more than very much
            biggest & thickest & kindest

            of ring & all one two three rings
            are cake & everything is protected by
            cellophane against anything(because
20   nothing really exists

pity this busy monster,manunkind,

not. Progress is a comfortable disease:
your victim(death and life safely beyond)

plays with the bigness of his littleness
5   —electrons deify one razorblade
into a mountainrange;lenses extend

unwish through curving wherewhen till unwish
returns on its unself.
      A world of made
10   is not a world of born—pity poor flesh

and trees,poor stars and stones,but never this
fine specimen of hypermagical

ultraomnipotence. We doctors know

a hopeless case if—listen:there's a hell
15   of a good universe next door;let's go

 "sweet spring is your
 time is my time is our
 time for springtime is lovetime
 and viva sweet love"

5 (all the merry little birds are
 flying in the floating in the
 very spirits singing in
 are winging in the blossoming)

 lovers go and lovers come
10 awandering awondering
 but any two are perfectly
 alone there's nobody else alive

 (such a sky and such a sun
 i never knew and neither did you
15 and everybody never breathed
 quite so many kinds of yes)

not a tree can count his leaves
each herself by opening
but shining who by thousands mean
20   only one amazing thing

(secretly adoring shyly
tiny winging darting floating
merry in the blossoming
always joyful selves are singing)

25   "sweet spring is your
time is my time is our
time for springtime is lovetime
and viva sweet love"

i thank You God for most this amazing
day:for the leaping greenly spirits of trees
and a blue true dream of sky;and for everything
which is natural which is infinite which is yes

5   (i who have died am alive again today,
and this is the sun's birthday;this is the birth
day of life and of love and wings:and of the gay
great happening illimitably earth)

how should tasting touching hearing seeing
10   breathing any—lifted from the no
of all nothing—human merely being
doubt unimaginable You?

(now the ears of my ears awake and
now the eyes of my eyes are opened)

l(a

le
af
fa

5   ll

s)
one
l

iness

i carry your heart with me(i carry it in
my heart)i am never without it(anywhere
i go you go,my dear;and whatever is done
by only me is your doing,my darling)
5   i fear
no fate(for you are my fate,my sweet)i want
no world(for beautiful you are my world,my true)
and it's you are whatever a moon has always meant
and whatever a sun will always sing is you

10   here is the deepest secret nobody knows
(here is the root of the root and the bud of the bud
and the sky of the sky of a tree called life;which grows
higher than soul can hope or mind can hide)
and this is the wonder that's keeping the stars apart

15   i carry your heart(i carry it in my heart)

Now i lay[1] (with everywhere around)
me(the great dim deep sound
of rain;and of always and of nowhere)and

what a gently welcoming darkestness—

5 now i lay me down(in a most steep
more than music)feeling that sunlight is
(life and day are)only loaned:whereas
night is given(night and death and the rain

are given;and given is how beautifully snow)

10 now i lay me down to dream of(nothing
i or any somebody or you
can begin to begin to imagine)

something which nobody may keep.
now i lay me down to dream of Spring

all worlds have halfsight,seeing either with

life's eye(which is if things seem spirits)or
(if spirits in the guise of things appear)
death's:any world must always half perceive.

5 Only whose vision can create the whole

(being forever born a foolishwise
proudhumble citizen of ecstasies
more steep than climb can time with all his years)

he's free into the beauty of the truth;

10 and strolls the axis of the universe
—love. Each believing world denies,whereas
your lover(looking through both life and death)
timelessly celebrates the merciful

wonder no world deny may or believe

[1]An allusion to the children's night prayer: "Now I lay me down to sleep./
I pray the Lord my soul to keep./ If I should die before I wake,/ I pray the
Lord my soul to take."

Hart Crane (1899–1932)

Harold Hart Crane was born in Garrettsville, Ohio, but grew up in Cleveland, where his father owned a candy factory. His father had difficulty in understanding his extremely sensitive son, and his mother demanded and drained a lot of emotional attention from him. The differences between his parents, and their divorce, created psychological tensions that the boy never resolved. After trips to Cuba and to France he alternated unhappily between jobs in his father's business and writing advertising copy in Manhattan. He finally moved to New York in 1920 to immerse himself in the literary scene and to try to live as a poet with the patronage of banker Otto Kahn and others.

White Buildings (1926) showed what Crane had learned from Eliot and others about the French *symbolistes* in poems whose power lay in elliptical concentration. Through his association with Waldo Frank's group of literary nationalists, he attempted to link the contemporary scene with traditional myths in "For the Marriage of Faustus and Helen," and by the mid-twenties he was working on a bolder scheme: a long epic called *The Bridge* whose mystical synthesis of past and present would create a native myth strong enough to project Whitman's prophecy into an industrialized and urban America and to defeat the impotent disillusionment for which Eliot was the most powerful spokesman.

Crane's fragile psyche continued to crack under the strain of alcoholism and homosexuality and under the pressure of writing *The Bridge*. He vacillated between manic excitement and despair over the poem and over his life. It appeared in 1929, its scheme uncompleted, but passage after passage attest to Crane's imaginative leap and grasp. He went to Mexico on a Guggenheim Fellowship in 1931 to plan an epic about Montezuma, but accomplished very little. "The Broken Tower" articulates the sense of failure and collapse that led him to jump off the ship bringing him back to the United States in 1932.

To intellectuals like Allen Tate and Yvor Winters he was a tragic lesson in Romantic folly. But to Crane, poetry was the vehicle for vision; he strove for an almost impossible goal: the moment of ultimate intensity that would break through rational categories so as to glimpse or project godhead in the compressed indirections of metaphor.

TEXT

Crane, Hart. *Complete Poems with Selected Letters and Prose.* Ed. Brom Weber. New York: Liveright, 1966.

REFERENCE

Crane, Hart. *The Letters of Hart Crane 1916–1932.* Ed. Brom Weber. Berkeley: University of California Press, 1965.

Horton, Philip. *Hart Crane: The Life of an American Poet.* New York: W. W. Norton, 1937.

Lewis, R. W. B. *The Poetry of Hart Crane: A Critical Study.* Princeton: Princeton University Press, 1967.

Unterecker, John. *Voyager: A Life of Hart Crane.* New York: Farrar, Straus and Giroux, 1969.

Weber, Brom. *Hart Crane: A Biographical and Critical Study.* New York: Bodley Press, 1948.

from **Voyages**

VOYAGES II

And yet this great wink of eternity,
Of rimless floods, unfettered leewardings,[1]
Samite[2] sheeted and processioned where
Her undinal[3] vast belly moonward bends,
5 Laughing the wrapt inflections of our love;

Take this Sea, whose diapason[4] knells
On scrolls of silver snowy sentences,
The sceptred terror of whose sessions rends
As her demeanors motion well or ill,
10 All but the pieties of lovers' hands.

And onward, as bells off San Salvador[5]
Salute the crocus lustres of the stars,
In these poinsettia meadows of her tides,—
Adagios[6] of islands, O my Prodigal,
15 Complete the dark confessions her veins spell.

Mark how her turning shoulders wind the hours,
And hasten while her penniless rich palms
Pass superscription of bent foam and wave,—
Hasten, while they are true,—sleep, death, desire,
20 Close round one instant in one floating flower.

Bind us in time, O Seasons clear, and awe.
O minstrel galleons of Carib[7] fire,
Bequeath us to no earthly shore until
Is answered in the vortex of our grave
25 The seal's wide spindrift[8] gaze toward paradise.

---

[1]Motion in the direction toward which the wind is blowing.
[2]Heavy silk interwoven with gold or silver.
[3]Undine: a water sprite who could earn a soul by marrying a mortal and bearing his child.
[4]The scale of a musical instrument.
[5]An island in the Bahamas.
[6]In music, a slow tempo; in ballet, an intricate section of the *pas de deux*.
[7]Caribbean.
[8]Wind-blown sea spray.

from **The Bridge**

PROEM: TO BROOKLYN BRIDGE

How many dawns, chill from his rippling rest
The seagull's wings shall dip and pivot him,
Shedding white rings of tumult, building high
Over the chained bay waters Liberty[1]—

5 Then, with inviolate curve, forsake our eyes
As apparitional as sails that cross
Some page of figures[2] to be filed away;
—Till elevators drop us from our day . . .

I think of cinemas, panoramic sleights
10 With multitudes bent toward some flashing scene
Never disclosed, but hastened to again,
Foretold to other eyes on the same screen;

And Thee,[3] across the harbor, silver-paced
As though the sun took step of thee, yet left
15 Some motion ever unspent in thy stride,—
Implicitly thy freedom staying thee!

Out of some subway scuttle, cell or loft
A bedlamite speeds to thy parapets,
Tilting there momently, shrill shirt ballooning,
20 A jest falls from the speechless caravan.

Down Wall,[4] from girder into street noon leaks,
A rip-tooth of the sky's acetylene;
All afternoon the cloud-flown derricks turn . . .
Thy cables breathe the North Atlantic still.

25 And obscure as that heaven of the Jews,
Thy guerdon[5] . . . Accolade thou dost bestow

---

[1]The Statue of Liberty off the end of Manhattan in the bay.
[2]For example, in a ledger or an accounting book.
[3]The Brooklyn Bridge, spanning the East River and joining Manhattan and Brooklyn, was the first suspension bridge to use steel-wire cables. Designed by John Roebling in 1867 and opened for traffic in 1883, it was at the time the world's longest bridge.
[4]Wall Street in lower Manhattan.
[5]Reward.

Of anonymity time cannot raise:
Vibrant reprieve and pardon thou dost show.

O harp and altar, of the fury fused,
30 (How could mere toil align thy choiring strings!)
Terrific threshold of the prophet's pledge,
Prayer of pariah,[6] and the lover's cry,—

Again the traffic lights that skim thy swift
Unfractioned idiom, immaculate sigh of stars,
35 Beading thy path—condense eternity:
And we have seen night lifted in thine arms.

Under thy shadow by the piers I waited;
Only in darkness is thy shadow clear.
The City's fiery parcels all undone,
40 Already snow submerges an iron year . . .

O Sleepless as the river under thee,
Vaulting the sea, the prairies' dreaming sod,
Unto us lowliest sometime sweep, descend
And of the curveship lend a myth to God.

[6]Outcast from society.

from **The Bridge**

POWHATAN'S DAUGHTER[1]

> "*—Pocahuntus, a well-featured but wanton yong
> girle . . . of the age of eleven or twelve years, get
> the boyes forth with her into the market place, and
> make them wheele, falling on their hands, turning
> their heels upwards, whom she would followe, and
> wheele so herself, naked as she was, all the fort over.*"

THE HARBOR DAWN

Insistently through sleep—a tide of voices—
They meet you listening midway in your dream,
The long, tired sounds, fog-insulated noises:
Gongs in white surplices, beshrouded wails,
5 Far strum of fog horns . . . signals dispersed in veils.

And then a truck will lumber past the wharves
As winch engines begin throbbing on some deck;
Or a drunken stevedore's howl and thud below
Comes echoing alley-upward through dim snow.

10 And if they take your sleep away sometimes
They give it back again. Soft sleeves of sound
Attend the darkling harbor, the pillowed bay;
Somewhere out there in blankness steam

Spills into steam, and wanders, washed away
15 —Flurried by keen fifings, eddied
Among distant chiming buoys—adrift. The sky,
Cool feathery fold, suspends, distills
This wavering slumber. . . . Slowly—
Immemorially the window, the half-covered chair,
20 Ask nothing but this sheath of pallid air.

And you beside me, blessed now while sirens
Sing to us, stealthily weave us into day—

Marginal notes:
400 years and more . . . or is it from the soundless shore of sleep that time

recalls you to your love, there in a waking dream to merge your seed

---

[1]Pocahontas, identified by Crane with the American land as mythological virgin—lover—mother. The quotation is from William Strachey's *History of Travaile into Virginia Brittanica* (c. 1615), which William Carlos Williams cited in *In the American Grain* (1925).

Serenely now, before day claims our eyes
Your cool arms murmurously about me lay.

25 While myriad snowy hands are clustering at the panes—

your hands within my hands are deeds;
my tongue upon your throat—singing
arms close; eyes wide, undoubtful
*   dark*
30 *   drink the dawn—*
a forest shudders in your hair!

The window goes blond slowly. Frostily clears.
From Cyclopean[2] towers across Manhattan waters
—Two—three bright window-eyes aglitter, disk
35 The sun, released—aloft with cold gulls hither.

—with whom?

The fog leans one last moment on the sill.
Under the mistletoe of dreams, a star—
As though to join us at some distant hill—
Turns in the waking west and goes to sleep.

Who is the
woman with us
in the dawn?
. . . whose is
the flesh our
feet have
moved upon?

VAN WINKLE

40 Macadam, gun-grey as the tunny's belt,
Leaps from Far Rockaway to Golden Gate:[3]
Listen! the miles a hurdy-gurdy grinds—
Down gold arpeggios[4] mile on mile unwinds.

Streets spread
past store and
factory — sped
by sunlight and
her smile . . .

Times earlier, when you hurried off to school
45 —It is the same hour though a later day—
You walked with Pizarro[5] in a copybook,
And Cortez rode up, reining tautly in—
Firmly as coffee grips the taste,—and away!

[2]Cyclops, a one-eyed giant (of a race of such giants) fought by Odysseus in
The Odyssey.
[3]That is, from Brooklyn to San Francisco.
[4]A rapid succession of notes that make up a chord.
[5]Francisco Pizarro (1470–1541) and Hernando Cortez (1485–1547) were Span-
ish explorers of the New World.

There was Priscilla's[6] cheek close in the wind,
50   And Captain Smith,[7] all beard and certainty,
And Rip Van Winkle[8] bowing by the way,—
"Is this Sleepy Hollow, friend—?" And he—

And Rip forgot the office hours,
          and he forgot the pay;
55   *Van Winkle sweeps a tenement*
            way down on Avenue A,—

The grind-organ says . . . Remember, remember
The cinder pile at the end of the backyard
Where we stoned the family of young
60   Garter snakes under . . . And the monoplanes
We launched—with paper wings and twisted
Rubber bands . . . Recall—recall
              the rapid tongues
That flittered from under the ash heap day
65   After day whenever your stick discovered
Some sunning inch of unsuspecting fibre—
It flashed back at your thrust, as clean as fire.

And Rip was slowly made aware
     that he, Van Winkle, was not here
70   *nor there. He woke and swore he'd seen Broadway*
       a Catskill daisy chain in May—

So memory, that strikes a rhyme out of a box
Or splits a random smell of flowers through glass—
Is it the whip stripped from the lilac tree
75   One day in spring my father took to me,
Or is it the Sabbatical, unconscious smile
My mother almost brought me once from church
And once only, as I recall—?

Like Memory, she is time's truant, shall take you by the hand . . .

[6]Priscilla Mullins, the beauty of Plymouth, who married John Alden after Alden failed in his plea for her hand for his friend Miles Standish. Longfellow recounted their story in *The Courtship of Miles Standish.*
[7]Captain John Smith (1580–1631): English explorer and adventurer who came to Jamestown, Virginia, in 1607 and, according to his story, was rescued from the Indians by Pocahontas.
[8]The chief character in the story in Washington Irving's *Sketch Book* (1819). Rip, a Dutch colonist shortly before the Revolution, went hunting in the Catskill Mountains, was given a potion by strange elfish men, and awoke only after twenty years to find his shrewish wife dead and the new nation, the United States. "Sleepy Hollow" is the setting of another Irving sketch about Ichabod Crane.

It flickered through the snow screen, blindly
80   It forsook her at the doorway, it was gone
Before I had left the window. It
Did not return with the kiss in the hall.

Macadam, gun-grey as the tunny's belt,
Leaps from Far Rockaway to Golden Gate. . . .
85   Keep hold of that nickel for car-change, Rip,—
Have you got your *"Times"*—?[9]
And hurry along, Van Winkle—it's getting late!

THE RIVER

Stick your patent name on a signboard
brother—all over—going west—young man
90   Tintex—Japalac—Certain-teed Overalls ads[10]
and lands sakes! under the new playbill ripped
in the guaranteed corner—see Bert Williams[11] what?
Minstrels when you steal a chicken just
save me the wing for if it isn't
95   Erie it ain't for miles around a
Mazda[12]—and the telegraphic night coming on Thomas

a Ediford[13]—and whistling down the tracks
a headlight rushing with the sound—can you
imagine—while an express makes time like
100   SCIENCE—COMMERCE and the HOLYGHOST
RADIO ROARS IN EVERY HOME WE HAVE THE NORTHPOLE
WALLSTREET AND VIRGINBIRTH[14] WITHOUT STONES OR
WIRES OR EVEN RUNNING brooks connecting ears
and no more sermons windows flashing roar
105   Breathtaking—as you like it[15] . . . eh?

. . . and past
the din and
slogans of the
year—

[9]*The New York Times.*
[10]Patented names of products. Tintex was a brand of dyes; Japalac, a brand of varnish.
[11]A Black vaudeville singer and comedian (1875–1922).
[12]A light bulb, named after a Zoroastrian deity.
[13]Thomas A. Edison (1847–1931), who invented the electric light bulb and Henry Ford (1863–1947), who designed and manufactured automobiles.
[14]The religious doctrine that states that through the power of the Holy Spirit, Mary conceived Jesus without loss of her virginity and bore Him as a virgin mother.
[15]Shakespeare's romantic comedy.

So the 20th Century[16]—so
whizzed the Limited—roared by and left
three men, still hungry on the tracks, ploddingly
watching the tail lights wizen and converge, slip-
110   ping gimleted and neatly out of sight.

                                •

The last bear, shot drinking in the Dakotas
Loped under wires that span the mountain stream.
Keen instruments, strung to a vast precision

to those whose   Bind town to town and dream to ticking dream.
addresses are   115   But some men take their liquor slow—and count
never near   —Though they'll confess no rosary nor clue—
The river's minute by the far brook's year.
Under a world of whistles, wires and steam
Caboose-like they go ruminating through
120   Ohio, Indiana—blind baggage—
To Cheyenne tagging . . . Maybe Kalamazoo.[17]

Time's rendings, time's blendings they construe
As final reckonings of fire and snow;
Strange bird-wit, like the elemental gist
125   Of unwalled winds they offer, singing low
My Old Kentucky Home and *Casey Jones,*
Some Sunny Day. I heard a road-gang chanting so.
And afterwards, who had a colt's eyes—one said,
"Jesus! Oh I remember watermelon days!" And sped
130   High in a cloud of merriment, recalled
"—And when my Aunt Sally Simpson smiled," he drawled—
"It was almost Louisiana, long ago."

"There's no place like Booneville[18] though, Buddy,"
One said, excising a last burr from his vest,
135   "—For early trouting." Then peering in the can,
"—But I kept on the tracks." Possessed, resigned,
He trod the fire down pensively and grinned,
Spreading dry shingles of a beard. . . .

                                Behind
140   My father's canner works I used to see

[16]Twentieth Century Limited, a transcontinental railroad train.
[17]Cheyenne, Wyoming; Kalamazoo, Michigan.
[18]Booneville: any one of the many towns named after explorer and scout
Daniel Boone (1734–1820), who crossed the Cumberland Gap and opened up
Kentucky for settlement.

Rail-squatters ranged in nomad raillery,
The ancient men—wifeless or runaway
Hobo-trekkers that forever search
An empire wilderness of freight and rails.
145   Each seemed a child, like me, on a loose perch,
Holding to childhood like some termless play.
John, Jake or Charley, hopping the slow freight
—Memphis to Tallahassee[19]—riding the rods,
Blind fists of nothing, humpty-dumpty clods.

150   Yet they touch something like a key perhaps.
From pole to pole across the hills, the states
—They know a body under the wide rain;
Youngsters with eyes like fjords, old reprobates
With racetrack jargon,—dotting immensity
155   They lurk across her, knowing her yonder breast
Snow-silvered, sumac-stained or smoky blue—
Is past the valley-sleepers, south or west.
—As I have trod the rumorous midnights, too,

*but who have
touched her,
knowing her
without name*

And past the circuit of the lamp's thin flame
160   (O Nights that brought me to her body bare!)
Have dreamed beyond the print that bound her name.
Trains sounding the long blizzards out—I heard
Wail into distances I knew were hers.
Papooses crying on the wind's long mane
165   Screamed redskin dynasties that fled the brain,
—Dead echoes! But I knew her body there,
Time like a serpent down her shoulder, dark,
And space, an eaglet's wing, laid on her hair.

Under the Ozarks, domed by Iron Mountain,
170   The old gods of the rain lie wrapped in pools
Where eyeless fish curvet a sunken fountain
And re-descend with corn from querulous crows.
Such pilfering make up their timeless eatage,
Propitiate them for their timber torn
175   By iron, iron—always the iron dealt cleavage!
They doze now, below axe and powder horn.

*nor the
myths of her
fathers . . .*

And Pullman breakfasters glide glistening steel
From tunnel into field—iron strides the dew—

[19]Memphis, Tennessee; Tallahassee, Florida.

Straddles the hill, a dance of wheel on wheel.
180 You have a half-hour's wait at Siskiyou,[20]
Or stay the night and take the next train through.
Southward, near Cairo[21] passing, you can see
The Ohio merging,—borne down Tennessee;
And if it's summer and the sun's in dusk
185 Maybe the breeze will lift the River's musk
—As though the waters breathed that you might know
Memphis Johnny, Steamboat Bill, Missouri Joe.
Oh, lean from the window, if the train slows down,
As though you touched hands with some ancient clown,[22]
190 —A little while gaze absently below
And hum *Deep River* with them while they go.

Yes, turn again and sniff one more—look see,
O Sheriff, Brakeman and Authority—
Hitch up your pants and crunch another quid,
195 For you, too, feed the River Timelessly.
And few evade full measure of their fate;
Always they smile out eerily what they seem.
I could believe he joked at heaven's gate—
Dan Midland—jolted from the cold brake-beam.

200 Down, down—born pioneers in time's despite,
Grimed tributaries to an ancient flow—
They win no frontier by their wayward plight,
But drift in stillness, as from Jordan's brow.[23]

You will not hear it as the sea; even stone
205 Is not more hushed by gravity . . . But slow,
As loth to take more tribute—sliding prone
Like one whose eyes were buried long ago

The River, spreading, flows—and spends your dream.
What are you, lost within this tideless spell?
210 You are your father's father, and the stream—
A liquid theme that floating niggers swell.

Damp tonnage and alluvial march of days—
Nights turbid, vascular with silted shale

[20]A mountain peak in southwestern Oregon.
[21]Cairo, Illinois.
[22]Peasant; man of the soil.
[23]The Jordan River in Palestine, where Jesus was baptized.

And roots surrendered down of moraine clays:
215 The Mississippi drinks the farthest dale.

O quarrying passion, undertowed sunlight!
The basalt surface drags a jungle grace
Ochreous and lynx-barred in lengthening might;
Patience! and you shall reach the biding place!

220 Over De Soto's[24] bones the freighted floors
Throb past the City storied of three thrones.[25]
Down two more turns the Mississippi pours
(Anon tall ironsides up from salt lagoons)

And flows within itself, heaps itself free.
225 All fades but one thin skyline 'round . . . Ahead
No embrace opens but the stinging sea;
The River lifts itself from its long bed,

Poised wholly on its dream, a mustard glow
Tortured with history, its one will—flow!
230 —The Passion spreads in wide tongues, choked and slow,
Meeting the Gulf, hosannas silently below.

THE DANCE

The swift red flesh, a winter king—
Who squired the glacier woman down the sky?
She ran the neighing canyons all the spring;
235 She spouted arms; she rose with maize—to die.

And in the autumn drouth, whose burnished hands
With mineral wariness found out the stone
Where prayers, forgotten, streamed the mesa sands?
He holds the twilight's dim, perpetual throne.

240 Mythical brows we saw retiring—loth,
Disturbed and destined, into denser green.
Greeting they sped us, on the arrow's oath:
Now lie incorrigibly what years between. . .

Then you shall
see her truly —
your blood
remembering
its first
invasion of
her secrecy,
its first
encounters
with her kin,
her chieftain
lover . . . his
shade that
haunts the
lakes and hills

[24]Hernando de Soto (1500–1542): Spanish explorer who discovered the Mississippi.
[25]New Orleans, which had been under the French, Spanish, and English.

There was a bed of leaves, and broken play;
245   There was a veil upon you, Pocahontas, bride—
O Princess whose brown lap was virgin May;
And bridal flanks and eyes hid tawny pride.

I left the village for dogwood. By the canoe
Tugging below the mill-race, I could see
250   Your hair's keen crescent running, and the blue
First moth of evening take wing stealthily.

What laughing chains the water wove and threw!
I learned to catch the trout's moon whisper; I
Drifted how many hours I never knew,
255   But, watching, saw that fleet young crescent die,—

And one star, swinging, take its place, alone,
Cupped in the larches of the mountain pass— ˙
Until, immortally, it bled into the dawn.
I left my sleek boat nibbling margin grass. . .

260   I took the portage climb, then chose
A further valley-shed; I could not stop.
Feet nozzled wat'ry webs of upper flows;
One white veil gusted from the very top.

O Appalachian Spring! I gained the ledge;
265   Steep, inaccessible smile that eastward bends
And northward reaches in that violet wedge
Of Adirondacks![26]—wisped of azure wands,

Over how many bluffs, tarns,[27] streams I sped!
—And knew myself within some boding shade:—
270   Grey tepees tufting the blue knolls ahead,
Smoke swirling through the yellow chestnut glade. . .

A distant cloud, a thunder-bud—it grew,
That blanket of the skies: the padded foot
Within,—I heard it; 'til its rhythm drew,
275   —Siphoned the black pool from the heart's hot root!

[26]A section of the Appalachian Mountains in northeastern New York.
[27]Mountain lakes.

A cyclone threshes in the turbine crest,
Swooping in eagle feathers down your back;
Know, Maquokeeta, greeting; know death's best;
—Fall, Sachem,[28] strictly as the tamarack!

280 A birch kneels. All her whistling fingers fly.
The oak grove circles in a crash of leaves;
The long moan of a dance is in the sky.
Dance, Maquokeeta: Pocahontas grieves . . .

And every tendon scurries toward the twangs
285 Of lightning deltaed down your saber hair.[29]
Now snaps the flint in every tooth; red fangs
And splay tongues thinly busy the blue air . . .

Dance, Maquokeeta! snake that lives before,
That casts his pelt, and lives beyond! Sprout, horn!
290 Spark, tooth! Medicine-man, relent, restore—
Lie to us,—dance us back the tribal morn!

Spears and assemblies: black drums thrusting on—
O yelling battlements,—I, too, was liege[30]
To rainbows currying[31] each pulsant bone:
295 Surpassed the circumstance, danced out the siege!

And buzzard-circleted, screamed from the stake;
I could not pick the arrows from my side.
Wrapped in that fire, I saw more escorts wake—
Flickering, sprint up the hill groins like a tide.

300 I heard the hush of lava wrestling your arms,
And stag teeth foam about the raven throat;
Flame cataracts of heaven in seething swarms
Fed down your anklets to the sunset's moat.

O, like the lizard in the furious noon,
305 That drops his legs and colors in the sun,
—And laughs, pure serpent, Time itself, and moon
Of his own fate, I saw thy change begun!

[28]Indian chieftain.
[29]The lightning, flashing from the hair, makes a pattern like a river delta.
[30]Subject to, like a vassal.
[31]Coloring.

And saw thee dive to kiss that destiny
Like one white meteor, sacrosanct and blent
310   At last with all that's consummate and free
There, where the first and last gods keep thy tent.

●

Thewed of the levin,[32] thunder-shod and lean,
Lo, through what infinite seasons dost thou gaze—
Across what bivouacs of thin angered slain,
315   And see'st thy bride immortal in the maize!

Totem and fire-gall, slumbering pyramid—
Though other calendars now stack the sky,
Thy freedom is her largesse, Prince, and hid
On paths thou knewest best to claim her by.

320   High unto Labrador the sun strikes free
Her speechless dream of snow, and stirred again,
She is the torrent and the singing tree;
And she is virgin to the last of men . . .

West, west and south! winds over Cumberland
325   And winds across the llano[33] grass resume
Her hair's warm sibilance. Her breasts are fanned
O stream by slope and vineyard—into bloom!

And when the caribou slant down for salt
Do arrows thirst and leap? Do antlers shine
330   Alert, star-triggered in the listening vault
Of dusk?—And are her perfect brows to thine?

We danced, O Brave, we danced beyond their farms,
In cobalt desert closures made our vows . . .
Now is the strong prayer folded in thine arms,
335   The serpent with the eagle in the boughs.

INDIANA

. . . and read
her in a
mother's
farewell gaze.

The morning-glory, climbing the morning long
Over the lintel on its wiry vine,
Closes before the dusk, furls in its song
As I close mine. . .

[32]Lightning bolt.
[33]Grassy plain.

340 And bison thunder rends my dreams no more
     As once my womb was torn, my boy, when you
 Yielded your first cry at the prairie's door. . .
        Your father knew

Then, though we'd buried him behind us, far
345   Back on the gold trail—then his lost bones stirred. . .
 But you who drop the scythe to grasp the oar
       Knew not, nor heard.

How we, too, Prodigal, once rode off, too—
     Waved Seminary Hill a gay good-bye. . .
350 We found God lavish there in Colorado
       But passing sly.

The pebbles sang, the firecat slunk away
     And glistening through the sluggard freshets came
 In golden syllables loosed from the clay
355   His gleaming name.

A dream called Eldorado[34] was his town,
     It rose up shambling in the nuggets' wake,
 It had no charter but a promised crown
       Of claims to stake.

360 But we,—too late, too early, howsoever—
     Won nothing out of fifty-nine—those years—
 But gilded promise, yielded to us never,
       And barren tears. . .

The long trail back! I huddled in the shade
365   Of wagon-tenting looked out once and saw
 Bent westward, passing a stumbling jade
       A homeless squaw—

Perhaps a halfbreed. On her slender back
     She cradled a babe's body, riding without rein.
370 Her eyes, strange for an Indian's, were not black
       But sharp with pain

---

[34]Legendary city or kingdom in Spanish America, fabled for riches and gold.
Literally, the golden land.

And like twin stars. They seemed to shun the gaze
Of all our silent men—the long team line—
Until she saw me—when their violet haze
375   Lit with love shine. . .

I held you up—I suddenly the bolder,
Knew that mere words could not have brought us nearer.
She nodded—and that smile across her shoulder
Will still endear her

380   As long as Jim, your father's memory, is warm.
Yes, Larry, now you're going to sea, remember
You were the first—before Ned and this farm,—
First-born, remember—

And since then—all that's left to me of Jim
385   Whose folks, like mine, came out of Arrowhead.
And you're the only one with eyes like him—
Kentucky bred!

I'm standing still, I'm old, I'm half of stone!
Oh, hold me in those eyes' engaging blue;
390   There's where the stubborn years gleam and atone,—
Where gold is true!

Down the dim turnpike to the river's edge—
Perhaps I'll hear the mare's hoofs to the ford. . .
Write me from Rio . . . and you'll keep your pledge;
395   I know your word!

Come back to Indiana—not too late!
(Or will you be a ranger to the end?)
Good-bye . . . Good-bye . . . oh, I shall always wait
You, Larry, traveller—
400   stranger,
                    son,
                        —my friend—

from **The Bridge**

CAPE HATTERAS[1]

> *The seas all crossed,*
> *weathered the capes, the voyage done . . .*
> —WALT WHITMAN[2]

Imponderable the dinosaur
       sinks slow,
             the mammoth saurian
                  ghoul, the eastern
5   Cape. . .
While rises in the west the coastwise range,
                 slowly the hushed land—
Combustion at the astral core—the dorsal[3] change
Of energy—convulsive shift of sand. . .
10 But we, who round the capes, the promontories
Where strange tongues vary messages of surf
Below grey citadels, repeating to the stars
The ancient names—return home to our own
Hearths, there to eat an apple and recall
15 The songs that gypsies dealt us at Marseille
Or how the priests walked—slowly through Bombay—
Or to read you, Walt,—knowing us in thrall

To that deep wonderment, our native clay
Whose depth of red, eternal flesh of Pocahontus—
20 Those contintental folded æons, surcharged
With sweetness below derricks, chimneys, tunnels—
Is veined by all that time has really pledged us. . .
And from above, thin squeaks of radio static,
The captured fume of space foams in our ears—
25 What whisperings of far watches on the main

---

[1]A promontory on Hatteras Island in the Atlantic off the coast of North Carolina.

[2]A line from Walt Whitman's "Passage to India," which celebrates technological triumphs as symbols, not just of man's mastery of matter but of the leap of his spirit to new frontiers and horizons. In "Cape Hatteras," Crane extends the effort to assimilate the radio, the dynamo, the telescope, the engine, and the airplane into poetry as the terms of man's imaginative and spiritual vision in the twentieth century.

[3]Forming a ridge like the back of an animal. The adjective looks back to the dinosaur and mammoth mentioned earlier; they sink to earth, extinct, as the earth lifts in mountain ranges suggestive of the prehistoric beasts.

Relapsing into silence, while time clears
Our lenses, lifts a focus, resurrects
A periscope to glimpse what joys or pain
Our eyes can share or answer—then deflects
30   Us, shunting to a labyrinth submersed
Where each sees only his dim past reversed. . .

But that star-glistered salver[4] of infinity,
The circle, blind crucible[5] of endless space,
Is sluiced by motion,—subjugated never.
35   Adam and Adam's answer in the forest[6]
Left Hesperus mirrored in the lucid pool.
Now the eagle dominates our days, is jurist
Of the ambiguous cloud. We know the strident rule
Of wings imperious. . . Space, instantaneous,
40   Flickers a moment, consumes us in its smile:
A flash over the horizon—shifting gears—
And we have laughter, or more sudden tears.
Dream cancels dream in this new realm of fact
From which we wake into the dream of act;
45   Seeing himself an atom in a shroud—
Man hears himself an engine in a cloud!

"—Recorders ages hence'"[7]—ah, syllables of faith!
Walt, tell me, Walt Whitman, if infinity
Be still the same as when you walked the beach
50   Near Paumanok[8]—your lone patrol—and heard the wraith
Through surf, its bird note there a long time falling. . .[9]
For you, the panoramas and this breed of towers,
Of you—the theme that's statured in the cliff.
O Saunterer on free ways still ahead!
55   Not this our empire yet, but labyrinth
Wherein your eyes, like the Great Navigator's[10] without ship,
Gleam from the great stones of each prison crypt
Of canyoned traffic . . . Confronting the Exchange,[11]

---

[4]Tray, plate.
[5]A vessel used for melting materials at high temperatures.
[6]Adam's joining Eve in the Original Sin, which lost mankind Paradise and brought him the imperfections of mortality.
[7]The title and first line of a poem in the "Calamus" section of *Leaves of Grass*, which celebrates the manly love of comrades.
[8]The Indian name for Long Island, as in Whitman's "Starting from Paumanok."
[9]A reference to Whitman's poem "Out of the Cradle Endlessly Rocking."
[10]Columbus, who was the speaker in the section of *The Bridge* entitled "Ave Maria," which comes between the "Proem" and "Powhatan's Daughter."
[11]The Stock Exchange in the financial district of Manhattan.

Surviving in a world of stocks,—they also range
60 Across the hills where second timber strays
Back over Connecticut farms, abandoned pastures,—
Sea eyes and tidal, undenying, bright with myth!

The nasal whine of power whips a new universe. . .
Where spouting pillars spoor[12] the evening sky,
65 Under the looming stacks of the gigantic power house
Stars prick the eyes with sharp ammoniac proverbs,
New verities, new inklings in the velvet hummed
Of dynamos, where hearing's leash is strummed. . .
Power's script,—wound, bobbin-bound, refined—
70 Is stropped to the slap of belts on booming spools, spurred
Into the bulging bouillon, harnessed jelly of the stars.
Towards what? The forked crash of split thunder parts
Our hearing momentwise; but fast in whirling armatures,[13]
As bright as frogs' eyes, giggling in the girth
75 Of steely gizzards—axle-bound, confined
In coiled precision, bunched in mutual glee
The bearings glint,—O murmurless and shined
In oilrinsed circles of blind ecstasy!

Stars scribble on our eyes the frosty sagas,
80 The gleaming cantos of unvanquished space. . .
O sinewy silver biplane, nudging the wind's withers![14]
There, from Kill Devils Hill at Kitty Hawk[15]
Two brothers in their twinship left the dune;
Warping the gale, the Wright windwrestlers veered
85 Capeward, then blading the wind's flank, banked and spun
What ciphers risen from prophetic script,
What marathons[16] new-set between the stars!
The soul, by naphtha[17] fledged into new reaches,
Already knows the closer clasp of Mars,—[18]
90 New latitudes, unknotting, soon give place
To what fierce schedules, rife of doom apace!

---

[12]Make a track or trail, like an animal.
[13]The rotating part of a dynamo, consisting of copper wire wound around an iron core.
[14]The high point of a horse's back at the base of the neck and the shoulders.
[15]A village in North Carolina; on a beach nearby Orville and Wilbur Wright made the first successful flight of a power-driven airplane in 1903.
[16]Originally, a 26-mile cross-country race in the ancient Greek Olympic Games; extended to mean any test of endurance.
[17]An obsolete word for petroleum.
[18]The planet named after the god of war.

Behold the dragon's covey—amphibian, ubiquitous
To hedge the seaboard, wrap the headland, ride
The blue's cloud-templed districts unto ether. . .[19]
95   While Iliads[20] glimmer through eyes raised in pride
Hell's belt springs wider into heaven's plumed side.
O bright circumferences, heights employed to fly
War's fiery kennel masked in downy offings,—
This tournament of space, the threshed and chiselled height,
100   Is baited by marauding circles, bludgeon flail
Of rancorous grenades whose screaming petals carve us
Wounds that we wrap with theorems sharp as hail!

Wheeled swiftly, wings emerge from larval-silver hangars.[21]
Taut motors surge, space-gnawing, into flight;
105   Through sparkling visibility, outspread, unsleeping,
Wings clip the last peripheries of light. . .
Tellurian[22] wind-sleuths on dawn patrol,
Each plane a hurtling javelin of winged ordnance,[23]
Bristle the heights above a screeching gale to hover;
110   Surely no eye that Sunward Escadrille[24] can cover!
There, meaningful, fledged as the Pleiades[25]
With razor sheen they zoom each rapid helix![26]
Up-chartered choristers of their own speeding
They, cavalcade on escapade, shear Cumulus—[27]
115   Lay siege and hurdle Cirrus down the skies!
While Cetus-like,[28] O thou Dirigible, enormous Lounger
Of pendulous auroral beaches,—satellited wide
By convoy planes, moonferrets[29] that rejoin thee
On fleeing balconies as thou dost glide,
120   —Hast splintered space!

                               Low, shadowed of the Cape,
Regard the moving turrets! From grey decks

---

[19]The regions of space beyond earth's atmosphere.
[20]Here, new and modern epics commensurate with Homer's.
[21]Planes, emerging from hangars, are compared to the hatching of larvae.
[22]Of Tellus, or Earth.
[23]Artillery.
[24]In World War I, a unit of airplanes, usually six.
[25]A group of stars in the constellation Taurus.
[26]Spiral.
[27]Cumulus and cirrus (below) are kinds of clouds.
[28]Whale-like.
[29]Ferrets were small animals used to search out the object of the hunt. Here the planes around the dirigible are like ferrets protecting it and like moons or satellites around it.

See scouting griffons[30] rise through gaseous crepe[31]
Hung low . . . until a conch of thunder answers
125 Cloud-belfries, banging, while searchlights, like fencers,
Slit the sky's pancreas of foaming anthracite
Toward thee, O Corsair of the typhoon,—pilot, hear!
Thine eyes bicarbonated white by speed, O Skygak, see
How from thy path above the levin's lance[32]
130 Thou sowest doom thou hast nor time nor chance
To reckon—as thy stilly eyes partake
What alcohol of space. . . ! Remember, Falcon-Ace,
Thou hast there in thy wrist a Sanskrit charge[33]
To conjugate infinity's dim marge—
135 Anew. . . !

But first, here at this height receive
The benediction of the shell's deep, sure reprieve!
Lead-perforated fuselage, escutcheoned wings
Lift agonized quittance, tilting from the invisible brink
140 Now eagle-bright, now

          quarry-hid, twist-

                   -ing, sink with

Enormous repercussive list-

          -ings down

145 Giddily spiralled

          gauntlets, upturned, unlooping

In guerrilla sleights,[34] trapped in combustion gyr-
Ing, dance the curdled depth

          down whizzing

150 Zodiacs,[35] dashed

          (now nearing fast the Cape!)

            down gravitation's

               vortex into crashed

. . . dispersion . . . into mashed and shapeless débris. . . .
155 By Hatteras bunched the beached heap of high bravery!

          •

The stars have grooved our eyes with old persuasions
Of love and hatred, birth,—surcease of nations. . .

---

[30]Griffon: a mythological beast with the body of a lion and the head and
  wings of an eagle.
[31]The gas fumes hang like a crepe, as a decoration or as a sign of mourning.
[32]Lightning bolt.
[33]A power as ancient and original and mysterious as is Sanskrit.
[34]Deceiving movements like the quick attacks of guerrilla warfare.
[35]Zodiac: the circle of planets and constellations in Astrology.

But who has held the heights more sure than thou,
O Walt!—Ascensions[36] of thee hover in me now
160   As thou at junctions elegiac, there, of speed
With vast eternity, dost wield the rebound seed!
The competent loam, the probable grass,—travail
Of tides awash the pedestal of Everest,[37] fail
Not less than thou in pure impulse inbred
165   To answer deepest soundings! O, upward from the dead
Thou bringest tally, and a pact, new bound,
Of living brotherhood!

                    Thou, there beyond—
Glacial sierras and the flight of ravens,
170   Hermetically past condor zones, through zenith havens
Past where the albatross has offered up
His last wing-pulse, and downcast as a cup
That's drained, is shivered back to earth—thy wand
Has beat a song, O Walt,—there and beyond!
175   And this, thine other hand, upon my heart
Is plummet ushered of those tears that start
What memories of vigils, bloody, by that Cape,—[38]
Ghoul-mound of man's perversity at balk[39]
And fraternal massacre! Thou, pallid there as chalk,
180   Hast kept of wounds, O Mourner, all that sum
That then from Appomattox stretched to Somme![40]

Cowslip and shad-blow,[41] flaked like tethered foam
Around bared teeth of stallions, bloomed that spring
When first I read thy lines, rife as the loam
185   Of prairies, yet like breakers cliffward leaping!
O, early following thee, I searched the hill
Blue-writ and odor-firm with voilets, 'til
With June the mountain laurel broke through green
And filled the forest with what clustrous sheen!

---

[36]The passage is filled with words and images important to Whitman: ascensions, eternity, grass, tides, tally, brotherhood.
[37]A peak in the Himalayas, the highest in the world.
[38]Civil War battles.
[39]Crane's coinage, perhaps meaning "blundering."
[40]Appomattox: the town in Virginia where General Robert E. Lee surrendered to General U. S. Grant in 1865, ending the Civil War; Somme: a river in France, the site of battles in World War I in 1916 and 1918.
[41]Also called shadbush, or Juneberry.

190 Potomac lilies,—then the Pontiac rose,[42]
And Klondike edelweiss of occult snows!
White banks of moonlight came descending valleys—
How speechful on oak-vizored palisades,
As vibrantly I following down Sequoia alleys
195 Heard thunder's eloquence through green arcades
Set trumpets breathing in each clump and grass tuft—'til
Gold autumn, captured, crowned the trembling hill!

Panis Angelicus![43] Eyes tranquil with the blaze
Of love's own diametric[44] gaze, of love's amaze!
200 Not greatest, thou,—not first, nor last,—but near
And onward yielding past my utmost year.
Familiar, thou, as mendicants in public places;
Evasive—too—as dayspring's spreading arc to trace is:—
Our Meistersinger,[45] thou set breath in steel;
205 And it was thou who on the boldest heel
Stood up and flung the span on even wing
Of that great Bridge, our Myth, whereof I sing!

Years of the Modern! Propulsions toward what capes?[46]
But thou, *Panis Angelicus*, hast thou not seen
210 And passed that Barrier that none escapes—
But knows it leastwise as death-strife?—O, something green,
Beyond all sesames[47] of science was thy choice
Wherewith to bind us throbbing with one voice,
New integers of Roman, Viking, Celt—
215 Thou, Vedic Caesar,[48] to the greensward knelt!

---

[42]Pontiac: an Indian chief of the Ottawas in Michigan and Canada. Crane is associating growing things with geographical areas across the continent, moving to the Canadian Klondike and the redwoods, or sequoias, of California.

[43]Crane probably thought this meant "Angelic Pan," thus linking material nature with spirit, pagan with religious image. It is actually Latin for "Angelic bread," and in Catholic liturgy and hymn refers to the Eucharist, the spiritualized bread of Communion.

[44]That is, the diameter of the circle, going through the middle to connect the two points on opposite sides.

[45]German: "master singer."

[46]"Years of the Modern" is the title of a Whitman poem; the second part of the line returns to the epigraph from "Passage to India."

[47]Not the herb, but the openings that science has made, as in "Open, Sesame" in the story of Aladdin.

[48]Caesar, because of Whitman's national power; Vedic (from the Hindu scriptures the Vedas), because of the strong mystical and visionary element in Whitman, as in "Passage to India."

And now, as launched in abysmal cupolas of space,
Toward endless terminals, Easters of speeding light—
Vast engines outward veering with seraphic grace
On clarion cylinders pass out of sight
220 To course that span of consciousness thou'st-named
The Open Road[49]—thy vision is reclaimed!
What heritage thou'st signalled to our hands!

And see! the rainbow's arch—how shimmeringly stands:
Above the Cape's ghoul-mound, O joyous seer!
225 Recorders ages hence, yes, they shall hear
In their own veins uncancelled thy sure tread
And read thee by the aureole 'round thy head
Of pasture-shine,[50] *Panis Angelicus!*

                                   Yes, Walt,
230 Afoot again, and onward without halt,—
Not soon, nor suddenly,—No, never to let go
    My hand[51]
           in yours,
                Walt Whitman—
235   so—

THE BROKEN TOWER

The bell-rope that gathers God at dawn
Dispatches me as though I dropped down the knell
Of a spent day—to wander the cathedral lawn
From pit to crucifix, feet chill on steps from hell.

5 Have you not heard, have you not seen that corps
Of shadows in the tower, whose shoulders sway
Antiphonal carillons launched before
The stars are caught and hived in the sun's ray?

The bells, I say, the bells break down their tower;
10 And swing I know not where. Their tongues engrave
Membrane through marrow, my long-scattered score
Of broken intervals. . . . And I, their sexton slave!

[49]Whitman's "Song of the Open Road."
[50]Again the suggestion is "Angelic Pan."
[51]A frequent image of comradeship in Whitman's poetry.

Oval encyclicals[1] in canyons heaping
The impasse high with choir. Banked voices slain!
15   Pagodas, campaniles with reveilles outleaping—
O terraced echoes prostrate on the plain! . . .

And so it was I entered the broken world
To trace the visionary company of love, its voice
An instant in the wind (I know not whither hurled)
20   But not for long to hold each desperate choice.

My word I poured. But was it cognate,[2] scored
Of that tribunal monarch of the air
Whose thigh embronzes earth, strikes crystal Word
In wounds pledged once to hope—cleft to despair?

25   The steep encroachments of my blood left me
No answer (could blood hold such a lofty tower
As flings the question true?)—or is it she
Whose sweet mortality stirs latent power?—

And through whose pulse I hear, counting the strokes
30   My veins recall and add, revived and sure
The angelus of wars my chest evokes:
What I hold healed, original now, and pure . . .

And builds, within, a tower that is not stone
(Not stone can jacket heaven)—but slip
35   Of pebbles—visible wings of silence sown
In azure circles, widening as they dip

The matrix of the heart, lifts down the eye
That shrines the quiet lake and swells a tower . . .
The commodious, tall decorum of that sky
40   Unseals her earth, and lifts love in its shower.

[1]A papal message.
[2]Related by origin or nature.

Allen Tate (1899–)

John Orley Allen Tate was born in Winchester, Kentucky, and attended Vanderbilt, graduating in 1922. There he became a member of the Fugitive Group around Ransom, bringing to the older members his incisive critical judgments and his intense interest in poets like Poe, Baudelaire, Rimbaud, and Eliot—all influences on his own work. *Poems 1922–1947* (1948) brought together earlier volumes—among them *Mr. Pope and Other Poems* (1928), *The Mediterranean and Other Poems* (1936), and *The Winter Sea* (1944).

Robert Lowell has said that from Tate he learned that "a good poem had nothing to do with exalted feelings of being moved by the spirit" or any such romantic nonsense; that it was rather "a piece of craftsmanship" which must "be tinkered with and recast until one's eyes pop out of one's head." The prevailing theme of these compacted poems is the living death of modern secular man without roots or faith. In 1950 Tate became a Roman Catholic, and in "The Buried Lake," a section from a projected autobiographical poem in *terza rima* added to the 1960 reprinting of *Poems,* there is the first expression of the deliverance of the agonized ego into the possibility of "enduring love."

Tate edited various journals, including the *Sewanee Review* from 1940 to 1946, and was an important figure in the New Criticism. He taught at several universities, most recently at the University of Minnesota. His achievement in various fields—his poetry and teaching and editing, the novel *The Fathers* (1938), the biographies of Stonewall Jackson and Jefferson Davis, the brilliant essays collected in *Essays of Four Decades* (1969)—have made him, to cite the title of one of his essays, "The Man of Letters in the Modern World." The latest and fullest collection of verse is *The Swimmers and Other Selected Poems* (1970).

REFERENCE

Cowan, Louise. *The Fugitive Group: A Literary History.* Baton Rouge: Louisiana State University Press, 1959.

"Homage to Allen Tate" Issue, *Sewanee Review,* LXVII (Autumn, 1959).

Meiners, R. K. *The Last Alternatives: A Study of the Works of Allen Tate.* Denver: Swallow, 1963.

Squires, Radcliffe. *Allen Tate: A Literary Biography.* New York: Pegasus, 1971.

Stewart, John L. *The Burden of Time: The Fugitives and Agrarians.* Princeton, N.J.: Princeton University Press, 1965.

AENEAS AT WASHINGTON[1]

I myself saw furious with blood
Neoptolemus, at his side the black Atridae,[2]
Hecuba and the hundred daughters, Priam[3]
Cut down, his filth drenching the holy fires.
5   In that extremity I bore me well,
A true gentleman, valorous in arms,
Disinterested and honourable. Then fled:
That was a time when civilization
Run by the few fell to the many, and
10 Crashed to the shout of men, the clang of arms:
Cold victualing[4] I seized, I hoisted up
The old man my father[5] upon my back,
In the smoke made by sea for a new world
Saving little—a mind imperishable
15 If time is, a love of past things tenuous
As the hesitation of receding love.

(To the reduction of uncitied littorals[6]
We brought chiefly the vigor of prophecy,
Our hunger breeding calculation
20 And fixed triumphs)
                  I saw the thirsty dove
In the glowing fields of Troy, hemp ripening
And tawny corn, the thickening Blue Grass
All lying rich forever in the green sun.
25 I see all things apart, the towers that men
Contrive I too contrived long, long ago.
Now I demand little. The singular passion
Abides its object and consumes desire
In the circling shadow of its appetite.

[1]In Vergil's *Aeneid* the Trojan hero Aeneas travels west after the fall of Troy, lands in Italy and becomes the ancestor of the founders of Rome. Here his westward journey is extended to the New World, specifically to the city of Washington on the Potomac River. Behind Aeneas' monologue lie correlations between the Roman republic and the American republic, and between the Trojan War and the Civil War.
[2]All Greek generals: the Atridae were the sons of Atreus, Menelaus and Agamemnon; Neoptolemus, the son of Achilles.
[3]Priam and Hecuba, the King and Queen of Troy; in most versions, Priam has fifty sons and fifty daughters by different wives.
[4]Food.
[5]Anchises.
[6]Shores.

30 There was a time when the young eyes were slow,
    Their flame steady beyond the firstling fire,
    I stood in the rain, far from home at nightfall
    By the Potomac, the great Dome[7] lit the water,
    The city my blood had built I knew no more
35 While the screech-owl whistled his new delight
    Consecutively dark.

                              Stuck in the wet mire
    Four thousand leagues from the ninth buried city[8]
    I thought of Troy, what we had built her for.

MOTHER AND SON

    Now all day long the man who is not dead
    Hastens the dark with inattentive eyes,
    The woman with white hand and erect head
    Stares at the covers, leans for the son's replies
5   At last to her importunate womanhood—
    Her hand of death laid on the living bed;
    So lives the fierce compositor of blood.

    She waits; he lies upon the bed of sin
    When greed, avarice, anger writhed and slept
10 Till to their silence they were gathered in:
    There, fallen with time, his tall and bitter kin
    Once fired the passions that were never kept
    In the permanent heart, and there his mother lay
    To bear him on the impenetrable day.

15 The falcon mother cannot will her hand
    Up to the bed, nor break the manacle
    His exile sets upon her harsh command
    That he should say the time is beautiful—
    Transfigured by her own possessing light:
20 The sick man craves the impalpable night.

[7]Of the Capitol.
[8]Archeologists have uncovered nine levels of construction on the presumed
site of Troy.

Loosed betwixt eye and lid, the swimming beams
Of memory, blind school of cuttlefish,[1]
Rise to the air, plunge to the cold streams—
Rising and plunging the half-forgotten wish
25 To tear his heart out in a slow disgrace
And freeze the hue of terror to her face.

Hate, misery, and fear beat off his heart
To the dry fury of the woman's mind;
The son, prone in his autumn, moves apart
30 A seed blown upon a returning wind.
O child, be vigilant till towards the south
On the flowered wall all the sweet afternoon,
The reaching sun, swift as the cottonmouth,[2]
Strikes at the black crucifix on her breast
35 Where the cold dusk comes suddenly to rest—
Mortality will speak the victor soon!

The dreary flies, lazy and casual,
Stick to the ceiling, buzz along the wall.
O heart, the spider shuffles from the mould[3]
40 Weaving, between the pinks and grapes, his pall.
The bright wallpaper, imperishably old,
Uncurls and flutters, it will never fall.

THE WOLVES

There are wolves in the next room waiting
With heads bent low, thrust out, breathing
At nothing in the dark; between them and me
A white door patched with light from the hall
5 Where it seems never (so still is the house)
A man has walked from the front door to the stair.
It has all been forever. Beasts claw the floor.
I have brooded on angels and archfiends
But no man has ever sat where the next room's
10 Crowded with wolves, and for the honor of man
I affirm that never have I before. Now while

[1]Squid-like mollusks.
[2]The water moccasin, a deadly snake.
[3]Mildew; also the molding at the top of the wall.

I have looked for the evening star at a cold window
And whistled when Arcturus[1] split his light,
I've heard the wolves scuffle, and said: So this
15 Is man; so—what better conclusion is there—
The day will not follow night, and the heart
Of man has a little dignity, but less patience
Than a wolf's, and a duller sense that cannot
Smell its own mortality. (This and other
20 Meditations will be suited to other times
After dog silence howls his epitaph.)
Now remember courage, go to the door,
Open it and see whether coiled on the bed
Or cringing by the wall, a savage beast
25 Maybe with golden hair, with deep eyes
Like a bearded spider on a sunlit floor
Will snarl—and man can never be alone.

THE SUBWAY

Dark accurate plunger down the successive knell
Of arch on arch, where ogives[1] burst a red
Reverberance of hail upon the dead
Thunder like an exploding crucible![2]
5 Harshly articulate, musical steel shell
Of angry worship, hurled religiously
Upon your business of humility
Into the iron forestries of hell:

Till broken in the shift of quieter
10 Dense altitudes tangential[3] of your steel,
I am become geometries, and glut
Expansions like a blind astronomer
Dazed, while the worldless heavens bulge and reel
In the cold revery of an idiot.

[1] One of the brightest stars; in the constellation Boötes.
[1] Arches.
[2] A vessel for melting materials, especially metals, at high temperatures.
[3] Touching and diverging from.

LAST DAYS OF ALICE[1]

Alice grown lazy, mammoth but not fat,
Declines upon her lost and twilight age;
Above in the dozing leaves the grinning cat[2]
Quivers forever with his abstract rage:

5   Whatever light swayed on the perilous gate
Forever sways, nor will the arching grass,
Caught when the world clattered, undulate
In the deep suspension of the looking-glass.

Bright Alice! always pondering to gloze[3]
10   The spoiled cruelty she had meant to say
Gazes learnedly down her airy nose
At nothing, nothing thinking all the day.

Turned absent-minded by infinity
She cannot move unless her double move,
15   The All-Alice of the world's entity
Smashed in the anger of her hopeless love,

Love for herself who, as an earthly twain,
Pouted to join her two in a sweet one;
No more the second lips to kiss in vain
20   The first she broke, plunged through the glass alone—

Alone to the weight of impassivity,
Incest of spirit, theorem of desire,
Without will as chalky cliffs by the sea,
Empty as the bodiless flesh of fire:

25   All space, that heaven is a dayless night,
A nightless day driven by perfect lust
For vacancy, in which her bored eyesight
Stares at the drowsy cubes of human dust.

---

[1]The heroine of Lewis Carroll's *Alice Through the Looking-Glass* (1871).
Here Alice, Narcissus-like, has turned in on herself and gone through the
mind's looking glass into a kind of abstraction that abandons external
reality—matter, flesh, experience—in a suspended paralysis of passion
and will.
[2]The Cheshire cat in *Alice's Adventures in Wonderland* (1865), whose body
gradually disappears and leaves only his grin hanging in air.
[3]Gloss, interpret (sometimes with the suggestion of false explanation).

—We too back to the world shall never pass
30   Through the shattered door, a dumb shade-harried crowd
Being all infinite, function[4] depth and mass
Without figure, a mathematical shroud

Hurled at the air—blesséd without sin!
O God of our flesh, return us to Your wrath,
35   Let us be evil could we enter in
Your grace, and falter on the stony path!

TO A ROMANTIC

(1924)

TO ROBERT PENN WARREN

You hold your eager head
Too high in the air, you walk
As if the sleepy dead
Had never fallen to drowse
5   From the sublimest talk
Of many a vehement house.
Your head so turned turns eyes
Into the vagrant West;
Fixing an iron mood
10   In an Ozymandias'[1] breast
And because your clamorous blood
Beats an impermanent rest
You think the dead arise
Westward and fabulous:
15   The dead are those whose lies
Were doors to a narrow house.

---

[4]Not just "proper or assigned activity," but the mathematical sense of "a variable so related to another variable that for each value of one there is a corresponding value of the other."

[1]Rameses II, Pharaoh of Egypt; the largest statue in ancient Egypt depicted him with the inscription: "I am Ozymandias, king of kings; if anyone wishes to know what I am and where I lie, let him surpass me in some of my exploits."

THE BURIED LAKE

Ego mater pulchrae dilectionis, et timoris,
et agnitionis, et sanctae spei.[1]

Lady of light, I would admit a dream[2]
    To you, if you would take it in your hand.
    Will you not let it in a gentle stream

Of living blood? How else may I remand
5   Your light if not as pulse upon your ear?
    Since I have dreamt this dream at your command,

If it shall bring my edge of darkness near
    I pray you do not let the edging slough
    To blind me, but light up my edge of fear.

10 The Way and the way back are long and rough
    Where Myrtle twines with Laurel[3]—single glow
    Of leaf, your own imponderable stuff

Of light in which you set my time to flow
    In childhood, when I tried to catch each flake
15   And hold it to deny the world of snow.

—The night was tepid. I had kept opaque
    Down deeper than the canyons undersea
    The sullen spectrum of a buried lake[4]

Nobody saw; not seen even by me;
20   And now I pray you mirror my mind, styled
    To spring its waters to my memory.

[1]"I am the mother of lovely choice, and fear, and knowledge, and holy hope" (Ecclesiasticus 24); used often in the liturgy of the Catholic Mass on a feast honoring the Virgin Mary. The woman figure in the poem appears as mother, lover, and saint.
[2]The poem takes its imagery from three dreams that Tate had.
[3]The laurel is associated with the poet's crown awarded by Apollo; myrtle, with the gift of true love granted by Venus. Art and love, creative energy and sexual energy are related throughout the poem.
[4]An image for the unconscious explored in dreams; suggests as well the Stygian Lake in Dante's *Inferno* (Tate chose as his meter the *terza-rima* of the *Divine Comedy*) and the lake from which the Mount of Purgatory rises.

I fumbled all night long, an ageing child
   Fled like a squirrel to a hollow bole
   To play toy soldier, Tiny Tim, or the mild

25   Babes-in-the-Woods: sunk in their leafy hole,
   The terror of their sleep I could not tell
   Until your gracing light reduced the toll.

I stumbled all night long on sand and shell
   By a lakeshore where time, unfaced, was dark;
30   I grazed with my left foot a pinched hotel

Where a sick dog coughed out a sickly cark[5]
   To let me in. Inside I saw no man,
   But benches ranged the wall as round a park—

Sputtering gas-jet, ceiling without span,
35   Where thinning air lay on my cheek like tin;
   But then exulting in my secret plan,

I laid my top hat to one side; my chin
   Was ready, I unsnapped the lyric case;
   I had come there to play my violin.

40   Erect and sinuous as Valence lace[6]
   Old ladies wore, the bow began to fill
   The shining box—whence came a dreaming face,

Small dancing girl who gave the smell of dill
   In pelts of mordents[7] on a minor third
45   From my cadenza for the Devil's Trill.

No, no! her quick hand said in a soft surd.[8]
   She locked the fiddle up and was not there.
   I mourned the death of youth without a word.

[5]Charge.
[6]Suggests Valencia in Spain and the Flemish town of Valenciennes, also famous for its lace.
[7]Pelts: rapid succession; mordents, in music a melodic passage in which a note is rapidly alternated with another note a half or a full step below.
[8]A voiceless sound.

And could I go where air was not dead air?
50   My friend Jack Locke,[9] scholar and gentleman,
      Gazed down upon me with a friendly glare,

Flicking his nose as if about to scan
      My verse; he plucked from his moustache one hair
      Letting it fall like gravel in a pan,

55   And went as mist upon the browning air
      Away from the durable lake, the blind hotel,
      Leaving me guilted on a moving stair

Upwards, down which I regularly fell
      Tail backwards, till I caught the music room
60   Empty, like a gaol without a cell.

"If I am now alone I may resume
      The grey sonata"—but the box was gone;
      Instead I heard three footfalls, a light broom

Dusting the silted[10] air, which now put on
65   (Like Pier Francesca[11] sunning a shady wall)
      A stately woman who in sorrow shone.

I rose; she moved, she glided towards the hall;
      I took her hand but then would set her free.
      "My Love," I said.—"I'm back to give you all,"

70   She said, "my love." (Under the dogwood tree
      In bloom, where I had held her first beneath
      The coiled black hair, she turned and smiled at me.)

I hid the blade within the melic[12] sheath
      And tossed her head—but it was not her head:
75   Another's searching skull whose drying teeth

Crumbled me all night long and I was dead.
      Down, down below the wave that turned me round,
      Head downwards where the Head of God has sped

[9]Possibly John Locke (1631–1704), the English empiricist philosopher.
[10]Filled with dust or silt.
[11]Piero della Francesca (1420–1492), painter of the Italian Renaissance.
[12]Lyric.

On the third day;[13] where nature had unwound
80   And ravelled her green that she had softly laved—
The green reviving spray now slowly drowned

Me, since the shuttling eye would not be saved.
In the tart undersea of slipping night
The dream whispered, while sight within me, caved,

85   Deprived, poured stinging dark on cold delight,
And multitudinous whined invisible bees;
All grace being lost, and its considering rite,

Till come to midmost May I bent my knees,
Santa Lucia![14] at noon—the prudent shore,
90   The lake flashing green fins through amber trees—

And knew I had not read your eye before
You played it in the flowing scale of glance;
I had not thought that I could read the score,

And yet how vexed, bitter, and hard the trance
95   Of light—how I resented Lucy's play!
Better stay dead, better not try the lance

In the living bowl: living we have one way
For all time in the twin darks where light dies
To live: forget that you too lost the day

100   Yet finding it refound it Lucy-guise
As I, refinding where two shadows meet,
Took from the burning umbrage mirroring eyes

---

[13]By ancient Christian tradition, Jesus descended to hell, between his burial and resurrection, in order to free into heaven all the virtuous who had been awaiting release and salvation since Adam's sin.

[14]Saint Lucy: a virgin-martyr at Syracuse in Sicily. Her name means "light," and by legend her executioners tore her eyes out. Hence she is patroness of eyesight and eye troubles, and is represented as holding her eyes in a dish with another set of eyes in her head. There are overtones from Dante as well. In *Inferno* the Blessed Virgin sends Saint Lucy to Beatrice, Dante's ideal love in Paradise, to bid her help Dante. Beatrice sends Vergil to guide him through Hell. Then they emerge on the shores of a lake, cross it to the Mount of Purgatory, and find they cannot enter. It is Saint Lucy who gains entrance to Purgatory for them.

Like Tellico[15] blue upon a golden sheet
    Spread out for all our stupor. Lady coming,
105   Lady not going, come Lady come: I greet

You in the double of our eyes—humming
    Miles of lightning where, in a pastoral scene,
    The fretting pipe is lucent and becoming.

I thought of ways to keep this image green
110   (Until the leaf unfold the formal cherry)
    In an off season when the eye is lean

With an inward gaze upon the wild strawberry,
    Cape jasmine, wild azalea, eglantine—
    All the sad eclogue that will soon be merry:

115 And knew that nature could not more refine
    What it had given in a looking-glass
    And held there, after the living body's line

Has moved wherever it must move—wild grass
    Inching the earth; and the quicksilver art
120   Throws back the invisible but lightning mass

To inhabit the room; for I have seen it part
    The palpable air, the air close up above
    And under you, light Lucy, light of heart—

Light choir upon my shoulder, speaking Dove.[16]
125   The dream is over and the dark expired.
    I knew that I had known enduring love.

---

[15]Tellico Plains, a town in Tennessee, or the Tellico River.
[16]The Holy Spirit is often represented as a descending dove, as at Jesus'
baptism.

Yvor Winters (1900–1968)

Arthur Yvor Winters was born in Chicago, moved to California with his family in 1904, and returned to Chicago in 1915. Withdrawing from the University of Chicago after a year because of tuberculosis, he spent some years in Santa Fe, New Mexico, before earning his M.A. from the University of Colorado. In 1926 he married Janet Lewis, the novelist, and the next year they went to Stanford, where, first as a graduate student and then as a professor, he remained, receiving his Ph.D. in 1934 and teaching until shortly before his death.

Winters' early poetry was in the Imagist mode of Pound, Williams, and Marianne Moore, but in the late twenties he began to write in more traditional forms, especially those of the Renaissance lyric poets. This change reflected his growing critical conviction that poetry should be a rationally controlled reflection on morally significant experience. By these standards most English and American poets since the Romantics wrote unfocused and subjective effusions without intellectual or moral coherence. His strongly argued views are contained in *In Defense of Reason* (1947)—which brought together *Primitivism and Decadence* (1937), *Maule's Curse* (1938), and *The Anatomy of Nonsense* (1943)—and in *The Function of Criticism* (1957) and *Forms of Discovery* (1967). *Collected Poems* (1952, 1960) preserved his choice from such earlier books as *The Magpie's Shadow* (1922), *The Bare Hills* (1927), and *The Giant Weapon* (1943). It was supplemented by *The Early Poems* (1966). With the student poets who worked with him at Stanford, Winters exerted a rigorous resistance to the prevailing literary attitudes. *Quest for Reality* (1969), an anthology done with Kenneth Fields, presents the Winters canon of poets.

THE UPPER MEADOWS

The harvest falls
Throughout the valleys
With a sound
Of fire in leaves.

5   The harsh trees,
Heavy with light,
Beneath the flame, and aging,
Have risen high and higher.

Apricots,
10 The clustered
Fur of bees
Above the gray rocks of the uplands.

The hunter deep in summer.
Grass laid low by what comes,
15 Feet or air—
But motion, aging.

THE MORALISTS

You would extend the mind beyond the act,
Furious, bending, suffering in thin
And unpoetic dicta; you have been
Forced by hypothesis to fiercer fact.
5 As metal singing hard, with firmness racked,
You formulate our passion; and behind
In some harsh moment nowise of the mind
Lie the old meanings your advance has packed.

No man can hold existence in the head.
10 I, too, have known the anguish of the right
Amid this net of mathematic dearth,
And the brain throbbing like a ship at night:
Have faced with old unmitigated dread
The hard familiar wrinkles of the earth.

THE INVADERS

They have won out at last and laid us bare,
The demons of the meaning of the dead,
Stripped us with wheel and flame. Oh, where they tread,
Dissolves our heritage of earth and air!
5   Till as a locomotive plunges through
Distance that has no meaning and no bound
Thundering some interminable sound
To inward metal where its motion grew—

Grew and contracted down through infinite
10 And sub-atomic roar of Time on Time
Toward meaning that its changing cannot find;
So, stripped of color of an earth, and lit
With motion only of some inner rime,
The naked passion of the human mind.

TO EMILY DICKINSON

Dear Emily, my tears would burn your page,
But for the fire-dry line that makes them burn—
Burning my eyes, my fingers, while I turn
Singly the words that crease my heart with age.
5   If I could make some tortured pilgrimage
Through words or Time or the blank pain of Doom
And kneel before you as you found your tomb,
Then I might rise to face my heritage.

Yours was an empty upland solitude
10 Bleached to the powder of a dying name;
The mind, lost in a word's lost certitude
That faded as the fading footsteps came
To trace an epilogue to words grown odd
In that hard argument which led to God.

APOLLO AND DAPHNE

Deep in the leafy fierceness of the wood,
Sunlight, the cellular and creeping pyre,
Increased more slowly than aetherial fire:
But it increased and touched her where she stood.
5   The god had seized her, but the powers of good
Struck deep into her veins; with rending flesh
She fled all ways into the grasses' mesh
And burned more quickly than the sunlight could.

And all her heart broke stiff in leafy flame
10   That neither rose nor fell, but stood aghast;
And she, rooted in Time's slow agony,
Stirred dully, hard-edged laurel, in the past;
And, like a cloud of silence or a name,
The god withdrew into Eternity.

THE SLOW PACIFIC SWELL

Far out of sight forever stands the sea,
Bounding the land with pale tranquillity.
When a small child, I watched it from a hill
At thirty miles or more. The vision still
5   Lies in the eye, soft blue and far away;
The rain has washed the dust from April day;
Paint-brush and lupine[1] lie against the ground;
The wind above the hill-top has the sound
Of distant water in unbroken sky;
10   Dark and precise the little steamers ply—
Firm in direction they seem not to stir.
That is illusion. The artificer
Of quiet, distance holds me in a vise
And holds the ocean steady to my eyes.

15   Once when I rounded Flattery, the sea
Hove its loose weight like sand to tangle me
Upon the washing deck, to crush the hull;
Subsiding, dragged flesh at the bone. The skull

---

[1]Paint-brush, lupine: wild flowers.

Felt the retreating wash of dreaming hair.
20 Half drenched in dissolution, I lay bare.
I scarcely pulled myself erect; I came
Back slowly, slowly knew myself the same.
That was the ocean. From the ship we saw
Gray whales for miles: the long sweep of the jaw,
25 The blunt head plunging clean above the wave.
And one rose in a tent of sea and gave
A darkening shudder; water fell away;
The whale stood shining, and then sank in spray.

A landsman, I. The sea is but a sound.
30 I would be near it on a sandy mound,
And hear the steady rushing of the deep
While I lay stinging in the sand with sleep.
I have lived inland long. The land is numb.
It stands beneath the feet, and one may come
35 Walking securely, till the sea extends
Its limber margin, and precision ends.
By night a chaos of commingling power,
The whole Pacific hovers hour by hour.
The slow Pacific swell stirs on the sand,
40 Sleeping to sink away, withdrawing land,
Heaving and wrinkled in the moon, and blind;
Or gathers seaward, ebbing out of mind.

ORPHEUS[1]

IN MEMORY OF HART CRANE[2]

Climbing from the Lethal dead,
Past the ruined waters' bed,
In the sleep his music cast
Tree and flesh and stone were fast—
5   As amid Dodona's wood[3]
Wisdom never understood.

Till the shade[4] his music won
Shuddered, by a pause undone—
Silence would not let her stay.
10   He could go one only way:
By the river, strong with grief,
Gave his flesh beyond belief.[5]

Yet the fingers on the lyre
Spread like an avenging fire.
15   Crying loud, the immortal tongue,
From the empty body wrung,
Broken in a bloody dream,
Sang unmeaning down the stream.

[1]The poet whose song had power over trees and rocks and animals. When Eurydice, his wife, died, he went to the underworld and so moved Persephone, the Queen of Hades, by his music and song that she allowed Eurydice to return to earth with him, on condition that he not look around during the journey back. When Orpheus, anxious and impatient for his wife, glanced back, she had to return to Hades.

[2]Crane committed suicide in 1932 by drowning himself. See headnote on Crane.

[3]A grove that was the seat of an oracle of Zeus, who expressed his will through the rustling of the leaves of an oak tree for interpretation by his priests and priestesses.

[4]The shade or spirit of Eurydice.

[5]According to one legend, Orpheus died at the hand of the Maenads, who were driven to tear him apart by the resentful and jealous Dionysus. His head and lyre floated down a stream to Lesbos, making music all the way. Here his death seems to be in grief over Eurydice.

TO THE HOLY SPIRIT

from a deserted graveyard
in the Salinas Valley[1]

Immeasurable haze:
The desert valley spreads
Up golden river-beds
As if in other days.
5   Trees rise and thin away,
And past the trees, the hills,
Pure line and shade of dust,
Bear witness to our wills:
We see them, for we must;
10   Calm in deceit, they stay.

High noon returns the mind
Upon its local fact:
Dry grass and sand; we find
No vision to distract.
15   Low in the summer heat,
Naming old graves, are stones
Pushed here and there, the seat
Of nothing, and the bones
Beneath are similar:
20   Relics of lonely men,
Brutal and aimless, then,
As now, irregular.

These are thy fallen sons,
Thou whom I try to reach.
25   Thou whom the quick eye shuns,
Thou dost elude my speech.
Yet when I go from sense
And trace thee down in thought,
I meet thee, then, intense,
30   And know thee as I ought.
But thou art mind alone,
And I, alas, am bound
Pure mind to flesh and bone,
And flesh and bone to ground.

[1]Near the Monterey peninsula in California.

35 These had no thought: at most
Dark faith and blinding earth.
Where is the trammeled ghost?
Was there another birth?
Only one certainty
40 Beside thine unfleshed eye,
Beside the spectral tree,
Can I discern: these die.
All of this stir of age,
Though it elude my sense
45 Into what heritage
I know not, seems to fall,
Quiet beyond recall,
Into irrelevance.

Langston Hughes (1902–1967)

James Langston Hughes was born in Joplin, Missouri, and after attending Columbia for a year graduated from Lincoln University in 1929. He worked as a seaman on voyages to Europe and Africa and lived in Mexico and the Soviet Union as well as on the Continent. His ebullient creative energy was devoted to translating the experience of American Negroes, those still living on the land and those crowded into city slums, into the rhythms of spirituals and blues and jazz. His many books of poems include: *Weary Blues* (1926), *The Dream Keeper* (1932), *Shakespeare in Harlem* (1942), *Montage of a Dream Deferred* (1951), and *The Panther and the Lash* (1967). He has done several anthologies, among them: *The Poetry of the Negro* (1949), *The Book of Negro Folklore* (1958), and *The Best Short Stories by Negro Writers* (1967). He wrote two autobiographies, *The Big Sea* (1940) and *I Wonder as I Wander* (1956), as well as fiction and plays. *The Langston Hughes Reader* came out in 1958 and *Selected Poems* in 1959. His popular success and wide recognition, as evidenced by his many awards, made Hughes the lyric voice of the black man in mid-twentieth-century America.

REFERENCE

Emanuel, James A. *Langston Hughes.* New York: Twayne, 1967.
Langston Hughes: Black Genius. Ed. Therman B. O'Daniel. New York: William Morrow, 1971.

THE NEGRO SPEAKS OF RIVERS

I've known rivers:
I've known rivers ancient as the world and older than the
    flow of human blood in human veins.

My soul has grown deep like the rivers.

I bathed in the Euphrates[1] when dawns were young.
5 I built my hut near the Congo and it lulled me to sleep.
I looked upon the Nile and raised the pyramids above it.
I heard the singing of the Mississippi when Abe Lincoln
    went down to New Orleans, and I've seen its muddy
    bosom turn all golden in the sunset.

I've known rivers:
Ancient, dusky rivers.

10 My soul has grown deep like the rivers.

DREAM VARIATIONS

To fling my arms wide
In some place of the sun,
To whirl and to dance
Till the white day is done.
5 Then rest at cool evening
Beneath a tall tree
While night comes on gently,
    Dark like me—
That is my dream!

10 To fling my arms wide
In the face of the sun,
Dance! Whirl! Whirl!
Till the quick day is done.
Rest at pale evening . . .
15 A tall, slim tree . . .
Night coming tenderly
    Black like me.

[1]The Euphrates River in Turkey, Syria, and Iraq; the Congo in Africa; the
Nile in Egypt.

FIRE

Fire,
Fire, Lord!
Fire gonna burn ma soul!

I ain't been good,
5   I ain't been clean—
I been stinkin', low-down, mean.

Fire,
Fire, Lord!
Fire gonna burn ma soul!

10 Tell me, brother,
Do you believe
If you wanta go to heaben
Got to moan an' grieve?

Fire,
15 Fire, Lord!
Fire gonna burn ma soul!

I been stealin',
Been tellin' lies,
Had more women
20 Than Pharaoh had wives.

Fire,
Fire, Lord!
Fire gonna burn ma soul!
I means Fire, Lord!
25 Fire gonna burn ma soul!

BAD MORNING

Here I sit
With my shoes mismated.
Lawdy-mercy!
I's frustrated!

OLD WALT

Old Walt Whitman
Went finding and seeking,
Finding less than sought
Seeking more than found,
5   Every detail minding
Of the seeking or the finding.

Pleasured equally
In seeking as in finding,
Each detail minding,
10   Old Walt went seeking
And finding.

MIDNIGHT RAFFLE

I put my nickel
In the raffle of the night.
Somehow that raffle
Didn't turn out right.

5   I lost my nickel.
I lost my time.
I got back home
Without a dime.

When I dropped that nickel
10   In the subway slot,
I wouldn't have dropped it,
Knowing what I got.

I could just as well've
Stayed home inside:
15   My bread wasn't buttered
On neither side.

STONY LONESOME

They done took Cordelia
Out to stony lonesome ground.
Done took Cordelia
To stony lonesome,
5 Laid her down.
They done put Cordelia
Underneath that
Grassless mound.
    Ay-Lord!
10   Ay-Lord!
          Ay-Lord!
She done left po' Buddy
To struggle by his self.
Po' Buddy Jones,
15 Yes, he's done been left.
She's out in stony lonesome,
Lordy! Sleepin' by herself.
    Cordelia's
      In stony
20   Lonesome
          Ground!

DOWN AND OUT

Baby, if you love me
Help me when I'm down and out.
If you love me, baby,
Help me when I'm down and out,
5 I'm a po' gal
Nobody gives a damn about.

The credit man's done took ma clothes
And rent time's nearly here.
I'd like to buy a straightenin' comb,
10 An' I need a dime fo' beer.

I need a dime fo' beer.

I, TOO

I, too, sing America.

I am the darker brother.
They send me to eat in the kitchen
When company comes,
5 But I laugh,
And eat well,
And grow strong.

Tomorrow,
I'll be at the table
10 When company comes.
Nobody'll dare
Say to me,
"Eat in the kitchen,"
Then.

15 Besides,
They'll see how beautiful I am
And be ashamed—

I, too, am America.

Robert Penn Warren (1905–)

From Guthrie, Kentucky, Warren went to Vanderbilt and became the youngest member of The Fugitive Group around Ransom, graduating in 1925. He did graduate work and as a Rhodes Scholar got a B.Litt. from Oxford in 1930. He taught at Louisiana State University in Baton Rouge, where he and Cleanth Brooks founded and edited the *Southern Review* from 1935 to 1942. Also with Brooks he did a number of anthologies that were instrumental in spreading the New Criticism throughout American universities.

Meanwhile Warren was establishing himself equally as a poet and a novelist. *Selected Poems* (1944) contains the early work, and was followed by *Brother to Dragons* (1953), *Promises* (1957), *You, Emperors, and Others* (1960), *Selected Poems New and Old* (1966), *Incarnations* (1968), and *Audubon: A Vision* (1969). His many novels include *All the King's Men* (1946), *World Enough and Time* (1950), *The Cave* (1959) and *Meet Me in the Green Glen* (1971). There are also *Selected Essays* (1958), and two books on race relations, *Segregation* (1956) and *Who Speaks for the Negro?* (1965). For some years he has been on the faculty at Yale.

Warren's awards include two Guggenheims, Pulitzer prizes in poetry and in fiction, and the Bollingen Prize. In 1924 Allen Tate dedicated a poem to him called "To a Romantic," and Warren's early "metaphysical" manner, full of the tightness and paradox cultivated by the New Criticism, soon gave way to a looser and more emotive expression of Romantic themes: the dilemma of the self facing death in time, the disparity between imagined ideals and experience.

REFERENCE

Cowan, Louise. *The Fugitive Group: A Literary History*. Baton Rouge: Louisiana State University Press, 1959.

Stewart, John L. *The Burden of Time: The Fugitives and Agrarians*. Princeton, N.J.: Princeton University Press, 1965.

Strandberg, Victor. *A Colder Fire: The Poetry of Robert Penn Warren*. Lexington: University of Kentucky Press, 1965.

BEARDED OAKS

The oaks, how subtle and marine,
Bearded, and all the layered light
Above them swims; and thus the scene,
Recessed, awaits the positive night.

5   So, waiting, we in the grass now lie
Beneath the languorous tread of light:
The grasses, kelp-like, satisfy
The nameless motions of the air.

Upon the floor of light, and time,
10   Unmurmuring, of polyp made,
We rest; we are, as light withdraws,
Twin atolls on a shelf of shade.

Ages to our construction went,
Dim architecture, hour by hour:
15   And violence, forgot now, lent
The present stillness all its power.

The storm of noon above us rolled,
Of light the fury, furious gold,
The long drag troubling us, the depth:
20   Dark is unrocking, unrippling, still.

Passion and slaughter, ruth,[1] decay
Descend, minutely whispering down,
Silted down swaying steams, to lay
Foundation for our voicelessness.

25   All our debate is voiceless here,
As all our rage, the rage of stone;
If hope is hopeless, then fearless is fear,
And history is thus undone.

Our feet once wrought the hollow street
30   With echo when the lamps were dead
At windows, once our headlight glare
Disturbed the doe that, leaping, fled.

---

[1]Pity, sorrow.

I do not love you less that now
The caged heart makes iron stroke,
35   Or less that all that light once gave
The graduate[2] dark should now revoke.

We live in time so little time
And we learn all so painfully,
That we may spare this hour's term
40   To practice for eternity.

THE WELL HOUSE

What happened there, it was not much,
But was enough. If you come back,
Not much may be *too much*, even if you have your old knack
Of stillness, and do not touch
5   A thing, a broken toy or rusted tool or any such
Object you happen to find
Hidden where, uncontrolled, grass and weeds bend.

The clematis that latches the door
Of the ruinous well house, you might break it.
10   Though guessing the water foul now, and not thirsting to take it,
With thirst from those years before
You might lean over the coping to stare at the water's dark-glinting
        floor.
Yes, that might be the event
To change *not much* to *too much*, and more than meant.

15   Yes, Truth is always in balance, and
Not much can become *too much* so quick.
Suppose you came back and found your heart suddenly sick,
And covered your sight with your hand:
Your tears might mean more than the thing you wept for but did not
        understand.
20   Yes, something might happen there
If you came back—even if you just stood to stare.

[2]By steps or degrees.

IN ITALIAN THEY CALL THE BIRD CIVETTA[1]

The evening drooped toward owl-call,
The small moon slid pale down the sky,
Dark was decisive in cedars,
But dust down the lane dreamed pale,
5   And my feet stirred that pale dust there—
Ah, I see that Kentucky scene
Now only behind my shut eyelids,
As in this far land I stand
At the selfsame ambiguous hour
10   In the heart's ambiguity,
And Time is crumpled like paper
Crushed in my hand, while here
The thin moon slants pale down the pale sky,
And the small owl mourns from the moat.

15   This small owl calls from the moat now,
And across all the years and miles that
Are the only Truth I have learned,
That other owl answers him;
So back from the present owl-call
20   Burns backward the blaze of Time,
And the passage of years, like a tire's scream,
Fades to nothing while the reply
Of a dew-damp and downy lost throat now
Quavers from that home-dark,
25   To frame, between owl-call and owl-call,
Life's bright parenthesis.
The thin moon slants pale down the pale sky:
The small owl mourns from the moat.

[1]Warren has lived in Italy; hence the continuity and discontinuity of time and place in the poem.

WHAT DAY IS

In Pliny,[1] *Phoenice.* Phoenicians,
Of course. Before that, Celts.
Rome, in the end, as always:
A handful of coins, a late emperor.
5   Hewn stone, footings for what?
Irrigation, but now not easy
To trace a flume-line.[2]

              Later,
Monks, Moors, murderers,
10   The Mediterranean flotsam, not
Excluding the English, they cut
Down olives, plucked vines up, burnt
The chateau.

            All day, cicadas,
15   At the foot of infinity, like
A tree, saw. The sawdust
Of that incessant effort,
Like filings of brass, sun-brilliant,
Heaps up at the tree-foot. That
20   Is what day is.

         Do not
Look too long at the sea, for
That brightness will rinse out your eyeballs.

They will go gray as dead moons.

[1]Roman historian, 23–79 A.D.
[2]The bed of a stream.

WHERE THE SLOW FIG'S PURPLE SLOTH

Where the slow fig's purple sloth
Swells, I sit and meditate the
Nature of the soul, the fig exposes,
To the blaze of afternoon, one haunch
5   As purple-black as Africa, a single
Leaf the rest screens, but through it, light
Burns, and for the fig's bliss
The sun dies, the sun
Has died forever—far, oh far—
10   For the fig's bliss, thus.

         The air
Is motionless, and the fig,
Motionless in that imperial and blunt
Languor of glut, swells, and inward
15   The fibers relax like a sigh in that
Hot darkness, go soft, the air
Is gold.

         When you
Split the fig, you will see
20   Lifting from the coarse and purple seed, its
Flesh like flame, purer
Than blood.

         It fills
The darkening room with light.

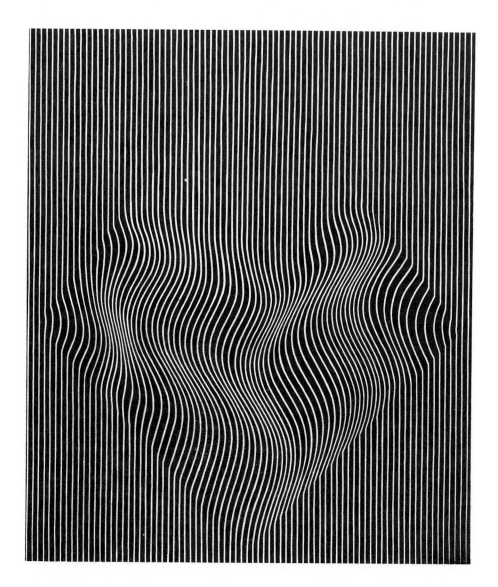

"Obsession," polymer tempera on canvas, 1965, by Julian Stanczak (1928–   ).
(Courtesy of Indianapolis Museum of Art, James E. Roberts Fund)

Part Four

THE CONTEMPORARY SCENE

Many of the poets who have emerged since 1945 have been connected with universities and colleges as teachers of literature or of creative writing. And many of these—for example, J. V. Cunningham, Richard Wilbur, and W. D. Snodgrass—are disciplined craftsmen for whom poetry implies professional mastery of the medium; for them form and technique are not empty exercises in insincerity, but the means to press normally slipshod language at once to the point of clarity and complexity of apprehension. It is also true that some of the most striking developments have come from poet-teachers. For example, Theodore Roethke, Robert Lowell, and John Berryman have moved to a greater freedom of structure and language than their first books indicated: Roethke, in the long psychological sequences strung together on rapid shifts of rhythm and dream-like leaps of imagery; Lowell, in the "confessional poetry" that finds its pattern not through the artifice of metaphors or meter, but through the reconstruction of autobiographical facts; Berryman, through an idiom and syntax so idiosyncratic that it can bear a range of comic and tragic refractions. Yet in these three poets the tendency to defined form has remained strong. To the end Roethke wrote as much in meter as in free verse; Berryman's most eccentric verse established and worked within its own conventions; of his more recent poems Lowell has made a notation that describes many contemporary poems besides his own:

> In the back of my head somewhere I am conscious that rhythm is usually made up of iambics, trochees, anapests and spondees. . . . Usually even in more or less free verse I set down restrictions: stanzas with the same number of lines (most often quatrains), rhymes or off-rhymes sometimes at random, sometimes with a fixed place in the stanza, lines of a more or less uniform length on the page, sometimes lines [that] are accentual and *will* scan, though this is a meter that allows great license, and the accenting of a syllable is often arbitrary.

The major programmatic resistance to the assumptions of academic poetry and criticism came from an academic community itself—at least from its fringes. Charles Olson had gone on from graduate study at Harvard to turn Black Mountain College in North Carolina, largely unknown and now defunct, into a vortex (to use Pound's word) of artistic activity during the fifties; moreover, his essay "Projective Verse" became the manifesto and point of departure for a group of loosely associated poets known now as "the Projectivist School" or "the Black Mountain School." With Pound and Williams in mind, Olson spoke of poetry not as a defined and structured statement, but as an "open field" of energy in motion, directed by the poet through the poem to the reader and spaced out in phrasal units organic to the sensibility and breath of the poet. In capital letters he proclaimed the Emersonian axiom: FORM IS NEVER MORE THAN AN EXTENSION OF CONTENT. For Robert Duncan, too, poetry is "not a fulfillment but a process," so that "my revisions are my new works, each poem a revision of what has gone before. In-sight. Re-vision." Denise Levertov speaks of organic poetry as "a *method of apperception*, that is, of recognizing what we perceive, and is based on an intuition of an order, a form beyond forms, in which forms partake, and of which man's creative works are analogies, resemblances, natural allegories."

The late fifties brought another focus of activity: the sudden emergence of the "Beat Generation," as Jack Kerouac called himself and his friends, coinciding and overlapping with the San Francisco Renaissance. The Beats voiced—none too concisely or articulately, some thought—a resurgent transcendental Idealism against materialistic affluence. Refusing to conform to the American "work ethic," they wandered in search of relationship and enlightenment. Jack Kerouac's "novels" in "spontaneous prose" are his song of the open road, and the visionary impulse of the group, which included Allen Ginsberg, Gary Snyder, Gregory Corso, and Lawrence Ferlinghetti, has become increasingly explicit. Their inspiration came from Williams and Whitman more than from Williams and Pound, and that fact suggests many of the differences in technique between the Beats and the Projectivists.

Associated with the Beats were several figures who preceded them on the California scene: Kenneth Rexroth, the dynamic paterfamilias of San Francisco poets; Robert Duncan; and William Everson (Brother Antoninus), whose free verse concentrated sound and rhythm into a massive rhetoric. The Beats were on the whole not as self-conscious as the Projectivists, not as concerned with describing themselves in the poetic process, but what they shared with the Projectivists is a sense of the immediate connection, almost equivalence, of poetry with one's inner and outer life, and consequently a sense of the poem as oral and oracular.

The rivalry between academic and nonacademic poetry is illustrated by two anthologies that have had wide circulation: *New Poets of England and America*, edited by Donald Hall, Robert Pack, and Louis Simpson, all poet-teachers, which virtually ignored open-form poetry; and Donald Allen's *The New American Poetry*, which included only open-form poetry, bringing together the Beats and the Projectivists with such New York poets as John Ashbery and Frank O'Hara. During the sixties, however, the sense of competition abated. The Projectivists and even some of the Beats found acceptance in the universities. In addition, other issues and factors captured the attention: a great outburst of Black poetry with LeRoi Jones in the vanguard; a new kind of woman poet in Denise Levertov, Adrienne Rich, and Sylvia Plath; a new political commitment in the work of poets as diverse as Lowell, Denise Levertov, Jones, Ginsberg, Ferlinghetti, and Adrienne Rich. But the most important factor was the general shift, in all but the most committed formalists, toward freer form, not just to draw more broadly on the data of lived experience, but also to allow the unconscious fuller play. Adrienne Rich described the change in her own assumptions and responses, but her words convey the prevailing tendency among poets in and out of universities:

> Without for one moment turning my back on conscious choice and selection, I have been increasingly willing to let the unconscious offer its materials, to listen to more than the one voice of a single idea. Perhaps a simple way of putting it would be to say that instead of poems *about* experiences I am getting poems that *are* experiences, that contribute to my knowledge and my emotional life even while they reflect and assimilate it. In my earlier poems I told you, as precisely and eloquently as I knew how, about something; in the more recent poems something is happening, something has happened to me and, if I have been a good parent to the poem, something will happen to you who read it.

This testimonial can stand as a summary and concluding statement about the direction of American poetry in the 1970's. The exact shape of the future is of course unclear. But almost surely the tensions and provisional resolutions, the oppositions and continuities that we have seen take different shapes over three hundred years of development, will provide much of the interest and excitement in the work already under way and in the work yet to be begun.

Theodore Roethke (1908–1963)

Roethke's parents were German immigrants who had settled in Saginaw, Michigan, and his father and uncle owned one of the biggest floral businesses in the state. The memories of these crucial early years inform many of Roethke's poems, especially the "greenhouse poems" at the beginning of *The Lost Son* (1948). That volume fulfilled the promise of *Open House* (1941) and marked Roethke's poetic maturity. He had graduated from the University of Michigan in 1929 and done graduate work at Harvard. He suffered the first of several mental breakdowns just as he was beginning to establish himself as teacher and poet, but he always bounced back with resilient energy. He taught at the University of Washington from 1947 until his death.

The long psychological sequence begun in *The Lost Son* was continued in *Praise to the End!* (1951) and completed in *The Waking* (1953). These open-form poems, which depended on the spontaneities and leaps of unconscious association to trace out the painful development of self-awareness, were archetypal as well as personal. Roethke's later volumes include *Words for the Wind* (1958) and the posthumous *The Far Field* (1964), in which his involvement with nature and with the psyche moved even more explicitly into a religious and mystical dimension. His honors include the Bollingen Prize, the Pulitzer Prize, two National Book Awards, two Guggenheims, and a Fulbright lectureship in Italy. He bought his own editions of Emerson and Thoreau at an early age, and the naturalism and mysticism that were the complementary sources of solace for his tormented spirit had deep American roots.

TEXT

Roethke, Theodore. *Collected Poems.* New York: Doubleday, 1966.

REFERENCE

Malkoff, Karl. *Theodore Roethke: An Introduction to the Poetry.* New York: Columbia University Press, 1966.

Roethke, Theodore. *On the Poet and His Craft: Selected Prose of Theodore Roethke.* Ed. Ralph J. Mills, Jr. Seattle: University of Washington Press, 1965.

Roethke, Theodore. *Selected Letters.* Ed. Ralph J. Mills, Jr. Seattle: University of Washington Press, 1968.

Seager, Allan. *The Glass House: The Life of Theodore Roethke.* New York: McGraw-Hill, 1968.

Theodore Roethke: Essays on the Poetry. Ed. Arnold Stein. Seattle: University of Washington Press, 1965.

CUTTINGS[1]

Sticks-in-a-drowse droop over sugary loam,
Their intricate stem-fur dries;
But still the delicate slips keep coaxing up water;
The small cells bulge;

5 One nub of growth
Nudges a sand-crumb loose,
Pokes through a musty sheath
Its pale tendrilous horn.

CUTTINGS

(later)

This urge, wrestle, resurrection of dry sticks,
Cut stems struggling to put down feet,
What saint strained so much,
Rose on such lopped limbs to a new life?

5 I can hear, underground, that sucking and sobbing,
In my veins, in my bones I feel it,—
The small waters seeping upward,
The tight grains parting at last.
When sprouts break out,
10 Slippery as fish,
I quail, lean to beginnings, sheath-wet.

---

[1]The poems from "Cuttings" through "Frau Bauman, Frau Schmidt, and Frau Schwartze" are from a sequence of "greenhouse poems," recalling Roethke's memories of the floral business that his father and uncle had when he was a boy.

ROOT CELLAR

Nothing would sleep in that cellar, dank as a ditch,
Bulbs broke out of boxes hunting for chinks in the dark,
Shoots dangled and drooped,
Lolling obscenely from mildewed crates,
5 Hung down long yellow evil necks, like tropical snakes.
And what a congress of stinks!—
Roots ripe as old bait,
Pulpy stems, rank, silo-rich,
Leaf-mold, manure, lime, piled against slippery planks.
10 Nothing would give up life:
Even the dirt kept breathing a small breath.

FORCING HOUSE

Vines tougher than wrists
And rubbery shoots,
Scums, mildews, smuts along stems,
Great cannas or delicate cyclamen tips,—[1]
5 All pulse with the knocking pipes
That drip and sweat,
Sweat and drip,
Swelling the roots with steam and stench,
Shooting up lime and dung and ground bones,[2]—
10 Fifty summers in motion at once,
As the live heat billows from pipes and pots.

WEED PULLER

Under the concrete benches,
Hacking at black hairy roots,—
Those lewd monkey-tails hanging from drainholes,—
Digging into the soft rubble underneath,
5 Webs and weeds,

[1]Cannas are tropical plants with broad leaves and bright flowers; cyclamen
are small and delicate plants that like shade and bloom in winter.
[2]Fertilizers.

Grubs and snails and sharp sticks,
Or yanking tough fern-shapes,
Coiled green and thick, like dripping smilax,[1]
Tugging all day at perverse life:
10 The indignity of it!—
With everything blooming above me,
Lilies, pale-pink cyclamen, roses,
Whole fields lovely and inviolate,—
Me down in that fetor of weeds,
15 Crawling on all fours,
Alive, in a slippery grave.

ORCHIDS

They lean over the path,
Adder-mouthed,
Swaying close to the face,
Coming out, soft and deceptive,
5 Limp and damp, delicate as a young bird's tongue;
Their fluttery fledgling lips
Move slowly,
Drawing in the warm air.

And at night,
10 The faint moon falling through whitewashed glass,
The heat going down
So their musky smell comes even stronger,
Drifting down from their mossy cradles:
So many devouring infants!
15 Soft luminescent fingers,
Lips neither dead nor alive,
Loose ghostly mouths
Breathing.

[1]A kind of climbing vine.

MOSS-GATHERING

To loosen with all ten fingers held wide and limber
And lift up a patch, dark-green, the kind for lining cemetery baskets,
Thick and cushiony, like an old-fashioned doormat,
The crumbling small hollow sticks on the underside mixed with
    roots,
5 And wintergreen berries and leaves still stuck to the top,—
That was moss-gathering.
But something always went out of me when I dug loose those
    carpets
Of green, or plunged to my elbows in the spongy yellowish moss of
    the marshes:
And afterwards I always felt mean, jogging back over the logging
    road,
10 As if I had broken the natural order of things in that swampland;
Disturbed some rhythm, old and of vast importance,
By pulling off flesh from the living planet;
As if I had committed, against the whole scheme of life, a desecration.

BIG WIND

Where were the greenhouses going,
Lunging into the lashing
Wind driving water
So far down the river
5 All the faucets stopped?—
So we drained the manure-machine
For the steam plant,
Pumping the stale mixture
Into the rusty boilers,
10 Watching the pressure gauge
Waver over to red,
As the seams hissed
And the live steam
Drove to the far
15 End of the rose-house,
Where the worst wind was,
Creaking the cypress window-frames,
Cracking so much thin glass

We stayed all night,
20   Stuffing the holes with burlap;
But she rode it out,
That old rose-house,
She hove into the teeth of it,
The core and pith of that ugly storm,
25   Ploughing with her stiff prow,
Bucking into the wind-waves
That broke over the whole of her,
Flailing her sides with spray,
Flinging long strings of wet across the roof-top,
30   Finally veering, wearing themselves out, merely
Whistling thinly under the wind-vents;
She sailed until the calm morning,
Carrying her full cargo of roses.

OLD FLORIST

That hump of a man bunching chrysanthemums
Or pinching-back asters, or planting azaleas,
Tamping and stamping dirt into pots,—
How he could flick and pick
5   Rotten leaves or yellowy petals,
Or scoop out a weed close to flourishing roots,
Or make the dust buzz with a light spray,
Or drown a bug in one spit of tobacco juice,
Or fan life into wilted sweet-peas with his hat,
10   Or stand all night watering roses, his feet blue in rubber boots.

TRANSPLANTING

Watching hands transplanting,
Turning and tamping,
Lifting the young plants with two fingers,
Sifting in a palm-full of fresh loam,—
5   One swift movement,—
Then plumping in the bunched roots,
A single twist of the thumbs, a tamping and turning,
All in one,

Quick on the wooden bench,
10   A shaking down, while the stem stays straight,
Once, twice, and a faint third thump,—
Into the flat-box it goes,
Ready for the long days under the sloped glass:

The sun warming the fine loam,
15   The young horns winding and unwinding,
Creaking their thin spines,
The underleaves, the smallest buds
Breaking into nakedness,
The blossoms extending
20   Out into the sweet air,
The whole flower extending outward,
Stretching and reaching.

CHILD ON TOP OF A GREENHOUSE

The wind billowing out the seat of my britches,
My feet crackling splinters of glass and dried putty,
The half-grown chrysanthemums staring up like accusers,
Up through the streaked glass, flashing with sunlight,
5   A few white clouds all rushing eastward,
A line of elms plunging and tossing like horses,
And everyone, everyone pointing up and shouting!

FLOWER DUMP

Cannas shiny as slag,
Slug-soft stems,
Whole beds of bloom pitched on a pile,
Carnations, verbenas, cosmos,[1]
5   Molds, weeds, dead leaves,
Turned-over roots
With bleached veins
Twined like fine hair,
Each clump in the shape of a pot;

[1]A kind of tropical plant with variously colored flowers.

10 Everything limp
But one tulip on top,
One swaggering head
Over the dying, the newly dead.

FRAU BAUMAN,
FRAU SCHMIDT, AND FRAU SCHWARTZE

Gone the three ancient ladies[1]
Who creaked on the greenhouse ladders,
Reaching up white strings
To wind, to wind
5 The sweet-pea tendrils, the smilax,
Nasturtiums, the climbing
Roses, to straighten
Carnations, red
Chrysanthemums; the stiff
10 Stems, jointed like corn,
They tied and tucked,—
These nurses of nobody else.
Quicker than birds, they dipped
Up and sifted the dirt;
15 They sprinkled and shook;
They stood astride pipes,
Their skirts billowing out wide into tents,
Their hands twinkling with wet;
Like witches they flew along rows
20 Keeping creation at ease;
With a tendril for needle
They sewed up the air with a stem;
They teased out the seed that the cold kept asleep,—
All the coils, loops, and whorls.
25 They trellised the sun; they plotted for more than themselves.

I remember how they picked me up, a spindly kid,
Pinching and poking my thin ribs,
Till I lay in their laps, laughing,
Weak as a whiffet;

[1] The three old German women who worked in the floral business become good witches, fairy godmothers, Fates. This poem was added to the "greenhouse poems" and serves as something of a concluding poem.

30   Now, when I'm alone and cold in my bed,
They still hover over me,
These ancient leathery crones,
With their bandannas stiffened with sweat,
And their thorn-bitten wrists,
35   And their snuff-laden breath blowing lightly over me in my first
sleep.

A FIELD OF LIGHT[1]

1

Came to lakes; came to dead water,
Ponds with moss and leaves floating,
Planks sunk in the sand.

A log turned at the touch of a foot;
5   A long weed floated upward;
An eye tilted.

Small winds made
A chilly noise;
The softest cove
10   Cried for sound.

Reached for a grape
And the leaves changed;
A stone's shape
Became a clam.

15   A fine rain fell
On fat leaves;
I was there alone
In a watery drowse.

---

[1]Roethke has described his psychological poems as attempts to render states of mind and feeling "dramatically, without comment, without allusion, the action often implied or indicated in the interior monologue or dialogue between the self and its mentor, or conscience, or, sometimes, another person." He uses various devices of indirection: an instinctive pattern of evolving associations, rapid shifts of metaphor and rhythm, rhetorical questions, and so on.

2

Angel within me, I asked,
20   Did I ever curse the sun?
Speak and abide.

Under, under the sheaves,
Under the blackened leaves,
Behind the green viscid trellis,
25   In the deep grass at the edge of field,
Along the low ground dry only in August,—

Was it dust I was kissing?
A sigh came far.
Alone, I kissed the skin of a stone;
30   Marrow-soft, danced in the sand.

3

The dirt left my hand, visitor.
I could feel the mare's nose.
A path went walking.
The sun glittered on a small rapids.
35   Some morning thing came, beating its wings.
The great elm filled with birds.

Listen, love,
The fat lark sang in the field;
I touched the ground, the ground warmed by the killdeer,[2]
40   The salt laughed and the stones;
The ferns had their ways, and the pulsing lizards,
And the new plants, still awkward in their soil,
The lovely diminutives.
I could watch! I could watch!
45   I saw the separateness of all things!
My heart lifted up with the great grasses;
The weeds believed me, and the nesting birds.
There were clouds making a rout of shapes crossing a
      windbreak of cedars,
And a bee shaking drops from a rain-soaked honeysuckle.
50   The worms were delighted as wrens.
And I walked, I walked through the light air;
I moved with the morning.

[2]A water bird called "killdeer" in imitation of his cry.

FOUR FOR SIR JOHN DAVIES'

1. THE DANCE

Is that dance slowing in the mind of man
That made him think the universe could hum?
The great wheel turns its axle when it can;
I need a place to sing, and dancing-room,
5   And I have made a promise to my ears
I'll sing and whistle romping with the bears.

For they are all my friends: I saw one slide
Down a steep hillside on a cake of ice,—
Or was that in a book? I think with pride:
10   A caged bear rarely does the same thing twice
In the same way: O watch his body sway!—
This animal remembering to be gay.

I tried to fling my shadow at the moon,
The while my blood leaped with a wordless song.
15   Though dancing needs a master, I had none
To teach my toes to listen to my tongue.
But what I learned there, dancing all alone,
Was not the joyless motion of a stone.

I take this cadence from a man named Yeats;
20   I take it, and I give it back again:
For other tunes and other wanton beats
Have tossed my heart and fiddled through my brain.
Yes, I was dancing-mad, and how
That came to be the bears and Yeats would know.

2. THE PARTNER

25   Between such animal and human heat
I find myself perplexed. What is desire?—
The impulse to make someone else complete?
That woman would set sodden straw on fire.

---

¹Roethke described this sequence as "among other things, a tribute to the
Elizabethan author of 'Orchestra' and to the late W. B. Yeats." Sir John
Davies (1569–1626) used the music of the orchestra and the dancing to its
music as a metaphor for the harmony that binds all things into cosmos. Yeats
(1865–1939) is felt here not only in the style but in his own use of the dance
metaphor, for example, in "Among School Children."

Was I the servant of a sovereign wish,
30   Or ladle rattling in an empty dish?

We played a measure with commingled feet:
The lively dead had taught us to be fond.
Who can embrace the body of his fate?
Light altered light along the living ground.
35   She kissed me close, and then did something else.
My marrow beat as wildly as my pulse.

I'd say it to my horse: we live beyond
Our outer skin. Who's whistling up my sleeve?
I see a heron prancing in his pond;
40   I know a dance the elephants believe.
The living all assemble! What's the cue?—
Do what the clumsy partner wants to do!

Things loll and loiter. Who condones the lost?
This joy outleaps the dog. Who cares? Who cares?
45   I gave her kisses back, and woke a ghost.
O what lewd music crept into our ears!
The body and the soul know how to play
In that dark world where gods have lost their way.

3. THE WRAITH

Incomprehensible gaiety and dread[2]
50   Attended what we did. Behind, before,
Lay all the lonely pastures of the dead;
The spirit and the flesh cried out for more.
We two, together, on a darkening day
Took arms against our own obscurity.

55   Did each become the other in that play?
She laughed me out, and then she laughed me in;
In the deep middle of ourselves we lay;
When glory failed, we danced upon a pin.
The valley rocked beneath the granite hill;
60   Our souls looked forth, and the great day stood still.

There was a body, and it cast a spell,—
God pity those but wanton to the knees,—

[2]Yeats' "Lapis Lazuli": "Gaiety transfiguring all that dread."

The flesh can make the spirit visible;
We woke to find the moonlight on our toes.
65 In the rich weather of a dappled wood
We played with dark and light as children should.

What shape leaped forward at the sensual cry?—
Sea-beast or bird flung toward the ravaged shore?
Did space shake off an angel with a sigh?
70 We rose to meet the moon, and saw no more.
It was and was not she, a shape alone,
Impaled on light, and whirling slowly down.

4. THE VIGIL

Dante attained the purgatorial hill,[3]
Trembled at hidden virtue without flaw,
75 Shook with a mighty power beyond his will,—
Did Beatrice deny what Dante saw?
All lovers live by longing, and endure:
Summon a vision and declare it pure.

Though everything's astonishment at last,
80 Who leaps to heaven at a single bound?
The links were soft between us; still, we kissed;
We undid chaos to a curious sound:
The waves broke easy, cried to me in white;
Her look was morning in the dying light.

85 The visible obscures. But who knows when?
Things have their thought: they are the shards of me;
I thought that once, and thought comes round again;
Rapt, we leaned forth with what we could not see.
We danced to shining; mocked before the black
90 And shapeless night made no answer back.

---

[3]In *The Divine Comedy* after emerging from the Inferno, Dante came to the Mount of Purgatory; and after that was allowed to proceed to Paradise, where his guide was Beatrice, the object of his Platonic love, the lady perfect in beauty and virtue and spirituality, now departed but still the image of his ideal.

The world is for the living. Who are they?
We dared the dark to reach the white and warm.
She was the wind when wind was in my way;
Alive at noon, I perished in her form.
95 Who rise from flesh to spirit know the fall:
The word outleaps the world, and light is all.

THE WAKING

I wake to sleep, and take my waking slow.[1]
I feel my fate in what I cannot fear.
I learn by going where I have to go.

We think by feeling. What is there to know?
5 I hear my being dance from ear to ear.
I wake to sleep, and take my waking slow.

Of those so close beside me, which are you?
God bless the Ground! I shall walk softly there,
And learn by going where I have to go.

10 Light takes the Tree; but who can tell us how?
The lowly worm climbs up a winding stair;
I wake to sleep, and take my waking slow.

Great Nature has another thing to do
To you and me; so take the lively air,
15 And, lovely, learn by going where to go.

This shaking keeps me steady. I should know.
What falls away is always. And is near.
I wake to sleep, and take my waking slow.
I learn by going where I have to go.

---

[1]The form of this poem is the villanelle: 19 lines of five tercets and a quatrain, with the first and third lines of the first tercets and joined in the quatrain as the concluding couplet. A favorite form of French, Italian and Provençal poets of the Renaissance.

THE LONGING[1]

1

On things asleep, no balm:
A kingdom of stinks and sighs,
Fetor of cockroaches, dead fish, petroleum,
Worse than castoreum[2] of mink or weasels,
5   Saliva dripping from warm microphones,
Agony of crucifixion on barstools.
    Less and less the illuminated lips,
    Hands active, eyes cherished;
    Happiness left to dogs and children—
10   (Matters only a saint mentions!)
Lust fatigues the soul.
How to transcend this sensual emptiness?
(Dreams drain the spirit if we dream too long.)
In a bleak time, when a week of rain is a year,
15   The slag-heaps fume at the edge of the raw cities:
The gulls wheel over their singular garbage;
The great trees no longer shimmer;
Not even the soot dances.

And the spirit fails to move forward,
20   But shrinks into a half-life, less than itself,
Falls back, a slug, a loose worm
Ready for any crevice,
An eyeless starer.

2

A wretch needs his wretchedness. Yes.
25   O pride, thou art a plume upon whose head?

How comprehensive that felicity! . . .
A body with the motion of a soul.
What dream's enough to breathe in? A dark dream.
The rose exceeds, the rose exceeds us all.
30   Who'd think the moon could pare itself so thin?
A great flame rises from the sunless sea;
The light cries out, and I am there to hear—

[1]The first poem of six in the "North American Sequence," from *The Far Field*.
[2]A smelly brown oil obtained from a gland in the groin of the beaver and related animals, used as a fixative in perfume.

I'd be beyond; I'd be beyond the moon,
Bare as a bud, and naked as a worm.

35 To this extent I'm a stalk.
        —How free; how all alone.
    Out of these nothings
        —All beginnings come.

3

I would with the fish, the blackening salmon, and the mad lemmings,
The children dancing, the flowers widening.
Who sighs from far away?
I would unlearn the lingo of exasperation, all the distortions of
        malice and hatred;
I would believe my pain: and the eye quiet on the growing rose;
I would delight in my hands, the branch singing, altering the exces-
        sive bird;
I long for the imperishable quiet at the heart of form;
I would be a stream, winding between great striated rocks in late
        summer;
A leaf, I would love the leaves, delighting in the redolent disorder
        of this mortal life,
This ambush, this silence,
Where shadow can change into flame,
And the dark be forgotten.
I have left the body of the whale, but the mouth of the night is still
        wide;
On the Bullhead, in the Dakotas, where the eagles eat well,
In the country of few lakes, in the tall buffalo grass at the base of the
        clay buttes,
In the summer heat, I can smell the dead buffalo,
The stench, of their damp fur drying in the sun,
The buffalo chips drying.

    Old men should be explorers?[3]
    I'll be an Indian.
    Ogalala?[4]
    Iroquois.

[3]T. S. Eliot, "East Coker," the second of the *Four Quartets*: "Old men ought to be explorers." The poem is an exploration of history—personal, cultural, and national.
[4]The Ogalala: a tribe of Sioux, who inhabited the Dakotas; the Iroquois, a group of tribes who inhabited an area around the Great Lakes. Here the point seems to be that the Ogalala are associated with the plains; the Iroquois, with water.

THE ROSE[1]

1

There are those to whom place is unimportant,
But this place, where sea and fresh water meet,
Is important—[2]
Where the hawks sway out into the wind,
5   Without a single wingbeat,
And the eagles sail low over the fir trees,
And the gulls cry against the crows
In the curved harbors,
And the tide rises up against the grass
10 Nibbled by sheep and rabbits.

A time for watching the tide,
For the heron's heiratic fishing,
For the sleepy cries of the towhee,[3]
The morning birds gone, the twittering finches,
15 But still the flash of the kingfisher, the wingbeat of the scoter,
The sun a ball of fire coming down over the water,
The last geese crossing against the reflected afterlight,
The moon retreating into a vague cloud-shape
To the cries of the owl, the eerie whooper.
20 The old log subsides with the lessening waves,
And there is silence.

I sway outside myself
Into the darkening currents,
Into the small spillage of driftwood,
25 The waters swirling past the tiny headlands.
Was it here I wore a crown of birds for a moment
While on a far point of the rocks
The light heightened,

---

[1]This is the concluding poem of the "North American Sequence."
[2]The allusions to Eliot's *Four Quartets*, felt through the Sequence, are particularly strong in this poem; Roethke is developing the rose symbolism of the *Quartets*, especially of "Little Gidding," but on his own, different terms. Cf. these lines from "Little Gidding":

> There are other places
> Which also are the world's end, some at the sea jaws,
> Or over a dark lake, in a desert or a city—
> But this [the chapel at Little Gidding] is the nearest, in place and time,
> Now and in England.

[3]The names in these lines are all of birds.

And below, in a mist out of nowhere,
30   The first rain gathered?

2

As when[4] a ship sails with a light wind—
The waves less than the ripples made by rising fish,
The lacelike wrinkles of the wake widening, thinning out,
Sliding away from the traveler's eye,
The prow pitching easily up and down,
The whole ship rolling slightly sideways,
The stern high, dipping like a child's boat in a pond—
Our motion continues.

But this rose, this rose in the sea-wind,
Stays,
Stays in its true place,
Flowering out of the dark,
Widening at high noon, face upward,
A single wild rose, struggling out of the white embrace of the
    morning-glory,
Out of the briary hedge, the tangle of matted underbrush,
Beyond the clover, the ragged hay,
Beyond the sea pine, the oak, the wind-tipped madrona,[5]
Moving with the waves, the undulating driftwood,
Where the slow creek winds down to the black sand of the shore
With its thick grassy scum and crabs scuttling back into their glisten-
    ing craters.

And I think of roses, roses,
White and red, in the wide six-hundred-foot greenhouses,
And my father standing astride the cement benches,
Lifting me high over the four-foot stems, the Mrs. Russels,[6] and
    his own elaborate hybrids,
And how those flowerheads seemed to flow toward me, to beckon
    me, only a child, out of myself.

What need for heaven, then,
With that man, and those roses?

---

[4]Eliot has several elaborate similes in "East Coker" and often develops the
  metaphor of a trip or journey in the *Quartets*.
[5]A tree common in the West.
[6]A kind of rose.

3

What do they tell us, sound and silence?
I think of American sounds in this silence:
60   On the banks of the Tombstone,[7] the wind-harps having their say,
The thrush singing alone, that easy bird,
The killdeer whistling away from me,
The mimetic chortling of the catbird
Down in the corner of the garden, among the raggedy lilacs,
65   The bobolink skirring from a broken fencepost,
The bluebird, lover of holes in old wood, lilting its light song,
And that thin cry, like a needle piercing the ear, the insistent cicada,
And the ticking of snow around oil drums in the Dakotas,
The thin whine of telephone wires in the wind of a Michigan winter,
70   The shriek of nails as old shingles are ripped from the top of a roof,
The bulldozer backing away, the hiss of the sandblaster,
And the deep chorus of horns coming up from the streets in early
        morning.
I return to the twittering of swallows above water,
And that sound, that single sound,
75   When the mind remembers all,
And gently the light enters the sleeping soul,
A sound so thin it could not woo a bird,

Beautiful my desire, and the place of my desire.

I think of the rock singing, and light making its own silence,
80   At the edge of a ripening meadow, in early summer,
The moon lolling in the close elm, a shimmer of silver,
Or that lonely time before the breaking of morning
When the slow freight winds along the edge of the ravaged hillside,
And the wind tries the shape of a tree,
85   While the moon lingers,
And a drop of rain water hangs at the tip of a leaf
Shifting in the wakening sunlight
Like the eye of a new-caught fish.

4

I live with the rocks, their weeds,
90   Their filmy fringes of green, their harsh
Edges, their holes
Cut by the sea-slime, far from the crash

[7]Probably not the Arizona mining town, but the lakes in Oregon.

Of the long swell,
The oily, tar-laden walls
Of the toppling waves,
Where the salmon ease their way into the kelp beds,
And the sea rearranges itself among the small islands.

Near this rose, in this grove of sun-parched, wind-warped madronas,
Among the half-dead trees, I came upon the true ease of myself,
As if another man appeared out of the depths of my being,
And I stood outside myself,
Beyond becoming and perishing,
A something wholly other,
As if I swayed out on the wildest wave alive,
And yet was still.
And I rejoiced in being what I was:
In the lilac change, the white reptilian calm,
In the bird beyond the bough, the single one
With all the air to greet him as he flies,
The dolphin rising from the darkening waves;

And in this rose,[8] this rose in the sea-wind,
Rooted in stone, keeping the whole of light,
Gathering to itself sound and silence—
Mine and the sea-wind's.

IN A DARK TIME

In a dark time, the eye begins to see,
I meet my shadow in the deepening shade;
I hear my echo in the echoing wood—
A lord of nature weeping to a tree.
5 I live between the heron and the wren,
Beasts of the hill and serpents of the den.

What's madness but nobility of soul
At odds with circumstance? The day's on fire!
I know the purity of pure despair,
10 My shadow pinned against a sweating wall.
That place among the rocks—is it a cave,
Or winding path? The edge is what I have.

---

[8]Eliot's rose symbolism culminates in "Little Gidding" in Dante's mystical Rose
at the center of Paradise.

A steady storm of correspondences!
A night flowing with birds, a ragged moon,
15   And in broad day the midnight come again!
A man goes far to find out what he is—
Death of the self in a long, tearless night,
All natural shapes blazing unnatural light.

Dark, dark my light, and darker my desire.
20   My soul, like some heat-maddened summer fly,
Keeps buzzing at the sill. Which I is *I*?
A fallen man, I climb out of my fear.
The mind enters itself, and God the mind,
And one is One, free in the tearing wind.

THE TREE, THE BIRD

Uprose, uprose, the stony fields uprose,
And every snail dipped toward me its pure horn.
The sweet light met me as I walked toward
A small voice calling from a drifting cloud.
5   I was a finger pointing at the moon,
At ease with joy, a self-enchanted man.
Yet when I sighed, I stood outside my life,
A leaf unaltered by the midnight scene,
Part of a tree still dark, still, deathly still,
10   Riding the air, a willow with its kind,
Bearing its life and more, a double sound,
Kin to the wind, and the bleak whistling rain.

The willow with its bird grew loud, grew louder still.
I could not bear its song, that altering
15   With every shift of air, those beating wings,
The lonely buzz behind my midnight eyes;—
How deep the mother-root of that still cry!

The present falls, the present falls away;
How pure the motion of the rising day,
20   The white sea widening on a farther shore.
The bird, the beating bird, extending wings—.[1]
Thus I endure this last pure stretch of joy,
The dire dimension of a final thing.

[1]Cf. the last lines of Wallace Stevens' "Sunday Morning."

Charles Olson (1910–1970)

Olson was born in Worcester, Massachusetts, but the family soon moved to Gloucester. He got an A.B. (1932) and an M.A. (1933) from Harvard, and taught there, and later at Black Mountain College in North Carolina. After becoming rector of Black Mountain in the early fifties, he made the college a center for creative artists. In reaction against academic verse and the New Criticism, Olson's essay "Projective Verse" (1950) became the manifesto of the "Projectivist School": among them, Duncan, Levertov, and Creeley. Developing his principles out of Pound and Williams, Olson saw the poem as an "open field" through which the poet transfers energy from his source to the receptive reader. The measure was not the metered line, but the breath unit of spoken phrases, and the disposition of the poem on the page was an integral part of its dynamic effect. Resisting abstraction, each poem evolved its own realization of the world.

Olson's major books of poetry are: *In Cold Hell, In Thicket* (1953), *The Distances* (1960), *The Maximus Poems* (1960), *Maximus IV, V, VI* (1968) and *Archaeologist of Morning* (1971). From an extended archaeological expedition to Mexico he wrote Creeley *The Mayan Letters* (1953). Other prose includes: *Call Me Ishmael* (1947), an experimental study of Melville, *A Bibliography on America for Ed Dorn* (1964), *The Human Universe and Other Essays* (1965), and *Poetry and Truth* (1971). His robust spontaneity made him a powerhouse on the platform and in the classroom.

Olson taught for several years at the State University of New York at Buffalo, but based himself in Gloucester, which became, as Paterson was for Williams, the geographical ground of reference for a long organic poem with "Maximus" as the shaping consciousness. Creeley edited *Selected Writings* in 1967. Olson's ideas about poetry probably had a more widespread effect on the writing of poetry in America after 1950 than any other single factor.

THE KINGFISHERS[1]

1

What does not change / is the will to change

He woke, fully clothed, in his bed. He
remembered only one thing, the birds, how
when he came in, he had gone around the rooms
5   and got them back in their cage, the green one first,
she with the bad leg, and then the blue,
the one they had hoped was a male

Otherwise? Yes, Fernand, who had talked
                             lispingly of Albers & Angkor Vat.[2]
10   He had left the party without a word.
                             How he got up, got into his coat,
I do not know. When I saw him, he was
                             at the door, but it did not matter,
he was already sliding along the wall of the night, losing himself
15   in some crack of the ruins. That it should have
                             been he who said, "The kingfishers!
who cares
for their feathers
now?"

20   His last words had been, "The pool is slime." Suddenly everyone,
ceasing their talk, sat in a row around him, watched
they did not so much hear, or pay attention, they
wondered, looked at each other, smirked, but listened,
he repeated and repeated, could not go beyond his thought
25   "The pool   the kingfishers' feathers were wealth   why
did the export stop?"

It was then he left

---

[1]A family of birds with crested heads.
[2]Josef Albers (1888–   ): German abstract painter, teaching with Olson at
Black Mountain College. Angkor Vat: an ancient and ruined temple in
Cambodia.

2

I thought of the E on the stone, and of what Mao[3] said
la lumiere"
30   but the kingfisher
de l'aurore"
          but the kingfisher flew west
est devant nous![4]
          he got the color of his breast
35   from the heat of the setting sun!

The features are, the feebleness of the feet
                    (syndactylism[5] of the 3rd & 4th digit)
the bill, serrated, sometimes a pronounced beak, the wings
where the color is, short and round, the tail
40 inconspicuous.

But not these things were the factors. Not the birds.
The legends are
legends. Dead, hung up indoors, the kingfisher
will not indicate a favoring wind,
45 or avert the thunderbolt. Nor, by its nesting,
still the waters, with the new year, for seven days.
It is true, it does nest with the opening
                    year, but not on the waters.
It nests at the end of a tunnel bored by itself in a bank. There,
50 six or eight white and translucent eggs are laid, on fishbones
not on bare clay, on bones thrown up in pellets by the birds.

          On these rejectamenta[6]
(as they accumulate they form a cup-shaped
                    structure) the young are born.
55 And, as they are fed and grow, this
          nest of excrement and decayed fish becomes
                    a dripping, fetid mass

---

[3]Mao Tse-tung (1893–   ): Chinese Communist revolutionary, writer, and
  head of state.
[4]"La lumière de l'aurore est devant nous!": French for "The light of dawn is
  before us!"
[5]Fusion of the digits.
[6]Things rejected or thrown up (literally, thrown back).

Mao concluded:
                    nous devons
60   nous lever
                            et agir!⁷

                              3

When the attentions change / the jungle
leaps in
              even the stones are split
65   they rive

Or,
enter
that other conqueror we more naturally recognize
he so resembles ourselves

70 But the E
cut so rudely on that oldest stone
sounded otherwise,
was differently heard

as, in another time, were treasures used:

75 (and, later, much later, a fine ear thought
a scarlet coat)

                  "of green feathers   feet, beaks and eyes
                  of gold

                  "animals likewise,
80   resembling snails

                  "a large wheel, gold,
                            with figures of unknown four-foots,
                  and worked with tufts of leaves, weight
                  3800 ounces

85   "last, two birds, of thread and featherwork, the quills
                  gold, the feet
                  gold, the two birds perched on two reeds
                  gold, the reeds arising from two embroidered mounds,

⁷French: "We must rouse ourselves and act!"

one yellow, the other
90   white.

"And from each reed hung
seven feathered tassels.

In this instance, the priests
(in dark cotton robes, and dirty,
95 their dishevelled hair matted with blood, and flowing wildly
over their shoulders)
rush in among the people, calling on them
to protect their gods

And all now is war
100 where so lately there was peace,
and the sweet brotherhood, the use
of tilled fields.

4

Not one death but many,
not accumulation but change, the feed-back proves,
105   the feed-back is
the law

Into the same river no man steps twice
When fire dies air dies
No one remains, nor is, one

110 Around an appearance, one common model, we grow up
many. Else how is it,
if we remain the same,
we take pleasure now
in what we did not take pleasure before? love
115 contrary objects? admire and / or find fault? use
other words, feel other passions, have
nor figure, appearance, disposition, tissue
the same?

To be in different states without a change
120   is not a possibility

We can be precise. The factors are
in the animal and / or the machine the factors are

communication and / or control, both involve
the message. And what is the message? The message is
125 a discrete or continuous sequence of measurable
                              events distributed in time

is the birth of air, is
the birth of water, is
a state between
130 the origin and
the end, between
birth and the beginning of
another fetid nest

is change, presents
135 no more than itself

And the too strong grasping of it,
when it is pressed together and condensed,
loses it

This very thing you are

II

140   They buried their dead in a sitting posture
serpent   cane   razor   ray of the sun

And she sprinkled water on the head of the child, crying
"Cioa-coatl! Cioa-coatl!"
with her face to the west

145   Where the bones are found, in each personal heap
with what each enjoyed, there is always
the Mongolian louse

The light is in the east. Yes. And we must rise, act. Yet
in the west, despite the apparent darkness (the whiteness
150 which covers all), if you look, if you can bear, if you can,
                              long enough

as long as it was necessary for him, my guide
to look into the yellow of that longest-lasting rose

so you must, and, in that whiteness, into that face,
155   with what candor, look

and, considering the dryness of the place
        the long absence of an adequate race

                (of the two who first came, each a conquistador,
                                one healed, the other
160   tore the eastern idols down, toppled
        the temple walls, which, says the excuser
        were black from human gore)

hear
hear, where the dry blood talks
165   where the old appetite walks

                        la piu saporita et migliore
                        che si possa truovar al mondo[8]

where it hides, look
in the eye how it runs
170   in the flesh / chalk

                but under these petals
                in the emptiness
                regard the light, contemplate
                the flower

175   whence it arose

                with what violence benevolence is bought
                what cost in gesture justice brings
                what wrongs domestic rights involve
                what stalks
180   this silence

        what pudor pejorocracy affronts
        how awe, night-rest and neighborhood can rot
        what breeds where dirtiness is law
        what crawls
185   below

[8]Italian: "the spiciest and best that can be found in the world."

III

I am no Greek, hath not th'advantage.
And of course, no Roman:
he can take no risk that matters
the risk of beauty least of all.

190   But I have my kin, if for no other reason than
(as he said, next of kin) I commit myself, and,
given my freedom, I'd be a cad
if I didn't. Which is most true.

It works out this way, despite the disadvantage.
195   I offer, in explanation, a quote:
si j'ai du goût, ce n'est guères
que pour la terre et les pierres[9]

Despite the discrepancy (an ocean   courage   age)
this is also true: if I have any taste
200   it is only because I have interested myself
in what was slain in the sun

I pose you your question:

shall you uncover honey / where maggots are?

I hunt among stones

THE DISTANCES

So the distances are Galatea[1]

and one does fall in love and desires
mastery
old Zeus—young Augustus[2]

---

[9]French: "If I have any taste, it is scarcely for anything except the earth and the stones."

[1]A statue made by Pygmalion; he fell in love with her and so ardently begged Aphrodite to bring her to life, that his wish was granted.
[2]Zeus: the chief of the Greek gods on Mount Olympus; Augustus: Gaius Octavius (44 B.C.–14 A.D.), the adopted son of Julius Caesar who became emperor after Caesar's death and adopted the title "Augustus" or "Imperial Majesty."

5 Love knows no distance, no place
                              is that far away or heat changes
          into signals, and control

                  old Zeus—young Augustus

          Death is a loving matter, then, a horror
10   we cannot bide, and avoid
          by greedy life

                      we think all living things are precious
                      —Pygmalions

                              a German inventor in Key West
15 who had a Cuban girl, and kept her, after her death
          in his bed
                              after her family retrieved her
          he stole the body again from the vault

          Torso on torso in either direction,
20   young Augustus
                              out via nothing where messages
          are
              or in, down La Cluny's³ steps to the old man sitting
          a god throned on torsoes,

25   old Zeus

          Sons go there hopefully as though there was a secret, the object
          to undo distance?
                              They huddle there, at the bottom
          of the shaft, against one young bum
30   or two loving cheeks,

                  Augustus?

          You can teach the young nothing
                              all of them go away, Aphrodite
          tricks it out,
35   old Zeus—young Augustus

---

³The ruined Benedictine abbey in the French town of Cluny.

You have love, and no object
                                    or you have all pressed to your nose
which is too close,

        old Zeus hiding in your chin your young
40   Galatea

the girl who makes you weep, and you keep the corpse live by all
your arts

            whose cheek do you stroke when you
                                    stroke the stone face
45   of young Augustus, made for bed in
                            a military camp, o Caesar?

O love who places all where each is, as they are, for every moment,
yield
            to this man
50   that the impossible distance
be healed,
            that young Augustus
            and old Zeus
be enclosed

55   "I wake you,
        stone. Love this man."

from **The Maximus Poems**

LETTER 6

polis[1] is
eyes

            (Moulton cried up that day,
            "Where'd you get those glasses?"
5   after, like a greenhorn,
            I'd picked three swordfish out of the sun-blaze
            where no regular could afford to look,
            to waste his eyes seeking a fin in that place

[1]Greek: city-state.

I have suffered since,
10   from that enthusiasm

            as my heart has never been so good
            as the day I'd be damned if that Englishman,
            and mountain-climber,
            would beat me
15   up the Bright Angel trail
                                I'd been the cannier
            in the descent, had a chocolate bar we all ate
            as we cooled our feet in the Colorado
                                            It was coming up
20   I spent myself, falling face-flat each step I managed,
            flopping in the fine dust which mules,
            wiser & wealthier persons rode,
            had ground the sandstone to)

    It is just such folly is not necessary, yet I have not noticed
25 that those who are sharp haven't got that way
    by pushing their limits
                        (above me,
            when Moulton hollered from the wheel,
            was Burke, humped over the masthead like the ball
30   on top of a weather-pole, he squatting in the canvas strap,
            the rest of us standing in the whale-rope rigging, all of us
            like birds in a cote, and he the leader
            as he well was, he was that good a professional, his eyes
            as a gull's are, or any Portygee's,[2]
35   and the long visor of his cap more of a beak
            than even the same we all wore

    It is of the matter that this Burke on land was a drunk
                                (though, one Sunday,
    I did see him on the wharf with his kids, showing them
40   the vessel, he
    in a blue suit, and the old stiff straw, the only time
                                        I did see him so,
            like the oval portrait hangs
            in so many living rooms
45   not at all the same grace of a man
    came up on deck at sea in oilskins (as Olsen,
                            two days out, would appear

---

[2]Portuguese, known for their sailing ability. Many emigrated to Gloucester
and engaged in the shipping business.

in a new white shirt and new fedora, Hyperion[3]
to the lump his men would have wheeled aboard,
50   at sailing time,
in a barrow)

It makes sense that these men

Burke was raising his family
in a shack out over the marsh,
55   and Olsen, they now tell me,
is carting fish, for Gorton-Pew,
the lowest job, Gloucester,
the job we all started with

young Douglas, who never went to sea,
60   he's different, is in the front office
at Gorton-Pew, was so good a ball player
he got moved up, and fast:

he gave me cans of cooked mackerel,
the last time I was home, "for the ride back"
65   he said, and I couldn't tell him I hate
picnics
                ("pick-nicks," Pound roared[4]
when Con suggested we have fried chicken,
and get him out of S'Liz for the afternoon,
70   eat alongside the tennis courts
out over the Anacostia
                                        I was against it
for another reason, because of the Navy planes
roar in just there, and the chatter of the patients
75   was more to my liking as background
for the great man, in his black coat and wide hat,
                                        the whole man
wagging, the swag
of Pound

---

[3]The sun god.
[4]Ezra Pound was kept at St. Elizabeth's Hospital in Washington, D. C., from 1945 to 1958 after he was found mentally unfit to stand trial for treason for his support of Mussolini and attacks on American policy during World War II. The Anacostia is a river in the District of Columbia joining the Potomac just south of Washington.

80 Eyes,
 & polis,
 fishermen,
 & poets
   or in every human head I've known is
85   busy
 both:
 the attention, and
 the care
   however much each of us
90   choose our own
   kin and
   concentration

     2

And the few—that goes, even inside the major
economics. It is not true that the many,
95 even in fishing, say, Gloucester,
are the gauge
   (where Ferrini,[5] as so many,
   go wrong
so few
100 have the polis
in their eye
   The brilliant Portuguese owners,
   they do. They pour the money back
   into engines, into their ships,
105   whole families do, put it back
   in. They are but extensions of their own careers
   as mastheadsmen—as Burkes

(the day we all stood around on the wharf examining the Laura
Dysart, the gash in her bow, and her foremast snapped off, where
10 the Magellan[6] had piled into her. And Dysart himself telling about
it, the thing still right in front of him, how neither he nor Captain
Rose would give way, both of them coming up on the same fish.

---

[5]Possibly Vincent Ferrini (1913–   ), a New England poet, who wrote a book
called *Sea Spring* (1949), published in Gloucester about sailing and fishing, and
who had earlier written socially concerned poems about the oppression of the
many by the few, as in *Blood of the Tenement* (1944).
[6]Ferdinand Magellan (1480–1521): Portuguese mariner and explorer, com-
mander of the expedition that first sailed around the world; here, a boat in the
Gloucester harbor.

What struck me was, Dysart's admiration, how the Magellan had
overtaken him, from the speed of her Diesels, and he saying he was
115   sure Rose had sighted the fish as soon as he had, aft of him though
she was, those island eyes that very damned good, and he, Dysart,
and his ship, witness to it

So few need to,
to make the many
120   share (to have it,
too)

but those few . . .

What kills me is, how do these others think
the eyes are
125   sharp? by gift? bah   by love of self? try it   by god? ask
the bean sandwich

There are no hierarchies, no infinite,
no such many as mass, there are only
eyes in all heads,
130   to be looked out of

Elizabeth Bishop (1911–   )

The same year as her birth in Worcester, Massachusetts, Elizabeth Bishop's father died and her mother was committed to a mental institution, so that she grew up with her maternal grandparents in Nova Scotia and with an aunt in Boston. Since her graduation from Vassar in 1934 she has traveled a great deal and lived in many places—since 1952 in Brazil. *Poems* (1955) brought together *North & South* (1946) with a new book, *A Cold Spring;* it won a Pulitzer Prize and confirmed her reputation for a keen eye and a craftsman's way with words. *Questions of Travel* (1965) was followed by *Complete Poems* (1969), which won the National Book Award. Her admiration for and her friendship with Marianne Moore are reflected in her precision, at once descriptive and suggestive. But her view of things is much colder and bleaker than Miss Moore's, and the deceptive simplicity and spareness of her style is her own. Poetry is her way of distancing and fixing her observations of the world she inhabits as an alien. without having to draw conclusions about it.

REFERENCE

Mills, Ralph J., Jr. *Contemporary American Poetry.* New York: Random House, 1965.

Stevenson, Anne. *Elizabeth Bishop.* New York: Twayne, 1966.

THE ARMADILLO

FOR ROBERT LOWELL

This is the time of year
when almost every night
the frail, illegal fire balloons appear.
Climbing the mountain height,

5   rising toward a saint
still honored in these parts,[1]
the paper chambers flush and fill with light
that comes and goes, like hearts.

Once up against the sky it's hard
10   to tell them from the stars—
planets, that is—the tinted ones:
Venus going down, or Mars,

or the pale green one. With a wind,
they flare and falter, wobble and toss;
15   but if it's still they steer between
the kite sticks of the Southern Cross,

receding, dwindling, solemnly
and steadily forsaking us,
or, in the downdraft from a peak,
20   suddenly turning dangerous.

Last night another big one fell.
It splattered like an egg of fire
against the cliff behind the house.
The flame ran down. We saw the pair

25   of owls who nest there flying up
and up, their whirling black-and-white
stained bright pink underneath, until
they shrieked up out of sight.

The ancient owls' nest must have burned.
30   Hastily, all alone,

---

[1]Rio de Janeiro.

a glistening armadillo left the scene,
rose-flecked, head down, tail down,

and then a baby rabbit jumped out,
short-eared, to our surprise.
35　So soft!—a handful of intangible ash
with fixed, ignited eyes.

Too pretty, dreamlike mimicry!
O falling fire and piercing cry
and panic, and a weak mailed fist
40　*clenched ignorant against the sky!*

SANDPIPER[1]

The roaring alongside he takes for granted,
and that every so often the world is bound to shake.
He runs, he runs to the south, finical, awkward,
in a state of controlled panic, a student of Blake.[2]

5　The beach hisses like fat. On his left, a sheet
of interrupting water comes and goes
and glazes over his dark and brittle feet.
He runs, he runs straight through it, watching his toes.

—Watching, rather, the spaces of sand between them,
10　where (no detail too small) the Atlantic drains
rapidly backwards and downwards. As he runs,
he stares at the dragging grains.

The world is a mist. And then the world is
minute and vast and clear. The tide
15　is higher or lower. He couldn't tell you which.
His beak is focussed; he is preoccupied,

looking for something, something, something.
Poor bird, he is obsessed!
The millions of grains are black, white, tan, and gray,
20　mixed with quartz grains, rose and amethyst.

[1]A small bird that frequents the seashore and beaches.
[2]William Blake (1757–1827): the English poet considered eccentric for his pro-
phetic visions. "Auguries of Innocence" begins with these famous lines: "To
see a World in a Grain of Sand/And a Heaven in a Wild Flower. . . ."

J. V. Cunningham (1911–   )
James Vincent Cunningham was born in Cumberland, Maryland, but grew up in Denver. After attending the Jesuit college in St. Mary's, Kansas, he went to Stanford University, living for a while in a place behind Yvor Winter's house. He got his A.B. in 1934 and his Ph.D. in 1945. He has taught at various universities, including Stanford and currently Brandeis. Cunningham is the most important of the poets to emerge from Stanford under Winters' influence, but he is closer in temper and technique to Ben Jonson or to Martial than to Winters' somber solemnity. The disciplined compression of his poems enunciates a deep scepticism, now in witty word play, now in the emotional reserve behind the abstract words and grammatical precisions. For Cunningham, rational control is the way to epitomize comment on a world flawed and incapable of transcendence. *Poems and Epigrams* (1971) collects *The Helmsman* (1942), *The Judge Is Fury* (1947), *Doctor Drink* (1950), *The Exclusions of a Rhyme* (1960), *To What Strangers, What Welcome* (1964), and *Aliquid Salis, or Some Salt* (1969). His prose includes: *Woe or Wonder: The Emotional Effect of Shakespeare's Tragedy* (1951), *Tradition and Poetic Structure* (1960), and *The Journal of John Cardan* (1964). Cunningham's verse has been gathered into *Collected Poems and Epigrams* (1971).

REFERENCE
Winters, Yvor. *The Poetry of J. V. Cunningham*. Denver: Swallow, 1961.

DREAM VISION

This dry and lusty wind has stirred all night
The tossing forest of one sleepless tree,
And I in waking vision walked with her
Whose hair hums to the motion of the forest
5   And in the orbit of whose eyelids' fall
The clouds drift slowly from the starry wharves.
I knew her body well but could not speak,
For comprehension is a kind of silence,
The last harmonic of all sound. Europa,
10 Iö, and Danäe:[1] their names are love
Incarnate in the chronicles of love.
I trace their sad initials which thy bark,
Gaunt tree, may line with age but not efface,
And carve her name with mine there. The tree is gnarled
15 And puckered as a child that looks away
And fumbles at the breast—prodigious infant
Still sucking at the haggard teats of time!
Radical[2] change, the root of human woe!

All choice is error, the tragical mistake,
20 And you are mine because I name you mine.
Kiss, then, in pledge of the imponderables
That tilt the balance of eternity
A leaf's weight up and down. Though we must part
While each dawn darkens on the fortunate wheel,
25 The moon will not soften our names cut here
Till every sheltering bird has fled the nest.
They know the wind brings rain, and rain and wind
Will smooth the outlines of our lettering
To the simplicity of epitaph.

---

[1]Three beautiful women loved by Zeus: Europa was possessed by Zeus in the form of a bull; Danäe, by Zeus as a shower of gold; Iö was turned into a white heifer by Hera out of jealousy that Zeus loved her.
[2]Pun: the eytmological root of "radical" is "root."

CHOICE

Allegiance is assigned
Forever when the mind
Chooses and stamps the will.
Thus, I must love you still
5   Through good and ill.

But though we cannot part
We may retract the heart
And build such privacies
As self-regard agrees
10   Conduce to ease.

So manners will repair
The ravage of despair
Which generous love invites,
Preferring quiet nights
15   To vain delights.

FOR MY CONTEMPORARIES

How time reverses
The proud in heart!
I now make verses
Who aimed at art.

5   But I sleep well.
Ambitious boys
Whose big lines swell
With spiritual noise,

Despise me not!
10   And be not queasy
To praise somewhat:
Verse is not easy.

But rage who will.
Time that procured me
15   Good sense and skill
Of madness cured me.

REASON AND NATURE

This pool in a pure frame,
This mirror of the vision of my name,
    Is a fiction
On the unrippled surface of reflection.

5   I see a willowed pool
Where the flies skim. Its angles have no rule.
    In no facet
Is the full vision imaged or implicit.

I've heard, in such a place
10 Narcissus[1] sought the vision of his face.
    If the water
Concealed it, could he, drowning, see it better?

I know both what I see
And what I think, to alter and to be,
15   And the vision
Of this informs that vision of confusion.

RIPENESS IS ALL[1]

Let us not live with Lear—
Not ever at extremes
Of ecstasy and fear,
Joy in what only seems,
5   Rage in the madman's hut
Or on the thunderous hill,
Crying *To kill, to kill!*
Nor in a blind desire
To sire we know not what
10 Ravish the eternal Will.

---

[1]The beautiful youth who was so enamoured of himself, that he embraced his image in the water and plunged to his death by drowning.

[1]Shakespeare's *King Lear* V, ii: After Lear's madness on the heath and in the hut in which he seeks shelter from the storm, and after Lear's capture by his evil daughters' army, Edgar says to his blinded father Gloucester: "Men must endure/Their going hence, even as their coming hither;/Ripeness is all."

APOLOGY

Simplicity assuages
With grace the damaged heart—
So would I in these pages
If will were art.

5 But the best engineer
Of metre, rhyme, and thought
Can only tool each gear
To what he sought

If chance with craft combines
10 In the predestined space
To lend his damaged lines
Redeeming grace.

CONVALESCENCE

I found that consciousness itself betrays
Silence, the fever of my harried days.

In the last circle of infirmity
Where I almost attained simplicity—

5 So to recite as if it were not said,
So to renounce as if one lost instead—

My unabandoned soul withdrew abhorred.
I knew oblivion was its own reward,

But pride is life, and I had longed for death
10 Only in consciousness of indrawn breath.

EPIGRAM

If wisdom, as it seems it is,
Be the recovery of some bliss
From the conditions of disaster—
Terror the servant, man the master—
5   It does not follow we should seek
Crises to prove ourselves unweak.
Much of our lives, God knows, is error,
But who will trifle with unrest?
These fools who would solicit terror,
10   Obsessed with being unobsessed,
Professionals of experience
Who have disasters to withstand them
As if fear never had unmanned them,
Flaunt a presumptuous innocence.

15   I have preferred indifference.

EPIGRAM: NIGHT-PIECE

Three matches in a folder, you and me.
I sit and smoke, and now there's only two,
And one, and none: a small finality
In a continuing world, a thing to do.
5   And you, fast at your book, whose fingers keep
Its single place as you sift down to sleep.

TO MY WIFE

And does the heart grow old? You know
In the indiscriminate green
Of summer or in earliest snow
A landscape is another scene,

5   Inchoate and anonymous,
And every rock and bush and drift

As our affections alter us
Will alter with the season's shift.

So love by love we come at last,
10   As through the exclusions of a rhyme,
Or the exactions of a past,
To the simplicity of time,

The antiquity of grace, where yet
We live in terror and delight
15   With love as quiet as regret
And love like anger in the night.

from **To What Strangers, What Welcome**

8

The night is still. The unfailing surf
In passion and subsidence moves
As at a distance. The glass walls,
And redwood, are my utmost being.
5   And is there there in the last shadow,
There in the final privacies
Of unaccosted grace,—is there,
Gracing the tedium to death,
An intimation? Something much
10   Like love, like loneliness adrowse
In states more primitive than peace,
In the warm wonder of winter sun.

9

Innocent to innocent,
One asked, What is perfect love?
Not knowing it is not love,
Which is imperfect—some kind
5   Of love or other, some kind
Of interchange with wanting,

There when all else is wanting,
Something by which we make do.

So, impaired, uninnocent,
10 If I love you—as I do—
To the very perfection
Of perfect imperfection,
It's that I care more for you
Than for my feeling for you.

10

A half hour for coffee, and at night
An hour or so of unspoken speech,
Hemming a summer dress as the tide
Turns at the right time.

5   Must it be sin,
This consummation of who knows what?
This sharp cry at entrance, once, and twice?
This unfulfilled fulfilment?

                            Something
10 That happens because it must happen.
We live in the given. Consequence,
And lack of consequence, both fail us.
Good is what we can do with evil.

15

Identity, that spectator
Of what he calls himself, that net
And aggregate of energies
In transient combination—some
5 So marginal are they mine? Or is
There mine? I sit in the last warmth
Of a New England fall, and I?

A premise of identity
Where the lost hurries to be lost
10   Both in its own best interests
And in the interests of life.

EPIGRAM: FOR A WOMAN WITH CHILD

We are ourselves but carriers. Life
Incipient grows to separateness
And is its own meaning. Life is,
And not; there is no nothingness.

CONSOLATIO NOVA:[1]
FOR ALAN SWALLOW

To speak of death is to deny it, is
To give unpredicated substance phrase
And being. So the discontinuous,
The present instant absent finally
5   Without future or past, is yet in time
For we are time, monads of purposes
Beyond ourselves that are not purposes,
A causeless all of momentary somes.
And in such fiction we can think of death.

[1]Latin: New consolation. Alan Swallow (1915–1966) was the poet's publisher
and friend.

William Everson (Brother Antoninus)

(1912–   )   Born in Sacramento, California, Everson grew up in the San Joaquin Valley, working as a farmer and rooting himself in nature and in his psychic depths. He had begun publishing pamphlets of his poems before World War II, when his refusal of military service forced him to spend those years in work camps for conscientious objectors, for the longest time at Waldport, Oregon.

The Residual Years (1948) brought a Guggenheim. In 1949 Everson converted to Catholicism, and two years later he became a Dominican lay brother as Brother Antoninus. Previously associated with Kenneth Rexroth in the San Francisco poetry scene, Antoninus emerged again with the Beat poets in the late fifties. A much enlarged Residual Years (1968) gathers all the pre-Catholic poetry of Everson, and the later volumes include: The Crooked Lines of God (1959), The Hazards of Holiness (1962), The Rose of Solitude (1967), and The Last Crusade (1969). After the death of his early master, Robinson Jeffers, he wrote an elegy, The Poet Is Dead (1964), and a critical book, Robinson Jeffers: Fragments of an Older Fury (1968). Everson left the Dominican Order in 1969, and now lives with his wife near San Francisco.

Everson's vision is mystical and erotic; he has assimilated Whitman's bardic power, Jeffers' pantheism, Lawrence's sexual life force, Jung's psychology of the unconscious, and Christian incarnational theology; and his poems are the bold record of his attempts to resolve the dislocations within himself so that he can surrender to love human and divine.

REFERENCE

"A Conversation with Brother Antoninus." Harvard Advocate Centennial Anthology. Ed. Jonathan Culler. Cambridge, Mass.: Schenkman Publishing Co., 1966.

Gelpi, Albert J. "The Rose of Solitude." Harvard Advocate, CII (March 1968).

Mills, Ralph J. Jr. Contemporary American Poetry. New York: Random House, 1965.

WE IN THE FIELDS

Dawn and a high film; the sun burned it;
But noon had a thick sheet, and the clouds coming,
The low rain-bringers, trooping in from the north,
From the far cold fog-breeding seas, the womb of the storms.
5 Dusk brought a wind and the sky opened:
All down the west the broken strips lay snared in the light,
Bellied and humped and heaped on the hills.
The set sun threw the blaze up;
The sky lived redly, banner on banner of far-burning flame,
10 From south to the north the furnace door wide and the smoke
    rolling.
We in the fields, the watchers from the burnt slope,
Facing the west, facing the bright sky, hopelessly longing to know
    the red beauty—
But the unable eyes, the too-small intelligence,
The insufficient organs of reception
15 Not a thousandth part enough to take and retain.
We stared, and no speaking, and felt the deep loneness of incom-
    prehension.
The flesh must turn cloud, the spirit, air,
Transformation to sky and the burning,
Absolute oneness with the west and the down sun.
20 But we, being earth-stuck, watched from the fields,
Till the rising rim shut out the light;
Till the sky changed, the long wounds healed;
Till the rain fell.

AUGUST

Smoke-color; haze thinly over the hills, low hanging;
But the sky steel, the sky shiny as steel, and the sun shouting.
The vineyard: in August the green-deep and heat-loving vines
Without motion grow heavy with grapes.
5 And he in the shining, on the turned earth, loose-lying,
The muscles clean and the limbs golden, turns to the sun the lips
    and the eyes;
As the virgin yields, impersonally passionate,
From the bone core and the aching flesh, the offering.

He has found the power and come to the glory.
10   He has turned clean-hearted to the last God, the symbolic sun.
With earth on his hands, bearing shoulder and arm the light's touch,
    he has come.
And having seen, the mind loosens, the nerve lengthens,
All the haunting abstractions slip free and are gone;
And the peace is enormous.

BARD

Sing it. Utter the phrase, the fine word.
Make the syllables shout on the page,
The letters form till the line glows and is ringing.
Pursue the illusion. It is sweet to the heart
5   To think of them listening, to think of them
Thumbing the leaves, the eyes avidly drinking.

You have in your nights the dreams of the older years:
Hearth-side bards in the great halls, singing,
Shouting the tale, chanting the lusty word and the rhyme,
10   While the warriors stared, the women hushed and not breathing.

It is fine for the heart to think of oneself as the Voice,
The Pointer of Ways.
It is warm in the chest to think of them listening.
Sing the phrase and fashion the line;
15   Hug the sweet dream in the lonely dusks when the far planes whine
    in the sky and the west deadens.
It is good to the heart, it is fine in the chest to think of them listening.

LAVA BED

Fisted, bitten by blizzards,
Flattened by wind and chewed by all weather,
The lava bed lay.
Deer fashioned trails there but no man, ever;
5   And the fugitive cougars whelped in that lair.
Deep in its waste the buzzards went down to some innominate[1] kill.

[1]Unnamed.

The sun fell in it,
And took the whole west down as it died.
Dense as the sea,
10 Entrenched in its years of unyielding rebuff,
It held to its own.
We looked in against anger,
Beholding that which our cunning had never subdued,
Our power indented,
15 And only our eyes had traversed.

THE RAID

They came out of the sun undetected,
Who had lain in the thin ships
All night long on the cold ocean,
Watched Vega down, the Wain hover,[1]
5 Drank in the weakening dawn their brew,
And sent the lumbering death-laden birds
Level along the decks.

They came out of the sun with their guns geared,
Saw the soft and easy shape of that island
10 Laid on the sea,
An unwakening woman,
Its deep hollows and its flowing folds
Veiled in the garlands of its morning mists.

Each of them held in his aching eyes the erotic image,
15 And then tipped down,
In the target's trance,
In the ageless instant of the long descent,
And saw sweet chaos blossom below,
And felt in that flower the years release.

20 The perfect achievement.
They went back toward the sun crazy with joy,
Like wild birds weaving,
Drunkenly stunting;

[1]Vega: the brighter star in the constellation Lyra (the Lyre). The Wain: another name for the Big Dipper because of its resemblance to a wagon as well; here also punning on "wane."

Passed out over edge of that injured island,
25 Sought the rendezvous on the open sea
Where the ships would be waiting.

None were there.
Neither smoke nor smudge;
Neither spar nor splice nor rolling raft.
30 Only the wide waiting waste,
That each of them saw with intenser sight
Than he ever had spared it,
Who circled that spot,
The spent gauge caught in its final flutter,
35 And straggled down on their wavering wings
From the vast sky,
From the endless spaces,
Down at last for the low hover,
And the short quick quench of the sea.

A CANTICLE TO THE WATERBIRDS

Written for the Feast of Saint Francis of Assisi, 1950

Clack your beaks you cormorants and kittiwakes,[1]
North on those rock-croppings finger-jutted into the rough Pacific
    surge;
You migratory terns and pipers who leave but the temporal clawtrack
    written on sandbars there of your presence;
Grebes and pelicans; you comber-picking scoters and you shorelong
    gulls;
5 All you keepers of the coastline north of here to the Mendocino
    beaches;
All you beyond the cliff-face thwarting the surf at Hecate Head;
Hovering the under-surge where the cold Columbia grapples at the
    bar;
North yet to the Sound, whose islands float like a sown flurry of
    chips upon the sea:
Break wide your harsh and salt-encrusted beaks unmade for song
10 And say a praise up to the Lord.

[1]All the birds named are waterbirds of the Pacific coast, as the geographical
references range north through California to the Pacific Northwest, the Colum-
bia River, and Puget Sound.

And you freshwater egrets east in the flooded marshlands skirting
 the sea-level rivers, white one-legged watchers of shallows;
Broad-headed kingfishers minnow-hunting from willow stems on
 meandering valley sloughs;
You too, you herons, blue and supple-throated, stately, taking the
 air majestical in the sunflooded San Joaquin,[2]
Grading down on your belted wings from the upper lights of sunset,
15 Mating over the willow clumps or where the flatwater rice fields
 shimmer;
You killdeer, high night-criers, far in the moon-suffusion sky;
Bitterns, sand-waters, all shore-walkers, all roost-keepers,
Populates of the 'dobe cliffs of the Sacramento:
Open your water-dartling beaks,
20 And make a praise up to the Lord.

For you hold the heart of His mighty fastnesses,
And shape the life of His indeterminate realms.
You are everywhere on the lonesome shores of His wide creation.
You keep seclusion where no man may go, giving Him praise;
25 Nor may a woman come to lift like your cleaving flight her clear
 contralto song
To honor the spindrift[3] gifts of His soft abundance.
You sanctify His hermitage rocks where no holy priest may kneel to
 adore, nor holy nun assist;
And where his true communion-keepers are not enabled to enter.

And well may you say His praises, birds, for your ways
30 Are verved with the secret skills of His inclinations,
And your habits plaited and rare with the subdued elaboration of
 His intricate craft;
Your days intent with the direct astuteness needful for His out-
 working,
And your nights alive with the dense repose of His infinite sleep.
You are His secretive charges and you serve His secretive ends,
35 In His clouded mist-conditional stations, in His murk,
Obscure in your matted nestings, immured in His limitless ranges.
He makes you penetrate through dark interstitial[4] joinings of His
 thicketed kingdoms,
And keep your concourse in the deeps of His shadowed world.

---

[2]A river in California flowing from the Sierra Nevada Mountains to the sea,
joining the Sacramento River near its mouth.
[3]Sea spray.
[4]With spaces between individual things or parts.

Your ways are wild but earnest, your manners grave,
Your customs carefully schooled to the note of His serious mien.[5]
You hold the prime conditions of His clean creating,
And the swift compliance with which you serve His minor means
Speaks of the constancy with which you hold Him.
For what is your high flight forever going home to your first
    beginnings,
But such a testament to your devotion?
You hold His outstretched world beneath your wings, and mount
    upon His storms,
And keep your sheer wind-lidded sight upon the vast perspectives of
    His mazy latitudes.

But mostly it is your way you bear existence wholly within the con-
    text of His utter will and are untroubled.
Day upon day you do not reckon, nor scrutinize tomorrow, nor
    multiply the nightfalls with a rash concern,
But rather assume each instant as warrant sufficient of His final seal.
Wholly in Providence you spring, and when you die you look on
    death in clarity unflinched,
Go down, a clutch of feather ragged upon the brush;
Or drop on water where you briefly lived, found food,
And now yourselves made food for His deep current-keeping fish,
    and then are gone:
Is left but the pinion-feather spinning a bit on the uproil
Where lately the dorsal cut clear air.

You leave a silence. And this for you suffices, who are not of the
    ceremonials of man,
And hence are not made sad to now forgo them.
Yours is of another order of being, and wholly it compels.
But may you, birds, utterly seized in God's supremacy,
Austerely living under His austere eye—
Yet may you teach a man a necessary thing to know,
Which has to do of the strict conformity that creaturehood entails,
And constitutes the prime commitment all things share.
For God has given you the imponderable grace to *be* His verification,
Outside the mulled incertitude of our forensic[6] choices;
That you, our lessers in the rich hegemony[7] of Being,
May serve as testament to what a creature is,
And what creation owes.

[5]Bearing, manner.
[6]Consisting in argument and debate.
[7]Order by rule or predominance.

70 Curlews, stilts and scissortails, beachcomber gulls,
Wave-haunters, shore-keepers, rockhead-holders, all cape-top vigi-
    lantes,
Now give God praise.
Send up the articulation of your throats,
And say His name.

THE SOUTH COAST

Salt creek mouths unflushed by the sea
And the long day shuts down.
Whose hand stacks rock, cairn-posted,
Churched to the folded sole of this hill,
5 And Whose mind conceives? Three herons
Gig their necks in the tule[1] brake
And the prying mudhen plies.
Long down, far south to Sur,[2] the wind lags,
Slosh-washes his slow heel,
10 Lays off our coast, rump of the domed
Mountain, woman-backed, bedded
Under his lea.[3] Salt grasses here,
Fringes, twigging the crevice slips,[4]
And the gagging cypress
15 Wracked[5] away from the sea.
God *makes.* On earth, in us, most instantly,
On the very now,
His own means conceives.
How many strengths break out unchoked
20 Where He, Whom all declares,
Delights to make be!

[1]Bulrushes.
[2]A promontory on the California coast.
[3]Lea: meadow.
[4]Crevasses or faults in rock.
[5]Ruined, wrecked; here referring to the sea drift, whose motion makes for the
choking or retching movement of the cypress.

THE POET IS DEAD

A Memorial for Robinson Jeffers

To be read with a full stop between the strophes, as in a dirge.

In the evening the dusk
Stipples with lights. The long shore
Gathers darkness in on itself
And goes cold. From the lap of silence
5   All the tide-crest's pivotal immensity
Lifts into the land.

●

The great tongue is dried.
The teeth that bit the bitterness
Are sheathed in truth.

●

10   For the poet is dead.
The pen, splintered on the sheer
Excesses of vision, unfingered, falls.
The heart-crookt hand, cold as a stone,
Lets it go down.

●

15   If you listen
You can hear the field mice
Kick little spurts in the grasses.
You can hear
Time take back its own.

●

20   For the poet is dead.
On the bed by the window,[1]
Where dislike and desire
Killed each other in the crystalline interest,
What remains alone lets go of its light. It has found
25   Finalness. It has touched what it craved: the passionate
Darks of deliverance.

●

At sundown the sea wind,
Burgeoning,
Bled the west empty.

[1]See Jeffers' poem "The Bed by the Window."

●

30   Now the opulent
Treacherous woman called Life
Forsakes her claim. Blond and a harlot
She once drank joy from his narrow loins.[2]
She broke his virtue in her knees.

●

35   In the water-gnawn coves of Point Lobos[3]
The white-faced sea otters
Fold their paws on their velvet breasts
And list waveward.

●

But he healed his pain on the wisdom of stone,
40   He touched roots for his peace.

●

The old ocean boils its wrack,
It steeps its lees.

●

For the poet is dead. The gaunt wolf
Crawled out to the edge and died snapping.[4]
45   He said he would. The wolf
Who lost his mate. He said he would carry the wound,
The blood-wound of life, to the broken edge
And die grinning.

●

Over the salt marsh the killdeer,[5]
50   Unrestrainable,
Cry fear against moon set.

●

And all the hardly suspected
Latencies of disintegration
Inch forward. The skin
55   Flakes loss. On the death-gripped feet
The toenails glint like eyeteeth
From the pinched flesh.
The caged ribs and the bladed shoulders,
Ancient slopes of containment,
60   Imperceptibly define the shelves of structure,
Faced like rock ridges

---

[2]See Jeffers' poem "Post Mortem."
[3]A promontory just south of Carmel, California, where Jeffers lived.
[4]See Jeffers' poem "The Deer Lay Down Their Bones."
[5]Waterbirds, called "killdeer" for their cry.

Boned out of mountains, absently revealed
With the going of the snow.

●

In the sleeve of darkness the gopher
65   Tunnels the sod for short grass
And pockets his fill.

●

And the great phallus shrinks in the groin,
The seed in the scrotum
Chills.

●

70   When the dawn comes in again,
Thoughtlessly,
The sea birds will mew by the window.

●

For the poet is dead. Beyond the courtyard
The ocean at full tide hunches its bulk.
75   Groping among the out-thrusts of granite
It moans and whimpers. In the phosphorescent
Restlessness it chunks deceptively,
Wagging its torn appendages, dipping and rinsing
Its ripped sea rags, its strip-weeded kelp.
80   The old mother grieves her deathling.
She trundles the dark for her lost child.
She hunts her son.

●

On the top of the tower[6]
The hawk will not perch tomorrow.

●

85   But in the gorged rivermouth
Already the steelhead[7] fight for entry.
They feel fresh water
Sting through the sieves of their salt-coarsened gills.
They shudder and thrust.

●

90   So the sea broods. And the aged gull,
Asleep on the water, too stiff to feed,
Spins in a side-rip crossing the surf
And drags down.

●

---

[6]Hawk Tower, which Jeffers built from the stone of the Carmel Beach, as he did
Tor House. The house and adjacent tower overlook the sea.
[7]Marine trout.

This mouth is shut. I say
95   The mouth is clamped cold.
I tell you this tongue is dried.

•

But the skull, the skull,
The perfect sculpture of bone!—
Around the forehead the fine hair,
100   Composed to the severest
Lineaments of thought,
Is moulded on peace.

•

And the strongly wrought features,
That keep in the soul's serenest achievement
105   The spirit's virtue,
Set the death mask of all mortality,
The impress of that grace.

•

In the shoal-champed breakers
One wing of the gull
110   Tilts like a fin through the ribbon of spume
And knifes under.

•

And all about there the vastness of night
Affirms its sovereignty. There's not a cliff
Of the coastline, not a reef
115   Of the waterways, from the sword-thrust Aleutians
To the scorpion-tailed stinger Cape Horn—
All that staggering declivity
Grasped in the visionary mind and established—
But is sunken under the dark ordainment,
120   Like a sleeper possessed, like a man
Gone under, like a powerful swimmer
Plunged in a womb-death washed out to sea
And worked back ashore.

•

The gull's eye,
125   Skinned to the wave, retains the ocean's
Imponderable compression,
And burns yellow.

•

The poet is dead. I tell you
The nostrils are narrowed. I say again and again
130   The strong tongue is broken.

•

But the owl
Quirks in the cypresses, and you hear
What he says. He is calling for something.
He tucks his head for his mate's
135 Immemorial whisper. In her answering voice
He tastes the grace-note of his reprieve.

●

If there is fog in the canyons
The redwoods will know what it means.
The giant sisters
140 Gather it into their merciful arms
And stroke silence.

●

When you smell pine resin laced in the salt
You know the dawn wind has veered.

●

And on the shelf in the gloom,
145 Blended together, the tall books emerge,
All of a piece. Transparent as membranes
The thin leaves of paper hug their dark thoughts.
They know what he said.

●

The sea, reaching for life,
150 Spits up the gull. He falls spread-eagled,
The streaked wings swept on the sand.
When the blind head snaps
The beak krakes at the sky.

●

Now the night closes.
155 All the dark's negatory[8]
Decentralization
Quivers toward dawn.

●

He has gone into death like a stone thrown in the sea.

●

And in far places the morning
160 Shrills its episodes of triviality and vice
And one man's passing. Could the ears
That hardly listened in life
Care much less now?

●

The great tongue

---

[8] A coinage for "negative."

165 Dries in the mouth. I told you.
The voiceless throat
Cools silence. And the sea-granite eyes.
Washed in the sibilant waters
The stretched lips kiss peace.

●

170 The poet is dead.

●

Nor will ever again hear the sea lions
Grunt in the kelp at Point Lobos.
Nor look to the south when the grunion[9]
Run the Pacific, and the plunging
175 Shearwaters,[10] insatiable,
Stun themselves in the sea.

IN ALL THESE ACTS

Cleave the wood and thou shalt find Me, lift the rock and I am there!
                                    —The Gospel According to Thomas[1]

Dawn cried out: the brutal voice of a bird
Flattened the seaglaze. Treading that surf
Hunch-headed fishers[2] toed small agates,
Their delicate legs, iridescent, stilting the ripples.
5 Suddenly the cloud closed. They heard the big wind
Boom back on the cliff, crunch timber over along the ridge.
They shook up their wings, crying; terror flustered their pinions.
Then hemlock, tall, torn by the roots, went crazily down,
The staggering gyrations of splintered kindling.
10 Flung out of bracken, fleet mule deer[3] bolted;
But the great elk, caught midway between two scissoring logs,
Arched belly-up and died, the snapped spine
Half torn out of his peeled back, his hind legs
Jerking that gasped convulsion, the kick of spasmed life,
15 Paunch plowed open, purple entrails
Disgorged from the basketwork ribs

[9]Small fish who move in schools and during spring high tides at the full of the
moon rush up on the Pacific beaches to spawn.
[10]Oceanic birds, which skim along the waves and feed in the sea.

[1]One of the apocryphal Gospels.
[2]Kingfishers, a family of crested birds.
[3]Also called "black-tailed deer."

Erupting out, splashed sideways, wrapping him,
Gouted in blood, flecked with the brittle sliver of bone.
Frenzied, the terrible head
20 Thrashed off its antlered fuzz in that rubble
And then fell still, the great tongue
That had bugled in rut, calling the cow-elk up from glades,
Thrust agonized out, the maimed member
Bloodily stiff in the stone-smashed teeth . . .

25   Far down below,
The mountain torrent, that once having started
Could never be stopped, scooped up that avalanchial wrack
And strung it along, a riddle of bubble and littered duff
Spun down its thread. At the gorged river mouth
30 The sea plunged violently in, gasping its potholes,
Sucked and panted, answering itself in its spume.
The river, spent at last, beating driftwood up and down
In a frenzy of capitulation, pumped out its life,
Destroying itself in the mother sea,
35 There where the mammoth sea-grown salmon
Lurk immemorial, roe in their hulls, about to begin.
They will beat that barbarous beauty out
On those high-stacked shallows, those headwater claims,
Back where they were born. Along that upward-racing trek
40 Time springs through all its loops and flanges,[4]
The many-faced splendor and the music of the leaf,
The copulation of beasts and the watery laughter of drakes,
Too few the grave witnesses, the wakeful, vengeful beauty,
Devolving itself of its whole constraint,
45 Erupting as it goes.

            In all these acts
Christ crouches and seethes, pitched forward
On the crucifying stroke, juvescent,[5] that will spring Him
Out of the germ, out of the belly of the dying buck,
50 Out of the father-phallus and the torn-up root.
These are the modes of His forth-showing,
His serene agonization. In the clicking teeth of otters
Over and over He dies and is born,
Shaping the weasel's jaw in His leap
55 And the staggering rush of the bass.

[4]An edge or rim on a wheel or pipe.
[5]T. S. Eliot, "Gerontion": The speaker says, "In the juvescence of the year/
Came Christ the tiger. . . . The tiger springs in the new year. Us he devours."

THE SONG THE BODY
DREAMED IN THE SPIRIT'S MAD BEHEST

I am black but beautiful, O ye daughters of
Jerusalem. Look not upon me because I
am black, because the Sun has looked upon me.
                    —THE CANTICLE OF CANTICLES

The Imagination, unable to grasp the reality
of pure Spirit, conceives of their union
under the modality of her own nature. Longing
to respond totally to the divine summons,
and convinced in faith that the Redemption has
rendered this possible, she struggles to
cast off all the inhibitions of original sin, and
evokes the deepest resources of her sensuality,
in order to achieve in shamelessness
the wholeness of being an age of shame has
rendered incomplete.

Call Him the Lover and call me the Bride.
Lapsing upon the couch of His repose
I heard the elemental waters rise,
Divide and close.

5   I heard Him tremble and I turned my head.
Behold, the pitiless fondness in His eyes;
Dark, the rapacious terror of the heart
In orgy cries.

His eyes upon me wanton into life
10   What has slept long and never known the surge;
Bequeath an excess spilt of the blood's delight,
And the heart's purge.

His lips have garnished fruits out of my breast
That maddens Him to forage on my throat,
15   Moan against my dread the finite pang
Of the soul's gloat.

He is the Spirit but I am the Flesh.
Out of my body must He be reborn,
Soul from the sundered soul, Creation's gout[1]
20   In the world's bourn.[2]

---

[1]Clot, blob.
[2]Term, bounds, limits.

Mounted between the thermals[3] of my thighs
Hawklike He hovers surging at the sun,
And feathers me a frenzy ringed around
That deep drunk tongue.

25   The Seal is broken and the Blood is gushed.
He does not check but boldens in His pace.
The fierce mouth has beaked out both my eyes,
And signed my face.

His tidal strength within me shores and brunts,
30   The ooze of oil, the slaver of the bitch,
The bull's gore, the stallion's famished gnash,
And the snake's itch.

Grit of great rivers boasting to the sea,
Geysers in spume, islands that leveled lie,
35   One snow-peak agonized against the bleak
Inviolate sky.

Folding Him in the chaos of my loins
I pierce through armies tossed upon my breast,
Envelop in love's tidal dredge of faith
40   His huge unrest.

But drifting into depth that what might cease
May be prolonged until a night is lost,
We starve the splendor lapsing in the loins,
Curb its great cost.

45   Mouthless we grope for meaning in that void
That melds[4] between us from our listening blood,
While passion throbs the chopped cacophony
Of our strange good.

Proving what instinct sobs of total quest
50   When shapeless thunder stretches into life,
And the Spirit, bleeding, rears to overreach
The buttocks' strife.

---

[3]Adjective used here as noun to indicate something hot and heated.
[4]Blends.

That will be how we lose what we have gained,
The incremental rapture at the core,
55   Spleened[5] of the belly's thick placental[6] wrath,
And the seed's roar.

Born and reborn we will be groped, be clenched
On ecstasies that shudder toward the crude birth,
When His great Godhead peels its stripping strength
60   In my red earth.

THE ROSE OF SOLITUDE

Her heart a bruise on the Christ-flesh suffered out of locked agonies
    of rebirth.
Her soul fierced inward upon the extravagant passion of woman cut
    between somber and radiant choices.
Her lips panting the Name of God as she thrusts out the tip of her
    tongue for one more drop of his nerving grace.

Solitary Rose! What wall could entomb her? She is all polish and
    ecstasy.
5   She is all passion, all fire and devotion. She is all woman, in love of
    God bitten by the rapture of God.
She sounds through my mind thirsting the inconceivable excellence
    of Christ.
I hear her feet like rain-clashes run the flat streets to do His will.

All ache. Her heart the glorified Wound. Her soul curls back on its
    pang as the toes of the Christ clutched back on that Nail.
In the stigmata[1] of His gaze her love coils like the flesh on its iron,
    the love-ache of the opening.
10   When she utters the Holy Name you could never doubt God died
    for the love of man.

---

[5]"Spleen" used as a past participle to mean "done or made with spleen, taken
as the seat of bitterness and bad temper in the body."
[6]The placenta is a membrane that develops in the womb of mammals during
pregnancy; it nourishes the fetus in the womb and is expelled as afterbirth.

---

[1]The marks of Jesus' crucifixion wounds, sometimes conferred on saints in an
extreme state of ecstatic or mystical identification with the crucified Jesus.

Solitary Rose! Unspeakable primacy! The masked and dangerous
    glint of implication!
The gleam of death in the knives of her desire! The crescendos
    thirsted in the strings of her passion!
I have seen in her eyes destinies expand and race out beyond the
    apogees[2] of perfection!

She catches them all! Birds beak for her! In the click of her teeth she
    bites little pieces!
15 Dance! Dance! Never stint that torrential heart, girl and mother,
    holy immolation,
Free as none else of the vice of the self: that narrow hoard of
    unbroachable stinkings!
In the lift of her head earth glints and sparkles! The seethe of her
    voice is pure as the ecstasy of fire in ice!

Solitary Rose! The Spanish pride! The Aztec death! The Mexican
    passion! The American hope!
Woman of the Christ-hurt aching in moan! God-thirster! Beautiful
    inviolable well-deep of passion!
20 In the fiercest extravagant love is the tangible source of all wisdom!
In the sprint of your exquisite flesh is evinced the awesome reckless-
    ness of God's mercy!

THE VISION OF FELICITY

       And the terrible
       Pang of the heart unhinged,
       Bereft of its sources.

       Out of the smashed
5   Light; out of the hard
       Unmalleable, abstract
       Ferocity of the streets;

       Out of the depraved
       Human face, horribly
10   Emptied of its beatitude—

---

[2]The point in the orbit of a satellite or moon when it is farthest from the earth.

I behold. I behold.

I behold the vision of felicity
And the insuperable human grace.

As one who after mindless torment
15 Sees surcease in the smile of gratitude,
The plenitude of peace.

Give me my love!
This cry, this cruciform.[1]

Give me back the beauty!

20 Give me my ache of love
Out of this emptiness!

From the belled
Hell, from the brass
Inferno:

25 Give me the center back
Of my soul!

New York City

---

[1]The form of a cross.

John Berryman (1914–1972)

Berryman was born in McAlester, Oklahoma, but the family moved to Florida, where his banker-father killed himself when the boy was twelve. After that the family settled in New York. With degrees from Columbia and from Clare College, Cambridge, he taught at various universities, including Harvard, Princeton, and finally Minnesota. His early writing in *The Dispossessed* (1948) contains some good poems, but is chiefly interesting as a preparation for his two long masterworks: *Homage to Mistress Bradstreet* (1956), a love poem for the first American poet that evokes her with great historical and imaginative force as a foil and inspiration to Berryman's modern *angst*; and *The Dream Songs* (1969), which put together *77 Dream Songs* (1964) and *His Toy, His Dream, His Rest* (1968). Through the persona of Henry the Dream Songs explore personal crisis against the enveloping sense of a society gone tragically and comically awry. Without falsifying the depth of the difficulties, both of his major poems strive to resist a final despair: to choose life over death and to affirm "savage and thoughtful/surviving Henry." In each poem Berryman has worked out a form flexible yet governed by its own complex conventions and an eccentric yet eloquent language to express the dislocations within and without.

Other books are *Berryman's Sonnets* (1967), *Short Poems* (1967), *Love and Fame* (1970), *Delusions Etc.* (1972), and a critical study of *Stephen Crane* (1950). *Love and Fame* concludes a sequence of autobiographical poems with "Eleven Addresses to the Lord," poem-prayers that pointed to Berryman's return to Catholicism shortly before his suicide in January 1972. Berryman won a Guggenheim, a Pulitzer Prize for *77 Dream Songs*, which may be the most original volume of verse to appear in the United States during the sixties; and the National Book Award and the Bollingen Prize for *His Toy, His Dream, His Rest*.

REFERENCE

"John Berryman Issue," *Harvard Advocate*, CIII (Spring 1969).

Martz, William J. *John Berryman*. Minneapolis: University of Minnesota Press, 1969.

Rosenthal, M. L. *The New Poets*. New York: Oxford University Press, 1967.

from **The Dream Songs**[1]

1

Huffy Henry hid   the day,
unappeasable Henry sulked.
I see his point,—a trying to put things over.
It was the thought that they thought
5   they could *do* it made Henry wicked & away.
But he should have come out and talked.

All the world like a woolen lover
once did seem on Henry's side.
Then came a departure.
10   Thereafter nothing fell out as it might or ought.
I don't see how Henry, pried
open for all the world to see, survived.

What he has now to say is a long
wonder the world can bear & be.
15   Once in a sycamore I was glad
all at the top, and I sang.
Hard on the land wears the strong sea
And empty grows every bed.

9

Deprived of his enemy, shrugged to a standstill[1]
horrible Henry, foaming. Fan their way
toward him who will
in the high wood: the officers, their rest,
5   with p. a.[2] echoing: his girl comes, say,
conned in to test

---

[1]*The Dream Songs* are about Henry in the first or in the third person. The poet
moves in and out of the persona of Henry.

[1]This Dream Song draws on the climax of the Humphrey Bogart movie *High
Sierra.*
[2]Public address.

if he's still human, see: she love him, see,
therefore she get on the Sheriff's mike & howl
'Come down, come down'.
10 Therefore he un-budge, furious. He'd flee
but only Heaven hangs over him foul.
At the crossways, downtown,

he dreams the folks are buying parsnips & suds[3]
and paying rent to foes. He slipt & fell.
15 It's golden here in the snow.
A mild crack: a far rifle. Bogart's duds
truck back to Wardrobe. Fancy the brain from hell
held out so long. Let go.

29

There sat down, once, a thing on Henry's heart
só heavy, if he had a hundred years
& more, & weeping, sleepless, in all them time
Henry could not make good.
5 Starts again always in Henry's ears
the little cough somewhere, an odour, a chime.

And there is another thing he has in mind
like a grave Sienese face[1] a thousand years
would fail to blur the still profiled reproach of. Ghastly,
10 with open eyes, he attends, blind.
All the bells say: too late. This is not for tears;
thinking.

But never did Henry, as he thought he did,
end anyone and hacks her body up
15 and hide the pieces, where they may be found.
He knows: he went over everyone, & nobody's missing.
Often he reckons, in the dawn, them up.
Nobody is ever missing.

---

[3]Beer.

---

[1]Jesus, imagined by Henry as a face in a Sienese painting.

48

He[1] yelled at me in Greek,
my God!—It's not his language
and I'm no good at—his is Aramaic,
was—I am a monoglot of English
5   (American version) and, say pieces from
a baker's dozen others: where's the bread?

but rising in the Second Gospel, pal:[2]
The seed goes down, god dies,
a rising happens,
10   some crust, and then occurs   an eating. He said so,[3]
a Greek idea,
troublesome to imaginary Jews,

like bitter Henry, full of the death of love,
Cawdor-uneasy, disambitious, mourning
15   the whole implausible necessary thing.
He dropped his voice & sybilled of
the death of the death of love.
I óught to get going.

75

Turning it over, considering, like a madman
Henry put forth a book.
No harm resulted from this.
Neither the menstruating   stars (nor man) was moved
5   at once.
Bare dogs drew closer for a second look

---

[1]Jesus speaking in the Greek of the Gospel texts, though he actually spoke Aramaic.
[2]Jesus' death and resurrection described as the rising of bread, the Communion that is a sharing in the mystery of love.
[3]In John 6: 51ff., when Jesus says, "The bread that I shall give is my flesh, for the life of the world," many Jews questioned this teaching. But Jesus insisted, "I tell you most solemnly, if you do not eat the flesh of the Son of Man and drink his blood, you will not have life in you." The institution of Communion at the Last Supper fulfilled the teaching and extended it through time. It is a Greek idea, because more intellectual and sophisticated than the more primitive Jews could accept—an idea developed by theologians from St. Paul to St. Thomas Aquinas, who were influenced by the Greeks and Greek thought.

and performed their friendly operations there.
Refreshed, the bark rejoiced.
Seasons went and came.
10   Leaves fell, but only a few.
Something remarkable about this
unshedding bulky bole-proud[1] blue-green moist

thing made by savage & thoughtful
surviving Henry
15   began to strike the passers from despair
so that sore on their shoulders old men hoisted
six-foot sons and polished women called
small girls to dream awhile toward the flashing & bursting tree!

77

Seedy Henry rose up shy in de world[1]
& shaved & swung his barbells, duded Henry up
and p.a.'d poor thousands of persons on topics of grand
moment to Henry, ah to those less & none.
5   Wif a book of his in either hand
he is stript down to move on.

—Come away, Mr. Bones.

—Henry is tired of the winter,
& haircuts, & a squeamish comfy   ruin-prone proud national
10   mind,   & Spring (in the city so called).
Henry likes Fall.
Hé would be prepared to líve in a world of Fáll
for ever, impenitent Henry.
But the snows and summers grieve & dream;

15   thése fierce & airy occupations, and love,
raved away so many of Henry's years
it is a wonder that, with in each hand
one of his own mad books and all,
ancient fires for eyes, his head full
20   & his heart full, he's making ready to move on.

[1]Bole: the trunk of a tree.

[1]Sometimes Henry talks to someone else, who calls Henry "Mr. Bones," the blackface minstrel character. Often the language shades in and out of a deliberate parody of Negro dialect.

from **Eleven Addresses to the Lord**

3

Sole watchman of the flying stars, guard me
against my flicker of impulse lust: teach me
to see them as sisters & daughters. Sustain
my grand endeavours: husbandship & crafting.

5   Forsake me not when my wild hours come;
grant me sleep nightly, grace soften my dreams;
achieve in me patience till the thing be done,
a careful view of my achievement come.

Make me from time to time the gift of the shoulder.
10 When all hurt nerves whine shut away the whiskey.
Empty my heart toward Thee.
Let me pace without fear the common path of death.

Cross am I sometimes with my little daughter:
fill her eyes with tears. Forgive me, Lord.
15 Unite my various soul,
sole watchman of the wide & single stars.

8

A Prayer for the Self

Who am I worthless that You spent such pains
and take may pains again?
I do not understand; but I believe.
Jonquils respond with wit to the teasing breeze.

5   Induct me down my secrets. Stiffen this heart
to stand their horrifying cries, O cushion
the first the second shocks, will to a halt
in mid-air there demons who would be at me.

May fade before, sweet morning on sweet morning,
10 I wake my dreams, my fan-mail go astray,

and do me little goods I have not thought of,
ingenious & beneficial Father.

Ease in their passing my beloved friends,
all others too I have cared for in a travelling life,
15   anyone anywhere indeed. Lift up
sober toward truth a scared self-estimate.

10

Fearful I peer upon the mountain path
where once Your shadow passed, Limner of the clouds
up their phantastic guesses. I am afraid,
I never until now confessed.

5   I fell back in love with you, Father, for two reasons:
You were good to me, & a delicious author,
rational & passionate. Come on me again,
as twice you came to Azarias & Misael.[1]

President of the brethren, our mild assemblies
10   inspire, & bother the priest not to be dull;
keep us week-long in order; love my children,
my mother far & ill, far brother, my spouse.

Oil all my turbulence as at Thy dictation
I sweat out my wayward works.
15   Father Hopkins[2] said the only true literary critic is Christ.
Let me lie down exhausted, content with that.

[1]Two of the Hebrew boys taken to the Chaldean court of King Nebuchadnezzar after he had conquered Jerusalem, and given the names Abednego and Meshach. With Daniel they passed the test of fasting, and with Shadrach they escaped the fiery furnace unhurt. See Daniel 1:6ff and Daniel 3:12ff.
[2]Gerard Manley Hopkins (1844–1889), the English poet and Jesuit priest.

Robert Lowell (1917–   )
Named after his father, Lowell was born in Boston and traced his New England ancestry back through the Lowell, Winslow, and Stark lines. He left Harvard College to study under Ransom at Kenyon College, graduating in classics in 1940. From Ransom Lowell learned the decorum of formal discipline, and from Tate, the ability to pack each line with sound and metaphoric complexity.

Burdened with the past, rebelling against the materialism that underlay and undermined the Puritanism of his successful forebears, Lowell became a Roman Catholic in 1940. The poems of *The Land of Unlikeness* (1944) and *Lord Weary's Castle* (1946), a Pulitzer Prize winner, insist that the transcendent Spirit break into and break down the temporal order to save it from its own crass destructiveness. By 1950 Lowell could not sustain his religious faith, and *Life Studies* (1959) presents poems that are boldly autobiographical and stripped of the ornamented formalism of the Catholic period. The poems seem to shape their meaning through associations and juxtapositions, as the mind sifts the details of memory, its conscious recognitions supplying their coherence. He had read Williams and his friends Elizabeth Bishop and Randall Jarrell, but the new style, colloquial yet elliptical, was his own. *For the Union Dead* (1964), *Near the Ocean* (1967), and *Notebook* (1970) enunciate more explicitly the public catastrophe behind personal anxiety. During the sixties Lowell became more active in political protest, especially against the war in Vietnam.

His other books include *The Mills of the Kavanaughs* (1951) and *Imitations* (1964), winner of the Bollingen Prize for translation, and several plays: *Phaedra* (1961), *The Old Glory* (1965), and *Prometheus Bound* (1969), all adaptations with a strong flavor of Lowell's sensibility. For several years he has lived in New York and commuted to Harvard to teach during half the year. The power of Lowell's language, enunciating an apocalyptic vision, has made him a prophetic presence—and perhaps the most influential American poet of the second half of the twentieth century.

REFERENCE

Cooper, Philip. *The Autobiographical Myth of Robert Lowell*. Chapel Hill: University of North Carolina Press, 1970.

Mazzaro, Jerome. *The Poetic Themes of Robert Lowell*. Ann Arbor: University of Michigan Press, 1965.

Robert Lowell: A Collection of Critical Essays. Ed. Thomas Parkinson. Englewood Cliffs, N. J.: Prentice-Hall, 1968.

Robert Lowell: A Portrait of the Artist in His Time. Ed. Michael London and Robert Boyers. New York: D. Lewis, 1970.

Staples, Hugh. *Robert Lowell: The First Twenty Years*. New York: Farrar, Straus and Cudahy, 1962.

COLLOQUY IN BLACK ROCK[1]

Here the jack-hammer jabs into the ocean;
My heart, you race and stagger and demand
More blood-gangs for your nigger-brass percussions,
Till I, the stunned machine of your devotion,
5 Clanging upon this cymbal of a hand,
Am rattled screw and footloose. All discussions

End in the mud-flat detritus[2] of death.
My heart, beat faster, faster. In Black Mud
Hungarian workmen give their blood[3]
10 For the martyre Stephen, who was stoned to death.

Black Mud, a name to conjure with: O mud
For watermelons gutted to the crust,
Mud for the mole-tide harbor, mud for mouse,
Mud for the armored Diesel fishing tubs that thud
15 A year and a day to wind and tide; the dust
Is on this skipping heart that shakes my house,[4]

House of our Savior who was hanged till death.
My heart, beat faster, faster. In Black Mud
Stephen the martyre was broken down to blood:
20 Our ransom is the rubble of his death.

Christ walks on the black water.[5] In Black Mud
Darts the kingfisher.[6] On Corpus Christi, heart,
Over the drum-beat of St. Stephen's choir
I hear him, *Stupor Mundi*,[7] and the mud
25 Flies from his hunching wings and beak—my heart,
The blue kingfisher dives on you in fire.

[1]A section of Bridgeport, Connecticut, which is a spit of land jutting out into
Long Island Sound. Lowell was serving time in prison there as a conscientious
objector during World War II. The poem was written for the Feast of Corpus
Christi, which celebrates God's incarnation in the Body of Christ.
[2]Rock worn down to rubble by abrasion.
[3]Many of the Hungarians who lived in Black Rock worked in the defense plants
in the area; here they are seen contributing to a blood drive for United States
troops held under the sponsorship of St. Stephen's church, a Hungarian parish.
There is a St. Stephen of Hungary and another St. Stephen, who was stoned to
death and became the first Christian martyr (see Apostles 6, 7).
[4]That is, my body, which is the dwelling place of the Savior.
[5]In Mark 6:45ff Jesus walks on the waters to help the Apostles, floundering in
a boat during a storm.
[6]The crested bird, whose name here suggests the King of the Fishers, Jesus, who
said to his fishermen-Apostles: "Henceforth you will fish for men."
[7]Latin: Splendor of the World.

THE QUAKER GRAVEYARD IN NANTUCKET[1]

(FOR WARREN WINSLOW, DEAD AT SEA)[2]

> *Let man have dominion over the fishes of the sea and the*
> *fowls of the air and the beasts and the whole earth and*
> *every creeping creature that moveth upon the earth.*[3]

I

A brackish reach of shoal off Madaket,—[4]
The sea was still breaking violently and night[5]
Had steamed into our North Atlantic Fleet,
When the drowned sailor clutched the drag-net. Light
5 Flashed from his matted head and marble feet,
He grappled at the net
With the coiled, hurdling muscles of his thighs:
The corpse was bloodless, a botch of reds and whites,
Its open, staring eyes
10 Were lustreless dead-lights
Or cabin-windows on a stranded hulk
Heavy with sand. We weight the body, close
Its eyes and heave it seaward whence it came,
Where the heel-headed dogfish barks its nose
15 On Ahab's void and forehead; and the name
Is blocked in yellow chalk.
Sailors, who pitch this portent at the sea
Where dreadnaughts[6] shall confess
Its hell-bent deity,
20 When you are powerless
To sand-bag this Atlantic bulwark, faced
By the earth-shaker,[7] green, unwearied, chaste

---

[1]An island off Cape Cod, Massachusetts.
[2]The poet's cousin, missing at sea during World War II.
[3]Genesis 9:1ff: These are God's words blessing Noah and his sons after the
flood has receded. The flood was retribution for man's violation of the ordered
harmony of creation, and now that God has cleansed the world for a new start,
He again charges man to reign off creation in harmony under a New Covenant
with God.
[4]On the Massachusetts coast.
[5]The imagery for this sentence is adapted from Thoreau's description of a ship-
wreck victim in the first chapter of *Cape Cod* (1865).
[6]Battleships.
[7]The Greek Poseidon or Roman Neptune, god of the sea.

In his steel scales: ask for no Orphean[8] lute
To pluck life back. The guns of the steeled fleet
25　Recoil and then repeat
The hoarse salute.

II

Whenever winds are moving and their breath
Heaves at the roped-in bulwarks of this pier,
The terns and sea-gulls tremble at your death
30　In these home waters. Sailor, can you hear
The Pequod's[9] sea wings, beating landward, fall
Headlong and break on our Atlantic wall
Off 'Sconset, where the yawing S-boats[10] splash
The bellbuoy, with ballooning spinnakers,
35　As the entangled, screeching mainsheet clears
The blocks: off Madaket, where lubbers lash
The heavy surf and throw their long lead squids
For blue-fish? Sea-gulls blink their heavy lids
Seaward. The winds' wings beat upon the stones,
40　Cousin, and scream for you and the claws rush
At the sea's throat and wring it in the slush
Of this old Quaker graveyard where the bones
Cry out in the long night for the hurt beast
Bobbing by Ahab's whaleboats in the East.

III

45　All you recovered from Poseidon died
With you, my cousin, and the harrowed brine
Is fruitless on the blue beard of the god,
Stretching beyond us to the castles in Spain,
Nantucket's westward haven. To Cape Cod
50　Guns, cradled on the tide,
Blast the eelgrass about a waterclock
Of bilge and backwash, roil the salt and sand
Lashing earth's scaffold, rock
Our warships in the hand

[8]The power of Orpheus' music won from Proserpina, Queen of Hades, permission for Eurydice, Orpheus' wife, to return to earth with him.
[9]The whaling ship, commanded by Captain Ahab, in Melville's *Moby-Dick* (1851).
[10]A kind of sailboat; reminiscent, too, of submarines that operated in the Atlantic during World War II.

55 Of the great God, where time's contrition blues
    Whatever it was these Quaker sailors lost
    In the mad scramble of their lives. They died
    When time was open-eyed,
    Wooden and childish; only bones abide
60 There, in the nowhere, where their boats were tossed
    Sky-high, where mariners had fabled news
    Of IS, the whited monster.[11] What it cost
    Them is their secret. In the sperm-whale's slick
    I see the Quakers drown and hear their cry:
65 "If God himself had not been on our side,
    If God himself had not been on our side,
    When the Atlantic rose against us, why,
    Then it had swallowed us up quick."

                    IV

    This is the end of the whaleroad and the whale
70 Who spewed Nantucket bones on the thrashed swell
    And stirred the troubled waters to whirlpools
    To send the Pequod packing off to hell:
    This is the end of them, three-quarters fools,
    Snatching at straws to sail
75 Seaward and seaward on the turntail whale,
    Spouting out blood and water as it rolls,
    Sick as a dog to these Atlantic shoals:
    Clamavimus, O depths.[12] Let the sea-gulls wail

    For water, for the deep where the high tide
80 Mutters to its hurt self, mutters and ebbs.
    Waves wallow in their wash, go out and out,
    Leave only the death-rattle of the crabs,
    The beach increasing, its enormous snout
    Sucking the ocean's side.
85 This is the end of running on the waves;

[11]IS: Being itself, as God identified himself to Moses in Exodos 3:14 as "I am who am." Ahab identified God's mystery with Moby-Dick, the white whale. In the New Covenant, which man repeatedly violates, IS indicates Iesus Salvator, Jesus the Savior. Ironically, even the pacifist Quakers hunt the whale.
[12]Psalm 130:1: "Out of the depths I have cried to you, O Lord." Here *clamavimus:* Latin for "we have cried."

We are poured out like water.[13] Who will dance
The mast-lashed master of Leviathans[14]
Up from this field of Quakers in their unstoned graves?

V

When the whale's viscera go and the roll
90 Of its corruption overruns this world
Beyond tree-swept Nantucket and Wood's Hole[15]
And Martha's Vineyard, Sailor, will your sword
Whistle and fall and sink into the fat?
In the great ash-pit of Jehoshaphat[16]
95 The bones cry for the blood of the white whale,
The fat flukes arch and whack about its ears,
The death-lance churns into the sanctuary, tears
The gun-blue swingle, heaving like a flail,
And hacks the coiling life out: it works and drags
100 And rips the sperm-whale's midriff into rags,
Gobbets of blubber spill to wind and weather,
Sailor, and gulls go round the stoven timbers
Where the morning stars sing out together[17]
And thunder shakes the white surf and dismembers
105 The red flag hammered in the mast-head.[18] Hide,
Our steel, Jonas Messias,[19] in Thy side.

[13]Psalm 22:14: "I am poured out like water."
[14]Suggests at once Ahab, and Odysseus lashed to the mast so as not to fall victim to the Sirens' fatal song.
[15]Woods Hole: near Falmouth, Massachusetts; Martha's Vineyard (below), an island off Cape Cod.
[16]Joel 4:1ff: God says "I am going to gather all the nations and take them down to the Valley of Jehoshaphat; there I intend to put them on trial for all they have done to Israel, my people and my heritage." There the apocalyptic Last Judgment will take place. The citation is the *Jerusalem Bible* translation; in the *King James Bible* the verses are 3:2ff.
[17]Job 38:1ff. God's answer to Job's complaints about his sufferings, spoken out of the whirlwind: "Who is this obscuring my designs with his empty-headed words? . . . Where were you when I laid the earth's foundations . . . when all the stars of the morning were singing with joy, and the sons of God in chorus were chanting praise?"
[18]Tashtego hammering the flag to the mast, the last glimpse of the *Pequod* sinking after being smashed by Moby-Dick.
[19]Jonah's being swallowed by the great fish and his return to land, told in the Book of Jonah, has been taken as a type, or symbolic foreshadowing, of Jesus the Messiah's death and resurrection, which secured the salvation of mankind though mankind crucified the Savior. Here, therefore, the poet prays that man's continued violations continue to work his salvation through God's mysterious design.

VI

OUR LADY OF WALSINGHAM[20]

There once the penitents took off their shoes
And then walked barefoot the remaining mile;
And the small trees, a stream and hedgerows file
Slowly along the munching English lane,
5   Like cows to the old shrine, until you lose
Track of your dragging pain.
The stream flows down under the druid tree,
Shiloah's whirlpools gurgle and make glad
The castle of God.[21] Sailor, you were glad
10   And whistled Sion by that stream.[22] But see:

Our Lady, too small for her canopy,
Sits near the altar. There's no comeliness
At all or charm in that expressionless
Face with its heavy eyelids. As before,
15   This face, for centuries a memory,
Non est species, neque decor,[23]
Expressionless, expresses God: it goes
Past castled Sion. She knows what God knows,
Not Calvary's Cross nor crib at Bethlehem
20   Now, and the world shall come to Walsingham.

VII

The empty winds are creaking and the oak
Splatters and splatters on the cenotaph,[24]
The boughs are trembling and a gaff
Bobs on the untimely stroke
25   Of the greased wash exploding on a shoal-bell
In the old mouth of the Atlantic. It's well;

[20]An old and popular English shrine to the Virgin Mary. Lowell has indicated that this passage is an adaptation of several paragraphs from E. I. Watkin's *Catholic Art and Culture.*

[21]Isaiah 8:6ff. God's prophecy to Isaiah: "Because this people has refused the waters of Shiloah which flow in tranquility . . . , the Lord will bring up against you the might and deep waters of the River . . . it will inundate Judah, flow over, pour out, flooding it up to the neck. . . ."

[22]Psalm 137, 1–2: "By the waters of Babylon we sat down and wept when we remembered Zion, hanging our harps on the poplars there." Zion: the Jewish homeland and the city of God.

[23]Latin: "There is neither beauty nor gracefulness."

[24]A monumental tombstone for a person whose remains are not there.

Atlantic, you are fouled with the blue sailors,
Sea-monsters, upward angel, downward fish:[25]
Unmarried and corroding, spare of flesh
30 Mart once of supercilious, wing'd clippers,
Atlantic, where your bell-trap guts its spoil
You could cut the brackish winds with a knife
Here in Nantucket, and cast up the time
When the Lord God formed man from the sea's slime
35 And breathed into his face the breath of life,
And blue-lung'd combers lumbered to the kill.
The Lord survives the rainbow of His will.[26]

CHRISTMAS EVE UNDER HOOKER'S STATUE

Tonight a blackout. Twenty years ago
I hung my stocking on the tree, and hell's
Serpent entwined the apple in the toe[1]
To sting the child with knowledge. Hooker's heels[2]
5 Kicking at nothing in the shifting snow,
A cannon and a cairn of cannon balls
Rusting before the blackened Statehouse, know
How the long horn of plenty broke like glass
In Hooker's gauntlets. Once I came from Mass;

10 Now storm-clouds shelter Christmas, once again
Mars meets his fruitless star with open arms,
His heavy saber flashes with the rime,
The war-god's bronzed and empty forehead forms
Anonymous machinery from raw men;
15 The cannon on the Common cannot stun
The blundering butcher as he rides on Time—

---

[25]In *Paradise Lost* I, 462–463, Milton describes the pagan god Dagon as "sea monster, upward man/And downward fish."

[26]The image of the rainbow suggests the rainbow at the end of the flood, which is, God tells Noah in Genesis 9:17, "the sign of the Covenant I have established between myself and every living thing that is found on the earth." It recalls as well, for ironic contrast, the story of the pot of gold at the end of the rainbow.

---

[1]The re-enactment of the temptation and sin of Eden.

[2]General Thomas Hooker (1814–1879) of the Union Army, who lost the Battle of Chancellorsville and whose bronze equestrian statue is on the lawn of the Massachusetts State House above the Boston Common.

The barrel clinks with holly. I am cold:
I ask for bread, my father gives me mould;

His stocking is full of stones. Santa in red
20   Is crowned with wizened berries. Man of war,
Where is the summer's garden? In its bed
The ancient speckled serpent will appear,
And black-eyed susan with her frizzled head.
When Chancellorsville mowed down the volunteer,
25   "All wars are boyish," Herman Melville said;[3]
But we are old, our fields are running wild:
Till Christ again turn wanderer and child.

BEYOND THE ALPS

*(On the train from Rome to Paris, 1950, the year Pius XII
defined the dogma of Mary's bodily assumption.)*[1]

Reading how even the Swiss had thrown the sponge
in once again and Everest[2] was still
unscaled, I watched our Paris pullman lunge
mooning across the fallow Alpine snow.
5   *O bella Roma!*[3] I saw our stewards go
forward on tiptoe banging on their gongs.
Life changed to landscape. Much against my will
I left the City of God where it belongs.

---

[3] Actually the line is from Melville's poem "The March into Virginia"—after the First Battle of Manassas.

[1] The Catholic doctrine that teaches that as a special grace to Mary, the sinless Mother of God, her body was assumed into heaven along with her soul immediately after death instead of having to wait until the Last Judgment. A traditional belief from the earliest Christian times, it was officially made dogma in 1950. It is an extension of the Incarnation (God's becoming man in the person of Jesus) and the Ascension of Jesus, body and soul, into heaven, and it asserts, through the signal instance of Mary, that man is saved not by transcendence of the human condition, but in his human condition, body and soul.

[2] A peak in the Himalayas, the highest in the world. The reference here is to a newspaper account of the latest unsuccessful attempt to scale its height.

[3] Italian: "O Lovely Rome." The City of God suggests the ironic disparity between Rome as the center of the Church and the image of the new Zion, the heavenly city, as expressed, for example, in St. Augustine's *The City of God*.

> There the skirt-mad Mussolini[4] unfurled
> 10 the eagle of Caesar. He was one of us
> only, pure prose. I envy the conspicuous
> waste of our grandparents on their grand tours—
> long-haired Victorian sages accepted the universe,
> while breezing on their trust funds through the world.

> 15 When the Vatican made Mary's Assumption dogma,
> the crowds at San Pietro screamed *Papa.*[5]
> The Holy Father dropped his shaving glass,
> and listened. His electric razor purred,
> his pet canary chirped on his left hand.
> 20 The lights of science couldn't hold a candle
> to Mary risen—at one miraculous stroke,
> angel-wing'd, gorgeous as a jungle bird!
> But who believed this? Who could understand?
> Pilgrims still kissed Saint Peter's brazen sandal.[6]
> 25 The Duce's lynched, bare, booted skull still spoke.
> God herded his people to the *coup de grâce*—[7]
> the costumed Switzers[8] sloped their pikes to push,
> O Pius, through the monstrous human crush. . . .

> Our mountain-climbing train had come to earth.
> 30 Tired of the querulous hush-hush of the wheels,
> the blear-eyed ego kicking in my berth
> lay still, and saw Apollo[9] plant his heels
> on terra firma[10] through the morning's thigh . . .
> each backward, wasted Alp, a Parthenon,[11]
> 35 fire-branded socket of the Cyclops' eye.[12]
> There were no tickets for that altitude

[4]Benito Mussolini (1883–1945), the Duce of Facist Italy, lynched by Italians in Milan at the end of World War II.

[5]San Pietro: the church and plaza of St. Peter, the center of the Vatican; Papa: Italian for "Pope" in his role of "Holy Father."

[6]The bronze statue of St. Peter within the church.

[7]The finishing blow delivered mercifully to the mortally wounded; literally from the French, "blow of grace, or mercy." Here there is an ironic pun on "grace."

[8]The Pope's Swiss Guards, with uniforms designed by Michaelangelo.

[9]Apollo: the sun god. Aurora: the goddess of the dawn; hence, "the morning's thigh."

[10]Solid land.

[11]The temple to Athena on the Acropolis in Athens.

[12]Odysseus blinded the Cyclops by driving a firebrand into his one eye.

once held by Hellas,[13] when the Goddess[14] stood,
prince, pope, philosopher and golden bough,[15]
pure mind and murder at the scything prow—
40   Minerva, the miscarriage of the brain.

Now Paris, our black classic, breaking up
like killer kings on an Etruscan cup.

GRANDPARENTS

They're altogether otherworldly now,
those adults champing for their ritual Friday spin
to pharmacist and five-and-ten in Brockton.[1]
Back in my throw-away and shaggy span
5   of adolescence, Grandpa still waves his stick
like a policeman;
Grandmother, like a Mohammedan, still wears her thick
lavender mourning and touring veil;
the Pierce Arrow[2] clears its throat in a horse-stall.
10   Then the dry road dust rises to whiten
the fatigued elm leaves—
the nineteenth century, tired of children, is gone.
They're all gone into a world of light;[3] the farm's my own.

The farm's my own!
15   Back there alone,
I keep indoors, and spoil another season.
I hear the rattley little country gramophone
racking its five foot horn:
"O Summer Time!"
20   Even at noon here the formidable

---

[13]The Greek name for Greece.
[14]Athena or Minerva, who sprang from Zeus' forehead full-grown in armor; the
goddess of intellect, wisdom, and war, and one of the most powerful of the
Olympian gods.
[15]Sir James Frazer's study of comparative mythologies and comparative reli-
gions, *The Golden Bough* (1890).

[1]A city in Massachusetts.
[2]An automobile, no longer manufactured.
[3]"They Are All Gone into the World of Light!", a mystical and Christian poem
by Henry Vaughan (1621–1695).

Ancien Régime[4] still keeps nature at a distance. Five
green shaded light bulbs spider the billiards-table;
no field is greener than its cloth,
where Grandpa, dipping sugar for us both,
25 once spilled his demitasse.
His favorite ball, the number three,
still hides the coffee stain.

Never again
to walk there, chalk our cues,
30 insist on shooting for us both.
Grandpa! Have me, hold me, cherish me!
Tears smut my fingers. There
half my life-lease later,
I hold an *Illustrated London News*—;
35 disloyal still,
I doodle handlebar
mustaches on the last Russian Czar.

WAKING IN THE BLUE

The night attendant, a B. U. sophomore,[1]
rouses from the mare's-nest of his drowsy head
propped on *The Meaning of Meaning*.[2]
He catwalks down our corridor.
5 Azure day
makes my agonized blue window bleaker.
Crows maunder on the petrified fairway.
Absence! My heart grows tense
as though a harpoon were sparring for the kill.
10 (This is the house for the "mentally ill.")

What use is my sense of humor?
I grin at Stanley, now sunk in his sixties,
once a Harvard all-American fullback,
(if such were possible!)

---

[4]French for "The Old Regime," referring to the monarchy and its way of life
before the French Revolution.

---

[1]The night attendant at McLean's Hospital, a sanitarium outside Boston, is a
sophomore (etymologically, "wise fool") from Boston University.
[2]An influential study of language and linguistics by I. A. Richards and C. K.
Odgen (1923).

15 still hoarding the build of a boy in his twenties,
as he soaks, a ramrod
with the muscle of a seal
in his long tub,
vaguely urinous from the Victorian plumbing.
20 A kingly granite profile in a crimson golf-cap,
worn all day, all night,
he thinks only of his figure,
of slimming on sherbet and ginger ale—
more cut off from words than a seal.

25 This is the way day breaks in Bowditch Hall at McLean's;
the hooded night lights bring out "Bobbie,"
Porcellian '29,[3]
a replica of Louis XVI
without the wig—
30 redolent and roly-poly as a sperm whale,
as he swashbuckles about in his birthday suit
and horses at chairs.

These victorious figures of bravado ossified young.

In between the limits of day,
35 hours and hours go by under the crew haircuts
and slightly too little nonsensical bachelor twinkle
of the Roman Catholic attendants.
(There are no Mayflower
screwballs in the Catholic Church.)

40 After a hearty New England breakfast,
I weigh two hundred pounds
this morning. Cock of the walk,
I strut in my turtle-necked French sailor's jersey
before the metal shaving mirrors,
45 and see the shaky future grow familiar
in the pinched, indigenous faces
of these thoroughbred mental cases,
twice my age and half my weight.
We are all old-timers,
50 each of us holds a locked razor.

---

[3]Porcellian is the most exclusive social club at Harvard. "Bobbie" was taken into Porcellian in 1929.

MEMORIES OF WEST STREET AND LEPKE[1]

Only teaching on Tuesdays, book-worming
in pajamas fresh from the washer each morning,
I hog a whole house on Boston's
"hardly passionate Marlborough Street,"[2]
5 where even the man
scavenging filth in the back alley trash cans,
has two children, a beach wagon, a helpmate,
and is a "young Republican."
I have a nine months' daughter,
10 young enough to be my granddaughter.
Like the sun she rises in her flame-flamingo infants' wear.

These are the tranquillized *Fifties*,
and I am forty. Ought I to regret my seedtime?
I was a fire-breathing Catholic C.O.,[3]
15 and made my manic statement,
telling off the state and president, and then
sat waiting sentence in the bull pen
beside a Negro boy with curlicues
of marijuana in his hair.

20 Given a year,
I walked on the roof of the West Street Jail, a short
enclosure like my school soccer court,
and saw the Hudson River once a day
through sooty clothesline entanglements
25 and bleaching khaki tenements.
Strolling, I yammered metaphysics with Abramowitz,
a jaundice-yellow ("it's really tan")
and fly-weight pacifist,
so vegetarian,
30 he wore rope shoes and preferred fallen fruit.
He tried to convert Bioff and Brown,

---

[1]After being sentenced in 1944 to a year and a day for refusing to comply with the draft law, Lowell was first sent to the West Street Jail in Manhattan. The most famous prisoner there at the time was Louis ("Lepke") Buchalter (1897–1944), the New York trade union racketeer, murderer, and gang boss whose gentle manner and family feeling belied the activities in which he was involved; he awaited execution. Lowell went from there to the Black Rock penitentiary and served five months of his term.

[2]Henry James' description of the fashionable street off the Public Gardens.

[3]Conscientious objector.

the Hollywood pimps, to his diet.
Hairy, muscular, suburban,
wearing chocolate double-breasted suits,
35   they blew their tops and beat him black and blue.

I was so out of things, I'd never heard
of the Jehovah's Witnesses.
"Are you a C.O.?" I asked a fellow jailbird.
"No," he answered, "I'm a J.W."
40   He taught me the "hospital tuck,"
and pointed out the T shirted back
of *Murder Incorporated's* Czar Lepke,
there piling towels on a rack,
or dawdling off to his little segregated cell full
45   of things forbidden the common man:
a portable radio, a dresser, two toy American
flags tied together with a ribbon of Easter palm.[4]
Flabby, bald, lobotomized,[5]
he drifted in a sheepish calm,
50   where no agonizing reappraisal[6]
jarred his concentration on the electric chair—
hanging like an oasis in his air
of lost connections. . . .

SKUNK HOUR

(FOR ELIZABETH BISHOP)

Nautilus Island's[1] hermit
heiress still lives through winter in her Spartan cottage;
her sheep still graze above the sea.
Her son's a bishop. Her farmer
5   is first selectman in our village;
she's in her dotage.

[4] Used as part of the service on Palm Sunday, the week before Easter, to commemorate Jesus' triumphal entry into Jerusalem shortly before his crucifixion and resurrection.

[5] A lobotomy is a surgical incision into the brain; one of the effects is to block off memory.

[6] A much-quoted phrase of John Foster Dulles, Secretary of State for President Eisenhower, in relation to a foreign-policy crisis.

[1] In Maine.

Thirsting for
the hierarchic privacy
of Queen Victoria's century,
10   she buys up all
the eyesores facing her shore,
and lets them fall.

The season's ill—
we've lost our summer millionaire,
15   who seemed to leap from an L. L. Bean[2]
catalogue. His nine-knot yawl
was auctioned off to lobstermen.
A red fox stain covers Blue Hill.

And now our fairy
20   decorator brightens his shop for fall;
his fishnet's filled with orange cork,
orange, his cobbler's bench and awl;
there is no money in his work,
he'd rather marry.

25   One dark night,[3]
my Tudor Ford climbed the hill's skull;
I watched for love-cars. Lights turned down,
they lay together, hull to hull,
where the graveyard shelves on the town. . . .
30   My mind's not right.

A car radio bleats,
"Love, O careless Love. . . ." I hear
my ill-spirit sob in each blood cell,
as if my hand were at its throat. . . .
35   I myself am hell;[4]
nobody's here—

---

[2]A Maine sporting-goods and sportswear store that puts out a mail-order cata-
logue, but fancier and more expensively stylish than most mail-order
catalogues.
[3]Lowell has commented: "all comes alive in stanzas V and VI. This is the dark
night. I hoped my readers would remember John of the Cross' poem [St. John
of the Cross (1542–1591), who wrote an account of his mystical experiences
called *The Dark Night of the Soul*]. My night is not gracious, but secular,
puritan, and agnostical. An Existential night. . . . Out of this comes the march
and affirmation, an ambiguous one, of my skunks in the last two stanzas."
[4]Satan's words in *Paradise Lost* IV, 75.

only skunks, that search
in the moonlight for a bite to eat.
They march on their soles up Main Street:
40 white stripes, moonstruck[5] eyes' red fire
under the chalk-dry and spar spire
of the Trinitarian Church.

I stand on top
of our back steps and breathe the rich air—
45 a mother skunk with her column of kittens swills the garbage pail.
She jabs her wedge-head in a cup
of sour cream, drops her ostrich tail,
and will not scare.

WATER

It was a Maine lobster town—
each morning boatloads of hands
pushed off for granite
quarries on the islands,

5   and left dozens of bleak
white frame houses stuck
like oyster shells
on a hill of rock,

and below us, the sea lapped
10 the raw little match-stick
mazes of a weir,[1]
where the fish for bait were trapped.

Remember? We sat on a slab of rock.
From this distance in time,
15 it seems the color
of iris, rotting and turning purpler,

but it was only
the usual gray rock

[5]Lunatic.

[1]A fence or woven obstruction placed in the water to catch fish.

turning the usual green
20   when drenched by the sea.

The sea drenched the rock
at our feet all day,
and kept tearing away
flake after flake.

25   One night you dreamed
you were a mermaid clinging to a wharf-pile,
and trying to pull
off the barnacles with your hands.

We wished our two souls
30   might return like gulls
to the rock. In the end,
the water was too cold for us.

FOR THE UNION DEAD

"Relinquunt Omnia Servare Rem Publican."[1]

The old South Boston Aquarium stands
in a Sahara of snow now. Its broken windows are boarded.
The bronze weathervane cod has lost half its scales.
The airy tanks are dry.

5   Once my nose crawled like a snail on the glass;
my hand tingled
to burst the bubbles
drifting from the noses of the cowed, compliant fish.

My hand draws back. I often sigh still
10   for the dark downward and vegetating kingdom
of the fish and reptile. One morning last March,
I pressed against the new barbed and galvanized

[1]Latin: "They left all to serve the Republic." As his epigraph Lowell adapted
the inscription composed by Harvard President Charles W. Eliot ("omnia reliq-
uent servare rem publicam" or "He left all . . . .") for the memorial honoring
Colonel Robert Shaw (1837–1863) who commanded the 54th Massachusetts
Volunteers, the first Negro regiment from the free states to serve in the Civil
War. Colonel Shaw was killed, with many of his men, in the battle at Fort
Wagner.

fence on the Boston Common.[2] Behind their cage,
yellow dinosaur steamshovels were grunting
15   as they cropped up tons of mush and grass
to gouge their underworld garage.

Parking spaces luxuriate like civic
sandpiles in the heart of Boston.
A girdle of orange, Puritan-pumpkin colored girders
20   braces the tingling Statehouse,[3]

shaking over the excavations, as it faces Colonel Shaw
and his bell-cheeked Negro infantry
on St. Gaudens' shaking Civil War relief,[4]
propped by a plank splint against the garage's earthquake.

25   Two months after marching through Boston,
half the regiment was dead;
at the dedication,
William James could almost hear the bronze Negroes breathe.[5]

Their monument sticks like a fishbone
30   in the city's throat.
Its Colonel is as lean
as a compass-needle.

He has an angry wrenlike vigilance,
a greyhound's gentle tautness;
35   he seems to wince at pleasure,
and suffocate for privacy.

He is out of bounds now. He rejoices in man's lovely,
peculiar power to choose life and die—
when he leads his black soldiers to death,
40   he cannot bend his back.

[2]For several years during the 1950's, the construction of an immense under-
ground garage for public parking under the Boston Common filled part of the
Common with excavations and machinery.
[3]The Massachusetts State House, an outstanding example of Federalist archi-
tecture by Charles Bulfinch (1763–1844), was undergoing repairs and renova-
tions at the same time as the construction of the garage. The State House is at
the top of Beacon Hill opposite and above the Common.
[4]The monument is a bas-relief by the American sculptor Augustus Saint-
Gaudens (1848–1907) and stands on the edge of the Common facing the State
House. It was unveiled in 1897.
[5]William James, the philosopher and psychologist, spoke at the dedication of
the Shaw monument and made this comment among his remarks.

On a thousand small town New England greens,
the old white churches hold their air
of sparse, sincere rebellion; frayed flags
quilt the graveyards of the Grand Army of the Republic.

45   The stone statues of the abstract Union Soldier[6]
grow slimmer and younger each year—
wasp-waisted, they doze over muskets
and muse through their sideburns . . .

Shaw's father wanted no monument
50   except the ditch,
where his son's body was thrown
and lost with his "niggers."

The ditch is nearer.
There are no statues for the last war here;
55   on Boylston Street,[7] a commercial photograph
shows Hiroshima boiling

over a Mosler Safe, the "Rock of Ages"
that survived the blast. Space is nearer.
When I crouch to my television set,
60   the drained faces of Negro school-children rise like balloons.[8]

Colonel Shaw
is riding on his bubble,
he waits
for the blesséd break.

65   The Aquarium is gone. Everywhere,
giant finned cars nose forward like fish;
a savage servility
slides by on grease.

[6]James's address also made the connection between this monument and others
to the Union dead.
[7]One of Boston's central streets; it runs along one side of the Common. The
advertisement for the Mosler Safe as the "Rock of Ages" with a photograph
of one that had survived the atomic blast in Hiroshima appeared on a billboard
above Boylston Street and the Common. "Rock of Ages" is the popular Protes-
tant hymn.
[8]In a television news report on one of the attempts to desegregate Southern
public schools during the late 1950's.

Robert Duncan (1919–   )
Duncan's mother died at his birth in Oakland, California, and he was adopted the next year. The name he chose for himself is a composite of the names given him by both sets of parents. He attended the University of California, Berkeley, at different times, studying in particular the civilization of the Middle Ages. He was active in the San Francisco poetry scene during the forties, and since the fifties has been linked with Olson, Levertov, and Robert Creeley in the "Projectivist School."

Among the Projectivists Duncan has been more deeply influenced by Pound than by Williams. For him, poetry is an extension of the process through which "unwittingly we achieve our form." Since poetry participates in the emergent design, it must be open-ended and ongoing: a magic invocation of the "correspondence between inner being and outer world." Like Pound, too, Duncan draws on myths East and West to celebrate his mysteries. His many volumes of poetry include: *Heavenly City, Earthly City* (1947), *Medieval Scenes* (1950), *Selected Poems* (1959), *The Opening of the Field* (1960), *Roots and Branches* (1964), and *Bending the Bow* (1968). The last volumes of poems contain the continuing sequences "The Structure of Rime" and "Passages." He has also written plays: *Medea at Kolchis* (1965) and *Adam's Way: A Play upon Theosophical Themes* (1966).

REFERENCE

Rosenthal, M. K. *The New Poets.* New York: Oxford University Press, 1967.

THE LAW I LOVE IS MAJOR MOVER

from which flow destructions of the Constitution.
No nation stands unstirrd
in whose courts. *I, John, testify:*
I saw.[1] But he who judges must
5   know mercy
as a man knows a woman
      in marriage,

for She is fair, whom we, masters, serve.

The Which, says John Adams,
10   "requires the continual exercise of virtue
      "beyond the reach
      "of human infirmity, even in its best estate."

Responsibility is to keep
      the ability to respond.
15 The myriad of spiders' eyes that Rexroth[2] saw
      reflecting light
are glamorless, are testimony
      clear and true.

The shaman[3] sends himself
20 The universe is filld with eyes then, intensities,
      with intent,
      outflowings of good or evil,
      benemaledictions of the dead,

      but
25 the witness brings self up before the Law.
It is the Law before the witness that
      makes Justice.

There is no touch that is not each
      to each   reciprocal.

30 The scale of five, eight, or twelves tones
      performs a judgment

[1]St. John identifies himself as witness to all the things in his vision at the beginning of the Book of Revelation.
[2]Kenneth Rexroth (1905–   ), the San Francisco poet.
[3]Inspired priest through whom the spirits speak in certain Asian sects; the medicine man in certain North American Indian tribes.

previous to music. The music restores
    health to the land.

The land? The Boyg
35   in Peer Gynt[4] speaks.
On the stage it was shown: a moving obscurity.

●

I try to read you, lad, who offer no text.
Not terror now, dumb grief it is,
diabolus[5]—but little devils
40   are garbled men that speak garble.
Your chosen place is less than hell,
nor hate nor love breeds. There,
disorder is not, order is not, not no
even simpleton need demands my ear.

45 Hear!

Hear! Beautiful damnd man that lays down his law lays down
        himself creates hell
a sentence unfolding healthy heaven.

Thou wilt not allow the suns to move
50   nor man to mean desire move,
nor rage for war and wine,
here where the mind nibbles,
nor embrace the law under which you lie,
that will not fall upon your face
55   or upon knees, all
but twisted out of shape, crippled
by angelic Syntax.

Look!   the Angel that made a man of Jacob[6]
        made Israël in His embrace

60 was the Law,   was Syntax.

Him I love is major mover.

[4]The Boyg is a troll monster in Henrik Ibsen's *Peer Gynt* (1867), who represents
the riddle of life and who for a while blocks Peer Gynt's progress while refus-
ing to fight him in a contest.
[5]Latin: devil.
[6]In Genesis 32, Jacob, son of Isaac, wrestled all night with a mysterious being,
sometimes called an angel, who changed his name to Israel at the end of the
struggle. Jacob had a dislocated hip but said "I have seen God face to face and
I have survived."

ANSWERING

(after CLARITAS by Denise Levertov)

A burst
of confidence. Confiding

a treasured thing

kept inside,
5   as if it were a burden,

worrying about money,
or were pride
and ambition struggling—

sings out.

10   It was a song I did not sing.

●

The men are working in the street.
The sound

of pick and pneumatic drill

punctuates
15   the chirrup a bird makes,

a natural will
who works the tossing dandelion head

—a sheaf of poems.

They are employd
20   at making up a joyous

possibility.

They are making a living
where I take my life.

●

With no more earnest skill
25   than this working song

sings
—as if the heart's full

responsibility
were in the rise of words

30   as momentarily
that bird's notes he concentrates

above the swaying bough,
the fluttering wings.

●

For joy
35   breaks thru

insensible to our human want.
Were we birds too

upon some blowing crown of seeds,
it would be so

40   —we'd sing as we do.

The song's a work of the natural will.
The song's a work of the natural will.

OFTEN I AM PERMITTED
TO RETURN TO A MEADOW

as if it were a scene made-up by the mind,
that is not mine, but is a made place,

that is mine, it is so near to the heart,
an eternal pasture folded in all thought
5   so that there is a hall therein

that is a made place, created by light
wherefrom the shadows that are forms fall.

Wherefrom fall all architectures I am
I say are likenesses of the First Beloved
10   whose flowers are flames lit to the Lady.

She it is Queen Under The Hill
whose hosts are a disturbance of words within words
that is a field folded.

It is only a dream of the grass blowing
15   east against the source of the sun
in an hour before the sun's going down

whose secret we see in a children's game
of ring a round of roses told.

Often I am permitted to return to a meadow
20   as if it were a given property of the mind
that certain bounds hold against chaos,

that is a place of first permission,
everlasting omen of what is.

TRIBAL MEMORIES PASSAGES 1

from the Emperor Julian,[1] *Hymn to the
Mother of the Gods:*

*And Attis[2] encircles the heavens like
a tiara, and thence sets out as
though to descend to earth.*

●

*For the even is bounded, but the
uneven is without bounds and
there is no way through or out of it.*

And to Her-Without-Bounds I send,
wherever She wanders,   by what
campfire at evening,

among tribes setting each the City where
5   we Her people are

[1]Roman Emperor of the fourth century A.D., known as "The Apostate" for at-
tempting to drive out Christianity and restore the pagan gods on the basis of
neo-Platonist philosophy.
[2]A descendant of the Phrygian fertility goddess Cybele who became himself a
spring fertility god; his yearly death and return to earth symbolized the con-
tinuity of natural process.

at the end of a day's reaches   here
     the Eternal
lamps lit, here   the wavering human
     sparks of heat and light
10   glimmer, go out, and reappear.

For this is the company of the living
and the poet's voice speaks from no
     crevice in the ground between
     mid-earth and underworld
15   breathing fumes of what is deadly to know,
     news larvae in tombs
     and twists of time do feed upon,

but from the hearth stone, the lamp light,
     the heart of the matter where the

20   house is held   •

yet here, the warning light at the edge of town!

The City will go out in time, will go out
     into time, hiding even its embers.
And we were scatterd thruout the countries and times of man

25   for we took alarm in ourselves,
     rumors of the enemy
spread among the feathers of the wing that coverd us.

                 •

Mnemosyne,[1] they named her, the
     Mother with the whispering
30   featherd wings.   Memory,

the great speckled bird[2] who broods over the
     nest of souls, and her egg,
     the dream in which all things are living,
I return to, leaving my self.

[1]Daughter of Uranus and Gaea; the earth goddess and the goddess of memory, who, by Zeus, became the mother of the Muses.
[2]A reference to the fundamentalist hymn that depicts the Bible as a great speckled bird.

35   I am beside myself with this
            thought of the One in the World-Egg,[3]
      enclosed,   in a shell of murmurings,

                        rimed round,
                        sound-chamberd child.

40   It's that first!   The forth-going to be
                        bursts into green as the spring
            winds blow watery from the south
      and the sun returns north.   He hides

            fire among words in his mouth

45   and comes racing out of the zone of dark and storm

                  towards us.

      I sleep in the afternoon, retreating from work,
      reading and dropping away from the reading,
      as if I were only a seed of myself,
50   unawakend,   unwilling
                  to sleep or wake.

AT THE LOOM   PASSAGES 2

                        A cat's purr
            in the hwirr thkk   *"thgk, thkk"*
      of Kirke's loom on Pound's Cantos
            "I heard a song of that kind . . ."[1]

5   my mind a shuttle[2] among
            set strings of the music
      lets a weft of dream grow in the day time,

---

[3]In many myths, creation began with the world-egg, from which all things were hatched.

---

[1]Canto 39 begins with Odysseus hearing the sound of Circe's loom, linked with a cat and with "the sharp sound of a song." The line quoted is from the Canto.

[2]An instrument used at the loom to pass the thread of the weft in and out through the threads of the warp. In weaving, the warp is the threads held in the loom, and the weft is the cross-threads woven through the warp to make the fabric.

an increment of associations,
luminous soft threads,
10   the thrown glamour, crossing and recrossing,
the twisted sinews underlying the work.

Back of the images, the few cords that bind
meaning in the word-flow,
the rivering web
15   rises among wits and senses
gathering the wool into its full cloth.

The secret!   the secret!   It's hid
in its showing forth.
The white cat kneads his paws
20   and sheathes his eyes in ecstasy against the light,
the light bounding from his fur as from a shield
held high in the midst of a battle.

What does the Worm work in His cocoon?

There was such a want in the old ways
25   when craft came into our elements,
the art shall never be free of that forge,
that loom, that lyre—

the fire, the images, the voice.

Why, even in the room where we are,
30   reading to ourselves, or I am reading aloud,
sounding the music,
the stuff
vanishes upon the air,
line after line thrown.

35   Let there be the clack of the shuttle flying
forward and back,   forward and
back,

warp, *wearp, varp:*   *"cast of a net, a laying of eggs"*
from **warp-* *"to throw"*

40   the threads twisted for strength
              that can be a warp of the will.

        "*O weaver, weaver, work no more,*"
        Gascoyne[3] is quoted:
        "*thy warp hath done me wrong.*"

45 And the shuttle carrying the woof I find
        was *skutill*   "*harpoon*"   —a dart, an arrow,
            or a little ship,

            navicula   *weberschiff,*[4]

crossing and recrossing from shore to shore—

50   prehistoric **skutil* **skut-*
        "*a bolt, a bar, as of a door*"
        "*a flood-gate*"   •

                        but the battle I saw
        was on a wide plain,   for the
55   sake of valor,
        the hand traind to the bow,
            the man's frame
        withstanding,   each side

        facing its foe for the sake of
60   the alliance,
        allegiance, the legion, that the
            vow that makes a nation
        one body not be broken.

        Yet it is all, we know, a mêlée,
65   a medley of mistaken themes
            grown dreadful and surmounting dread,

[3]George Gascoigne (c. 1530–1577), Elizabethan poet. The lines quoted are from
"The Complaint of the Greene Knight."
[4]Navicula: Latin for "little ship"; Weberschiff: German for "shuttle," literally
"weaving-ship."

so that Achilles may have his wrath
and throw down
the heroic Hektor[5] who raised
70   that reflection of the heroic

in his shield . . .

WHERE IT APPEARS   PASSAGES 4

I'd cut the warp
to weave that web

in the air

and here

5   let image perish in image,

leave writer and reader

up in the air

to draw

momentous

10   inconclusions,

ropes of the first water
returnd by a rhetoric

the rain swells.

Statistically insignificant as a locus of creation
15   I have in this   my own

intense

area of self creation,

the Sun itself

insignificant among suns.

20   The magi of the probable
bring forth a mirror,   an

[5]The Trojan prince equal to Achilles among the Greeks in heroism, who is killed
by Achilles in combat after rousing Achilles' wrath by killing Patroclus,
Achilles' close friend.

iridescence,   an ocean

which I hold in the palm of my hand   •

as if I could cast a shadow   •

25   to surround   •

what is boundless   •

as if I could handle   •   this pearl   •   that touches

upon every imagination of what

I am   •

30   wrong about the web,   the

reflection,   the lure of the world

I love.

THE MOON   PASSAGES 5

so pleasing   a light

round,   haloed,   partially

disclosed,   a ring,

night's wedding signet   •

5   may be

a great lady drawing

her tide-skirts up   •

in whirls

and loosening to the gilt

10   shore-margins   of her sea-robes

•   or he,   his consent

releasing dreams,

the dazzling path remaining

over the waves,

15   a lord too,   lunar moth king

Oberon[1]   •   gleaming amidst clouds.

[1]In folklore, the king of the fairies.

From what source

the light of their faces,   the

light of their eyes,   the dark

20   glance that illumines,   the kindling look

as if over the shimmer of the lake

his flesh radiant   •

My Lord-and-Lady Moon

upon whom

25   as if with love

the sun at the source of light

reflects   •

Lifted   •

Mount Shasta[2] in snowy reverie

30   •   floats

---

[2]A mountain in the Cascades of Northern California.

Lawrence Ferlinghetti (1919–)

Born in Yonkers, New York, Ferlinghetti spent part of his youth in Paris. He received a B.A. from the University of North Carolina, an M.A. from Columbia, and a doctorate from the Sorbonne in 1950. After serving in the Navy during World War II, he worked for *Time*. Settling in San Francisco in 1951, he founded the City Lights Bookstore and made it a center for Beat poets during the San Francisco Renaissance of the fifties. City Lights Books published many experimental open-form poets, including Ferlinghetti and Ginsberg. Ferlinghetti's books and readings have been immensely popular. The earlier books—*Pictures of the Gone World* (1955), *A Coney Island of the Mind* (1958), and *Starting from San Francisco* (1961)—combine a jazzy impressionism and wacky humor, and *The Secret Meaning of Things* (1969) is increasingly incantatory and visionary. Ferlinghetti has also written a novel, *Her* (1960), and two books of plays: *Unfair Arguments with Existence* (1963) and *Routines* (1964).

STARTING FROM SAN FRANCISCO[1]

Here I go again
crossing the country in coach trains
(back to my old
lone wandering)
5   All night Eastward . . . Upward
over the great Divide and on
into Utah
over Great Salt Plain
and onward, rocking,
10 the white dawn burst
across mesas,
table-lands,
all flat, all laid away.
Great glary sun—
15 wood bridge over water. . . .
Later in still light, we still reel onward—
Onward?
Back and forth, across the Continent,
bang bang
20 by any wheel or horse,
any rail,
by car
by buggy
by stagecoach,
25 walking,
riding,
hooves pounding the Great Plains,
caravans into the night. Forever.
Into Wyoming.
30 All that day and night, rocking through it,
snow on steppes and plains of November,
roads lost in it—or never existent—
back in the beginning again, no People yet,
no ruts Westward yet
35 under the snow. . . .
Still more huge spaces we bowl through,
still untouched dark land—
Indomitable.
Horizons of mesas

---

[1]Cf. Whitman's "Starting from Paumanok." Ferlinghetti is reversing Whitman's westward journey.

40 like plains of Spain high up
   in Don Quixote country—
   sharp eroded towers of bluffs
   like windmills tilted,
   "los molinos"[2] of earth, abandoned—
45 Great long rectangular stone islands
   sticking up on far plains, like forts
   or immense light cargo ships
   high on plains of water,
   becalmed and rudderless,
50 props thrashing wheat,
   stranded forever,
   no one on those bridges. . . .
   Later again, much later,
   one small halfass town,
55 followed by one telephone wire
   and one straight single iron road
   hung to the tracks as by magnets
   attached to a single endless fence,
   past solitary pumping stations,
60 each with a tank, a car, a small house, a dog,
   no people anywhere—
   All hiding?
   White Man gone home?
   Must be a cowboy someplace . . .
65 Birds flap from fences, trestles,
   caw and caw their nothingness.
   Stone church sticks up
   quote Out of Nowhere unquote
   This must be Interzone
70 between Heaven and Brooklyn.
   Do they have a Classified Section
   as in phonebooks
   in the back of the Bibles here?
   Otherwise they'd never find Anything.
75 Try Instant Zen.[3] . . .
   Still later again,
   sunset and strange clouds like udders
   rayed with light from below—

[2]Spanish: The windmills. The mesas of the Western deserts are compared to the windmills that Don Quixote, the comic caricature of the chivalric knight in Cervantes' novel, tilted at in vain.
[3]Zen Buddhism: a school of Buddhist thought that stresses meditation and contemplation.

some God's hand sticks through,
80 black trees stand out.
The world is a winter farm—
Cradle we rocked out of—[4]
prairie schooners[5] into Pullmans,
their bright saloons sheeted in oblivion—
85 Wagon-lits[6]—bedwagons over the prairies,
bodies nested in them,
hurtled through night,
inscrutable. . . .
Onward still . . . or Backward . . .
90 huge snow fields still, on and on,
still no one,
Indians all gone to Florida
or Cuba!
Train hoots at something
95 in the nowhere we still rock through,
Dingding crossroads flicker by,
Mining towns, once roaring,
now shrunk to the railhead,
streetlights stoned with loneliness
100 or lit with leftover sun
they drank too much of during the day. . . .
And at long last now
this world shrunk
to one lone brakeman's face
105 stuck out of darkness—
long white forehead
like bleached skull of cow—
huge black sad eyes—
high-peaked cloth cap, grey-striped—
110 swings his railroad lantern high, close up,
as our window whizzes by—
his figure splashed upon it,
slanted, muezzin-like,[7]
very grave, very tall,
115 strange skeleton—
Who stole America?

Myself I saw in the window reflected.

[4]Cf. Whitman's "Out of the Cradle Endlessly Rocking."
[5]Covered wagons.
[6]French name for "Pullman berths"; literally, "wagon-beds."
[7]Muezzin: the crier who calls the Mohammedan faithful to prayer five times
daily.

Richard Wilbur (1921–   )

Born in New York, Wilbur got his B.A. from Amherst in 1942 and his M.A. from Harvard in 1947, with service in the infantry during World War II between degrees. He has taught at Harvard, Wellesley, and now at Wesleyan in Middletown, Connecticut. Wilbur's sense of things is religious, but not rhapsodic or mystical. His theme is the tribulations of spirit trying to realize itself in a fallen world. The graceful decorum, the wit and cerebral precision of the poems, express his faith in, or hope for, a form underlying the fractures of the natural order. The titles of the books are: *The Beautiful Changes* (1947), *Ceremony* (1950), *Things of This World* (1956), *Advice to a Prophet* (1961), and *Walking to Sleep* (1969). He has won a Guggenheim, a Pulitzer Prize, the National Book Award, the Prix de Rome, and the Bollingen Prize for Translation for his version of Molière's *Tartuffe* (1963).

REFERENCE

Hill, Donald L. *Richard Wilbur*. New York: Twayne, 1967.
Mills, Ralph J. Jr. *Contemporary American Poetry*. New York: Random House, 1965.

"A WORLD WITHOUT OBJECTS IS A SENSIBLE EMPTINESS"[1]

The tall camels of the spirit
Steer for their deserts, passing the last groves loud
With the sawmill shrill of the locust, to the whole honey of the arid
    Sun. They are slow, proud,

5   And move with a stilted stride
To the land of sheer horizon, hunting Traherne's
Sensible emptiness, there where the brain's lantern-slide
    Revels in vast returns.

O connoisseurs of thirst,
10   Beasts of my soul who long to learn to drink
Of pure mirage, those prosperous islands are accurst
    That shimmer on the brink

Of absence; auras, lustres,
And all shinings need to be shaped and borne.
15 Think of those painted saints, capped by the early masters
    With bright, jauntily-worn

Aureate plates, or even
Merry-go-round rings. Turn, O turn
From the fine sleights of the sand, from the long empty oven
20   Where flames in flamings burn

Back to the trees arrayed
In bursts of glare, to the halo-dialing run
Of the country creeks, and the hills' bracken tiaras made
    Gold in the sunken sun,

25   Wisely watch for the sight
Of the supernova[2] burgeoning over the barn,
Lampshine blurred in the steam of beasts, the spirit's right
    Oasis, light incarnate.

---

[1]Adapted from a statement in a prose meditation by the metaphysical poet Thomas Traherne (1638–1674): *Second Century*, Meditation 65, from his *Centuries of Meditations*.
[2]The explosion of a star.

LOVE CALLS US TO
THE THINGS OF THIS WORLD

The eyes open to a cry of pulleys,
And spirited from sleep, the astounded soul
Hangs for a moment bodiless and simple
As false dawn.
5   Outside the open window
The morning air is all awash with angels.

Some are in bed- sheets, some are in blouses,
Some are in smocks: but truly there they are.
Now they are rising together in calm swells
10 Of halcyon feeling, filling whatever they wear
With the deep joy of their impersonal breathing;

Now they are flying in place, conveying
The terrible speed of their omnipresence, moving
And staying like white water; and now of a sudden
15 They swoon down into so rapt a quiet
That nobody seems to be there.
                              The soul shrinks

From all that it is about to remember,
From the punctual rape of every blessèd day,
20 And cries,
          "Oh, let there be nothing on earth but laundry,
Nothing but rosy hands in the rising steam
And clear dances done in the sight of heaven."

Yet, as the sun acknowledges
25 With a warm look the world's hunks and colors,
The soul descends once more in bitter love
To accept the waking body, saying now
In a changed voice as the man yawns and rises,

"Bring them down from their ruddy gallows;
30 Let there be clean linen for the backs of thieves;
Let lovers go fresh and sweet to be undone,
And the heaviest nuns walk in a pure floating
Of dark habits,
                keeping their difficult balance."

DIGGING FOR CHINA

"Far enough down is China," somebody said.
"Dig deep enough and you might see the sky
As clear as at the bottom of a well.
Except it would be real—a different sky.
5   Then you could burrow down until you came
To China! Oh, it's nothing like New Jersey.
There's people, trees, and houses, and all that,
But much, much different. Nothing looks the same."

I went and got the trowel out of the shed
10   And sweated like a coolie all that morning,
Digging a hole beside the lilac-bush,
Down on my hands and knees. It was a sort
Of praying, I suspect. I watched my hand
Dig deep and darker, and I tried and tried
15   To dream a place where nothing was the same.
The trowel never did break through to blue.

Before the dream could weary of itself
My eyes were tired of looking into darkness,
My sunbaked head of hanging down a hole.
20   I stood up in a place I had forgotten,
Blinking and staggering while the earth went round
And showed me silver barns, the fields dozing
In palls of brightness, patens[1] growing and gone
In the tides of leaves, and the whole sky china blue.
25   Until I got my balance back again
All that I saw was China, China, China.

ADVICE TO A PROPHET

When you come, as you soon must, to the streets of our city,
Mad-eyed from stating the obvious,
Not proclaiming our fall but begging us
In God's name to have self-pity,

5 Spare us all word of the weapons, their force and range,
The long numbers that rocket the mind;

[1]A plate or disc of metal, used at Mass to hold the Eucharist.

Our slow, unreckoning hearts will be left behind,
Unable to fear what is too strange.

Nor shall you scare us with talk of the death of the race.
10   How should we dream of this place without us?—
The sun mere fire, the leaves untroubled about us,
A stone look on the stone's face?

Speak of the world's own change. Though we cannot conceive
Of an undreamt thing, we know to our cost
15   How the dreamt cloud crumbles, the vines are blackened by frost,
How the view alters. We could believe,

If you told us so, that the white-tailed deer will slip
Into perfect shade, grown perfectly shy,
The lark avoid the reaches of our eye,
20   The jack-pine lose its knuckled grip

On the cold ledge, and every torrent burn
As Xanthus[1] once, its gliding trout
Stunned in a twinkling. What should we be without
The dolphin's arc, the dove's return,

25   These things in which we have seen ourselves and spoken?
Ask us, prophet, how we shall call
Our natures forth when that live tongue is all
Dispelled, that glass obscured or broken

In which we have said the rose of our love and the clean
30   Horse of our courage, in which beheld
The singing locust of the soul unshelled,
And all we mean or wish to mean.

Ask us, ask us whether with the worldless rose
Our hearts shall fail us; come demanding
35   Whether there shall be lofty or long standing
When the bronze annals of the oak-tree close.

---

[1]The chief city of ancient Lycia in Asia Minor. In the sixth century B.C., when the city was besieged by the Persians, the men gathered wives, families, slaves, and treasure into the Acropolis, burned it down, and went out to fight and be slain without a survivor.

IN A CHURCHYARD

That flower unseen, that gem of purest ray,[1]
Bright thoughts uncut by men:
Strange that you need but speak them, Thomas Gray,
And the mind skips and dives beyond its ken,

5   Finding at once the wild supposèd bloom,
Or in the imagined cave
Some pulse of crystal staving off the gloom
As covertly as phosphorus in a grave.

Void notions proper to a buried head!
10   Beneath these tombstones here
Unseenness fills the sockets of the dead,
Whatever to their souls may now appear;

And who but those unfathomably deaf
Who quiet all this ground
15   Could catch, within the ear's diminished clef,
A music innocent of time and sound?

What do the living hear, then, when the bell
Hangs plumb within the tower
Of the still church, and still their thoughts compel
20   Pure tollings that intend no mortal hour?

As when a ferry for the shore of death
Glides looming toward the dock,
Her engines cut, her spirits bating breath
As the ranked pilings narrow toward the shock,

25   So memory and expectation set
Some pulseless clangor free
Of circumstance, and charm us to forget
This twilight crumbling in the churchyard tree,

---

[1]Thomas Gray (1716–1771), "Elegy Written in a Country Churchyard," which
contains the quatrain:
   Full many a gem of purest ray serene,
     The dark unfathomed caves of ocean bear:
   Full many a flower is born to blush unseen,
     And waste its sweetness on the desert air.

Those swifts or swallows which do not pertain,
30   Scuffed voices in the drive,
That light flicked on behind the vestry pane,
Till, unperplexed from all that is alive,

It shadows all our thought, balked imminence
Of uncommitted sound,
35   And still would tower at the sill of sense
Were not, as now, its honed abeyance crowned

With a mauled boom of summons far more strange
Than any stroke unheard,
Which breaks again with unimagined range
40   Through all reverberations of the word,

Pooling the mystery of things that are,
The buzz of prayer said,
The scent of grass, the earliest-blooming star,
These unseen gravestones, and the darker dead.

SEED LEAVES[1]

HOMAGE TO R. F.[2]

Here something stubborn comes,
Dislodging the earth crumbs
And making crusty rubble.
It comes up bending double,
5   And looks like a green staple.
It could be seedling maple,
Or artichoke, or bean.
That remains to be seen.

Forced to make choice of ends,
10   The stalk in time unbends,
Shakes off the seed-case, heaves
Aloft, and spreads two leaves

[1]The first leaves to appear from the sprouting seed, different from the later and distinctive leaves of the particular kind of plant.
[2]Robert Frost.

Which still display no sure
And special signature.
15 Toothless and fat, they keep
The oval form of sleep.

This plant would like to grow
And yet be embryo;
Increase, and yet escape
20 The doom of taking shape;
Be vaguely vast, and climb
To the tip end of time
With all of space to fill,
Like boundless Igdrasil³
25 That has the stars for fruit.

But something at the root
More urgent than that urge
Bids two true leaves emerge,
And now the plant, resigned
30 To being self-defined
Before it can commerce
With the great universe,
Takes aim at the sky
And starts to ramify.

³In Norse mythology, the Great World Tree that holds earth, heaven, and hell
together.

Jack Kerouac (1922–1969)

Jean-Louis Lefris de Kérouac was born of French-Canadian parents in the factory town of Lowell, Massachusetts. His football prowess in high school brought him to Columbia, but he did not graduate. After stints in the Navy and the Merchant Marine he traveled around the United States, and in the fifties, with Ginsberg and Ferlinghetti, became a major figure in what he dubbed "the Beat Generation." His novels are episodes in a long autobiographical chronicle improvised in "spontaneous prose" out of his prodigious memory. Among them: *On the Road* (1957), *The Dharma Bums* (1958), *Visions of Gerard* (1963), *Desolation Angels* (1965), *The Vanity of Duluoz* (1968). His poetry includes *Mexico City Blues* (1959), *The Scripture of the Golden Eternity* (1960) and *Scattered Poems* (1971).

He wrote freely and fast, refusing to revise on vatic as well as aesthetic grounds: the artist is an oracle filled with inspiration beyond words, and any attempt at conscious control or improvement only interferes with the flow. Beyond the hard living and restless movement, Kerouac's Catholic spirit moved into Buddhist meditation. His innocence marked not just his limitations but his strength: at once a source of ecstasy and a judgment on the society he dropped out of. Kerouac demonstrates the links between the Beats and the nineteenth-century Transcendentalists: like Thoreau he saw most men in society as leading desperate lives; like Emerson he saw material forms dissolve in the totality and nothingness of spirit.

from **Mexico City Blues**

66th CHORUS

Dharma law[1]
   Say
  All things is made
     of the same thing
5   which is a nothing

  All nothings are the same
         as somethings
         the somethings
         are no-nothings,
10   equally blank

 Blank
    bright
       is the whole scene
      when you let your eyes
15   wander beyond the mules
    and the fields and carpets
    and bottles on the floor
    and clean mahogany radios,
dont be afraid
20 the raid hasnt started
panic you not
     day the better
     arriveth soon
And the gist of it Nothing-ness
25   SUCH-NESS

195th CHORUS

The songs that erupt
Are gist of the poesy,
Come by themselves, hark,
Stark as prisoners in a cave
5 Let out to sunlight, ragged
And beautiful when you look close

[1]In Buddhism, the ultimate law of all things to which the individual should conform.

And see underneath the beards
the holy blue eyes of humanity
And brown.

10 The stars on high sing
songs of their own, in motion
that doesnt move, real,
Unreal, singsong, spheres:—

But human poetries
15   With God as their design
        Sing with another law
          Of spheres & ensigns
                And rip me a blues,
                Son, blow me a bop,
20   Let me hear 'bout heaven
                In Brass Fluglemop[1]

228th CHORUS

Praised be man, he is existing in milk
      and living in lillies—
And his violin music takes place in milk
      and creamy emptiness—
5 Praised be the unfolded inside petal
      flesh of tend'rest thought—
      (petrels on the follying
      wave-valleys idly
      sing themselves asleep)—
10 Praised be delusion, the ripple—
Praised the Holy Ocean of Eternity—
Praised be I, writing, dead already &
      dead again—
      Dipped in ancid inkl
15   the flamd
              of T i m
      the Anglo Oglo Saxon Maneuvers
      Of Old Poet-o's—
            Praised be wood, it is milk—
20   Praised be Honey at the Source—
Praised be the embrace of soft sleep

---

[1]A telescoping of fluglehorn and the popular bebop song "Raggmopp."

—the valor of angels in valleys
of hell on earth below—
Praised be the Non ending—
25   Praised be the lights of earth-man—
Praised be the watchers—
    Praised be my fellow man
    For dwelling in milk

A PUN FOR AL GELPI

Jesus got mad one day
at an apricot tree.[1]
He said, "Peter, you
of the Holy See,[2]
5   Go see if the tree is ripe."
    "The tree is not yet ripe,"
    reported back Peter the Rock.
"Then let it wither!"
Jesus wanted an apricot.
10   In the morning, the tree
    had withered,
Like the ear in the agony
of the garden,[3]
Struck down by the sword,
15   Unready.
    What means this parable?
Everybody
    better see.
You're really sipping[4]
20   When your glass
    is always empty.

[1]The incident is told in Matthew 21:18–22 and in Mark 11: 12–14, where it is a fig tree.

[2]"See" here in the sense of the "seat of a bishop." The Holy See refers to the central authority of the Pope as supreme bishop. In Catholic belief, Jesus appointed Peter the first Pope when in Matthew 16: 18–19 he changed Peter's name from Simon with these words: "You are Peter and on this rock I will build my Church."

[3]When the soldiers surrounded Jesus to arrest him in the garden of Gethsemane, Peter struck off the ear of Malchus, the high priest's servant, with his sword. But Jesus said: "Put your sword back in its scabbard; am I not to drink the cup that the Father has given me?"

[4]Kerouac's note indicates that the major pun comes here with "sipping/slipping."

Denise Levertov (1923–   ) Denise Levertov's

mother was English and her father was a Russian Jew who became an Anglican priest; she was born in Ilford, Essex, and was educated mostly at home. Her training in ballet ended with World War II, during which she served as a civilian nurse in London. In 1946 she published *The Double Image*—in her own words as a "British Romantic with almost Victorian background." After the war she met Mitchell Goodman, an American writer in Europe on the G.I. Bill; they were married and came to the United States in 1948.

Her poetry is indisputably "American" from this point on. She learned a lot from Williams and from Olson's "Projective Verse" about the shape and idiom of poetry, and she became a close friend of such members of the Projectivist School as Duncan and Creeley. In an essay in *Poetry*, September 1965, she described her sense of organic form as proceeding from "an intuition of an order, a form beyond forms, in which forms partake, and of which man's creative works are analogies, resemblances, natural allegories" drawn out by realizing our unconscious intuitions in the precisions of language and metaphorical association.

For years the Goodmans lived in Manhattan; they have a house in Maine and have taught at various universities. Her principal volumes of poetry are: *With Eyes at the Back of Our Heads* (1959), *The Jacob's Ladder* (1961), *O Taste and See* (1964), *The Sorrow Dance* (1967), *Relearning the Alphabet* (1970), *To Stay Alive* (1971) and *Footprints* (1972). The later volumes are darker than the earlier ones, troubled by personal loss and public grief over the war in Vietnam. First published in America by Ferlinghetti in the City Lights Series, Denise Levertov is a popular figure on campuses; her sense of the openness and exactness of language, of form as organic yet achieved, places her at the center of the contemporary poetic scene.

REFERENCE

Howard, Richard. *Alone with America*. New York: Atheneum, 1969.

Mills, Ralph J., Jr. *Contemporary American Poetry*. New York: Random House, 1965.

Rosenthal, M. L. *The New Poets*. New York: Oxford University Press, 1967.

Wagner, Linda W. *Denise Levertov*. New York: Twayne, 1967.

NIGHT ON HATCHET COVE

The screendoor whines, clacks
shut.   My thoughts crackle
with seaweed-seething diminishing
flickers of phosphorus.   Gulp
5   of a frog, plash
of herring leaping;
                              interval;
squawk of a gull disturbed, a splashing;
pause
10   while silence poises for the breaking
bark of a seal: but silence.
                              Then
only your breathing. I'll
be quiet too. Out
15   stove, out lamp, let
night cut the question with profound
unanswer, sustained
echo of our unknowing.

SONG FOR ISHTAR[1]

The moon is a sow
and grunts in my throat
Her great shining shines through me
so the mud of my hollow gleams
5   and breaks in silver bubbles

She is a sow
and I a pig and a poet

When she opens her white
lips to devour me I bite back
10   and laughter rocks the moon

In the black of desire
we rock and grunt, grunt and
shine

[1]The Babylonian goddess of love and fertility.

THE ACHE OF MARRIAGE

The ache of marriage:

thigh and tongue, beloved,
are heavy with it,
it throbs in the teeth

5 We look for communion
and are turned away, beloved,
each and each

It is leviathan[1] and we
in its belly
10 looking for joy, some joy
not to be known outside it

two by two in the ark of
the ache of it.

CLARITAS[1]

i

The All-Day Bird, the artist,
whitethroated sparrow,
striving
in hope and
5 good faith to make his notes
ever more precise, closer
to what he knows.

ii

There is the proposition
and the development.
10 The way
one grows from the other.
The All-Day Bird
ponders.

[1]Whale.

[1]Latin: light, clarity.

iii

May the first note
15 be round enough
and those that follow
fine, fine as
sweetgrass,
                prays
20 the All-Day Bird.

iv

Fine
as the tail of a lizard,
as a leaf of
chives—
25 the *shadow of a difference*
falling between
note and note,
a *hair's breadth*
defining them.

v

30 The dew is on the vineleaves.
My tree
is lit with the
break of day.

vi

Sun
35 light.
        Light
light light light.

THE GROUND-MIST

In hollows of the land
in faults and valleys
                the white fog
bruised
5   by blue shadows
a mirage of lakes

and in the human
faults and depths
                    silences
10 floating
              between night and daybreak
illusion and substance.

But is illusion
so repeated, known
15   each dawn,
silence
          suspended in the
mind's shadow

always, not substance
20 of a sort?
                the white
bruised
          ground-mist the mirage
of a true lake.

O TASTE AND SEE

The world is
not with us enough.[1]
O taste and see[2]

the subway Bible poster said,
5 meaning *The Lord*, meaning
if anything all that lives
to the imagination's tongue,

grief, mercy, language,
tangerine, weather, to
10 breathe them, bite,
savor, chew, swallow, transform

---

[1]"The World Is Too Much with Us," a sonnet by William Wordsworth (1770–1850).
[2]Psalm 34:18: "O taste and see that the Lord is good."

into our flesh our
deaths, crossing the street, plum, quince,
living in the orchard and being

15   hungry, and plucking
the fruit.

THE GARDEN WALL

Bricks of the wall,
so much older than the house—
taken I think from a farm pulled down
           when the street was built—
5   narrow bricks of another century.

Modestly, though laid with panels and parapets,
a wall behind the flowers—
roses and hollyhocks, the silver
pods of lupine, sweet-tasting
10   phlox, gray
lavender—
           unnoticed—
                      but I discovered
the colors in the wall that woke
15   when spray from the hose
played on its pocks and warts—

a hazy red, a
grain gold, a mauve
of small shadows, sprung
20   from the quiet dry brown—

                      archetype
of the world always a step
beyond the world, that can't
be looked for, only
25   as the eye wanders,
found.

THE CAT AS CAT

The cat on my bosom
sleeping and purring
—fur-petalled chrysanthemum,
squirrel-killer—

5   is a metaphor only if I
force him to be one,
looking too long in his pale, fond,
dilating, contracting eyes

that reject mirrors, refuse
10 to observe what bides
stockstill.
            Likewise

flex and reflex of claws
gently pricking through sweater to skin
15 gently sustains their own tune,
not mine. I-Thou, cat, I-Thou.[1]

A LAMENTATION

Grief, have I denied thee?
Grief, I have denied thee.

That robe or tunic, black gauze
over black and silver my sister[1] wore
5   to dance *Sorrow*, hung so long
in my closet. I never tried it on.
           And my dance
was *Summer*—they rouged my cheeks
and twisted roses with wire stems into my hair.
10 I was compliant, Juno de sept ans,[2]

---

[1]Martin Buber (1878–1965), the Jewish existentialist philosopher, argued for an "I-Thou" relationship, in which individuals could meet and come to know one another as each individual was in himself.

---

[1]Olga Levertoff (1914–1964).
[2]French: "Seven-year-old Juno."

betraying my autumn birthright pour faire plaisir.[3]
Always denial. Grief in the morning, washed away
in coffee, crumbled to a dozen errands between
busy fingers.

15   Or across cloistral shadow, insistent
intrusion of pink sunstripes from open
archways, falling recurrent.

Corrosion denied, the figures the acid designs
filled in. Grief dismissed,
20 and Eros[4] along with grief.
Phantasmagoria swept across the sky
by shaky winds endlessly,
the spaces of blue timidly steady—
blue curtains at trailer windows framing
25 the cinder walks.
There are hidden corners of sky
choked with the swept shreds, with pain and ashes.
                                Grief,

have I denied thee? Denied thee.
30 The emblems torn from the walls,
and the black plumes.

PSALM CONCERNING THE CASTLE

Let me be at the place of the castle.
Let the castle be within me.
Let it rise foursquare from the moat's ring.
Let the moat's waters reflect green plumage of ducks, let the shells
    of swimming turtles break the surface or be seen through the
    rippling depths.
5 Let horsemen be stationed at the rim of it, and a dog, always alert on
    the brink of sleep.
Let the space under the first storey be dark, let the water lap the
    stone posts, and vivid green slime glimmer upon them; let a
    boat be kept there.

---

[3]French: "to make pleasure."
[4]The Greek god of love, the Roman Cupid; also in psychology, the self-preserv-
ative instincts, as opposed to Thanatos, the self-destructive instincts.

Let the caryatids[1] of the second storey be bears upheld on beams that
    are dragons.
On the parapet of the central room, let there be four archers, look-
    ing off to the four horizons. Within, let the prince be at home,
    let him sit in deep thought, at peace, all the windows open to
    the loggias.[2]
Let the young queen sit above, in the cool air, her child in her arms;
    let her look with joy at the great circle, the pilgrim shadows,
    the work of the sun and the play of the wind. Let her walk to
    and fro. Let the columns uphold the roof, let the storeys uphold
    the columns, let there be dark space below the lowest floor, let
    the castle rise foursquare out of the moat, let the moat be a
    ring and the water deep, let the guardians guard it, let there be
    wide lands around it, let that country where it stands be within
    me, let me be where it is.

CITY PSALM

The killings continue, each second
pain and misfortune extend themselves
in the genetic chain, injustice is done knowingly, and the air
bears the dust of decayed hopes,
5 yet breathing those fumes, walking the thronged
pavements among crippled lives, jackhammers
raging, a parking lot painfully agleam
in the May sun, I have seen
not behind but within, within the
10 dull grief, blown grit, hideous
concrete façades, another grief, a gleam
as of dew, an abode of mercy,
have heard not behind but within noise
a humming that drifted into a quiet smile.
15 Nothing was changed, all was revealed otherwise;
not that horror was not, not that the killings did not continue,
not that I thought there was to be no more despair,
but that as if transparent all disclosed
an otherness that was blessèd, that was bliss.
20 *I saw Paradise in the dust of the street.*

---

[1]Columns carved in the form of figures.
[2]Roofed but open galleries.

A VISION

'The intellectual love of a thing is the understanding of its perfections.'
Spinoza, quoted by Ezra Pound

Two angels among the throng of angels
paused in the upward abyss,
facing angel to angel.

Blue and green glowed the wingfeathers
5 of one angel, from red to gold the sheen
of the other's. These two,

so far as angels may dispute, were poised
on the brink of dispute, brink of
fall from angelic stature,

10 for these tall ones, angels
whose wingspan encompasses entire
earthly villages, whose heads if their feet touched earth

would top pines or redwoods, live by their vision's harmony
which sees at one glance
15 the dark and light of the moon.

These two hovered dazed before one another,
for one saw the seafeathered, peacock breakered
crests of the other angel's magnificence,
different from his own,

20 and the other's eyes flickered with vision of
flame petallings, cream-gold grainfeather glitterings,
the wings of his fellow,

and both in immortal danger of dwindling, of dropping
into the remote forms of a lesser being.

25 But as these angels, the only halted ones
among the many who passed and repassed,
trod air as swimmers tread water, each gazing

[1]The vision described in the poem came to the poet in a dream and was recorded
immediately thereafter.

on the angelic wings of the other,
the intelligence proper to great angels flew into their wings,
30   the intelligence called *intellectual love*, which,
understanding the perfections of scarlet,

leapt up among blues and greens strongshafted,
and among amber down illumined the sapphire bloom,

so that each angel was iridescent with the strange newly-seen
35   hues he watched; and their discovering pause
and the speech their silent interchange of perfection was

never became a shrinking to opposites,

and they remained free in the heavenly chasm,
remained angels, but dreaming angels,
40   each imbued with the mysteries of the other.

ADVENT 1966

Because in Vietnam the vision of a Burning Babe
is multiplied, multiplied,
                    the flesh on fire
not Christ's, as Southwell[1] saw it, prefiguring
5   the Passion upon the Eve of Christmas,

but wholly human and repeated, repeated,
infant after infant, their names forgotten,
their sex unknown in the ashes,
set alight, flaming but not vanishing,
10   not vanishing as his vision but lingering,

cinders upon the earth or living on
moaning and stinking in hospitals three abed;

because of this my strong sight,
my clear caressive sight, my poet's sight I was given

---

[1]Robert Southwell, S. J. (1561–1595), the Jesuit poet executed for his Catholic activities under Queen Elizabeth I, whose poem "The Burning Babe" depicts the Christ child burning with flames in the midst of Christmas snow as a foreshadowing of His future redemptive suffering and death.

15 that it might stir me to song,
    is blurred.
                There is a cataract filming over
    my inner eyes. Or else a monstrous insect
    has entered my head, and looks out
20 from my sockets with multiple vision,

    seeing not the unique Holy Infant
    burning sublimely, an imagination of redemption,
    furnace in which souls are wrought into new life,
    but, as off a beltline, more, more senseless figures aflame.

25 And this insect (who is not there—
    it is my own eyes do my seeing, the insect
    is not there, what I see is there)
    will not permit me to look elsewhere,

    or if I look, to see except dulled and unfocused
30 the delicate, firm, whole flesh of the still unburned.

Edgar Bowers (1924–   )

Born in Rome, Georgia, Bowers served in the Army from 1943 to 1946, part of the time in Germany. In 1947 he got a B.A. from the University of North Carolina and in 1953 a Ph.D. from Stanford, where he studied with Yvor Winters. Now he teaches at the University of California, Santa Barbara. He has been at different times a Fulbright and a Guggenheim Fellow. His two books of poems are *The Form of Loss* (1956) and *The Astronomers* (1965). For Bowers, rational and technical control provides the distance and focus needed for self-comprehension and self-expression, and thereby fixes whatever is recoverable from the waste of time and passion.

REFERENCE
Howard, Richard. *Alone with America.* New York: Atheneum, 1969.

TO THE READER

These poems are too much tangled with the error
And waste they would complete. My soul repays me,
Who fix it by a rhythm, with reason's terror
Of hearing the swift motion that betrays me.
5   Mine be the life and failure. But do not look
Too closely for these ghosts which claim my book.

THE STOIC:

FOR LAURA VON COURTEN

All winter long you listened for the boom
Of distant cannon wheeled into their place.
Sometimes outside beneath a bombers' moon
You stood alone to watch the searchlights trace

5   Their careful webs against the boding sky,
While miles away on Munich's vacant square
The bombs lunged down with an unruly cry
Whose blast you saw yet could but faintly hear.

And might have turned your eyes upon the gleam
10   Of a thousand years of snow, where near the clouds
The Alps ride massive to their full extreme,
And season after season glacier crowds

The dark, persistent smudge of conifers.
Or seen beyond the hedge and through the trees
15   The shadowy forms of cattle on the furze,
Their dim coats white with mist against the freeze.

Or thought instead of other times than these,
Of other countries and of other sights:
Eternal Venice sinking by degrees
20   Into the very water that she lights;

Reflected in canals, the lucid dome
Of Maria dell' Salute at your feet,

Her triple spires disfigured by the foam.
Remembered in Berlin the parks, the neat

25 Footpaths and lawns, the clean spring foliage,
Where just short weeks before, a bomb, unaimed,
Released a frightened lion from its cage,
Which in the mottled dark that trees enflamed

Killed one who hurried homeward from the raid.
30 And by yourself there standing in the chill
You must, with so much known, have been afraid
And chosen such a mind of constant will,

Which, though all time corrode with constant hurt,
Remains, until it occupies no space,
35 That which it is; and passionless, inert,
Becomes at last no meaning and no place.

AMOR VINCIT OMNIA[1]

Love is no more.
It died as the mind dies: the pure desire
Relinquishing the blissful form it wore,
The ample joy and clarity expire.

5 Regret is vain.
Then do not grieve for what you would efface,
The sudden failure of the past, the pain
Of its unwilling change, and the disgrace.

Leave innocence,
10 And modify your nature by the grief
Which poses to the will indifference
That no desire is permanent in sense.

Take leave of me.
What recompense, or pity, or deceit
15 Can cure, or what assumed serenity
Conceal the mortal loss which we repeat?

The mind will change, and change shall be relief.

[1]Latin: "Love conquers all."

THE VIRGIN MARY

The hovering and huge, dark, formless sway
That nature moves by laws we contemplate
We name for lack of name as order, fate,
God, principle, or primum mobile.[1]
5　But in that graven image, word made wood
By skillful faith of him to whom she was
Eternal nature, first and final cause,
The form of knowledge knowledge understood
Bound human thought against the dark we find.
10　And body took the image of the mind
To shape in chaos a congruent form
Of will and matter, equal, side by side,
Upon the act of faith, within the norm
Of carnal being, blind and glorified.

AN AFTERNOON AT THE BEACH

I'll go among the dead to see my friend.
The place I leave is beautiful: the sea
Repeats the winds' far swell in its long sound,
And, there beside it, houses solemnly
5　Shine with the modest courage of the land,
While swimmers try the verge of what they see.

I cannot go, although I should pretend
Some final self whose phantom eye could see
Him who because he is not cannot change.
10　And yet the thought of going makes the sea,
The land, the swimmers, and myself seem strange,
Almost as strange as they will someday be.

[1]Latin: "first mover."

from **Autumn Shade**

1

The autumn shade is thin. Grey leaves lie faint
Where they will lie, and, where the thick green was,
Light stands up, like a presence, to the sky.
The trees seem merely shadows of its age.
5 From off the hill, I hear the logging crew,
The furious and indifferent saw, the slow
Response of heavy pine; and I recall
That goddesses have died when their trees died.
Often in summer, drinking from the spring,
10 I sensed in its cool breath and in its voice
A living form, darker than any shade
And without feature, passionate, yet chill
With lust to fix in ice the buoyant rim—
Ancient of days, the mother of us all.
15 Now, toward his destined passion there, the strong,
Vivid young man, reluctant, may return
From suffering in his own experience
To lie down in the darkness. In this time,
I stay in doors. I do my work. I sleep.
20 Each morning, when I wake, I assent to wake.
The shadow of my fist moves on this page,
Though, even now, in the wood, beneath a bank,
Coiled in the leaves and cooling rocks, the snake
Does as it must, and sinks into the cold.

9

In nameless warmth, sun light in every corner,
Bending my body over my glowing book,
I share the room. Is it with a voice or touch
Or look, as of an absence, learned by love,
5 Now, merely mine? Annunciation, specter
Of the worn out, lost, or broken, telling what future,

What vivid loss to come, you change the room
And him who reads here. Restless, he will stir,
Look round, and see the room renewed, and line,
10   Color, and shape as, in desire, they are,
Not shadows but substantial light, explicit,
Bright as glass, inexhaustible, and true.

10

My shadow moves, until, at noon, I stand
Within its seal, as in the finished past.
But in the place where effect and cause are joined,
In the warmth or cold of my remembering,
5   Of love, of partial freedom, the time to be
Trembles and glitters again in windy light.
For nothing is disposed. The slow soft wind
Tilting the blood-root keeps its gentle edge.
The intimate cry, both sinister and tender,
10   Once heard, is heard confined in its reserve.
My image of myself, apart, informed
By many deaths, resists me, and I stay
Almost as I have been, intact, aware,
Alive, though proud and cautious, even afraid.

Robert Creeley (1926–   )

Creeley was born in Arlington, Massachusetts, and attended Harvard without graduating both before and after serving in the American Field Service in Asia during World War II. After living for a time in Europe, he got an A.B. from Black Mountain College in 1955, taught there at Olson's invitation, and edited the *Black Mountain Review*. Subsequently he has taught at various places, including the State University of New York at Buffalo, and he has a house in the New Mexico desert. *For Love* (1962) brought together the verse of the previous decade and has been followed by *Words* (1967) and *Pieces* (1969). The titles are significant; his poems are scaled down: prismatic fragments of language that refract through the subtle shifts of tone and rhythm the difficulties of human perception and communication. Wry where Olson, Duncan, and Levertov are visionary, Creeley sees as the link among the members of the Projectivist Group "a common feeling that verse was something *given* one to write, and that the form it might then take was intimate with that fact." Creeley now lives part of the year near San Francisco.

REFERENCE
Howard, Richard. *Alone with America*. New York: Atheneum, 1969.
Rosenthal, M. L. *The New Poets*. New York: Oxford University Press, 1967.

THE RIDDLE

What it is, the literal size
incorporates.
       The question
is a mute question. One is
5 too lonely, one wants
to stop there, at the edge of

conception. The woman

imperative, the man
lost in stern
10 thought:

give it form certainly,
the name and titles.

THE DISHONEST MAILMEN

They are taking all my letters, and they
put them into a fire.

               I see the flames, etc.
But do not care, etc.

5 They burn everything I have, or what little
I have. I don't care, etc.

The poem supreme, addressed to
emptiness—this is the courage

necessary. This is something
10 quite different.

THE IMMORAL PROPOSITION

If you never do anything for anyone else
you are spared the tragedy of human relation-

ships. If quietly and like another time
there is the passage of an unexpected thing:

5   to look at it is more
than it was. God knows

nothing is competent nothing is
all there is. The unsure

egoist is not
10 good for himself.

THE DEATH OF VENUS

I dreamt her sensual proportions
had suffered sea-change,

that she was a porpoise, a
sea-beast rising lucid from the mist.

5   The sound of waves killed speech
but there were gestures—

of my own, it was to call her closer,
of hers, she snorted and filled her lungs with water,

then sank, to the bottom,
10 and looking down, clear it was, like crystal,

there I saw her.

FOR FEAR

For fear I want
to make myself again
under the thumb
of old love, old time

5   subservience
and pain, bent
into a nail that will
not come out.

Why, love, does it
10   make such a difference
not to be heard
in spite of self

or what we may feel,
one for the other,
15   but as a hammer
to drive again

bent nail
into old hurt?

FOR LOVE

FOR BOBBIE[1]

Yesterday I wanted to
speak of it, that sense above
the others to me
important because all

5   that I know derives
from what it teaches me.
Today, what is it that
is finally so helpless,

[1]The poet's wife, Bobbie Hall.

different, despairs of its own
10 statement, wants to
turn away, endlessly
to turn away.

If the moon did not . . .
no, if you did not
15 I wouldn't either, but
what would I not

do, what prevention, what
thing so quickly stopped.
That is love yesterday
20 or tomorrow, not

now. Can I eat
what you give me. I
have not earned it. Must
I think of everything

25 as earned. Now love also
becomes a reward so
remote from me I have
only made it with my mind.

Here is tedium,
30 despair, a painful
sense of isolation and
whimsical if pompous

self-regard. But that image
is only of the mind's
35 vague structure, vague to me
because it is my own.

Love, what do I think
to say. I cannot say it.
What have you become to ask,
40 what have I made you into,

companion, good company,
crossed legs with skirt, or
soft body under
the bones of the bed.

45 Nothing says anything
but that which it wishes
would come true, fears
what else might happen in

some other place, some
50 other time not this one.
A voice in my place, an
echo of that only in yours.

Let me stumble into
not the confession but
55 the obsession I begin with
now. For you

also (also)
some time beyond place, or
place beyond time, no
60 mind left to

say anything at all,
that face gone, now.
Into the company of love
it all returns.

THE LANGUAGE

Locate *I*
love you some-
where in

teeth and
5 eyes, bite
it but

take care not
to hurt, you
want so

10 much so
little. Words
say everything,

I
love you
15 again,

then what
is emptiness
for. To

fill, fill.
20 I heard words
and words full

of holes
aching. Speech
is a mouth.

GEMINI[1]

Two eyes, two hands—
in one two are given.

The words
are messages

5 from another,
not understood but given.

●

Neither one, nor the other
nor of a brother—but in

the one, two, restless,
10 confined to a place ruled

by a moon, and another one
with messages, rather, sequences

of words that are not to be understood
but somehow given to a world.

[1]A constellation of the twins Caster and Pollux; also the third sign of the
Zodiac.

15 All this dances in a room,
two by two, but alone.

●

From one to two,
is the first rule.

Of two minds the twin
20 is to double life given.

●

What it says is that one
is two, the twin,

that the messenger comes
to either, that these fight

25 to possess, but do not
understand—that if the

moon rules, there is
"domestic harmony"—but if the blood

cry, the split so divide,
30 there can be no

company for the two in one.
He is alone.

In secret
the out's in—

the wise
surprised, all

5 going coming,
begun undone.

Hence the fool dances
in endless happiness.

●

A circling with
10 snake-tail in mouth—

what the head was
looked *forward,*

what backward is,
then guess.

15 Either way,
it will stay.

"Time" is some sort of hindsight, or else rhythm of activity
—e.g., now it's 11 days later—"also alive" like they say.

●

Where it is
was and
5 will be never
only here.

●

—fluttering as
falling, leaves,
knives, to
10 avoid—tunnel
down the
vague sides . . .

●

—it
it—

W. D. Snodgrass (1926–   )

William DeWitt Snodgrass was born in Wilkinsburg, Pennsylvania; after service in the Navy during World War II he got his A.B., M.A., and M.F.A. from the State University of Iowa, and has since taught at a number of universities, now at Syracuse. His first book, *Heart's Needle* (1959), won the Pulitzer Prize and wide acclaim in the United States and England. The sequence that bears the book's title is "confessional," dedicated to his daughter between a painful divorce from her mother and Snodgrass' remarriage. The best poems of *After Experience* (1968) demonstrated again his disciplined skill in objectifying autobiography into finished aesthetic expression. The form, imagery, and metaphors are precisely scaled to the substance; there are no loose ends, no lapses, no extraneous details, as the poem fulfills the terms and limits it has set for itself.

REFERENCE
Howard, Richard. *Alone with America.* New York: Atheneum, 1969.

THE MARSH

Swampstrife and spatterdock[1]
   lull in the heavy waters;
some thirty little frogs
   spring with each step you walk;
5 a fish's belly glitters
   tangled near rotting logs.

Over by the gray rocks
   muskrats dip and circle.
Out of his rim of ooze
10   a silt-black pond snail walks
inverted on the surface
   toward what food he may choose.

You look up; while you walk
   the sun bobs and is snarled
15 in the enclosing weir[2]
   of trees, in their dead stalks.
Stick in the mud, old heart,
   what are you doing here?

from **Heart's Needle**

1

Child of my winter, born
When the new fallen soldiers froze
In Asia's steep ravines and fouled the snows,[1]
When I was torn

5 By love I could not still,
By fear that silenced my cramped mind

---

[1]Both aquatic plants.
[2]Interwoven fence placed in a stream to catch fish.

---

[1]The Korean War (1950–1953) in which the United Nations forces, with the United States predominating, defended the Republic of Korea against invasion from Communist North Korea.

To that cold war² where, lost, I could not find
My peace in my will,³

All those days we could keep
10   Your mind a landscape of new snow
Where the chilled tenant-farmer finds, below,
His fields asleep

In their smooth covering, white
As quilts to warm the resting bed
15   Of birth or pain, spotless as paper spread
For me to write,

And thinks: Here lies my land
Unmarked by agony, the lean foot
Of the weasel tracking, the thick trapper's boot;
20   And I have planned

My chances to restrain
The torments of demented summer or
Increase the deepening harvest here before
It snows again.

7

Here in the scuffled dust
is our ground of play.
I lift you on your swing and must
shove you away,
5   see you return again,
drive you off again, then

stand quiet till you come.
You, though you climb
higher, farther from me, longer,
10   will fall back to me stronger.

²Pun on the Cold War—that is, the political and ideological, but not military,
struggle that developed after World War II between the communist world
under Soviet Russia and the capitalist-republican world under the United
States.
³A rewriting of Dante's famous maxim: "My peace in His [God's] Will."

Bad penny, pendulum,
   you keep my constant time

to bob in blue July
   where fat goldfinches fly
15 over the glittering, fecund
   reach of our growing lands.
Once more now, this second,
   I hold you in my hands.

MEMENTOS, 1

Sorting out letters and piles of my old
   Canceled checks, old clippings, and yellow note cards
That meant something once, I happened to find
   Your picture. *That* picture. I stopped there cold,
5 Like a man raking piles of dead leaves in his yard
   Who has turned up a severed hand.

Still, that first second, I was glad: you stand
   Just as you stood—shy, delicate, slender,
In that long gown of green lace netting and daisies
10   That you wore to our first dance. The sight of you stunned
Us all. Well, our needs were different, then,
   And our ideals came easy.

Then through the war and those two long years
   Overseas, the Japanese dead in their shacks
15 Among dishes, dolls, and lost shoes; I carried
   This glimpse of you, there, to choke down my fear,
Prove it had been, that it might come back.
   That was before we got married.

—Before we drained out one another's force
20   With lies, self-denial, unspoken regret
And the sick eyes that blame; before the divorce
   And the treachery. Say it: before we met. Still,
I put back your picture. Someday, in due course,
   I will find that it's still there.

LOBSTERS IN THE WINDOW

First, you think they are dead.
Then you are almost sure
One is beginning to stir.
Out of the crushed ice, slow
5   As the hands of a schoolroom clock,
He lifts his one great claw
And holds it over his head;
Now, he is trying to walk.

But like a run-down toy;
10   Like the backward crabs we boys
Splashed after in the creek,
Trapped in jars or a net,
And then took home to keep.
Overgrown, retarded, weak,
15   He is fumbling yet
From the deep chill of his sleep

As if, in a glacial thaw,
Some ancient thing might wake
Sore and cold and stiff
20   Struggling to raise one claw
Like a defiant fist;
Yet wavering, as if
Starting to swell and ache
With that thick peg in the wrist.

LEAVING THE MOTEL

Outside, the last kids holler
Near the pool: they'll stay the night.
Pick up the towels; fold your collar
Out of sight.

5   Check: is the second bed
Unrumpled, as agreed?
Landlords have to think ahead
In case of need,

Too. Keep things straight: don't take
The matches, the wrong keyrings—
We've nowhere we could keep a keepsake—
Ashtrays, combs, things

That sooner or later others
Would accidentally find.
Check: take nothing of one another's
And leave behind

Your license number only,
Which they won't care to trace;
We've paid. Still, should such things get lonely,
Leave in their vase

An aspirin to preserve
Our lilacs, the wayside flowers
We've gathered and must leave to serve
A few more hours;

That's all. We can't tell when
We'll come back, can't press claims;
We would no doubt have other rooms then,
Or other names.

Allen Ginsberg (1926–   )
Ginsberg was born in Paterson, New Jersey, graduated from Columbia, and had a range of jobs from dishwashing to market research before emerging as the guru of the Beat Generation of the fifties and of the Hip Generation of the sixties. He once described his intentions by saying: "If I look funny or get up in public and say I am homosexual, take drugs, and hear Blake's voice, then people who are heterosexual, don't take drugs, and hear Shakespeare's voice may feel freer to do what they want and be what they are." *Howl* (1956), a sensation when issued by Ferlinghetti's City Lights, and *Kaddish* (1961), an elegy for his mother, are scatological attempts to purge himself of his personal and family demons and of the demons of urban America, in order to free himself into ecstasy, often by mind-expanding drugs. *Planet News* (1968) and *Ankor Wat* (1968) are more consistently visionary; all things are holy because all things are projections of Spirit struggling to shine through bodies. In Ginsberg the Hebrew prophet, Dionysus, and Buddha meet. He has been in India and Japan as well as in Europe, and travels through the United States speaking out as mediator between the Establishment and the hippie subculture. Whitman is Ginsberg's point of departure, not only as a seer to America but as an experimenter with "the formal organization of the long line" of free verse. He revered Williams as a powerful older local poet, and Williams supplied the Introduction to *Howl* when it appeared.

REFERENCE
Howard, Richard. *Alone with America*. New York: Atheneum, 1969.
Kramer, Jane. *Allen Ginsberg in America*. New York: Random House, 1969.
Merrill, Thomas F. *Allen Ginsberg*. New York: Twayne, 1969.
Rosenthal, M. L. *The New Poets*. New York: Oxford University Press, 1967.

A SUPERMARKET IN CALIFORNIA

What thoughts I have of you tonight, Walt Whitman, for I walked
    down the sidestreets under the trees with a headache self-
    conscious looking at the full moon.
In my hungry fatigue, and shopping for images, I went into the
    neon fruit supermarket, dreaming of your enumerations!
What peaches and what penumbras! Whole families shopping at
    night! Aisles full of husbands! Wives in the avocados, babies
    in the tomatoes!—and you, Garcia Lorca,[1] what were you doing
    down by the watermelons?

I saw you, Walt Whitman, childless, lonely old grubber, poking
    among the meats in the refrigerator and eyeing the grocery
    boys.
5   I heard you asking questions of each: Who killed the pork chops?
    What price bananas? Are you my Angel?
I wandered in and out of the brilliant stacks of cans following you,
    and followed in my imagination by the store detective.
We strode down the open corridors together in our solitary fancy
    tasting artichokes, possessing every frozen delicacy, and never
    passing the cashier.

Where are we going, Walt Whitman? The doors close in an hour.
    Which way does your beard point tonight?
(I touch your book[2] and dream of our odyssey in the supermarket
    and feel absurd.)
10 Will we walk all night through solitary streets? The trees add shade
    to shade, lights out in the houses, we'll both be lonely.

[1]Federico Garcia Lorca (1899–1937), Spanish poet and dramatist.
[2]From Whitman's poem "So Long!":
    Camerado, this is no book,
    Who touches this touches a man,
    (Is it night? are we here together alone?)
    It is I you hold and who holds you,
    I spring from the pages into your arms—
        decease calls me forth.

SUNFLOWER SUTRA[1]

I walked on the banks of the tincan banana dock and sat down under
the huge shade of a Southern Pacific locomotive to look at the
sunset over the box house hills and cry.
Jack Kerouac sat beside me on a busted rusty iron pole, companion,
we thought the same thoughts of the soul, bleak and blue and
sad-eyed, surrounded by the gnarled steel roots of trees of
machinery.
The oily water on the river mirrored the red sky, sun sank on top of
final Frisco peaks, no fish in that stream, no hermit in those
mounts, just ourselves theumy-eyed and hungover like old
bums on the riverbank tired and wily.
Look at the Sunflower, he said, there was a dead gray shadow against
the sky, big as a man, sitting dry on top of a pile of ancient
sawdust—
5 —I rushed up enchanted—it was my first sunflower, memories of
Blake[2]—my visions—Harlem
and Hells of the Eastern rivers, bridges clanking Joes Greasy Sand-
wiches, dead baby carriages, black treadless tires forgotten
and unretreaded, the poem of the riverbank, condoms & pots,
steel knives, nothing stainless, only the dank muck and the
razor sharp artifacts passing into the past—
and the gray Sunflower poised against the sunset, crackly bleak and
dusty with the smut and smog and smoke of olden locomo-
tives in its eye—
corolla[3] of bleary spikes pushed down and broken like a battered
crown, seeds fallen out of its face, soon-to-be-toothless mouth
of sunny air, sunrays obliterated on its hairy head like a dried
wire spiderweb,
leaves stuck out like arms out of the stem, gestures from the sawdust
root, broke pieces of plaster fallen out of the black twigs, a dead
fly in its ear,
10 Unholy battered old thing you were, my sunflower O my soul, I
loved you then!
The grime was no man's grime but death and human locomotives,
all that dress of dust, that veil of darkened railroad skin, that smog
of cheek, that eyelid of black mis'ry, that sooty hand or phallus
or protuberance of artificial worse-than-dirt—industrial— mod-
ern—all that civilization spotting your crazy golden crown—

[1]Sutra: In Buddhism, a scriptural narrative.
[2]William Blake (1757–1827), the English visionary poet.
[3]The petals of a flower.

and those blear thoughts of death and dusty loveless eyes and ends
and withered roots below, in the home-pile of sand and saw-
dust, rubber dollar bills, skin of machinery, the guts and innards
of the weeping coughing car, the empty lonely tincans with
their rusty tongues alack, what more could I name, the smoked
ashes of some cock cigar, the cunts of wheelbarrows and the
milky breasts of cars, wornout asses out of chairs & sphincters
of dynamos—all these
entangled in your mummied roots—and you there standing before
me in the sunset, all your glory in your form!

15   A perfect beauty of a sunflower! a perfect excellent lovely sunflower
existence! a sweet natural eye to the new hip moon, woke up
alive and excited grasping in the sunset shadow sunrise golden
monthly breeze!
How many flies buzzed round you innocent of your grime, while
you cursed the heavens of the railroad and your flower soul?
Poor dead flower? when did you forget you were a flower? when did
you look at your skin and decide you were an impotent dirty old
locomotive? the ghost of a locomotive? the specter and shade of
a once powerful mad American locomotive?
You were never no locomotive, Sunflower, you were a sunflower!
And you Locomotive, you are a locomotive, forget me not!

20   So I grabbed up the skeleton thick sunflower and stuck it at my side
like a scepter,
and deliver my sermon to my soul, and Jack's soul too, and anyone
who'll listen,
—We're not our skin of grime, we're not our dread bleak dusty
imageless locomotive, we're all beautiful golden sunflowers
inside, we're blessed by our own seed & golden hairy naked
accomplishment-bodies growing into mad black formal sun-
flowers in the sunset, spied on by our eyes under the shadow
of the mad locomotive riverbank sunset Frisco hilly tincan eve-
ning sitdown vision.[4]

Berkeley 1955

---

[4]Ginsberg's comment: "But how sustain a long line in poetry (lest it lapse into prosaic)? It's natural inspiration of the moment that keeps it moving, disparate things put down together, shorthand notations of visual imagery, juxtapositions of hydrogen juke-box—abstract haikus sustain the mystery and put iron mystery back into the line: the last line of *Sunflower Sutra* is the extreme, one stream of single word associations, summing up."

AMERICA

America I've given you all and now I'm nothing.
America two dollars and twentyseven cents January 17, 1956.
I can't stand my own mind.
America when will we end the human war?
5   Go fuck yourself with your atom bomb.
I don't feel good don't bother me.
I won't write my poem till I'm in my right mind.
America when will you be angelic?
When will you take off your clothes?
10   When will you look at yourself through the grave?
When will you be worthy of your million Trotskyites?[1]
America why are your libraries full of tears?
America when will you send your eggs to India?
I'm sick of your insane demands.
15   When can I go into the supermarket and buy what I need with my
      good looks?
America after all it is you and I who are perfect not the next world.
Your machinery is too much for me.
You made me want to be a saint.
There must be some other way to settle this argument.
20   Burroughs[2] is in Tangiers I don't think he'll come back it's sinister.
Are you being sinister or is this some form of practical joke?
I'm trying to come to the point.
I refuse to give up my obsession.
America stop pushing I know what I'm doing.
25   America the plum blossoms are falling.
I haven't read the newspapers for months, everyday somebody goes
      on trial for murder.
America I feel sentimental about the Wobblies.[3]
America I used to be a communist when I was a kid I'm not sorry.

I smoke marijuana every chance I get.
30   I sit in my house for days on end and stare at the roses in the closet.
When I go to Chinatown I get drunk and never get laid.
My mind is made up there's going to be trouble.
You should have seen me reading Marx.

---

[1]Followers of Leon Trotsky (1877–1940), Russian Communist revolutionary, banished in 1929 and assassinated in Mexico.
[2]William Burroughs (1914–   ), American writer expatriated to Tangiers.
[3]The Industrial Workers of the World, a militant labor organization strong in the thirties.

My psychoanalyst thinks I'm perfectly right.

35 I won't say the Lord's Prayer.

I have mystical visions and cosmic vibrations.

America I still haven't told you what you did to Uncle Max after he
      came over from Russia.

I'm addressing you.

Are you going to let your emotional life be run by Time Magazine?

40 I'm obsessed by Time Magazine.

I read it every week.

Its cover stares at me every time I slink past the corner candystore.

I read it in the basement of the Berkeley Public Library.

It's always telling me about responsibility. Businessmen are serious.
      Movie producers are serious. Everybody's serious but me.

45 It occurs to me that I am America.

I am talking to myself again.

Asia is rising against me.

I haven't got a chinaman's chance.

I'd better consider my national resources.

50 My national resources consist of two joints of marijuana millions of
      genitals an unpublishable private literature that goes 1400 miles
      an hour and twentyfive-thousand mental institutions.

I say nothing about my prisons nor the millions of underprivileged
      who live in my flowerpots under the light of five hundred suns.

I have abolished the whorehouses of France, Tangiers is the next to go.

My ambition is to be President despite the fact that I'm a Catholic.

America how can I write a holy litany in your silly mood?

55 I will continue like Henry Ford my strophes are as individual as his
      automobiles more so they're all different sexes.

America I will sell you strophes $2500 apiece $500 down on your
      old strophe

America free Tom Mooney[4]

America save the Spanish Loyalists[5]

America Sacco & Vanzetti must not die[6]

---

[4]Tom Mooney (1884–1945); labor leader sentenced to death for killings in the
San Francisco Preparedness Parade in 1916; sentence commuted to life im-
prisonment by President Wilson because of suspicion of perjured testimony,
until he was pardoned in 1938.

[5]Supporters of the republican government during the Spanish Civil War against
Franco's Fascist forces during the 1930's.

[6]Nicola Sacco (1891–1927) and Bartolomeo Vanzetti (1888–1927): two Italian-
born anarchists executed for murder after a trial that caused a great outcry of
injustice because of questionable evidence and the prejudice of the judge.

60   America I am the Scottsboro boys.[7]
America when I was seven momma took me to Communist Cell
     meetings they sold us garbanzos a handful per ticket a ticket
     costs a nickel and the speeches were free everybody was an-
     gelic and sentimental about the workers it was all so sincere
     you have no idea what a good thing the party was in 1935 Scott
     Nearing was a grand old man a real mensch Mother Bloor made
     me cry I once saw Israel Amter plain.[8] Everybody must have
     been a spy.
America you don't really want to go to war.
America it's them bad Russians.
Them Russians them Russians and them Chinamen. And them
     Russians.
65   The Russia wants to eat us alive. The Russia's power mad. She wants
     to take our cars from out our garages.
Her wants to grab Chicago. Her needs a Red Readers' Digest. Her
     wants our auto plants in Siberia. Him big bureaucracy running
     our fillingstations.

That no good. Ugh. Him make Indians learn read. Him need big
     black niggers. Hah. Her make us all work sixteen hours a day.
     Help.
America this is quite serious.
America this is the impression I get from looking in the television
     set.
70   America is this correct?
I'd better get right down to the job.
It's true I don't want to join the Army or turn lathes in precision
     parts factories, I'm nearsighted and psychopathic anyway.
America I'm putting my queer shoulder to the wheel.

---

[7]Negroes, charged with raping two white girls in a famous 1931 trial in Scotts-
boro, Alabama; the trial became a center of controversy and a cause for
Northern liberals. Some were convicted, and there were appeals and retrials.
[8]Scott Nearing, Ella Reeve ("Mother") Bloor and Israel Amter were all politi-
cally active in Socialist and radical causes. Mensch: German for "man."

KRAL MAJALES[1]

And the Communists have nothing to offer but fat cheeks and eye-
glasses and lying policemen
and the Capitalists proffer Napalm and money in green suitcases to
the Naked,
and the Communists create heavy industry but the heart is also
heavy
and the beautiful engineers are all dead, the secret technicians con-
spire for their own glamor
5   in the Future, in the Future, but now drink vodka and lament the
Security Forces,
and the Capitalists drink gin and whiskey on airplanes but let Indian
brown millions starve
and when Communist and Capitalist assholes tangle the Just man is
arrested or robbed or had his head cut off,
but not like Kabir,[2] and the cigarette cough of the Just man above
the clouds
in the bright sunshine is a salute to the health of the blue sky.
10   For I was arrested thrice in Prague, once for singing drunk on
Narodni street,
once knocked down on the midnight pavement by a mustached agent
who screamed out BOUZERANT,[3]
once for losing my notebooks of unusual sex politics dream opinions,
and I was sent from Havana by plane by detectives in green uniform,
and I was sent from Prague by plane by detectives in Czecho-
slovakian business suits,
15   Cardplayers out of Cézanne, the two strange dolls that entered
Joseph K's room at morn[4]
also entered mine, and ate at my table, and examined my scribbles,
and followed me night and morn from the houses of lovers to the
cafés of Centrum—
And I am the King of May, which is the power of sexual youth,
and I am the King of May, which is industry in eloquence and action
in amour,

[1]King of the May, elected by the students of Prague to rule over the spring
celebration of the May Parade; in 1965 Ginsberg was elected Kral Majales by
the students and was, as the poem tells, expelled from Czechoslovakia.
[2]Kabir (1450?–1518), Indian religious leader who preached love as the means
for the emotional integration of the individual with divinity.
[3]A Czechoslovakian term of abuse to a homosexual.
[4]The painting of card players by Paul Cézanne (1839–1906); Joseph K.: the
protagonist and victim in *The Trial* by the Austrian novelist Franz Kafka
(1883–1924).

20   and I am the King of May, which is long hair of Adam and the Beard
     of my own body

and I am the King of May, which is Kral Majales in the Czechoslo-
     vakian tongue,

and I am the King of May, which is old Human poesy, and 100,000
     people chose my name,

and I am the King of May, and in a few minutes I will land at London
     Airport,

and I am the King of May, naturally, for I am of Slavic parentage and
     a Buddhist Jew

25   who worships the Sacred Heart of Christ the blue body of Krishna
     the straight back of Ram[5]

the beads of Chango the Nigerian singing Shiva Shiva in a manner
     which I have invented,

and the King of May is a middleeuropean honor, mine in the XX
     century

despite space and the Time Machine, because I heard the voice of
     Blake in a vision,[6]

and repeat that voice. And I am King of May that sleeps with teen-
     agers laughing.

30   And I am the King of May, that I may be expelled from my Kingdom
     with Honor, as of old,

To shew the difference between Caesar's Kingdom and the Kingdom
     of the May of Man—

and I am the King of May, tho paranoid, for the Kingdom of May is
     too beautiful to last for more than a month—

and I am the King of May because I touched my finger to my fore-
     head saluting

a luminous heavy girl trembling hands who said "one moment Mr.
     Ginsberg"

35   before a fat young Plainclothesman stepped between our bodies—I
     was going to England—

and I am the King of May, returning to see Bunhill Fields and walk
     on Hampstead Heath,

and I am the King of May, in a giant jetplane touching Albion's[7] air-
     field trembling in fear

as the plane roars to a landing on the grey concrete, shakes & expells
     air,

[5]Krishna and Rama: Incarnations of Vishna, who with Brahman and Shiva
make up the Hindu divine triad.
[6]William Blake (1757–1827): the English visionary poet and artist.
[7]Albion: England. Blake wrote a prophecy "Visions of the Daughters of
Albion."

and rolls slowly to a stop under the clouds with part of blue heaven
    still visible.

40   And *tho* I am the King of May, the Marxists have beat me upon the
    street, kept me up all night in Police Station, followed me thru
    Springtime Prague, detained me in secret and deported me from
    our kingdom by airplane.

Thus I have written this poem on a jet seat in mid Heaven.

May 7, 1965

Adrienne Rich (1929–   )

Adrienne Rich was born in Baltimore, Maryland, and graduated from Radcliffe College in 1951. That same year her first book, *A Change of World,* won the Yale Younger Poets Award and was published with an introduction by W. H. Auden, whose influence on her early work is clear. After *The Diamond Cutters* (1955) the poems in *Snapshots of a Daughter-In-Law* (1962) show at once a new openness and a new concentration, as she assimilated certain things from Williams and from Lowell to her own techniques. The poem became not an elegant comment on experience, but an experience in itself, whose pressures and penetrations constitute the act of comprehension. She lives in New York with her three sons and teaches at City College. In *Necessities of Life* (1966), *Leaflets* (1969), and *The Will to Change* (1971), mind and passion focus to an unsparing but cleansing intensity. The recent poems are both political and psychological, spacing out dream-like images in cinematic montages. She sees sex and politics as the twin and related modes of oppression in our patriarchy, and envisions a breakthrough which will deliver us into ourselves, women and men, and so into a society rooted in individual wholeness. The direction and coherence of these poems emerge from the faceted phrases and from the silences that separate and link them.

REFERENCE

Gelpi, Albert. "Adrienne Rich: The Poetics of Change," in *American Poetry Since 1960.* Ed. Robert Shaw. Cheshire: Carcanet Press, 1973.
Howard, Richard. *Alone with America.* New York: Atheneum, 1969.

THE KNIGHT

A knight rides into the noon,
and his helmet points to the sun,
and a thousand splintered suns
are the gaiety of his mail.
5   The soles of his feet glitter
and his palms flash in reply,
and under his crackling banner
he rides like a ship in sail.

A knight rides into the noon,
10   and only his eye is living,
a lump of bitter jelly
set in a metal mask,
betraying rags and tatters
that cling to the flesh beneath
15   and wear his nerves to ribbons
under the radiant casque.

Who will unhorse this rider
and free him from between
the walls of iron, the emblems
20   crushing his chest with their weight?
Will they defeat him gently,
or leave him hurled on the green,
his rags and wounds still hidden
under the great breastplate?

THE ROOFWALKER

FOR DENISE LEVERTOV

Over the half-finished houses
night comes. The builders
stand on the roof. It is
quiet after the hammers,
5   the pulleys hang slack.
Giants, the roofwalkers,
on a listing deck, the wave
of darkness about to break

on their heads. The sky
10 is a torn sail where figures
pass magnified, shadows
on a burning deck.

I feel like them up there:
exposed, larger than life,
15 and due to break my neck.

Was it worth while to lay—
with infinite exertion—
a roof I can't live under?
—All those blueprints,
20 closings of gaps,
measurings, calculations?
A life I didn't choose
chose me: even
my tools are the wrong ones
25 for what I have to do.
I'm naked, ignorant,
a naked man fleeing
across the roofs
who could with a shade of difference
30 be sitting in the lamplight
against the cream wallpaper
reading—not with indifference—
about a naked man
fleeing across the roofs.

IN THE WOODS

"Difficult ordinary happiness,"
no one nowadays believes in you.
I shift, full-length on the blanket,
to fix the sun precisely

5 behind the pine-tree's crest
so light spreads through the needles
alive as water just
where a snake has surfaced,

unreal as water in green crystal.
10   Bad news is always arriving.
"We're hiders, hiding from something bad,"
sings the little boy.

Writing these words in the woods,
I feel like a traitor to my friends,
15   even to my enemies.
The common lot's to die

a stranger's death and lie
rouged in the coffin, in a dress
chosen by the funeral director.
20   Perhaps that's why we never

see clocks on public buildings any more.
A fact no architect will mention.
We're hiders, hiding from something bad
most of the time.

25   Yet, and outrageously, something good
finds us, found me this morning
lying on a dusty blanket
among the burnt-out Indian pipes

and bursting-open lady's-slippers.
30   My soul, my helicopter, whirred
distantly, by habit, over
the old pond with the half-drowned boat

toward which it always veers
for consolation: ego's Arcady.[1]
35   leaving the body stuck
like a leaf against a screen.—

Happiness! how many times
I've stranded on that word,
at the edge of that pond; seen
40   as if through tears, the dragon-fly—

only to find it all
going differently for once

[1]Arcadia, poetically taken as a place of rustic harmony and contentment.

this time: my soul wheeled back
and burst into my body.

45 Found! ready or not.
    If I move now, the sun
    naked between the trees
    will melt me as I lie.

THE TREES

The trees inside are moving out into the forest,
the forest that was empty all these days
where no bird could sit
no insect hide
5 no sun bury its feet in shadow
the forest that was empty all these nights
will be full of trees by morning.

All night the roots work
to disengage themselves from the cracks
10 in the veranda floor.
The leaves strain toward the glass
small twigs stiff with exertion
long-cramped boughs shuffling under the roof
like newly discharged patients
15 half-dazed, moving
to the clinic doors.

I sit inside, doors open to the veranda
writing long letters
in which I scarcely mention the departure
20 of the forest from the house.
The night is fresh, the whole moon shines
in a sky still open
the smell of leaves and lichen
still reaches like a voice into the rooms.
25 My head is full of whispers
which tomorrow will be silent.

Listen. The glass is breaking.
The trees are stumbling forward
into the night. Winds rush to meet them.
30 The moon is broken like a mirror,
its pieces flash now in the crown
of the tallest oak.

LIKE THIS TOGETHER

FOR A.H.C.

1

Wind rocks the car.
We sit parked by the river,
silence between our teeth.
Birds scatter across islands
5 of broken ice. Another time
I'd have said "Canada geese,"
knowing you love them.
A year, ten years from now
I'll remember this—
10 this sitting like drugged birds
in a glass case—
not why, only that we
were here like this together.

2

They're tearing down, tearing up
15 this city, block by block.
Rooms cut in half
hang like flayed carcasses,
their old roses in rags,
famous streets have forgotten
20 where they were going. Only
a fact could be so dreamlike.
They're tearing down the houses
we met and lived in,
soon our two bodies will be all
25 left standing from that era.

3

We have, as they say,
certain things in common.
I mean: a view
from a bathroom window
30 over slate to stiff pigeons
huddled every morning; the way
water tastes from our tap,
which you marvel at, letting
it splash into the glass.
35 Because of you I notice
the taste of water,
a luxury I might
otherwise have missed.

4

Our words misunderstand us.
40 Sometimes at night
you are my mother:
old detailed griefs
twitch at my dreams, and I
crawl against you, fighting
45 for shelter, making you
my cave. Sometimes
you're the wave of birth
that drowns me in my first
nightmare. I suck the air.
50 Miscarried knowledge twists us
like hot sheets thrown askew.

5

Dead winter doesn't die,
it wears away, a piece of carrion
picked clean at last,
55 rained away or burnt dry.
Our desiring does this,
make no mistake, I'm speaking
of fact: through mere indifference
we could prevent it.
60 Only our fierce attention
gets hyacinths out of those
hard cerebral lumps,
unwraps the wet buds down
the whole length of a stem.

"I AM IN DANGER—SIR—"[1]

"Half-cracked" to Higginson,[2] living,
afterward famous in garbled versions,[3]
your hoard of dazzling scraps a battlefield,
now your old snood

5   mothballed at Harvard[4]
and you in your variorum monument
equivocal to the end—
who are you?

Gardening the day-lily,
10 wiping the wine-glass stems,
your thought pulsed on behind
a forehead battered paper-thin,

you, woman, masculine
in single-mindedness,
15 for whom the word was more
than a symptom—

a condition of being.
Till the air buzzing with spoiled language
sang in your ears
20 of Perjury[5]

and in your half-cracked way you chose
silence for entertainment,[6]
chose to have it out at last
on your own premises.[7]

[1] Emily Dickinson responding to Higginson's criticism of her technique in a letter: "You think my gait 'spasmodic'—I am in danger—Sir—you think me 'uncontrolled'—I have no tribunal."

[2] Thomas Wentworth Higginson (1823–1911), essayist and critic, was a correspondent of Emily Dickinson and met her in a couple of brief visits to the Dickinson family house in Amherst. He once referred to the poet in a letter as "half-cracked."

[3] Until the variorum edition of Dickinson *Poems* edited by Thomas H. Johnson (1955), previous editors smoothed out and regularized the poems to some extent.

[4] In the Emily Dickinson Room of the Houghton Library at Harvard.

[5] Poem 1768 in the Johnson edition reads: "Lad of Athens, faithful be/to Thy-self,/and Mystery—/All the rest is Perjury—"

[6] Dickinson's decision not to publish during her lifetime.

[7] Pun: on your own terms and, as a recluse, on the premises of the Dickinson home.

FOCUS

FOR BERT DREYFUS

Obscurity has its tale to tell.
Like the figure on the studio-bed in the corner,

out of range, smoking, watching and waiting.
Sun pours through the skylight onto the worktable

5 making of a jar of pencils, a typewriter keyboard
more than they were. Veridical[1] light . . .

Earth budges. Now an empty coffee-cup,
a whetstone, a handkerchief, take on

their sacramental clarity, fixed by the wand
10 of light as the thinker thinks to fix them in the mind.

O secret in the core of the whetstone, in the five
pencils splayed out like fingers of a hand!

The mind's passion is all for singling out.
Obscurity has another tale to tell.

5:30 A.M.

Birds and periodic blood.
Old recapitulations.
The fox, panting, fire-eyed,
gone to earth in my chest.
5 How beautiful we are,
he and I, with our auburn
pelts, our trails of blood,
our miracle escapes,
our whiplash panic flogging us on
10 to new miracles!
They've supplied us with pills

---

[1]Accurate, expressing the truth.

for bleeding, pills for panic.
Wash them down the sink.
This is truth, then:
15 dull needle groping in the spinal fluid,
weak acid in the bottom of the cup,
foreboding, foreboding.
No one tells the truth about truth.
that it's what the fox
20 sees from his scuffled burrow:
dull-jawed, onrushing
killer, being that
inanely single-minded
will have our skins at last.

NIGHTBREAK

Something broken   Something
I need   By someone
I love   Next year
will I remember what
5 This anger   unreal
yet
has to be gone through
The sun to set
on this anger
10   I go on
head down   into it
The mountain pulsing
Into the oildrum   drops
the ball of fire.

15 Time is quiet   doesn't break things
or even wound   Things are in danger
from people   The frail clay lamps
of Mesopotamia
row on row under glass
20 in the ethnological section
little hollows for dried-
up oil   The refugees
with their identical
tales of escape   I don't

25 collect what I can't use   I need
what can be broken.

In the bed the pieces fly together
and the rifts fill   or else
my body is a list   of wounds
30 symmetrically placed
a village
blown open   by planes
that did not   finish the job

The enemy has   withdrawn
35 between raids   become invisible
there are
      no agencies
            of relief
the darkness becomes utter
40 Sleep   cracked and flaking
sifts over the shaken   target

What breaks   is night
not day   The white
scar   splitting
45 over the east
The crack weeping
Time for the pieces
            to move
dumbly back
50   toward each other.

THE BURNING
OF PAPER INSTEAD OF CHILDREN

I was in danger of verbalizing my moral impulses out of existence.
—*Fr. Daniel Berrigan, on trial in Baltimore.*[1]

1.   My neighbor, a scientist and art-collector, telephones me in a
state of violent emotion. He tells me that my son and his, aged
eleven and twelve, have on the last day of school burned a mathe-
matics text-book in the backyard. He has forbidden my son to come
to his house for a week, and has forbidden his own son to leave the
house during that time. "The burning of a book," he says, "arouses
terrible sensations in me, memories of Hitler; there are few things
that upset me so much as the idea of burning a book."

Back there: the library, walled
with green Britannicas
Looking again
in Dürer's *Complete Works*[2]
for MELANCOLIA, the baffled woman

the crocodiles in Herodotus[3]
the Book of the Dead[4]
the *Trial of Jeanne d'Arc*,[5] so blue
I think, It is her color

and they take the book away
because I dream of her too often

love and fear in a house
knowledge of the oppressor

I know it hurts to burn

[1] Father Berrigan was tried and convicted, with others, of destroying draft-board
records in Catonsville, Maryland, in protest against American involvement in
the Vietnam War.
[2] Albrecht Dürer (1471–1528), German painter and engraver.
[3] Greek historian, fifth century B.C.
[4] Both the Tibetan and the Egyptian *Book of the Dead* are instructions for the
afterlife.
[5] St. Joan of Arc (1412–1431), visionary who led the French army against the
English and was burned as a heretic by the Inquisition.

2.   To imagine a time of silence
or few words
25   a time of chemistry and music

the hollows above your buttocks
traced by my hand
or, *hair is like flesh,* you said

an age of long silence

30   relief

from this tongue   the slab of limestone
or reinforced concrete
fanatics and traders
dumped on this coast   wildgreen   clayred
35   that breathed once
in signals of smoke
sweep of the wind

knowledge of the oppressor
this is the oppressor's language

40   yet I need it to talk to you

3.   "People suffer highly in poverty and it takes dignity and intelli-
gence to overcome this suffering. Some of the suffering are: a child
did not had dinner last night: a child steal because he did not have
money to buy it: to hear a mother say she do not have money to buy
45   food for her children and to see a child without cloth it will make
tears in your eyes."

(the fracture of order
the repair of speech
to overcome this suffering)

50   4.   We lie under the sheet
after making love, speaking
of loneliness
relieved in a book
relived in a book
55   so on that page
the clot and fissure
of it appears

words of a man
in pain
60 a naked word
entering the clot
a hand grasping
through bars:

deliverance

65 What happens between us
has happened for centuries
we know it from literature

still it happens

sexual jealousy
70 outflung hand
beating bed

dryness of mouth
after panting

there are books that describe all this
75 and they are useless

You walk into the woods behind a house
there in that country
you find a temple
built eighteen hundred years ago
80 you enter without knowing
what it is you enter
so it is with us

no one knows what may happen
though the books tell everything

85 *burn the texts*   said Artaud[6]

5.   I am composing on the typewriter late at night, thinking of
today. How well we all spoke. A language is a map of our failures.
Frederick Douglass[7] wrote an English purer than Milton's. People
suffer highly in poverty. There are methods but we do not use them.

[6]Antonin Artaud (1896–1948), French surrealist poet, actor, and critic.
[7]American Negro abolitionist (1817–1895) and author of *Narrative of the Life
of Frederick Douglass* (1845).

90   Joan, who could not read, spoke some peasant form of French. Some
of the suffering are: it is hard to tell the truth; this is America; I
cannot touch you now. In America we have only the present tense.
I am in danger. You are in danger. The burning of a book arouses
no sensation in me. I know it hurts to burn. There are flames of
95   napalm in Catonsville, Maryland. I know it hurts to burn. The type-
writer is overheated, my mouth is burning, I cannot touch you and
this is the oppressor's language.

PIERROT LE FOU

1

Suppose you stood facing
a wall
        of photographs
from your unlived life

5   as you stand looking at these
stills from the unseen film?

Yourself against a wall
curiously stuccoed

Yourself in the doorway
10   of a kind of watchman's hut

Yourself at a window
signalling to people
you haven't met yet.

Yourself in unfamiliar clothes
15   with the same eyes

2

On a screen as wide as this, I grope for the titles.
I speak the French language like a schoolgirl of the 'forties.
Those roads remind me of Beauce and the motorcycle.
We rode from Paris to Chartres in the March wind.
20   He said we should go to Spain but the wind defeated me.

France of the superhighways, I never knew you.
How much the body took in those days, and could take!
A naked lightbulb still simmers in my eyeballs.
In every hotel, I lived on the top floor.

3

25 Suppose we had time
and no money
living by our wits
telling stories

which stories would you tell?

30 I would tell the story
of Pierrot Le Fou[1]
who trusted
not a woman
but love itself

35 till his head blew off
not quite intentionally

I would tell all the stories I knew
in which people went wrong
but the nervous system

40 was right all along

4

The island blistered our feet.
At first we mispronounced each others' names.
All the leaves of the tree were scribbled with words.
There was a language there but no-one to speak it.
45 Sometimes each of us was alone.
At noon on the beach our shadows left us.
The net we twisted from memory kept on breaking.
The damaged canoe lay on the beach like a dead animal.
You started keeping a journal on a coconut shell.

---

[1]Pierrot the Madman; Pierrot is a character in French pantomime, desperately in love with Pierrette, who does not return his love. Also a movie by French director Jean-Luc Godard.

5

50   When I close my eyes
other films
        have been there all along

a market shot:
bins of turnips, feet
55   of dead chickens

close-up: a black old woman
buying voodoo medicines

a figure of terrible faith
and I know her needs

60   Another film:
        an empty room stacked with old films
I am kneeling on the floor
It is getting dark
        they want to close the building
65   and I still haven't found you

Scanning reel after reel
tundras in negative,
the Bowery
        all those scenes

70   but the light is failing
        and you are missing
from the footage of the march
the railway disaster
the snowbound village

75   even the shots of the island
miss you
        yet you were there

6

To record
in order to see
80
        if you know how the story ends
why tell it

To record
in order to forget

85
                      the surface is always lucid
                      my shadows are under the skin

To record
in order to control

                      the eye of the camera
                      doesn't weep tears of blood

90
To record
for that is what one does

                      climbing your stairs, over and over
                      I memorized the bare walls

                      This is my way of coming back

Gary Snyder (1930–   )

Born in San Francisco and brought up on a farm, Snyder got a degree in anthropology from Reed College in Oregon. He was a friend of Kerouac, Ginsberg, and others of the Beat Movement of the fifties. He combines political radicalism, harking back to his parents' activities in the I. W. W. (International Workers of the World) during the Depression years, with the religious discipline of Zen Buddhism, which he studied in a Japanese monastery (1956–1964, 1965–1968). Now he lives with his wife, Masa, and their two sons in the foothills of the Sierras in northern California. His verse includes: *Myths and Texts* (1960), *Riprap and Cold Mountain Poems* (1965), *Six Sections of Mountains and Rivers Without End* (1965), *The Back Country* (1967), and *Regarding Wave* (1970). *Earth House Hold* (1969) contains journal excerpts and essays on subjects religious, poetic, political, and ecological. In fact, Snyder sees ecology—the balance of the total process of creation, including man's harmonious place in that process—as the center in which the individual and society and earth, philosophy and religion and politics are conjoined. Here his poems turn on the primitive rhythms of nature and of man's work in nature, as mind and the elements inform each other in the Zen All, which is Emptiness.

REFERENCE

Howard, Richard. *Alone with America*. New York: Atheneum, 1969.

REVOLUTION IN THE REVOLUTION
IN THE REVOLUTION

The country surrounds the city
The back country surrounds the country

"From the masses to the masses"[1] the most
Revolutionary consciousness is to be found
5 Among the most ruthlessly exploited classes:
Animals, trees, water, air, grasses

We must pass through the stage of the
"Dictatorship of the Unconscious" before we can
Hope for the withering-away of the states
10 And finally arrive at true Communionism.

●

If the capitalists and imperialists
are the exploiters, the masses are the workers.
and the party
is the communist.

15 If civilization
is the exploiter, the masses is nature.
and the party
is the poets.

If the abstract rational intellect
20 is the exploiter, the masses is the unconscious.
and the party
is the yogins.[2]

& POWER
comes out of the seed-syllables of mantras.[3]

---

[1]The technique, enunciated by Chairman Mao Tse-tung (1893–   ), the Chinese
Communist revolutionary leader, whereby the revolutionary listens to the
people in order to formulate the principles and programs, which he then ar-
ticulates back to them as their basis for action.
[2]Plural of yogi, one who practices yoga, the Hindu discipline for higher states
of consciousness.
[3]A Hindu sacred formula or prayer thought to possess divine and magic powers.

RUNNING WATER MUSIC

under the trees
under the clouds
by the river
on the beach,

5   "sea roads."
    whales   great sea-path beasts—

       salt;   cold
         water;   smoky fire.
steam, cereal,
10   stone, wood boards.
bone awl, pelts,
       bamboo pins and spoons.
unglazed bowl.
a band around the hair.

15   *beyond wounds.*

sat on a rock in the sun,
watched the old pine
wave
over blinding fine white
20   river sand.

MEETING THE MOUNTAINS

He crawls to the edge of the foaming creek
He backs up the slab ledge
He puts a finger in the water
He turns to a trapped pool
5   Puts both hands in the water
Puts one foot in the pool
Drops pebbles in the pool

He slaps the water surface with both hands
He cries out, rises up and stands
10   Facing toward the torrent and the mountain
Raises up both hands and shouts three times!

Kai[1] at Sawmill Lake VI.69

BEFORE THE STUFF COMES DOWN

Walking out of the "big E"[1]
Dope store of the suburb,
   canned music plugging up your ears
   the wide aisles,
5   miles of wares
   from nowheres,

Suddenly it's California:
Live oak, brown grasses

Butterflies over the parking lot and the freeway
10   A Turkey Buzzard power in the blue air.

A while longer,
Still here.

LONG HAIR

Hunting season:

Once every year, the Deer catch human beings. They
do various things which irresistably draw men near them;
each one selects a certain man. The Deer shoots the man,
5   who is then compelled to skin it and carry its meat home
and eat it. Then the Deer is inside the man. He waits
and hides in there, but the man doesn't know it. When

[1]Snyder's young son.

[1]The advertising nickname for the Emporium, a department store with many
branches in northern California, often in shopping centers.

enough Deer have occupied enough men, they will strike
all at once. The men who don't have Deer in them will
10   also be taken by surprise, and everything will change
some. This is called "takeover from inside."

•

Deer trails:

Deer trails run on the side hills
      cross-country access roads
15   dirt ruts to bone-white
      baard house ranches,
      tumbled down.

Waist high through manzanita,
Through sticky, prickly, crackling
20   gold dry summer grass.

Deer trails lead to water
Lead sidewise all ways
Narrowing down to one best path—
And split—
25   And fade away to nowhere.

Deer trails slide under freeways
      slip into cities
      swing back and forth in crops and orchards
      run up the sides of schools!

30   Deer spoor and crisscross dusty tracks
Are in the house: and coming out the walls:

And deer bound through my hair.

Sylvia Plath (1932–1963)

Sylvia Plath was born in Boston, where her father taught biology at Boston University; she graduated from Smith College in 1955, and got an M.A. from Newnham College, Cambridge, as a Fulbright Scholar. Her extremely fragile sensitivity fills her autobiographical novel of adolescence, *The Bell Jar* (1963). In 1956 she married Ted Hughes, the English poet, and after living in the United States for a while they moved to England (first London, then Devon), where their two children were born. She committed suicide in 1963.

The violent and enthralling lure of death filled the poems of *The Colossus* (1962), the rhymed and metered stanzas crammed with sound and metaphor. During the last months of her life she wrote and revised with furious passion poems whose dislocations and concentrations are as disturbing as they are disturbed. They were published posthumously as *Ariel* (1966), with an introduction by Robert Lowell (who had come to know her when she audited his poetry course at Boston University in the late fifties), *Crossing the Water* (1971) and *Winter Trees* (1972). In the end she found the frantic rhythms and wild leaps of association to convey the hellish and ecstatic states of mind that consumed her.

REFERENCE

Howard, Richard. *Alone with America*. New York: Atheneum, 1969.
The Art of Sylvia Plath. Ed. Charles H. Newman. Bloomington: Indiana University Press, 1970.

LADY LAZARUS[1]

I have done it again.
One year in every ten
I manage it—

A sort of walking miracle, my skin
5 Bright as a Nazi lampshade,[2]
My right foot

A paperweight,
My face a featureless, fine
Jew linen.

10 Peel off the napkin
O my enemy.
Do I terrify?—

The nose, the eye pits, the full set of teeth?
The sour breath
15 Will vanish in a day.

Soon, soon the flesh
The grave cave ate will be
At home on me

And I a smiling woman.
20 I am only thirty.
And like the cat I have nine times to die.

This is Number Three.
What a trash
To annihilate each decade.

25 What a million filaments.
The peanut-crunching crowd
Shoves in to see

---

[1]Jesus raised Lazarus from the dead. See John 11.
[2]Ilse Koch, wife of Colonel Karl Koch, commander of the concentration camp at Buchenwald, had lampshades made from the skins of some of the people executed there.

Them unwrap me hand and foot—
The big strip tease.
30   Gentlemen, ladies

These are my hands
My knees.
I may be skin and bone,

Nevertheless, I am the same, identical woman.
35   The first time it happened I was ten.
It was an accident.

The second time I meant
To last it out and not come back at all.
I rocked shut

40   As a seashell.
They had to call and call
And pick the worms off me like sticky pearls.

Dying
Is an art, like everything else.
45   I do it exceptionally well.

I do it so it feels like hell.
I do it so it feels real.
I guess you could say I've a call.

It's easy enough to do it in a cell.
50   It's easy enough to do it and stay put.
It's the theatrical

Comeback in broad day
To the same place, the same face, the same brute
Amused shout:

55   'A miracle!'
That knocks me out.
There is a charge

For the eyeing of my scars, there is a charge
For the hearing of my heart—
60   It really goes.

And there is a charge, a very large charge
For a word or a touch
Or a bit of blood

Or a piece of my hair or my clothes.
65   So, so, Herr[3] Doktor.
So Herr Enemy.

I am your opus,
I am your valuable,
The pure gold baby

70   That melts to a shriek.
I turn and burn.
Do not think I underestimate your great concern.

Ash, ash—
You poke and stir.
75   Flesh, bone, there is nothing there—

A cake of soap,
A wedding ring,
A gold filling.

Herr God, Herr Lucifer
80   Beware
Beware.

Out of the ash
I rise with my red hair
And I eat men like air.

---

[3]The German masculine address of politeness, equivalent to "Mister."

CUT

FOR SUSAN O'NEILL ROE

What a thrill—
My thumb instead of an onion.
The top quite gone
Except for a sort of a hinge

5　Of skin,
A flap like a hat,
Dead white.
Then that red plush.

Little pilgrim,
10　The Indian's axed your scalp.
Your turkey wattle
Carpet rolls

Straight from the heart.
I step on it,
15　Clutching my bottle
Of pink fizz.

A celebration, this is.
Out of a gap
A million soldiers run,
20　Redcoats, every one.

Whose side are they on?
O my
Homunculus,[1] I am ill.
I have taken a pill to kill

25　The thin
Papery feeling.
Saboteur,
Kamikaze man[2]—

[1]Little man.
[2]During World War II, a Japanese pilot who made a suicidal crash attack into his target.

The stain on your
30 Gauze Ku Klux Klan[3]
Babushka[4]
Darkens and tarnishes and when

The balled
Pulp of your heart
35 Confronts its small
Mill of silence

How you jump—
Trepanned[5] veteran,
Dirty girl,
40 Thumb stump.

ARIEL[1]

Stasis in darkness.
Then the substanceless blue
Pour of tor[2] and distances.

God's lioness,
5 How one we grow,
Pivot of heels and knees!—The furrow

Splits and passes, sister to
The brown arc
Of the neck I cannot catch,

10 Nigger-eye
Berries cast dark
Hooks—

Black sweet blood mouthfuls,
Shadows.
15 Something else

[3]A secret society organized after the Civil War to defend white supremacy,
even by violent means.
[4]Kerchief, or woman's head scarf.
[5]Trapped.

[1]The poet's horse, named after the airy sprite of Shakespeare's *The Tempest*.
[2]A rocky peak.

Hauls me through air—
Thighs, hair;
Flakes from my heels.

White
20 Godiva,[3] I unpeel—
Dead hands, dead stringencies.

And now I
Foam to wheat, a glitter of seas.
The child's cry

25 Melts in the wall.
And I
Am the arrow,

The dew that flies
Suicidal, at one with the drive
30 Into the red

Eye, the cauldron of morning.

DADDY

You do not do, you do not do
Any more, black shoe
In which I have lived like a foot
For thirty years, poor and white,
5 Barely daring to breathe or Achoo.

Daddy, I have had to kill you,
You died before I had time—
Marble-heavy, a bag full of God,
Ghastly statue with one grey toe
10 Big as a Frisco seal[1]

---

[3]Godiva (1040–1080): the benevolent wife of the Earl of Mercia. The fictitious
legend says that, as a condition for her husband's freeing his peasants from
heavy taxes, she rode through Coventry naked, clothed only in her long hair,
the townspeople having been forewarned to close their shutters and remain
inside.

---

[1]On the Seal Rocks at San Francisco.

And a head in the freakish Atlantic
Where it pours bean green over blue
In the waters off beautiful Nauset.[2]
I used to pray to recover you.
15   Ach, du.[3]

In the German tongue, in the Polish town
Scraped flat by the roller
Of wars, wars, wars.
But the name of the town is common.
20   My Polack friend

Says there are a dozen or two.
So I never could tell where you
Put your foot, your root,
I never could talk to you.
25   The tongue stuck in my jaw.

It stuck in a barb wire snare.
Ich, ich, ich, ich,[4]
I could hardly speak.
I thought every German was you.
30   And the language obscene

An engine, an engine
Chuffing me off like a Jew.
A Jew to Dachau, Auschwitz, Belsen.[5]
I began to talk like a Jew.
35   I think I may well be a Jew.

The snows of the Tyrol,[6] the clear beer of Vienna
Are not very pure or true.
With my gypsy ancestress and my weird luck
And my Taroc pack and my Taroc pack[7]
40   I may be a bit of a Jew.

---

[2]Harbor on the east coast of Cape Cod, Massachusetts.
[3]German: Ah, you (the personal, intimate form of "you"). Here again, Sylvia
  Plath associates the masculine authority figure with the Nazi and herself with
  his victim, Pole and Jew, in World War II.
[4]German: I.
[5]Nazi concentration camps where millions of Jews were murdered.
[6]A province of Austria in the Alps.
[7]Tarot pack of cards used in fortune telling.

I have always been scared of *you*,
With your Luftwaffe,[8] your gobbledygoo.
And your neat moustache
And your Aryan[9] eye, bright blue.
45 Panzer-man, panzer-man,[10] O You—

Not God but a swastika[11]
So black no sky could squeak through.
Every woman adores a Fascist,
The boot in the face, the brute
50 Brute heart of a brute like you.

You stand at the blackboard, daddy,
In the picture I have of you,
A cleft in your chin instead of your foot
But no less a devil for that, no not
55 Any less the black man who

Bit my pretty red heart in two.
I was ten when they buried you.
At twenty I tried to die
And get back, back, back to you.
60 I thought even the bones would do.

But they pulled me out of the sack,
And they stuck me together with glue.
And then I knew what to do.
I made a model of you,
65 A man in black with a Meinkampf[12] look

And a love of the rack and the screw.
And I said I do, I do.
So daddy, I'm finally through.
The black telephone's off at the root,
70 The voices just can't worm through.

---

[8]The Nazi German air force; literally, "air weapon."
[9]For the Nazis, a Caucasian gentile, especially of Nordic extraction.
[10]Panzer: German for "armor." Used during World War II for Nazi armored military units.
[11]The ancient cosmic symbol of a cross with bent arms, adopted as the emblem of the Nazis.
[12]Adolf Hitler's *Mein Kampf* (*My Battle*) published in 1924–1926, which is the manifesto of the Nazis.

If I've killed one man, I've killed two—
The vampire who said he was you
And drank my blood for a year,
Seven years, if you want to know.
75 Daddy, you can lie back now.

There's a stake in your fat black heart[13]
And the villagers never liked you.
They are dancing and stamping on you.
They always *knew* it was you.
80 Daddy, daddy, you bastard, I'm through.

FEVER 103°

Pure? What does it mean?
The tongues of hell
Are dull, dull as the triple

Tongues of dull, fat Cerberus[1]
5   Who wheezes at the gate. Incapable
Of licking clean

The aguey[2] tendon, the sin, the sin.
The tinder cries.
The indelible smell

10   Of a snuffed candle!
Love, love, the low smokes roll
From me like Isadora's scarves,[3] I'm in a fright

One scarf will catch and anchor in the wheel.
Such yellow sullen smokes
15   Make their own element. They will not rise,

---

[13]The only way to kill a vampire.

---

[1]The three-headed dog guarding the entrance to Hades.
[2]Suffering from ague, or chills and fever.
[3]Isadora Duncan (1878–1927), American dancer, killed when her scarf caught in the wheels of an automobile.

But trundle round the globe
Choking the aged and the meek,
The weak

Hothouse baby in its crib,
20 The ghastly orchid
Hanging its hanging garden in the air,

Devilish leopard!
Radiation turned it white
And killed it in an hour.

25 Greasing the bodies of adulterers
Like Hiroshima ash and eating in.
The sin. The sin.

Darling, all night
I have been flickering, off, on, off, on.
30 The sheets grow heavy as a lecher's kiss.

Three days. Three nights.
Lemon water, chicken
Water, water make me retch.

I am too pure for you or anyone.
35 Your body
Hurts me as the world hurts God. I am a lantern—

My head a moon
Of Japanese paper, my gold beaten skin
Infinitely delicate and infinitely expensive.

40 Does not my heat astound you. And my light.
All by myself I am a huge camellia
Glowing and coming and going, flush on flush.

I think I am going up,
I think I may rise—
45 The beads of hot metal fly, and I, love, I

Am a pure acetylene
Virgin
Attended by roses,

By kisses, by cherubim,
50   By whatever these pink things mean.
Not you, nor him

Not him, nor him
(My selves dissolving, old whore petticoats)—
To Paradise.

LeRoi Jones (Amiri Baraka) (1934–   )

From Newark, New Jersey, Jones graduated from Howard University in 1954. After a visit to Castro's Cuba in 1960, his poetry began to move from a pained personal lyricism to a vehement, deliberately shocking diatribe against the black man's plight in contemporary America, as Jones became increasingly involved in black militant protest. He lives in Newark again, at Spirit House, the community center that he founded and that has been instrumental in organizing black power in the city. He was arrested for illegal possession of a weapon during the 1967 race riots in Newark, was convicted and then acquitted on a retrial. Jones is now a Black Muslim with the name Amiri Baraka and bears the minister's title Imamu.

His poetry includes *Preface to a Twenty Volume Suicide Note* (1961), *The Dead Lecturer* (1964), *Black Magic* (1969) and *In Our Terribleness* (1970). *Dutchman* and *The Slave* (1964) have been successful on the stage. He has written other prose: a novel, *The System of Dante's Hell* (1965), *Home: Social Essays* (1966), *Tales* (1967), and *Raise Race Rays Raze: Essays Since 1965* (1971). Jones has addressed himself more and more exclusively to a black audience. He sees his poetry as moving from death and suicide, as a result of being a black man and a Beat poet in a white society, to a prophetic affirmation of the beauty and spirit of black people. Poetry is a vehicle for attack and an invocation: black magic, as the title of his recent book states; and the poet is the voice expressing and creating his people's sense of themselves.

AN AGONY. AS NOW.

I am inside someone
who hates me. I look
out from his eyes. Smell
what fouled tunes come in
5   to his breath. Love his
wretched women.

Slits in the metal, for sun. Where
my eyes sit turning, at the cool air
the glance of light, or hard flesh
10   rubbed against me, a woman, a man,
without shadow, or voice, or meaning.

This is the enclosure (flesh,
where innocence is a weapon. An
abstraction. Touch. (Not mine.
15   Or yours, if you are the soul I had
and abandoned when I was blind and had
my enemies carry me as a dead man
(if he is beautiful, or pitied.

It can be pain. (As now, as all his
20   flesh hurts me.) It can be that. Or
pain. As when she ran from me into
that forest.
            Or pain, the mind
silver spiraled whirled against the
25   sun, higher than even old men thought
God would be. Or pain. And the other. The
yes. (Inside his books, his fingers. They
are withered yellow flowers and were never
beautiful.) The yes. You will, lost soul, say
30   'beauty.' Beauty, practiced, as the tree. The
slow river. A white sun in its wet sentences.

Or, the cold men in their gale. Ecstasy. Flesh
or soul. The yes. (Their robes blown. Their bowls
empty. They chant at my heels, not at yours.) Flesh
35   or soul, as corrupt. Where the answer moves too quickly.
Where the God is a self, after all.)

Cold air blown through narrow blind eyes. Flesh,
white hot metal. Glows as the day with its sun.
It is a human love, I live inside. A bony skeleton
40 you recognize as words or simple feeling.

But it has no feeling. As the metal, is hot, it is not,
given to love.

It burns the thing
inside it. And that thing
45 screams.

THE DANCE

The dance.
        (held up for me by
an older man. He told me how. Showed
me. Not steps, but the fix
5 of muscle. A position
for myself: to move.

Duncan[1]
told of dance. His poems
full of what we called
10 so long for you to be. A
dance. And all his words
ran out of it. That there
was some bright elegance
the sad meat of the body
15 made. Some gesture, that
if we became, for one blank moment,
would turn us
into creatures of rhythm.

I want to be sung. I want
20 all my bones and meat hummed
against the thick floating
winter sky. I want myself
as dance. As what I am
given love, or time, or space
25 to feel myself.

[1]Robert Duncan, the poet.

The time of thought. The space
of actual movement. (Where they
have taken up the sea, and
keep me against my will.) I said, also,
30   love, being older or younger
than your world. I am given
to lying, love, call you out
now, given to feeling things
I alone create.

35   And let me once, create
myself. And let you, whoever
sits now breathing on my words
create a self of your own. One
that will love me.

A POEM SOME PEOPLE
WILL HAVE TO UNDERSTAND

Dull unwashed windows of eyes
and buildings of industry. What
industry do I practice? A slick
colored boy, 12 miles from his
5   home. I practice no industry.
I am no longer a credit
to my race. I read a little,
scratch against silence slow spring
afternoons.
10   I had thought, before, some years ago
that I'd come to the end of my life.
        Watercolor ego. Without the preciseness
a violent man could propose.
        But the wheel, and the wheels,
15   wont let us alone. All the fantasy
        and justice, and dry charcoal winters
All the pitifully intelligent citizens
        I've forced myself to love.

        We have awaited the coming of a natural
20   phenomenon. Mystics and romantics, knowledgeable

workers
of the land.

But none has come.
(Repeat)
25   but none has come.

Will the machinegunners please step forward?

W.W.

Back home the black women are all beautiful,
and the white ones fall back, cutoff from 1000
years stacked booty, and Charles of the Ritz[1]
where jooshladies turn into billy burke[2] in blueglass
5   kicks. With wings, and jingly bew-teeful things.
The black women in Newark are fine. Even with all that grease
in their heads. I mean even the ones where the wigs
slide around, and they coming at you 75 degrees off course.
I could talk to them. Bring them around. To something.
10   Some kind of quick course, on the sidewalk, like Hey baby
why don't you take that thing off yo' haid. You look like
Miss Muffett in a runaway ugly machine. I mean. Like that.

KA 'BA

A closed window looks down
on a dirty courtyard, and black people
call across or scream across or walk across
defying physics in the stream of their will

5   Our world is full of sound
Our world is more lovely than anyone's
tho we suffer, and kill each other
and sometimes fail to walk the air

[1]The fancy beauty salon.
[2]Actress and movie star of the thirties and forties, with blonde hair, blue eyes,
and a baby-doll face, who played the Good Witch in the movie *The Wizard
of Oz.*

We are beautiful people
10   with african imaginations
full of masks and dances and swelling chants
with african eyes, and noses, and arms,
though we sprawl in grey chains in a place
full of winters, when what we want is sun.

15   We have been captured,
brothers. And we labor
to make our getaway, into
the ancient image, into a new

correspondence with ourselves
20   and our black family. We need magic
now we need the spells, to raise up
return, destroy, and create. What will be

the sacred words?

THE SPELL

The Spell The SPELL THE S P E L L L L L L L L L L L !
Away and sailing in warm space. The eyes of God-our on us
in us. The Spell. We are wisdom, reaching for itself. We are
totals, watch us, watch through yourself, and become the whole
5   universe at once so beautiful you will become, without having
moved, or gone through a "change," Except to be moving with
the world,
at that incredible speed, with all the genius of a tree.

PART OF THE DOCTRINE

RAISE THE RACE RAISE THE RAYS THE RAZE RAISE IT RACE RAISE
ITSELF RAISE THE RAYS OF THE SUNS RACE TO RAISE IN THE RAZE
OF THIS TIME AND THIS PLACE FOR THE NEXT, AND THE NEXT RACE
OURSELVES TO EMERGE BURNING ALL INERT GASES GASSED AT THE
5 GOD OF GUARDING THE GUARDIANS OF GOD WHO WE ARE GOD IS
WHO WE RAISE OUR SELVES WHO WE HOVER IN AND ARE RAISED
ABOVE OUR BODIES AND MACHINES THOSE WHO ARE WITHOUT GOD
WHO HAVE LOST THE SPIRITUAL PRINCIPAL OF THEIR LIVES ARE
NOT RAISED AND THEIR RACE IS TO THEIR NATURAL DEATHS NO MATTER
10 HOW UN-NATURAL, WITHOUT SPIRIT WITHOUT THE CLIMB THROUGH SPACE
TO THE SEVENTH PRINCIPLE WITHOUT THE PURE AND PURITY OF, THE
SPIRIT. TO RAISE THE EYES TO RAISE THE RACE AND THE RAYS OF
OUR HOT SAVAGE GODS WHO DISAPPEARED TO REAPPEAR IN THE BODY
IN THE ARM MOVE THROUGH THE GOD OF THE HEAVEN OF GOD WHERE
15 WE RAISE THE RACE AND THE FACE THROUGH THE EYE OF SPACE
TO RAISE AND THE RAYS OF THE RACE WILL RETURN THROUGH ALL SPACE
TO GOD TO GOD TO GOD TO GOD TO GOD TO GOD TO GOD, GOD GOD GOD
GOD GOD GOD GODGOD GOD GOD GOD GOD GOD GOD GOD GOD GOD GOD GOD
GOD GOD GOD GOD GODGODGODGODGODGODGOD GODGODGOD GODGODGODGODGOD
20 GODGODGODGODGODGODGODGOD GODGODGODGOD GODGODGODGODGODGODGODGOD

To Suns raise, to raise the sons and the old heat of our truth
and passage through the secret doctrinaire universe. Through
God. We are raised and the race is a sun sons suns sons first
out of heaven to be god in the race of our raise through perfection.

LEROY

I wanted to know my mother when she sat
looking sad across the campus in the late 20's
into the future of the soul, there were black angels
straining above her head, carrying life from our ancestors,
5 and knowledge, and the strong nigger feeling. She sat
(in that photo in the yearbook I showed Vashti) getting into
new blues, from the old ones, the trips and passions
showered on her by her own. Hypnotizing me, from so far
ago, from that vantage of knowledge passed on to her passed on
10 to me and all the other black people of our time.
When I die, the consciousness I carry I will to
black people. May they pick me apart and take the
useful parts, the sweet meat of my feelings. And leave
the bitter bullshit rotten white parts
15 alone.

Wendell Berry (1934–   )

Berry was born in Henry County, Kentucky, and got his A.B. and M.A. from the University of Kentucky, where he now teaches while living with his wife and children on a riverfront farm near Port Royal. Like the man himself, Berry's poetry is rooted in place and in earth, stripped of metaphors and artifice and drawing its quiet, steady strength from the recognition of man's place in the natural cycle: mortal but capable of love in the humble acceptance of his mortality. Berry's books of poems are *The Broken Ground* (1964), *Openings* (1968), *Findings* (1969), and *Farming: A Handbook* (1970). His prose includes two novels, *Nathan Coulter* (1960) and *A Place on Earth* (1967); *The Long Legged House* (1969), and *A Continuous Harmony* (1972), essays; and a study of racism in America, *The Hidden Wound* (1970). Against society's degradation of man and earth, Berry's naturalistic faith emerges not from Emersonian optimism but from a Southerner's stoicism, its gravity lightened by joy and humor.

THE PEACE OF WILD THINGS

When despair for the world grows in me
and I wake in the night at the least sound
in fear of what my life and my children's lives may be,
I go and lie down where the wood drake
5 rests in his beauty on the water, and the great heron feeds.
I come into the peace of wild things
who do not tax their lives with forethought
of grief. I come into the presence of still water.
And I feel above me the day-blind stars
10 waiting with their light. For a time
I rest in the grace of the world, and am free.

THE DEAD CALF

Dead at the pasture edge,
his head is without eyes, becalmed
on the grass. There was no escaping
the heaviness that came on him,
5 the darkness that rose
under his belly as though he stood
in a black sucking pool.
Earth's weight grew in him,
and he lay down. As he died
10 a great bird took his eyes.

Where is the horror in it?
Not in him, for he came to it
as a shadow into the night.
It was nameless and familiar.
15 He was fitted to it. In me
is where the horror is. In my mind
he does not yield. I cannot believe
the deep peace that has come to him.
I am afraid that where the light
20 is torn there is a wound.
There is a darkness in the soul
that loves the eyes. There is a light
in the mind that sees only light
and will not enter the darkness.

25 But I would have a darkness
in my mind like the dark
the dead calf makes for a time
on the grass where he lies, and will make
in the earth as he is carried down.
30 May all dead things lie down in me
and be at peace, as in the ground.

ENRICHING THE EARTH

To enrich the earth I have sowed clover and grass
to grow and die. I have plowed in the seeds
of winter grains and of various legumes,[1]
their growth to be plowed in to enrich the earth.
5 I have stirred into the ground the offal
and the decay of the growth of past seasons
and so mended the earth and made its yield increase.
All this serves the dark. Against the shadow
of veiled possibility my workdays stand
10 in a most asking light. I am slowly falling
into the fund of things. And yet to serve the earth,
not knowing what I serve, gives a wideness
and a delight to the air, and my days
do not wholly pass. It is the mind's service,
15 for when the will fails so do the hands
and one lives at the expense of life.
After death, willing or not, the body serves,
entering the earth. And so what was heaviest
and most mute is at last raised up into song.

A WET TIME

The land is an ark, full of things waiting.
Underfoot it goes temporary and soft, tracks
filling with water as the foot is raised.
The fields, sodden, go free of plans. Hands
5 become obscure in their use, prehistoric.

---

[1]French: vegetables.

The mind passes over changed surfaces
like a boat, drawn to the thought of roofs
and to the thought of swimming and wading birds.
Along the river croplands and gardens
10   are buried in the flood, airy places grown dark
and silent beneath it. Under the slender branch
holding the new nest of the hummingbird
the river flows heavy with earth, the water
turned the color of broken slopes. I stand
15   deep in the mud of the shore, like a stake
planted to measure the rise, the water rising,
the earth falling to meet it. A great cottonwood
passes down, the leaves shivering as the roots
drag the bottom. I turn like an ancient worshipper
20   to the thought of solid ground. I was not ready for this
parting, my native land putting out to sea.

THE SATISFACTIONS
OF THE MAD FARMER[1]

Growing weather; enough rain;
the cow's udder tight with milk;
the peace tree bent with its yield;
honey golden in the white comb;

5   the pastures deep in clover and grass,
enough, and more than enough;

the ground, new worked, moist
and yielding underfoot, the feet
comfortable in it as roots;

10   the early garden: potatoes, onions,
peas, lettuce, spinach, cabbage, carrots,
radishes, marking their straight rows
with green, before the trees are leafed;

raspberries ripe and heavy amid their foliage,
15   currants shining red in clusters amid their foliage,

---

[1]A persona for the poet in a sequence of poems; his "madness" is a sign of the
sanity of a nonconformist and visionary.

strawberries red ripe with the white
flowers still on the vines—picked
with the dew on them, before breakfast;

grape clusters heavy under broad leaves,
20 powdery bloom on fruit black with sweetness
—an ancient delight, delighting;

the bodies of children, joyful
without dread of their spending,
surprised at nightfall to be weary;

25 the bodies of women in loose cotton,
cool and closed in the evenings
of summer, like contented houses;

the bodies of men, competent in the heat
and sweat and weight and length
30 of the day's work, eager in their spending,
attending to nightfall, the bodies of women;

sleep after love, dreaming
white lilies blooming
coolly out of my flesh;

35 after sleep, the sense of being enabled
to go on with work, morning a clear gift;

the maidenhood of the day,
cobwebs unbroken in the dewy grass;

the work of feeding and clothing and housing,
40 done with more than enough knowledge
and with more than enough love,
by men who do not have to be told;

any building well built, the rafters
firm to the walls, the walls firm,
45 the joists without give,
the proportions clear,
the fitting exact, even unseen,
bolts and hinges that turn home
without a jiggle;

50 any work worthy
    of the day's maidenhood;

    any man whose words
    lead precisely to what exists,
    who never stoops to persuasion;

55 the talk of friends, lightened and cleared
    by all that can be assumed;

    deer tracks in the wet path,
    the deer sprung from them, gone on;

    live streams, live shiftings
60 of the sun in the summer woods;

    the great hollow-trunked beech,
    a landmark I loved to return to,
    its leaves gold-lit on the silver
    branches in the fall: blown down
65 after a hundred years of standing,
    a footbridge over the stream;

    the quiet in the woods of a summer morning,
    the voice of a pewee passing through it
    like a tight silver wire;

70 a little clearing among cedars,
    white clover and wild strawberries
    beneath an opening to the sky
    —heavenly, I thought it,
    so perfect; had I foreseen it
75 I would have desired it
    no less than it deserves;

    fox tracks in snow, the impact
    of lightness upon lightness,
    unendingly silent.

80 What I know of spirit is astir
    in the world. The god I have always expected
    to appear at the woods' edge, beckoning,
    I have always expected to be
    a great relisher of the world, its good
85 grown immortal in his mind.

Al Young (1939–   ) From Ocean Springs on the Mississippi Gulf Coast, Al Young grew up in the North and the South. He began writing about the age of ten, and became associated with various black magazines even before going to the University of Michigan. After leaving Michigan, he went to California, graduated in Spanish from Berkeley, earned a Stegner Writing Fellowship at Stanford, and teaches in the Creative Writing Program there. His books of poems are *Dancing* (1969) and *The Song Turning Back into Itself* (1971); *Snakes* (1970) is his first novel. Young celebrates the sacredness of life; his exuberance and humor enable him to express, beyond the tensions of the racial crisis, an abiding love of people and of things.

A DANCE FOR MILITANT DILETTANTES

No one's going to read
or take you seriously,
a hip friend advises,
until you start coming down on them
5   like the black poet you truly are
& ink in lots of black in your poems
soul is not enough
you need real color
shining out of real skin
10   nappy snaggly afro hair
baby grow up & dig on *that!*

You got to learn to put in about
stone black fists
coming up against white jaws
15   & red blood splashing
down those fabled wine & urine-
stained hallways
black bombs blasting out real white estate
the sky itself black with what's to come:
20   final holocaust
the settling up

Dont nobody want no nice nigger no more
these honkies man that put out
these books & things
25   they want an angry splib
a furious nigrah
the dont want no bourgeois woogie
they want them a militant nigger
in a fiji haircut
30   fresh out of some secret boot camp
with a bad book in one hand
& a molotov cocktail in the other
subject to turn up at one of their conferences
or soirees
35   & shake the shit out of them

THE DANCER

When white people speak of being uptight
theyre talking about dissolution & deflection
but when black people say uptight
they mean everything's all right.
5   I'm all right.
The poem brushes gayly past me
on its way toward completion,
things exploding in the background
a new sun
10   in a new sky
cantaloupes & watermelon for breakfast
in the Flamingo Motel
with cousin Inez
her brown face stretching & tightening
15   to keep control of the situation,
pretty Indian cheeks
cold black wavelets of hair,
her boyfriend
smiling from his suit.
20   We discuss concentration camps
& the end of time.
My mustache
wet with cantaloupe juice
would probably singe
25   faster than the rest of me
like the feathers of a bird over flame
in final solution of
the Amurkan problem.
Ah, Allah,[1]
30   that thou hast not forsaken me
is proven by the light
playing around the plastic slats
of half-shut venetian blinds
rattling in this room on time
35   in this hemisphere on fire.
The descendants of slaves
brush their teeth
adorn themselves before mirrors
speak of peace & of living kindness &
40   touch one another

[1]God in the Mohammedan religion.

intuitively & in open understanding.
"It could be the end of the world,"
she says, "they use to didnt be afraid
of us but now that they are
45   what choice do they have
but to try & kill us?"
but she laughs & I laugh & he laughs
& the calmness in their eyes
reaches me finally
50   as I dig my spoon into the belly of a melon

LEMONS, LEMONS

Hanging from fresh trees
or yellow against green
in a soft blaze of afternoon
while I eat dutifully
5   my cheese & apple lunch
or the coolness of twilight
in some of these California towns
I inhabited a lifetime ago

Hung that way
10   filled up with sunlight
like myself ripe with light
brown with light & ripe with shadow
the apple red & gold & green with it
cheese from the insides of
15   sun-loving cows

Sweet goldenness of light
& life itself
sunny at the core
lasting all day long
20   into night
into sleep
permeating dream shapes
forming tingly little words
my 2¢ squeezed out
25   photosynthetically[1]
in hasty praise
of lemon/light

[1]Photosynthesis is the process by which plants convert light into energy.

INDEX

The names of the poets are given in capitals. The titles of poems are given in italics. The first lines of poems are given in roman type.

1 2 3 4 5 6 7 8 9 10